ROUTLEDGE LIBRARY EDITIONS:
THE BRONTËS

Volume 4

THE WORKS OF PATRICK
BRANWELL BRONTË

THE WORKS OF PATRICK BRANWELL BRONTË

Volume 2, 1834–1836

Edited by
VICTOR A. NEUFELDT

Routledge
Taylor & Francis Group

LONDON AND NEW YORK

First published in 1999 by Garland Publishing, Inc.

This edition first published in 2015
by Routledge
2 Park Square, Milton Park, Abingdon, Oxon OX14 4RN

and by Routledge
711 Third Avenue, New York, NY 10017

Routledge is an imprint of the Taylor & Francis Group, an informa business

British Library Cataloguing in Publication Data
A catalogue record for this book is available from the British Library

ISBN: 978-1-138-92982-1 (Set)
ISBN: 978-1-315-68086-6 (Set) (ebk)
ISBN: 978-1-138-92915-9 (Volume 4) (hbk)
ISBN: 978-1-138-92918-0 (Volume 4) (pbk)
ISBN: 978-1-315-68135-1 (Volume 4) (ebk)

Publisher's Note
The publisher has gone to great lengths to ensure the quality of this reprint but
points out that some imperfections in the original copies may be apparent.

Disclaimer
The publisher has made every effort to trace copyright holders and would welcome
correspondence from those they have been unable to trace.

The Works of
Patrick Branwell Brontë
Volume 2, 1834–1836

Edited by
Victor A. Neufeldt

Garland Publishing, Inc.
A member of the Taylor & Francis Group
New York and London
1999

Library of Congress Cataloging-in-Publication Data

Brontë, Patrick Branwell, 1817–1848.
    [Works. 1999]
    The works of Patrick Branwell Brontë : an edition / edited by
Victor A. Neufeldt.
        p.   cm. — (Garland reference library of social science ; v. 1238)
    Includes bibliographical references and index.
    ISBN 0-8153-0225-8 (alk. paper)
    I. Neufeldt, Victor A. II. Title. III. Series.
PR4174.B23 1999
828'.709—dc21   97-11630
                                                      CIP

Printed on acid-free, 250-year-life paper
Manufactured in the United States of America

To Audrey

CONTENTS

ACKNOWLEDGEMENTS

It is with pleasure that I acknowledge the cooperation and assistance of the many persons and agencies without whose generous help this work would not have been possible.

For their generous financial assistance in the form of research grants I wish to thank the Social Sciences and Humanities Research Council of Canada, and the Office of Research Administration of the University of Victoria, and for its generous secretarial assistance, the Department of English at the University of Victoria.

For their support during my pleasant term as a Visiting Fellow at Clare Hall, University of Cambridge, I wish to thank Gillian Beer, President, and the staff of Clare Hall.

For their permission to reproduce the texts of manuscripts, transcriptions, and letters held by them it is my pleasure to acknowledge the following libraries and individuals: the family of the late C. K. Shorter; the Council of the Brontë Society; the Brotherton Collection, the Brotherton Library, University of Leeds; the British Library, Department of Manuscripts; the Trustees of the National Library of Scotland; the Robert H. Taylor Collection, Princeton University Library; the J. Alexander Symington Collection, Special Collections and University Archives, Rutgers University Libraries; the Henry W. and Albert A. Berg Collection, New York Public Library, Astor, Lennox, and Tilden Foundations; the Pierpont Morgan Library; the Harry Ransom Humanities Research Center, University of Texas at Austin; Roger W. Barrett.

For their assistance in locating and making available materials and answering my numerous queries, I wish to acknowledge the following individuals: Juliet R. V. Barker; Jane Sellars, Mike Hill, Kathryn White, Anne Dinsdale at the Brontë Parsonage Museum; Christopher D. W. Sheppard and staff at the Brotherton Collection, University of Leeds, the Keeper and staff, British Library, the Keeper and staff, National Library of Scotland; Mark R. Farrell and Charles Greene at the Taylor Collection, Princeton University; Edward Skipworth and staff at Special Collections and Archives, Rutgers University; Rodney Philips and staff at the Berg Collection, New York Public Library; Robert E. Parks, Christine Nelson, Inge Dupont, Vanessa Pintado, Sylvie Merian at the Pierpont Morgan Library; Cathy Henderson, Pat Fox, Rachel Howarth, Barbara La Borde-Smith at the Harry Ransom Humanities Research Center, University of Texas; George MacMinn, Clerk of the British Columbia Legislative Assembly; staff of the McPherson Library, University of Victoria; and colleagues and friends Elizabeth Archibald, Lionel Adey, Edward

Berry, Mariel Grant, Patrick Grant, Elizabeth Grove-White, Michael Hadley, Kathy Kirby-Fulton, John Money, Joan and John Noble, Karen Smith, Peter Smith, Lisa Surridge, Henry Summerfield. I wish also to thank Juliet Barker, Christine Alexander, Jane Sellars, and Margaret Smith for the assistance they have provided with their recent publications.

Finally, for their unflagging help in the preparation of the text and the annotations, I wish to thank the indefatigable Robin Cryderman, and my wife, Audrey, who declines to be listed as co-editor.

LIST OF ABBREVIATIONS

Alexander CB	*An Edition of the Early Writings of Charlotte Brontë*, vols. I and II, ed., Christine Alexander, Oxford: Basil Blackwell, 1987 and 1991
Alexander EW	*The Early Writings of Charlotte Brontë*, by Christine Alexander, Oxford: Basil Blackwell, 1983
Alexander & Sellars	*The Art of the Brontës*, by Christine Alexander and Jane Sellars, Cambridge: Cambridge University Press, 1995
Barker Brontës	*The Brontës*, by Juliet Barker, London: Weidenfeld and Nicholson, 1994
Berg	Berg Collection, New York Public Library
BL: Ashley	British Library: Ashley Collection
BPM: Bon	Brontë Parsonage Museum: Bonnell Collection
BPM: BS	Brontë Parsonage Museum: Brontë Society's Collection
Brotherton	Brotherton Collection, Brotherton Library, University of Leeds
Gérin PBB	*Branwell Brontë*, by Winifred Gérin, London: Hutchinson & Co., 1967
Hatfield Papers	The papers of the late C. W. Hatfield, at the BPM, containing notes, transcriptions, and correspondence
HRC	Harry Ransom Humanities Research Center, University of Texas, Austin
Neufeldt Bibliog	*A Bibliography of the Manuscripts of Patrick Branwell Brontë*, ed., Victor A. Neufeldt, New York: Garland Publishing Inc., 1993
Neufeldt PBB	*The Poems of Patrick Branwell Brontë*, ed., Victor A, Neufeldt, New York: Garland Publishing Inc., 1990

Neufeldt PCB	*The Poems of Charlotte Brontë*, ed., Victor A. Neufeldt, New York: Garland Publishing Inc., 1985
Neufeldt PBB Works I	*The Works of Partrick Branwell Brontë*, vol. I, ed., Victor A. Neufeldt, New York: Garland Publishing Inc., 1997
PML	Pierpont Morgan Library, New York
SHB LL	*The Brontës: Their Lives, Friendships, and Correspondence*, (The Shakespeare Head Edition), ed., Thomas J. Wise and John Alexander Symington, 4 vols., Oxford: Basil Blackwell, 1932
SHB Misc	*The Miscellaneous and Unpublished Writings of Charlotte and Patrick Branwell Brontë*, (The Shakespeare Head Edition), ed., Thomas J. Wise and John Alexander Symington, 2 vols., Oxford: Basil Blackwell, 1936 and 1938
Smith Letters	*The Letters of Charlotte Brontë*, 2 vols., ed., Margaret Smith, Oxford: Oxford University Press, 1995
Taylor	Taylor Collection, Princeton University Library
Winnifrith PBB	*The Poems of Patrick Branwell Brontë*, ed., Tom Winnifrith, Oxford: Basil Blackwell, 1983

INTRODUCTION

Volume one of this edition covered 1827-33, in which Branwell was mainly concerned with the creation of the Glass Town Confederacy, and with the establishment of Rougue/Alexander Percy/Elrington as his protagonist. This volume covers 1834-36, during which Branwell focuses on the creation of Angria, and on the growing conflict between Alexander Percy, Earl of Northangerland, and Arthur Wellesly, Duke of Zamorna and King Adrian of Angria.

In these three years Branwell produced the largest, most sustained body of written work of any comparable period in his literary life, totaling approximately 300,500 words of prose, and 42 (37 extant) poems. All the poems have previously appeared in my 1990 edition of Branwell's poetry. Of the prose, approximately 241,000 words are published here for the first time.[1] None of the previously published prose texts retain Branwell's original spelling, punctuation, sentence structure, and paragraphing. All have not only been normalized, but also contain significant misreadings, "revisions," and omissions; and all are fragments, taken out of context, offering the reader little sense of how and where they fit into the larger whole, and therefore little sense of how much Branwell had written or what he was attempting to achieve.

Branwell's script and punctuation have obviously created difficulties for would-be editors, including this one. Almost all of the manuscripts through 1839 are written in minute print writing, which in most cases must be read through a magnifying glass. His abandonment of the minute print in 1839 coincides with his abandonment of the Angrian saga. While he used the tiny pages for which the Brontë children have become famous only through 1832, then fairly consistently used pages taken from notebooks measuring approximately 9 x 15 cm., 11 x 18 cm., or 18 x 24 cm., Branwell continued to cram as many words as possible onto a page, up to approximately 2500 on an 11 x 18 cm. page, making reading extemely difficult and interlinear additions or revisions at times impossible to decipher. Added to these difficulties is Branwell's erratic punctuation. Essentially, the only punctuation he uses in the prose manuscripts is the full-stop, which while scattered liberally throughout his prose, is seldom used to signify the end of a sentence. Sometimes it serves as a comma or other type of natural pause, but more often it indicates nothing more than Branwell resting his quill while trying to think what his next word(s) should be. Nor does he always capitalize the first word of a sentence.

The intention of this edition, therefore, is both to correct the effects of previous misreadings and "improvements," and to provide the reader with what remains of the actual text that Branwell produced. All of the texts in this edition are based on my own transcriptions of the manuscripts. It has not been possible

---

[1]   This figure does not include the many pages of manuscript in facsimile in SHB Misc I and II.

to retain the original page breaks, or the original lining in the case of prose works except for lists, tables, titles, title-pages, and contents pages. In all other respects the text offered is the text as Branwell left it, except in the matter of his revisions, where only major canceled lines or passages have been reproduced. In the case of uncanceled variants, the latest variant is given in the text; other variants appear in the notes. Editorial insertions have been added in square brackets where necessay for the sake of clarity. Titles in square brackets are ones indirectly supplied by Branwell. In the case of Branwell's idiosyncratic spelling, I have labeled with "[sic]" only those spellings that might strike the reader as particularly strange or misleading. Doubtful readings due to manscript deterioration, blotting, or the impossiblity of reading the minute print writing appear in <   >.

As I indicated in the previous volume (p. xxviii), from the age of eleven on, Branwell saw himself as published author/editor. The reproduction of the text exactly as he left it allows the reader to trace clearly both Branwell's adoption of various authorial personae and his mode of composition.[2] Doing so increases the difficulty of reading the text and might well lead to a wish that Branwell had written less more carefully and legibly. It should be remembered, however, that the poems and chronicles until early 1836, when he sent his poem **Misery** to *Blackwood's*, were never meant for actual publication. They are the result of childhood play and adolescent fantasy, often written in the headlong rush of feverish composition. Thus the quality of the work is uneven, yet these volumes also reveal a Branwell who, when at his best, carefully revised his poems (up to four versions of some are extant) to achieve his goal of becoming a published poet, a goal he achieved five years before his sisters did.

The organisation of this volume has proved much more problematical than that of the first. In it, with few exceptions, the items appear in chronological order. Such an ordering is not entirely possible in this volume for a number reasons. First, throughout the three years covered by this volume, Branwell was working on two or even three projects simultaneously. With four exceptions—the "Greek" poems and **The CXXXVII Psalm** in 1834, **The Spirit of Poetry** in 1835, and **Misery** in late 1835/early 1836—Branwell's energies were focused on tracing the history and fortunes of the Percy family and on delineating the creation and fortunes of Angria. He completed **The Wool is Rising** between February and June 1834, and **The Life of Percy** between Spring 1834 and late 1835 or early 1836.[3] At the same time, he began [**Angria**

---

2   The practice of standardizing and "correcting" the grammar, punctuation and spelling of the original script has created a false impression of childhood and adolescent writing much more polished and carefully written than it was in reality.

3   Volume I of **The Life of Percy** is undated, but the two poems it contains are both dated Spring 1834 in the 1837 notebook in which he reworked them (see volume III). It is likely, therefore, that Branwell began **The Life**

and the Angrians] in May 1834 and continued work on it into 1839. Second, the manuscripts have been fragmented, scattered, and portions of them lost. As a result, for example, only portions of **[Angria and the Angrians]** are extant today and even these are fragmented and widely scattered.[4] The title appears in square brackets because it is partially conjectural. The first portion **(I a)** is missing at least two pages at the beginning, but the narrator refers to the work by this title on at least three occasions—see p. 278, n. 2. I have chosen, therefore, to print the two works concerning the Percies consecutively, then **[Angria and the Angrians]**, and to interweave the other materials with them, so as to create the least possible disruption of chronlogical order and continuity, and to provide the best possible sense of Branwell's literary progress.

---

immediately after completing **The Wool is Rising** on June 26, 1834, about the same time that he began **[Angria and the Angrians]**.

[4]   The reasons for the fragmentation and dispersal of Branwell's manuscripts are discussed in my edition of his poems and in my Bibliography of his manuscripts. However, Branwell himself may be responsible for some of the missing bits of **[Angria and the Angrians]**, as well as the early versions of five poems in this volume, discarding the first version when he revised poems for his 1837 manuscript notebook of poems—see vol. III.

THE WORKS OF
PATRICK BRANWELL BRONTË

To the horse black Eagle which I rode at the battle of Zamorna[1]

Swart steed of night, thou hast charged thy last
O'er the red[2] war-trampled plain
Now fallen asleep is the battle blast
It is stilled above the slain[3]

Now hushed is the clang of armour bright[4]
thou willt never bear me more
to the deadliest press of the gathering fight
through seas of noble gore

And the cold eyes of midnight skies shall
Shall not pour their light on thee
When the wearied host of the conqueror lies
On a field of victory

Rest now in thy glory noble steed[5]
Rest all thy wars are done
True[6] is the love & high the meed
Thou from thy lord hast won

---

[1] Half-page manuscript leaf, 9.8 x 6.8 cm, in the Berg Collection. On the reverse is part of a road or trail map. Undated and unsigned, but the battle of Zamorna began January 22, 1834—see vol. I, pp. 443-46 and pp. 22 and 32 below—so early 1834 seems the likely time of composition. For an earlier reference to Black Eagle, see vol. I, p. 445. The title is preceded by two canceled lines:
> Fallen asleep is the battle blast
> It is hushed on each war trampled plain

[2] "gory" altered to "red."

[3] Two canceled lines follow:
> Thunder clad shall it wake once more
> Will thou hear the trump again

[4] A canceled line follows:
> Through to the thickest of the gathering Fight

[5] The line originally read:
> Rest thunder clad, Sleep noble steed.

[6] "Strong" altered to "True."

In daisied lawns[7] sleep peacefully
Dwell by the quiet wave
Till death shall sound his signal cry
And call thee to thy grave.

---

7   "mead" altered to "lawns."

And is this Greece is this the land I sing[1]
These Mountains hoar and this tempestous land
Yes this is Greece Behold in gathered ring
Beneath yon dreary brow that little band
Helms on each had and lances in each hand
The wild waste round them and the <bleak> <fire>
Sole light amid them flashing while they stand
On each <Iron> front white clouds of smoke aspire
Above their crested helms and still ascending higher
Why gathering thus on Pindus[2] stormy steep
Why <assembling> thus in daylights dim decline
War sounds not in these <gusts> which round you sweep
Greece may be robed in light <or> wrapt in storm
little avails it <to> her sons <laid> there

---

[1]   These faintly penciled lines, undated and unsigned but in Branwell's hand, appear on the endpaper of a Greek Prayer Book in the PML (MA 2696) that belonged to Mr Brontë. Originally belonging to Mrs. Jane Morgan, the book was presented to Mr. Brontë by William Morgan as a memorial of his wife on September 29, 1827. The lines would seem to describe the band surrounding Leonides at Thermopylae, although the last two lines seem to refer to the battle's aftermath; the handwriting suggests that they were added later. Both these lines and the following set seem to be trial lines for **The Pass of Thermopylae**, p. 6 below, thus likely composed January/February 1834.
[2]   A rugged mountain range in northwestern Greece, separating Thessaly from Epirus.

Now[1] the sweet[2] Hour of closing day
Draws down from Heaven her latest smile
And Evenings beams have ceased to play
    Round Scyros[3] lofty Isle.
Thermopylaes commanding height
Looks oer the silent march of Night
And wide benea[t]h it Grecia lies
As still and silent as the skies
A moveless shadow dim and blue
Spreads oer her Hills one deathlike hue[4]
And wide Thessalia far away
Spreads her deep shadows cold and grey
From far Euboea[5] wild and lone
Why hear I note[sic] the shepheards tone
Why do his shrill notes dying afar
Cease to soothe the twilight air
Where is the twinkling lamp of night
Which used to flash on Phocias height
And down the Peneus brawling stream
Glint the lone travellers warning beam

Where dost thou ask., through smiling[6] Greece
Have fled these signs of life and peace
Where is the youth of the old man gone
Why hath the joy of the Hop[e]less flown
Where is the light in the closing eye
Of the wretch in sickness stretched to die
And why have the sweet sounds of Evening time
Sunk into the silence through Hellas clime

---

1   These lines, undated and unsigned, cover most of the verso of a single leaf (13x21 cm) in the BPM: BS 113. See also p. 8, n. 1, and p. 9, n. 1.
2   "calm" altered to "sweet."
3   An island off Thessaly where Theseus was slain and buried; sanctuary of Achilles.
4   Two canceled lines follow:
        And where Thessalia's champaign lies
        Slowly the mists of Evening rise
5   The largest island of the Greek archipelago where the Greeks won a great naval victory over the Persians in 480 B. C.
6   "silent" altered to "smiling."

I said that. spent with Iron pain
The Dying man may not complain
I said that to the erring sight
Deaths gleam may seem Hopes beamy light
A Charnel vapour oft may shine
As fair as Luna's light divine

Well now All Grecia seems to sleep
In peaceful twilight dark and deep
Where is the wild red fire of war
No cries of Anguish fill the air
No clash of arms no battle cry
And not one. lightning from the sky
Can thus a mighty Nation die

The Pass of Thermopylae.[1]
Fifty six lines.
P.B. Brontë

Thermopyla[e]'s tremendous hight
Has lost the Evenings fading light
And each tremendous mountain round
Seems blackning in the shades profound
Alike wild waste and ocean wild
Dark as those hills around them piled
Lie gloomy as they neer had worn
The sunshine of a summer morn
Above the moonbeams fitful light
Breaks shivering through the heavy night
And as the stormy rack sweeps by
Fades lost amid the troubled sky
At times that moon so sadly now
Glints on Thermopyla[e]'s stern brow
Where bloody grass and trampled heath
Lie soaked beneath their loads of death
Where shattered rocks with mossy head
Form many a warriors dying bed
And many a dim and darkning eye
Now gazes on this stormy sky
    Sleep Noble Soldier sleep alone
The whistling wind your burial moan
The bloody rock your bed of death
Your shroud grey grass and tangled heath
The Mountains lofty brow ye have
At once your monument and grave
    O Glorious dead sleep peacfully
Your name your fame shall never die
By you your country saved from chains

---

1   The fourth of five poems in BPM: BS 117-5—see vol. I, p. 203, n. 1. In the 1837 revised version of the poem in vol. III, Branwell dates the original version January 19, 1835; either he was confused or an intermediate version dated January 19 has been lost. The Battle of Thermopylae clearly fascinated Branwell during 1834/35—see pp. 10-16 below. The pass provided the only route from Thessaly into central and southern Greece (Achaia). In 480 B. C. Leonides and 300 Spartans made a heroic defense here against the army of Xerxes, king of Persia, but were defeated when the Persians through treachery discovered a path over the mountain, enabling them to attack the Greeks from the rear.

Still, free, unconquered Greece, remains
And not one drop of all that blood
Which curdles now in Peneus[2] flood
No Not one drop is lost in vain
For every drop dissolves a chain
And each cold hand and nerveless arm
Which never more that blood can warm
Have while they slew their meanest foe
Given Susa's domes[3] a fatal blow
There may proud Persias legions stay
For darkness clouds her future way
Thermopyla[e] thy conquered dead
Have bent to earth even Xerxes head
    Arise ye Spartan heroes rise
Come seize your sceptres in the skys
There from your everlasting throne
Behold the wonders you have done
Not Phocias[4] mountains dark and hoar
Not all you Grecias classic shore
Not distant Persias sorrowing reign
Not Alpine hill or Roman plain
Shall limit your great leaders name
Or eer confine your lasting fame
    Never did Trumpets loudest voice
Rouse the feirce soldier to rejoice
As now will yon ensanguined pass
And that one word Leonidas!.

          P B Brontë
          March 3[d]
          A D 1834

---

[2]   The chief river in Thessaly.

[3]   The capital of the ancient Persian Empire and site of the royal palace.

[4]   A district in central Greece containing Parnassus and Delphi. During the Persian invasion the Phocians helped oppose the Persians, but their irresolute conduct at Thermopylae contributed to the defeat of Leonides.

Sing for the power of thy foeman hath gone[1]
Quenched in the sun beam that smiles round thy throne
Raise higher and louder your voices to sing
Angria Our Country Zamorna our King
River whose waves through the wide desart winding
    Bearest thy streams to the home of our pride
Each weary waste of thy glory reminding
    Rise and spread round thee thy glittering tide
O All ye proud Mountains which high from afar
Crown your blue brows with the wandering star
Tell you your torrents and deep shadowed plain
Zamorna hath triumphed oer Angria to reign
    Aye tell ye the North with its storms and its snow
    Tell ye the South where the ocean gales blow
    Tell ye the East in its Summer Sun glow
       Angria and Arthur are shining again
       Mid night and tempest may darken in vain
         Foes may arise
         & Fate may suprise
Dust on a mountain and drops in the main
Sing for the sun hath arisen on creation
    Sound ye the Trumpet to herald its dawn
Rise Man and Monarch and City and Nation
    Away with your Darkness and hail to your Morn
Sound the Loud Trumpet oer land and oer sea
    Join tongues hearts and v[o]ices rejoicing to sing
    Afric hath risen hath sworn to be free
Glory to Angria and GOD SAVE OUR KING

According to his 1837 volume of poems (see vol.III), Branwell wrote the first draft of **The CXXXVII[th] Psalm** (no longer extant) in the Spring of 1834. As, according to Branwell, it was composed by Percy for his motet, "The Captivity," it may have been intended as part of **The Life of Percy**—see p. 92.

---

[1]   These lines, undated and unsigned, appear on the recto of a single leaf (13x21 cm) in the BPM: BS 113, and constitute the earliest version of **Sound The Loud Trumpet**. For the two subsequent versions, see p. 204 and vol. III. As the second version precedes a January 2, 1835 date in the manuscript, and Branwell assigns a composition date of "Spring 1834"in the revised 1837 version, May 1834 seems a likely date for the composition of these lines. For a possible source, see Moore's "Sound the loud timbrel o'er Egypt's dark sea."

(a)When on the thorny bed of Death[1]
   The wasted sick man quivering lies
His breast scarce heaving with his breath
   And cold his brow and quenched his eyes
Then when as hopelessly he dies
   In that forlorn and dreary hour
Oh what a host of feelings rise
   To imbitter death with darker power
Then Death and darkness round him lower
   He see his children round him stand
   And cannot even lift that hand
   Which gave them bread and strength and life
   While they in Anguished hopeless strife
      Pour out the unavailing shewer

(b)When on the thorny bed of death
   The wasted victim spent with pain
His breast scarce heaving to his breath
   Still clings to bitter life in vain
When moveless powerless to complain
   All—hope—and voice and eyesight—gone
And dark and deep the livid stain
   Leaves each frozen member cold as stone
Then as he turns his sightless eye
With bitter anguish to the sky
   And strives with hollow tone
One word—But now the <cleaving> tongue
But that death rattle can prolong
   It sinks and he is gone

---

[1]   These trial lines for the first version of **Misery**, Scene II, ll. 149-61 (see p. 490) appear on both sides of the leaf described on p. 4, n. 1. The first set, probably the earlier of the two, appears upside down at the bottom of the recto, separated from the trial lines for **Sound The Loud Trumpet** by sketches of gothic windows, a mythical creature, a profile of a trumpeter, a castle on a rocky outcrop with river and buildings below. For further details, see Alexander and Sellars, p. 314. The second set appears at the top of the verso, preceeding the lines on p. 4. Early 1834 would seem a likely date of composition.

Thermopylae, PBB

Book I[st]
Ten stanzas,.217 Lines[1]

I
18
Now morning rises broad & bright
Above the Egean sea
And gives to heaven returning light
While hill and valley plain & height
Roll of the iron shroud of night
And welcome in the day
Awake Egean wake from sleep
Behold the sunlight dawn
Come join thy waves in glittering light
To hail the rising morn
All Grecias shores beneath the sun
With golden lustre glow
And heaven reflects a dazzling light
From thy wild waves below
High oer the vapours curling off
The Argolic Mountains[2] rise

---

[1]   Hand-sewn booklet without covers, 9.5x15.5 cm, of 14 pages in BPM: Bon 142. Although Branwell used the same lined paper as for his notebook of poems—see p. 444, n. 1—the poem seems to have been bound separately. Despite the "Book 1st", there is no evidence of further books having been written, but the late Everard Flintoff of Leeds University believed that Branwell originally planned poems covering the morning before the battle, the battle itself, and the battle's aftermath at dusk, a very plausible suggestion in light of the poems and fragments on pp. 3-7. Although both Gérin BB and Winnifrith PBB suggest that Branwell read Glover's *Leonides* in the Ponden House library, all the basic information on the Persian/Greek conflict was also available to him in Mavor's *Universal History* (see vol I, p. 100, n. 3). Branwell's use of ordinary long-hand script rather than the miniature print-writing here and for the five poems in BPM: BS 117-5 may well be related to Charlotte's "public" volume of poems begun in December 1833—see Neufeldt PCB, pp. xxxvi-vii.
[2]   The peninsula of Argolis in the district of Argos in the eastern Peloponnesus. The Argives were friendly to Persia and took no part in the war against Xerxes.

And Attica[3] her arid ridge
    Rears far amid the skys

II
18
Now all around this smiling sea
One swelling champaign sweeps away
Shewn in this early morning light
With streams and trees & temples bright
    Beyond its eastern bound
Rise the dark hills of Thessaly
Above it beetling awfully
As proud its guardian walls to be
    They gird the champaign round
Rise up oh hills still sterner rise!
Still blacker frown against the skys
This morning dawns how fair & gay
How shore and ocean seem in play
    To hail returning life
But has not oft and outside fair
A forehead seeming smoothed from care
Striven to conceal a hearts despair
    And inward burning strife

III
25
A gnawing worm hath Grecia now
    Though sumer like all round her lie
Beneath Thessalia's frowning brow
    Her soft vales smiling on the sky
Behold! far outward round the plain
Yon mighty host of moving men
Slow as they wheel in line on line
Their helms and arms & armour shine
Still pressing on each trodden place
Still closing round each vacant space
And still as farther on the sight
Forth flashes up this newborn light
For mile on mile across the plain
Moves on this mighty warrior train
Behold them joined, one glisttering mass
Thermopylae's tremendous pass
    Above them beetling lone

---

3   The district around Athens.

While neath it, village feild or tree
The eyesight strives in vain to see
All calmer scenes of nature flee
    As that huge host rolls on
The sudden shout the long drawn hum
The Trumpets blast the thundring drum
Like smoke oer mountains rolling come
    With mixed and mu[r]mering tone

IV
20

Now far & wide the Ensigns fliy
Like thousand flashes mid the sky
Thier silken folds all fluttering bright
Make wide heaven quiver with varying light
Behold yon broad bright crimson shown
In gold emblazed its gilded sun
Great Mithra[4] with a borrowed glow
Blazes along the closing row
A thousand suns this fated day
In Oceans breezes glance & play
And sunny helm and suntipped spear
Above each mountain gorge appear
Greece! let me drop one tear for thee
    Where hath thy light of freedom gone
I know thy sons will perish free
Yet what avails a glory flown
And when thy Children all are gone
    Where will that light of Freedom be
Where!—Thou struck, blasted, lying alone,
Must feel this huge hosts tread & wither neath its throne

V
12

I said a mountains stormy hight
Hung beetling oer that Army bright
Yes! there thou frownst Thermopylae
Stern standard of the brave & free
High oer rough Peneus roaring flood
Oer swelling hill & shadowed wood
Thy huge rocks starting to the sky
Swell forth a barrier broad & high

---

4   The ancient Persian god of light and truth, supposed to be the sun or Venus Urania.

And seems as rent by thunders stroke
Between the ribbed and frowning rock
That path which upward from the shore
Winds high above the torrents roar

VI
17

Now all beneath that bulwark high
The whole wide champaign sounds with joy
And Oh! in what unnumbered lines
Yon mighty army shades & shines
First breath[e]s the spearlight oer the hill
Then seems its flash the vale to fill
And still oer all that wide expanse
One broad bright sunbeam seems to glance
Hark to the roar of revelry!
Hark to the ceaseless shouts of joy!
See! how the rising morning wind
        Swells up each banners glorious fold
See! how before around behind
        Flames forth in crimson & in gold!
        Yon long long ranks of war unfold
Lo how they crowd in burnished ring
Around the standard of their King!

VII
20

That King upon his golden throne
High oer the Tumult shines alone
Their Xerxes with insatiate eye
Roams oer the hosts which round him lie
Parthians & Medians[5] beneath him stand
Glittering in purple a kinglike band
Aye many a Monarch is in yon train
Doomed to the sun his beams to wane
Where far mid the desart the Nile flows on
Egypt hath given her shaven son
The sunscorched Arabian stands haughtily there
The Parthian lifts his wandering spear
And glorious Indias clime's unknown
Sends her dark hostage round that throne
Aye there they crowd a jewelled throng

---

5   Iranian tribes, part of the Persian Empire. The Parthians excelled as as archers on horseback.

Loud notes of triump[h] on each tongue
Yet all in thrice redoubled ring
Prone kneeling neath their lord the King!
He rising, lord of Glory stands
And spreads toward heaven his sceptred hands

VIII
54.

Ha! Mithra thou in glory now
Mayst shed thy halo round my brow
To thee I vow a sacrifice
Such as hath never to the skys
          Blazed in accepting flame
To thee yon Grecian army dies
To thee I vow its obsequies
A Hecatomb,[6] ye favouring skys!
          Accept the whole Grecian name!
Gods have a band of traitorous men
Thus braved the lion in his den
Lo twice ten thousand Persians lie
To stiffen neath a Grecian sky
And yet Achaia's[7] evil star
Can shine a[s]cendant through the air
Well twice I have seen my warriors fall
Beneath yon heaven erected wall
Twice have my troops in vain assayed
To force yon rocks tremendous shade
But not a third time never more
Shall we roll backward on the shore!
          Thou saidst a Goatherds step might find
          A path which up yon dark hills brow
High toward Thermopylae may wind
          To 'oerlook the Traitor host below
          Tis well now Persians strike your blow
Mardonius[8] seize thy trustiest brand
Thou boastedst oft lead thou the band
          To storm yon heaven built wall
Let all our choicest troops advance

---

6   In ancient Greece, the slaughter of 100 cattle at one time as an offering to the gods.
7   Achaea is a district on the northern coast of the Peleponnesus, but in Homer and for the Romans, it referred to Greece generally as Branwell uses it here.
8   One of the chief Persian instigators of the expedition against Greece.

Take Parthian javelin Persian lance
          And heaven for Xe[r]xes call
Vengeance on Greece aye let them know
That what hath stayed the coming blow
Shall only force it on our foe
          With heavier dint to fall
The meanest cloud which spots the sky
May hide even Mithras light on high
Yet when again breaks out the day
How those vain vapours fade away
          Now thou who hast betrayed to me
                Thy country and thy home
          Tis meet that I should show to thee
                Thy own reward to come
Ha! base Trachinian[9] deemst thou then
          Because I seize thy way
That I will weigh three hundred men
          Against thy craven clay
Go slave and know a Persian eye
Though it accept the Treachery
          The Traitor casts away
Thou hast shown my way to victory
Oer the dead corses of the free
And death base slave I shew to thee

                    IX
                    8

The Traitor wr[e]tch is born away
He casts a wild glance round the sea
But dares not face Thermopylae
          On thy betrayed brow
He who to the proud spoilers hand
Hath given the bravest of his land
Beneath the glad receivers hand
          Rolls headless breathless now

                    X
                    25

Just then the sun with sudden light
Burst full on yon far fronting height
And flashing back in golden lines
Wide oer the champaign streams and shines

---

9   An inhabitant of Trachis in Thessaly who showed the Persians the path over
the mountain that enabled them to attack Leonides' troop from behind.

Lo all along yon brazen sea
How flame the bright arms gallantly
See how they spread from side to side
Forth streaming oer the champaign wide
And what a cloud of standards stare
Lighten and darken through the air
For Victory for Victory
Roars high above the living sea
Aye ye may shout proud Persians now
For all hopes garlands bind your brow
Aye ye shall gain yon mighty height
And fight and conquer in that fight
　Oh Greece in this dark hour of gloom
When round thee yawns one bloody tomb
Think through destructions dreariest day
Freedom can shine with brightest ray
That in the Tyrants might[i]est hour
One godgiven sword may shake his power
Now bid thy armed children see
On thy huge heights Thermopylae
Three hundred fight gainst millions three

August 9[th] 1834.
P B Bronte[10]

According to his 1837 volume of poems (see vol. III), Branwell composed an earlier draft of **Thermopylae** (no longer extant) on January 19, 1835. Unless Branwell has his dates confused, this was a revision of the version on p. 6.

---

[10] The poem covers pp. 1-13 of the manuscript booklet; p. 14, so badly rubbed as to be indecipherable, seems to contain five quatrains having to do with Angria—see p. 199.

meeting[1] of some of our liberal and moderate. Members of Parliament. at the residence of my freind Sir R W Pelham. I[2] therefore took my hat and determinded. upon walking along the harbour quay. to his House. The Night though cloudy was still and the lights in the streets shone brilliently. I paced along the broad. bustling space. round the Harbour but amid the wagons and carts and lights and lading and merchandise and tar and. horses and sailors. I could scarce get one glimpse of the wide and. ship laden Bay. erelong I to shorten the way. turned up a dark passage between the Gables of two huge old warehouses and picking my steps in the moonlight amid "muckmiddens."[3] carts and lumber. passed upward allong a narrow filthy lane till I reached a comparitivly wide. courtyard formed by. the Back settlements of a tavern. the end of an old wall. the rear. of a desolate factory and the front of a ruinous combing shop.[4] above amid the dark murky air the vast chimneys of. half a dozen old mills puffed out their black smoke against. the yellow stifled heavens. through the whole of the humble. square. no human being scarcly a trace of one existed. and. in the combing shop I above mentioned alone did the light of lamp or candle. brighten the poverty of all around me unhappily. my acquaintance with this place being but slender. its apertures and their directions where unknown to me and the reasons for my entering it seemed very likly to be frustrated. in fact as more

---

1   A two-page manuscript fragment, 11.2x18.5 cm, in the Brotherton Collection. The fragment seems to be part of an early draft of **The Wool is Rising**, p. 24 below.

2   Sir John Flower.

3   Refuse heaps.

4   Branwell had first-hand knowledge of wool combing shops. According to the Babbage Report of 1850, "Many of the occupants of Haworth pursue the occupation of combing wool for the factories." The work was both unpleasant and unhealthy; an account written in 1845 states, "The wool-combers assort the wool cheifly in an apartment of their own dwelling. The work is done over a fire of charcoal which sends forth volumes of carbonic acid gas, and the work people are obliged to keep their windows open in all weathers to prevent or to mitigate the evil effects of the gas. They are roasted to perspiration on one side, and have often a current of cold air rushing upon them from the window. They look pale and cadaverous and are short-lived, few reaching fifty years of age." (E. Lipson, *A Short History of Wool and Its Manufacture*, Cambridge, Mass., 1953, pp. 121-22)

In a letter to parliament, July 1840, the Bradford Woolcomber's Association representative stated combers were "compelled to work from 14 to 16 hours per day, and with all this sweat and toil we are not able to procure sufficient of the neccesaries of life wherewith to subsist on" (James Burnley, *The History of Wool and Woolcombing*, London, 1889, p. 177). Not surprisingly, these conditions led to major strikes in Yorkshire and Lancastershire 1825 and 1832.

haste makes less speed. my wish to gain sooner the place. of my destination had now I perceived only tended to fix me in that worst of quagmires. a stuck path a bewildered. pr[o]gress hearing voices and seeing forms moving across the light of the combing shop before me I stepped up to its entrance eager to gain more certain intelligence of my route. and as I neared its cracked. lintel. the voices within tended to inspire me with a desire to know who were the inmates astir and and working so late at night. The curious mixture of an industrious bustle. and a wrangling conversation. prepared me for the scene I witnessed on entering. —tubs of wool ranged on each hand. formed a passage into the middle of a confined heated and dilapidated apartment. the slates almost of[f] the rafters almost rotten in the roof and every inch of plaster. departed from the walls. 3 combing pots filled the cheif part of the place and. the. sickly light of the lamps the close air of the apartment and the. stinking smell of wool and oil. made no pleasant impression on the olfactory nerves of one just entered from the fresh moonlight air. "Whose there" called on[e] of the three combers at work as he turned round. and hastily strode to the door "My lads I have almost lost my path here" I answered while the man stood before me with an unwelcoming visage. I did not here[sic] his grumbling answer for his appearance. fixed all my attention he was a young man 21 very tall and slender habited in the usual attire of his trade. corduroy trousers. shirt and bare elbows. But his countenance—that strange compound of curled hair feminine nose scornful lips and unquiet eye. seemed at once the youthful imprint of a well known Nobleman. and. the form of his fellow workman behind him habited like him. but lower slighter and. yet. with just his aspect. strength[en]ed my conjecture before hastily formed that these two. young men were Sons of Northangerland. of whom we had just been conversing. "Edward Percy" I said unconsciously "Whisht. I tell you. Sir John. for I see you are him You I hope dont intend to tear the life from the hearts of two industrious workmen do you. I say. what are you wanting at this time of night. coming staring at our doghole be off or. well stripe you with a comb or two. —Silence I say there Timothy. we'll have none off your puritanical howling." Edward Percy turned feircely round to the third comber present a droll specimen of humanity sallow squat and greasy with lank hair upturned eyes and. a mouth opened to the utterance. of a solemn psalm or. methodistical sermon. there was an expression of settled cunning on this worthys sanctimonious countenance which settled on him a character beyond. his youthful years and. commonplace figure. Edward Percy turning to me said "Who I am its useless to say. yons my Brother William thats Mr Timothy Steaton son of. the steward of Elrington Hall. a goodly company and an <circl[e]> here we are placed under the Ban and curse of Him there Him that is—our. —dad. —Hem. hem. — well we deprived of house and home plack and penny[5] have just as you observe set up in a small way and in a smaller corner for ourselves beginning here as combers on our own account with capital of 9£ among us. we intend. through a course of

---

5   i.e., everything, down to the last farthing (Scots and northern dialect).

labour and honesty. (hem) to rise as it were from our present position to large trade wealth and. consequence. If such sequels do not follow the course of Edward (by right.) Lord Viscount Percy. the Honorable William Percy and. Timothy Steaton Esqr. Attorney at law. why. may HE. catch us thats the humour of it. now weve told you our tale. tell us yours or. <death> and—." as he spoke his Brother and Steaton stepped up and stood between me and the door the first. swaggering the last sighing like a furnace. "Realy gentlemen you know who I am. I have lost my way amid these doleful lanes and have entered this house to ask the direction from hence to Georges Street." "Georges figs." interrupted Edward. "I tell you Sir if you come disturbing three honest combers in this way well roast you in the ovens thats all now <moot> this scene to Him! you know who and. why I know what'll be the end of you. —you see that door out of it this instant. tramp off for a great mole blind fool. Tim clap the door to or Ill baste you. —" Timothy instantly. as Edward Percy turned back. slammed the door full in my face with a "Oh may you be blessed" and. as I. staggered back. out of doors he struck up inside a real nasal psalm tune. I walked of as I best could inwardly cursing such a suspicious and. wanton insult. but comforting myself with the noise of a sudden quarrel. which as I walked from the yard I heard rise in the interior of this most singular combing shop.

		Feb. 18.
haworth		1834.
	haworth[6]	P B B.

Our last scene was laid in a combing shop in the back. slumms of the Verdopolitan Harbours our next we shall place in the interior of the House of Peers in the aristocratic heart of Verdopolis.[7] It was on the Evening of Monday. Feb. 8 that this august Assembly were met as usual. for discussion of buisness in their Noble and splendid Hall. The great chandeliers threw a golden light all over the galleries thronged with political characters. the benches filled with Kings and Noblemen and the wide open area. in the midst of that arena. of strife and discussion This evening the House was unusually well filled and the. crowds of Opposition commoners who sat gathered in the Gallerys with the alert watchfulness of the Lords on the same side of the benches betokened on their part that some measure of importance. was to come out that night. Ere any other person could rise to speak on any subject. up started. the Most Noble. Duke of Zamorna. and advanced into the middle of the House. He stood and cast his eyes hastily round the assembled Noblemen while his youthful fire and. magnificent person. inspired. in his freinds behind him as much confidence and energy as any speech could have done. With a haughty bow to his auditors he began.

My Lords, your Majestys, I am perfectly well. aware of how many there are among you how many even among the highest the very highest rank.

---

6   The "haworths" are in longhand.
7   Compare with pp. 31-34 of **The Wool is Rising**.

who however. much they may wish to hurry forward their workmen. in any of their undertakings. however willing then to speak. of the evils of procrastination the benifits of Industry. do yet when the hour of payment arrives. at once draw in their horns. trifle with those workmen. procrastinate and. shuffle and delay. They my Lords have no feeling but for the masters They wish others for them to work. they for others will never construe to pay.

To me my Lords this the Exordium[8] of my speech is at. least. well founded. and. exhibits only <thruth>. But I did not rise. to detain you with proverbs and truisms. I did not intend. to reproach you for your imperfections I. rose. to claim a right to claim my wages to demand justice to demand my own. Arthur Wellesly has not for the last quarter of a year. consented to live amid danger left his native city left his personal property put in constant peril his life. and delivered his soul up to the salvation of his country to be cast again on the successful conclusion of his struggles. into his past obscurity to be pushed once more behind his equals or to be as usual trampled underfoot by his inferiors. You my Lords know what during the course of the present war I have done what. My Noble Freind. beside me has done. what. General Thornton and General Castlereagh. and Mr Warner. and Mr Montmorency. and a hundred others. all have done. and since you know all I should not act as a fool were [I] to employ a night. aye. or a minute. in repeating over to you the hundred times told story of our perils and victorys. I shall just say, we have saved our country. and. <Gov> the days of abstract patriotism and unalloyed generosity are past. we do here demand. the wages of our. labour. Do you think. can you for one moment suppose that a couple of titles that a rank or two of. promotion or a couple of purses of copper. can satisfy myself. or Lord Northangerland. No. my Lords these toys will not satisfy us. and I demand we demand. a recompense more substantial. Their Majestys, Stumphs. and Moncay. are Sons of 12s. They are Kings. What have they done. I am A Son of a 12. I am not a King—what have I not done.? My Lords time wears late. moments press hard. much may yet be said. Then let me come to a conclusion. Hear me Kings and Noblemen of Verdopolis. I have rejoined a shattered Government. I have conciliated a divided army I. have. reconquered this City from its Enimies I have. totaly defeated. 200 000 foes. —Oh. your Majestys I have brought (booty)[9] into the Exchequer. 5 000 000£ of money—Hah! —Now. for these services rendered by me to my country. I demand from it the possession of my Feilds of battle I. demand. my Lords the provinces of Angria. Calabar. and Northangerland. and Gordon. to be yeilded up to me unconditionally and immediatly. in. just right to myself and my heirs and successors. in due and rightful sovereignty now and hereafter and. to this Effect I move that to morrow night February the 9th A D. 1834. a bill be brought forward in the Commons House of Parliament for the. direct conferring of the Kingdome of Angria upon his Grace the Most Noble Arthur Augustus

---

[8]   In classical rhetoric, the opening part of a speech, treatise, etc.
[9]   Branwell's parentheses.

Adrian. Wellesly. Duke of Zamorna Marquis of Douro and Lieut. General in the Verdopolitan Army."

The Orator as he concluded this singular speech looked round him triumphantly and. calmly resumed his seat. his Noble features wearing an expression of serene contempt as he surveyed the consternation and suprise. which reigned in the soul of every Nobleman present. except indeed his Noble freind and father in law the Earl of Northangerland. who smiling at the kindred character displayed in the speech just delivered. arose. ere any other Peer could occupy the floor of the house.

"My Lords Do you like Honesty? you say you do. well I will suppose you do. Ought it to be a violent supposition? —it is—well. if you like Hon[e]sty you like an honest speech you must like an honest man you must like the speech just delivered you must like its speaker you must like the Duke of Zamorna. Dont flinch my Lords for if you retract. an inch in this case. you must renounce. your admiration of frankness of plain dealing. That of course you will never do But perhaps. however you may like the <frankness> with which my My Noble freind who has just addressed you has delivered his opinions you yet may not like those opinions themselves. I grant this. yet hear me. Is not an open enimy better than a concealed foe. Is not an antagonist who tells you what he is about to do. preferable to the man who works against you in deceit. and will you not be more inclined. to believe that such a man. in spite of his seeming opposition does mean you no harm then should he silently attempt to undermine and covertly overthrow you. would you not at least. without anger receive his affirmation of "Gentlemen you think I war with you—I do not. You war with me. I wish you well. —I act for your good. walk with me. —" If you did answer to him. "No Sir We see your actions we see from where they rose to were they tend. You cannot favour us." You would not be able to say. "You are a Traitor and have conspired against us. You are not a boxer but an assassin." Now then my Lords I have gained t[w]o points in my argument You think my freind Honest in his intention be it good or bad. and you. should he prove that he means you no harm. will willingly believe him. My task then be it to prove it. then it is yours to believe.

How can the workman mean his master harm when after having done that masters bidding he comes to receive. his rightful wages. How can a Ministry mean the people harm when after having laid plans for the prosperity of their country they demand from that country means for carrying those plans into execution. How can a General mean his country harm. when after fighting for it from youth to age after endangering life and. loosing limb. in its service he comes to receive from it his hard earned reward I say how can Arthur Wellesly mean. Verdopolis harm when after casting himself as a sheild before his country in its hour of peril he turns round. to receive from her one kiss of love and gratitude. Come Verdopolis thou art young in years and fair in person. Thou art the queen of Nations and the pride of this Century. Thou art. the noblest of the Noble. the fairest of the fair. Ha! Verdopolis thou hast received and received too smilingly Old Men and hoary men of rude speech and. understanding. scarred men of war. I have seen thee. smile upon beings just ready to drop into their graves. And How my Queen canst thou now then frown upon that young and noble prince who has now thrown himself at thy feet to worship thee Thou art a woman Verdopolis and a lovely one. So being I can shape thy character I can measure thy. esteem. thou must favour Verdopolis thy noble Duke of Zamorna. —Ha but perhaps thou hast Guardians Keepers Duennas[10] Old Women. Ha! old women placed by thy Father to watch over thee and to keep thee in all thy ways.[11] Ha! thou queenly Damsel shall thy Noble Suitor then pine and sigh in hopeless despondency—hast thou not a will hast thou not means for exercising that will is womans ingenuity dead within thee. Wilt thou submit to a set of old dames. Come then thou canst. evade thy guardians thou canst oppose thy Duenna's thou wilt. oppose thy Duenna's thou wilt receive thy King!

My Lords you believe. that the Duke of Zamorna has done you service you believe that he deserves reward for that service. you think that. hes the son of a King he. can receive a Kingdom. and were there only these grounds to proceed upon you readily would give him a Kingdom. —But can we trust a whole people to our untried Sovereign. Can the Duke of Zamorna be fit to reign over the men of Angria. has he abilitys to weild a sceptre has he a character to pass him through the page of history. remember the words of our Constitution. a Baby can never reign over a Verdopolitan.

"Noblemen of. Africa. I saw the battle of Zamorna. I saw that dark and stormy evening when all around all the circle of a depopulated country the cannon of invading myriads threatened front and flank and rear of the Verdopolitan Armys I and[sic] experienced soldier shrunk when I heard the Artillery of Napoleon roar out their defiance. from the Batterys of Northangerland. till the longs lines of Zamorna took up the contest and swelled up in a doubled thunder. along the ranks of an advancing foe. Then my Lords. when all through a misty and windy night. our soldiers had to withstand. the Bayonets of Massena and Soult and. Ney and Lannes[12] and NAPOLEON when

---

[10] A chaperon or governess.

[11] Compare Psalm 91:11.

[12] For Massena and Soult, see vol. I, pp. 13, 369, 376.

Michel Ney, Duc d'Elchingen, Prince de la Moskova, marshal of France (1769-1815) was one of Napoleon's most respected Generals. He was instrumental in the victory at Elchingen, the surrender of General Mack at Ulm, and the victory at Friedland. He distinguished himself at the battle of Moskova and commanded the French rear-guard in the retreat from Moscow. After the Restoration he was made a peer, and in 1815 given command of the army sent to check Napoleon after his escape from Elba, but defected at the sight of his old leader. At Waterloo he commanded the last charge of the Old Guard. In December 1815 he was found guilty of treason and executed.

Jean Lannes, Duc de Montebello, marshal of France (1769-1809) rose from working-class origins to become a distinguished soldier in Italy and Egypt under

from every feild and hedge and high road dashed on us the fiery cavalry of. Murat.[13] then when. the strongest features of war seemed writhing in their wildest contortions and when everything that can distract the senses and. disorganise the mind stood fronting with a terrible array around us. I made it an essential buisness of mine to watch the behaviour and conduct of my fellow commander of my future King and what conclusions did I draw from that conduct and behaviour Why I. saw him in the darkest hour of Battle. cheer and rekindle the courage of a harrassed Army call back hope and rejoicing over. despair and doubting present a cheerful and. intrepid front to every point of Danger and. fight and defeat and rout and massacre. a huge host of inveterate and tyger hearted foes.

Gentlemen the Duke of Zamorna is made for extremes and up to this moment A splendid exterior of appearance. and. kingly loftiness of character and. mind formed on the model. of a conqueror. a life of brilliant performances. have all crowned the fate. of. the man destined as Africas cherished and darling hero. Come my Lords do your Saviour justice. or there is another bar to appeal to. you may pass upon the Duke of Zamorna an adverse sentence. you may vote him. unworthy the Kingdom of Angria But—"respice finem"[14] we will show your sentence to your country we will present your verdict to that tribunal. and. then looking to that other and higher Authority where will you and your. malice fall. Take then upon yourselves the credit of a good action. for you know how a forced favour looks from the wretch who gives it. Give to the Duke of Zamorna the Kingdom of Angria. and. my Lords that favour shall yeild you a glorious Harvest. a sevenfold return

I cordially second the the motion brought for ward by my Noble freind that A Bill for the Bestowal &c. —shall be brought before the House of Commons on February the 9th instant."—

A speech like this and spoken by such a speaker did not fall to the ground unheeded <During> all the time. that the Earl of Northangerland addressed the House you might indeed have heard a pin fall to the floor.[15]

Napoleon, becoming a General and commandant of the consular guard. He demonstrated great leadership at the battles Marengo, Austerlitz, Jena and Frieldland. In 1808 he was made commander-in-chief of French forces in Spain, but was mortally wounded during the retreat at Aspern in the failed attempt to cross the Danube, and died at Vienna.

[13] See vol. I, pp. 22, n. 4; 52, n. 12; 378, n. 27. For the battle referred to, see vol. I, pp. 374-400; 440-446.

[14] "Look to the end" or "Look before you leap."

[15] The text is followed by a sketch of the sun rising over land and water, with a ship and figures in the foreground—see Alexander and Sellars, p. 313.

THE.
WOOL IS RISING[1].
OR::
THE ANGRIAN ADVENTURER.
= A Narrative of the proceedings
= Of the Foundation of the —
= Kingdom of Angria ʃʃʃ

By

THE RIGHT HONOURABLE ˙ʃ˙
JOHN .ʃʃ˙
Baron Flower and Viscount Richton
Secretary of State for
Foreign Affairs::
Ambassador to the Court
of Angria FLS. &c &c
[Drawing of a
figure of Justice]

———————

Verdopolis printed and
published by.
Seargt Tree. =

And sold by all other Booksellers=

P B Brontë
June. 26. A D 1834.

[Drawing of the rising sun][2]

---

1   A hand-sewn booklet in blue paper covers, 11.5x18.5 cm, 24 pages (one blank) in the BL: Ashley 2469. Along the right-hand margin, opposite the title, in long hand appear the words "My Country." Presumably, Branwell is claiming proprietership of the Angrian narrative. In October, Charlotte began her narrative entitled "My Angria and the Angrians"—see Alexander CB, II, part ii, especially her sarcastic description of its founding on p. 240. Although June 26 is the date of completion, Branwell began the work in May—see the 1837 revised version of the poem in vol. III, entitled "The Rover."
2   The emblem of Angria.

CHAPTER I.

A Bright blazing Fire bickered[3] up the chimney and glittered upon the marble mantelpeice of. a snug and hansome study in Elrington Hall. The ample and closed velvet curtains the. thickly clustered. Bookshelves the rich carpet strewn with voulumes. the. glowing warmth of that fire above mentioned and. the soft fair light shed round the room from the glittering Luster which hung from the ceiling all contributed to give this apartment a strangly mingled air of Aristocratic splendour. and. calm country comfort. it was quite cheering to see the. blaze which glowed over the rich turkey rug[4] and upon the. glossy and well laden table. a great Newfoundland Dog sat cosily warming himself. by the fire his back casting its long dark shadow over the carpet into the very middle of the room even till met by the bright spot of light wich spread the floor just under the chandelier. upon the well cushioned. sofa. which united on the. left of the Door the fireplace whith table. while a corresponding seat closed in this sanctum on the right sat leaning back with his eyes fixed on the fire and his head on his hand the only human occupant of this cheery room cheery it might be to others it did not seem so to him. There he sat or rather reclined. one hand immersed in the curls of his hair the other small and aristocratic passed once or perhaps twice over his as aristocratic forehead. where two calm blue eyes gazed slowly and languidly round the room and his small and well chiselled mouth seemed only capable of assuming one single expression a settled but unobtrusive sneer This gentleman might be about 40 years of age. was very tall & thin his plain black dress and. quiet manner only seemed to give additional effect to a countenance which once seen could never be forgotten. I need not tell my readers his name. or station it was of course the Right Honourable Alexander Earl of Northangerland and Viscount Elrington. just visited with a fit of melancholy and shutting himself up to the solitude of his study From the "Dim sounds heard far remote[5] it was evident that his splendid. house was occupyied by some large and splendid party But the only sound of consequence which seemed to reach his ear were the soft. and most distant notes of music from the concert room and at once. the the. deep boom of the great bell of St Michaels tolling without the Hour of ten. his attention to the first sound was confined to a languid smile as a long solemn chord stole. on his ear. the second. voice. of the cathedral. roused [him] to a change of posture. a change merly to place one leg across the other and to take one arm from his head to his table. where while his hand fingered the leaves of some finely bound book and his face gazed calmly on the rousing fire he broke

---

3 To bicker means to quiver or flicker.
4 i.e., a turkish rug.
5 The phrase seems to be Branwell's.

into a few half connected sentences a few words or thoughts rather. expressed by the voice and intended for no ones ear not even for his own.

"What is it which has made me. so gloomy tonight I believe Im scarce. well—Ive shut myself here alone. with out cause or reason. I have slid from a gay and enlivening circle and am come. here to luxuriate in thoughts and feelings which I can never call sweet but often bitter. Now I know they say I am Misanthropic-I am not. they judge falsly. Some will cry I feel remorse—Ha here is a mistake a mistake indeed. I am neither. Simply it is I cannot always enjoy what always I would enjoy—for what should I feel a misanthrope I do not hate. man. certainly "Man delights not me"[6] but he does not plague me. I know that in all that party in all this city in all this country there is not one man whom I feel a freindship for. not one for whom on the score of feeling alone I should feel very greived. did I hear the cathedral bell just now tolling for his funeral. There is one of them that fiery young Duke.[7] for whom I sometimes catch myself. Fancying a freindship. but I catch myself on the sands I feel solicitous about him because my present fortunes are bound up with him I. do heartily wish him well because as he is so must I be. I like to see him exhibit all his pride and. splendour and. prosperity because. even If I may be a tool in his hands for his ends I know that he too [may] be a tool in my hands for mine. —for mine. —I care nothing about men in detail. in general I do for I know that it is only among them among their energy of character strength of nerve. tone. of feeling their rousing pursuits and paths of unquiet buisness that I can at all rouse myself into any height or sink myself to any depth with them only can I use my reason or unfold my character. Of me I know women have never had cause to complain. Men I admire hate and cannot live without. cannot could not exist without—But however I may smile at the general character of women yet to women In generall I feel as to woman in particular and there is not one Lady in the saloons I have left. from. 18 to —— come come dont mention ages Alexander whom I don't pretty passably. after all the sums are run to a total. Love. true I while down in the rooms this evening havent spoken a word to one of them But only have conversed with Zamorna Fidena Warner Montmorenci. &c Yet this does not in the slightest degree alter my sentiments They think me cold and dead but they do not think truely. —yet now perhaps I am. I know that I have been just opposite and many of them know it too. but am I cold now I dont think that I. that my mind can be. the outer covering the. flesh is, that is beyond all doubt. but because I disbeli[e]ve in religion because I scorn morality and justice and benevolence because I am not generous or warm hearted because to many I am unsocial because I sneer to all. I dont think that. I—am to be plunged amid ice and winter. and agedness. among Ladies truely I let Zamorna "the princly Zamorna" take the shine compleatly out of me and without on my part a struggle or sigh—Well I too have had my day and I would lengthen that day now

---

6   Compare Shakespeare's *Hamlet*, II, ii, 328.
7   The Duke of Zamorna.

till evening but the sun has set beyond all my power to rise. Hah. but though the Earth the Body has lost its beams. yet do they still glow and brighten. in the mind in the sky. If the earth. preserve this hard cold crust of clay yet there are men to be found yet who urge that in its centre all is molten heat and raging flame. though Northangerland. appear a freezing cheerless Nobleman. yet he himself can declare that he is a fiery ardent Ambitionist. aye thats a word. -and can Ambition exist without youth without the principal of youth. I dont know how a coal can give warmth without fire. were I not now rather otherwise than well I should feel "glory and joy around me shine"[8] tonight this night in the House of peers while in the act of doing what others what all others would be ashamed to do. in the act—in the act of. vindicating injustice of holding a sheild of brass of robbing my benefactors of. hah. of doing an act of benevolence. of benifiting a fellow man.!!! Fah.! of proving myself a tool of Zamorna. of proving Zamorna a tool of me. In the Late war they say I seemed miserable. and I beli[e]ve them but. Volo I was not miserable at least not always. my cold and wretched outside. covered a delight in the scenes of men around me in the scenes of tumult and danger and destruction I knew that I must here fall or rise that I could not stand still. the earth was rocking all round me and my stance shakes as all round me shakes. well this—this state is my Elysium Hah its the only Paradise I shall ever see—I may then be constantly harassed with fears of death. a little defeat may enrage me. the advancement of an opponent a rival an enemy a Fidena. may half madden me and yet there is enough <lightness> to keep the ship from sinking enough sunshine to warm me in this winter the horrors of actual conflict produce a silent quiet joy the. thoughts future steps gained points accomplished produces a tumultous excitement. —Hah-Faugh! —Hang me. and the world too!"

Northangerland dragged a book toward him across the table. opened at a blank leaf and taking a pen began to scribble. lines as fast as his practised hand could move

> Backward I look upon my life.
> And see one waste of storm and strife
> One wrack of sorrows hopes and pain.
> Vanishing too arise again.
>   That life has passed through evening where
> Continual shadows veild my sphere
> From youths horizon upward rolled
> To lifes meridian dark and cold.
> The gathering clouds of vengeance. form.
> In many a sudden pouring storm.
> Yet forming in the Silence of the tomb.
>   Save when the sudden lightning flash

---

8   Compare Luke 2:9, and the hymn "While Shepherds watched their flocks by night."

Save when the awakning Thunder crash.
Rolled through the desert heart or glanced across its gloom
Yes prides, hates, lightning and ambitions thunder.
Alone could rend that Iron heart asunder.

I would not praise myself or deem
Me greater, better, than I seem.
I know that I am dead and cold.
My fortunes black my spirit old

Yet there are echoes in my heart that well
Can answer to the awakning Bugle's swell.
There is a feeling in me which can warm
In the stern senates strife or ocean storm
Gods wrath mans hatred my own misery
A Foemans glance a womans smiling eye.
All these may fall may centre all on me

64   Yet like yon Niger surging to the sea.
128   Can only swell the torrent of my soul
33   Can only urge me faster x x x x x x x x
                x x x x x x x x x x x x x

Northangerland stopped here for an instance and again commenced scratching the
paper seemingly on a new train of thought.

Why do I thus my spirit guage and scan
Am I then other than a common man
I am——Volo! an Idiot. ——
            x x x x x x x

Sail fast sail fast my gallant ship thy ocean thunder round thee
At length thour't in thy paradise thine own wide heaven around thee.
The morning flashes up in light and strikes its beams before
Where yon wide streaks of lustre bright lie like a fairy shore.
The day presages storm and strife yet what need. percy care.
Thy deck hath born him through the storm shall bear him through the war
The Thundering winds are swelling up and whistle through thy shroud
Yet overhead in the iron. sky how sullen sleeps each cloud.
Lo! yon feirce blast hath swept the seas and covered them with foam
Yet shall it force the[e] on thy way wherever thou mayst roam.
The rich but feebled Merchant ship may quiver to this gale.
For it shall guide thee to thy prey and swell thy eager sail
    When Night and tempest gather up and shroud the stormy sky
The timid sheep may look to heaven with an imploring eye.
But while they flock. in frightend. haste and. crowd the narrow way
What cares the lordly Lion then who pounces on his prey.
The storm has but his reaper been to gather in his grain.
And thus to thee my ship shall be this hoarse resounding main.
Look Look beneath yon thick black cloud. on yon dark line of water.
A fair and clustered Argosie just gathered for the slaughter

See how the spread sails glimmer white. as scudding far before.
They steering in one steady line fly oer the watery roar.
     Now rouse ye then my gallant men. rouse up with hearty cheer.
Quick clear the deck crowd all your sail your cannon bring to bear
My arms my arms my trusty pike. of quick and bloody blow.
My pistols black my sabre white. -then onward for the foe.
Ha! Connor Gordon steer ye right the winds confuse them now
As 'mid the geese an eagle's flight. amid them drive my prow
I stand upon my steady deck. around me flies the foam
My pirate ship[9] skims in the blast across her ocean home
The fleet, the Argosie before. with furled or shivered sail.
Like helpless swans together crowd and tremble to the gale
Now light your matches. —from a smoke bursts up one crash of thunder
Rebellows from the clouds above and the white surges under.
They know us then! They know the Hawk. But dread hath paled each
     [brow]
Furl in your sails. your irons cast we are full. upon them now.
And fastned by our trusty hooks yon freighted galleon lies.
Her heisitating broadside bursts in thunder to the skies
We heed it not. I. forward rush upon her shaking deck.
And. all my band of gallant hearts have followed at my beck.
Now mid the thickning smoke and sleet one mighty tumult reigns
The sparkles flash across each eye. the blood boils through the veins
Man dashed on man. in trampled blood. strew thick each groaning plank
Unheard unseen the sabres clash amid each gory rank.
Where am I. dashed into the hold upon a strangling foe.
All men and smoke and shouts above. a writhing wretch below.
He dies I. rise and grasp a rope—am on the deck once more.
And Percys arm and Percys sword still bathe that deck with gore.
An hour of tempest passes by the Galleon blazes now.
And. smoke and slaughter crowds the deck. and heaps the bending prow
Our swords seem grown into our hands our eyes glance fiery light.
And heaped beneath us scattered lie the wrecks of that wild fight
"Ye have done your work most gallantly-that precious merchandise.
In haste convey upon our deck, our just and well earned prize.
Then fire the ship and follow me to our own deck again
To chase the coward wanderers across yon stormy main."
     The evening sinks in sullen light across the heaving sea.
And sees the "Rover" oer its waves plough on her gallant way.
While far behind across the surge a blaze of blood red light.

---

9   Percy is recalling his days as a pirate on the "Rover"—see **The Pirate** in
vol. I. See the 1837 revised version of the poem, entitled "The Rover," in vol.
III.

Drifts on to windward. shrouding round. the relic of that fight.
I see a—far the blackned masts stand gainst the flaring flame.
And high in heaven the heavey smoke curls oer its blazing frame
Those fires discharge its cannonry with sullen sounding boom
Till like a bloodred Moon it sets behind its watery tomb.

Northangerland had written thus far when he yawned, stopped, and without taking one glance at what he had written. turned again to the fire. one hand remaining on the table gathering up its fingers to tear out the fly leaf from the book in which he had been scribbling when he felt it arested by a slender hand from behind. turning hastily round his eyes met those of His Lady the Countess. whose majestic figure presented itself. before the yet more majestic one of the young Duke of Zamorna quizzing him through an eyeglass "Take your finger from that trash Zenobia" said the Earl to the Countess but upon her silent refusal he calmly resigned it to her with a sort of incipient sneer at his own performance.one would have thought him the most obedient spouse on record. but when the Duke tapped him on the shoulder he started up as if to dare him by his own even superior stature."Well brazen dog and what are you pestering me here for" It was to flee from your abominable countenance that I left the room." "Ah a wise action truly. I am come sir upon a brazen buisness. My lord be pleased to create Angria."[10] "Hah. hang Angria create it! Deluge it-redeem it! destroy it. Follow me."So muttering he. strode out of the room. "Well Zenobia what have you got there." asked the [Duke of] Zamorna laughing to the Countess whose attention seemed concentred upon what she held in her hand. She handed it to him in silence and he after an attentive perusal laid it on the table. "An abominable handwriting" then after a pause. "A strange man. Have you got anything else of this sort. Zenobia" "Oh no Arthur" was the reply. I do indeed wish I had. how grieved I am you cannot tell that Elrington has not based his fame or at least part of it like the Heroes of antiquity like the heroes of literary greatness." "Why Zenobia the man cannot write 6 lines on end without running himself into instant contradiction to what he has said before" "Ah but mark that when he has got full into a subject there are no collisions no stops. the fight of the pirate sweeps on as resistlessly as its <u>hero</u> as I may term the vessel its subject." The Duke again looked at the paper. and then said "Well Zenobia let us hear more of him. more of me. —Drive to the house of peers This night must the Angrian creation be concluded or destroyed To say the truth our struggles through the day have been desperate to beat up recruits and now on the last reading the sixth. day. as Northangerland has it. our fate must be decided I suppose. However I expect your divine prescence to shed light upon our deliberations." Zamorna. left the apartment and prepared to depart. His carriage was ready and mounting it he drove off. wheeling along the crowded and brilliant streets till. the. House of Peers presented its imposing screen of columns to the

---

[10] That is, the kingdom of Angria.

gas light and moonlight around him. The square in which it stood was choked with an eager and excited multitude. amid whose wedged woven lines even the Duke of Zamorna himself. could scarcly force his way. Yet upon the splendid chariot and dashing Horses of the Duke being recognised amid the confusion. a shout rose which rang through the clear midnight and rattled against the lofty buildings with. a true applauding thunder. The moving of arms and waving of hats swung the whole crowd from side to side and tossed them like a sea in a tempest. and upon. the Dukes alighting at the front of the steps and. turning his noble countenance to them with glad and approving smile. the clapping and shouting and fighting was recommenced. and the Darkness was forced again to return its echoe. For himself Zamorna entered the Hall. and walked unconcernedly to his place. that Hall through its whole. vast and domed circle. glittered in one blaze of light. the dark uneven pavement of black. and crowded Nobility. rising like an amphitheatre almost to the floor of the gallerys. nobly set off. the superstructure of white and shining wall and dome starred with its clusters of light. Far before at the upper end. five gorgeous seats[11] attracted instant attention the middlemost. and. largest which held a globe suspended over it. unoccupied. but in the others a Verdopolitan eye could with a glance recognise the bald and lofty brow of the northern the calm artful eye of the Southern and the frank if it dared be countenance of the Rossian potentate. beneath or almost on a level with these. a hundred Aristocrats countenances were turned up with half disguised but breathless attention to the person then addressing the House. In whose pale features and tall black figure. Zamorna right soon distinguished his trusty fere Northangerland.He had latly seen [him] sitting in his own study out of humour with all men and employed in scribbling lines on paper and. now. he beheld him giving laws to the nation and railing upon the Nobles of Verdopolis "My lords" he was saying when Zamorna first caught his loud impetous voice.

   "My lords can the workman mean his master harm when after having done that masters Bidding he comes to receive his rightful wages How can a Ministry mean a Nation harm when after having laid plans for the prosperity of their country they should from that country demand means for carrying those plans into execution How can a General mean his Army harm when after having concerted a series of maneuvres. to defeat his enimy he should but request from that Army the action of all their energys when that action would free them from defeat disgrace raise them to honour to advancement. And I say to you how can Arthur Wellesly mean the country harm when after having cast himself. as a sheild before his country in her hour of peril he but—the hour of defeat averted. —turns round to beg from her one kiss of love and gratitude Come Verdopolis thou art young in years and lovely in person thou art the queen of Nations and the Pride of thy Century thou art the Noblest of the Noble the fairest of the fair. —Ha Verdopolis thou hast received and received too smiling Old men and hoary

---

[11] The seats of the four kings and the Archbishop of the Verdopolitan Union.

men. of rude speech and understanding scarred men of war I have seen thee smile upon beings just ripe for their graves. and how my Queen canst thou now frown upon that young and Noble Prince who has just thrown himself at thy feet to worship thee Thou art a woman Verdopolis and a lovely one but so being I can gauge thy character I can measure thy esteem Thou wilt favour—Verdopolis— thy noble Duke of Zamorna—Ha but perhaps thou hast Guardians keepers duennas old women yes my lords old women. placed by thy father too watch over thee and keep thee in all thy ways[12] Ha thou queenly damsel shall thy noble suitor then pine and sigh in hopeless despondency—Hast thou not a will hast thou not means for exercising that will is a womans ingenuity dead within thee wilt thou then submit to this company of old dames come then thou canst evade thy guardians thou canst oppose these Duennas thou wilt oppose these keepers thou will receive thy King—!

"My lords you believe that the Duke of Zamorna has done you service you believe that he deserves reward for that service you believe that he is the son of a King and that thus he is qualified to receive a kingdom. and as in this case these are the only true grounds to proceed upon you would you would readily give to him a kindgom But can we trust a whole people to an untried sovereign is the Duke of Zamorna qualified to reign of[sic] the people of Angria Has he the abilitys to weild a sceptre has he character to pass him through the ordeal of the future—remember the words of our Constitution "A baby can never rule over a Verdopolitan."

"My lords I saw the Battle of Zamorna. I saw that rough and stormy evening when round all the circle of a depopulated country the cannon of invading thousands threatned front and flank and rear of Verdopolitan Armies when with the spirit of Napoleon before us a harassed and uncombined army around us and an unsettled and divided city behind us. we the Generals of Verdopolis were forced to bear up against the overwhelming and victorious numbers of the advancing foe. Then my Lords when through a misty and gloomy night our soldiers were assailed by the Bayonets of Ney and Soult and Lannes and Massena. when from every hedge and highroad dashed in upon us the serried cavalry of a Murat then when the strongest features of war seemed writhing in their wildest contortions and when everything that can distract the senses and disorganise the mind stood fronting with a terrible array around us then had I not noble scope to judge of the behaviour and conduct of my fellow commander of my future King and what conclusion did I draw from that conduct and behaviour—Why when I saw him in the darkest hour of battle cheer and rekindle the exhausted courage of his army call back hope to the despairing and plant Life over death when I beheld him in one short night defeat and crush and. dissipate all the plans of Napoleon then my Lords I knew that I saw a son of Wellington a man destined to be a KING

---

[12]   See p. 22, notes 10 & 11.

My lords the Duke of Zamorna is made for Extremes and up to this hour a splendid exterior of appearance and a mind formed in the mould of a conqueror a Force and loftiness of character and a life of Brilliant performances have all contributed to crown the fate of him destined as Africas cherished and darling hero

My Lords do you your Saviour justice or there is another bar to appeal to pass upon the Duke of Zamorna an adverse sentence vote him unworthy to be your king But—respice finem—I will show your verdict to a higher tribunal I will present your sentence to your country and then before the judgment of that authority where will you and your mandates fall—Take then to yourselves the credit of a good action for well you know how a forced favour looks from the wretch who bestows it—Present to the Duke of Zamorna the Kingdom of Africa[13] and that one favour shall yeild you a sevenfold Harvest of return. —"

The most deafning cheers from the Angrians even from the Gallery and the square followed the conclusion of this speech and Northangerland sat down wiping his forehead with his white handkercheif. and stunned with the applause which rung above and around him.

Zamorna now started up. he advanced into the middle of the House & with a haughty bow to his auditors thus began "My Lords, your Majesties, I am perfectly well aware of how many there are amongst you, who, however much they may wish to hurry forward their workmen in their undertakings however willing then to speak of the evils of procrastination, the advantages of industry, do yet when the hour of payment arrives at once recoil, trifle with those workmen, shuffle procrastinate & delay. Come my Lords this the exordium of my speech is at least well—founded, and exhibits only the truth; but I did not rise to detain you with proverbs & truisms, I rose to claim, a right, to take my wages, to ask justice, to demand my own; Arthur Wellesly has not for the last quarter of a year consented to live amid dangers absent, from his native city from his personal property, his life in continual peril his very soul delivered up for the salvation of his country, to be cast from successful conclusion of his struggles into his ancient obscurity, to be thrust again behind his equals to be trampled underfoot once more by his inferiors. You my Lords know what during the course of the late war I did, what my noble relative beside me did what Thornton, & Castlereagh, & Warner, & Montmorency and a hundred others did, & since you know it, it would be folly to employ a night, aye or a minute in telling over to you the oft repeated story of our dangers & sufferings & victories. I shall just say we have saved our country, & (for the days of abstract patriotism and unalloyed generosity are past) we come now to demand the wages of our labour. Do you think that a pair of titles or a lift or two on the ladder of promotion or a couple of purses of copper can satisfy myself or Lord Northangerland No. my lords these toys will not satisfy us & we demand a recompense more substantial. Their Majesties Stumpz and Moncai are sons of Twelves they are Kings. what

---

13 "Angria" obviously intended.

have they done? I am the son of a Twelve and I am no King. What have I not done? My lords the night wears late, Time presses hard let me then come to a conclusion, Hear me Kings & nobles of Verdopolis! I have re-joined a shattered Government I have conciliated a divided army, I have ransomed a Kingdom from its captors I have utterly defeated 200,000 foes! O your Majesties, I have brought booty into the exchequer 5,000,000 of pounds sterling. Hah! Now for all this I demand my fields of battle, I demand the provinces of Angria, Calabar & Zamorna to be yielded up to me in uncontrolled sovereignty in just right for myself & my heirs now & for evermore, And to this effect I move that tomorrow night February 4 AD 1834 a bill be brought forward in the Commons house of Parliament for the direct conferring of The Kingdom of Angria upon Field-Marshal the most Noble Arthur Augustus Adrian Wellesly, Duke of Zamorna, Marquis of Douro & Lieutenant of the Verdopolitan Armies.

The Noble Orator as he concluded this unparrarelleled. speech looked round him triumphantly and then coolly resumed his seat his Magnificant features wearing an expression of serene contempt as he surveyed the consternation and suprise which seemed in a greater or less degree to rule the countenance of every on[e] present except indeed his noble freind and father in law the Earl of Northangerland. who smiling at the kindred character displayed in the speech just delivered again rose ere another peer could occupy the floor of the house.

"My lords do you like Honesty you say you do—well Ill suppose you do—ought it to be a violent supposition? —it is." (a violent cough from Zamorna) Well if you like Honesty you like an honest speech you like an honest man you like the speech just now delivered you like its speaker. you like the Duke of Zamorna. —Dont flinch Dont flinch. for retract a step in this case you must retract all. and-the Noblemen of Verdopolis the Kings of Verdopolis hate frankness and plain dealing! —what will the world. say. —Hah. should that world here[sic] of it it will be unpleasant for me for self. in the first instance. because ere the first burst of suprise be over I shall irredeemably be branded as a tale bearer and false witness. The Noblemen and Kings of Verdopolis—practice double dealing this would be to improb[ab]le an assertion—one too little countena[n]ced by past conduct to to gain credence. untill. I its first promulgator. should. be. irretreviably sunk in the worlds opinion. —(a loud cheer from the freinds of Zamorna. —met by a countercheer from the. Ministerial benches)— well then Im right. you all applaud me. So my lords. for your own sakes for my own sake I do implore you not to reject my first proposition not to reject our Duke of Zamorna. and you say you dont with that I am satisfied. I know to well the always manly and open decision of your conduct ever to doubt your first word. and assertion. I say I am satisfied you will give Angria to Zamorna. and for your timely Determination I do return you my most fervent acknowledgement. —My Lords let the Question be put."

Here as the Noble speaker resumed his seat a deafning shout of question Question arose from Zamorna's party. but met by the most vigorous No No from the numerous and Influential ministerials. Earl St Clair arose.[14]

"My lords I do deplore this spirit of. indecourous and irrational spirit which seems from what inlet I will not say to have crept in among us. ere the question upon this Bill be put ere we give any opinion upon its merits or demands let us calmly and coolly consider and weigh those merits or demerits. I ask you all shall we the highest department of the Verdopolitan Legisllature put our signature to and pass in to law a measure framed and calculated not only to dismember the Kingdoms of Africa for the present generation not only to put a premium upon insubordination rebellion and immorality but to give to the whole world for all time to come one huge undying precedent to the violation of rights and laws and constitutions." (tremendous cheering and dissapprobation) The Premeir went on to show the important consequences which wether good or bad must inevitably flow from the passage of this bill now before the house. He pointed out first the danger which must result from a new and sudden excitement arising in a nation only just recovering from the horrors of invasion and the fever of war of. the great commercial speculation and almost certain following Bankruptcy which would arise from the sanguine eagerness to throw money into this new channel of commerce and circulation. He adverted to the nest of demagogues and traitors which would certainly be formed in a country so new so unsettled and so insubordinate as Angria would be He affirmed that the eastern side of Verdopolis was already by far to insecure and exposed to too much danger from invaders beyond it to be given into the hands and placed under the Government of anyone save the great general Dynasties He apologised for his venturing to touch on a topic of such nicety and delicacy but he really must pause to reflect upon the madness and the folly of. giving in free grant a country placed under such circumstances and with such prospects into the despotic hands of a young man scarcly yet of age and well known for qualities far from allied to prudence and discretion (loud cries of Order cheering and confusion) Noble lords called. to order but he affirmed himself not out of order he was pointing to them in all its bearings the course and consequences of the question before them then he strongly animadverted upon the characters of the probable corulers of the unborn Kindgom and perdicted to a measure arising from dissatisfied Ambition conducted by Headstrong impetouosity and crowned by utter violation of the Verdopolitan Constitution a fate which always has been and allways will be the ruin of such eager wild and undigested projects ruin not only to the originators but to all things around them. "My lords" said the Earl after citing a variety of

---

[14] Branwell seems to have forgotten that he had St Clair executed in vol. I— see pp. 428-29—but then he also ressurected Alexander Rougue—see vol. I, p. 240, n. 2. Charlotte seems to have ignored the execution, for the Earl appears in "High Life in Verdopolis," written in February and March 1834—see Alexander CB, II, part ii.

passages from our statutes and constitution which went incontestibly to prove that to dismember and divide the Kingdoms would be to overthrow a fundamental principle in our Government "My lords perhaps what I have now said may yet prove of no Office to you perhaps however you agree to the truth of these our facts and assertions You may think that old age is worthless and old institutions are not to be regarded but I tell you take heed how you spurn at the foundations of all your own power and priveliges But I will think better of you I will think better of your country and however strongly I reprobate the conduct of a rash and insolent traitorous faction I do hope and believe that you the Noblemen and citizens of Verdopolis will yet determine to arrest the progress of unblushing profligacy to uphold your al[t]ars and your thrones Yes my Lords the waves of the Atlantic do often dash upon the shores of Africa but never yet did they rage so wildly as does now the tide of Innovation around the Antient Institutions of Africa But as the white cliffs[15] of Verdopolis have hitherto withstood the fury of the tempests so may hereafter the far whiter and purer bulwarks of the Constitution in like manner withstand the wild swell of popular madness and the hoarse Howlings of Democratical innovation"

The Noble Premeir sat down amid a perfect chaos of. hisses and cheering and long before the uproar had subside[d] Viscount Castlereagh was upon his legs In a vigorous and energetic speech he characterised the words of the Prime Minister as the hesitation and <rapacity> of greedy and retaining senility and ceased by recommending to the house one only course of safty. the course of concession.

Continued uproar followed the Noble Viscounts speech. and scarcly subsided even when the Duke of Fidena arose This great man. in a speech of great length which we do greave it our utter inability to insert. and in words all flowing with the deepest sagacity and most commanding eloquence Advocated the concession to the Duke of Zamorna of his Demand of the Angrian Kingdom but only on condition that it should not as was stated in the Bill be considered as no part or parcel of the Glasstown country but should yet remain like Monkeys and Stumps lands complete in Government but. yet united to the General Union The Duke strengthened his position by a number of Arguments of surprassing weight and decision he concluded by proposing to that effect an Amendment The feeling produced by Fidena's Astonishing speech was overwhelming 20 different speakers got up and spoke after wards but they positivly were not even heard so powerful was the confliction of sentiment upon the Amendment and bill. The Aristocrats were enraged at Fidenas motion. the Angrians scarcly less so at last up starts the Earl. [of] Northangerland himself. and in a short speech. of <ut most> energetic Argument. <embellishes> and fixes his seal to Fidena's Amendment concluding however by a Nauseous string of sneers at the Duke himself."Hang thee" he concluded "thy Amendment thou fool and tyrant has saved us and ruined thee Vote for us my freinds and we conquer." The Duke of

---

[15]   An adaptation of the symbolic nature of the white cliffs of Dover.

Zamorna. also concurred with an eager. appearance in the Earls opinion he boldly
put the question Strangers were directly excluded and after a long time spent by
those without in intense and breathless agitation the doors were again thrown
open after the rush of entrants was over dead silence reigned through the Hall the
Chancellor in a clear voice read the numbers of the division for the Bill—O."
against it. 230. For Fidenas Amendment. 270. Majority 20. Thus passed the
Amended Angrian bill. Fidenas motion was paradoxical though wise by it
Verdopolis was saved from anarchy the Angrian faction from immediate defeat
and future Bloody triumph. The city received the news in a storm of confusion

CHAP II

Among the vast crowds which poured forth from the hot and steamy
atmosphere of Parliament into the cold. raw air of the nightlike morning. and
surrounded their respective carriages or drove off through the multitude. with
wheels of aristocratic thunder. it was easy for the thousands gathered round that
House to view their two heroes and champions Zamorna and Northangerland.
The statly chariots of the Kings and Ministers swept past ungreeted by look or
murmur but the moment the plumed crest and. bold bright eye of Zamorna. or
the hatted head. and. sensitive nose of Northangerland were distinguished amid
their attendant crowd of freinds and supporters one. hearty vehement cheer from
all that vast square and its long lanes and. <feeders> proclaimed with trumpet
voice the joy of universal Verdopolis. There stood on the great steps the KING
OF ANGRIA. and well indeed did he beseem his dignity his triumphant features.
his marble forehead shadowed by the black military Bonnet his mouth. smiling
with. unfeigned joy in victory. his statuesque and Appolo-like form. —truly
on[e] could almost fancy him shining with the light of present and future
victory. And then when the highborn and. Noble crowd of beauty. which had just
ornamented the gallery. during the debate. and whose chariots were now waiting
to receive them. surrounded. him. under that mighty portico. and. beamed from
so many radiant eyes and breathed from so many lips. of. loveliness. their
unaffected and ardent. and enthusiastic joy at his. sudden and proud elevation
Then Indeed who could refuse to the young King of Angria his title. Conqueror.
and lord of Venus and Victory. The lily hand of one Princes[s] or Duchess or
Countess. following another Insinuated itself within his. own to awaken him to
the. silver voiced congratulation which followed its touch but while he thus
stood in the full enjoyment of his morning of conquest. his fellow labour[er] and
distinguished supporter Northangerland. had strode downward a few steps from
the pillared. platform. to converse with his freinds the. Angrians from the
Commons house. who in knots of 2 or 3 Dozens were wedging through the
crowd. from their just dissmissed assembly to meet here their King and. director.
The slender figure of W H Warner. his pale feautures restless with anxiety the
tall. brawny. height of Montmorenci with opened brow. and sini[s]ter feature the
squat ungainly but sagacious Morley. and the. firm hearty. countenance of
General Thornton. these were the forms which surrounded and conversed with

Northangerland. The almost only smile of Delight which dawned on that mans features was when he cast his eye on the two lines of men which trooped from their apex the great Door of the house. and diverged on each side of the animated group of Zamorna and his own anxious cluster These were the Ministerials passing to their carriages with black looks and. downcast faces. and a sight like this could and did awaken the feeling of. triumph in Northangerland. which joy and congratulation could seldom raise. he turned to them with a whitened face and a more ghastly sneer and then again plunged. into plans and consultations with his fellow statesmen.

But while the head and right arm of Angria were thus engaged. upon the. steps. a feeling if possible of greater enthusiasm reigned among the crowds below incessant shouting and clapping of hands intermixed as usual in Verdopolis with a turn up "turn out." pitching bit" leap frog" or tossing match" kept all that wide chaos of humanity in one round of roaring confusion. and just as the Duke of Zamorna and his freind Northangerland. prepared to dismount the steps. one simultaneous rush was made to ward their carriages the horses were taken of and a hundred brawny arms. were instantly on the traces and. while the torrent hurried Northangerland and Zamorna into the glossy vehicles they were. both. whirled along the street with a rattle and a voice of thunder.

It was now grey morning the sun had not risen but the lamps were out. and the still sharp air sleeping hitherto in cold dead slumber. hang of[16] all this mighty city. but in the streets which swept away toward Wellesly House and Elrington Hall their inhabitants could hear coming from afar. a noise gathering and. swelling like the sound of a torrent far remote among the wild hills of Central Africa. anon detached groups and masses of Fellows. began to rush past down the pavement then. at the upper bend of the magnificent parade. a great black mass blocked up the. road from side to side. sending forth. before it its feelers in thicker and broader masses. instantly and ere it approached. the Victoria Square was on[e] sea of shouting heads the rails in front of its lordly Mansions were. hung with people. and. as the great tide of populace burst into this magnificent estuary and crushed to the wall its former occupants. on[e] long loud clear and unbroken shout the very topmost voice of a city rang up and echoed as if from iron against the the clear stern heaven above. ere it could die into silence. that voice was taken up and. swelled again by the thousands who pressed forward from the streets far beyond. LONG LIVE THE KING OF ANGRIA. "Long live. the Noble Zamorna. and Hurra for Northangerland long live Northangerland. —were the universal watchwords of that huge jarring multitude. The noble object of all this gratulation had. dismounted from his chariot and now stood on the steps of his own magnificent mansion. turning unplumed. toward that Ocean. with his own bright hair wreathed round features flushed with. triumph and animation. he spoke to these his enthusiastic admirers. "This morning my brave fellows has proved a glorious commencement of my reign and. I assure

---

[16] "hung over" obviously intended.

you that it shall be my study henceforward. to follow a pathway. as noble as the gate which has led to it. You this morning have proved that you have not forgotten Arthur Wellesly. and though. he may forget his Kings and. your aristocracy Arthur Wellesly will prove that he can never never forget you." as Zamorna uttered these words with an animation of tone and feeling which thrilled through all round him he. turned to welcome as Queen of Angria. the lovely being. which advancing from the Noble portico now stood beside him. —But so soon as the immense crowd perceived. her. a new shout rose up and a new tumult thundered along the huge bulks of buildings which frowned round this lively tempest and when. the grand uproar began to die. away and the voices to become audible at least his own to each respective shouter. the cries of Long live. the Duchess of Zamorna. long live the Daughter of Northangerland. joy to the wife of our Hero. Long reign the Queen of Angria". broke upon the ear in mixed and melodious confusion. The Beautiful object of all this applause Apollo's own favourite Goddess. advanced a few steps forward. and the cries sank instantly. her Percian countenance. was. animated almost like her Noble Husbands and her silver voice trembled with emotion as she said. yet with clear and. distinct emphasis. "The applauses you have bestowed on my Husband should have proved amply sufficient for me. But, since you have. found me deserving or a seperate applause. I must let my future actions show that gratitude which I know my plain words can never do." So speaking and with a graceful inclination of her. beautiful head. she retired to the side of. the. Duke. that. pride and. glory of Verdopolis.

But an ominous countenance now appeared. —The Earl. stood in his open chariot. and That pale face those flashing eyes. the expanded nostril and the. lip. curled in its inimitable sneer. —presented an appearance. —looked like a meteor which had so often amid such crowds as these. portended. bloodshed and. havoc and and wide wasting misery. when that tall statly figure and that. ominous countenance appeared above the crowd one could on beholding it have fancied they [heard] the cannon thundering behind them and. the cavalry dashing in among. them. "Hah!" said Northangerland in tones that would be heard "Ha. you are ready my freinds in your applauses—can the arm second the tongue— well happiness fall on you for your services this day. I see those services were not feigned and when the bold hearts around one beat so strongly I know that they never beat in vain. well. you have given us your countenance. in this our hour of prosperity—would you have done the same in an hour of discomfiture. you have thundered out you[r] united plaudits upon the King of Angria would you have done so upon the Duke of Zamorna. The House of Peers has. by dint of argument and reason and threatning and scorn of reason at length recognised the right of that young General to the throne of the country which his valour saved from death. and you with you[r] united voices seal that recognisance to [be] sure. but say had the House. of Peers. sent to its benches Deaf men men who would not hearken who could not hear and would not understand. had the Duke of Zamorna by them been refused his claim and been denied his Kingdom. why what would you have said then. but saying would have mattered little. What would you have done then—Aye what would have done then. Ha. Ill tell you what you would have done. what you should have done. you would have raised the price of pears. —you would have devoured such a number of fruit that a scarcity would have followed. well and there stands a Physician who would have preserved you from Cholera Morbus.[17] Ha however this has not happened and let those enjoy their lives who if they do not deserve them do yet seem so wishful to secure them.

Verdopolitans. (this word was uttered with sudden and stirring vehemence. Rogue was on a new tack)—Verdopolitans. you are slaves. you are in Africa. you are in Egypt. Ha. are you yourselves then Egyptians I see a small and chosen company who with their pillar of fire above them. are even now about to depart from among you to pass Eastward. and. reach the land of promise. their Caanan of rest. —Well I speak not to them though I am one of them. They have gained their desire. I speak to you to my countrymen. yet lying in darkness and oppressed by their relentless taskmasters. Oh. my countrymen. it was to the East that the Israelites journeyed when leaving Egypt. for a happier resting place. It was from the East. that. the light of. promise rose and broke of a dark and. dying world. —So has it been so will it be. it is to the East that I journey that that young General journeys toward his resting place. —And—It shall be from the East that. He will dispense. a hope and a promise over benighted Africa. Look. Verdopolitans look over the buildings of your city look toward Angria. See that bright sun just rising on the horizon. rising I know now on the fair plain and. bright river of our Jordan Our Calabar. —Look Verdopolitans Look. toward the East. Look toward Angria. See that bright Pheobus.that bright Zamorna.just rising on the horizon. rising over the fair plain and bright river of our Jordan our Calabar. I have often talked to you of morning and here at last is morning come. from the West. sunk your Evening sunk long ago and. a night of darkness has followed in its wake but. now I may fairly say. the daylight dawns once more. where then is the man so blind as not to see it the man so foolish as not to take advantage of it w[h]ere is he who will cling to night and will strive now to up hold the Darkness.

Moses left not an Israelite behind when he left Egypt for Palestine.

Zamorna must leave a million Glasstowners behind when he leaves Twelves Land for Angria. —Must he Glasstowners. no he must not. rise up and fear not. What is it you fear. Ha.! truly I had forgot. The firstborn must be slain. A RED SEA MUST BE PASSED ERE YOU REACH YOU CANAAN AND VICTORY—!"[18]

The Satanic Orator. sat down in his chariot with a bitter sneer he only looked round to see that he had done his work. and then amid the most deafning

---

[17] According to the OED, a disorder attended with bilious diarrhoea, vomiting, stomach ache, and cramps, generally occuring in the late summer and early autumn. Also known as "British" or "Summer" cholera.

[18] Compare Exodus, chapters 5-14.

and unceasing shouts from the excited and enthusiastic multitude he was whirled of through the choked up streets to his Noble Elrington Hall. He alighted amid those shouts three or four times repeated. turned on the steps to the Multitude and with the words "Remember your Land of promise" turned round and walked into the Hall. Here while the applauses and tumults still thundered round the building he strode hastily into the Breakfast room and violently shut the door behind him The Countess who just returned from the House of Peers and and the company of Zamorna. stood at one of the great Embayed windows gazing upon the tossing waste of Humanity below her turned round and advanced as she saw the Earl her. Noble countenance and dark eyes animated with a perfect flash of triumph an Exultation. "Oh Percy. Angria gained and victory won this night have ensured me I should hope one day of delight and. pleasure. yes the Day is already passed for the hours which must elapse ere sunset can prove only minute. compared to the mighty 3 o clock of this morning."—Northangerland stood with both hands resting on a table. he attempted to reply to his Lady But his face turned. white. as ashes and his voice stopped. "Alexander you are ill the exertion has proved too strong. is the Day to be long yet then." The Earl still silent walked to the window. and Zenobia saw that. contrary to its general effect when unwell that walk did not render him paler. —he gazed with a distorted glance at the crowd below. and striking with violence. the edge of a sideboard he. vehemently broke out. —"A curse upon you! Villains begone! Then turning to the Countess who stood petrified at the feeling which could prompt him to such language at such a moment. "Oh Zenobia I wish I were dead! —miserable is this hour which can. give me food and tear my teeth out. I wish this Roof might fall and crush me. thousands round me excitement and devotion to me in Verdopolis too and. yet no struggle. no attempt to reach. it. all to return as they came and if they do rise I must damp them must quell them. Volo. I had rather die than do so. —But. Hang Angria. —Zamorna curse him shall look to something higher than thee. And was I forced to veil my hints under Biblical expressions. was I— Ha if I spare now Ill smite. at last. —Why had I dared the attempt had he curse him dared aid me He should ere sunset have been King of VERDOPOLIS. —Ha if the time is not now arrived if this [is] but the dawn of morning yet a sun. shall arise. a daylight. shall appear he shall not stay in Angria He shall reign in Verdopolis." during the latter part of these sentences Northangerland. strode rapidly about the room. His strikingly expressive features concentred in one appearance of demoniacal despair and misery.

The Countess who was acquainted fully with all the. darkness and. contrariety of his strangly constituted mind. yet did indeed feel startled. at. this ebullition of passion. She stood just as she had stepped from the window on his entrance. and when his eye fixed upon her at the conclusion of his speaking. and he noticed the. expression of simplicity and. wonder which sat so curiously upon her handsome and haughty features he first sneered then smiled. and taking her hand in his said "Truely My Dear Zenobia I. feel wretched I want hope now then do not kill me by the expressionless timidity of those. Lovely eyes of thine. Shall my only hope be from myself. Ha there only in general. during my life has it been and must I only say from my own heart. that I still will look to the day when thy hand may be held. in that of a greater than. [a] mere Premeir of Angria. —" "Ah Percy. it is held now in a hand greater than that of a <u>mere</u> Premeir of Angria." Northangerland smiled again as he looked at. the slender Grecian fingers. which reposed in his own Aristocratic palm and then suddenly turned round to leave the room. ere he gained the door. his despair seemed to return. he looked back on the Countess with a bitter curl of the lips. "EN you may have them grasped by another than the premeir of Angria now and then I suppose. Hang me! —My carriage again for Victoria Square."—"Waiting my lord. at the door" said an officious menial. Percy. mounted. thundered "Drive off." and was whirled out of the square in an instant.

Now whilst affairs were taking this turn. among the. Great ones of the City. every street was crowded with groups of <people> disputing and conversing on the events of the night. in Inns and. Galleries. with knots of. Gentlemen. all whose conversation turned upon the same topic. One universal feeling of triumph seemed to pervade both the lower and middle classes or rather all those who had nothing to lose. for among these men. it is that Zamorna or Northangerland or any other lion of the day find their most trusty supporters. as for the substantial and monied men. these. shook their heads at the affair. cried "we can not see what will become of it and plunging their hands into their pockets with their brains at work guessing in what could they profit by this movement they passed thoughtfully on. Of course this class of citizens. are slippery and unstable supporters where the sun shines there their heads will turn. It must by other aid than theirs that a faction can climb. partly did the Angrians find that aid with the commonal[i]ty and "rare apes" of the country for in that country Zamorna is omnipotent. partly with the younger branches of the Aristocracy all the sons of Peers all the young Noblemen clung to his cause with a courage worthy of their country a thoughtlessness. inseperable from their years But for the Aristocracy of Verdopolis the Kings the. Peers the Noblemen. bitter bitter indeed is the feeling these maintain and undecided. the opposition these afford to all new arrivals to. the Duke of Zamorna. to the Earl of Northangerland to the Angrian Creation bill. But if they Hate the Angrians the Angrians hate them their own Heirs hate them their peasantry their countrys pride can in a moment be led to hate them. and this day ample proof was given of how by a little exertion. the leaders of the Angrians could rouse insurrection against them.

We know that they had been defeated that night upon this just decided bill and we have seen into what an excitement Verdopolis had plunged. How its thoroughfares. were. choked with. a daring multitude. How 10s of thousands had gathered round Zamorna and Northangerland with untiring and enthusiastic plaudits. We have shown too the. Demoniacal hint which the last named person had flung forth to his hearers. a whet for their appetite till dinner might arrive. Now this hint the populace were not slow to take. and had it been laid more stress on had Zamorna and Warner followed it up. Verdopolis would ere midnight have flowed in blood. and now whilst matters <stood> in rest. while the.

Angrian politicians while Arundel and Castlereagh. Warner and Montmorency and. each supporter of this new born faction was the instant his carriage was recognised deafned by the approving shouts and encouraging voices of the sweet toned multitude. attended each to his mansion by a < > of admiring thousands. —Then and on the morning the moment the carriage. of an Aristocrat or. King follower was beheld yells groans and menaces were showered upon him hisses followed him and in several cases his chariot or horse was stopped and himself personally insulted or threatened. to take one instance from a Number The Duke of Fidena. who had never proved himself. hostile to Zamorna who in private had been his most intimate freind. was riding down. Elrington Square. from the House of Peers on horseback and unattended. His statly figure and calm Noble countenance seemingly unmoved and unruffled by the riot and uproar around him when. as he checked his steed to allow its passing quietly amid the press of men. first looks then whispers were circulated amid that concourse "Yons the Traitor as Rougue said." "Thats Fidena. and a bitterer hand we couldnt meet with." These and such expressions were spread like wild fire. by a knot of thorough rascals. fellows who belong to Northangerlands private cutthroats [and who] now stood huzzaying and gloriing round his mansion. roused by those experienced bands the crowd first sullenly refused to open to let the Duke of Fidena pass. then. began to close firmer in and at last when he rather too proudly said. "Open my lads. those carcases are distasteful." then. 3 or 4 huge. dangerous looking bandits of the true Percian aspect rushed upon his steed grasped the bridle and. fired the mob by shouts of."Kings man Aristocrat—Angrian hater down with him the hide of a bug." Their comrades with yells and hooting lifted their shillela[g]hs[19] and bore down one over the other upon their Noble prey. he reined in his steed stood erect in the stirrups and pulling forth a pistol discharged the contents into the brains of the nearest rioter The Verdopolitans are naturally hot tempered—a wretched little old man[20] with a knife between his teeth. struck the Dukes horse. with his heavy handled whip across the forelegs it fell directly and the crowd rushed forward thundring over the Prince. like falling houses. That moment might have proved his last. —but a fine tall young Gentleman[21] of vast power and activity. rushed from amid the crowd. discharged. a couple of pistols and. hurled the old wretch who was grappling at the Dukes throat. over the heads of a dozen fellows. then with his strong flexible arm thrusting back the furious crowd and warding the blows aimed at his own. person. he. made a momentary space round Fidena. That Nobleman sprung up and. stood unflinchingly amid his haters. Two such. Active and superior looking fighters were not to be despised but the Multitude. were Verdopolitans opposition only roused them and yet though meditating bloodshed their natural hearty spirits. still clung to them They respecting the. appearance of the doomed ones. did not

---

[19] An Irish term meaning a thick stick or cudgel.
[20] S'death.
[21] Edward Percy.

dastardly rush in with pikes staves and. clamour but. a hundred brawny arms were. unsheathed in a twinkling and [the] whole front of stout fellows stood watching. who the two assailed they would signalise among them for a pitch up. but. Fidena stood sternly one hand on a pistol the other on the rein of his just risen horse. and his companion. looked round and over the mob with a gaze of passion and threatning. The old villain before mentioned was creeping forward again with his knife This champion espyed him and with "Ho Sdeath. to death." he spitted him on to a pike and dashed him forwards amid the rioters. [The] instant he was again upon him. Fidena mounted and dashed in the breach. They burst together through the press and. the Duke galloped. down the street.

CHAP III

We shall not show our reader into a splendid state room of a Verdopolitan Palace or the unappeased Tumult of a Verdopolitan Square.[22] But here he must enter. a. a snug little apartment. decently carpetted and papered. a bright fire blazing in its appropriate recess. and. a large framed. Glasstown Almanack[23] suspended above the chimney peice. The windows of this room look out on the manufacturing district of Verdopolis and. all round the millyard just below. gables of warehouses perforated mill fronts great smoking chimneys and. a wild chaos of vast shapeless masses. toss away into the dim murky distance and yellow choking sky. This very apartment it is evident. from the tremulous feeling of. all its furniture and the sudden burst of sound ensuing on a neighbouring door being opened. is in or closely adjacent to a thriving factory and the uses for which its snug sanctorum are intended are ascertained by the two clean raw deal desks of such ample. dimensions which stand side by side ranging down the room. The desk nearest the fire and. closest to the dark corner. contains an occupant. a low. broad backed fellow. with. a not very scrupulous brown coat. its protruded elbows. having formed most productive shores for wool and fleece—rather greased trowsers and. not particularly refulgent shoes. however although his outward man seems squat mean and slovenly the ardour with which he applies himself. to his work of writing for never even when to obtain ink does that grizzly brown shock rise above his coat collar. and the perfectly professional articles which cover his desk proclaim him at once indefatigable and industrious. I have heard the Earl of Northangerland affirm that you must examine a mans study table to examine his mind. and truley from the appearance. here beheld I should agur the <intellect> of this described one. to be perfectly agreeing with his proffession. on the upper part of the desk. a pile of red clasped. ledgers present their scarcly inviting sallowness on one side. lies. a

---

[22] Compare Branwell's focus here with that of Charlotte in **High life In Verdopolis**, written in March 1834, Alexander CB II, part ii, 4-5.

[23] An annual table containing a calendar of months and days, with astronomical data and calculations, ecclesiastical and other anniversaries.

sheet price current. a small almanack. above it. another price current above this
and a small black greasy creature of a volume. over all. What this abortion may
be is not apparent it is evidently the owners private reading the mysterious title
"Wesleys Hymns"[24] appears lettered on the back.

But we have spent too much time in painting this figure. and. if its
dingy plodding aspect may have wearied the spectator let him turn to the desk
beside it. here. before an apparatus altogether newer and smarter is seated. a
figure. in as striking contrast to the one just abandoned. he is bent to his writing
therefore his face we cannot see. but if we can judge by. a slight and elegant
figure. light curled hair and. a very small white hand. whose fingers move across
his paper with all the easy grace of a ready writer We should consider him in this
room as a hen swimming or a goose flying not at all in an appropriate situation.
a pile of invoices and trade orders lyes beside him for copying or endorsing but
alas his private reading seems composed of three very suspicious looking post
octavos[25] whose light aspect. white leaves and blue and white binding augur but
poorly indeed for their interior solidity. toward these books his head is often
directed and again as if by an effort he turns it to his work of drudgery.

Yet of these two we could not call the last master of the first or the first
of the last. For their superior one must seek elsewhere.There is a table of
mahogany. in the middle of the room. and on it is placed at the left of the door
and near the fire a handsome portable desk of the like material. beside it on a
chair turned to the chimney. is. seated. a Gentleman. whose. tall and finely
proportioned figure. promise. great bodily strength and activity. a pair of.
handsome legs are stretched cosily on the rug toward the blaze. a delicate hand.
but with a wrist (for his cuff is turned back while writing) of strength sufficient
for most purposes. is while the elbow rests on the desk supporting his head and.
its fingers. are embedded in the soft curls of reddish auburn hair which in thick
ringlets covers his head. his eyes for his back is turned from the door seem
directed in thought to the Almanack over the chimney peice and. his desk is not
covered with the every day work books of the counting house but with the
superior and more theoretical Reviews Magazines and Newspapers in this
Gentlemans person there cannot be found although he seems slender and young.
anything of that slimness and slightness which characterize. the figure at the
desk near the door. No. he rises up from the chair and looking hastily round the
room walks to the window. Then we see. in his tall stature. active limbs and.
springy tread. the true tokens of one yet unbroken by the world and fitted to pass
through its stormiest scenes. but if one admires the figure let them start at the
countenance. Lo the. calm fair forehead the delicate retroussé nose. the Light
complexion and the restless mouth of a genuine PERCY but in this handsome

[24] The BPM has a copy of Wesley's Hymns owned by the Brontë family.

[25] "Post" refers to the size of the paper used in printing; "octavo" refers to
folding one sheet of paper three times to produce eight leaves—16 pages. The
three volumes suggest he is reading a novel.

face is wanting that. feminine eye. and Satanic sneer of the Great Northangerland. or the. cheerful glance and winning smile of the Duchess of Zamorna. But in place of these. a. haughty arrogance in the eye. an aspect of active apprehension in buisness and. an appearance. of. incessant. employment vigour of thought inflexible determination and an abominable disposition. gives by turns an animated or repulsive aspect to the well chiselled countenance of. =EDWARD PERCY ESQ^r= Such my readers must have guessed this Gentleman to be and They might have discovered. in him the very person who that morning had so signally exerted the above mentioned qualities of vigour decision and. activity in rescuing the Duke of Fidena from a ferocious and blinded multitude.

Edward Percy Esqr. as all know is the Eldest son of the. Right Honourable Alexander Earl of Northangerland But the moment he was born that strange Nobleman delivered him to Old Sdeath his Lieutenant with strict injunction for his death instantly and decidedly Old Sdeath for motives known only to himself. did convey him away but. secreted him. and. caused his life to be preserved. and when upon the birth of another son. (that young man whom we have described sitting at the desk beside the broad back scoundrel.) the Earl also gave him to Sdeath to destroy but the old fellow also conveyed him away. with life.[26] The course of existence pursued by these two young men I cannot describe but after a childhood and youth spent in unmitigated hardships destitution and wickedness. after being tossed all round Africa after trying all means to rise wether robbing swindling gambling or pilfering. they or rather the oldest whose firm intellect. alas not united with a spark of goodness had born him through every disaster. determined to set up in Verdopolis on his own account first as a working wool comber then to mount if successful through every stage even as his own audacity planned it to the very highest attainable. —For such a course as this he was eminently fitted and his own quick wit. fertile imagination active talent and unshrinking hardihood and arrogance. he well knew would carry him allike through the fair stream of prosperity and the labyrinths of dishonest crime. he set up his trade in an obscure hole in partnership with his younger brother William Percy. and a wretch, by name. Timothy Steaton (the above mentioned squat industry.) a cast of and. abandoned son of Charles Wyndham Steaton Esqr. the Earl of Northangerlands steward. a fellow young in years but old in wickedness meanness treachery and Hypocrisy. The trio in a month or two from the mere possession of. a wretched combing shop had mounted to the employment of many hands and a decent floating capital Ere long they bought a mill. employed workmen. set up. a <de[c]ided> mercantile concern and found themselves working gradually to riches Edward Percy now with the audacity and keenness peculiar to himself <claimed> the whole management of the concern. Instantly the spirited but weak. William and the. mean and grovelling Timothy were under him. were subordinates he was the sole head and director. he began to appear at the Cloth Halls wool sales and. and

---

[26] For the death of the third son, Henry, see Alexander CB II, part ii, 139.

peice Markets. Here all the Men of Buisness soon noticed him he was young and seemingly Hot. hearted ergo. a hundred shearers were upon him a hundred fleecers and swindlers seemed to unite to do for him. alas they had caught a Porcupine. and Edward Percy the stuff manufacturer. and the son of the great Northangerland. was soon noticed as the. keenest bite the most enterprising trader and the most active young man in the whole market. all saw his abilities and the. awful cognomen YOUNG ROUGUE! was soon well known through all the East end of the City.

It is at this time when aged 22 propietor of a mill and possessed of capital amounting to perhaps 20 or 30000£ that I have introduced him and his gang to my readers in their counting house and. sitting room. employed at their buisness

Edward Percy after looking for an instant out of the window bent his eye upon his two partners (partners?) "Timothy. put that silly Wesley in your pocket. Sir! —William.!" The addressed started as [if] he were galvanised. "William what is it we see there. my nose! and is this the manner in which you mean to forward your buisness—come I can have little play here. work or starve. Sir. not so many flourishes in your work. a mercantile hand is short and clean. —" He again returned to his seat and sat down turning over the leaves of the last magazine. but his eyes directed on vacancy and his forehead corrugated with thinking.

"Timothy." said he after a long silence. "you know that in many quarters trade owing [to] the shattered state in which the last war left it is bad indeed and that the thousands of French prisoners. whom the Government distributed among the Manufactury are now out of employ. wandering about in a state of. perfect idiotism Now—Steaton—" Here Edward arose and. walking to Steatons desk leant his hands upon it. while Timothy regarded him [with] looks of sagacity and. intrest not often excited in his broad glimmering visage. — "what sayest thou to a little-speculation. a little Jewism. a little of the Hebrew. —thou Israelite indeed in whom there is no-good. —well. Tim. I mean to send thee instantly among the most destitute of these. workers. mind keep clear of the rare lads they are fending for themselves-but pick out the most miserable of the others-offer them but with thy native tenacity. first the sum of. 1^S per week for every peice they bring in to the counting house of. "Percy Steaton and Co" a little loaf is better than no meat. but if gasping Nature shrinks at so. feeble. a tenure why you may augment the offer. to perhaps 2—6^d but you are your own judge here. However not one farthing more! not a farthing more! —now by this means you can see Tim—I shall have laid up in the warehouse. several thousands of peices. which when a return of trade flows back I can then deliver on the market. at. half at even half the price. usually given for them and yet ensure to myself a return in intrest of double the sum I gave for them 1000. peices bought by me. at. 2^S each. Tot. —100£ I shall dispose of at. $6^{S.}$ each. Tot. 300£ Thus gaining 2 to 1 upon my outlay and yet being a whole half price beneath the market. —verily Percy. bustle and thou shalt be fed. —!27 Timothy turned his face to the ceiling and. elevated his not scrupulously clean hands in. a fit of perfect ecstasy. "Oh. now. may the work prosper it is the Lords.!" "Is it Timothy the lord Harrys[28] perhaps." "Oh thou my shepherd shalt provide and feed me with a shepherd's care.!"[29] —"Death and destruction." broke in Mr Edward in a fury and is this all the sense I am to procure from thee. speak like a man or Ill fell thee to the floor." The passion in which Mr Percy spoke. made. poor William at the counter wince and shrug. while Timothy. no whit dismay[ed] rose up and. as he said to "Bless the Lord for. this mercy vouchsafed to him. —actually knelt down in prayer in the middle of the room. and while. his master stood storming over him poured forth his soul in a blessed exercise of thanksgiving. William sat at his desk with his hand to his mouth. striving to smother that laughter. which had his brother heard might have perchance. in its effect have smothered himself. —Edward threatned loudly that the instant Mr Timothy arose he would fell him down again a menace which his excited eye the grasped poker and the firm Iron arm. rendered both. awful and certain. in effect. But honest Timotheus had his own way of avoiding this chastisment. he broke out aloud at concluding his exercise. "And I thank thy providence for its gracious mercy. appertaining the case of the sheep. and as shown in this affair of the lambs. —Oh save poor sinners Amen. —" "Timothy what was it you were jabbering about? eh sheep" Timothy winked at his own adroitness he wished to turn his masters attention from the chastisment to Buisness. and after. spitting upon the floor and hemming twice or thrice he pulled a visage of incredible length and commenced. "Now while engaged in that comfortable wrestling. and while thanking the Lord for his abundant loving kindness. a light as that which fell upon Saul. of Tarshish[30] broke in upon my mind. I bethought me at a venture. upon the lost sheep of the house of Israel. and I said to my soul Truely it hath pleased the Lord. to send rain upon the earth. whereby perchance many of his creatures have been delectated and many. damaged. but as his mercy endureth for ever[31] he hath so ordered it that none of this damage shall if we use the sense he has given us fall upon the head of sinful and erring man. now peradventure there shall have been in this wet season a plenitude of sheep and lambs of his fold found upon the pasturage seized with the rot. and that to them frail mortals death shall have come thereby now greedy and lucreloving mortals. may at first sight of this case feel cause to mourn but. thou a ministering angel flys. and.

---

27 Compare Psalm 37:3.

28 i.e., the devil.

29 I have been unable to locate a source for Timothy's words here; they are likely Branwell's.

30 Compare Acts, chapter 9.

31 Compare Psalm 106:1; 107:1; 118:1; 139:1; I Chronicles 16:34; II Chronicles 5:13; 7:3 and 6.

chases misery from their soul. I said to my soul oh frail tenant of a frail clay. why art thou not awake to sing thy creators praise Lo may not my master. perchance sojourn into the far country and gather together as sheaves into a garner all the fleeces of sheep fallen through the rot. These fleeces can he take at. a small trifle and resell at and[sic] enlarged. sum. I forbear to enlarge providence we see will provide May we be saved. Now touching our sins and theire cons— ". "Oh" cried Edward. "stop thus far but no farther. well Tim I warrant you hoped to cover with this spice. a dose of phisic to tack to the tail of this welcome dialogue. a long sermon. My!. well however theres sense contained in that. hint. pray after this fashion Tim and you may pray till doomsday. Sheep—rot—a shilling or two a fleece sold to me under on my part a pretence of there being made into rugs. dressed and. combed and carded. and out comes a rare fine peice of. stuff—hem. Ill think of this. Tim! Thy hint is worth thine ears. and. said I to my soul are not those large enough. verily remain with me and thou shalt be fed."

In an instant was Mr Edward. at his table paper before him. his brows knit and his whole soul evidently immersed in plans and calculations. upon this notable scheme and the one before mentioned. For an hour deep silence reigned through this room of industry a stillness only interrupted by. an occasional sigh from Timothy or a cough from William. while Edward had in that short space of time with a versatility strongly characteristic of his energetic race. written calculations and. accounts and letters over. 3 or 4 sheets of paper. made and mended and thrown away almost a dozen of pens. read or skimmed over. a score of articles. in the Magazines before him scratched their pages over with short and energetic. sentences in argument or condemnation of opinions contained in them. made sketches of the two underlings seated at the windows and. ere they were half completed. threw them into the fire with a real air of contempt. at being found engaged on any thing so worthless.

Then he leant back in his chair looking out of the window at the scene of traffic without. then at the ladylike hand and pugilistic wrist[32] on the table then. at the pair of active. handsome legs. before him then again his forehead clouded and again he seemed buried in thoughts and visions within. till his quick ears caught a step without. the door opened he turned round. "Ha Sdeath" "Why —" The figure which entered was not Robert the great. but. a scoundrel servant of the house he bore a letter adressed to "Edward Percy Esqr. No 1. Wagon Yard. Grenvilles Wharf. Verdopolis. The moment the man had placed it on the table. Edward motioned impatiently and he withdrew. as impatiently tearing of the envelope our hero opened the note. "Humph some Lordlings work this. heh what. usury Tim—Stop no.

                                                    The Fidena. P[a]lace.
                                                    Verdopolis.

---

[32] For Branwell's interest in boxing, see vol. I, pp. 178 and 294.

Sir.

His Grace the Duke of Fidena having discovered Mr E Percy as the person who this morning so generously risked his life in defence. of his Grace. —I. am directed to inform you that. his Grace. desires. your company this evening at. the Fidena Palace. to dinner.

By Order of his Grace.

J Jhonstone Macdonald MacPride.

"Ha ha. MacPride indeed"—said Edward as withouth[sic] the the least expression of anger. or joy. or gladness or scorn he got up and left the room. "Eh Tim are we to have a holiday—" asked William eagerly. "Oh is it not now a holy day." "Stuff ass. I mean a little relaxation from buisness" "pray for relaxation from sin" "Tim I'll cleave your. bullet coated skull into thous—" here Edward again entered and all was still as death. he appeared at the door his tall handsome figure attired in an elegant evening costume of Blue and white a hat and (for I adore particulars) a pair of white kid gloves in his hands. —"Timothy you scoundrel" he said. "stick to your work and force William to His. —leave of coughing there. —I shall not return till midnight and at that time I <u>must</u> see the arrears cleared up then when I return we will speak of. the buying of goods and the rot affair till perhaps 2 or 3 at morning when I expect that you and William will be sent out to the country for orders and &c. —" Timothy received this sketch of proceedings as ones laudable and praisworthy industry—William more naturaly turned red as scarlet—Will I obey you Will I turn your slave. Ill die rather. he made an effort to rush past Mr Edward and gain the door—Edward stood with a cold smile and as he passed him dealt him such a blow on the temples as felled the young man like a shot. and gave ample evidence of the power of the dealers arm. Tim was already busy plodding at the desk. William lay almost breathless on the carpet. and Edward shutting the door with a scornful laugh strode along the passage to the door and there springing on to the back of as handsome a steed as is usually seen he snatched the bridle from old Sdeath its holder who stood bye the bye. his head patched and. his visage elongated a rueful image of that mornings deeds. Edward I have said snatched from this doughty groom the reins and cantered dashingly down the broad and ample street. —

CHAP. IV.

Upon the same Evening as that whose events I have just been detailing. the bright fire of a handsome apartment in the Fidena Palace shed warmth and comfort on the social circle. gathered round its. bright and glowing environs. That circle consisted of His Lordship the Premier of Africa. Sir R Pelham Mr Sydney the Home Secretary Col Bud Capt Tree. and myself. all stout and conscientious supporters of [the] existing Government and of things as they are. Our Host the Noble Duke of Fidena. had lately left the room upon some buisness of importance regarding [the] Government. and we had just plunged into deep and anxious conversation upon the mighty the allabsorbing topics of the day. the late momentous descision in Parliament the future prospects of Zamorna of Angria and of Verdopolis engrossed all our thoughts and all our attention. Earl St Clair. sat the superior of the fire side and his Noble Countenance wore an expression of deep unfeigned embarrasment as he surveyed in his mind the present difficulties of Government and the shadows of evil to come Mr Sydney sat next to him by the fire and its blaze. here was cast upon a corrugated and restless countenance. ever animated by political difficulties and. glittering with the light. of. national agitation; Mr Bud. occupied his arm chair in a manner at once philosophical and. social thinking indeed on the wild waste of the future but knowing himself now embosomed in a warm and sheltered present—Tree the unhappy little Literary captain. sat on his seat as if upon pins restless. anxious eager to talk to exhibit and to display. My Honoured friend Sir R W Pelham. whose seat was the sofa beside me. seemed surveying all his freinds with a calm searching eye. his handsome but rigid features varied by one smile of half shrewd half wooden meaning. but our tongues one and all struck the single ominous note of Angria and the Angrians Lord St Clair had just concluded a striking and finished portrait of the character and views of the newly created Monarch and Mr Sydney was dilating in strong and alas too true terms upon the views and proceedings of his associate the Earl of Northangerland. when a servant opened the door and there entered a new visitor—a Tall young Gentleman whose feature[s] and appearance imposed an instants silence over every tongue present. Our eyes were directed one to another mutely inquiring "who is yon" we none of [us] knew him but we all knew his countenance. That figure dislayed all the bearing and features and expression of a youthful Northangerland save that the eye. was. feircer the aspect more restless. the. action devoid of that finished grace which were said to mark the person of. Alexander Rougue. and yet there was a haughtiness and an eagerness of expression a searching fearlessness in the glance which well beseemed the well known name I have just mentioned. I have just said that we none of us were acquainted with this new visitor but for that he little seemed to care. His first words as he strode to the cheerful seat which Fidena had latly left. were. "I had intended to see the Duke your host but. it seems my intention is not yet to be gratified I stepped into this room hoping to meet either with solitude or civility but when I meet with neither when in the Fidena Palace I encounter the staring gazers at a country puppet show I am truely astonished and indignant. —Who do you think I am Gentlemen that you in this manner look at me I am not your master but only one like yourselves of his very humble. and obedient servants. —I know you all and I see no reason why you should not also know me. I am. Edward Percy. of right. Lord Elrington. of necessity. a stuff manufacturer—And so now my Lord and Governor. my honourable Home Secretary my most excellent freinds of the S[t]ationery and you my would be Brother in law. either shut your. gaping mouths or open them to a Christian and rational purpose." as he said these words in a rather loud and overbearing voice. the astonishment of myself and my freinds changed into a feeling of suprise and intrest. here we had lighted upon the son of Northangerland and. and one too who well beseemed his race—

"Well" He said taking a seat on the sopha. beside Sir R Pelham "well I should be able to guess what it is that now occupies the thoughts which linger on the tongue. of all you around me. The wounded soldier must think on the Battle the defeated pugilist must reflect on his conqueror. Well the Aristocrats too must ponder over the Angrians. —My Lord St Clair I am not an Angrian I dont follow the Duke of Zamorna. But neither am I an Aristocrat of a surety I wont follow destruction. If you heard one tythe of what I hear or could see a fraction of what I see you would shrink from your party and principles as I would from plague and pestilence!"

"Alas" answered Mr Sydney raising his hand to his forehead. "Alas I know not what can prevent the tide now round us from rising over every stone and pebble we can raise. Oh my country if thou couldst be saved If thou canst yet be supported well thou knowest that all the exertions all the strength of this feebled arm and this wasted frame have been spent to strengthen thee and have fallen to uphold thee"

Mr Edward gave no answer to the Senator but looked at his Neighbour and laughed in derision—a short period of silence then ensued. Mr Sydney was to much offended to speak again Earl St Clairs aristocratic temper had been ruffled by the unceremonious entrance of the visitor Sir R Pelham could scarcly stomach the sneer respecting. his would be relationship. Captain Tree was collecting his ideas in search of a subject wherewith to overwhelm us. Col Bud was employed in meditation on the forthcoming dinner. I sat intent upon observation of the faces around me. Mr Percy stood. leaning on one side of the mantle peice his han[d]some countenance curled in contempt and his eye glancing in derision of the company around him. The cold wind of constraint played all through the apartment.

At this critical juncture of affairs our host the Duke of Fidena again returned And the statly walk and benignant gesture with which advancing forward he welcomed our intractable fellow visitor Almost restored a harmony into the somewhat too aristocratical circle. "This young Gentleman" said the Duke turning to the visibly clouded countenance of St Clair. "has only a few hours since preserved I beli[e]ve the life and I am sure the saf[e]ty of the. Heir to your country. and whether the act is advantageous. to that country it is so to its Prince. for this reason I have—" "Beg your pardon my lord Duke for untimely interruption but in order to prevent mistakes I think it best to inform you that there are more than one threads in a hank of cotton. and there are more resons than one in a good action Your Grace is of course aware that had any untoward event taken place in Elrington Square the Landlord of the Zamorna Arms up at the top of it would have felt. three times as glad as I could wish *him* to feel. —" Fidena smiled slightly at this declaration. Sir R Pelham. stroked his face with his hand. Mr Sydney rubbed his fingers and Mr Tree cocked his nose. all more or less gratified by the apparent hostility entertained by this Young Adventurer to the faction at present so formidable and so strong. Mr Edwards quick glances assured him of the feeling in the company he abruptly said. there are two stones in the road both dirty and rugged. a man is invited to rest upon one Volo he

wont but is it certain that hell take the other? no I think he'll walk forward and
seat himself on a—nother and. better block even if it be a bit farther on." —To
this equivocal allusion Mr Sydney "rose to reply" and just as he had risen as if
"on the floor" and was twisting his paper and countenance together—our Noble
Host with his accustomed tact. changed the conversation "now Clair let us
descend from these Highlands Sydney let us. ascend to the Upper House Bud let
us go a-foraging. Mr Percy I have invited you to dinner." —The door was
thrown open and servants conducted us in to the Dining Hall. The Duke having
introduced Mr Percy to the Duchess and the Duchess having elegantly
acknowledged his mornings services. and Mr Percy having unaffectedly and
polit[e]ly acknowledged her Graces condescension. we sat down to table. of
course I need not particularise the well known and faultless entertainments of the
Fidena Palace. or speak of the ease and freedom of its refined. and aristocratic
circle. I must cheifly confine myself to my hero. Mr Percy. as some among us
sat rather silent and probably reflecting on the events of the morning he ran over
our countenances eager to find some striking expression of greif or dismay.
unhappily Mr Sydney with his pale puckered visage and. thin trembling fingers
attracted most of his too apparent eagerness for ridiculing. —Mr Sydney. it is
said that I have saved the Duke of Fidenas life. —well I know who has saved
yours—" "I dont understand you Sir" "Probably not." "Really." "aye truly.
—Why ha arnt you engaged on public affairs " The hands this aching forehead
must witness for me." "And do not public concerns when oppressive on you
prove that oppression." "what the—Honourable Gentlem—Ah. I—What. you
have asked my former answer must prove." "Eh. well And has not the late. wild
maneuvre of the Angrian kingdom hugely proved threatning and oppressive" "Oh
my country thou knowest—" "Well and is not this stage over " "Yes. alas!" "and
does not relief from labour invigorate the weary." "I hope so for other wise. I am
lost." Ah then have you not. been released by the passing of the Dukes bill. and
has not the Duke passed it." "Sir." "And if the Duke has passed it has he not.
revived you." I appeal to—" "Your spouse" said Edward laughing in allusion to
the not very elegant. language of Mr Montmorency during the agitations of the
late war.[33] Sydney. dashing his hair back from his forehead in evident agitation
the Duke of Fidena. gazed on him with evident. polit[e]ness. "Sydney—Buisness
distracts you you cant recognise you[r] best friends. The dish before you is
untouched and its contents form the apotheosis of a brace of. unequalled green
Ducks. Sydney transfered his attack from Percy to the Ducks and wisely judging
that. they being two were yet preferable as prisoners. to the opposite and
intractable one. he. seized captured and executed them with laudable and. truly
heroic expedition. Conversation sharpened by. as. (Edward termed it)
"edification" (from edo not aedifico)[34] flowed on in that. broad. noble channel
which one would naturally expect from. the confluence of so many mighty and

---

[33]   See vol. I, pp. 416ff.
[34]   i.e., to bring forth, to divulge, to spread, rather than to erect, to establish.

well watered streams. St Clair lent his High polish and aristocratic character. Mr Bud. his deep erudition and recondite reading. Sir R Pelham his deep and cool knowledge of character. Mr Tree his smart conversational Talent And the Duchess of Fidena was far from behindhand with. the offerings of a mind naturaly both extensive and elegant and adorned with education much deeper than can be found in the rank too which she has shown herself worthy of being raised. However on our parts most interest was excited by our guest. and. difficult was it at times to avoid feeling as if in company with that man whom we were certain of all men in the world most hated that house and all it contained. there. There sat on the sofa (for dinner had departed) the changing and varying figure which yet ever and anon flashed upon us the living image of a youthful Northangerland. There was the tall. form the. golden hair the "peculiar" nose and the lofty forehead. There was the never to be forgotten delicate hand spread upon the knee. and the small springy foot. so conspicuosuly[sic] thrown out to the view of the beholder but Edward Percy was free from the apparent melancholy the ill humoured frozen indifference which so frequently marks the presence of the Earl of Northangerland. The eye glanced as haughty but a far freer and feircer light the mouth was curled into as sarcastic but more heartily sarcastic smile. and the voice allas it had not the double refined purified and. sneering calmness of the sleeping tongue of the father. no it was eager firm and toned with an energetic precision and when contradicted. his eye lightened the lip curled up the hand. was outspread on the table. the other clenched on his knee. and he sneered and argued and hectored at his enemy with perfect dictatorial impetuosity. He seemed through the whole evening to glory in exhibiting to us his total want of principal contempt of everything noble scorn of all restraint and determined reliance upon himself and his own rescources.

Ere long our circle received a new and brilliant addition. in the course of the evening there entered in the appartment. a young Lady. whose tall youthfull figure was habited in a dress of rich and splendid satin and whose. dark. eyes. "dark even with excessive bright."[35] shed light and lustre over a gay but haughty countenance. and gave double keenness to her expression of inexhaustible and irrepressible archness. She was accompanyed by a Gentleman. of a tall and well proportioned form. dressed in blue with epauletted shoulders. This young Noblemans countenance though possessing claims to be called even. decidedly handsome. could not also with equal reason be termed as decidedly agreeable. his light hair and complexion his uncertain eye and. its glance of hesitating calculation. the put on smile and. mock welcome of the mouth. the brooding ill humoured forehead. and the hand helld partially forth in welcome. did but very ill suit with. the. upright step black neckercheif and the blue uniform of a royal sailor.

However questionable to the reader may be the identity of these two new comers it was not so to the company when they entered all rose from their

---

[35] Compare Milton, *Paradise Lost*, III, 380.

seat[s] and while the young Lady commenced instant and unscrupulous appropriation of her share of the Apartment the young Gentleman was surrounded by the company with "I rejoice to see you from your cruise Arthur." "Lets have your Budget Admiral." "Oh My Lord Marquis you have arrived at an unfortunate crises." "Now lets have an evening Ardrah."—He muttered his returns in a nasal laugh and took his seat with an ill conditioned glance at the uncongratulatory figure who stood having bowed to his companion Lady Maria Sneachi. "Ha" said the Duke of Fidena. "I must introduce to you Arthur and I suppose to you Maria. a young Gentleman who has this morning saved my life and. defended our liberties. to Mr Edward Percy a son—a Gentleman of this city." "Ha" said the Marquis of Ardrah bowing stiffly. a son of the Earl of Northangerland Im vastly obliged in your company Sir" "Oh" said Lady Maria. "a son of your own works I know Sir well I am really obliged to see you. after hearing of the deed you have done. and you know that in a case like yours one so very peculiar and interesting ones sensibility must be really excited when one reflects on the generosity and courage you have shown. Really Mr Percy believe me you are quite interesting." Mr Percy upon so flattering a reco[g]nition bowed smiled and said "Indeed My lady I am in this situation quite interested. and must confess I have found my last congratulation by far the most delightful."—Lady Maria bowed and rather haughtily took her seat. Conversation now again began to flow forward but. Mr Percys eager eye. was kept fixed on the. look and even voice of the Marquis of Ardrah and. lighted with a keenness for mis[c]heif whenever the Prince of Parrys Land. uttered a sentence which Edwards sharp sneer might contrive to fix itself on. at each of the still calculating maxims and double dealing well weighed sentences which so often garnish the conversation of the Son of His Southern Majesty. he opened his fire of sneering contradiction and irony. The Marquis first replied with double stiffness and. increased frigidity. but as the sarcasm increased upon him he. compressed his lips fixed a dishonest look in his eye and seemed inclined not to resent or hurl back the attacks of his neighbour oh. no. too fix them and register them in the inmost recesses of his tenacious and. unamiable heart. The Duke of Fidena with his accustomed address and high breeding. constantly attempted to avert this collision but the aggressive young stuff spinner. as he termed himself. look[ed] feirce hectored and proceeded The Prince of Parrys land. looked sullen dogged and pale with. malice. The Duke of Fidenas sister Lady Maria all the time gazed on the affair with evident and undisguised mirth and satisfaction not all the chiding glances of her Noble Brother could prevent her from throwing in every now and then her own bright and witty sallies in aid of Mr Edward and against the Marquis of Ardrah whom she evidently delighted to see embarrassed and irritated. "Well my lord" said Edward "As I was saying. wether is Bunting[36] made of wool or cotton." "Sir you are more likely to know than I." "Eh how so Im no sailor. really. my Lord

---

36 Thin cloth used in the making of flags, banners, holiday decorations, etc.

you do me too much honour. "Ne sutor ultra crepidam."[37] you know but assuredly if a cobbler shouldnt look beyond his last he should look the closer at it. but I suppose my Lord you though you are a sailor being too high in rank and consequence never look above you knowing that there is nothing above you. otherwise I really cannot account for the fact that a young man should have been all his life at sea and never have know[n] that the sails which bore him on. were made. of. real stout. unbleached well beaten flax. —Ha I beg your pardon My Lord Marquis I mean no disrespectful allusions and when I speak of flaxen sails above one I really did not once reflect that upon some occasions I might be speaking to one with flaxen <u>hair</u> above one. —now this flaxed hair is I can prove it. the very type and emblem of all that is great noble and exalted. —but as I mean nothing personal and in saying so can not possibly allude to your Lordship—(Ha.) Ill e'en pass on. to say that a real. Northern Mariner is—" "Sir" said Ardrah severely "do you dare to be personal." "Of course not my Lord. but to go on such a one may be. and perhaps has been. everything good and great and noble. I once for all disclaim all personality. and mean no allusion to your Lordship

"Silence Sir." "No no" said Lady Maria "Mr Percy I beg you'll proceed and my Lord Marquis you know. that as this Gentleman is now engaged in praising sailors. without of course in so doing any particular allusion. I who do so foolishly dislike them may be converted to his evident opinion" "Ha. My Lady." said Edward I can plainly perceive that you are in my opinion now

He went on mingling with much nonsense and much that was coarse out of taste and very Roughish. a sufficient quantity of information knowledge and energy of language to make all the topics he touched on eminently pleasing and delightful. Yet unhappily his unbearable. ill temper having once got the scent did every minute in spite of all precaution turn round snap and snarl at the sour and disaffected Marquis of Ardrah Edward saw that he did not like him and to one who did not like him Edward threw down the gauntlet and declared never ending war. This evening such sentences. as "I dont like the sea. it is treacherous and it loves treachery" "light things are always the most dangerous the light waves are the stormiest light spirits are the most fiery. light hearts the most cowardly light heads the most silly. and. those articles on the summit of the head. I. dont allude to life but vegetation are when light methinks the tokens of. an intellect. as boisterous as the wave as silly as the brain as cowardly and[sic] as their heart." "How light is Scotch whiskey and how nauseous." Such sentences as these kept up through the whole evening a spirit of hesitation in the company and of. bitter feeling in the Prince at whom they were pointed The Lady Maria Sneachi alone for reasons best known to herself. seemed to rejoice and be gratified with them and to add fresh point and vigour to them. and often by her. own "spiritual emanations" she called down a darker and more brooding frown over the forehead of the Marquis of Ardrah. at length Percy said. "Now its

---

37 "Let the cobbler stick to his last"—Pliny.

strange Mr Sydney. all cutaneous diseases the leprosy the Scurvy and especially the Scotch itch.[38] once introduced into a family become hereditary and cannot be eradicated. Oh. how like in this respect is the Scotch temper to the Scotch fiddle.! I love consistency." This was barely said when the Marquis of Ardrah. arose and bowing to his host and hostess very properly left the room. Earl St Clair accompanied him. Edward Percy glanced round eagerly and without speaking to any one rose from his chair and allso departed. smiling as he left the apartment at. the short sharp shocked exclamation of Mr Sydney and the. slight coquettish laugh sinking into silence through pride of the Lady Maria Sneachi—

CHAP V.	June 12::
	AD 1834.
	P B B—te

My Reader ought to be well aware that the serie[s] of chapters which I am now engaged in inditing neither can have nor pretends to have the slightest claims to the character of a tale or Novel Plot or entanglement unravelling or denouement he is not to expect from me my simple design in the work I lay before him is to portray and describe if I can the character mind and entrance into society of a man as remarkable in my mind as any one who has within my experience risen above the Verdopolitan Horizon. The person to whom I allude is indeed young in years and has been deserted by fortune he is indifferent in principle and. not formed to fir[e] our admiration. but despite all this and much more than this I. think that I do most clearly perceive in his present track all the signs and indications of a long a high and an encrgetic light amid the storms and dangers and successes. of an active and conspicous existence Many of my Reader[s] who now scarce know his existence will perhaps ere long awake to a hundred actions and feelings and associations at the name or presence of. Edward Percy Esq[r]. Stuff manufacturers of Verdopolis.

We left him [in the] last chapter departing from Fidena. Palace from the house of a prince and the company of. nobility. from the prescence of some of the principal characters of the mighty city and we must seek him again in the modest and buisness like purlieus of Grenvilles Wharf. and his well ordered counting house. awaking from dreams of splendour and scenes of princly magnificence. as he touched the well known steps he. gave his horse to the clerk. and. his forehead corrugated into lines thinking he. advanced stooping his fine height into the little snug mill parlour. There he flung a feirce look at its occupants. Timothy his industrious carcase bent into a perfect curve sat scratching his papers with indefatigable pertinacity William sat too at his desk but alas the keen glance of his Brother espyed his hand hastily thrust into a load

---

[38] A very derogatory term denoting the prevalence of scabies amongst the Scots, the result of malnourishment, impoverished living conditions, and, presumably, personal uncleanliness. Compare Alexander CB II, part ii, 319.

of papers as he entered the room. Walking up to the confused William he turned over these papers took therefrom a small. blue and white post Octavo and hurled it with a laugh of scorn into the warm blazing fire William half choked with awe and anger rose and spurned his seat from him but his Tyrannical superior at once opened against him all that full torrent of. threats and hectoring and. fury which have so often caused that room to ring Struggles against him were useless and only procured to him the harsh tidings "If it isnt 3 o clock at morning. its as good and better too so you had best at once. don your team mount the gig and away." with Edward a suggestion once made is soon put into practise he rang the bell violently and ordered the above mentioned vehicle to be brought forth. it was vain that William cried "Why youre mad Edward its only 12 at night." "all the better said the inexorable Egyptian. and commenced gathering the Notes Cash Papers etc necessary for William to go—his journeys with as Traveller to the firm of. "Percy Steaton and Percy." "Go now" he said. and "get yourself ready" William murmuring and cursing to himself left the room. Edward then stepped up to Timothy and the industrious earthworm. arose with a twinkle in his glimmering optics. "With the Lords blessing am I not to search after the lost sheep of Israel." "Yes Tim and you get of now " I must first implore a blessing from on high over a slight repast of. ale and cheese." "Go then. and be hanged to you." Tim departed into the kitchen. till the two worthys return[ed] Edward hurriedly paced the apartment and. when they again entered he gave William strict and minute instructions how to proceed with the various bankers manufacturers and tradespeople whom he was to visit and. entered deeply with Timothy into the manner in which he was to creep through the dark dirty ways of the screwing plan and the rot concerns. and then he hurried them both to their two vehicles saw them drive off the one fretful and discontented the other patient and perservering through the lamplighted streets of Verdopolis. Edward having despatched this buisness turned back and gained his room with the stride of a master calling by the way for a tumbler of hot brandy and water. and the glass being placed steaming and shining on the table with its appropriate appendages of bottle jug sugar basin and waiter he closed the parlour door pokered the fire. trimmed the candles and seated himself in his armchair. his brows bent and his lips compressed to think and run over all his schemes and plans and deep diving paths of. Ambition.

Let us change our scene to daylight and while the bright Sun shines gloriously from a blazing sky. upon that huge sunny waste of. walls and windows and chimnies and steeples ycleped Verdopolis and upon the millions of men and beasts and carts and chariots which shoal along its thousand streets and block up its hundred marts we must confess that. amid all that huge waste of. bustle and tumult and activity there did not one soul one head or arm exist amid them more capable of. stemming and buffet[ing] with this mighty torrent than that. young man whom we may see standing under the portals of the Hall of Commerce surrounded by the busy knot of anxious and wealthy Merchants all men of experience and capital yet all owning the power of a superior mind and all looking up to him for a single sentence on the topics of conversation. It was in this situation and considered in this light that we must look on Edward Percy. Days passed by and buisness went and came. but he was still noticed by the mercantiles. ever active energetic fertile in s[c]hemes. always able to command a handsome capital. constantly buying up and selling out. exposing goods unrivalled in even sterling quality and. steady. comfortable price. All men wondered that with his known daring character "young Rougue" did not enter and participate in their speculations afloat. but they little knew that he was engaged in other and surer ones of his own. —Ere many days William returned laden with orders and. bearer of the tidings of extended connections. and soon after him returned the more anxiously expected Timothy. the fruits of whose expedition were seen in the huge waggon loads of closely packed. fleeces which in their great unweildy vehicles soon appeared in Grenvilles Wharf. and which were so hurriedly taken in and stowed in the roomy recesses of "Young Rougues" warehouse. and next in the great crowds of half insane and half. starved Frenchys who appeared at the "livering in"[39] with their completed peices and who departed content with the shillings and half crowns which Timothy so sparingly doled out among them. gradually by these means were those Ware and storehouses filled with Merchandise. and on the first great stuff and peice market. held when. from the continuance of the peice[sic] and the restoration of public credit buisness and manufactur[e]s had begun to flow again straight forward in the tide of improvement. —when the buyers and sellers saw the long stacks. of peices. and great piles of wool packs. lettered "P.S.& P." and heard the incredibly low prices and the strong rapid sale of these same piles and packages they were filled with wonder and saw the fruits of successful speculation. Edward with his unfailing sagacity brought out his sales at the just nick of time. and such was the demand for his. "rolled" wool and his hard wrung peices that on the Evening of the last of the 3 sale days. Edward Percy could write himself down with between 60 and 70000 pounds!

Now Edward felt it necessary to extend his concerns but he did not do so by. having a new and handsome house and removing to a more. fashionable part of the City. no his strong sagacity saw in such a course diminshed credit and. exhausting expenditure. he stuck to his old lodgings. but. Bought a capital new factory. set at work several hundreds of new looms. hired 2 or 3 assistant clerks and. established Travellers to the principal cities of the kingdom. he. also for he could perceive the rising prosperity of Angria laid in a few thousands in shares of building ground at the newly founded City of Adrianopolis. at the Exchange he was now a man of note. he was 2 or 3 times observed in conversation with Grenville and Bellingham remarked to me of him as one of the "best goods in the market". In Edwards person these advances produced no effect but. that of increasing his keenness of look. determination of manner. and quick ene[r]getic decision of voice and action. in his private economy. I believe it it determined him to two new things to buy a first rate blood horse and to sit for his portrait.

---

[39] A Yorkshire expression, meaning to bring in, to deliver, to unload.

The first he had long in his mind the last he alway[s] said he would defer till he could pay a crack sum for a crack picture as his head was not to be thrown away. Now being able to accomplish his end in this respect he one fine Afternoon. at a time when he was not oppressed with buisness and. could spare a few hours of Idleness. repaired to the studio of. the great Sir Edward de Lisle. our noblest portrait painter and most gentlemanly Artist one whose polished manners and connsumate ability have raised him from the hearthstone of an Alehouse to the Halls of Kings Palaces. Mr Edward. on entering the house haughtily demanded to see "the painter"[40] A colour grinder presented himself and in answer said something in so hurried a tone that Edward could not catch his meaning. This grinder was a fellow of singular aspect he was a Lad of perhaps 17. years of age but from his appearance he seemed at least half a score years older and his meagre freckled visage and. large Roman nose thatched by a thick. matt of red hair constantly. changed. and. twisted themselves into an endless variety of incomprehensible movements. As he spoke instead of looking his auditor streight in the face he turned his eyes which were further beautified by a pair of spectacles. either toward his toes. nose or fingers. and while one word issued stammering from his mouth it was straightway contradicted or confused by a chaos of strange succeding jargon. "Hillo" cried Mr Edward grasping the handle of his riding whip. "what have ye here Sirrah. shew me the way to the painter."—"Haw." replied the scraping and bowing grinder. "Im—that is—Oh of course Ill show you Sir. but—that is, this is the way Sir. that is My Master that is a Lady I mean a Lady. is-but follow me Sir and I'll show you the way" "Oh if your Master is at all particularly engaged I can wait. Scoundrel what is it you mean."—"Haw only—I mean. that is. a Lady is sitting for her portrait and. my master that is my master he told me to-to not to I mean. not to let any body into the painting room. Sir—but then. that is you can go Sir come this way Sir. this way." "Volo and I will go this way. My nose! I think it is not such as you who are to lock me out of a painters "daubing hoyle" The terrified grinder cringing before him—ushered him through an Ante room filled with the rare and beautiful in art But whose contents only raised a smile of scorn on Edward[s] countenance and. opened after vast hesitation the door of the studio. Into this classic ground let us take a peep.

Classic indeed it seemed. it was an apartment of moderate dimensions and lofty roof. lighted by a small dome of glass above. for the walls without windows were covered with. large. Oil Sketches. unfinished portraits and several paintings whose brilliancy of effect and colour. far outshone the splendid frames in which they were enshrined. in the recesses formed by the four corners of the Apartment. stood. beautiful. statues. and casts the from the Antique. round the ceiling were tastefully disposed variously arranged drapery and. costly suits of Armour. but what rendered it propable[sic] that this was rather an Apartment for receiving the more distinguished Sitters than the artists own private. snug

---

[40] Five canceled lines follow.

painting room was the fact that with the exception of a large rosewood Easle. and a marble slab heaped with palette brushes pencils knives. oils and. crayons. none of the usual vast and miscellaneous litter. invariably. found to crowd the nest of an Artist here covered and accumulated over the unincumbered an[d] close matted floor. The occupants of this handsome apartment consisted first in a tall Elegant looking Gentleman attired rather proffessionally in a close fitting jacket and pantaloons of. fine grey fustian. This was Sir Edward the Artist. and he stood before the easel pencil in hand sketching over the large sheet of canvass the first free outline or as beautiful a face as the eye of Painter ever gazed on, The owner of that face sat on a highly raised and costly seat used by Artists to place their most distinguished sitters and. one glance at the august and brilliant image told. Edward Percy this Lady on whom he had intruded was no other than the Princess Maria of Sneachi's land. There she sat her raven ringlets curled over a forehead of. marble. purity and though her swanlike and swelling neck and her robes of such rich and flowing drapery. did so well suit the manner in which she sat on the now doubly thronelike chair and cast so proud and lofty an air over her whole. unshadowed aspect yet <as one> gazed at the unconscious smile which seemed only to linger on her lips and to the changing lustre of those dark brilliant eyes which ere while so animated so quenchless their glance and sparkle did use to shed light and joy and cheerfulness on all arround her but now. so softened and so saddened was their shining so often did the snowy lids half veil the glory of those. too ever melancholy eyes Edward knew not how to account for this changing aspect but he did know and did believe that she might be placed in the darkest midnight. in the wildest scenes. and among the roughest storms yet would it seem as if all that darkness that wildness that tempest must <laugh> and. leave their threatenings around her he could believe in his admiration that were that dome over this windowless apartment closed up and darkened she yet must still shine in her own unborrowed and unequalled light "My lady" he said advancing without looking at two other persons who occupied the room "to you at least my apology is imperatively due for the unthinking manner in which I have intruded on the apartment which you might have appropriated but I can apologise no farther for as all must be aware. I did not know before whose prescence I might appear. and permit me here to tender to yourself. my warmest acknowledgements for your. own. condescension. and. what was more to me your own presence. aye your even single smile of welcome. with which you may have greeted me upon my visit last night to your brothers palace. My lady. I do never flatter and however you may have been accustomed to the incinserity of. the. court butterflys or—court spoilers—who hang about you however improper may be this place and prescence for the expression of a stronger sentence than one warranted by the etiquettes yet I shall tell you that when last night I saw you in that palace. I felt as if till then enterprise through my life had never yet lightened my spirit or Hope. amid all my actions had never cheered my way" He spoke these words without alas a single bow or genuflection erect and haughty but his fine face and passioned eyes kindled and flushed with the warmth of. his true feelings as he gazed on the queen of Beauty who sat before him. at once abruptly she turned to Sir Edward De Lisle who stood not know[ing] his new visitor but amazed at "the likeness" and hesitating as to his admission "Sir I ask you not to speak a single word. upon my entrance into this apartment. I have apologised as far as I will do lay your anger on the back of your colourgrinder I. —but. —" Here his eye caught the figure of. the Marquis of Ardrah who it seemed had accompanyed the Lady Maria as cavalier and servant to the Artists and who now stood sinister and frozen to resent the "persons" intrusion. "Death Sir. Ill have none of thee" said Mr Edward "I tell thee between thee and me their is a great gulf fixed neither will I who am on this side pass over to thee neither dare thou who art on that side come over hither to me!" Here Edward his face convulsed with scorn left the Marquis and looked at the third person. him he could not mistake and knew that he gazed on the magnificent figure. and glorious countenance of the youthful Sun of Angria There stood the Duke of Zamorna at an altar like. table in the recess of the room gazing with almost boyish eagerness at a huge portfolio of drawings sketches studies and all the heaped up riches of a great Artists brain The Dukes all quenching eyes shone brighter as while he rapidly turned over the drawings one hit his unerring fancy and his diamond ringed finger was instantly placed upon it it was deemed his own but for the last few minutes he had been standing with that hand resting on the pictures and. all the mingled expressions of his godlike countenance centered upon the haughty and passionate figure of Edward Percy who stood eyeing the apartment with an air as if he would find fault with every stone in the walls The Marquis of Ardrah. likewise stood. his hand on the back on his chair and his unsmiling countenance pale with rage. he looked as if wishful to call a servant to turn the intruder from the house. Sir E De Lisle too with his painting stick hanging neglected in his hand was gazing with his cool keen eyes with full apparent intrest on the uncommon vision which in "Young Rougue" was presented to his view Lady Maria seated on her throne. totally disposs[ess]ed of her usual arch and malicious coquettry had roused her fair features from their expression of languor to one of suprise. and wonder. a slight smile and a fitful lighting of the eye. spoke of the rising. godess of smiles who might have shone forth had it been her pleasure to have done so

I must remark that although this studio now contained the a[u]gust prescences of a King a Prince and a Princess. yet as all these visits were made quite incog. and without bustle Sir E—s mansion had not shewn symptoms of the honour conferred upon it nor had Edward till he entered had any knowledge of it. True he saw two handsome carriages bearing the arms of Zamorna and Sneachis land waiting at the great door but he had either never bestowed a thought upon them or had supposed them the carriages of some officers of the household. as to Zamornas entrance that is not at all to be wondered at what great Artist in Verdopolis is their who cannot boast of having seen the majestic plume of Zamorna bowed to enter his portal "Edward Percy" said Zamorna breaking the silence "can this be you. Keeper of the gates of Paradise you have yet your flaming sword![41] My Brother in law I am glad to see thee! Whence comest thou and whither art thou going" Edward. turned round he knew the Duke directly as who does not. and had been aquainted with him (after a sort) while he held the office of doorkeeper at the Elysium But now holding the doctrine that he would never associate with a man higher than himself he seemed shy of the Dukes aquaintance and only said. "From Grenvilles wharf and to the wharf again. you say you are my brother in law I am sorry for your relationship and hope you will never have cause to repent it—Sir Edward De Lisle my buisness in calling on you at so unseasonable a time is merely to arrange with you for a whole length of. my self. to be executed in your best style and at your speediest rate name your price. and dont dare to impose upon me" "Why Sir the price we charge for a whole length life size. is from 250 to 300 guineas." of course you dont dare to ask guineas for ready money." "Art" replied the Artist while an expression of scorn pervaded his intelligent features. "Art can never be bargained for" "Be more explicit." "Hem! —credit and ready money are not in the Artists province. The price once fixed cannot be changed." "I believe that Artists <u>do</u> know little of ready money aye and less of <u>credit</u> too I think. Ha. —Well Sir this is not the time for settling. I shall be here again in the evening at perhaps. 7 or 8 o clock." with these words Mr Edward Percy turned quickly from the artist. cast a bitter look at. the Marquis and. without heeding the "Mighty" he. bowed gracefully to Lady Maria and quitted the room. Ere many moments had elapsed it seemed evident from the wretched stuttering jabbering and shufflings heard below that he had quenched his ungovernable temper on the bones of the confounded colour grinder. directly after he was beheld trotting past the house on his new and handsome steed.

"Who <u>can</u> this be" said Sir Edward De Lisle turning astonishedly to the Duke of Zamorna The same eyes the same forehead the same nose the very curl of the lip the bitter voice. —" "Prove him to be what he is, the true son of. the Earl of Northangerland answered the Duke. "But Maria he seems aquainted with you. how did you attain that distinguished honour" "Oh. Arthur is not the meanest daisy often accquainted with the sun. —? He gained my notice in the usual way. yesterday morning amid the troubles which pervaded the city. and all too arising from that fount of troubles from as I have heard or at least shall very like hear My servant. the Mariner here call you that Ocean of Misery Arthur Adrian Augustus Wellesly oh now you have made me lose myself. as alas you have made a hundred more silly than I do—well amid these shoutings and mobs and landlubbers. my Brother the Duke. attracted the invidious notice of a crowd of scoundrels sufficient in number to pull him from his horse and threaten to kill him a threat which I fear they might have been incited to fullfil had not this young Gentleman come up and taking my brothers cause. laid prostrate round him the most insolent and frantic of the rioters. they thus joining arms. drove

---

[41] See vol. I, pp. 289ff. It is, of course, also an ironic refenence to Genesis 3:24.

the traitors before them and. my Brother invited his deliverer to the Palace that evening. here it was that I saw him and here too if I mistake not Neptune heard him. O Arthur I know him to be a strange young man I can see it and I know not who can pass him by." "Will you return to the Palace" interrupted the Marquis of Ardrah in a tone of decided sullenness. "Not till the sea is calm" answered the <coy> Maria a flash of something like pride darting from her brilliant eyes She was offended at the sullenness of the Marquis question. and went on "Sir Edward. shall I instruct you how to paint the sailors portrait." "Ah. My Lady did I often receive instructions from one like you I should believe the muse of Painting to have descended from heaven. to teach. me." "and why not Sir Edward has not. the God of Poetry [h]as not Apollo. himself done so and shall we wonder if the Muses follow their Guardian—and De Lisle what beneath a goddess can instruct you how to paint a God. Jove himself need not disdain to speak of his brother Neptune. Let us behold then upon your forthcoming canvass The billows assuaging upon the ocean and the clouds all rolling of from the sky. In that sky the sun himself must appear but in colour of a light gray. thereby to contrast and elevate the bright and glorious circles of. the Sea Gods golden hair Neptune must appear in the foreground. and his eyes turned inward toward each other as too resplendent to shine on the mean humble sights around. at his feet must kneel a wretched and dripping sailor just cast from the vortex of the storm but from whose. vulgar grasp the the glorious God must be gracefull[y] turning inward his refulged knees. thereby De Lisle prefiguring the Honourable badge of a mariner which among man receives an insolent and degraded name. around Neptunes feet. beams barrels bottles bags jewels purses copper silver and gold must unceasingly be cast up on to the beach from the storm and over the pure because inanimate articles Neptune shall augustly and protectingly spread forth his uncontaminated hand [with] which he severly snatches a no doubt stolen neckcloth from the throat of the justy half drowned sailor he must himself (and mark the far different disinterestedness of his own intention) be engaged in quickly placing one foot upon a particularly full purse of guineas and securing it no doubt to deliver to its own rightful owner now behind this—oh but alas I forget a portrait so worthy of its subject would approach in cos[t]liness to an Historical painting. and alas alas My Ardrah would never never consent to fling forth so much money into the hands of. a mere mechanical mercenary craven who should aspire thus to add new glory to his unapproachable and everlasting name." The words so strongly and bitterly satirical. did. Lady Maria run oer with an air of. pleasure and delight and an eye glistening with satisfied. victory. and when she had concluded and the Marquis striving though his face was pale with his well known deep sunk. Anger. to conceal his black and malicious sullenness under a forced and hollow laugh when so doing he arose and they all three. (id est with the the king of kings and lord of lords)[42] left the apartment. Marias speaking eye was turned from the Marquis to the Duke with an expression which

---

[42] Compare with the "Hallelujah Chorus" from Handel's *Messiah*.

shewed that a feeling deeper than mere thoughtless gaiety was she forced amid all her enlivening cheerfulness to harbour and hold within.

CHAP VI

Now while the rapid torrent of Edward Percys fortune was flowing onward in the course and manner which I have above described far different events must agitate the huge and restless billows of the vast Zamorna'n sea we have seen how the triumphal passage of the Bill for the Angrian kingdom was received by the people by the vast mass of the Inhabitants Sensations quite as enthusiastic directly spread over the whole country and from the mouth of the Gambia to the waves of the Calabar one shout of "Zamorna. and Angria." arose over an enraptured and according land. The young monarch himself while Marquis of Douro had long since. gained over by his generous dashing and splendid qualities. all the feelings and affections of our bold hearted peasantry and while these. present events assuredly did not tend any farther to estrange them they brought over in a moment. vast reinforcements of the adventurous daring and needy the men of strong ability and weak morality to stick to the wheel of fortune and worship the rising sun Then. also there was now firmly united to the Banners of Zamorna. a whole faction a great party which when even alone and unaided had often found itself able to shake and alarm whole Dynasties and Kingdoms. a faction comprising all the stern and reckless spirits who confiding entirely on their own. vast. ability undaunted. hardihood and. awestriking principle. could at any time. boldly plunge out without sail or compass. into all the confusing billows of a rough and stormy sea.

Now when these two mighty factions the Angrians and the Democrats. were united so firmly together and led on by. Arthur Wellesly and Alexander Percy marshalled by. Warner Warner and Hector Montmorency <embod[y]ing> all the young Nobility and the rising talent of the age under the guidance of. a Castlereagh and a Morley swelled by all the strength of a million Laurys and Scrovens. fronted by youthful hope and arising glory. backed by the fear or the good wishes of a mighty country what obstacle I ask could possibly arise to oppose them at what limits dare I fix their goal? Theire o[b]stacle. I show forth in the old Aristocracy of Africa their goal in the boundarys of the world.

The Sun of Angria risen in such a glorious morning we may be assured shone forth with un clouded brilliancy. all that country denominated by the name I have mentioned and stretching in a broad fertile region from the Gordon Mountains in the North to the mouths of the Calabar in the South. bounded on the West by the long ridge of the glass town valley and the eastern skirts of. Verdopolis and on the east by the rapid. <Nowrnone> and. the huge wastes of eastern Africa. All this wide stretch of country forming the whole eastern portion of the Great Glasstown Country. and measuring about 400 miles in length and nearly 300 in breadth. was now by one sweeping act of Parliament given into the hands of the young Duke of Zamorna as his due and rightful kingdom. Now Angria is a naturally very fertile Province abounding in rivers and prairies of vast extent and magnificence but it is though ancient and stored with classic spoil as yet thinly and scatteringly populated but that population though far from numerous is entirely made up of bold rough hardly Old Glasstowners. stern and unsophisticated in their character ardent and warlike in temprament and. proud and independent in principle The internal power of the country is and always has been confided to the hands of a haughty class of Gentry. commonly Esquires in title but Noblemen in all besides The men are of vast wealth and of habits not likly to lose it They mix but little with the gaietys of the capitol and. only court publicity in times of war. The very prince and cheif of all this class of men is Warner Howard Warner Esqr of Warner Hall in the Hills of that name which form the heart of this country This Gentleman. by his surprassing ability. unwearied activity. and intense ambition united to a lofty Ancestry enormous wealth and a character unstained in honour and veracity has arisen in spite of his youth and want of strength to be the Dictator of the Angrian Gentlemen. and the third. despot of the Angrian Faction. The Duke of Zamorna has found him in the house of commons to be one of his most ardent and eloquent supporters—And the inhabitants of his country consider him as (under their King himself) their only other Head and Dictator[43]

I have here now shortly enumerated the conditions of the new kingdom and the power and support commanded by its[sic] but let not my reader suppose that because he can pour forth so mighty a torrent his channel must there fore be even and unchafed. by rocks. alas no! Zamorna and Northangerland at every step had to face a hundred difficulties and a thousand cares I shall state explicitly that with the exception of the Duke of Wellington. every one of the 7 kings is determinedly opposed to them all the Ministry of Verdopolis is against them all the Old and long vested. Aristocracy. are against them. (I exclude every soul of their devoted followers the young and rising noblemen) The popular and power full John Duke of Fidena frowns upon them. and Quashia! the awful the tremendous Quashia! Quashia the Prince of the Africans. he with all the gathered forces of his inumurable myriads of expatriated and ferocious Negroes occupies all that mighty and unexplored territory horrid with heat and desolation which lies along all the unprotected east of Angria there the young Lion couches and there he hopes to rush down upon the unsettled country overwhelm all the power of his intensly hated foster brother Zamorna and from thence rush down on Verdopolis and regain his long long occupied throne against him and his indefatigable savages it will require in that waste and unprotected frontier. all the splendid resistlessness of Zamorna all the unfathomable ablility of Northangerland. all the indefatigable activity of Warner all the courageous sagacity of Thornton all the bold high blooded bravery of the Angrian people to defend their bulwarks and stem the inundating sea.

---

43 Alexander suggests that Warner is based Sir Robert Peel—see CB II, part i, p. 345, n. 54.

During the first month. (May) after the Foundation of the Angrian Kingdom its monarch and champions in Verdopolis were incessantly engaged in laying down. the basis of a Constitution partitioning out. province[s] and settlements. forming a Ministry and Government. organising a vigorous Army fixing the site of a huge metropolis. receiving all the unfailing tide of inflocking Adherents. strengthning their position in this great Verdopolis laying hold of the huge. machines the public press filling as far as they were able parliament with their Adherents. and in a thousand other ways laying the basis of a firm and Despotic sway. Zamorna himself the young the Glorious the godlike Zamorna was on the very pinnacle of splendour he was adored wherever he appeared cheered by an applauding populace surrounded by a resistless young Nobility. worshipped fairly and decidedly worshipped by. a mighty and. heavenly galaxy. of all the titled and untitled Beauty of Verdopolis. Nay I do not even know wether there are in all our mighty city 10 women who are not in heart and soul devoted and enthusiastic Angrians. And while he blazed out in all his own unquenchable. majesty the pole star the guider the crown of all. His strange and unfathomable righthand companion. the dark deep treacherous but unconquered. Northangerland. controuled all the movement regulated all the marching of the swelling tide of. a victorious faction. Without one solitary smile of pleasure without a word or gleam of triumph but with cold and sceptic brow and languid and bitter and melancholy aspect. this Immortal Nobleman devoted day and night all his hours and thoughts and choicest imaginings to the advancement and perfection of this his latest and dearest paln[sic] of Ambition. what though he continually affronted his brother leaders though he forever decried and abused his son in law and monarch he yet spent all his strength and energy his very life and reason in upholding and increasing and continuing his glory, Zamorna and Angria with him was all in all Now amid all these huge revolutions and strange paths of events when the course of history seemed about to change and a new era to open upon us. who is there who could suppose that Edward Percy the young talented Energetic and hot spirited Edward Percy could for a moment shut his eyes to or turn his face from these. incidents so glorious and hopeful to a young and Ambitious and enthusiastic mind No Edward gazed on the progress of the Angrian kingdom with intense eagerness of feeling and as intensly did he long to commit his whole life fortune. and. prospects to that. glorious and dazzling bark. But here lay his hindrance. how could he do so without. coming under the notice of its lieutenant. the Earl of Northangerland his own tremendous father. Northangerland who had sworn to slay him the day he was born and who failing in that and other attempts had yet kept unwithered and unsoftened that horrible and infernal determination. and who should he now attain the knowledge of Edwards fortune and habitation would again rush onto the scent of death with unnatural and bloodhound ferocity. Under his Notice. the coolness and. caution of our Hero determined him not to come but how otherwise he was to attain his beloved and cherished prospect of Father of the Angrian Commerce he neither could guess or comprehend! one Afternoon a week after the visit above recorded to the studio of De Lisle. Edward was standing with his elbow resting against a wool pack. in the large room of his principle Warheouse[sic]. he had been superintending the placing of a huge arrival of fleeces from the mountains the last drafts of his favourite rot. scheme. In the yard without stood a long line of emptying waggons and up the sides of the great building were <apilling> by the aid of cranes and pulleys the great brown unweildy sheets. laden with all this mighty heap of "Deaths loathsome leavings of mortality"[44] while the creaking [of] the cranes and the shouts of the craners the trampling of the horses and the curses of the carters. resounded from without the heavey stamping over the wooden flooring and the heavey sound of the deposited wool sheets accompanyed by the unresting and contradictory orders of the overlookers kept up a still more echoing and discordant noise within. The long lofty room was dark and gloomy its walls unplastered and its roof unceiled admitted the beams of an afternoon sun through its yellow oilstained skylights up and along even to the very rafters were piled the hundereds of stone of fleeces all pinned in their coarse wool sheets and arranged and lettered. two great grinning mastiffs chained and kennelled guarded the two sides of the widely expanded door. but all egress was much more effectually secured by. the fact that that door did not unfold straight on to a well paved and solid mill yard but unto the wide void of air 20 feet over that said delightful square and on pressing through the crowd of workmen who garnished its massy portals you only looked down on to a half dozen of. suspended packs swinging upwards through wide air to their dolesome and. oily resting place. within.

Here. in the interior of this bustling warehouse Edward Percy as I have said was standing in a recess and reclining against an unplaced pack sheet. his face wore an expression of the deepest thoughtfulness and while under the knotted brows his calm blue eyes gazed unconsciously on the broad squat form of Timothy Steaton bustling about and directing the whole order of affairs yet his firmly compressed lips and motionless attitude. at once prohibited all intrusion and interruption to his reverie—no one dare at this moment either speak to or look at him after remaining nearly an hour in this position he started up and paced through the room to the door here he met William his brother who hat in hand and breathless with agitation had just mounted the ladder and stepped on to terra firma. "Huzza" cried William joyfully they have been talking about you at the Hall of Commerce this noon your peices went off like lightning and to crown the whole. Mr Bellinghame after saying let no one fear to buy from or partnerize with "young Rougue" hell make his way" he ordered by me on this note of hand. Thirty two thousands stone of best mountain wool.!! he said he'd call on you to morrow to settle terms" "Now Providence be blessed" cried Timothy elevating his hands in rapture. "Now you be hanged." retorted Edward in contemplation "let me see 32000 stone[45] at 8^S the stone. will amount to 12800£. Hem. well and he shall have it of the reall mountain breed Timothy.

---

44 I have been unable to locate a source for this quotation.
45 A stone equals 14 pounds.

Volo now I got this stuff for 2800. 500 per cent. of profit is something at least. it will take all the sheets I have on hand. —S'death and vengeance. I will fix Angria." with these words and his eye lighted with triumph he dashed down the ladder mounted his steed and trotted out of the yard. a quarter of an hours smart ride through the crowded streets of Verdopolis carried him straight to the front of the Aristocratical Victoria Square. and he here cast a hasty look at the gorgeous front of the Palace of the King of Angria. and the Queen. his own royal sister. he rode up flung himself from the horse gave the reins to a footman and hurried up the gorgeous flight of marble steps to the wide and high overarching portal "I ask an immediate interview with His Grace your master" "May I. ask your buisness." "What is that to thee." he answered the servant. "Then follow thou me." Edward strode through the entrance hall with a loud laugh at the readiness of the menials <   >. His card was sent up and an answer was returned stating that the Duke would be happy to receive him the menial directly ushered [him] up to the Monarchs private study and. Edward with a haughty stride entered under its portal. Now I always love to make my reader accquainted as far as I can with the locum the scene of my action obscurity must allways wrap round events when we know not how or where they were preformed

This study then was like the studies of others of the principal Noblemen of Africa save that. its contents were more frequently looked into and its arrangements were more exquisitly classical. it would be wrong to describe it in general terms as being filled with beautiful and costly furniture. To the spectator who attentivly considered that furniture he would perceive that there was positivly not a single article the choice of which was not dictated by the finest taste and most princly. munificence. The rosewood shelves which surrounded the walls were crowded with volumns in the most costly bindings well so were the shelves in a dozen other studies in the city. Yes but here there was not a volumn which was not of the brightest and most sterling quality in other. librarys the books are confused costly. mingled and partly worthless Zamorna had caused all his vast stores of rare antiquarian. or fashionable or modern or tales published or long since printed or miscellaneous or multifarious publications to be stored in that large and kingly collection which is now become one of the finest Librarys in Africa. in this Apartment the envious visitor would run his eyes over the private prey of the young Tygers mind the chosen and oft devoured companions of his studies. and it has struck me on comparing it with Northangerlands sanctum. to find the now so very few and particular works which saving the periodicals Northangerland ever glances over. and here the wondrous chaos of conflicting wisdom. which the far more ardent Zamorna has fixed in his keen and fiery mind. I dare say that the Dukes Librarian has some trouble when the fit is on his Grace to keep his masters shelves in order I dont know why I have as long been lecturing you upon the book cases of this perfection of studies in the noble Architectural mantle peice the pyramidical ornaments which rose in varied apex above it in the splendid cabinet peice which shone over those in the two chef d' oeuvres of Chantry[46] which stood in niches flanking the Grecian window in the costly publications of art which lay on the floor in the alas most wearisome shudder exciting and headach[e] given heaps of papers which piled in hideous rows on rug and table claimed the undivided notice of their monarch or his secretaries as the first fruits of his Angrian Kingdom and in the tall Apollo like athletic young (Gentleman)! who sat on the sofa close to the table. his thickly curled hair wre[a]thed over his forehead that forehead. now <uncalmly> concentered as it were between the eyes. those eyes covered by the ey[e]lids and lashes of such Ladylike whiteness and darkness the youthful lips concentered in an air of military decision and the white hands one grasping a pen and laid on a sheet of gilt edged paper the other its slender fingers spread. in an agony of disgust over the hideous yellow looking scrawl of parchment which hung so far down over the edge of the dark and shining cabinet. in these thing[s] I say would the observer of things find by far the most pleasure to gaze and remember.

Edward Percy on his entrance scarce took however so much time to observe as I have to relate he was standing in a moment on one side of the table Zamorna who had risen standing on the other There they stood two god like forms of youth daring and energy the one so eager so angry and athletic the other so statly and ardent and Heroic Edward leant his hands upon the table and surveyed his superior with a sneer of. feigned contempt and an eye of unfeigned earnestness. Zamorna. who just started from his seat had placed one hand backward on the arm of the sofa. retorted back his look with an eagle and fiery glance which flashed from the soul within "You wondered" said Edward Percy abruptly "to find me here I had treated you with scorn at the painters but Ive thought better on it since." "My freind" answered Zamorna with more of a sneer than his visitor "how could I wonder to see my father in law at his own sons mansion." "Curse you dare you use my weapons hang him whom you term your father in law hang you too" "hem and is thy[sic] the blessing you intreat on your Hosts threshold. ungodly heathen." "Why volo I come to ask my host to intreat a blessing on me" "And to prove how you heed blessings you show him how you are laden with curses." "Ha well. but—" "Come Edward Percy I know you take that sofa and speak of what you came for" So saying Zamorna resumed his seat and Edward Percy assumed his "Your Majesty" he began with a sneer "must be aware that I hold you to the relation if not of father in law at least of brother in law I am your wife's brother and I greive to say it. I have entered into the paths of trade and in the space of half a year have amassed the sum of nearly 100000£ 20000 of which has been gained this month and 10000 more I expect to gain this day with prospects so encouraging dont fear in your pride to disown me. for curse you and myself likewise" "Be more lavish of your christianity Mr

---

[46] Sculptures by the Verdopolitan sculptor, Sir Henry Chantry, named after Sir Francis Chantry (1781-1841), a celebrated scupltor of portrait statues and busts, a friend of Byron—see Alexander CB II, part i, 254 and 369.

Percy" "Destruction am I come to receive lessons in divinity from you you profligate Dare not to interrupt me. I was about to say had you not so infernally stopt me that as I have begun so will I will go on and Sdeath! by Arithmetical progression too why by the Genii ere half another year has passed Ill be worth 500000 or Ill be at the Gallows foot." "Ten to one on the latter Mr Percy" "Ill fling you out of the window if you dare interrupt me and myself after you" "Ha Ill give you the precedence. "Hum Good. too well by fair means and foul by fraud and force you see Duke what I have done and by the teeth of a < > you shall see too what I will do But do you think that I while such a rare game as the Angrian Adventure is going on before my very eyes do you dare to think that I will neglect it or delay the participation in it no Sir I never was know[n] for procrastination or leaving my chance till the last nor by all that[s] earthly will I be known for it now. I will this moment plunge head over ears. into the deepest entanglements of your glorious bubble." "Edward Percy" said the young Duke in return. "I intreat you to leave off this Hectoring language you came here I believe to ask a favour—" No by Heaven No a fair <feild> and no favour" "Hem Sir a fair feild granted by me I consider as a favour" "Do you then let me tell you youre—" "Be calmer Per—Edward Percy Believe ME Ill try my strength with you if you prolong your madcap language Now Edward I tell you I am fully at this moment aware of all your energy talent and abilities I know the enormous assistance which a man like yourself. for we are all headstrong and all young. would be to our Noble and cheerful hearted enterprise We are going to found a new kingdom and new Empire and though we do found it in the face of a thousand obstacles though we have in founding it met with almost unconquerable difficultys though we have seen men base enough to stop us to thwart us shackle us, us whom the[y] could not and dare not quell. yet—(here Zamorna arose his fiery eye kindled with enthusiasm) yet If I have life and. health. never Sir never amid all my trials. and encounters and conflicts shall the brave fellows who have committed themselves with me find reason to accuse and brand me with the charge of cowardice irresolution and flight and discomfiture never shall that sun which I have chosen for my crest be doomed to fail its beams before the clouds and darkness and difficultys of an insolent and inveterate Faction" While Zamorna spoke these words with an indescribable emphasis and triumph of feeling. these two children of the Sun both stood their eyes sparkling their minds aroused in the enthusiasm of their enterprise They seemed two noble specimens of youthful mortality I heartily wish I had been there with my own eyes to have seen them I have thought how different would have proved that sight had the Duchess of Zamorna and. —why any other—Lady Julia Sydney stood opposite to each other in the first suprise of sudden acquaintance. How different then to see the two forms of grace and beauty those sylphlike and slender figures those beings whom seemingly no sorrow could touch nor time nor winter wither with decay preserved from the assaults of age by their own ethereal lovliness to see their fair eyes shining in the light of. graceful (if not unfeigned courtesy) their lips the fit of modulation of their voices of well tuned silver and the air the highborn and faultless air of each neither increased nor diminished by her splendid personal decoration her golden curls or her robes of such costly trim in this sight all seen and heard would prove of that heavenly and celestial beauty that seems not of this earth—nor I think in the case of those two of heaven either. —shall I say of Elysium perhaps I have struck the right chord. let it vibrate. Well however different feelings must influence him who looked on the sight that did here present itself a sight where all alas all. was of this earth earthy where every look every gesture every accent breathed forth in fire the lords and rakes of this world. the eyes glowing with human passions the hand clenched with human energy the forms of human strength and enduring human tempests the voice alas the voice expressing all the Ambition and fire and anger and wicked and driving recklessness of all those truly human feelings which for 6000 years have added such pages of glory and misery to the chapter of humanitys.[sic] They stood and spoke and looked very pictures of the greatness and weakness of Humanity Oh what a sermon might be preached upon the minds of Arthur Wellesly and Edward Percy.

The Duke of Zamorna stood silent perhaps because his mind was too deeply engaged upon his subject to admit of the distraction consequent upon the excercise of speech Edward Percy had caught up his feelings and looked in answer to Zamornas sentiment. let not my reader suppose for a moment that a single generous or freindly feeling mingled in this agreeing enthusiasm. Zamorna I fear care[d] little what Edward thought and Edward a[s].little what Zamorna might feel Each looked to himself to his own path and considered the Angrian subject as a glorious road to exercise his own prowess and his future fortune. "Duke" said Edward eagerly "what do you mean to do here indeed you have <materials> to make or mar you volo and they shall make or mar. me. Ive told you I possess a capital already of 100000£ and 60000 of this Ill directly devote to shares in this projected city of yours that is Ill build Sir Three grand mills their of 20000£ value each they shall stand side by side and. in each Ill start a running upon 10000£ a mill. This 30000 will be laid out directly and thus my whole property will directly be on start and heres the game shall it run upward or downward—up if this arm can push it. —now it will be your intrest that I should rise for if I suceed your city will reap the benifit of my sucess and I look forward to vast eminence on the shores of the Calabar. Ill be. the Grenville of Adrianopolis—aye and something more. —a little more "Edward" exclaimed Zamorna who had been attentivly gazing on him—Edward I like your plan. it will advantage me. and should you embark body and soul in the Angrian adventure <u>you</u> will prove far from the least of the Angrian Adventurers.—" Edward ere this had risen from his seat and was pacing with rapid strides across the room he turned "No Duke Ill. not. build three mills directly Ill build one with 30000 and a fund of trade of 50000 more and every 100000£ I get up by its side shall start another and another mill you make[sic] guess my fortune by looking at my mills go to a million. Death! Ill begin" "Edward Percy you must remain to dinner" "Never—till I have consequence to sit at the upper end of the board. never unless you and the Duch—Mary. hang her—be alone." "Well I think we shall be alone except I believe Mr Warner who will call The city think I have set out for Angria. But I

and Mr Warner. have not yet nor shall till evning then you shall go with us" "I will Ill put Timothy to complete Grenvilles bargain and I will set of to the foundation of Adrianopolis Ill choose a site for my mills and then I commence. Sir you dont I hope expect. him—ah. —North—the—the huge monster here do you" Zamorna laughed "Oh no he is to busy in settling our affairs to stir from Sneachis town where he now is regulating the affairs in that quarter" "I dread him" "and he you" So speaking the young Duke arose and motioned Edward Percy to follow him the haughty young man who hated the bare idea of superiority in one so near his own age was speedily up with him and. side by side. they entere[d] into a large airy saloon which opened in a long row of windows on to the green lawn of the grounds which stretched down even to the banks of the mighty Niger The Afternoon was glorious and the unclouded sun blazed full on the bright glittering waters and on the vast terraced structures whose almost marble fronts shone all along its rippling edge The light from that sun and sky beamed also into this cool and sunny Hall and the extreme lightness and airy character of its structure. and furniture did contrast most refreshingly with the heat and sultriness of the day on their entrance this Noble Saloon contained one occupant the Duchess the haughty lofty cheerful condescending DUCHESS. the wife of Alexander the daughter of Scylla[47] She was attired in a costume of that light and graceful character that well did suit this scene and while gazing on the noonday sunshine she looked like a seraph just lighted from her native air as she stood before the open fold of the great window that like a door opened on to the lawn the splendid African flowers bending as in homage at her feet a bright ray of sunshine fell on her lovely features gilding with <double> light her fair large eyes and glittering on the abundant curls of her golden hair lightly and joyously she turned when the statly form of Zamorna entered the saloon and with a step of delight she left the forgotten landscape but when she noticed the figure accompanying him the young man so like herself., her father, but so reckless so eager his lips so convulsed with scorn his eye threatning her with such ominous light. she gazed on him with a countenance glorious in its perfect paleness all the passion which in a signal instance has been known to blaze out with such blasting and lasting effects. "Mary" broke forth Edward impetously placing one hand with haste on Zamornas shoulder extending the other closed toward her "Shew none of your cursed pride to me. I despise you and hang your rank and —" here a deliberate grasp on the collar and the organ tone of the monarch. warned him that he was treading on a volcano. "Edward beware. drop this language or drop yourself. Mary" turning to his Duchess and how different was that name when pronounced in the angry curse of Percy and the full musical tone of Wellesly sound[ing] through the room "your Brother will remain to dinner. Where is Warner." "Ah Arthur Warner is quicksilver and can never remain long in one stay. See him walking in the grounds with Montmorenci For

---

[47] The narrator's comment seems somewhat confused, as Mary is the wife of Adrian and the daughter of Alexander.

yourself Edward I should be happy to see you here. Indeed no one can know how happy I could be did not your insolent and overbearing temper go far to quench all feeling or regard" "I want no regard from you save the regard of your father" "Dont mention that name you have too often spoken it in a manner which I have never born to hear to make it a matter of pleasure to me that you should mention it now" "And you shall hear it again." "If she does it must be shouted from the bottom of the Niger. again interposed the Duke Edward turned directly toward him and I know not between two such fiery and youthful spirits what might have ensued had not Mr Montmorenci and Mr Warner entered the saloon from the shrubbery And while the first looking for a moment at Edward Percy turned round with a particular wink and shouted to the full pitch of his thundering voice "Northangerland. thy cub" the latter glanced with lightning restlessness round the room and halted hurriedly throwing his hand back on a flower vase beside him "Who is this" asked he with that impatient abruptness which his veriest spirit so often scintillates "And[sic] Angrian Warner a sworn brother" replied Zamorna smiling away the frown which had clouded his forehead. "Ah a sworn son rather" "What witty Warner toward me" "Hey" said Mont turning round "Warner joking My word—again Warner" But Warner was not joking and with his fair forhead knotted into lines of thought and his blue eyes hurrying over young Percy he stood gazing now at him then at the Duchess till she spoke "Mr Warner you perhaps never knew that I had a brother I have two have had 3."[48] She said these words in a tone of rather saddened feeling and her hazel eyes shone with unusual emotion "perhaps Sir few have before been placed in my circumstances and such a fact must excuse me from uncertainty how to act in them." While she so spoke she turned toward the lofty young Duke as to one whom she relied on as powerful to direct and guide "Mary" he answered "and you Gentlemen Edward Percy is young and gifted with ability to work his way he has joined or will join the Angrian Faction is rapidly rising in the world and to us his assistance can not be considered indifferent with his fathers unhappy hatred to him we are all accquainted and with it we have little to do if he joins us we need not be involved with that father till he is able to defend himself against him." "and that is at present said Edward feircely For you Gentlemen I have heard of your characters and for you Sir (turning to Montmorenci) I know or at least may have known you otherwise and now too you Mary you know that I know you and that likewise I dont love you curse you for a little impudent upstart thou hast pushed me from house and home birthright and heritage but in so doing thou shall see that the trouble thou hast given me will recoil not on my head though it well may on thine and erelong I by the sucessful endeavours of this own right hand shall have attained an eminence and glory which I never could have seen had I sat down content with [th]at paltry portion thy father has given to thee" "Then you Edward have gained your desire and I mine. And—but for Heavens sake Edward leave the room My father—" She said no more but ran quickly to the Door and

---

48 See note 26 above.

flung it herself wide open her Brother laughing scornfully and muttering threats as he went departed saying he would again be with Zamorna to accompany him to Angria." Just as a servant had closed the door after him A figure whose voice the Duchess had heard in the gardens walked up the lawn and the tall Dark melancholy Northangerland stalked in at the low Door window and in his silent abstraction took his seat on a sofa without speech or sign

CHAP VII

Arthur Parry Marquis of Ardrah; is the Only son of his Majesty William Edward King of Parrysland And therefore He of course is heir to the throne of that wide and fertile kingdom. He was born in the 1st year of his fathers accession to the throne and is therefore now about 26 years of age at the age of 16 he was sent to sea as a midshipman and here I must allow the young prince of parrysland met with no partial or servile treatment it was his Majestys pleasure that he should attain his distinctions by merit of some kind or another and though the young heir of Royalty did really rise fast in his proffession it was not so much by omnipotent influence and his dazzling rank as through his own genuine ability and true Caledonian prudence in all his conduct through several long voyages active service and. many engagements with pirates and Frenchmen he shewed a cool cautious intrepidity a calm attention to his proffession a readiness of thought and a depth of nautical knowledge seldom indeed attained or exhibited by a Prince of a mighty kingdom to these qualitys were allied in him a great deal of sagacity in discrimination of character a disposition which accomodated itself to the company it found him in and a prescenc[e] of mind which amid a hundred scrapes perils and predicaments never compelled him to divorce from his features their singularly stony and calculating expression in finishing that sentence last written I think I have made up the list of his good qualitys and must proceed now to enumerate his exceptionable ones I am aware Im dealing with a prince and so know I must be cautious Well Ardrah knew that he was a prince and this knowledge gave him a stiffness and pride and and bigotry which ill harmonizes with a very disagreeable and creeping cunning a cunning that was commonly employed to shroud and conceal all little slips scrapes and peccadilloes that he might have fallen into It was also currently reported that His royal Highness hands were far from being considered with a close dishonest and grasping spirit of avarice a greediness which kept him ever on the watch for means to gratify it and far from over scrupulous in the uprightness or integrity of the paths which he made to obtain them. Often were the Officers wages clipped. under fines levied and provisions curtailed on board the "Africa" to gratify her commanders Northern cupidity often too were there prizes made only half accounted for and customs inquired into with a secrecy that admitted of much filtration. Now to cover the accidents consequent upon this unlucky disposition a large fund of Deceit and Hypocrisy was brought into view of those who studied their future monarchs character and to complete the portrait a cold undistinguishing manner a heartless desertion of Old freinds and companions a deference to the rich and mighty and a scorn of the poor and humble. did too often shew it self in the actions and conversation of the Marquis to attract much warm affection from freinds or sincere respect from his enimys

But as I have said in spite of all these great defects of character the prince of parrysland rose rapidly in his proffession and on various trying occasions his Ability and sagacity shone forth over the wide waste of cold rotten and heartless deceitfulness ere 9 years had elapsed he had during a most active naval service attained the highest oceanic dignity in the kingdom that of Admiral of his fathers fleets and the beginning of this present year and the conclusion of this last French war beheld him crowned with distinguished sucess at sea and gifted with the higher honour of Lord High Admiral of the Glasstown Confederacy a title which gives him the principal use and government of the whole direction and laws of all our fleets of all our kingdoms true he cannot in war either command the sailors or direct the promotions of any vessel but his own but he can controul expenses overlook the erection and in a great measure introduce his mind into the internal management of every flag in the Verdopolitan Union.

The Marquis of Ardrah now at the age of 26 having attained a dignity due far rather too his real Ability than the influence of his Birth and being possessed of immense wealth and an inclination to preserve it has set up an (of course splendid though of course also niggardly) establishment in Verdopolis his sagacity has placed him as one of the principal and his Bigotry as one the most inveterate rulers of the Aristocratical Faction and with an outward familiarity with the Noble Duke of Fidena. an inward detestation of the Arch ruler of Angria and a detestation and fear of the Earl of Northangerland he has contrived to make himself one way and another one of the very principal men in this age very unflattering [to] Verdopolis.

Placed as he was in this lofty situation and forming the second grand base on which to build their future aspirations the principal Noblemen of the Aristocratical party looked round for a firm bond of conciliation between their first stay [the] Great House of Sneachi and their second the Opulent House of Parry The Marquis of Fidena was as yet unmarried and peers and Politicians alike queried that an union with the Lady Maria Sneachi <   > of the House of the North would cement the stones of their tower of strength in a manner that no force or artifice could destroy.

Maria Sneachi is the youngest Daughter of his Majesty Alexander King of Sneachisland and a princess of the Blood royal of Verdopolis She is now 19 years of age and to a person of Dazzling beauty joins a mind of quite equally Dazzling vivacity She was born and nursed amid all the splendour of a powerful court and with a stern father and a watchful mother over her a wise and Noble Brother to guide her and a lofty and strong minded sister to advise her she passed through her first years of infancy without I dare say much lasting or stinging pain in Early youth the persecution and final expulsion from the royal family of her next Brother the now well known and respected General Thornton[49] gave her some uneasiness and passingly roughed the surface of her brilliant sea In truth her character was to generous and open to coincide in the cruel and unwarranted treatment bestowed alike by the unyeilding Monarch the ungracious queen the scarcly just prince royal and the agreeing Princess royal on a young man [who] whatever his faults might have been was yet a son and a brother and a hearty and generous one too. However the disagreement consequent in the Royal family upon this untoward occasion in a while cleared up and the "Low Polar Star" shone out with an <added> brilliancy Lady Maria at this time appeared at Court and in public and her extreme youth her raven curls her dazzling eyes her bewitching smile and her every look and gesture of such Hebe like grace and loveliness: turned all eyes in delight upon her and crowned her the Northern Queen of May I well marked her first open appearance at the vast circles of Verdopolitan Aristocracy and while I saw the Native spirit of Her lofty house rise fully in her pride and haughtyness in that moveless forehead and swan like Neck. yet I guessed from her cheerful and enthusiastic smile her cordial delight for all things which touched on her fancy. her graceful and easy flow of sparkling conversation that underneath all a proud and unbending air of exclusiveness shone a heart of <that> true and natural youthfulness. Of course with such qualitys and such a station Lady Maria did directly raise. as with magic wand a vast circle of Lovers and servants among the highest and the wealthiest Aristocracy and there was not hardly a single young heir to a coronet. or Marquisate or Earldom or Lordship who in a greater or less degree did not kneel and sigh before the all presiding goddess of beauty and majesty But alas Maria was a Coquette a proud but still accomplished Coquette and little sorrow did it give to her when she glanced her large dark eye round the circle of her thousand admirers to know that from Prince to Viscount from the Man of Fame to him of fashion there was hardly one underneath the age of 30 who did not bow their hearts in slavery before the Name of the Princess Maria Sneachi In the multitude of coun[s]ellors saith the Prophet is safty[50] and I well know that in the multitude of anything is confusion Maria knew this too and amid the hundred sacrificers of Heart and Fortune there was not one which did not meet with a thousand objections in her too inextricably puzzled mind. and then the marriage of a Daughter of the House of Sneachi who but a Prince or at least a Duke Dare think of such a thing who anyhow dare put it into execution a few seasons of further scorn and petition or offering and demanding might have passed on beyond the present one had nott those awful <arbitrators> of a ladys satisfaction the grim rulers of the Verdopolitan politics cast their eyes round for a firm bond of unity between the cheif rulers of the Regal Parties. They had just beheld the King of Angria more firmly unite to his fortunes the Earl of Northangerland by marrying that Noblemans lovely daughter and they believed that the best plan for

---

49 See vol. I, p. 409.
50 Compare Proverbs 11:14; 24:6.

their intrest[sic] would be that the Heir to the throne of Parrysland should be united to a Princess of the Throne of the North. Lady Edith the Princess Royal had already received the hand of the young Earl of Arundel[51] and the Princess Maria next stood fairly in the eye of the politicians. Earl St Clair and the cheifs of the Ministry of Verdopolis consulted with the Earl of Arran[52] and the Ministry of Sneachisland and the Earl of Arran and the Ministry of Parrys land Lord Macara Lofty and Mr Secretary Pelham were despatched to the Southern Court where his Majesty gave his consent and his son his aquiescence to the matter thence they posted with a train of secretarys to the north where after deep consultation the King of the Mountains nodded his agreement and the Duke his son the great director of all our ongoings his brow first saddening and then reflecting ratified the compact by his omnipotent will. Now the matter was first broken to the victim of the Nations good to the princess Maria Sneachi The Royal father commanded the Royal Mother directed the Royal sister advised and the all powerful brother in his persuasive voice represented the matter in few and laconic words settled!— The Princess like a dutiful girl looked at the certainty. of grandeur present and royalty to come. then at the crowds of suitors whom certainty might kill and then at her own inclination and last at the Marquis of Ardrah.

Meantime the intelligence of the probable union by marriage of two illustrious familys had run the round of the whole country had been obscured by the <hints> of the officials applauded by the gratified Aristocrats sneered and ridiculed by Northangerland and-I really dont know what done to by the Zamorna. -I know that at a grand party at Wellesly House the Duke (par excellence) when standing by the princess Marias sofa after actually showering on her the light of his Godships countenance. said in a pitying tone. and with a deep decided

---

51   Henry Fitzalan, 12th Earl of Arundel (1511?-1580), was the only son of of the 11th Earl by his second wife, Lady Anne Percy, daughter of Henry Percy, 4th Earl of Northumberland. After distinguished service in the war with France, he was appointed Lord Chamberlain. He was active in allaying the Scots Rebellion of 1549, but was sent to the Tower in the same year for committing felonious acts with the Duke of Somerset. He set up and betrayed Northumberland over Mary's ascension to the throne, was appointed lieutenant general and captain of the forces for the defense of the kingdom. He also served Elizabeth in various capacities, but conspired against her vis-a-vis her marriage, was imprisoned, and died after his release, the last earl of his family.

52   James Hamilton, 2nd Baron Hamilton and 1st Earl of Arran (1477?-1529), signed the treaty between England and Scotland for Henry VIII in 1509. He was appointed generalissimo of the kindom, and commanded the expedition to aid the King of France in 1513. In 1517 he was appointed provost of Edinburgh, and joined the council of regents in 1522.

emphasis "Alas Iphigenia"![53] To which His right. Hand Northangerland with a sneer which ruffled the whole melancholy of his brightened countenance. added. gazing on the Marquis of Ardrah "She was sacrificed to the Ocean!" This sally ran through the saloons. Poor Iphigenia looked thoughtful after it and the Ocean looked deadly and grim.

Well time wore on Maria did not cast off her vanitys or much lightened her gai[e]ty. Ardrah steadily worked upon the subject of the tapis.[54] Zamorna Became King of Angria Edward Percy saved Fidena's life. was introduced to the family of the North insulted the Marquis of Ardrah and was patronized by the smile of Lady Maria Then she met him at. De Lisles the Artists and. he too met her but. his obscure and unknown situation his arrogant and haughty manners and his whole air of watchful and determined recklessness was scarcly calculated at first sight to be dwelt on with a smile by the young. and hau[g]hty princess. however none of that arrogance was dared against her and he had what she could not forget he had saved her Brothers life and he had insulted twice the offensive Ardrah The look too which the nameless adventurer cast upon her as he left her prescence could not leave her mind and. the fortunes of the strangly situated Son of the Mighty Northangerland the. being deprived of Title of fortune of. opportunity of everything but life struggling up through unnumbered difficultys overcoming them one by one and finally dawning on the world in a morn of huge hop[e]ful prosperity. I say these things the Princess Maria was forced to reflect on and her Intimate freind the Duchess of Zamorna contributed innocently to strengthen these remembrances by eagerly asking of her. (Maria) details of what. Her brother Edward Percy had said or done when she saw him. (this was ere Edward had introduced himself to the Duchess and when a long and total separation had effaced in her susceptible heart all trace of his earlier insolence though not of his earlier persecutions.

But my reader will ask. are their not Other Noblemen in this city of. personal appearance equal to Percy and of Splendour of Mental qualitys at first sight above him remember he is unknown and a manufacturer.

Aye I answer I know that but he is a son of Percy the great and a Percy is different from most other men. what Lady who beheld long since the youthful and. melancholy Pirate has ever forgotten him.

The Evening of June 1st. 1834. shone glorious over the glorious Glasstown Valley. and nowhere in all that wide land of unfading fertility did his beams glow brighter than on the lawns and partteres of. Northwood Park. a country estate of. his Majesty. the King of Sneachis land. Northwood Park is perhaps 20 miles from Verdopolis and its statly and Lofty Mansion is concealed amid a dense grove of statly trees which spread all their dark luxuriance of foliage

---

[53] The daughter of Agamemnon, offered by him as a sacrifice to Artemis and saved by the goddess, who made her a priestess—see Euripidies' *Iphigenia in Taurus*.

[54] Tapestry used as a curtain, table cloth or carpet.

wide and high over the hill sides above the many columned Hall. Far round it the rich and bright green lawns stretched on toward the Niger. that evening green indeed or yellow in the beams of the declining sun. the Enormous River flowed gloriously down toward the smoke of Verdopolis deeper and deeper in its blue profundity but up the vale and toward the sun its colour changed like magic from blue to white and from white to a dazzling and glittering gold. beyond it its own. gilded halo. quenched the far of hills and valleys in a sea of splendid light. and it was not till the country on each side of its banks began to wheel downward from the sun that all its beauty and verdure shewed themselves out full to the. astonished eye overhead the sky glowing with an Italian fervour was thickly ornamented with a vast fold of swelling cloud. rolling mass over mass in lights of crimson and violet and and gold till fairly lost and quenched in the lustre of Apollo's own declining beams.

A pleasant breeze rustled through the foliage of Northwood Park and while all the Hall and dark green woods beyond it were almost to the sight eaten away by the lower and appropriating sunbeams the foreground of close shorn velvet green and young trees. guarded by the protecting paling and stags spotting the expanse like cattle. and a broad path smoothed by the so thick strewn marks of carriage wheels gave at once. a life and tranquility to the scene which seemed in exquisite Harmony with all the joyful and glowing Nature But if the scene proved so enrapturing when only decked with inanimate nature. what must it be like when. surrounding a star of pure and brilliant <illumination.> That Evening this noble lawn was pressed by the footstep of the Princess Maria the Princess of Light. the Northern Queen of May. Herself the Earl. of Aroundel. and Her sister His Countess had a day before arrived at Northwood on a visit to the Queen then. residing temporarily at. the seat. That Afternoon Lady Maria was called to the Apartment of her Imperial Mother and their in the prescence of her Elder sister the Queen admonished her that the time for the connsumation of her marriage would ere long arrive that the Day was perhaps even now fixing and that It behoved herself to think. directly upon that event which must soon and inevitably arrive She eulogised the Marquis of Ardrah in the highest terms and declared that nothing could render her happier than the possession of such a son in law. Lady Arundel. seconded her mothers admonition and Lady Maria turned pale at its conclusion. The advice having been most explicitly repeated Maria obtain[ed] leave to withdraw She did so and hurried either to repress or give vent to her feelings into the wide and sunny park. here alone. she walked amid its shadowed alleys and open. green woods with a shade of sorrow on her countenance which one would greive to see settled on one so young and so lovely. and so lofty. "I hate him she said half. in meditation and half aloud to herself. as she stood looking but without admiring on the glorious sunset before her "I hate him and am I to form another Instance of the cruel sacrifice of a Affection to expediency of the feelings to Politics the Heart to a crown. My Brother has escaped this fatal Altar as has my sister. So has the Duke of Zamorna. and alas I only. am doomed to suffer what I least should like to bear. They tell me I am a Coquette If I am. I have found no sorrow in it. no harm in it. They say I am proud. but let them turn to their Mirror for pride Oh but I am obstinate and now because I refuse to give up all my happiness to them they brand me with a name they should take to themselves-to themselves only—I am a Princess and I know not where to look for hope.

   She seated herself. on a rural seat of. vine twigs and there reclined under the shadow of a noble chestnut. her hand supporting her head and. hid in the glossy curls of her luxuriant hair she cast her large eyes erewhile so bright and lively to the setting sun with a sigh of real and unaffected sadness. and while the arch smile had forsaken her lips she ran over in her mind and now and then repeated in a low tone her dislike of Ardrah and the hopelessness of her situation. "If I speak of it to Edith she will bore me with her detestable. canting if I look at John he will put on to please me one of his resolved unpitying smiles if to my mother oh what hopelessness is there and my father—I dare not speak of my feelings to him Lady Julia too will tell me. "A King for a husband so glorious even prospect" The Duchess of Zamorna will. pretend to know nothing on earth—Arthur Arthur I suppose will mutter his detestable "Iphigenia" and then smile his cruel selfish smile. and that horrid Northangerland—I almost wish Arthur were here.—" She looked again at the sun. "Ah I suppose my happiness is as low as thou It touches the horizon-hovers over the. sea." "If it is Morning it does" said. a firm voice behind her She started up and instantly regained her haughtiness. "Sir I demand the reason of your intrusion" "And you shall have it" said the person whom she addressed It was Edward Percy. He stood before her his tall symmetrical figure and handsome and haughty countenance seeming instinct with passion and energy. "his eye and forehead had a look of. deep thought and once he looked on the princess with a smile of strangely seeming pity his voice is usually harsh and menacing in first addressing any one It was now deep and softened in its feeling. "Maria" he said with. an air which however did not brook interruption "Do you wish to know why I am here to see you. —I am returning to Verdopolis from a journey taken in company with the Duke of Zamorna to the New founded capital of Angria. he has either passed on toward this house or the city I know not which but I knowing from the papers that you were here determined to see and speak to you." "And what Sir can prove your reason for desiring to speak to me the present is neither a fitting time nor place" said the Princess offendedly and about to turn away "It is both" returned Edward with a calmness which chained her to the spot. "It is both and I could not desire another spot for speaking to you than the one we now stand on Maria! you have stepped on the threshold of an important crisis of your life and wether shall it be the threshold of happiness or misery you just now compared your happiness to the sun—I know nothing of the truth of that comparison but this I do know your life is not like that sun. No Maria you are yet on the Horizon of morning and look now on all this wide blue expanse of Heaven see the long long course from East to West from Dawn to twilight. will you not shudder to think of adding oer all that Sky without happiness? —in clouds? —a sun of misery. are you living in the east and your happiness sinking in the west.? Oh Maria has it so far got the start of thee. No believe me it need not be so? —It is said you are about to be as they call it united to His royal Highness the Marquis of Ardrah. If that be true you of course know better than I wether your twilight is not now begun. but you need not take a step which you can never desire to do turn child and place thy fair foot if thou canst on thy only path to happiness." He smiled as he so spoke with a strange a singular smile he seemed to look into her soul. The Princess stopped she scarcly knew how to depart. She looked at him with more awe than often appeared in her lovely features. and answered in a voice trembling slightly. in the commencement. "Sir you act unfairly in addressing me here and now. I intreat you to dep—" "Maria dont interrupt me." —was the stern solemn reply. "They are going to make a queen of you yes they mean to decorate their victim" he stopped and smiled that strange smile again "I know Princess what you feel just now. and thy soft voice can never deceive me—But look at me Maria and remember you see one who can never fall one who must rise—or die. you see a man who has left obscurity for ever and who must be eminent. ere long you know I dont boast and you must believe me. Then hear me. —I love you and have so done since I first saw you. You think me presumptous—No not so I can mark my aim and fear not to shoot beyond. it or to shoot below it. —A month since I loved you and determined to have you Mine Maria was no cold or heartless love it is not a plodding and settlement seeking love it is not a sigh and goosebrain love it [is] A love of character which in proportion as it rises so much the more evident in me is so much the stronger you are aware of my impetous character and you may be aware that I am one thing to all one on my career thoughts of yourself or thoughts of that infernal Ardrah—Ah but I do know. I do know that during the last 4 weeks amid varied and rapidly passing scenes of life amid the trouble and bustle of commerce and the solitude of my own walks and rides and the <tumultous> feeling of rapid and swelling sucess there is one person and only one who has had power to shine forth like a watch fire and guide me to glory thou knowest Maria that that one person is thee and know too that the confession just made is the first of its kind which has yet escaped the lips of Edward Percy You I suppose have many admirers a vast host of—lov—of—of—lovers You may count in your train Princes and Nobles and Warriors and Statesmen but <hear me> Maria Sneachi dost thou know of a soul who is able to add one sunbeam to thy home-save one-and that one stands now before thee. —you may think that my tone of voice my rather <chagrining> mode of speech the absence (but I hope you cannot be so blind) of fond and endearing expressions. the look of my eyes may not augur more favourably for the ardour of so imperious a suitor—If you do think so open your eyes I intreat you for hear-that one word "Maria" sounds sweeter to me. than any other in this world and the mere pronouncing of it I love better than to mouth out a wild chaos of Queen Heavenly love dearest life and the like in <fatheaded> nonsense. and if I know what I am and I believe that I am. a man If refuse to bend and bow and flatter and offer my life and liberty and my soul at your hands it is Maria because I believe thee too high to accept such unworthy adulation and myself too high to plea thee it So far I will say that I am prouder of myself when I can think. that thou perhaps mayst yet be proud of me. —So far I have spoken of my own feelings Now I will speak Maria of thine. and I know that their beats not in all these our native countrys a heart more generous and high born or refined or warm than thine no none in thy sex so much so this language is not flattery it is praise which thou dost not often hear and hear me praise is not indifferent even to a princess when proceeding from the soul of a Percy." As Percy spoke these words he kept the glance of his keen eye ever on the countenance of the Princess and while he stood before her the very life and soul of repressed but unquenchable passion the picture of haughtiness and intrepid daring his forehead calmed in to smooth ivory his lips changed into a thousand flexible expressions and his voice in speaking was so firm so decided sometimes spoken through even his closed teeth. yet did it sound so sweet and impassioned that it ended on the ear like the last note of nervous but heavenly music. The single word "Maria" though addressed by a titleless young Nobleman to a lofty Princess did each time it was spoken thrill through the heart of his <beauteous> listner. She was to proud to betray many marks of confusion to depress her head or avert her eye but on his concluding to speak she stood erect her face forehead and neck blushing with royal blood her eyes sparkling with unrestrained feeling she pointed toward the distant Hall of Northwood and would have spoken but for a moment the words trembled on her lip without her having power to utter them. Percy stood opposite not relinquishing his haughty attitude bloodless cheek and fiery and peircing eye "Sir" she said almost distrusting her own voice to convey her thoughts "you have chosen a strange opportunity to speak to me on the subject you have alluded to you guess rightly when you speak as you have done of the step which I fear must be taken ere long by me. My father Sir the Queen my whole house the Aristocracy that city are all bent upon my—my" "Dont mention it." "And how in heaven or earth can I avert or avoid should I take a step a single step without their consent to what extremity to what inveteracy resentment will rise I cannot guess or tell. Oh No Sir my feelings my opinions are not and can never be my own leave this Hall. and do not see me again for I dare not even now think that you may be noticed and how dare I look forward upon the step you wish me to take." "If you wish me" said Edward "to relinquish my determination change that voice for its silver tone sounds like a trumpet of Defiance to me." Maria smiled but mournfully. "Sir truely this subject is both painful and difficult to speak of and for myself I am acting madly in staying a moment here. Oh Edward I am lost in a maze of misery." "And see the clue which alone can extricate you. Maria Shortly I shall see thee again I am not so rude as to force the untimely expression of your feelings. I am not so supine as to tear an advance expression of them. but by Heaven if the stability of this countrys Aristocracy depends upon the marriage of Maria Sneachi and Arthur Parry it must be sealed by in that case the hearts blood of Edward Percy and if that blood be necessary to seal it Oh that sacrifice shall never ascend to heaven that union shall never never happen And thou thyself. Maria shalt. be—the Wife of one whose love will only be extinguished with his life-whose fame will be long-long ere it die! That sun has set and with it shall sink thy sorrows for while this arm can grasp its weapon defiance shall never approach thee or degradation or sorrow assail thee. or one ray one single ray of light ever darken from thy own unequalled form." Edward spoke these words with his own unbridled energy he clasped the Princess to his heart and imprinting on her lips one ardent kiss threw himself on to his Horse which was. grazing in the copse. and without a backward look or gesture galloped furiously down the Avenue. and plunged out of sight "Hey Edward" cried Zamorna whom he crossed on gaining the road "Now whither away so fast." Edward only answered by a furious curse and galloped yet more swiftly along the road. "Warner" said the Duke more thoughtfully "you may ride on I *must*. call at Northwood Hall" as he spoke the young Monarch turned his steed to the park gates and motioned his page to follow behind.

CHAP VIII

Edward Percy reached his own house strode rapidly through the Hall into his sitting room ejected from it with a loud oath William and Timothy and shutting the door furiously behind them he. threw himself on to a fireside sopha. "There he sat or rather reclined his head leaning on his hand and his handsome countenance illumined by a thousand expressions of triumph and exultation. Those who might have passed him on his ride home would suppose some frightful event to have happened to him but they little knew Young Percys character joy made him always solitary and hope made him savage He. now though it was dark midnight and he propably[sic] had not slept for several nights back exhibited no signs of exhaustion or fatigue or heaviness he sat their all night. thinking rapidly over his prospects considering means to put a decided stop to the Royal Marriage determining himself to use his utmost exertions to rise directly to riches and distinction and then he said starting from his sopha. "then Maria Sneachi shall be mine I know what she feels and I am satisfied" When the light of morning dawned and the hundred mill bells began to tinkle out their gathering sound Edward sprung up opened the Door and on with his hat and down to the mills This morning his behaviour to the work. people was almost insufferable curses and threats and maledictions he poured out without mercy. As he stood at the Door of his counting house. Timothy came up with 3 or 4 Gentlemen of great wealth and distinguished among the Mercantile circles. He knew them and they Him. Therefore profiting by their knowledge they at once opened their advances. "Mr Percy we congratulate you this morning on your accustomed sucess. We form a deputation from the Council of the Commercial Hall. [and] think it proper to premise that during your abscence this week. Sir John Flower Member for. the west end of Verdopolis Division 1st. has been promoted to the peerage. and His freind our Banker James Bellinghame has taken that seat for that quarter of the City thus leaving vacant. our own part. the first Division of the East end and Manufacturing Division of the City. Now Sir. you know that. our Guild or Company of the United Commercial Hall exercises undoubted sovereignty in this part and that its member is alway[s] looked on as our representative[55] we therefore held a meeting yesterday at the Hall itself to decide on the choice of a member and as the time is now arrived when owing to the changes taking places in the country and the measures constantly moving over the face of trade. a member is wanted for us not. only of real wealth and capital but of active talent and rising abilitys. we looked round for such a one among us and we would inform you Sir that our choice almost unanimously fell upon Edward Percy Esqr Grenville Wood East End. you may guess the object of the present deputation. we met the Duke of Zamorna this morning and he told us our choice had been perfect." as the speaker concluded Edwards eyes glowed with light. "Mr Sydenham and Gentlemen you have done me a honour this day which it must be the study of my life to repay you have all deemed me worthy of. a seat to represent your body in the House of Commons. and in what way can I so well repay your distinguished favour as by accepting that seat and exerting myself when in it to preserve to increase and to perpetuate your just rights and principles—when Sir have you fixed the nomination" "Tomorrow evening Commercial Hall" "Then be assured I will there be present and will there on this subject in full adress you." The Deputation in a little while departed Edward looked triumphant—Timothy came up. "By the Lords kind mercy I was enabled the Day before yesterday to complete the Bargain with Colonel Grenville respecting the providentially gotten fleeces. on such terms as to obtain you a merciful profit." Edward seized the Note of receipt for his fleeces and saw there a bargain by which he had gained 15000£

I think it right to inform my readers that a few days before this event. the Ministry and their Majestys knowing that the present state of the Upper house of Parliament required the addition of a Man from the lower House of tolerable command of temper decent knowledge of public affairs and practical accquaintance with political buisness after a deliberation upon the choice of a person skilled in these essentials they did me the great and acknowledged Honour of conferring the post upon me and. as I. was inured to the life of a Ministry and possessed property quite sufficient to support the rank. their Majestys. were pleased to confer upon me the rank and title. of Baron Flower and Richton of Richton Castle and Flower hall.

But to conclude my own affairs and proceed with my Neighbors.

ON the Evening of June 3^d I was present at a splendid entertainment given at Welle[s]ly House. and fairly one of the finest in the season. I took my station of observation a[t] the. sounding board of a Noble Piano. and in the recess of an Ample Window over whose rich velvety curtains the soft lamps shed a mild and regal light Here enthroned in social comfort the New Lord Flower surveyed through the Telescope of his Mind all that unexplored Galaxy of Nobility and beauty congregated in the gorgeous saloons of the God of Fashion the Princly Zamorna. This Night in that August Heaven arose a star of the first

---

[55] Such an appointment was possible before the reforms of 1832, when some boroughs were controlled by corporations such as guilds.

magnitude a star as yet unseen unknown. but when once it had flashed on the eyesight of the Wondering Gazers destined to remain for ever in their minds and memorys. This Night there entered the rooms along with his Grace the Duke of Zamorna and Her Grace his lovely Duchess a Gentleman of erect and daring aspect who was introduced to the haughty company by the Name. The Right Honourable Edward Percy MP for Eastern Verdopolis—I myself beheld Mr E G Sydney turn to the Earl of Arran saying "My goodness and is it come to this and have these-Angrians attained another column to support their dome." to which my Noble freind the Marquis of Ardrah replied with bitterness. "Aye Sydney. a son of Northangerland." and Sir R W Pelham. remarked suavely "Certainly His Lordship and he will scarce drive forward together." "Humph" interrupted the Hon W S Lascelles.[56] "I bet 10 to a dozen how they slap hands at first meeting. "What do you think that Northangerlands such an addlehead as to kick off such a rum one as yon." "True William" said I "But will Northangerland see his ability" "L— I dont know"[57] was the lucid reply. It was evident to me that every Aristocrat present engaged himself in keen observation of this New Comer and almost every Aristocrat glanced with anger at the [Duke of] Zamorna when they beheld all the Youth Energy and Ability of the country passing over to his engrossing party The Cheif leaders of the Angrian faction also engaged themselves in endeavours to penetrate the sentiments and gauge the abilities of their unbroken Ally and numbers[58] were the crowds of noted and weighty leaders who gathered round him and strove to draw him into conversation

In the Glorious Galaxy of Beauty which crowded those Halls young percy was not unnoticed and his mysterious History his known high birth and his polished and handsome person. procured him a reception which I fear all his Talent and energy and commercial popularity could scarcly otherwise have done.

Amid this splendid Assemblage Edward Percy moved. wrapt up in his own thoughts he had entered the saloons with a stride of Haughtiness and he never relaxed it to the gay strut of the courtier A smile was often on his lips but it was one of sarcasm and his voice was fixed in a tone of Angry Determination he did not seem to love conversation he scowled at his sister and for the first half hour took. a seat in a recess and there. looked thoughtfully on the company There was one figure which his eye followed most restlessly round the room the.

---

56 Henry Lascelles, 2nd Earl of Harewood (1767-1841), was elected Tory member of parliament for Yorkshire in 1796 and reelected in 1802, but not in 1807, the first contested election in 66 years, memorable for the great expenses that occurred. He was elected for the town of Northallerton in 1818, and in 1831 declared himself a moderate reformer, in favour of the extension of representation but opposed to the Reform Bill. Harewood House, north of Leeds, is the home of the Lascelles family.

57 At this point there are seven canceled lines, upside down, dated March 17 PBB 1834.

58 "numerous" probably intended.

tall not ungracful but strangly sinister. figure of the Marquis of Ardrah as he
neared him Percy bent on him a frown of hatred and the Prince returned it by a
curious expression of compounded Pride and fear and. cunning

Among the fair Deitys who presided over the scene I saw one at least
whose observation of Edward Percy was neither unfrequent nor undistinguishing
and this one was the August and Awful Countess of Northangerland. Heavens
how her statly and. magnificent person and her dark complexioned but animated
features. seemed instinct with aversion as she saw him pass her with a slight
bow and an inimitable sneer. her kindled eye pursued him into the next
apartment and then she turned it back to the great Door opposite praying I dare
say in her heart that Northangerland might that moment enter but Alas
Northangerland was all that day lying on a hill side out of the road to Angria his
horse feeding beside him and himself thrown on the grass in an unmingled and
immitigable fit of black bitter Melancholy Oh had he that evening entered
Wellesly House I know not wether his soul could have born the sight. Edward
Percy standing with bitter smile and haloed brow young and tall and athletic the
picture of a renewed and embellished Rougue the youthful image of himself
standing now in the full pride of sound political ability declaring in strong
pointed and Eloquent language his often asked opinions of Angria and the state
of Africa he vented all his bitterest sneers and sarcasms upon the Aristocrats.
praised and became enthusiastic on the fortunes of the Angrian Adventurers and
cursed his father and insulted his hearers then again to view him his sneer
softning to a smile his voice softened in tone but his eye far far more wandering
far more unsettled in his gaze. surrounded by a heavenly circle of Beauty. the
Countess of Arundel (innocently) condescending to a smiling conversation the
Marchioness of Wellesly frightning him If such a character could frighten him
which I fear is far from the case. with a full display of her unnatural and languid
affectation Lady Julia Sydney really amusing him with her buoyant rattle and
cheerful and high bred spirits or the Countess his Step Mother Angering him and
drawing blood from his face with her awful and really detesting frown. —But, it
was to another being than any of those just named that Edward that night turned
a gaze of true and unfeigned illumination it was to the Princess Maria Sneachi
that he so often and so sternly looked in that splendid saloon she seemed sunk in
thought. her cheek was paler and her eye even brighter than usual she had forgot
all her accustomed high spirits and Royal Coquetry all but her royal pride and
allmost the only active interest she took in the evenings Gai[e]ty was to avoid
studiously to avoid the company of the Marquis of Ardrah who certainly was
very far from pressing it upon her but who passed composedly among the
Aristocrats now scowling at Edward Percy and his Host then recovering and to
Harlaw and. sneering down the Angrians the Duke of Zamorna often gave his
Notice to the Princess smiled his august smile or spoke in his godlike voice of
persusaion he once or twice mentioned Edward Percy and in terms of highest
Deference and he was not slow to mark the changing and agitated expression of
her generous features. he more than once or twice turned on her one of his
strange looks of half. unconcern half deep pity and she once started at hearing

something like the words "poor lamb" whispered emphatically in a solliloquy. A group had gathered round the splendid piano where I [the] greater part of the Evening had placed myself Lady Maria was called upon for one of her own highland airs of mingled grace and fire and tenderness. She was reluctantly and slow[ly] turning with her fair fingers the leaves of. the open music when Edward Percy one of the expecting listners sternly opened the page at a noble peice by Purcell.[59] and in cool firm accent said "Her ladyship will perhaps oblige me with. the one before her."

> I saw her in the Crowded Hall
> High plumes were waving there
> But mid those statly thousands all
> Were none like her so fair
>
> I saw the Ivory of her brow
> The diamonds in her hair
> I saw her swanlike neck of snow
> Her bright form shining there.
>
> Yes wake thee Maiden wake thee
> Thy fate frowns oer thy brow
> That neck which sorrow never bent
> Must bend to anguish now
> Oh loftiest of the lofty
> Fairest of the fair
> Can one dark shade pass oer thee
> Hast *thou*! shaken hands with care.
>
> Oh where in heaven or where in earth
> Can I behold a tearless mirth
> Alike the man of stormy life
> Long used to battle blood and strife
> Alike thou Beauteous queen of May
> In woes wild waste must mourn
> Must weep your glimpse of gladness gone
> And never to return.
> Then cease my lyre thy wailings cease
> Lingering quivering die in peace

The sound of the music faded into silence and the exquisitly plaintive melody sadden[ed] for a moment the hearts of the hearers. but ere long they were all gone and. gazing with delight over some novel or fashionable playthings Lady Maria alone. sat at the instrument one hand passivly laid one[sic] the less dazzling keys

---

59 The song is Branwell's, not Purcell's.

her eye gazing unconsciously on the opened page. "Never hesitate" said a
startlingly soft but stern voice in her ear. "resolve or be lost. —resolve and be
lost—resolve and be happy Maria they have fixed the hour" "Have they." she
answered turning paler at the approach of a dreaded moment. "And I have fixed it
too Wilt thou likewise have thy settlement Oh you are a Daughter of a royal line
I am the Descendant of a Noble one you are a lovely in mind and person I am
resolved in the one and can bear in the other can Do in both. will do in either—"
Here. the Marquis of Ardrah strode to the piano. his naturally fine countenance
darkened by a shade of the deepest hatred. "It is not my pleasure Sir that you
should attend this lady." "It is mine that I should attend thee." "Mr Percy leave
this place I command you" "Now by my own right hand Ill cut his head off.
Infernal scoundrel be gone from my sight." As Edward spoke He turned round to
the Marquis with [a] scowl of deep defiance. —His Royal Highness put on a face
of stony Caledonianism "You trespass on the bounds of Decorum" "You Lie"
was the ready Answer Ardrahs own natural courage could not bear this Affront
"Explain Sir" was his reply "you have told me a falshood" said Percy "Harlaw"
called the Prince Edward laughed sneeringly at the slight accent which expres[ed]
the last syllable and. called. in the full pitch of his trumpet voice. "Zamorna"
The Duke was directly on the spot Edward pointed feircely to the Marquis and
with the words "We have weapons" the whole 3 with young Marquis Harlaw left
the room the remainder of the company were ignorant except a few sharp eyed.
well understanding Gentlemen of the ominous transaction and its causes and
effects.
    I must change my scene abruptly and will not apologise it is my
custom convenience alone regulates my pages. it is on that same night but in a
different palace that these lights shed their halo round a whole statly and solemn
room dark hangings and a vaulted roof give a sort of Royal grandeur to its
appearance which suits well with the house of which it forms an apartment it is
a hall in the Elimboss Palace. and just risen from a richly carved seat at the
upper end of a long dark table stands a statly old man very tall in stature but
slightly stooped through age. his high bald forehead and silver haffets[60] his stern
eye brow and the whole Iron contour of his statly countenance show a man
neither of common rank or character Beside him stands a Lady advanced in life
but of features which if they have lost the more perishing <aspects> of beauty
still preserve all their pride and haughtiness and queenly severity a much younger
Lady of exquisite grace and be[a]uty but of quite as exclusive a deportment is
seated near the latter and a young Man a very picture of youthful wisdom of calm
philosophical state and Nobility is running over several papers and documents
which are placed upon the table where these stand. Several Gentlemen of
polished look and manners sit at a sort of Desk. their countenances marked with
cool political sagacity and their foreheads knotted in thoughtful speculation.
Maria Sneachi young beautiful but pale and melancholy is seated alone upon a

---

[60] The side of the head above the ear; the temples.

sofa and retired from the main group of persons. The occupants of this Apartment are high indeed in rank and dignity. Yon is His Majesty Alexander of Sneachisland who looks so sternly at the head of the room His Queen sits beside him near her is the Countess of Arundel the Duke of Fidena stands looking more in sorrow than anger at his younger sister and the Ambassadors from Parrysland with Mr Sydney and Sir R Pelham sit apart in deep diplomatic conference on the marriage settlements of the Prince of Parrysland and the Princess of the North.

"Has the Princess" said the stern voice of Her Royal Father "as yet given her distinct acquiescence in the settlements proposed" "Speak Maria" said the Queen "It does not become you to delay any longer" The Princess arose pale as death and much agitated "Your Majesty must excuse my silence" she said with a voice whose firmness increased as she proceeded "I have not yet given my acquiescence to the measure now in progress nor can I now through my whole life I have as yet known nothing of that sorrow with which I now behold you[r] eager pursuance of a plan which I cannot and dare not and I confess will not ratify.—" all present were silent for a moment. Lady Arundel spoke. "Maria are you Insane what reason can you have for hesitating at a matter involving the safty of these kingdoms" "With your leave sister" answered the Princess in something like a beam of her natural spirit "I cannot see how any matter so connected with my humble self can in any manner affect the intrests of a mighty empire. Edith above all persons it least becomes you to speak to me on this subject you have had your own inclination and you have given your hand to one of your own choice. and so have you John nor can either be better than one I could choose then why am I alone doomed to be singled out as the victim of expiation to a Nations sins Why must I only suffer in misery at being united to a person whom I could neither reverence admire or love This state alliance has never before been practiced in this kingdom and I will not be the first victim to its unjust decrees you may crush me but you shall not persuade me—you may oppress me but you shall never force me. I will die rather than degrade my dignity or ruin my happiness." She ceased and her forehead shone with unusual brightness her raven curls were thrown back and her dark eyes sparkled with a martyr like brilliancy Her father frowned and threatened her with the severest effects of his anger. her mother seconded and added force to his words with additional severity Edith reproached her bitterly and the Diplomatists entered into a long and alarming detail of the frightful consequences of her resolution The Duke of Fidena alone paced the room in deep and thoughtful silence. A scene of Royal Bitterness ensued which passes description and a bitterness of language was heard almost beneath the regal dignity The young Princess although her naturally proud and haughty spirit bore her up against this injurious attack yet at length wearied and frightened with the increasing violence of her opponents burst into a flood of tears "Oh Edward" she passionately exclaimed "I wish indeed you were here." "And I am here" said a stern voice. as the Member for Verdopolis entered the room. "Death what do I see Your Majesty I had come to accquaint you with a short peice of news. but I see a scene which calls straight for my first attention—What is it you are Daring to do Ive shot your scoundrel of a Prince and Maria come thou with me this is not home for you let these attend their wounded sparrow" he laughed sarcastically took the Princess's arm and led her almost stunned with astonishment to a noble chariot which he had waiting at the Door They both mounted The coachman was told thunderingly to Drive on and the carriage dashed rapidly away down Elimboss Square.

       A week after the incident above related I received an invitation to dinner at Edwardston Hall in the Kingdom of Angria near Verdopolis and the country seat of the Right Hon Edward Percy Esqr M P for Eastern Verdopolis and. president of the Board of Trade in the Government of the King of Angria on my arrival at the New and Noble Mansion I found there assembled a splendid party to greet the Nuptials of the Haughty young owner of the seat with the distinguished and beautiful Princess Maria of Sneachis land this I was aware of the marriage with its singular circumstances had spread through Verdopolis—Here I saw congregated the most noble and distinguished Leaders of the Angrian Faction the splendid young Monarch Arthur Duke of Zamorna with his Duchess the sister of the rising statesman. Viscount and Viscountess Castlereagh the Honourable W H Warner and his Lady H M M Montmorenci Lords Roslin Abercorn Molineux. &c with a splendid circle of attendant fashion and beauty among them all I failed not to Notice Timothy Steaton Esqr radiant though ill at ease in a bran[d] new suit of gorgeous olive brown. The Proud and Haughty Host dispensed with polished grace the Hospitalitys of his station and the statly and lovely Hostess on her part won all hearts by her grace and beauty and condescension Zamorna himself ruled lord of glory and gave his tone to all the festival.

       N B The Marquis of Ardrah is rapidly recovering from the wound he received in the unhappy affair on the 3 of June his Antagonist E Percy Esqr it is supposed will not be proceeded against as it might not only <create> much inconvenience to the country but would be totaly opposite to the usages and customs of Verdopolis.

Flower. and Richton

———————

P B Bronte

P B Bronte ——
Finished June 26. A D
1834.

The Life of feild Marshal the Right Honourable
ALEXANDER PERCY.[1]
Earl of Northangerland
Lord Viscount Elrington Lord Lieutenant of Northangerland
Premeir
of Angria Major General in the Verdopolitan Service &c &c &c--
By
| John | CHAPTER I[st] | BUD. |

VOL I

I am just about to commence writting an account of the life and character of the most extraordinary man of this century For amid all the Monarchs Warriors Statesmen Poets and Philosophers whose Stars have blazed and twinkled on the heavens of the last hundred years we the Inhabitants of Africa turn always from the lights of a Marlbourough Johnson Bonaparte Byron Nelson Scott or a "Georgius"[2] to look at the red troubled uncertain flashings of an Alexander Percy we look back through all the changes of time to the favorite luminarys of Greece and Rome. back even to Israel and Egypt. and in vain we seek for a being of so strange and wonderful Mystery as the one whom I have chosen for my hero his life and character though himself be one of the very leading men of Verdopolis is so uncertainly known to her Citizens that I deem it the duty of the man who has it to produce the key and unlock that casket is it not right that we whose every public action is involved in the actions of another should know the tenour of those actions and the source from whence they spring True but who is the man who has this secret I could name several persons fitted to weild so important a secret and there is one now alive who has known Northangerland from his boyhood who has entered into all his public machinations who has drunk of his draught both for good and evil who has mind and talent fitted to grasp his subject and who could write a life of Alexander

---

1 Manuscript in three volumes, without covers, 34 pages, 11.5x18.5 cm, in the Brotherton Collection. Volumes I and II are complete, but have been disassembled, and each leaf set into a sheet of paper. Only a two-page fragment of volume III is extant, but the existence of the volume is attested to by Branwell's footnote in BPM: Bon 149, leaf five: "Buds Life of Percy Vol III[d] p 1st"—see [Angria and the Angrians] IV (k) in vol. III. Volume I is undated, but in the 1837 revisions of the two poems it contains (see vol. III) Branwell dates both as having been composed in Spring 1834. It is likely, therefore, that he began this work immediately after completing **The Wool is Rising** in June 1834.

2 The Duke of Marlborough, who defeated the French at Blenheim (1704); Samuel Johnson; Napoleon; Lord Byron; Admiral Nelson; Sir Walter Scott; King George.

percy but now I fear that. Africa must resign all hope of having this work accomplished by him for politics have taken a turn which seperates the two confederates and widly alienates the mind of Mr H Montmorenci There is another person too in my eye whose brilliant genius and all powerful Intellect. could grasp the vision with magician hand who has a heart to respond and a head to understand all the varyings of this strange eventful history but the Duke of Zamorna's time is now swallowed up in the whirlpool of ambitious imaginings and. had he an hour to spare from the March of Angria he is yet in the dark respecting the first years of his Prime Minister My Noble and admirable freind. Lord Rirchton[sic] I know all my readers will suggest as the one remaining man fitted to encounter this difficult labour. But though I feel astonished at his deep accurate knowledge of. Percys character at his wide and varied information regarding his private and public ongoings though I. cannot to warmly express my gratitude for the vast stock of information he has afforded both yourselves and myself on every thing connected with this subject I yet must feel that Richton alas knows little of. [the] birth childhood and youth of. Northangerland.

Seeing then that the great champions of literature do not appear to take up arms against Goliath permit one to arise for you who though he knows he has all Davids untried weakness yet trusts that in this subject he may attain some of Davids unhoped suceess

From the Earl of Northangerlands early childhood to the time in which he entered before the world on the career which he is now accomplishing I was his Tutor and watched over his opening intellect. I was well accuainted with his fathers family and. knew every event relating [to] their origin for a natural turn to antiquarian research had qualified me for exploring the roots. of Genealogys. and since the fiery torrent burst from the confines of such a restricting valley as myself. I yet above it could. view and mark and wonder at that vast tortous course below. from that day till now I have not ceased noting the life of shall I feel proud or sorrowing to write my pupil. I also possess at present a great variety of papers and manuscripts written by or relating to Northangerland which are of great importance but which no other knows of. or possesses Do not let My Readers think for an instance that I possess or ever did possess one atom of the freindship of Lord Northangerland No I watched over his youth and. to one guilty of such a hideious offence never yet did he extend his freindship or pardon. the documents I do possess are not obtained from him but the[y] form the collection which when some years since. his whole fortune was brought under the hammer Lady Helen Percy requested me to procure and. save from the eyes of the public some others I have caught from destruction at various times during my accquaintance with him but did he know I possessed these he would. hate me and injure me. not a lines[sic] save of a political character that ever dropped from his pen did the Earl ever of his own consent caause[sic] to transpire.[3]

---

[3]   i.e., to become known, leak out or emerge from secrecy.

With these advantages then which none other can possess I come forward with some degree of. confidence before the public to present. Angria with the life of her Prime Minister and Verdopolis with the character of her Arch Agitator.

The ancient family of the Percys in the North of England. was descended from a branch of the great and powerful House of Northumberland.[4] A younger brother of Old Earl Percys. it is said sometime in the 14 century having been driven from his fathers Castle through his lawless and outrageous character. built for himself a sort of strong hold. in one of the western valleys of the Northumbrian Cheviots here he and his sons and immediate descendants for more than a hundred years held their seats as the half lord half robber of a wide and trembling district but when the times began to brighten a little from Feudal and outlawed oppression this tryannous and rebbellous house was forced to rein in its unwarranted. and oppressive. plundering during the. 15 century feauds[sic] with their Neig[h]bours the Scotch wranglings with the superior branch of Northumberland headlong gambling in the game of York and Lancaster[5] fully occupied the hands of the. dangerous.

> "Percies of Raystracke cladde in mail
> Belted and branded and horsed for warre
> Never knew thai fro ye. death to faill
> Readyye to do but lothe to bear"

From the settlement of the national quarrel to the union of the rival Crowns I know little of their ongoings but. when. James first ascended the throne of England.[6] Archibald Percie of Rayestracke. fastned his worn. out fortunes on court favour and. strove to mend in the South what his family had lost in the North When the heavy threatning of misfortune began to threaten round the throne of Charles First <rebellion> again sent forth all its minions alert for destruction and amid the most alert ther[e] issued out the dwellers of. Rastrick hall. they espoused the part of the Puritans and aided in the overthrow of the

---

[4] This elaborate delineation of Percy's ancestry suggests that Branwell was not satisfied with Charlotte's attempt to provide Percy with an aristocratic pedigree in "The Green Dwarf"—see Alexander CB, II, part i. The Brontë children would have read the legend concerning the Percies and Alnwick Castle which Scott both recounts and refutes in *Tales of a Grandfather*. According to this legend, when Malcolm III of Scotland invaded England, Robert de Mowbray brought him the keys of Alnwick Castle suspended on his lance. Handing the from the wall, he thrust his lance into the King's eye, whence he received the honorary name "Pierce-eye." The Brontës also knew of the Percies through their reading of Shakespeare's *Henry IV, Part I*.

[5] i.e., the Wars of the Roses. "Raistrick" is a long established name in Haworth.

[6] From the end of the Wars of the Roses to the accession of James I (James VI of Scotland) in 1603.

Monarchy but their reckless dispositions did not stand in good odour with the ascendent party and Archibald with his followers was fain to retire to his Hall in the Cheviots. here his descendants remained and I know nothing again of their history untill 1715 when. Henry Percy Esqr of Rastrick house plunged into all the troubles of the pretenders invasion[7] with characteristic effrontery abetted the attempt of that man whose Grandfather his Grandfather had aided to dethrone and. as characteristically he escaped out of the struggle with the loss of half his lands and hertiage[sic] upon which he gave himself up to dark and secluded parsimony shut himself up in the Old hall and. there after several years of. monastic severance from society he died in 1783 leaving a rescusitated property to his eldest son Edward. who recalled from France the country of his education entered upon his fathers estates and though very young and almost unknown to his tenantry. at once conciliated their applause and good wishes. Edward Percy. was a Gentleman. both in manners and appearance. and his handsome person. uncommon command in learning and <keen> polished. understanding. made him respected. for awhile by all his wide aqquaintance. but this was the white wash of <the plaster washed of> dead mens flesh and bones. prolifigate and dissolute habits a dark revengeful disposition and a constitution formed to bear much yet break not threw Mr Percy into a wild whirl of. riot and extravagance. he raised his rents. drove down to London gave his vote for Wilkes[8] played high and fought several duels. till a harrassed steward. a starving tenantry and an empty rentroll. called him. back to Northumberland. the moment he entered Raystrick house ruin stared him in the face so he. threw up all his property brought hall and house and heritage to the hammer and pocketting the proceeds of. a family downfall. he. fought a duel with a lord [and] carried off a Lady

"And soe to Irelonde"[9]

In this new country our Abraham set up his wandering sojourn and in Dublin he found few competitors in the race he was running those who knew Mr Percy in Africa can hardly believe the extent of his dissolute abandonment. his property would soon have evaporated save that he replenished now and then the cistern by the proceeds of deep and varied gambling and one of the fairest fountains from which he drew the water was Gerald Earl of Mornington[10] father of our great Duke of Wellington a Nobleman of high and brilliant Talents but. one whose lawless conduct had overseen the destruction of hundreds of his

---

7 James Francis Edward Stuart (1688-1766), the "Old Pretender."

8 John Wilkes (1727-97), radical reformer in Parliament.

9 The phrase seems to be Branwell's, but is possibly adapted from Shakespeare's *Richard II*, II, i, 219.

10 The actual name and title of the historical Duke of Wellington's father; also the title of the Duke's older brother, Richard, first Governor General of India. It was during his Governorship that Arthur Wellesley gained fame as a military leader.

ancestral acres. with this Man. Percy formed a deep card table race course freindship and. like all such freindships his time he employed in plotting the complete ruin of the New associates property to perform such a labour. He employed. a heart and hand associate The Earl of Caversham a Nobleman whose great landed estates and connections with the Wellesly family had only added a prominency to distorted talent and. coldhearted prolifigacy this man with his freind Mr Percy involved the Earl of Mornington in a maze of. extravaganc[e] losses depts[sic] and usury and the net then being drawn around their victim they rested awhile as sure of their play. meantime Mr Percys handsome figure and commanding intellect had secured to him the love of. a young lady of. high birth and. of a mind as noble as her person was beautiful He married Lady Helen Beresford and. returned to the completion of his scheme. Alas Morningtons eyes were opening the victim was struggling he had seen a little into the mass of knavery and. treachery with which he was surrounded and so had begun a little proceeding which was threatning to open up a hundred such <vain. manuvrings> the two Confederates concluded that there remained only one way by which to quash proceedings so detrimental to their projects they called into their councils Robert Patrick King the Valet of. Mr Percy a native it was supposed of Yorkshire and who had been in the service of the Percy family for. thirty years. the age of this servant was perhaps then as near as they could guess. 50 or 55. and of his life. though. Percy had so long known him he was very little acquainted an air of strange and impenetrable mystery hung over the fellows course. and stories were not wanting respecting him which might make the hair of ones head stand up with horror. so far all knew of his character—that there was no thought however foul no deed however monstrous no word however perjured which he would not say or do or. think for. —money and the love of. seeing his any mans death struggle[11] a hundred Men in the Metropolis of all ranks and titles had employed this Man as the Instrument of their crimes while in London he had. attained the proud eminence of general tutor of Vice. among the young and now in Dublin he was activly employed as its instument among the old. To such a spirit of evil Percy and Caversham had recourse in the time of their difficulty he taught them at once a ready method of removing the "Inconvaniense" and after insinuating himself into the confidence of the Earl of Mornington that Nobleman was one day found dead in his dressing room his features blackned and distorted by. some sudden struggle. he was buried with all the usual honours and. for a while all suspicion seemed laid at rest but his Lady the Countess. believed rather in death by the visitation of Man than by any <other> visitation whatever She again instituted an enquiry into the causes of this event. and erelong matters had come to the inauspicious pass that the Earl of Caversham Mr Edward Percy and. Mr John O Connor began to look oftener toward the Atlantic Ocean than the hills of Ireland.

---

[11] This rather contorted syntax was created by Branwell's emendations, the intended meaning being "for love of seeing any man's death struggle."

At this time 1790 the fame of our rising Empire in Africa had spread itself. abroad through the whole of Europe and all men heard with astonishment of. vast conquests and the rapid rise of a few military Adventurers whose leaders had 20 years before sailed from England without exciting one word or sign of notice from her whole population and though very lately one of these heroes had. delivered Europe from Slavery[12] and had departed for Africa with 50000 followers yet no one had hope that. in so short a time the 12 would have beheld. the whole course of the Niger the Gambia and the Senegal their own kingdom and. their own people But Now. All in Europe when they saw the light. of Fortune waning in their Hemisphere looked on Africa alone as the New seat of her capricious reign. every one who had heart and enterprise whose hands and purse were empty and his shoulders both broad and bare now embarked with joy for his Canaan[13] and promised land. that enthusiam with which 300 years ago Europe looked on America was now rekindled with triple ardour when she gazed towards Africa

Toward this shore so hopeful for the future. the three blood stained confederates directly turned their eyes and gathering together in haste all his lawless gains Mr Edward Percy fled to London from immediate apprehension and next early in 1790 set sail from England with his Newly wedded Bride Lady Helen Percy more than 100000£ in his purse and. His Tutor in crime R P King following faithfully at his back. but so close I understand where the Officers of Justice after the Criminal that the worthy Valet only escaped being whirled back to Ireland by levanting[14] in the night of departure from Portsmouth jail. The Earl of Caversham and Mr O Connor being both Irishmen had just before set sail for that part of Africa lying westward toward the Atlantic and known to be under the sovereignty of the Duke of Wellington Here too Mr Percy directed his wanderings though in so doing he knew he should place himself in the power of the son of the man he had murdered but his desperate character hardly brooked caution and muttering "Its best to sit near the fire when the chimney smokes" he anchored after a tolerable voyage at the mouth of the Noble Gambia My readers must know that 40 years ago 100000£ was no mean matter in Africa and let them not wonder if. however bad his character Mr Percy when he landed established himself on a high footing in his newly adopted country. his wealth his own Able and energetic character. the high station beauty and accomplishments of his Lady. opened to him a fair reception at court. He entered as Member of the general parliament for Wellingtons Town bought an old house. built by the English of AD 1500. amid the woodlands east of the capital and adding new fronts and gables to it he christened it Percy Hall and made it his familys country seat.

---

[12] i.e., Wellington at Waterloo.

[13] The promised land of the Israelites leaving Egypt under Moses' leadership was called Canaan—see Genesis 12, 13, 17; Exodus 23; Joshua 1.

[14] To steal away, bolt, abscond, especially of a betting man or gamester.

In 1790 Africa presented a very different appearance from what it does now the White Inhabitants comparitivly few in Numbers all most all soldiers ever bearing Arms and possessing a rough Iron and ambitious character ruled with haughty despotism over a lately vanquished and half unexplored region of burning Africa. Verdopolis itself almost the only great City of Consequence towered on the Niger the very Queen of our dominion and her population a vast whirlpool of. mingled YOUNG MEN. French Spaniards Americans Italians Moors Turks Persians Burmese and. Egyptians all inured to bloodshed alien from each other and each ambitious for supreme sword gain[ed] dominion. general awe only of the English Adventurers the 12s. prevented the other nations from throwing the confusion into absolute chaos and. while the young men kept up a desperate warfare against the French. all the remaining bands persecuted and worried each other. while over all things the GENII. small and great. wandered over all the continent oppressing and exacting demon malignity The Man who in those days beheld Verdopolis at Midnight would fancy he saw the streets of a stormed city so frequent and outrageous were the feauds fights and. murders amid its varied Inhabitants when just at this time arose the Great Rebellion against the the Genii[15] which shook Africa to its Centre. for nearly a year. I know that it was only the. undaunted energy of the Adventurers which kept them from the conviction that every thing about them was verging to everlasting ruin

The picture I have drawn of Africa at the end of the 18th century is a strange one but as true as strange. I was then in my 20th year a soldier in the Armies of the Young men and day and night I was occupied in a series of such battles as would have given a surfeit to many a gallant spirit But my mind naturally inquisitive and attentive to learning and accquirement was always observing things around me. and I for one among thousands only saw in the anarchy the Noble struggles of a rising Empire. In 1793 I received a temporary discharge from my military duties and hastened to Wellingtons town to visit my parents who resided near its suburbs I remember when I. turned up the road which led toward the scenes of my childhood. with what wonder I looked over the wide expanse of newly planted wood. and great sweeps of just clipped verdure. all circled by the park walls and poplars of that years erection and planting. I could not but wonder at the creation for it had spread leviathan like over many a spot and many a nook of. cherished boyhood recollection and I know that I hardly liked to see the old. house on the knoll of woodland now transformed into a great gentlemans Hall. half hidden among its massy <columns> one of the first questions I asked when I reached home was to whom belonged that fine domicile that had sprung up. since I left home over Alderwood Shaws. and woodlands. The answer which I received was. That the park and house belonged to Edward Percy Esqr. a Gentleman who had landed two or three years ago. and who was said to be worth a great deal of money and whose wife was a distant connection of the Kings. that this Mr Percy was a great man that

---

[15]   See **Letters From An Englishman**, vols. III-VI in vol. I.

he lived very high but was extremely proud and haughty he strained his tenantry as hard as they could bear and if the rents were not brought in exactly on the day appointed the unfortunate defaulter was at once cast into jail he never gave one farthing in charity and. if he knew of a poacher tresspassing upon his Manors it was hard indeed with the culprit. He would hang him if he dared though he only had stolen an egg In short the character of this Gentleman was drawn to me as that of a man whose life of dissipation and extravagance having begun to turn led his hardened mind into an extreme of selfish and grinding tyranny

In shuch[sic] esteem was held Edward Percy Esqr MP. of Percy Hall in Wellingtons land. But he little cared himself what another man thought of him so that he could find room for his revenge upon the thinker. But I have lingered to long over times and people who might have been dispatched in a much shorter space. I must hasten to be ready for an Advent of Importance far above <the> appearance of all I have yet spoken of and I fear Africa must mark with a black. cross the year AD 1793 for then. on the First of December in a bleak stormy morning was born at Percy Hall his countrys pride and. scourger

ALEXANDER PERCY

CHAPTER II^d

I have said that the birth of Northangerland was marked by a rough and stormy day. certainly their appeared no prodigy either on heaven or earth. But clouds and wind and rain beat around the ancient Hall when its young lord. first opened his eyes upon that life which for him [h]as seldom been one of happiness His Father and Mother were proud indeed of their Infant Son and the Domestics and retainers talked greatly of. his beauty and "wonderful wit" yet in despite of the strange anecdotes told by Nurse or Servant. little Alexander was at first like any other child. —and as No feast or entertainments would Mr Percy give in celebration of the birth of his Infant Son as he did not release a single deptor[sic] or give back one penny of rental as the christening was void of all show or ostentation. the. Tenantry and. people around him soon began to forget almost that their young master was alive in the world. Amid the Old Oaks and elms around him his Infancy past on in silence and seclusion. watched over and guided by the fond and anxious affection of a statly and Noble Mother. Cherished as the pride and glory of. his Nurse and attendants gazed on now and then with complacency often with out notice by his dark and haughty father. Alexanders first year or two exhibited all the little joys and sorrows of early Infancy and when he could speak and walk was often carried out round the park and to the houses of his Attendants acquaintance that they might see the young heir in all his rising glory I remember his favorite Nurse used very frequently to bring him down to My fathers house. where I myself. (Oh how different since) was his especial delight and attraction. I had just returned from war was young and active could tell him stories of battles and play and rattle with him to his hearts contents I fancy now I can see. Ellen Hope coming in at the garden gate with her charge in her arms. a wild rosy cheeked bright. eyed. little fellow of 3 year[s] old his large straw hat covering his light golden hair and his voice raised in a cheerful scream as he was born by some high waving lily or pretty flower hang[ing] almost within his reach over the hegge or paling he always sat down on the grass by me to hear about some bloody battle with the Frenchys and though he ever began to listen with all the fire and enthusiasm of a military hero yet I cannot recollect that on any of those occasions he ever came forth with any astonishing display of brilliant genius or far sighted sagacity no the cat or dog or his young Nurse or. a horrible shreik for a sight of my sword and gun. generally diverted the future rebel from the dark detail of. Battle and murder and sudden death. However upon the conclusion of my narratives "Mr Bud do take me to see the Duke of Wellington" or. "I will be a General wether Papa says so or not" formed the fervent aspiration of my aspiring listener.

And yet even in those times of childish gaity there was one tone in Alexanders mind which presaged something of his future strain of feeling One fair bright Afternoon as I sat with him at the honeysuckled door of my fathers dwelling delineating all the horrors and bloodshed of. the storm[ing] of. Doverham.[16] an Italian minstrel came up to the garden gate. one of the band of natives of that country who existed at that time amid the babel [of] confusion of Africa. This man. had only in his hand a simple flute on which he played the airs of .his native Apennines however ere he had concluded the first peice Alexander who had. lifted up his head in deep attention to the music dropt it again and covering his face with his hands burst into a long fit of weeping he sat in tears till after the music was done and the man had left the gate and then raising his eyes he looked hastily round him and rising run with all speed out at the gate and down the gravel walk his Nurse who hearing his crying had hastned to reach him now ran after him and found little Alexander fighting vigourously with the Minstrel for possession of the attractive Instrument. home he was carried weeping and chattering by turns or biting his nurse and struggling to recommence his attempted robbery from this moment Music formed the cheif passion of his soul all thought the child would never heed any thing else and his father cursed him for a silly Idiot. perched upon the Music stool of a large Harpsichord of Lady Helens he sat. spreading his small fingers over the keys and imitating every snatch of a song or bar of a tune which he had chanced to hear— with instinctive prescision daily and hourly he was plaguing his Mamma to teach him the mystery of his adored music and almost the first question which he asked of every Lady who visited the Hall was "can you play" or will you teach me to play." The Ladys themselves attracted by his beauty and cheerfulness always were glad for amusements sake to attend to his question and shew their powers on the Instrument and many a time has the Countess of Caversham or the Countess de Segovia or Lady Tracy and many [an]other fair visitor taken him into her chariot for a drive to some concert at Wellingtons City Music was his

---

[16] See vol. I, p. 386. Named after Dover, Doverham lies on the west coast, across from Calais in Frenchyland.

sole delight and of all airs the slow solemn funereal one best pleased him and made his fingers tremble with excitement when listning to the Organ at his Fathers Church I have often seen him clasp his hands together and look more like a little Seraph than any mortal child.

At this time when he had attained his Fourth year. The war with the Frenchys and Americans[17] again broke out most furiously I was recalled to the army and bid adieu for at time to my native scenes and aqquaintances on. the morning of my departure as I stood with my Bundle in my hand. my Elzevir Vergil[18] in one pocket and my half collected Songs of the young men tied up in tape in the other Little Alexander Percy came running before Ellen Hope toward me. crying that "He would go to fight with me under the Duke of Wellington and he didnt care for Papa any more than if he was a Frenchy and he was sure that Mamma could never like him worse for coming back dressed in scarlet and gold—and if Ellen would only leave off holding him he would marry her when he got back and make her a generals Wife."—

My Buisness here is not to write a life of myself but one of the Great Northangerland and therefore I must pass over without a word all my toils and travels and warfare in the 3^d War with the Frenchys from 1796 to 1800.[19] when hostilitys being concluded I again returned to Woodchurch[20] raised to the rank of Captain and resolved for a while to rest from the fatigues of service During this interval of four years. however often thoughts of home recurred to my mind the confusions and changes of constant fighting all conspired to drive far from me many ideas unconnected with my nearest and dearest imaginings and among the repulsed feelings Alexander Percy of courses[sic] faded in my remembrance my acquaintance with that little child however pleasant was of far too light and casual a character to bide the brunt of Battle and sieges When I reached my home raised in consequence and circumstances I dont recollect that ever I asked about the Fates of the heir of Percy Hall

One evening. [in] August 1800. as I sat in my study at home engaged in the delightful task of correcting the sheets of the 4th edition of my lately published and maiden work. "Leafs History with Commentaries"[21] a production which had spread my name through much of Africa. Betty stepped in announcing

---

[17]   Presumably, Branwell meant "Ashantees."

[18]   The edition seems to be ficticious. The printing and bookselling house of Daniel Elsevier existed from 1626-80.

[19]   A war not previously referred to in Glass Town/Angrian history. The dates correspond closely to those of the Second Coalition War, 1798-1801, in the Napoleonic Wars.

[20]   There is an actual Woodchurch in Kent, near the Romney Marsh.

[21]   Presumably a reference to Leaf's history of the early settlement of Africa by the Young Men, *The acts of the Twelves*—see vol. I, p. 164. Leaf also wrote the *Autobiography of Captain Leaf*—see Alexander CB I, 341.

a fine Gentleman as desirous of speaking with me—and much to my astonishment ere she had half finished her message. the said fine Gentleman himself. with out further staying walked into the Apartment not over and above pleased with his excess of familiarity I. gazed at him with considerable resentment as demanding the reason of his Insolence but that gaze soon convinced me that what I had taken for familiarity was in right directly contrary The stranger seemed a Lucifer of Pride Coldness Revenge and despotic Tyranny was shadowed strongly on every lineament of his handsome and haughty features and the averted twist of the eye and sunken corner of the mouth told me I might add to these pleasant qualitys present or past dissipations of the wildest character this Man whose tall form and dark attire carried forth his aspect as a Gentlemen turned a chair to the fire and seating himself began. "I understand you are my Tenant—Bud is you name I suppose""

"May I ask" I answered "Who I have the honour of being addressed by"

"And. you are the same person as the Man who wrote the History latly published." continued the Stranger without noticing my question. however I guessed who this should be. and spoke

"Mr Percy for I believe Sir you as my Landlord claim that name. I should certainly demand on account of my profession a different stile of language from the one you Sir have chosen to adopt"

"If you are my Tenant I shall either require you to accept the station of Tutor to my son or I will turn you from your property without delay your work shows much sense learning and information. and its writer perhaps may prove a man fitted for the office I mention remember Sir I am not to be trifled with and if I think. you as I do qualified to teach the heir. to my estates I require you either to obey me or Ill. make you repent it"

Now the pleasure felt by a young author flattered by a person so much above him. was just sufficient to repress my inclination to rise and turn this intruder from the door and when I reflected that this Gentlman could do much of what he threatned the share of prudence which I always have possessed determined me to refrain from a harsh answer to his tyranny. I told him that as he was my Landlord as I always had felt a regard for his son as it was not inconvenient to me to accept the station I would consent to enter upon the engagement he wished me too stipulating that in case of one word or action used to me which becomes not one Gentleman to another I. would leave his House directly as I had an Independance of my own which secured me from de[s]potism.

"Fudge" he said. "you have nothing to do with regard for my son? Train him to have a regard for Me. or at any rate to act as if he had. and as too your treatment Sir dont dictate to me." he then mentioned a very handsome sum as salary told me that the Hall must be my home appointed a day for my arrival there and without giving me time to answer left the room I heard his horse trot off. directly after.

Now reader in this strange Interview do not suppose that Mr Percys conduct was the bluntness of honesty or the unceremoniousness of. ample wealth. it was the real. Sour Insolent Tyranny of. his own mind. and as such it did not suprise me who by report had long been acquainted with my Landlords character. viewing it in this light I thought It folly to resent it and as the situation was really excellent and highly respectable. as I knew I should be treated as I deserved like a Gentleman by all save the Master of the Hall. as I should thus enter society were I fancied my abilities would find there way and as I. realy now recollected my future pupil as a cheerful handsome and intelligent child. I. obeyed the assignment and. on. the first of next month. set forth from my. dwelling for the great House over the Park before me.

As I passed through the long stretches of short green verdure and by the great masses of dark thick foliage and saw the great extent of the grounds and high order they were kept in and when I. looked up at the broad irregular but statly and imposing edifice before me and above all when I entered its magnificent apartments adorned with every thing which could make life a paradise I held a high opinion of the opulence of the owner of the Mansion. Upon my being shown < > statly Hall. < >[22] did not appear but a Magnificently dressed Lady of about 30 years of age. entered the Apartment His Wife Lady Helen. her now still majestic. and then eminently beautiful countenance. expressing not dark. brooding pride but. statly and queenlike condescension. to say that Lady Helen did not look haughty would be to talk like a fool She looked very haughty but with this look there shone intellect and. grace and condescension in every feature. She knew in what office I appeared she knew my proffession and the humble abilitys I had shown and she directly made me feel myself at ease and at home. after preliminary conversation where however Queenship and. aristocracy were never absent. she smilingly said. "I believe Captain that you will naturally ask from me a little insight into the character of. your future pupil you will certainly whish to know your ground before you advance on it But I fear I can hardly satisfy you as I ought to do. His mind has puzzled myself who I believe must know him as well as any one. I can hardly tell you Sir wether he will prove affectionate to those who like him or if he will regard authority however exerted. he wanders strangly is bent upon certain things at times and badly neglects every thing unconnected with his capricious pursuits he is passionate too and as yet only 2 persons have been found to quiet his passion and as I fear Both myself and. his immediate attendants deluded by his most frequent disposition have sadly indulged him those noxious weeds have acquired a root which render them very difficult to extract. but remember Sir that you are appointed the gardener of this Garden I must trust to you its management and you know that it will not become you to neglect it For the eradication of his bad qualitys I look to you Sir but I also know what human nature is and I do not expect more from you than you will be able to perform. I hope you have been told Captain to make this house your home and now Ellen where is Alexander."

---

[22] Much of the top line of the manuscript page has been concealed as a result of the page being set in.

"In his own room My Lady he would not come out with me."
"Then tell a servant to shew Mr Bud there."
So saying Lady Helen bowed graciously and left the room
I entered a handsome little apartment filled with a confused heap of all the playthings and gewgaws which children usually admire and in its first appearance presenting little difference from the studio of any indulged child of aristocracy but to one who looked further than first appearances there could something be seen which in these places we do not usually see I walked to the upper end of the room and as Master Percy could not be found here the servant went to fetch him Meanwhile my notice had been attracted to a beautiful Organ of fairy dimensions which stood before me a book of Music upon the front opened at a "Stabat Mater Dolorosa" "Veni Creator" and "Dies Irae" and upon the keys a sheet of paper scored over in a childish and unformed hand with a succesion of Breve's Semibreves and minims. in an Andante movement which the writer was adapting to the words[23]

> We leave our bodies in the tomb
> Like dust to moulder and decay
> Then while they waste in coffined gloom
> Our parted spirits where are they
> In endless night or endless day

underlined between the staffs till met by the lines

> Buried as our bodies are
> Beyond all earthly hope and Fear
> Like them no more to reappear[24]

written in an elegant and feminine handwriting. A Little Bible lay open on a music stool with. Eccles V—I—Remember thy Creator in the days of thy youth.[25] marked in pencil. "I shall arrange this"—And around. the carpet. were scattered five or six engravings of Battles a whole collection of Hymn books many odd volumns from a vast variety of works odd little drawings in pencil a little fife Millers Jest Book and a much fingered copy of Jewels Sermons Amid

---

[23] The titles refer to three medieval Latin hymns or plainsongs on the sorrows of the Virgin Mary at the crucifixion, on the coming of the creator, and on the Day of Judgment. A "breve" is a note equal to two whole notes, a minim is equal to a half note.

[24] See the revised 1837 version in vol. III.

[25] Actually XII:1. The jest book is *Joe Miller's Jests; or the Wits Vademecum, Being a Collection of the most Brilliant Jests; the Politest Repartees; the most Elegant Bon—Mots, and the most pleasant short stories in the English Language*, edited by John Mottley in 1739, into its tenth edition by 1759. According to the *DNB*, "Joe Miller's name has long been a synonym for a jest or witty anecdote of ancient flavour." "Jewels Sermons" refers to the sermons of John Jewel, Bishop of Salisbury, 1582-1607, whose most famous work was the *Apologia pro Ecclesia Anglicana*, 1562.

this ludicrous heap of. morsels I naturally remembering the errand for which I came looked for Grammars accidences[26] and the usual stepping stones to learning but alas I sought but could not find it true there was a leaf of a spelling book. but it floated like a boat in a vase of. water where a little well fitted ship was resting with its tiny silken sails.

At the fire side I saw a very little but very luxurious satin Sopha piled with soft cushions a pair of gloves and a brass cannon sharing the seat and a warm Indian shawl thrown over the back. If I mistake not thought I my pupils Intellect has received many impressions since I last beheld him but to what I can permanently direct his mind save music and luxury I at present cannot tell.

Of Alexander himself I saw nothing that Afternoon he could not be found by his Atendants and I was left to amuse myself. and survey my own apartments till evening. when I was called to tea. I recollect as I entered the room being struck first not by the rich and splendid furniture or the princly service of silver on the table. but by the Owner of these vanities who presided at their head I could hardly leave noticing Mr Percy as he sat gloomy and lowering his dark eyes fixed on any one who happened to be moving or speaking with such a look of bitter habitual malice that though very likly quite unintentional it gave the idea of his really hating every one about him and next to him I saw the Earl of Caversham whose high shining forehead bald before its time. and. statly Aristocratic person gave at first sight a very different impression from that which you owned after attentivly noting the athwart glances and mean craftyness of his countenance and the unrestrained unprincipaled sentiments of his conversation the. half worn out prolifigate Sullivan O Connor and the handsome statly Lady Caversham who sat next to the still more statley but as condescending as proud. Lady Helen Percy completed this small party of a few of those Aristocratic and wealthy familys in this part of the country who acknowledged. the Sour Ambitious and dishonest Edward Percy as their political guide and companion Of course amid such high company my buisness was rather to hear than speak and although (and let me indulged[sic] the vanity of an author) the fame of the work I had just published attracted me to more notice than I expected I. that evening employed myself cheifly in noting the character of the turbulent spirits who sat before me. And I know that soon as what I saw began to settle in my mind I felt that dreary ominous feeling steal over me which we experience in our recollections of these Old haunted Mansions and the predestined fates of their dark. evil guided childern the miserys and glamour of the Old Romances and tales which claimed our youthful admiration[27] All the sentiments and paths of action of my Master and his Associates seemed form[sic] the conversation so twisted so blackened and dangerous that ruin and downfall stepped in as their unparted companions nay ere the company parted my imagination had. pictured the room

---

[26] Works dealing with the inflections of words, as distinguished from word formation.

[27] Branwell is presumably referring to his own childhood reading.

hung round with sable the statly Mistress robed in mourning her look fixed and despairing Mr Percy. dead and coffined. the Earl Caversham chained and prisoned all fallen to ruin and predestined to decay Withall and in many respect[s] how just have been those Forebodings how true have lighted these fortunes. yet in one case I did not prophesy right I did not point out the author of this woe. No truly my suspicions were far from alighting on the head of the handsome boy who burst into the room as the company were concluding their repast his face looking so wild and excited his hair fallen back from his forehe[a]d and his eyes wandering round the room with such an earnest glance of comprehension he ran to Lady Helen and grasping the hand she held out to him leant against her knee gazing at every one as if unconscious of their prescence."

"My dear Alexander" said his Mother alarmed "What is the matter with you?"

Her son only started as if appalled at her voice but a servant who had entered after him answered. "My Lady young master had just returned from we dont know where. he came running into the Hall. and without noticing any one made directly for this apartment."

"Sirrah Sir What is this! answer your mother.!" cried Mr Percy angrily and with violence Alexander roused by this spoke. "I have seen the Angels" he said and his face assumed a ghast[l]ier paleness than before.

"Trash!" was his fathers harsh answer. "have done with this nonsense Sir! what have you been talking to him about such stuff for Helen? hes fit for nothing"

"Why Percy your son is strongly excited" remarked Caversham earnestly

"he'll be mad before twenty" said O Connor. and all three left the room for Wellingtons town leaving Lady Helen Lady Caversham and myself with the alarmed excited child. The moment his father and the other two departed Alexander leant his head on his mothers lap and burst into tears it was long ere he could be prevailed on to raise his head speak or attend to any one. but he hid his face in the folds of Her gown grasped her hands convulsivly and seemed to shudder if he was touched at last he again looked up and gasped suddenly.

"Mamma—I have seen the Angles.[sic]—I was playing on the Organ at the Church it was quite dark I had only a candle by me and Sdeath was blowing behind the Instrument—I was trying something of my own it was the thing Augusta had set words to[28] —I. had got <a much> grander music in my head— while I was playing from my own thoughts I shuddered and felt a coldness in my cheeks I could hardly see the paper and had to gasp for breath I was quite shivery and looked back hastily—" Here he stopped with a look as if reason had left him— —I—I saw them in the dark. standing just at my back. quite white and very high-they reached to the roof and looked down on me smiling like spirits—

---

[28] S'death was pumping the bellows of the organ. The "thing Augusta had set words to" is presumably the lines on p. 104, but it is not clear who the Augusta referred to is.

there were a great many of them and one had its hand on the seat behind me it pointed its finger to the paper on the keyboard and the others waved their wings impatiently—I—I couldnt speak. So—I began to play and played far far better than ever I did before but I dont know What I did—they all sighed and stooped down their heads from high—I couldnt bear it so I screamed out got up. I dont know any farther—They were all so white and solemn!—Oh Mamma! Mamma!" he clung to Lady Helen and shut his eyes in apparent agony his Mother carried [him] from the room

"This child" said Lady Caversham to me when they were gone "is a very singular one he is exceedingly engaging but I fear he wont live. I have often noticed him and wondered sometimes at his vivacity and cheerfulness and next at his silent abstraction If I take him with me in my Carriage for a while I can not satisfy him with carressing and attention but erelong his sits wrapt in his own dreams and starts if I speak to him he is constantly excited and I suppose this night he worked himself into delerium by his enthusiasm for the music he had hit upon indeed that art fixes all his delight he plays and sweetly too for hours together and is quite uncertain in any thing else he learns or toys at. I cannot tell his disposition at times it seems cruel careless and vindictive he would kicks[sic] a little dog or strike a child if they stood before him and is so proud that he affronts the attendants who take notice of him and his father increases his wanderings by his angry manner of noticing and checking his peculiaritys You Mr Bud must be cautious in your plan of. dealing with him I cannot think the boy will last long"

This strange vision the result of excited imagination produced such a violent illness in Alexander Percy that for many days it was totaly impossible for me to make him show the least sign of acquaintance with me and of course I could not commence my duties as Tutor to him. After some time however he recovered the usual tone of his mind and became himself again Alexander was now 8 years old. but his mind had been left intirly to itself what he knew he knew unassistedly for though his Mother was a woman of the clearest and strongest understanding yet her great affection for her ownly[sic] son seemed by himself to be taken advantage of to secure him that unlimited indulgence which affection is too often prone to give and now I found his temper much worse that it had been 4 years before. at this age he was often passionate revengeful and. headstrong and when I as in duty bound attempted to Inculcate on his mind those studies which youth are in general first initiated in the drugery and labour of the first lessons were not all forgotten in those that followed wayward to the last degree my pupil so obstinatly persisted in refusing to learn that at length I almost began to consider him incpacitated to understand one afternoon I I had been remonstrating with him on his Idleness at some length

"Mr Alexander" said I "at this age you ought certainly to be able if not to understand wisdom at least to know that she ought to be understood you are heir to a large property and will one day or other enter upon a station in which he who is poor in mind however wealthy in estates must be poor indeed. Your advancing age also calls upon you to work hard while the daylight is before you for remember child that the youth who sets to learning Latin or Greek when he ought to be employing learning already acquired looks laughable and. lamentable likewise"

"I know it all you've said so twenty times before" answered Percy pettishly

"Yes and if you hearken no more to it I must say so twenty times again Sir will you commence your lessons now or loiter their any longer? get up from the Sopha and throw down that hymn book directly Sir"
I was rather irritated for Alexander had been rolling on a pile of cushions for two or 3 hours doing little but singing and sleeping and asking a hundred strange questions on a hundred different subjects returning on his part for my answers such astonishing peices of information as "I have asked for wine after dinner Bud and am going to have it" "I'm going to sleep now" And "I have asked Mamma to tell Papa to be off to the City that I may have plenty of time to range over the park and country but she wont sir" At last I rose and said stepping toward him

"I'll tell your father If you dont set to work this minute He at least will not suffer you to neglect that for which he pays so much that you should attain"

"He's going to strike me! Bud if you offer to touch me I'll tear your tongue out you dirty half pay[29] I dont care for either you or Papa I'll do nothing!" this announcement was followed by a summary protest of a cushion delivered into my face in earnest I walked to the door but he arose and running before me crying out I'll tell Mamma he has struck me" flew as quick as a greyhound out of the room and half through the house—I returned destining for him a stern message from his Father when Young Alexander again entered the room his cheeks pale and his eyes flashing holding by the hand of a low mean looking blackguard of 70 habited in an ancient brown coat and whose shuffling gait insolent adress and malignant countenance. I at once recognised as the distinguished attributes of Mr R P King Mr Percys valet rentscrewer and man of all work. an hoary headed villain who was detested by all the tenantry around him

"Naa" ejaculated this precious ancient with a squirt of tobacco and a look of insolence "Naa 'What wor' yaw saying to young Measter? —it fits yaw sure enough to be hodding up yer head and hectoring and doctoring about th' place. at this time o' day—! Yaw wornt brought into th' hoyle to rule ower him nor ower me nother." here followed another <dr[e]ncher> of spittle and a dash across the mouth with his coat sleeve. "Aw'd hev ye to knaw that Aw'm the Maister o' this raam and noab[o]dy else. Aw'm this lads preceptor and Aw think its myseln that should point him his larning and noane o' yar <noise> Aat of th' haase un' smartly or you'll live to repent ont! aat mun!

"Mr Sdeath I believe I—"

---

29 A reduced allowance paid to an officer in the army or navy when not in actual service, or after retirement.

"Silence Aw say! What have yaw to do with th' lad indeed! come hither marry aw know how to diddle the like of yaw" and here the mean looking old rascal clenched his fist grinned with his exaggerated features and cast on me such a look of demoniacal malignity that I dont know whether I could for a minute have restrained myself from felling him to the ground As it was I had not the trial. Mr Percys stern voice was heard below "Sdeath—King here this instant!" The speaker followed his message directly dark angred and scowling "What in heavens name have you let the fool slip for Why I could have made 10000£ out of soul body and estate How dared you Villain to neglect the law case. To the jail with him directly and to —" Here Mr Percy cast an enquiring glance of ill humour on me and of rage upon his minion who boldly faced him with a loud expectoration

"Naw Maister Awm moan the man thaw taks me for do yaw think Awll be bothered with cases and judgements when Aw've getten sich a case o' me awn to look after Aw say to ye mun do you see what yaw'n sarved me with here— Here while aw hev labboured heart un hand at yon hight (pointing his skinny fingers to the City) and warked me poor old conscience till it creaks like a cart wheel. yawve disposessed me of my darling office at hoam and capped me i the matter of yawr young hopeful here wi an old prigmadainty book larned chap like yon"(another vehement ejection) Aw willnt have it nor will yaw nother" and here he stroked the curls of his young pupil who shook his head back and laughed at me with real contempt "Naw" continued the Senior "thaw sees the drift Mester Percy Hey Thaw sees what I want thaw knows what thaws done and—and mind Sir if I dont remember you for such conduct as this" With a feindish sneer first at Mr Percy and next at Alexander Mr R P 'Sdeath (or King) dashed his old hat over his brow and strode croaking out of the room Percy himself cursed me with an oath knocked his son down with his riding whip and followed his servant directly Alexander got up in tears certainly but bitterly hating myself and declaring he would obey Sdeath whatever he told him to do My feelings I had rather imagine than describe

Well under such auspices Time swept unstayingly on Alexander Percy saw birthday after birthday pass over him and every year beheld him taller and handsomer than before but while his expressive and beautifully chiselled features ripened in a loftier animation his mind and disposition seemed to grow constantly more strange and dark and impetous Music at all times formed his cheif amusement but it had ceased to be his chief employment truly his Learning was only taken up by starts and goaded as it were towards its goal but there were other thoughts and employments which exerted all his opening facultys and kept his fine forehead at all times corrugated with thought The first strong pulse of Ambition beat through his veins and roused every fibre to enthusiasm to be a great man to equal or eclipse all those great characters he was constantly reading of in his delightful "History"[30] to be the mover and controller of vast events to

---

30   See note 21 above.

send his name down time renowned either for good or evil seemed day and night
to be his great wish and endeavour he was constantly think[ing] of his future life
and picturing to himself its changes and greatness questioning me upon all
manner of subjects which he whish[ed] to lay hold on for this journey and
listning with delight and excitement to the tales and speeches of his constant
companion Old Sdeath. But amid all his wild and wandering desires and ever
extending yearnings of Ambition Religion that. subject that name was first and
foremost to claim his wrapt attention Oh how often I have seen him seated on
his favorite sopha his hand supporting his for[e]head and his elbow buried in the
cushion his own Bible spread upon it and his calm blue eye wandering over its
pages for hours together and sermons and strange old works of divinity he read
through and questioned me on almost daily and often where no mortal could
answer him "Mr Bud where shall we go when we die" "What are our Spirits like
Sir" "I wonder where (naming some one latly dead) is now" "do those who are
dead know any thing of the people of this world Mamma." "Can any one tell
what Christ was like when he came into this world" "What is the world why isnt
it swallowed up to day or to morrow why doesnt the judgement day come now
when men are so wicked" "I should like to live till the judgement day to see the
world destroyed and the end of time." "How can people tell that the Bible was
written or not written and how were those who wrote inspired" "it isnt written is
it Sir it is just the setting down of the strange things that happened long ago"[31]
"Oh how I should like to have lived in the days of the Bible and seen Christ or
David or Abraham and the patriarchs and the Angels—Bud—Mamma! are Angels
about us if they are they know how I want to see them Why Why dont they
appear." And then he would remain thinking and picturing to his mind the
sublime events he had spoken of or reading and rereading the holy volumn he
grasped in his hand or singing or playing for an hour or two together his favorite
hymns [32]

>"Twas on that dark that doleful night."
>"Why did my God and Savior bleed"
>"When I can read my title clear"
>"There is a land of pure delight"

or any such song or composition of sacred and solemn tone But what deeply
greived me to notice was the gradual manner in which as he grew older he left of
speaking of Religion by degrees and from questioning every one at any time
upon this Subject in a few years hed so changed as never to give the slightest
hint or speak a single word to any person upon any thing connected with it to
maintain the sternest and most inflexible silence upon his own opinions and
indeed to shrink absolutly if any one made an allusion to them Now I do not

---

[31] Branwell seems familiar with the sorts of questions that gave rise to the
Higher Criticism movement in Biblical studies.

[32] All hymns by Isaac Watts; the Brontë family's copy of his hymns is in the
BPM.

think that at this time young Percy was either deist[33] or Atheist or that he
thought less of death or eternity No far from that his thoughts had become deeper
more intense more absolutly delightful to himself though to think them always
made him both gloomy and sad and vindictive he had grasped the subject
altogether in his opening mind but alas that mind was always <subject> to error
and sorrowing and Religion never for a moment having acted as a guide to his
steps as a hope for an hereafter or as a beacon of the world before him he at last
unable to prove it true so as to satisfy his own yearning and over strained mind
dashed from his <parted lips> and trampled underfoot in despair Here Here indeed
the overmuch unassisted thinking of an Impassioned melancholy and unbridled
mind produced the crisis from which that mind revolted with horror and affright
fixed and hopeless and rayless Atheism.[34]

But I am straying far forward in my subject in his early years this cloud
had not darkended over Percys expanding intellect and only his own wild solemn
and unsettled imagination wandered unstayed through the sublime expanse of
heaven and eternity

Well—I was greived to know that however Alexander delighted in such
a subject it never for an instant operated beneficially on his capricious affections
vindictive pride or unbridled passionateness of disposition No men on noticing
in a cursory manner the youthful Heir of Percy Hall—beheld then a slender but
active boy tall of his years and possessing a countenance whose constant play of
varying expression shewed in every light its eminently handsome features they
in general thought him conscious of his aristocratic beauty and though a lad
rather disagreeably vain of it yet on observing him some were struck with
effeminacy and girlishness the expansive forehead the anxious eye and the
sensual lip the hasty abruptness of his general manner and the harsh daring tone
of his conversation all tended to shew them a proud handsome illtempered and
indulged boy one who it seemed could dash through life and oppose all who
opposed him the seraphic sweetness of Alexanders childhood had left him in his
youth and by the time he had reached his 15th year his vindictive haughtiness
had shaken from his freindship every one save those Ladies with whom he was
acquainted and to these the fair and lofty visitors of his Fathers Noble Hall—an
instantly assumed ease of manner a very pleasing and polished aspect and that
warm ardent tone of thinking which here glowed in openly expressed admiration
of themselves passionate fondness for Music and all loftier feelings of humanity
shone round and adorned him with such a delightful grace and poetry that few
there were of the Ladies of the Metropolis who left him unprepossessed in his
favour My readers may think I am describing nothing but contradictions but I
tell them this Percy was contradiction itself to me he seemed a living paradox

---

33 The belief that reason is sufficient to prove the existence of God, with the
consequent rejection of revelation and authority.

34 The intended meaning would seem to be "and fixed on hopeless and rayless
Atheism."

and I could trace none of his various feelings and actions to any common sources save generally and widly taken to Ardent and tumultous passions with an exquisitly sensitive Nervous conformation acting upon a mind from its earliest dayspring totally destitute of religious restraint or moral principle

I know that often and deeply I sorrowed to see my pupil wandering about by himself through the park of his Fathers Hall miserably sunk in a chaos of his own imaginations perhaps having rushed out of his Fathers prescence in a violent anger at Mr Percys stern Harsh tempered check of his errors or deep angry threat of future punishment and then running over in his own mind that and the like too frequent scenes cherishing the poison so often instilled into his soul by his own chosen Mr Sdeath thinking of Myself either with impatience or dislike and chafing and spurning at the unavoidable obstacles which lay between him and his hundred faroff but favorite attainments often thinking when should he know what he wished to know when he could do what he wished to do next striving to look into his future life and to chalk out future paths to power and glory amid the crimes and darkness which he conjured up before him from this he would ask himself what was he and where was he and think on Religion and the State of Nature and of the future world its creator and his favorite and cherished subject death and eternity He would form in his heart stanzas and passages leading upon this train of thinking would run over and listen to his self created strains in imaginary bursts of music and snatches of harmony till the color had left his face and tears had dimmed his sight and then Evening perhaps drawing on himself far from home he would return toward where he had started and enter abruptly into the confusion of a splendid entertainment harsh and resentful and gloomy to meet the black threatning frown of his enraged and vindictive father

CHAPTER III^d

Percy Hall and the splendid domains around it stretching wide over the woodlands of Wellingtons town formed to the stranger the principle and noblest feature in that direction East of the Metropolis where on every side of its spacious parks. along the banks of the Gambia north to the wild hills of the frontier and south to Alderwood and Rio Grande the numerous seats and possesssions of a proud and wealthy Aristocracy presented attractions hardly second to itself in the scenery of the Environs of the Capital But noble as were the features of the scenery they like many things beside were only pleasant to the eye their merits could not stand the test of reason for here in this portion of the kingdom was lodged a nest of Ambition crime and treachery from which that huge culture Democracy has since flown the scourge and curse of all Africa Aye here under the eye of the Duke of Wellington himself. Edward Percy Esqr M P reigned the prince and ruler of a band of men whose cheif wish and aim was revolution and anarchy and blood. Fitzgerald Earl of Caversham a few miles South of Percy Hall held his abode in the Noble Mansion of Ravensworth House[35] Sir William Streighton on the other side [of] the river claimed the lands of Riverton Hall The Earl of Jordan in the North resided at the foot of the mountains and Sullivan O Connor nearer town while Mr Henry Montmorency Richard MacArthur Philip St John and Carey and Gordon spread their statley Houses over the well peopled countryside All these men I have mentioned lived in a first rate style kept up splendid establishments plunged headlong in play and dissipation and in consequence grasped every penny they could lay their hands on and wrung without mercy all the savings of their harrassed tenantry In every thing they did however Edward Percy was pre eminent His expenditure his Avarice the dishonest and extorting means he used to gain money his tyranny over his tenants his dabblings in the darkness of politics. all formed the most perfect and highly finished portrait of. an Ambitious unprincipled and Tyrannical Opressor

Well these wicked and unprincipled men Have met with the punishment of their wickedness and of all persons whose names I have enumerated there is not one now a[l]ive. No the short space of twenty years has swept them all from the earth and they have long heard their eternal sentence and entered on their eternal doom—their own deeds destroyed them and their own children hastened their end. At this time 25 years ago almost all these Aristocrats of Wellingtons town had sons and successors. and young Caversham young Montmorenci young O Connor young Carey and many other lads and men of from 15 to 30 years old seemed now likly enough to perpetuate and strengthen their Ancestral qualitys If Mr Percy ruled among the fathers certainly his son did among the children and young Alexander from his fifteenth year upwards led from mischeif to crime those whom since he has led from crime to death. And I have forgot to mention as the Great Mentor the infallible Oracle in all thoughts and actions R P Sdeath as he was now called that Robert King who accompanied Mr Percy from England and Ireland and If Earth hold a Feind more infernal than this hoary old villian Earth has darker tenants than ever I could think on

But such writing as this takes me from my immediate subject and I must now strive to regain my narrative though at the loss of some years of Northangerlands existence I will again catch a glimpse of this brilliant but ominous meteor and reintroduce to my readers Alexander Percy now in his 17 year.

Alas when I saw him at that age I saw clouds gathering thicker over his sky all the best of his strange character deepning and darkning and his future dreary wilderness of life beginning to close its horrors fast around. him

Alexander at this age from a pretty little child had shot up into the grace and energy of springtime youth. his height equalled that of many men and his fine figure polished manners and ever impassioned express[i]on with that voice whose melancholy sweetness. melancholy without intention or meaning I can even at

---

[35] The village of Ravensworth lies just north of Richmond in the Yorkshire Dales.

this distance of time distinctly remember gave everywhere to his first appearance. an air of refin[ed] and noble Aristocracy—I shouldn't have said every where for often very often all these graces were hidden in him by morose silent gloomyness and harsh passionate impetuosity and the youth "Whose bright blue eyes"[36] seemed now suffused with the light of love and thought and poetry would next moment oppose to an angry Father scowls of threatning sullenness kick an unoffending spaniel from him till it ran howling out of his prescence and beat a restless horse with all the unfeeling brutality of a savage But if anyone attempted to aid or instruct him on his conduct sneers of contempt or a pointed insult might chance to be the payment of their ill timed kindness. Percys information in excursive reading was at this age prodigious beyond description an exquisite memory and a power of getting a sense of an Author in a glance united to an ardent eager thirst for books of any discription stored his mind with [a] mass of knowledge and information which has aided him since in all he has attempted in Languages the same qualitys of mind had done the same service and Greek and Latin with all their noble Authors were as familiar to him as his mother tongue Modern Languages he attained proficiency in immediatly but as for Mathematics his warm imagination could not fix. itself on that stern study of reason till years of unhappiness a contempt of all human enjoyment and a strange yearning after some thing certainly true after some thing on which he could rest his harrassed mind as immovable by the paltry will and not resting on the shallow arguments of man urged him against whom abstract Religion seemed for ever closed to seek in her sister philosophy a final shadow of omnipotent truth Alexander Percy at 17 cared nothing for Mathematics though Alexander Rougue of 30 was the finest Mathematician in Africa[37]

But let me now proceed in the relation of this strange eventful history and although I cannot attempt to detail every event and incident of Northangerlands boyhood for my space will even be too limited for a mention of the deeds of his manhood yet ere I bring Percy into active and public life I must describe to my readers that scene and incident which struck that keynote of his life whose chord had never since ceased to vibrate

On a wild Autumnal evening in AD 1810 (when Alexander was in his 18th year) the wind howled in mournful gusts round the walls of Percy Hall as if chafed and angry at its vain attempts to spoil the splendid rooms within the private parlour was lit up and the Great red Velvet curtains flowing down before the windows the gilt or mirrored walls and the rich Turkey Carpet all received a

---

[36] Compare Byron, *Childe Harold's Pilgrimage*, Canto I, l. 176.

[37] Thomas Elrington (1760-1835), a distinguished Irish mathematician, became professor of mathematics at Dublin University in 1795, provost of Trinity College in 1895, and Bishop of Limerick in 1820. His edition of Euclid was still being used as a textbook at Dublin University some forty years after his death. His name may well be the source of one of Percy's titles. There is also a town named Elrington in Northumberland, near Hexam.

redder <   >[38] and richer glow from the bright warm blazes which roared up
the ample and flashing fireplace—Why cannot man be happy The Owner of this
splendour sat in the full radiance of its shining on soft luxurious sopha his feet
resting on the warm hearthrugh[sic] and himself apparently with nothing to do
but listen to the voice of his chimney or think on his weal[t]h and <   >. but
yet as Mr Percy sat his face turned to the fire and his hands rested on his knees. I
never recollected to have seen a countenance more expressive of troubled and
tumultous feeling of a harrassed and exasperated mind than that over whose high
dark forehead the flame flung its strange flickering glow A heart ill at ease and a
soul scoured by the distractions of Ambition shewed all their clouds and misery
in that haughty handsome face. —But why should I proceed thus writing down
like a notary the furniture or persons of an apartment I cannot hope to give my
reader a living image by such a dead manner of painting And if I could hit on a
brighter colouring I would fain spread it on my canvass as it is let me work out
by laboured touches that idea which exists in my memory in such broad indelible
masterstrokes that evening and in that parlour there sat opposite Mr Percy and
beside his Lady a form which once looked on you would behold wether absent or
present a Woman it was and such a one Oh I feel I cannot describe to my readers
Lady Augusta Romana di Segovia[39] Only daughter of the late Earl of Jordan She
was then in her 24th year and her Father and mother being both dead she was left
sole guardian and director of her young Brother and untill his majority of his
great and princely fortune Descended from a High Florentine Family and born in
Italy every thought and feeling of her mind breathed of the sweet and sunny
South High birth high wealth high Intellect and high Passions centered in a form
of the highest the loftiest beauty surrounded from childhood to youth by wealth
and admirers early being bereaved of all natural or parental protection given to
life with a soul determined to take life and able to enjoy it all this had made her
what she was Noble lovely dazzling in mind and person warm as Italy itself in
all her thoughts and actions but beyond this all was wild waste and desolated
Religion shackled her feelings and bound her to dutys and humility therefore she
was a determined and unthinking Atheist Atheism showed her fears no refuge and
held out no real cure for the conscience and so she flew at times into
superstitious Popery Society and customs imposed on her certain rules. of
conduct and decorum So she trampled on and despised the world but without
Society she could no more shine than a taper in vacuity beyond it her mind felt
no ease in contemplation therefore she grasped with passion on the world its
glare its vanity and its dissipations and her burning and passionate feelings
kindled a fire in her heart which at once illumed and consumed her I knew
nothing of the extent of that passion nor the power of her pride nor the wild

---

[38] This blank and the one below contain unreadable interlinear emendations.

[39] The name "Augusta" may well have been borrowed from Byron's half-sister,
with whom the poet was deeply involved and for whom he named his own child
Augusta Ada.

waste of her prolifigacy. But I do know that when I beheld her in her usual magnificent drapery seated on that sopha. which took from those grand folds of velvet the aspect of a regal throne [regarded] her statly swelling neck and the light of deep emotion which quivered in her large dark eyes and black arching eyebrows when I heard her rich voice of melody and the warm enthusiasm of her language it cost me no struggle to keep in the background that dreary conviction that the meanest peasant girl in Africa might have more hope of peace here and happiness hereafter than Lady Augusta Romana di Segovia

I have said that amid a luxurious Apartment and the rich glow of fires and tapers there sat this night a gloomy distraction on the features of Mr Percy. the aspect of deep concern on the noble countenance of his Lady and a glow of excitement on the soft cheek of their Lofty Visitor In truth Young Alexander Percy had been absent from the house 2 or 3 weeks no one knew where but all supposed that he had run to sea. The Autumn was unusually wild and stormy of late especially the wind and rains had risen to an Hurricane and now they were blowing and beating most mournfully round the old and sheltered Hall. I had stood at the window with the curtain drawn back looking over the tempest till Lady Helen desired me to close it round again for it only added to her depression to view the wild waste of clouds drifting over the moon and piling in the dark dreary sky Her Ladyship had naturally an almost Spartan command over her feelings but often this evening I beheld her eyes lighten with a look of agony when her husband informed her that if Alexander were at sea then he must be under it and not above for it was hardly possible that any vessel could live on the water amid such a whirlwind as the day had past in. Lady Percy gave no way however to expressions of greif but servants had been despatched to all the ports adjacent and a very short time would clear the doubt wether the youthful wanderer was alive or dead. A short time did clear it just as I returned to assume my seat. I was stopped by hearing a well known voice in the Hall and raised too in a tone of exasperation the door opened and in dashed Alexander Percy drowned in the rain his handsome face shining and his hair all dripping over his forehead as he gazed hurriedly over the room he crimsoned through the paleness of exhaustion up to the eyes as they fell on the form of the Luxurious Augusta. But ere any one could speak Mr Percy who had risen with a tremendous scowl of threatning demanded angrily

"Sirrah. how dare you leave the Hall unpermitted you are come back but I wish to heaven you had dashed your brains out against the sea bottom: Begone fool—!"

"Edward" exclaimed Lady Percy "pray be silent anger cannot prove useful now Alexander you might have guessed that I could not feel easy in your absence amid such dreadful weather why did you depart so suddenly love"

"Why Mamma I cared as much for the sea in fine weather as I do for blustering nonsense in foul and Now that I could grasp a rough rageing Atlantic I would. take advantage of it I would not cause you a single tear uncared for but. never drop one over me I cannot die yet I will dare twice as wild an ocean to morrow without heeding it. Stuff what care I for blustering."

"Silence Sir" broke in Mr Percy impetously "silence your nonsense. I tell you that if you leave the Hall again without my express premission[sic] be it for a day or a month I will decide at once wether you can die or not die."

Lady Augusta had sat no unmoved spectator of this scene her dark eyes flashed with animation and as her beautiful lip curled in a sneer she said emphatically
"Mr Percy your son Alexander loves a storm do not act like a fool and caress him when he disobeys you punish him with a calm Sir."

"Do you say so Lady Segovia" asked young Percy turning to her with eager excitement

"Yes and I think much more Alexander" was the answer and its tone of music thrilled through the heart of him it was addressed to he turned round with a lightning glance of triumph. "Then I don't care whάt you say Sir!"
Mr Percys broad black eyebrows centered in a scowl of hatred. he fixed his countenance with the ghastliness of a dying man and muttered determinedly "Dare you speak so Sir"
Alexander faced His Father with a feirce vindictive flashing of his eye and a curl of defiance on his whitened lip. "Aye and think more too"

With a dreadful execration His Father dashed his closed fist in his face. but he warded the blow with his hand and turning with a strange look to Mr Percy sprung from the room
He did not stop till he reached the Hall and there he sat down wearied with the days wild weather. exhaustion and excitement combining spread a deathlike paleness over his face and [he] could have dropt from the seat unless roused by a coarse. sneering cough behind him he turning round and saw the hideous figure of Old Sdeath his little eyes flaming and his feindish features writhed with sarcastic laughter. "Naw what ailes thee Mun" asked the Old Villain "Sdeath I have been treated as by Heaven I'll never be treated again"—"Aw knaw Aw knaw But what'l ta do lad" "Ill never speak to him again" "That'l be nought. and wor nor nought" "What shall I do Sdeath" "Kill him mun" "Kill you" cried his pupil with a loud oath at the suggestion. But the Tutor dashing his greasy cuff across his misshapen Nose. came up to young Percy with a chuckle of. delight. "Aw'll tell thee what young man thaw's a gooid lad and a clever thaw weddnt deny it and thaws shewn as mich sperit this evning as would fill a score o' Hogsheads And awll tell thee what they's no way for thee but one. Thaw mun look to the lord man and abide by his will. Theres a providence ower were heads which alluss provides for the best and what says the Scripture. come unto me all ye that are heavy laden and I will give you rest. and agean though your sins be as scarlet yet they shall be as white as wool.[40] Naw them texts were never intended for ought but the help of the needy and Aw hev often and often thought on Em as aw read that blessed book. theres as mich store of comfort atween the two bords of the Bible as have lasted me. fro the rocker o' the cradle to the brink o' the grave. and

---

[40] Compare Matthew 11:28 and Isaiah 1:18.

Aw say that though aw have been young and now em Old. yet aw have nower seen the Righteous wanting or his seed begging their bread. And aw wad hev ye look to this betimes and think ont ere the hour cometh when no man can think[41] Aw hev brought yaw up from Infancy and aw 've thought many a time to myseln that aw wad nevver let ye go. and naw Alexander naw that times are lighting hard and vexations affright ye naw is the hour of trial and naw look to aloone un ever Aw spak look for thy deliverance cometh!"

As the Ancient Feind spoke thus with a godly sanctity diffused over his puckered features. the door opened and a young man stepped into the hall. who with an air of familiarity threw his hat and cloak aside and strode toward the fire He seemed a tall muscular young man about 6 and 20. with a brawny frame red wiskers and handsome wicked looking features. this new comer stretched his arm to Alexander shook. the clenched hand unoffered to him and asked between sneering and earnest "Heyday Percy what now say you?" Alexander with all the energy of hatred told him of the language and blows his father had bestowed on him and concluded. "Hector Ill never stay another night under this roof while he's alive" "No more should you come clear up. What Sir theres a way to use such an affair as you[rs]. Sdeath has the walls ears just now" "Noane at present aw think." "Hum well Just sit down a moment and listen to a fairer freind than Elihu.[42] was I fancy the little knowledge I have of law affairs will just aid me so far as to know the treatment of a business like you[rs]. Tut man of course youll never touch this doorstone yet a while why your 17 and its time to set up yourself." Young Percy caught the idea with lightning quickness he started up and said. "you mean. that I should borrow money dont you? and I will where shall I do't" "Hem very satisfactory but not so loud. and on second thoughts it were best to tell you under another roof than this Old House. so we'll just take a ride to Wellingtons town its a midding night and I can show you a cask that'll tap as freely as any one. Sdeath will have our horses in a twinkling" as he spoke Alexander ran out to the stable brought out two he vaulted onto one while his advisor mounted another and both. then galloped quickly down the avenue till lost in the wild howling night.

The Gentleman I have introduced to my readers was no other than Hector Matthias Mirabeau Montmorency son of William Daniel Henry Montmorency Esqr M P. of Derrinane Abbey.[43] and the very man who may be found at this moment diving in the wildest Ocean Of Our Countrys politics. 23 years ago however he was only known as a young Lawyer of. Astonishing Learning and Ability. burning with Ambition and fast for the top of the tree. but his reckless habits squandering extravagance and total want of principle kept him down from

---

[41] Compare John 9:4. For a possible source for the combination of Yorkshire dialect and religious cant, see Barker Brontës, 206-207.

[42] See Job chapters 32-37.

[43] Derrynane House, in County Kerry, Ireland, was the residence of Irish patriot Daniel O'Connell, who won Catholic Emancipation in 1829.

the height on which was fixed his most anxious wishes. he was a deep confidante of Alexander Percy and observed with wonder his young Freinds. fast opening Intellect overwhelming impetousity and eager alertness in crushing all marks of. goodness or principle. Well Alexander Percy accompanied by his firm freind Hector and followed by their common Father Sdeath hastened to Verdopolis and entered under the portals of. The Right Honourable the Earl of Caversham This Noble they found sitting alone as calmly and quietly as a Christian Anchorite but "there was that within that did not shew"[44] for a very little conversation and a short explanation of the scene above described drew forth first from his unspotted soul a gentle and soothing condolence and a moderate endeavour to heal all disagreeable difference. but when he saw the distaste whith which his words were received when he saw his young Visitor break into a passionate fit of cursing the instant reconciliation was mentioned he quietly put by all such useless artifice and at once sounded him on the subject he appeared to come for. Money for the purpose of. dashing on by himself money to squander in all the wildest riotings and gamblings and extravagance was what Alexander just now wanted and this the Earl of Caversham determined he should have He knew that Mr E Percys huge estates were entailed[45] upon his son and that now if he lent him a good round sum he could be sure hereafter to get it back again he was known through all Africa as a <black> and pitiless Usurer for Caversham however dissolute and abandoned he might be had allways an eager greediness of avarice and a cold calculating craftiness which made him lay by all the pride of Aristocracy and proceed with exquisite skill in his detestable proffession The wealth he gained by this conduct was immense but it was all lying in the hands of poor wretches to whom he had lent at enormous intrest and whom he snatched from the verge of Bankruptcy only to plunge into deeper and more hopeless ruin But the essay of this night might be classed among the most sucessful bits of buisness he had ever had a hand in here is the moument of his villainy

> "I Hereby promise to advance to Alexander Percy Esqr the sum of 25000£ upon the security of the entailed estates of his father E Percy Esqr an at an interest of 20 per cent per annum. to be paid either yearly or along with the principle when he arrives to his paternal property but in such case. burdened with an additional interest of 20 per cent upon the accumulated interest of the principle to fill up the loss sustained by the lender from not having that superior interest in his hand to traffic in

Signed	Caversham
Witness	{R P Sdeath
	{H M M Montmorency

---

[44] Compare Shakespeare's *Hamlet*, I, ii, 85.

[45] That is, the son was designated as sole heir.

Alexander the moment this paper was signed and all things settled in due legal formality Drafted a bill on the Earls Banker and as soon as he was satisfied took his hat and left the town Though that night was Dark and bleak and stormy and though he himself was dreadfully fatigued by the journey from the sea shore and the constant restlessness of his ongoings when now round home yet the conflicting passions of his mind so harrassed him as intirely to <drive> underneath observation all the faintness and weariedness of body He mounted his Horse and urged it madly through the streets till the spurred and frighted beast brought him straight before the banks of the Gambia and then he recovered recollection of where he was sufficiently to guide it upward along the road which winds north toward the Boundarys of Wellingtons Country He cared nothing about where he was going to or what hour of night it was or wether calm or stormy or wind or rain but all his thoughts were fixed on that situation and aspect of life into which his own wild passions had so suddenly and irretreivably plunged him Nay the very word "Life" alone was enough to make him start for that morning he had been only [a] wild spoiled passionate and headstrong boy residing at his fathers house all his prospects watched over by parents and his footsteps guarded as those of an inexperienced child practically what did he know of the world. what had he to do with the ongoings of men he certainly possessed a wide circle of companions and acted as the very prince of a host of. humanity But these acquaintances were youths and schoolboys or if men yet acting as his Mentors and teachers in frolic rioting and Boyish extravagances and truely too that morning he was only just returning from an expidition alone through the country to the sea and among strange scenes unaided and unwatched over but all this was nothing more than an outburst of unfledged daring and wild imagination it had been in reckless play with the tempests of nature and much relished buffeting with the waves or weather truely too he had thought much before this night but his thoughts were entirely exe[m]pted from the influence of the worlds events the mere creations and paintings of his own opening and unbrindled mind. He himself knew that it was nowise what the world calls thought and though much of his musing was on the future it was all just so little foresight. He knew that he did think intensly of his early childhood of his present. scenes of what was in store for him hereafter he weighed his own powers his own splendid mind and fastly widning stores of information that he was determined to be known in the world and that he cared for no one who shou[l]d ever arise to thwart him he was well aware that he did possess within himself such a soul such powers such immensity of talent and genius that he must if he lived gain at some period the emminence he looked for he knew too (and few know that) what he was where were his deeply rooted faults and what were those qualitys that were likely to ruin him he knew his extreme violence of passions his headstrong and unreasonable pettishness (for by that name could he call it) his total want of governing principle and his scorn and contempt for all the various aspects of goodness. he saw all that black melancholy which has since so miserably embittered his cup and which even then with its strange poisoned draught deranged his soul with its first bewildering fumes—But though he saw all this he could not tell how to amend it and when amendment was suggested to his mind he fiercely and contemptously repulsed it he knew that all was wrong with him but he gloried in that wrong he cherished it and laughed and scorned at the idea of setting his heart aright—Here then we have the key to that bitter mood with which this night he regarded all thoughts of his father no thought of Revenge presented itself openly to his mind but he determined never more to attend too or live with or in any wise obey him as a father He thought too of his Mother but her he loved and he knew that she loved him and if one tear was dropped by him that night it was over the feelings of long rooted affection the memory of his early childhood the image of her who had watched over him with the unchanged endurance of a Guardian Angel who had attended to all his capricious wishes had nursed him in sickness. and smiled on him in health whose voice he always heard and whose countenance still present looked at him in all his often repeated visions of that which to him was never again to return These feelings Percy has always felt with the most utter intensity and now in this present lonly stormy night the[y] filled his heart with an agony which no pen or tongue can describe And when he looked at the return he was now going to give for 18 years of unchanged unwearied affection that he was going to seperate himself at once from his mother to pass into a life were she could neither smile on him or advise him and which must certainly embitter all her thoughts for him and cause to her many a weary thought and many an unavailing tear When he thought of all this and felt that his spirit would not let him change or soften the keenness of seperation he just stopped his horse and with clenched teeth he shook his hand up to the sky and cried with a horrid curse—"He would that he might that moment be struck dead for ever!"

As he wildly looked round for the bolt which should strike him into annihilation an object passed his sight which in a manner forced him from the illusion of his agony A decrepit old man on a grey horse trotted up and. though the night was so Black and stormy touched his shoulder with a coarse greeting of familiar recognition "Who the D—l are you?" asked young Percy vehemently "Naaw" returned his fellow journeyer with a disgusting nasal laugh of derision—

"Its a braw cheild that doesnt knaw its own feyther thwart greeting to part wi thy Daddie Aw guess and doesnt knaw that Here he is beside thee and—lad—that thaw can <u>nivver</u> part wi him eh?. Hold up thy Heart child If aw am for thee what care ah who's agean thee.[46] and sure enough thaws the guid will o' heaven above thee for am noane clear that sich a blessed height have aw ever been aat in above what tha'rt fair clothed with sunbeams with aat and. glowing wi happiness within! sich a look aat for thee aw've gotten lad. Hold up thy head for Ill be hanged if I do not see a crown ower it a crown of white my lad silver I should guess and plaited into as many rays as there is hairs o' thy head and. thaas robes of white too but they muffle thy feet and hands sadly and thy face look[s] to resigned and pure lad. and thaa's a carraige just ahint thee nabbut its rayhter o'

---

46 Compare Romans 8:31.

the smallest and as black as the midnight. and thaw mun lie in't instead o' sitting ont. and thy palace isn't as large as some is. but what o' that 6 feet is as mich as thaa'l need an awll warant thee. —Naa! Naa what naao!" cried the old blackguard as his exasperated listner pulled out a pistol and fired it with an oath in his face. the feind drew back let his his young master proceed forward and followed him jeering at the unsteady aim he had taken

"What thaa's all of a fluster has thy father stricken thy wits asto or aart 'ta thinking o' thy mother lad nivver heed her say aw nivver heed her But happen thaw thinks Old Cavershams taken thee hold by the thrapple[47] ower this 30000£ thaw's gotten it and aw' say never heed that too aw say thaw hev getten it and that[s] enough to heed one while but lad aw'll tell thee what it is Aw have trotted me old bones so far for it ta make of a neight. Aw've News to tell thee and what'l tha give for em news as gooid as gold. ane better than some gold that aw hev knawn for their true news and noane coined ones—Aw say lad what does tha think o'—Lady Augusta?"

"I think you are the D—l." Shouted Alexander turning round on his tempter with a feirceness that might have start[l]ed anyone but this narrld old Sinner

"And aw Am" he shouted in return "And thaws made wor[se] guesses nor that and Aw made falser answers too But what says Scripture that a man shall leave Feyther and Mother and cleave unto—"[48]

"By Heaven Sdeath!—"

"Noa Noa Heavens nought to do with 't matter nor earth nauther. But Leddy Segovia.!"

"Ho you blasted villian will you drive me mad—Ha Im mad already—But Old Scoundrel. silence with your hateful—your—"

"Yawr what na? Yaw wad saw sommut sweet waddnt yaw But aw do say that She's as wild as yaw are and a bonny handsome couple yaw'll make and a good and. a decent and am sure yawll both live will I nill I.[49] as the saying is and for that matter yawll both die and be buried and—why after that rest your souls for I'm sure they'll both need rest wither they'll get it is another question Ha Ha Ha—But mind lad yaw be at the fayte at the Duke of Wellingtons to morn at neight. theres a card for ye lying at yere feythers. and look weel abaat ye there. and—goid Neight tye my Son."

"And eternal night to you Old Satan" exclaimed Alexander as R P Sdeath turned his old horse round and trotted off. toward the city amid the wild rain and wind and darkness. But the appearance and the conversation of the hoary rascall. had chainged[sic] somewhat the current of Percys feelings or at least had made an outlet to their intensity Determined now to cast off all vain melancholy

---

[47] "throat" or "windpipe"—Scots dialect. Branwell seems confused over the amount Percy received from Caversham—see p. 119 above.

[48] Compare Mark 10:7.

[49] i.e., willy nilly.

to crush all thoughts of Old associations and as usual to laugh at every idea of Religion and rectitude. he turned his horses head toward the city and rode forward thinking of the readiest mode of opposing his father and shewing him that he would live on without him and cut out his own scheme of life so that every event should prove what Mr Percy might hate and wish otherwise

"Curse the frenzied Tyrant" said Alexander to himself. "As truly ought to be his own dear freinds will play the double part and underhand will cherish what he himself will urge them to crush he may rave and storm at his will now but he shall feel I have the upper hand of him 30000£ in my purse. and from the pocket of his best associate too is a glorious begginning even though I myself will smart for the fingering of it but Hang it shall I regret the interest I have to pay for this foundation of my future fortune I think its the very picture of human life no blessing without ten times its weight of cursing not a step to climb but I've a dozen yards to fall for it. Oh curse that too its as bad as my father and I wish him and all such work was even now at the bottom of the Gambia. However I must so act as to seem all careless of the future I will hire to day a nest in the Western Hotel and daily and nightly I'll issue forth from my stronghold and blaze away at fetes and balls and entertainments and the opera and the Theatre and—mind lad—at the Gaming house too how in the world am I to pay up the interest of the cash I have laid hold on except I stake chance after chance as fast as I can lift my hands up one risk over another comes on till either I blow my brains out or the mercy of providence hold out hope of rescuscitation—What a fool I am always overlooking the bright side—or till I find my purse progressing in the best arithmetical manner that Old Bud ever pointed out or spoke or dreamed of. Old Bud! Old Fool! old before his time the scoundrel shall leave his lobster hold on me. What I learn I'll learn without his aid and I'll let that pedantic coxcomb feel the punishment of his disgusting hypocrisy does he suppose that he knows more than me that his brain is better furnished than mine Ah Captain your conceit could never carry you so far—But what need is there to trouble myself about him have at the world now and leave metal buckled schoolmasters to their hornbook and accidence[50] Hang me am I turned fool myself to be riding on here trieng[sic] to deceive myself into lightness and heedlesness Stupidity's at a high water mark I think. and I am careering full sail in the deepest off it—No No I am entered at last on what men call the ocean of life and if every[sic] anyone had a sailor a rudder or a chart or a compass—I have not—nor shore or harbour either"

So he went on trieng as he owned to himself to blind his own eyes to consequences and keep of his sight the stern reality of his prospects till Morning rose through the storm and he entered again the crowded Metropolis of Wellingtons land

---

50 A primer or an elementary text and the part of a grammar book that deals with inflections of words.

That Night Alexander Percy appeared at a splendid Feté given by His Grace the Duke of Wellington at the palace and many of those present remembered afterwards when his ongoings rose before the public attention. what a singularly a reckless and distracted air a look between feirceness and misery. was cast over his features through that gay and gorgeous night. His fine person and stature so much above his years. with a face of such varied expression and such refined and fascinating manners gained him always in public far more notice than his youth and his fathers enmity to Government could otherwise have given him But he hardly ever seemed to care for this notice and that evening least of all. he wandered apart from the spendid throng and sat down on a sopha in the most silent and empty saloon and past an hour of inward thinking unconscious almost of every thing around him at length the familiar aspect of a Grand piano which stood open opposite roused him to rise and step toward it his fingers once placed on the keys he could not think for a while of taking them off and so he sat running over the sheets of music and playing by starts each bit longer than the other till he fairly had launched out into the tide of some passage of Ancient and Sacred Harmony Those who had ears within hearing could not fail soon to catch the tones of such exquisitly skilfull playing and as it was affirmed "Young Percy was playing" that name (so well was his extraordinary musical genius known) directed the foot of many a lord and lady toward [the] room from where these sweet sounds proceeded. A certainly Aristocratical circle was soon [undecipherable line][51] on him with such general looks of admiration as his performances one forefinger pointed to an opened leaf and a voice itself of music desired him to play some peice whose title I have long since forgot He turned to the speaker and as he looked on Lady Augusta di Segovia all saw his changed expression and the bewildered stare when he resumed his playing in a minute after a half connected prelude he struck his fingers impatiently from the keys and said confusedly "I cannot play" left the instrument and the room together Lady Augusta herself smiled derisivly at those who turned to her for an explanation of this conduct her dark eyes seemed almost to say "The Deer is struck and well you depart in envy of the Huntress"[52] to those fair faces who returned looks of reproach and astonishment She answered with only a triumphant and insulting glance which soon subsided to her own look of Italian fervour.
Now far indeed was Lady Augusta from a Coquette her character had none of this surface of lightness and vanity Her almost solemnly musical voice her serious earnest smile the expression of her Dark and lustrous eye all most vividly shewed forth a character far indeed removed from the every day silliness of

---

[51] The top line of the manuscript page has been covered over as a result of the page being set in.

[52] I have been unable to find a source for this quotation. It may be a reference to the myth of Acteon, who happened upon Artemis bathing in a spring. Fearing he would report the incident, Artemis splashed water on his face and transformed him into a stag and he was torn to pieces by his own hounds.

frivolity and giddiness. and she knew that Alexander Percy had a spirit far too like her own to be enslaved by nonsensical airs of goddesship and caprice and disdain she knew that one hour of such a display would rouse him only [to] <hatred> and contempt. and her own Arts and Wiles and Snares were of an order. far other than those which excited all her scorn when she saw them employed round her <they> <assured> her more malice animosity and inveterate hostility than fell to the lot of any other <court> Star of Western Royalty

When morning dawned the guests departed and Alexander Percy entered on the wild irregular life which he had chosen out for himself. Since he had hardly yet numbered his eighteenth year fixed and melancholy misery could not for ever dwell on his mind and the task of driving it off was easier then for him than it would have proved in later life—His mornings he generally spent at the proffessors of boxing fencing and such athletic exercises in whose rooms he learnt all the art of Defence aquirred ideal skill and strength and repaired or warded off the inroads which the life he led was making on his naturaly strong and springy constitution then during the day the prescence company and ongoings of young Caversham Montmorency O Connor or Gordon and Old Caversham and Old Sdeath and a hundered of the like prolifigate villains of the city afforded him a vast instruction and amusement and completed the days course of study in the art of holy living and dying Every night the countless feastings and gaitys and splendour of a Wealthy Royal and Aristocratical City swallowed him irretreivably in its whirl of dissipation except now and then when the hours of midnight were spent in sullen gloomy thinking or fitful intermitted study such a round of existence as this he well knew accumulated vast materials for bitterness but he felt that it chased away the present heart burning and so he eagerly flung himself into its vortex and left future time to future thinking

Among all the many splendid edifices which thronged the capital and illuminated its streets with the blaze of their nightly assemblies none stood more eminent than the Noble Segovia Palace for in a couple of hours after sunset its pillared front was sure to be surrounded with equipages and its long rows of windows to fling forth the blaze of glaring light certainly the nominal owner of this Aristocratic Mansion fully bore out the truth of Zamorna's maxim that No man is so little Master as at his own hearthside. For in the unhappy looking youth all clothed in silks and velvet and possessing a countenance coloured so like the keys of "My Grandfathers harpsichord[53] who might be seen lounging about on the sophas of some secluded saloon no one could have thought to find the Right Hon John Earl of Jordan it was his statly sister Lady Augusta who held all the sovereignity of his lands Castle palace and revenues she controlled every thing as she wished and through her own profuse expenditure would soon have drained all her brothers immense wealth yet she possessed scources from which to aquire new. Well at the Segovia Palace and its far renowned entertainments Alexander Percy was seldom absent Augusta had never dreamed of better sucess than over

---

[53] I have been unable to track down this title.

this wild and wandering creature of his own passions and for himself he loved her enthusiastically So did she also in like manner love him and neither of the two were among those pale faced beings whose life and wishes are ever wafted off in the breath of a sigh who cannot know themselves and dare not take a step in life without being hurried on by the power of fate and circumstances No Augusta herself laughed at both fate and circumstances she cared little to what end her course was tending and Alexander—why he cared certainly for his aim was to force his life straight against both fate and circumstance. When I think of this[sic] two—Beings of minds so noble and of forms and feelings so calculated to adorn and exalt the world and life they moved in when I look back to twenty years ago and picture them as they were. placed in such lofty station and so much the admiration of a great and Royal Capital and think of their reckless determined headlong course of ruin the race which each seemed most desirous to run to death. and their troubled and bewildered life and (of one at least) the sudden and melancholy end I turn from the strange eventful History with a mind more strongly impressed than by the Wild unreal Romantic fiction that my ear ever listened too No one can hardly look on the present estate of Northangerland with such extraordinary interest as I can for few so well as myself know what that Nobleman has caused done and past through—But I am running out of the exact course of my subject the countless crowds of visitors at the nightly Fetes of Segovia Palace. as they entered into its splendid and glowing saloons were allways in a while sure to be received not only by the Well Known admired and detested Lady Augusta. but by "Young Percy" the remarkably tall handsome young Man attired in such scrupulous and fashionable elegance (for this was before the Northangerland clothed in solemn black) with such an extremly proud and haughty an air yet ever <   > and <breaking> through all his exclusiveness in to fits of passionate impetouosity. politicians weighed in their minds his demoniacal Father and his noble expectations and remarked one to another that the tyger of opposition was in his spirit and those who lived would soon very likely view his ravages, people of keen observation thought him a young man of uncommon personal and mental endowments But—and they shook their heads at the aspect of his character and rumours of his conduct As for the Ladies of Wellingtons land he allmost held the place then as it regards them which the "Sun of Angria" holds now his natural elegance was the perfection of grace his extreme passionateness of temper his fiery animation his well founded utter melancholy was indeed the quality which placed the capstone of his character the halo which shone around him and deified him But when the sharp observers. noticed his frequent appearance and gracful Lordliness at the Segovia Palace. and how his manner altered and his blue eye lightened in the prescence of its spendid Mistress they one and all deplored and compassionated his destiny and vilified and execrated the spells of the much hated Enchantress. There were not wanting in Wellingtons town many fair Heroines who I believe both would attempt and could suceed to save him from the toils for who could fail to notice how when the <very> earnest solicitation of some Lovely and Aristocratic Circle had prevailed on him to shew his admirable powers and genius on organ or piano as he sat at the splendid instrument creating its varied an[d] noble harmony he would look upon the statly plumes and raven or yellow curls. and heavenly faces which bent over him, with a rapture and excitement not all I know derived from the music he was playing and it was then that he seemed capable of feeling pleasure undashed by some bitter weight of care but when he entered those saloons where more sombre attire more anxious countenances deeper and sterner voices showed the prescence of beings of another discription feelings too of another discription seized on his soul and brought down again over his spirit black depressing thoughts and dreary outlooks for the future in his position with the circle I have mentioned he triumphed and gloried but here though he cared precious little for their good will he wished longed and burned for distinction among them to lead them or oppose them in all the walks of fame and empire to command in the feild and senate and rousing and employing all his energies with them or against them to carry on his schemes of Ambition and establish his course [as] the highest and most celebrated man of his time but the bitter consciousness had come over him that the life he was now leading though it might ensure him favour among the Women it could never give him sovereignty among the men of Africa.

But I must make a vigourous effort to proceed with my narrative or the life of Percy may linger in thoughts and reflections. Lady Augusta. saw that there might some time be a little danger of her enchantments loosing[sic] their power while Alexander was left at his own wild will as now. So in the month of May 1811. there [was] announced through the City the Marriage of Alexander Percy. Esqr with Lady Augusta Romana di Segovia. the fashionable circles immediatly resounded with hints innuendoes and violent invective. uttered perhaps with a sweet voice but certainly with most bitter feeling However there was one in Africa whose voice was not very sweet though his feelings were bitter indeed on the ocasion

My Readers may have wondered why since Alexander was yet a minor being only in his 19th year. His Father did not enter and put a stop by the strong hand of the Law to his rebellious and unauthorised conduct. against him. to do this was most certainly Mr Percys fixed resolution but unfortunatly only a day or two before Alexander had left Percy Hall one of Mr Edward Percys numerous Deptors[sic] a Gentleman who had been one of his associates and to whom he had lent large sums on usury which he proved quite unable to pay after a long and miserable imprisonment was freed by insolvency and now desperate at the mean greediness of the man who had thus ruined and persecuted him and seeing all his prospects through life destroyed by Mr Percys cruel avarice. publicly abused and insulted him under very aggravated circumstances with the intent to bring on a duel. with him Mr Percys cold blooded hardened feelings would have laughed at and despised the challenge but his black and revengeful passions urged him to punishment of the offender Nature contended against Nature till the skilful Old Valet Sdeath represented to him that he had seen Mr Sullivan (the unhappy insolvent) and that. "his hands trembled uncommon there wad be 90 to 1 agean his hitting" this hint succeded Mr Percy accepted the challenge and the two had a meeting where he shot Sullivan right through the heart. a duel in Africa neither was or is considered any thing very henious[sic] but in this case the freinds of the slain man took it up and pursued Mr Percy in an action for murder on the grounds of unfair play which were very apparent in the transaction for Old Mr Gordon a true fellow of the "Justice" acted as Sullivans second and suspicions were afloat that the gold had drawn that unfortunate wretches bullet from his pistol while "The Justice was know[n] to have used two in his own. Men believed all this as very likly to happen so as matters looked desperate at present the Magistrate of Percy Hall fled from it in hot haste and took refuge over the seas in Stumpsland till the storm should blow over. however it thickened and blackened till on a sudden as if by a blast of wind it had dissapeared and men heard no more of the prosecution for murder. In real truth Mr Percy had employed his old agent Money at a liberal rate to quash the Zeal of the freinds of the deceased and it seems he perfectly suceeded So after 3 months absense from Wellingtons town he again arrived at his seat in the beggining of June. but during his temporary exile it was that all these events happened with regard to his son Alexander and the news of his marriage with Lady Augusta saluted the ears of his Father as he passed through the Metropolis on his way to the Hall. When he arrived there I for one saw directly that the feind of passion held full possession of his heart He called his Lady apart and when in an hour or two she left the room I was commanded to appear the moment I entered I was saluted with "Fool Traitor Toad" and a host of the like decorous epithets he was in a towering passion abused me for conniving at the conduct of his son said he would hang me if I did not care for it and then threatened Alexander himself with the most dreadfull effects of his parental affection So soon as I departed Old Sdeath was ushered in and the two Master and Man remainded closeted together all the evening. at first it was said abusing and storming and cursing each other in the most unmeasured violence but all the rest of the time in deep secret and anxious consultation. Now this wretch Sdeath during the whole period of Mr Percys abscence had been at Verdopolis aiding Alexander and hurr[y]ing him on to all manner of vice and dissipation but when the Father returned he repaid this aid by informing against the Son and suggesting all the means for stopping his courses at night Councillor Daniel Montmorency Mr Percys Lawyer was called for and Early in the Morning Our Master accompanied by Sdeath and 5 or 6 trusty servants left the Hall. on horseback. for Wellingtons town

Alexander was <out> riding toward town on his return from a shooting excursion among the hills when Old Sdeath met him and persuaded him to take a short cut toward the city unthinking of treachery Percy followed his advice and they cantered forward through a large plantation belonging to his father. at a sudden turn of the road Sdeath blew his nose with portentous loudness and as Percy turned his steed to give him a blow for the din 6 mounted men burst suddenly through the thicket seized hold of his steed by saddle and bridle and laid hands on him to pull him to the earth Alexander with a succession of oaths fired his pistols into the faces of two and exerting all his uncommon muscular agility had nearly suceeded in freeing himself from the grasp of all of them but with a horrible curse from a well known voice another man burst upon him and threw him onto the ground Alexander knew his father directly who had grasped him with desperate violence and now the other servants except two disabled by the sons tremendous resistance. secured him and hurried him into a covered carriage which stood horsed and waiting not far off. his Father himself bound his hands with most painful tightness thrust him into the chaise and entering with Old Sdeath and an Athletic Attendant ordered the coachman to drive forward. —While these 4 remained in the carriage a profound silence was observed Alexander sat as pale as marble with hatred and exhaustion and it was not till after many hours furious driving that when the vehicle drew up at an inn in the Harbour of Wellingtons town that Mr Percy informed his son "I have stopped your opposition to my will at length marry whom you like. What the—has dared you act as you have done fool. what will you be fit for think you Man I here have you and off you must directly go for the Philosophers Isle While I was away I had settled all things for your reception But D—l I little thought to find you married when I returned. however to College you shall go or die for it and you'll embark this very evening aboard [th]is vessel just now weighing anchor your berth is secured and—bid adieu to your Lady if you can Sdeath is to accompany you there and after you're fixed he returns again away with him Servants away with him off begone!" —Alexander only uttered the words "You D—l." and was hurried out into the vessel and into a cabin ready prepared the ship weighed set sail and left Africa with the future Earl of Northangerland thus rudely snatched from the life he had chosen and his Goddess like Augusta to drudge in a far off College along the usual rough road to learning advancement and distinction in the world

CHAPTER IVth

My readers in perusing the account of Alexander Percy's youth which I have just concluded will perhaps be inclined to wonder at the few apparent traces which it exhibits of all those vast powers of Genius ability and natural and accquired knowledge By which he has arisen through life to the rank and station which he now holds in the Affairs of Africa But I must tell them that if this is their judgement it is a weak and. shortsighted one—I know that in all the pages just finished I have detailed no vast exertion of bodily or mental capabilitys no huge strides made toward power and importance no sudden plunge and rapid rise in the warlike or political events on[sic] the time The Warrior the Statesman the Rebel and the legislator have not yet appeared in any act or aspiration of the Soul of the future Earl of Northangerland I have only described the caprices and wanderings of an indulged and passionate child the vice and errors of an unbridled and impetous youth plunging now into a chaos of dissipation and folly then led by others to ruin and crime. This melancholy train of events has formed the staple the main plot of my Narrative but what is it that constituted the by play the under plot that portion which is usually by far the most interesting and important portion of a Novel or tale. Why it has been the gradual ripening and opening of an imperious temper ungovernable passions excitable feelings undaunted recklessness of purpose—Yes but what truly great Genius ever appeared in this world without a character like this and does not this character contain the seeds of. a powerful imagination mental energy fixed resolution and that spring and life blood of all Noble actions unquenchable untiring Ambition and must Not a Mighty genius possess all these—Yes also but if the Greatest Genius have all these and yet have not a determined line of conduct to pursue and an immediate a constant system of acting on that course he has taken. he will spend all his powers in vain may perhaps astonish the world for a moment but erelong must vanish

Like a bright exhalation in the evening

And no man see him more[54]

All this I know and I know that while Alexander Percy possessed all these powers of Intellect he also had fixed on some tangible mode in which to strengthen and bring them into action. He was yet only in his nineteenth year till this time he had done nothing thought of nothing to any tangible purpose or with any determination to proceed But Now—Now when he landed on the shores of the Philosophers Isle forced by his Father and deprived of all hope of escaping when he saw distinctly that only two ways were left for him to act either to remain at College and relenquish for the present all the pleasures he had left in Wellingtons land or by flying to that country again relenquish forever all hope of power and glory in life to come if he fled a short troubled life of dissipation awaited him to be followed by an early end If he stayed labour exertion and absence from what he loved but—(and here was the reward which so firmly chained his feelings) to be followed by vast information and knowledge acquired probable elevation and distinction at the Noble University he studied in and when he returned to Africa all the means and <appliance> at least. for arising to the topmost height of any station any aim he might fix his heart on All this Alexander Percy saw most vividly he knew what he wished to be and he felt that now was the hour for fitting himself to accomplish that wish for how through the wild life he. was sure to plunge in on his return could he attain any degree of eminence in any of the knowledge that men set value on he saw that it was now or never and so he instantly put his hand to the plow his shoulder to the wheel What were Alexanders feelings upon his arrival the the Philosophers Isle may best be gathered from his own writing and that my readers may have at least some insight into their wild and wayward character I feel it to be my duty to present them with the following letter addressed by him shortly after he landed to His Wife Lady Augusta Percy It has been in my possession ever since the wreck of his Fortune made in 18 .[55] and I have always considered it a most striking example of his thoughts and feelings before these terrible storms of Misfortune came upon him to cover all his spirit with their own oppressing gloom.

---

54 See Shakespeare's *Henry VIII*, III, ii, 226-27.

55 Branwell left the date blank.

Philosophers Isle
February. 1812.

Don't think Augusta when you receive this letter that I wrote it from a feeling of the necessity of making my Wife accquainted with my sudden and unexpected departure from herself and my house and country or that I felt anxious to quiet all your well grounded fears for my safty and uncertainty of where I may be or even that my anxiety arose from a very proper desire to know how yourself were and to bewail with you over our sudden separation No Augusta none of these thoughts influence me for you must be by this time well aware of the causes of our seperation I for my part will not bewail over what for 11 months to come I am determined to endure and as to my safty. I. at least know how little I care for that and how very little I care wether yourself be assured of it—I write to you Augusta. as I would speak to you. Because. wherever I am or whatever I may be thinking on you are always present to my mind and you seem to be present to my eye. Have no fear Augusta that I shall soon forget you for perhaps if I so constantly recurred to your recollection as you do to mine you would think in good truth the words were literally fullfilled that we two are made one.

Augusta how strangly rapid is the flight of time and what changes it is for ever bringing over our destinies it does seem to me not one day since with thee I laughed at home and parents and prospects and the future and just determined to make sure of pleasure in this life <jilting> pain till the life to come when if there be nothing of that sort in waiting for us pain must go about its own buisness if there be why we shall have plenty of it when I was with thee I did not feel it and when absent from thee. two or three <lesser> insignificant sensations such as hatred revenge etc prevented it from entering to my mind and since we two are one. was not this the case with you. I can answer that you have felt the delights of Hatred and Revenge as often perhaps as strongly as I have. —Well Augusta take up the pleasures again and I intreat you—feel them now. —I forsee that through this letter I shall be acting as I have been doing all my life wandering and digressing (write transgressing) continually. Come then let me shake of all ceremony. If I judge your heart aright (and it is not so easy to guess where its right lies) you will not seek for any thing more than my own thoughts and feelings expressed to you as the[y] occur to me and if when I give you them they appear erroneous and unintelligible let the fault lie on those thoughts and not on my head for writing them. Augusta—I HATE. my Father. I hate him he is a demon he has through all my life and through 19 years of his own made it his constant aim and endeavour to thwart and oppress and crush me. I have beheld nothing about him but his Black Bilious passion Brutal temper and base crafty dishonesty It cannot shock you to hear me speak thus of him for you have heard me speak so before you know I speak the truth and you yourself have received from him the dislike that I have done and you yourself feel toward him as I have felt. then listen to me Augusta think of him—Remember him I know you love revenge and excercise that revenge on him in any plan you may have for injuring and shackling him. I shall always be ready to assist you to the utmost of my power—what did I say—to Assist! to lead you to direct you not to bind the victim to the Altar But to stick the knife into its hearts<pine> Write to me If you observe any change in his health of all things I most wish him to die he is worth 30000£ a year and out of that 15000 is entailed on me Augusta you know that a property of 30000£ certain in spite of all his endeavours to devolve me is what neither yourself or myself will affect to turn from and before I am twenty one I see that I must either possess it or run myself into desperate embarrassment. (Ha I have done that already) And as to your own property Augusta I know you require it all and it must in a few years devolve on the pitiful creature your brother the fatted calf[56] curse him. If I return I'll give that into him which it will be long ere he is cured of It seems to me as if nothing but trouble is waiting to hail me on my majority—Yet among all the clouds in waiting there is one thought to give me delight. Thou too art in waiting I am not going to fill my paper with idle protestations of. "constancy affection" and all that sort of trash. But Augusta I love thee and thou knowest that I love thee you are the heaven on which all my hopes in the hereafter turn the paradise in which every pleasure I can trust on is centred I know well that you are as bad as I am that you are almost (as men say) as bad as you can be. but this does not matter a straw you are Augusta di Segovia. my brightest light of the past. you are Augusta Percy my only Hope of the future a minute ago I said that you know I love you and now I say I know that you love me and it is a love as warm and unthinking and inconsiderate on your part as on mine I could not trust you one moment I could not look forward to one bright day before me. but that I am certain you cannot leave me you want Augusta to make me [your] prisoner without committing yourself. for ever but you fell into the gulph you wished for me and when you wanted only to clasp my hand you found that I had as firmly clasped your own Oh when shall I clasp it in reality when shall I see thee again the woods and hills of Africa her noble rivers and her crowded metropolis the statly towers of Jordan Castle and the Noble Saloons of the Segovia palace they have no pleasure of recollection in my heart but what they derive from thy Italian eye and Raven curls and—satanic soul—Yet there is one other whom I greive to part with one other whom I do wish to behold again and that one Augusta. is My Mother. She I know loves me and what ever of goodness my soul possesses I owe it all to her. I cannot forget my childhood and in every thought connected with those times and their feelings my Mothers form my Mothers voice mingle in the dream and give it half its charm and all its comfort. Childhood to me seems to have been a period of unmingled happiness as I view it now contrasted with the storms of my later youth all looks like the Sabbath. all seems like those Sunday evenings in Summer when the sun was setting in golden light over the glades and dark green trees of the park it[s] yellow lustre flung over the wide spread lawns and shining with such soft and glowing light on the front of the Hall and the golden glittering windows and the sides of the white cows which spotted over the grass And My Mother then would walk with

---

[56] See Luke, chapter 15.

me alone. sometimes trying to call my wandering mind to a little sense of what I had heard at church. that day checking my as wandering feet from the countless objects of interest which distracted my attention and made me run every moment from her hand till satisfied curiosity brought me back again I might seem then heedless wild spoiled and incontrollable but in truth if I cared for no one else I did for her and she seldom had to reprove me twice in one day for the same fault though all her caution was forgotten on the morrow while I remembered it I heeded it. or at least often—but it was not in attending to what she said that I showed my affection for her but rather in unconscious delight in walking with her in sitting beside her in chattering to her and crying when separated from her when away from her I was passionate wilful cross and troublesome. when with her delighted. and far milder and calmer than children often are But when my father joined us as he sometimes did I caught a faster hold of her hand shrunk closer to her side and several times she caught me making apish grimaces at him. it was then only that I would willingly leave her and run to my nurse. when Ellen found in me at once a considerable pleasure and a very considerable plague. —But curse all this what am I doing Oh I forgot, writing down my thoughts as they occur and you must een take them as they occur I know you. dont like my Mother I know you wont like to hear of any pleasant days of mine if unconnected with you. you want only to hear of my thoughts of yourself and remembrances of the Noble girl the wicked Italian the glorious Enchantress who made my later days one stream of fevered excitement Ah. Augusta these feelings are different indeed from my dreams of childhood these fill my eyes with fire and those with tears and now when I think on these thoughts [they] bring suddenly upon my mind a host of different beings yet who have had almost as much to do with my later life as thou Ha I begin to feel the demon within me I begin to feel those burnings sensations which called from His Grace the Duke his short prophecy. that I should. through[sic] Africa into as great a fever as I seemed in myself. Come let me give way too the inspirations of the Deity within let me ask how are my noble freinds my hands my weapons My Noble Caversham and Montmorency and Sdeath and Simpson and St John and all the rest of the everlasting tribunal of immortality How are they and how do they get on they have my life in their hands and I theres in mine we are linked together but I am yet above them and I will yet be far above them. But I look to them as the swords werewith[sic] I shall slay the foe as the weapons of my arm Yes Augusta here I sit in my secluded study in one of the solemn Cloisters of St Patricks College in the Philosophers Isle What am I. A young Gentleman of considerable expectations snatched by his father from an imprudent marriage and sent here to complete his education for the life of an independent <   > and perhaps future Member of Parliament Ha is this so. Nay. A young—a young—why let us say for courtesy a young man. retired of his own private accord (wether hurried by force or not) into these accustomed precincts of learning with a determination to sit down and study night and day to plunge in to the most recondite mysterys of the Classics Languages Mathematics practical science. political economy the Art Naval and Military all the wide range of History and all the treasures of ancient and modern literature to study them indefatigably and unceasingly untill—a high degree. victory over all his fellows students the honour of Senior Wrangler[57] send him from the Island the wonder and respect of all the university his Mind strengthed and furnished with all the storys and accquirments of Learning armed at all points his weapons sharpened and his spirit fortified—To—Do that which he is determined to do—to fulfill his destiny to obey his own Soul. to spread his Name Fame words and actions wherever there is a world to spread them in and one single human being who can feel or hear. Augusta. do you know nothing of AMBITION. if so you know nothing of my heart. —Ambition that single word will rouse me when no other thought or feeling can It drives away joy and sorrow love and hatred crime or religion. drives them away or makes them bend instantly to serve its own ends and work what it imagines If ever human being[s] had the feeling I have it and all its fullest force is resistlessly centred in me—I cannot describe to you what I feel or how it affects me Augusta. the influence is really irresistible. My Ambition is not that pure and heavenly feeling which prompts a man to do what will prove to the glory of God and the benefit of his fellow men it is not that effervescence of youth which makes a man admire great actions and strive to imitate them it is not the generous ardour which prompts him to distinguish himself among heroes and sages which catches fire from Poetry or accident and which can rest content with a station and a name. It is not that sordid passion which directs the energies to the accumulation of pain and the accquirement of wealth and luxury—No By Heaven Augusta it is none of these. —Oh that I had the powers that my spirit longs for that I could tell you in living letter what it is I say it is none of these but it may be all of these and I think it is and twenty times as much besides. My Bodily conformation is excitable my nerves acutly sensible and they work on my brain till my feelings can be roused like gunpowder I have a mind naturally from these causes sensible of the strongest and most constantly recurring and most unquenchably raging emotions of Love, Hatred, Sorrow, and Anguish, But its Exaggerated tone though it can be driven almost to madness by these feelings cannot be moved at all by freindship respect. kindheartedness. platonism[58] the ties or religion or the customs of the world. The feind with in me drives me over all such feeble barriers and tramples upon these the passions of the cool reason and reflection. You see all my actions in this fight proceed from the Animal from the natural conformation and so they do nothing can be plainer I have all these nervous feelings and all the—the. —let the first word stand—all these nervous feelings which other human beings have But excited to a tenfold degree of intenseness.

---

[57] The student with the highest marks in his class at Cambridge. Patrick Brontë placed in the first class throughout his studies at Cambridge—see Barker Brontë, 9-10.

[58] The philosophy of Plato, especially insofar as it asserts the ideal forms as the absolute and eternal reality of which the phenomena of the world are an imperfect and transitory reflection.

As a vast deal of the mind really lies in the nerves as the brain could only be called the seat of the soul in as much as it is the rallying point of the nerves.[59] so since my nerves are naturally dreadfully excitable my imagination is to the highest degree vivid and burning I see every thing in a far stronger and more distinct light than others around me see them wether they be naturall objects they[sic] emotions which arise from the sight of scenery of the sky or the earth or the sea. or from their glorious and godlike associations. the thoughts which must rise when I gaze on the star spangled heaven of midnight or the stirring whirl of the city at midday and from hence Religion with its mysterys and associations has such effect on me that I am in daily agony that my searches shall find it to be untrue. Oh that day (and come it will) that day shall I lament to see. nay that is not strong enough but—away with this and hence. Music has allways had so irresistable a charm for me. and Hence the vehemence of my feelings has always shewn me forth like one mad with pride passion and waywardness. and hence I am what I am—Insane—a Madman. —But in order that I may prove a curse to the world that I may exercise my powers where if I was left to my personall feelings and my own organization I should spend a short life in a whirlwind and die at 20 of. pure old age. shaking like an aspen leaf! Burnt to white ashes! God if there be a God. Chance if there is none. has gifted me with. —An Intellect. strong vigourous powers of reason and thinking. —Ha and it is from thence from this Mind uniting with this Body. that I am what I am Not a mere madman not a mere prolifigate not a mere enthusiast. or poet or painter or Musician or Soldier. not one whose spirit is bent upon one subject and guided by one feeling or one whose reason is upset by his nerves and who is driven by all manner of feelings or one who is hurried into a waste of prolifigacy and has no thought for any thing else. But Augusta. I am—Alexander Percy. —Aye for by no other name can you call me. unless I be (following the doctrine of Pythagoras and it may be so for his metamorphoses forget their former life) a Bodily incarnation of Lucifer himself! Augusta if there be a Satan I am He.!.[60]

Oh why today when I was wandering by the sea shore why did I stop so before the full front of the Atlantic. and gaze over the mighty deep rolling with its thousand wild weltering waves and <gaze> on the clouds rising far beyond it and the sunlight on their sides and their deep black shadows and changing fleeting masses driven over all the soft azure sky and why did I listen so to the wind coming over the sea and whirling through my hair and to the roar of the Ocean dashing on the Beach and surging so ceaselessly all around the shore. What for was it that my feelings felt so roused and my mind was so filled with thick

---

[59] Compare with the views expressed on pp. 547-48.

[60] The association of Percy with Lucifer becomes standard in his later life—see, for example, pp. 259, 364, and 556. Pythagoras is said to have introduced the doctrine of the transmigration of souls into Greece, which was adopted by Plato. See Barker Brontë, 207 for a possible source in the conception of Percy.

coming fancys why did I feel at once so unutterably miserable and roused to such a pitch of energetic—Ambition yes then I felt even as I do now and what—what has my Ambition to do with the clouds and skies and seas of the shores of the Philosophers Isle why did I not speculate on what I saw on the mighty works of creation and the greatness of the Creator or on the nature and qualitys of that sea on the causes of its tides on the mystery of its formation the unknown depth of its waters and the shores, round, which they may flow—I have imagination why did I not think. on things like these—But no—I dreamed first over thee Augusta first all my feelings dwelt on thee. and then they dwelt on all the West of Africa and on all my prospects and all scenes of my past life. on Percy Hall and on Wellingtons town and all old times past marshalled before me. till. on a sudden like a true strong wind the thoughts of still older times swept through my mind and without my being able to guess well how the times about the Flood or after Egypt Nineveh Babylon the mighty Nations of Old their Empires conquests and the strange dreamlike feelings of their might and glory But I knew they had long past away as finally as the waves which rolled over the sands before me and how—by two powers the force of death and the power of man Sosostris and Israel and Cyrus and Persia and the Greeks and Alexander. must een appear to my sight and I could not but ask and what were these and for what did they live and what did they do. Carthage Rome Hannibal Sylla Ceasar. appeared with them and then still mightier and still more powerful. Napoleon and the War I could almost hear. the thunder of. Aveola Marengo the pyramids Austerlitz Jena Wagram Borodino the mighty struggle of 14 and the resurrection of 15[61] Close after this and while sights and sounds created by my own soul were yet hovering before my eyes and lingering in my ears. Our own Nation its rise the foundation and ongoings of the African Kingdoms the people the days the events among which I was born and which had not yet lapsed into the mere pictures of remembrance. but existed now and were now cabable of being acted on by the Human hand and mind, These thoughts rush upon my mind and shut out directly every other thought unless they connect it with themselves, what am I. I ask myself and I am not long in finding an answer and what shall I do in this world and what is this world what are its 1000000000 of inhabitants what have they been doing from the Creation till now and what are they going to do. what will the next 20 years bring forward and what shall I be at the end of that time Our Nation cannot

---

[61] Sesostris was a legendary Egyptian king to whom were ascribed great conquests in Africa and Asia. Though based on several rulers of the Twelfth Dynasty, he became the embodiment of the ideal of Egyptian kingship. Cyrus the Great, beginning in 550 B.C., fought a series of campaigns that led to the creation of the Persian Empire. Carthage, etc., all have to do with the creation of the Roman Empire. The final group of names, beginning with Aveola, contains the names of battles fought by Napoleon, his defeat in 1814 and his return in 1815. However, since it is only 1812, Percy could not have known about Napoleon in 1814 and 15.

stand still it is now rising and hurr[y]ing forward either upward or downward. mighty events are every day unfolding themselves and I know that Africa is the cradle of a new era. In history, and is it for me to sit down and see the world directed by the coarse minds of 12 northern Adventurers or by the routine intellect of 1200 Southern Noblemen or by the mere fate of events over which no one man has any controul. and shall I return to Africa and settle at Percy Hall (Oh I forgot my father is alive) well at Wellingtons town enter Parliament under the auspices of His Grace the Duke give a silent vote live splendidly perhaps enter the army and die Col Percy or Viscount Alnwick. a member of the Western Aristocracy or shall I [be] reconciled to my dear Father fight under his banner in the house of commons for a seat in the Ministry and as he would do having become Home Secretary die a—why like the other picture—a member of the Western Aristocracy—Do you think can you believe that such will be my Lot. —No By Heaven—No—Oh Sdeath, Oh Caversham, Old and young, Oh Streighton, Montmorency, Gordon, Simpson, Oh Well may you hope for my life and preservation it is you my fathers phalanx which I trust to make the stepping stone the weapon of my advancement. But Oh Wellingtons land Parrys land Rosses land Sneachis land Verdopolis. ye desarts of the east and Mountains of the north and woods of the west and plains of the south. thou City of Verdopolis thou land of the French ye Islands of the sea. I know what you are now but what is your future course and will you be ever doomed to be cursed with the name of Percy. and if you why not look at All Africa Asia America Europe, All the World! For all the world is open to me. may not all the world be mine? —When I look at the world at its state of blinded stupidity its mighty shackles of Religion the vast trammels of customs laws kings kingdoms Aristocracys factions manners morals. Faugh. Hence away with them all earth to earth to earth dust to dust ashes to ashes. all creation groaneth and travaileth in pain[62] untill now it is one D—d Ulcer which how can I hope to cure?

But I will cure it by My heart I will. Oh Augusta Augusta would that you knew what at this moment I feel I am a heap of wretched contradictions thinking of impossibilitys Dreaming—and waking to a consciousness that. all which I have felt and thought and seen and read of all the past the present the future is a slough of despond—Misery and dissapo[i]ntment, and hope without fullfillment and labour without recompense and Religion without righteousness and—sorrowing without end.

Well what is the future to me Augusta or the past. what do I care for aught but thee. —When shall I see thee again thou knowest how thou hast enchanted me and willingly I bear thy enchantment—

> Augusta though I am far away
> Across the dark blue sea

---

[62] See the service for the burial of the dead in the Book of Common Prayer and Romans 8:22.

Still eve and morn and night and day
    Will I remember thee

And though I cannot see thee nigh
    Or hear thee speak to me
Thy look thy voice thy memory
    Shall not forgotten be

I stand upon this Island shore
    One single hour alone
And view the Atlantic swell before
    With sullen surging tone

And high in heaven the full moon glides[63]
    Above the breezy deep
Unmoved by waves or winds or tides
    That far beneath her sweep

She marches through the midnight air
    So silent and divine
With not one wreath of vapour there
    To dim her silver shine

For every cloud through ether driven
    Has settled far below
And round the mighty skirts of heaven
    Their whitned fleeces glow

They join and part and pass away
    Beneath the heaving sea
So mutable and restless they
    So still and changless she

Those clouds have melted into air
    Those waves have sunk to sleep
But clouds renewed are rising there
    And now waves rouse the deep

How like the Chaos of my Soul
    Where visions ever rise

---

[63] In the left-hand margin opposite this and the next two stanzas appears a sketch of a figure with a club.

And thoughts and passions ceasless roll
And tumult never dies

Each fancy but the formers grave
And germ of that to come
While all are fleeting as the wave
That chafes itself to foam

I said yon full moon glides on high
Howeer the world repines
And in its own untroubled sky
Forever smiles and shines

So darkning oer my anxious brow
Though thicken cares and pain
Yet in my heart Augusta—thou
Shalt still for ever reign

And thou are not yon wintry moon
With its melancholy ray
But where thou shinest is summer noon
And bright and perfect day

The Moon sinks down as sinks the night
Thou ever beamest on
She shines only with borrowed light
But thine is all thine own![64]

And now Augusta fare thee well till thou meetest Again and roused to strength and energy thy Alexander Percy

I have given the whole of this young letter because I think it elucidates Northangerland[s] character and feeling at this time better far than any thing I could say of them myself. We see displayed in it all that enthusiastic spring of mind that ardent ambition which melancholy and greif had not yet withered within him and all those ideas of the world and its condition and ideas of what he should accomplish in it and how he should attempt it which have since so direfuly operated and which he is now endeavouring to carry further into effect. There runs also through this letter the strain of contradictory thinking of himself the overpowering glimpses of this worlds vanity and vexation which laid the foundation for his after miserable depression. —But I have lingered long enough over this interesting mirror of his strange character Let me now proceed with the details of its practical development

---

[64] See the 1837 revised version of this poem in vol. III.

The instant that Alexander found himself fairly transplanted into this new academic soil of the Philosophers Island he laid such effectual restraint upon his wayward wildness as to enter his class and pursue his studys with a vehemence and vigour that speedily brought down his fine healthy complexion into the true tint of student paleness all the day and half the night for the whole of the first month he was incessantly plunged into Greek Latin. Mathematics and every branch of learning and science that his capacious intellect could grasp on His Tutor Dr Chillcott.[65] an intimate friend of myself and since that time the respected prelate of Wellingtons town. thus writes to me. in March.

"You told me my dear Bud that my new pupil would prove almost impossible to controul I believe impossible was your very expression and when he walked into my study one morning and abruptly announced himself as "A D—l of the brood of Percy come to receive lessons in the art of destruction" I must say I looked at him with some feeling of unquietness on reflecting that I was to have charge of such a desperate young fellow as he seemed to be without waiting till I told him he took his seat beside the fire and asked with another oath "What the —— was he to do to be saved."[66] I said "Leave of swearing Sir and your chance will be improved." with a third exclamation he cried "I did not come here to bandy words with you or by G—d to be taught religion either. —I say Doctor Bolus. I want a prescription a tincture of humane letters my brain is as empty this morning as your brandy bottle was at the end of last night" Seeing that it was useless to grapple directly with his humour now I. determined to follow it and without answering him I wrote down in the form and language of a prescription the studies he was to enter upon and the amount in which each dose of learning was to be taken per day he perused the paper with a moody look. which cleared up once or twice into a sneering laugh and in conclusion said. "Are you fit to teach me these trifles for I <hear> some good fellows of your parts have their bellies lined a D—d deal better than their skulls—have you eaten your Brains Master. eh I'll not be humbugged" "Sir" I said "I am fitter to teach you than you are to learn." "How do you know that" was his answer. and so I told him distinctly and firmly that. His manner and language must be presently altered to me or he would not do long here I pointed out to him the consequences which would follow obdurate conduct. disgrace and expulsion from college. a character broken self respect in himself and the respect of others toward him all fallen away life begun without a single prospect of honour or happiness and then I asked him what would. follow "I'm the D—l." he said "and I know what you say is true. Doctor I'll call again this night" and so he rose and departed from the room. At evening he returned again and sat with me for 3 or 4 hours engaged in conversation respecting the course he was to pursue the branches of learning he was to follow and what he already

---

[65] Samuel Chilcote, curate of All Saints' Church in Cambridge, was one of Patrick Brontë's sponsors for ordination after he graduated from Cambridge.
[66] Compare The Acts of The Apostles 16:30.

knew in them. I was truly astonished to see his powers of conversation the wide extent of his information and the depth of his knowlege in Languages and History I told him that with the foundation he already had gained nothing but energetic attention was required to enable him to soar to the highest branches of human acquirements but attention I perceived (I told him) was what above all things must be exacted from him for I feared his character was neither so calm or so steady as I could wish it. "Why do you think so" he asked rather sharply "Your father Sir has informed me so and given me proof of it" "What proof." "Your marriage—" I didnt think that this string was one which could vibrate so the word marriage was hardly out of my lips when he started up and cursed and swore at me for a "D—d Old Fool who would be minding every bodys buisness but my own" told me to be D—d with my advice and left the room in a fury of rage. However as you had informed me of His character I determined to stomach this and I have since had reason to believe that all his inflammable restlessness of reproof arises from the sting left in his mind by his fathers harsh manner of sending him to this island for from this first week of his arrival to the present time a period of 5 or 6 weeks he has not for one moment relaxed from the most intense and ardent study night and day he is plunged in the very deepest fount of learning and his astonishing application has reduced him almost to a paleness and tenuity of a Senior Wrangler. he is struggling for a station in the July examination and truly I think he will obtain a high one I have entreated him to rest for a moment. But no he only curses me if I speak of it he says "I will be first or die for it" and indeed no pleasure no dissipation seems to possess power over his unshaken perseverance I think Bud you erred in describing him as you did in your last letter. at least such is not the opinion which 3 months experience enabled me to form of him I think him to be a young man of stern inflexible mind ardent and resolute in his determination to gain distinction and having an astonishing command over a fiery and impetous temper. his religious principle judging from his behav[i]our at devotions seems far more serious than those of the generality of our students for a look of more real and unaffected seriousness I seldom see or an aspect of deeper attention he associates with no body and is as temperate and frugal as a Spartan. Bud he will be a great man and I hope a good one"

"Such were the fruits of My excellent friends three months experience. well many a man has been almost as much as deceived as this. —At the conclusion of another three months when the summer examination came on Alexander Percy in spite of some awkward rumours which had spread among the Colleges still maintained among the heads of the University that character which has just been given of him and on the awful day of trial He bore the questioning and crossquestioning firmly showed such rapid progress and astonishing acquirments in Greek Latin Hebrew. Mathematics History and the Science of War. demeaned himself with such ready alertness calm scholarlike possession and with so triumphant a succes in all the examinations that. He was unanimously called the First Freshmen on the list[67] and though several students were then from priority of time etc. considerably in advance of him yet every body saw that efforts for another term like those for the one past would carry him up to the top of the tree

Such sucess was not in the nature of events likly to pass of without detractors instead [of] the rumours. which were afloat being quashed by this victory they only thickened and wandered on the ears like motes which the stronger the light the faster thicken over the eye. they were disregarded for a time as the mere suggestions of envey and malice—and so in truth they were but they were not the less well founded Dr Chillcotts letters to me however soon began to show some signs of doubt as it regards the character of his pupil. in the Month of August. a synod of the Grand University Council was suddenly called by the president Manfred and after a long deliberation during which Sundry Officers entered the Hall with several persons from the Philosophers town in custody. among others an Old Man who had latly settled there and who was supposed to have more to do with the students than was at all warrantable. these cust[o]dees not reappearing but being placed under lock and key. the meeting broke up and. Lo an Order was issued for the immediate apprehension and imprisonment of. "Alexander Percy of. St Patricks College. with.

Arthur O Connor	M Narmsworth
St J G Streighton	P St John
G J Gordon	L Caversham
J Gordon	and 100. Students from
N Gordon	various Colleges

No sooner was this order promulgated than the Officers proceeded to act upon it and amid dismay and su[s]pence on the part of all the University the Deliquents were apprehended and secured. But when the role of numbers came to be told it was found that all the persons mentioned in the list above were given were wanting. absconded clean evaporated 500£ reward was offered for the body of any one of them and 5000 for that of Alexander Percy Such an event as this was unprecendented and accordingly the excitement it occassioned was unprecedented among those apprehended were many of the heirs and representatives of the highest and most noble familys in the countries and others the most talented and brilliant of all its rising genius. the blight had particularly fallen on the youth of Wellingtons Country. As it would not do to keep everything in this suspense long His Highness Manfred promulgated the following Manifesto.

"In Consequence of various reports and rumours from many quarters and all them tending to afix suspicion upon many of the most distinguished young men in the University I on the first of August 1812 deemed it my duty to call a Grand Secret Synod of the Council of the Philosophers Isle. where were examined several of those men to whom the rise of the reports could cheifly be traced and among them a highly suspicious and illdisposed person who within

---

[67]   See n. 57 above.

the last 6 months has settled in the Island this man upon [being] promised. a reward and immunity declared he would declare the truth of all which he knew respecting the subject we were met to consider Having given in his name as Robert Patrick King. of Wellingtons town He upon oath deliberately and advisedly taken Swore that.

There exists at present in the Philosophers Island A Society composed of a number of the students and scholars of the whole University whose object and intent will best be given in the oath which he declared that each member took upon his entrance into this Society and which runs as follows.

"I swear in the name of all Nature that from this day henceforth without drawback or subterfuge I Devote my whole Soul and Body with all my Mind and energy to Firstly

The utter Extermination of all Religious creeds and modes of belief

Secondly the overthrow of the Whole Religion and Theocracy of the Verdopolitan Union[68]

Thirdly the utter extermination of all kingly Governments

Fourthly the overthrow of the present Constitution and Twelveship of Africa

That in order to accomplish these ends I enter as a member of the Society for the Creation of the World. the members of which society have sworn the oath which I do here swear and are as determined as I am to

Keep this Association a profound secret to all the world

To consider each member when he leaves this Island still a member wherever he may settle or whatever he may do.

To pay yearly into the funds of this society 50£ of current money

To keep up a constant communication with the president and council of the year running

To leave all the regulations of the Society to that president and co[u]ncil so long as they continued in office. and I swear to perform all that I have promised so help me. my mind

Futhermore the deponent declared that. this Society had elected Officers who were to hold office annually that the headquarters of the Society were to be fixed wherever its President resided that all the Members were to strive to enter parliament as soon as the[y] could legally do it and that the president must be in parliament at 21 and that there he should controul their movements subject to the decision[s] of the Council and whatever it should determine.

Futher more the deponent swore that the intent of the Society was to form a Nucleus among the rising men of the empire for the spread of Revolutionary and Republican opinions That they were determined to proceed in their open courses legally and as if acting indepedently as thinking and

---

[68] P. B. Shelley was sent down from Oxford in 1811 after circulating a pamphlet on "The Necessity of Atheism."

reflecting men while under hand they should form a compact well ordered and energetic association

Upon being pressed to declare the names of the Officers and originators and members of this Society. the Deponent demurred till as he expressed himself "Good terms were settled with him" upon this being settled he declared further upon Oath that. The originator of the Association was Alexander Percy. of St Patricks that it was formed in May. of the present year that the Council was composed of (Here the Manifesto enumerated the names of those heirs of. Wellingtons land whom I have above given) and of the members he gave a written list of which the following is a copy. (this copy comprising 100 names of course I cannot give) that they met once every month. in the vaults under St. Michaels Church. and the Council 3 times a week. at Mr Percys Rooms.

Deponent demurred to givin[g] the names of the Societys Treasurers as they were not members of the University and therefore we had no power over them. his demurrer was accepted.

Upon examining crossexamining and searching into all the minutiae of this buisness I found that The whole of what this Witness stated was substantially and perfectly correct he was thereupon ordered instantly to quit the Island now and for ever and Orders were promulgated by me for the detention and imprisonment of every man mentioned in his examination

Judgement will be given on the case on the 17th of August 1812

MANFRED.[69]

This affair was truly awful as it showed the tremendous character of the future premier of Angria and the effects which his wild ambition had wrought in secret. Yes reader here were the effects of the Noble and enthusiatic spirits that before developed in the Letter I quoted in a page back. All the University I may add all Africa was struck with horror at the wild and extravagent madness displayed by this hundred of her youthful and risings suns. I cannot tell what were my feeling when the news reached Africa. all the thoughts which had filled my mind on the future course of my strange pupil now flashed on me with resistless vehemences. I rem[em]bere I dropt the paper and cried out "What will he do next." However As he and the Officers of the Society could not he foundout. judgement was delayed till they could be secured by the civil Power of any Kingdom they might be lodged in and on August the 17[th] judgement was given to the following effect. That all the Members of the Society be fined 5000 each and be imprisoned 6 months in the University Dungeons or in default of payment they suffer expulsion from the University and the erasure of all their degrees titles or honours therein That the Members of the Council be fined 10000£ with 6 months imprisonment or instant expulsion from <their

---

[69] The name was likely borrowed from Byron's *Manfred*, which we know Charlotte had read by 1834—see Alexander EW, 22.

college with the erasure of their degrees> honours and <titles>[70] That the
President. Be either imprisoned one year with after expulsion and incapacity to
attain any Parliament public office or orders in the Church Army or Navy of
Africa. —or that he pay a fine of 50000£ and Be degraded from all the last terms
Honours and Station."

The announcement of this terrible sentence was followed by instant
action 20 of the members paid their fines. 80 were expelled from the College as
to the Council and the President all waited in suspense to see how they would
act their punishment was tremendous. —In the latter part of August a letter was
received from the Goverment stating No one knew where they were or what
the[y] could do in the matter and their assigned consequence was so high as to
envolve <varied> consequences in either sentence. But I must now relate how
they acted.

On the First 5th day[71] of August 1812 there was assembled a party in
one of the Saloons of Lady Augusta Percy at her mansion in Wellingtons Town
which if not numerous was certainly striking in its character and aspect as could
well be imagined

This saloon then a spendid and mirrored room was closely closed in the
great curtains hanging before the windows and the Luster from the ceiling
sheding its rich yellow light all over the hangings and furniture of the Noble
Apartment On an elevated sopha reclined the statly Augusta Percy the Wife of
the Revolutionary Student. her splendidly attired form and sparkling Italian eye
giving back her own aspect of Juno like grace and dignity near her the Earl of
Caversham with his bald forehead and suspicious courtliness of manner sat
looking with a hard cold and unaristocratic keeness. Mr Thomas Steaton the
steward of Mr Percy stood smiling sardonically. Mr William Montmorency and
the Counsellor looking ditto at him as if the two execrable traitors were
laughing at the Judas like conduct for their dear freind or masters interest
Counsellor Hector and Sir Thomas Streighton at the table over a pile of written
papers and ledgerlike red backed volumns was standing looking eager and aghast
at a little shriveled Old Man in a top coat and top boots of the shabbyest order
who remained near the door talking in a coarse hasty and impudent manner
garnishing his discourse by the comfortable flourish of the fingers and nose and
a more than due admixture of oaths and exercrations. As he went on in his
declamation the company waxed more and more aghast till as he said "And aw
aloon em escaped to tell ye" All looked at each other with an appearance of
blank dismay

---

[70] The top line of the manuscript page is partially covered as a result of the
page being set in.

[71] Branwell apparently changed his mind about the date but canceled neither.
However, in view of the date of Manfred's judgement on the previous page, both
are incorrect.

"Come" said Lady Augusta rising while her dark eyes seemed to flash literal fire as she spoke "Come now rouse yourselves you see what has transpired you see the detestable treachery of this infernal old villian but what is done you know cannot be undone what is to be done is what we must here decide upon Alexander is ruined for ever you Caversham lose 30000£ Simpson loses 20000. you Gentlemen lose your own sons I lose—but we know our losses so let us know our gains too Oh that you felt as I do and that execrable Master of yours Steaton would not live another day Sdeath will you—" "ess ess ess say aat say att Aw will aw will a commission a commission hullaballoo" "No No No" cried the company at once Lady Augusta seemed about to transfer her anger onto the company present when the Earl of Caversham spoke "Now I am Treasurer of the Society its funds are in mine and Simpsons hands If we pay the fines they will amount to all[sic] loss on our part of 100000£ If we do not pay we lose 60000 our sons Alexander our hope and glory and all the prospect of unlimited joys in the world to come. you all know <well about> young Percy['s] 50000 payable with smashing interest on the death of his father Now if we dont pay his fine on this D—d occasion he will be debarred from title to his fathers estates the usury comes to the ground and all is blown up between him and us for ever You see how the case stands—But If we do pay the fines we shall lay it to his account 100000 more well lay. lent on interest mind and payable on the death of his father the estate can afford the loss of a cool 200000£ mark you all this eh".

All present did mark it and Augusta said. "And his father shall die soon that I declare to you." A paper was drawn up stating that Lord Caversham had lent Mr Alexander Percy 100000£ on interest of 20 per cent per annum payable by instalments or on the estates of his father as soon as he should inherit them. Mr Sdeath was despatched with the bills to Stumps Isle where Alexander lay hid with the members of the Council and on the first of October Alexander delivered himself and themselves up to justice paid the fine of 50000 himself and 50000 for them to the perfect[ly] electrified astonishment of all present and upon laying down these terrific bills he said "And now D—n you all Heads and Feet together I'll enter as a student again and see if next January I dont again bear away the palm Oh Manfred indeed you have ruined me privatly but publicly you have made me great in deed." —Truly did this strange young man speak for he saw the dreadful embarrassment the payment of his debt must occasion at his fathers death and he felt in his own heart an intensity of hatred to the lenders Caversham and Simpson when he saw the crafty manner in which they had made good buisness of this dreadful discovery.

Alexander was now known emphaticaly in the University he was watched with the utmost vigilance but he shut himself up and this literally day and night studied to recover the ground he had lost and to gain so much more as to satisfy his revengeful feeling when he thought how they would be forced to give him the palm to whom of all they would most willingly refuse it. The Society was quite blown up now but. matters were [h]ushed after the exaction of the tremendous fines amounting in all to 200000£ No one knew how these fines were paid so readily no one knew the strange ramifications of this conspiracy against Africa and no one knew what years of blood and tumult it would ultimatly occasion no and No one knows this now

On the first of January 1813 Alexander Percy came up to the examination almost fainting deathly pale emaciated to a skeleton and his eyes almost fired as with insanity. It was at this expense that he. that. day Astounded all the most learned men in Africa distanced the most able competitors and in that Hall of perfect impartaility. though feared and hated and usually frowned on he for his splendid sucess in Languages Mathematics History and all Accquirements of Learning he received the splendid honour of SENIOR WRANGLER for the year 1812 in the University of the Philosophers Isle. he did not hear this word pronounced for he had fallen fainted from the fatigue of the successive examinations of 3 days superadded to his almost superhuman exertions since the fatal month of August.

Feild Marshal the Right Honourable
ALEXANDER   PERCY.
Earl of Northangerland
Lord Viscount Elrington Lord Lieutenant of Northangerland
Late Prime Minister of Angria Major General in The
Verdopolitan Service
&c &c &c &c
By Sir John Walter Bud Bart. Major General in the Verdopolitan
Ser[vice]

CHAPTER Ist   June 3^d 1835
VOL 2

I Now reader commence the second Volumn of my Life of Northangerland and I commence it at a time when your interest in it will be stronger than the work itself will warrant.

I know that no person looks with greater interest upon the present situation of Northangerland no one knows more of it than I do now and when I see this terrible ending to so long a career of misery this last fatal wreck of all power and hope and happiness it makes me look upon him at this time with a shuddering sensation at his agony and upon his life with wonder at its stormy darkness And now then feeling as I do the desolatness of his present existence torn at once from all power and distinction deserted by every one of the millions who lately looked up to him as their saviour proclaimed to the world as the convicted and degraded traitor forbid on a penalty which makes an attempt immpossible to touch or look on any of his only scources of ambition and exertion the scornful execrations of all men ringing in his ears the triumph of his slaves or enimies flashing on his eyes and the bitter upbraidings of an evil conscience rending his heart and all the Despair of his stricken spirit poisoning every feeling of his mind—I say that when I so strongly feel all of what he is I recurr with a double sorrow and astonishment to the recital of what he has been whether the cup of agony shall pass away from Northangerland or be filled again I know not But Truly he was already drunk of it often and deep and long

Now miserable as at present all the world sees Northangerland to be yet when I look back over all the events in his life which I am now about to detail I know myself and I must let my readers know that he has before this been as miserable and more despairing still Indeed when I run over in my mind the heads of the chapters in his Life I wonder how he has at all survived its events—How he is able now to face pain or sorrow.

With the commencement of this Volumn readers I am about to commence a detail which it will be most disagreeable to me to write or to think about through all the last Volumn you saw that I was cheifly engaged in describing the expanding mind and feelings of Alexander Percy latterly only in his Marriage with Lady Segovia and his unsuccessfull association of Republicans just entering upon a glimpse of the train of events to which that mind and those feelings were bearing I just dimly showed among what a set of

freinds and helpers he had got entangled but Now I shall shew something more
And Oh what tongue can tell what pen can write[1] the latter and dreadful
wickedness of the Higher classes around Wellingtons town. Yet all their crimes
shall shortly fade before the blackness of Percys own—I latly in conversation
heard a foppish person of this city declare that to seek true poetry it is necessary
to shut oneself out from Humanity from the stir and bustle of the world from the
commonplace wearisomness of its joys sorrows and greatnesses to look in
solitude into ones own soul and conjure up there some visionary form alien from
this worlds fears or sympathies I have heard another person of the weaker sex say
that it is the music of humanity which constitutes the essence of poetry but it is
a music in which Trumpet & Organ must have no sound where every thing real
in this worlds ongoings must give place to some pretty tale of true or false love
or the Orisons of some simple maiden or the gambols of fairies in a flowery
vale. I have heard too of another person and of the shorter sex too who though I
could not clearly understand her notions yet seemed from her likes and dislikes in
poetry to believe that every thing is to be placed below that rambling story of
versification which doles out by the 1000 lines descriptions of nature clouds
rocks and ruins wild forms and mighty visions of half forgotten times and people
dim old traditions—but nothing not a glimpse of real life or real feelings not a
wind not a breeze of that glorious Humanity which carrys with it some Soul
rousing or heart depressing vision of what a mortal may feel or see some flash of
that stir and glory which every age has presented to us something of the actual
shadow or sunshine which I know to be the greatest fountain of what I call
poetry.[2] —Well let these three classes of people think a little more and they will
sur[e]ly see the littleness of their doctrines I for one will always fly from the
sickly tales of mental concoctions or monstrositys sentimental decoctions or airy
fairyism and shadowy fancies of what has never been a Barmecideal feast[3] which
can never satisfy my hunger—To what has been is and will be to what I am now
writing to this very life take it in public or private to this very Man to the
greatest the mightiest poetry Alexander Percy and the History of Africa during
the last eventful 20 years Reader excuse this digression But it was forced upon
my mind when I thought that Here through all the ensuing pages there will he
no visionary legend no wild tradition for the imagination to rise on. Nothing of
light lyric fancy nothing of mere mental bubble blowing I shall detail nothing
but the stern misfortunes and coldnessess and blight of ordinary life the struggles
of a great mind bowed down and often prostrated beneath the world. with a glance
at the mighty ongoings of Empires and politics and war. My reason for speaking

---

1   Compare Shakespeare's *Loves labour Lost*, IV, iii, 41.
2   Bud's comments here are obviously directed at Branwell's three sisters, and
opposed to Branwell's own views about poetry which follow.
3   An illusory feast that appears plentiful—from the name of a noble Persian
family, one of whom served a beggar an imaginary feast in the *Arabian Nights*, a
work the Brontës knew well.

at all about Poetry Now is My knowledge of the fact that Poetry is something in language which rouses or sways the mind to itself. Northangerlands life does so therefore Northangerlands Life is poetry—To begin then—

My First Volumn concluded with a chapter which described the consequences of Alexander Percys education in the Philosophers Isle and shewed the discovery of that wild scheme of the Revolutionary Association which I am convinced was first set foot by the Earl of Caversham Old Montmorency Gordon Simpson and all the circle of the fallen spirits in the west These authorized Mr Sdeath to give Young Percy the sketch of the institution and that mind so fertile in the cultivation of evil produced the secret Society for the Creation of the World I need not again detail the consequences of this conduct. How Old Sdeath discovered the whole to the President of the University what vigorous measures the Grand Synod took to root out the evil and how the sentence past wrung 200000£ from Young Percys future property and expelled from college. 80 of the principle Young Men in Africa. Then I have brought into notice the diabolical manner in which Caversham Steaton and Simpson wound the coils round their victim By releiving him from the terrible embarrasment of fines which he could never pay. disbursing all themselves and agreeing with him to repay themselves with an usurious interest when he should come into possession of his fathers estates Percy saw that that wished for day would now prove a day of double gloom for then at a blow half his property must fall into the hands of the usurers and leave the claims of rank station extravagance. and waste to eat up right soon the rest.

This Volumn I must commence with another and yet darker subject where my praise cannot be heard for the blood which cries for vengeance and it is with extreme reluctance that I approach this year of Percys life and take my pen to indite nothing but crime and misfortune. Oh how soon how shortly after its rising was that Sun of brightness hidden in clouds and storms! After the Disclosure and punishment of the secret Society in the Autumn of 1812 little was heard farther in Africa of Alexander Percy save that he had reentered into his studies with even greater earnestness [than] before He hardly wrote to any one except His Mother and his Lady communications to the last of course I did not see but Lady Helen often.knowing the interest I felt in him and the time I had bestowed on him shewed me extracts from those that were addressed to her. I have forgot to mention that about a week after Alexander had left for the Philosophers Isle and while I was preparing for my departure from the Hall Mr Percy called me too his study. as I entered the Old Scoundrel Sdeath was concluding a tissue of bitter falsehoods respecting me and without telling me to sit down Mr Percy rose and furiously swore that "You are a D—d Rascal eating of my bread and drinking of my wine without the shadow of a service rendered to me You have afforded facilities for my D—d sons D—d marriage and you wish to live on me now when your pupil has been taken away from you Do you mean to teach me next Sirrah!" "No Sir my Rival tutor here seems to have taught you too well" "Begone Sir! I say be gone." And as the Master concluded the Man broke out "And Aw say begone yaw insolent upstart its yaw thats done mischeif and misguided. —" "Silence King" interrupted his Master "the fool misguided himself." "No Sir" I replied It was you two who misguided him" and so saying I left the room and house together

From that moment my connection with the Family of the Percys was dissolved—But my interest in their fate was undimminished and my eyes kept gazing upon them as before

I have mentioned that during the winter of 1812. the fears and hazards consequent upon the Discovery and punishment of the Society for the creation of the world had apparently subsided though deeply indeed had they sown the seeds of sorrows and dangers to come Alexander pursued his studies with impetous fervour at the University and his freinds and connections dived downward in their schemes of wickedness at home

In the last page of the former volumn of this life I shewed my reader a glimpse of the Interior of that splendid pile the Segovia Palace Wellingtons town and the transactions there in progress regarding the freeing (eh?—!) of Alexander Percy from the vengeance of law must add a new proof to the truth of that proverb which says that a fair outside often conceals loathsomeness within now in the same pillared and lighted Mansion I must open Scene the First of the Forthcoming Tragedy

It was wild and wintery in a dark January night but neither storm or darkness could enter the Magnificent Saloon where Lady Augusta Percy reclined on a sopha by a glowing fire and beneath the radiance of a noble chandelier The still solemn folds of the great curtains and Hangings of Velvet from cornice to carpet shut out all the storm whose dreary gusts were howling through the western Metropolis Her Ladyship sat in solitary luxuriousness with one of her youthful Husbands letters in her hand She had just perused it and now her soul seemed absorbed in reflecting on it yet wether her thoughts were pleasant or mournful could hardly be understood from those dark lustrous eyes whose glance either in joy or sorrow beamed with the same fervent glow But if I speak of Lady Augusta I can hardly restrain myself from entering into prolix minuteness and speaking with too much enthusiasm of one whose virtues I fear have long since been found wanting in the balance But my Reader must bear with me when he reflects upon what I am and how these thought[s] must affect me I have attained an age in which man is fonder of looking back than forward I am an Old retainer of the Percy family. and before I had attained the station I now move in—for years <I served Mr> Percy well (preserving <   > with pride[4] my honesty and independence and few know how difficult it was to do so) But yet looking up to these people I write of as my superiors and as among the loftiest in the Western Aristocracy but more at heart and to the point Whoever has not felt it can hardly know the feelings with which an Old Retainer looks back to the days he spent in the service of a great family and during the boyant morning of his life there

---

[4]   Again, much of the top line of the manuscript page has been obscured by the page being set in.

Antiquity their traditions their person their mariages and intermarriages and secret history and strange whispers and gloomy glimpses all are wrapt up in his Soul with his own nearest thoughts and imaginations. I always could readily feel these impressions and was not the PERCY FAMILY. calculated to inspire them was not its fate calculated to keep them alive untill my dying day While I lived at the Hall and the town Residences of Mr Percy much indeed I suffered cal[c]ulated to leave bitter feelings on my mind but the rememberances of these feelings NOW leaves sensations which I cannot very readily describe. —does not my reader enter into what I feel? And in spite of those scenes though rather perhaps aided by them the Noble heart the unvarying condescension of Lady Helen Percy the wondrous spirit of her unhappy son the mysterious family. the impassioned fervour of his Italian wife these things bound me to those chequered days The total breaking up of the Percy family when Alexander left Africa with my leaving the West at the same time to reside in Verdopolis have seperated all this first portion of my life from this Second and this too has added (how strongly!) to throw the solemn feeling over Old "Bygone" times How long could I run on in what I am digressing about. How I could describe the tales I have to tell of. these high and Ancient houses as a servant who remembers the personages he held communion with as if higher than any he sees around him now. The great Dukes family. the Wellesly House with the Dark Pakenham that double marriage which then was so much spoken of the youthful Brides one especially our gracious Queen. The Humes. whom another pen than mine[5] and engaged on later by not lower subjects has since thrown to other minds the same troubled poetry that they have in mine. —But. I must end this digression which I began by apologizing for my language respecting Lady Augusta Percy My apology is before my readers such a being so lofty so lovely despite her many and reckless crimes is she not one of the very cheif of these visions which are passing before me. Her life her death. —but let me hasten to detail them and that Dreary Tradgedy whose scenes I trembled to behold.

"Does he say that he cannot return as yet that he is involved beyond extrication! He shall return if what he speaks of alone hinders him I know its difficulty. But—O—My Dear Alexander What would I do to see thee once more! —and who knows thee who is worthy to love thee but me. I know how many in this City and in Verdopolis hate me for taking what they would industriously vie for but I have seized this prize from them like others and I laugh in my soul at their envious dissapointment it is the old cry again. "She indeed! how insolent" and. "What a fool he is" —what fools they are! —and how many of those haters have made their calls on me this morning—and would fill this house to night if I said the word

---

5   i.e., Charlotte's. The "Dark Pakenham" refers to Kitty Packenham, in real life, the Duke of Wellington's wife. See Alexander CB II, part i, p. 40, n. 67.

So Augusta spoke to herself her full rich voice giving bitter earnestness to her words. her lips curling in a smile of derision till again she gazed on the letter and her Dark eyes filled with impatient tears

As she sat leaning her forehead on her arm and tracing the hurried lines. which lay opened on the sopha A young lady suddenly entered the room wrapt in a large shawl that sparkled with rain.

"O Augusta" she said "it is a wild night. but I am come to tell you news which when I heard. I directly put on my Hat and a Shawl. and Hastened here through the streets with only a footman to guide me I could not think of waiting for the carriage. and my Father with the others will be here directly— what a spectacle I shall be!"

So standing before a large mirror she took of her hat. shook the rain drops from her hair and arranging it again, proceeded with what she had to say.

But it is fit first that I should speak some thing of one whom well I knew and [to] whom often have I told stories too while sitting on my knee

Miss Harriet O Connor. was the eldest daughter of Sullivan O Connor Esq[r]. and only sister of the unfortunate Arthur O Connor whose life has just so miserably ended[6] Mr O Connors other childern were by a later Wife. these two by his first Miss Woodfall Old Mr Percys first cousin. Harriet was now about 18 years of age a handsome Girl with red hair and commanding features She had always been her fathers favorite was hated by her stepmother and grew up amid constant scenes of quarrelling with her and crossings from her half sisters her Brother Arthur with all his culpable wildness and evil principles had a sort of good nature which he never used abroad but rattled through with at home and as he stood by "Mr Harry" in all the tempests at Woodfall House "Mr Harry" in return stood by him till his father sent him to the College School at Verdopolis. Then Mr or I ought rather to say Miss Harriet was left alone. Poor Girl she had not what she much needed a director and a Real freind when I think of her and her life I can hardly keep down a sigh her father indulged her and her mother treated her harshly for the first she felt grateful the last she laughed at and forgot. I used often to call at Woodfall House or their Residence in town. and my attention from the time she was eight years old was always attracted to the little girl with the curled Red hair. who if she came in crying was sure to go laughing out. —But when several years after she returned permanently from school (for her Step Mother succesfully resisted her having a Governess at home) when she returned with [the] finished form and rising grace of 17 I began to think more deeply of her prospects and mind. and from that time my forebodings were never bright concerning Harriet O Connor. At first sight the impression she produced on strangers was not intirly agreeable she was totally without pride and animated and cheerful but sometimes blunt and sudden in her address and though of most pleasant conversation still her egotism even when ridiculing herself. and many

---

6   Branwell offers no explanation for O Connor's death, who has been mysteriously resurrected after having been executed—see vol. I, pp. 216-17.

erroneous and unusual notions which she constantly repeated sometimes offended those who did not know her. she greived those who did But the freindly look of her eye and the odd way in which she shook her acquaintance so heartily by the hand with her evident pleasure in seeing those again whom she had seen before. forced many to feel toward her otherwise than harshly and though she was possessed somewhat of vanity and thought well of herself her plain dark frock and pearl necklace most seldom intruded it on others But this is only the surface of her character there was something lying underneath this seeming impossibility of feeling angry this complete freedom from pride this unguarded abruptness. was not the strongest feature of her mind She was not altogether what she seemed for underneath lay a heart filled with strong impressions a mind overgrown with eradicable errors habits of constant thinking which always ended in thinking wrongly. But also and mark the folly of judging intirly from outward appearances feelings always stretched and far too often troubled and restless and melancholy. I am convinced that her mind was of the highest order but. rendered useless through want of training to the right. I mean not as regard[ed] education for her information was remarkably extensive—One night as I was proceeding toward the House I met her on the lawn looking steadfastly up to the stars after her "Ah Mr Bud how do you do" she said "In what direction should Christians turn to pray?" I answered "Miss Harriet I hope you are not scoffing" "Scoffing! do you think I do not believe?" "You have often spoke[n] wrongly on the subject" "Indeed what should I do if I did not believe in Religion I should have no where to look to often. and I cant afford to part with my only Refuge—but Sir I can not call it a refuge because if the Bible is true it is no refuge for me and again Not for all the Bibles or Religions in the world would I give up the opinions I hold. I have prayed to be guided right and have afterwards found that nothing could guide me but where I wished." At another time she confessed "I am very melancholy Sir—for I feel as if I was not made to be what I am every thing that I do from my heart changes from what I wish it to be and I can see that nobody thinks of me as they should do no body knows me. I do not care for my mothers scoldings or the ill will of any body else. and yet there is nothing I so much want nothing I feel so glad for as any person's good will If I can feel sure that any one no matter how low thinks well of me it is to my mind a delightful pleasure. but it is one I seldom feel I am not quite sure wether all who know me do not hate me. I say that I was not meant to be what I am! —and because no one does know me is it well do you think.

'To be alone on earth as I am now?'

But Sir at any rate as the Author of that line says

'Before the chastner humbly let me bow

Our <u>hearts</u> <u>divided</u> and our <u>hopes</u> <u>destroyed</u>!'[7]

---

7   Compare Byron, *Childe Harold*, II, XCVIII, 921-23.

And so she turned away while ere another hour I saw her among her Mother and Sisters harshly abused by them answering in a most bitter passion but shortly declaring she would give in to them and consider herself worse than they did

A page back I mentioned her twice under the name of Mr Harry rather than Miss Harriet And for this reason it came upon my ears while writing in the very tone of those who used it as the well remembered name bestowed on her. when she was seen associating with such freinds and meddling with such matters as she did. who was her Guide and directer? Augusta di Segovia! This Lofty and wicked woman saw what Harriet was and Harriet knowing her talents and admiring her splendour and as was her usual custom captivated with her mode of setting the world aside in scorn at its customs and reproaches spoke her mind to her with double freedom defended her in company with reddened cheek and sparkling eye not by extenuating her faults but by praising them till the smiles of one half the room and the frowns of the other threw her (and more than once did I see it) completly of her guard in a passion of embarrassment. In Lady Augusta's society she could not long be without being in a society which truely she ought to have kept out of But this she could not do and accordingly Lord Caversham Mr Montmorency Sen[r] and Jun[r] Mr Macarthur Lord Edward Vernon these she spoke of and to as Freinds and Acquaintances and if a caution was breathed to her respecting them the usual shewing up and exaggerating Vices as Virtues stopped the mouth of freindship in complete dismay Nor was this all the danger which covered the path of one who was formed in a higher mould than hundreds happier than her. There was another thing which I saw soon and when others perceived it they counted her little else than lost—Always where the Lady and the Gentlemen I have above mentioned were there was one other among them the one whose life I am now wrighting[sic] Different from what men are now. Young Men most noble in form breathing in all that restless whirl of feelings whose settling has left the dreary waste we see. I recall vividly to my mind how when I was seated in the Drawing room at Mr O Connors town Residence conversing with Miss O Connor Her attention seemed constantly directed to the group where Young Mr Percy with manner different from the person who will recurr to my Verdopolitan Readers was talking earnestly and rapidly to Augusta Segovia and Lord Edward Vernon in a little while he advanced towards us and then Harriets face turned pale and he said "Now Hal why so shy this morning" She exclaimed emphaticly "Why D'ye call me Hal Percy[8] I might as well call you Alexandrina you have no right to do it—I get called enough for you—bored and scolded—while I act far wiser than my advisers. Dy'e really think my name's Henry—If it were I should know what to do" "eh—call him out perhaps?" interjected Lord Edward lounging lazily against the Mantel peice— "Stuff—But I must call myself in!" answered Harriet and Percy who had stood in thought muttered sotto voce "D—ation" and strode to the piano A short silence ensued when Harriet cried "Forgive me Sir I have spoken harshly. I **did not** mean it!" "It is I who ought to ask forgivness" he

---

8   Branwell seems to be echoing Shakespeare's *Henry IV*.

replied seriously but the entrance of other company put a stop to the subject and I left the room not admiring the acession of Visitors Certainly you will think that Miss Harriet O Connor ought to have been silent to those to whom Captain Bud did not think proper to speak But No and with fervour I say it Mr Jeremiah Simpson Mr Charles Steaton and Mr Robert Sdeath had buisness with Alexander which Miss O Connor very fully understood and very warmly entered into

On looking over what I have written I find that I have digressed so much and to such little purpose that it is incumbent upon me to resume the Course of my Narrative

"Now" said Harriet turning from the Glass "Now then I am handsome again as I can be at any rate although—But what is that Augusta? —A letter eh? —From whom? Alexander? —Do give it me do let me look at it.!"

"My Dear Harriet what made you visit me in a night so wild as this you forget yourself what is Sullivan coming for and who beside?"

"Why I have the most delightful news to tell—you could imagine that Old Scoundrel—but do let me see the letter how is he?"

"What is the letter to thee?. he is ill and I know not how to cure him"

"Ill! What both at once."

"Art thou ill or am I which dost thou join as both."

"The Old Rascal has broken his head!"

"What! Who? The Old D—l do you mean!"

"Yes He was fox hunting this morning and the ground being so splashy from the sleet as he was checking his Horse to threaten a farmer guilty of slaying a fox tother night in his poultry yard His Horse missed his footing in the sludge. and down he came with his rider beneath him they took him up completly sensless and he was conveyed through the city in a chaise this Evening to Percy Hall He never spoke and they say he's dead but the D—l is hard to kill at any time Would to Heaven he may be!

"Sancta Maria! I would die to have it so! Hast thou deceived me child— Oh Jesus when do they come?"

Lady Percy rose and paced through the room with clasped hands while Harriet bending over the table was eagerly perusing the Letter and as she laid it down saying—

"What would he have done! this comes just in the nick of time" the Door opened to admitt a servant announcing Visitors these followed close on the Announcement A Great Dark Man with a squint and Lord Vernon Lord Caversham Mr O Connor and Young Montmorency

"By G—d!" swore the harsh leader of the Group "Its done at last and My old freind has nabbed him however!" —"What Mr Simpson then youve been dead yourself if Deaths an old freind of yours!" But "Be silent Harriet" interrupted Lady Percy "Simpson! Caversham! is it true! —O Vernon is he dead indeed?"

"Dead as a door nail" answered the Earl of Caversham "I saw him lifted into the carriage white as a sheet where he was he black as a Thunder cloud.

"If he is not we shall soon see" said Mr Simpson "for we have despatched our dearly beloved Sdeath up to the Hall after the carriage and he promised to bring us down a faithful report of how the balance stood besides if doubtful a shrewd guess as to which would kick the beam But by the powers of Villainy we are likly to get our money sooner than I expected—But what's Miss Harriet walking about so troubled for? Felt a little twinge of affection for the deceased—heart broken—eh? —

"No Sir No Mr Simpson but—But I thought after reading that letter is Alexander to remain in ignorance of this event so long—so many days? How miserable and him so surrounded with fears I was thinking that he sha'nt and Sir For Gods sake let us give him intelligence directly let us think about nothing else Something may happen if we delay I—Ill Go myself! and that directly Ill go tomorrow!"

"Well thats considerate now! Ha ha ha the young D—l let him find it out himself But "A Dios'! doesnt thou know theres shuch an art as that of letter writing

"Oh It wont tell all or half!"—"Which I want to tell him" thrust Lord Vernon—"Stuff my Lord Who'll go Cannot I go—Augusta—nay Well Caversham!" "What. Harriet" "How will you send him word?"

"Segovia Mr Henry wants to set sail to morrow for the Philosophers Isle to acquaint your Innocent Infant with the Demise of his father and give him a little Fraternal admon[i]tion as to the manner he should bear it!"

"What is that Girl! Wither do you want to go have your senses fled up with the sins of that Scoundrel Know child that If any one in particular shall go to the Philosophers Isle it shall be Myself and not thee! —Your ignorance or insolence to the great—"

"I will not be silent now I will write to him this instant He shall not suffer from your cold blooded selfishness!—"

"Thou young fool do you know that I am in the room? —But she <demanded> "My Dear Caversham when does King arrive I cannot feel easy till he be here Oh If the wretch be dead that that is all I want I pray for nothing more!"

"You forget yourself Madam" said Simpson "I trust you dont pray for even that. By Satan! A Bishop himself would swear that such a prayer would lack an answer and so will I on my heart—but Here he comes"

A tantalizing Hawing and scraping was heard at the door the Gentlemen stood still the two Ladies were ready to fly and throw the door open The Ugly Old Feind they wished for entered. Wiping his nose with his coat cuff. he began with a satanic leer.

"Soa yaw're met to consult. are ye but yaw'd better gat away hoam He's nother dead nor like to be dead he opened his maath an spaak. just aft[e]r Aw'd getten into 'th roam. But Oh he wor beside himsell! He did talk wide! He swure! eh how he did swear! Yaw me leddy and yar bonny husband—He d——ned ye as oft as he oppened his maath. Theres no body i this roam but he titled off to 't fur spot i' the emptying of a pint pot. Dr Duncan. Bled him abaat temples and when aw left he wor mending fearful weel. Yaw better be agoing for there'll nought be done this last. yAw're fit for so little that theres no use trying on ye yaw mun sleep ower't as weel's ye can my Leddy for Aw sudnt wonder but he'll be stirring by this week end!

"By this week end!" Augusta said unconsciously and with eyes to which tears would have given relief."

"By me soul he will. and I'll stick by it and dee it ("Hang 'em they ernt worth a rotten filbert! "*sotto voce*)"

Simpson whose shaggy eyebrows had bent blacker while Sdeath spoke burst in a loud and contemptous fit of laughter

"Simpson" said Harriet weeping "dare you rejoice at it! you know How embarrassed Alexander is and you ought to know how this turn must dissapoint us."

"And I do Miss. But I laughed at the Old Gentleman here I'm guessing at his meaning! eh Old Boy? we are aquainted arnet we?"

""Aw knaaw nought abaat it Do not trouble me Yawr all fooils thegither Od! Awm plauged at o' me life ower ye."

"Good God" said Augusta passionatly. "And was the event so near completion only to pass off and leave me more miserably defeated than before Was I to feel such hope and see such a glimpse of happiness only to be hurried again into dissapointment and suspense It cannot be! I will not bear such a sucession of evils I will overcome so unnatural a tyrant. let them not speak to me of religion and laws I care for neither I have trampled on both ere now and yet never for such a cause as this Shall I hesitate when all I care for is concerned do I feel cowardice when I am to save Alexander from ruin? myself from utter ruin? Oh if <u>thou</u> wert here if <u>thou</u> couldst know what I am thinking if I should find aid equal to the enterprise! Yet without thee I will do what could but be done even with thee. and it shall be done to aid thee. —Old man you look as if you comprehended me I can trust your heart of steel. I feel that I can rely on you If I know you Simpson. —But I rashly venture my self among those who really hate me Oh that others could possess my mind that old customs old superstitions would weigh as light that fear would be as absent that. feelings and impulses of the heart which is the only mind would burn as strong and as brightly with them as with me! But we should have Hell in the world should we not! Jesus! and can there be a deeper pit than men have dug in it already! Oh if I were alone and could do my bidding with a wish. where should my path be taken and by means should it be made! —Am I to receive him then with the account of. happiness having knocked at the door but passing by ere it was opened of. a great good thing let to slip through the hand. and is he silently and within his own heart to blame me for losing the opportunity of vengenance for perpetuating all the countless evils to come? Oh if there were an Evil Spirit here I would entreat of him some counsel—But there IS an Evil Spirit! —Old man can I trust thee.?

"To DEATH. Madam!'

"You speak well. And I <u>will</u> trust you to DEATH!. Yes Robert. you know your young Masters difficultys you—you know what would end them What *alone*. would end them. —Ha do not mention the word I wish it to be

uttered by myself. —Yes I will repay him with My lord Cavershams interest for
the Misery he lent or attempted to give to me. But I am not formed for misery
and I will shake it from me I care not for the risk. or hazard—But then Why do I
hesitate you say? You are all known to me—Sirs! WE MUST KILL MR
PERCY !"
Amid another company horror would have compelled silence when Augusta
ceased. here the minds of all present were too well used to sin to start at the
suggestions of the tempter

      "My Soul" said Sdeath with emotion "But you have spoken well this
day! Aye when I brought em together I knew what they were and what they
would do! Oh thou art something like a woman!"

      "Eh Bob is she? —between ourselves—but no matter! A good move by
G—d! But what says our freind the Lord Harry? Liker a woman still perhaps.
eh?"

      "Lord Vernon By my Soul This is no time for nonsense Harriet sees the
affair more seriously than you But your Ladyship has thrust home. and your
words shall not fall to the ground."[9]

      "Stop Caversham" said Sdeath "Stop Lets see about this spot of work
and get it settled to our minds Oh But thourt the Queen of Heaven and I shall
never forget thee for this! Sit there for the best seat in the room is thine and My
Old Freind Jerry Simpson sit thou on her right hand Sblood but thourt true steel
and Ive known thee as many a day Caversham sit thou on her left. Stand ye
round now and for myself why Sdeath Im but a servant and een must kneel
before her."

      The Old Wretch fell upon his knees and while the fire glanced from his
withering eyes. he grasped a long knife he had drawn from his coat and extending
it toward them continued in a tone different from his usual mode of speaking

      "I neednt tell ye how the virtues of this old blade. but if ye want
anything doing sure and short. heres the thing that'll do it for ye and I need'nt tell
ye what this iron has accomplished for this is not just the hour for cracking over
old tales of sports that have been had but its the time to scheme a play that is to
come on and which God grant may be the merreist we've played since we opened
our eyes in the world. My Soul but thoust done well woman! but trust me for
doing better yet—"

      "But the knife" said Augusta. "the knife it leaves marks such a death—
will not appear to have been received in the hunting his cursed Wife will
discover it."

      "Trust me for that I merely hold out my old blade as the symbol of my
office My soul. must it not be these very old hands which dandled him when a
baby that shall handle him when a man did not these old bones hold him before
he couldnt walk. and shall not they HOLD. him now when he cant walk. By
G—d But I will give him an Embrace at parting one grasp of the hand ere he sets

---

9   Compare Luke 8:18.

sail on the voyage from whence no man returneth He's oft black in the face with passion and shuch a fall as he has getten may well bring on apoplexy. By G— d!"

"Now let it be done soon" cried Harriet do not delay. for the sooner it is finished the less suspicious will it seem."

"Your right Miss" said Simpson "My Old Freind ought to have him in limbo before this week end and roasted as black as a bilberry.[10] Ill furnish you gratis with the suit to rig him out for his journey. he sent his son on a voyage Let him go now on one himself. Gad! a thought strikes me Caversham shant we go and see our old chum By Jove. a good move. lets up and condole him over his misfortune. and prognosticate a speedy recovery and talk to his Lady of. a change for the better!

"And let Harriet go" said Lord Vernon "it will perfect her in the only sin she is not accomplished in—Hypocrisy.! Ha ha!"

"Never My Lord.! Oh God have I not sinned enough already!" and as she spoke with hands clasped she shed tears of bitterness But Augustas Italian eye smote her soul and she dried them to drown conscience in the passions of that bloody hour. She gazed on Lady Percy with awe when she viewed her in the fire of untamed nature with her black eye brows corrugated by Hatred and her Majestic form erect in the triumph of revenge she extended her white statue like arm as if grasping the Magic dagger while she said to the malignant Sdeath. "What thou doest do quickly"[11] And that wretched old man donning his tattered hat. answered by a sneering laugh of satisfaction. To Harriets excited mind the statly lighted saloon seemed to contain only feinds from the infernal pit. The Wife of Percy with her voluptuous form and dilating eye. Caversham with that high Noble forehead and scanty silver hair shining above his mean greedy eyes and a coldly treacherous smile. Vernon whose very smoothness of aspect shewed the deep villainy that lay beneath. Montmorency—Young Montmorency. (not now young. nor then young in crime) him she looked at often for he stood backward spoke little though laughing at every peculiarity in the conversation but with those features Massy even in youth. fixed in deep thought his brown hair falling over his knotty brow and his grey eye. some times bent on her with such a searching strangly gleeful glitter—and old Sdeath who paced to and fro with his hat struck over his brows his hands plunged in his pockets and croaking satisfiedly over the Misery that seemed ready to come. —while the rest were talking together in a low voice over their projected deed of blood. Hariet again took up Alexander Percy's Letter and gazed at it as if its pages hid some unfound meaning as her eyes dwelt on the very form of the hastily written words their impassioned meaning stole insensibly on her soul "I know not at all wether I am miserable or happy nay nor wether I have the materials for being either I fancy that I cannot receive one good without I lay down another Can I love any one

---

[10] A shrub of the heath family, with dark blue berries.

[11] Compare Shakespeare's *Macbeth*, I, vii, 1-2. Note also "Dr Duncan" earlier.

but thee? and yet my Augusta forms and feelings crowd around me which are not of thee. wether I am with thee or from thee!" As she read those words she looked up and half started at the look with which Montmorency was regarding her as he leant with folded arms on his yellow cane. Lady Augusta who had been speaking to Simpson extended her arm to him with a motion for silence Old Sdeath slouched down with his ear toward the door and as he sprung up with an emphatic Oath it flew open and <u>Alexander Percy</u> strode wildly into the Apartment!

He stopped when he saw who were in the Saloon But in a moment Augusta was in his Arms.
Affrightedly she gazed on his face where she saw his ghastly and emaciated look But convulsivly repressing all sign of joy and motioning her to keep silence he said looking hurriedly round him

"My God! What are you hatching here? Why gathered and with such an expression? By Heaven Tell me what you are doing!"

The Son of him they were about to murder had appeared among them with the suddenness of a thunderbolt. Lady Percy did not answer because in gazing on that unexpected form she had forgot every thing and every sound. <besides> poor Harriet was in tears for when Percy entered she sprung unconsciously to meet him and the sneer with which Montmorency beheld her had harshly called her back to reality The others present dare[d] not speak the awful answer Save two Simpson and Sdeath whom nothing could appall. and these both replied in a breath.

"We are murdering your Father!"

"Murdering my What Sirs!"

"Your Father"

"By heaven I will not be jested with!"

"And By H—l we will not jest! —But Good Sir" said Simpson "you give us no time to pay our respects on your sudden and unlooked for return"

To death with respects! I see you are on some infernal buisness—Mr Satan explain!"

"Ha ha ha a good move! But you're mistaken Satan has only entered this moment and knows as much of the matter as you do But we are only met on our usual buisness finding a "new way to pay old depts"[12] —Your father on hunting this morning fell from his horse and has injured himself so severly as to cause hopes of his death for two or three hours on end We hurried to your Lady to have a bit of chat over the news and Old Bob my freind was packed up to see how his master got on. as we were all speculating upon the expected catastrophe above there Bob pops in and tells us its no go and alls blown over like a sea sickness. such news struck us on a heap. but your good Lady who lives in a sort of "Inferno" and is not so soon frozen fast arose and gave us a hint which we are

---

[12] "debts" obviously intended. The phrase may have been derived from the title of Massinger's play *A New Way to Pay Old Debts*.

not slow to improve on says her Ladyship "We must Kill Mr Percy!" says Bob we must throttle him. says I We mu[st] get in our monies and say you they shall be paid every stiver!"

"Alexander" said Lord Caversham "Here were an opportunity which must be improved on—if not—why you pay up interests and lose principals we remain without our capital and your father lives on refusing your allowance or shuffling off the Entail."

"Do not persuade him" interrupted Sdeath "let the Lad take his own mind he'll come abaat ya'e see." and the Old villain stood regarding his pupil with a gleam of feindish satisfaction Percy stood still in utter silence he looked on the ominous faces about him almost recoiled from their expressions gazing steadfastly on Harriet he said with emphasis "And do *you* approve it too!" She could not reply but answered by her kindled eyes. "Sdeath" said Percy turning to the old man "Attend in my dressing room to morrow morning—Gentlemen meet me then at Breakfast here. go now—and to H—l with ye all!"

"Good night my Lord and Lady Macbeth." said Montmorency "we'll produce our Habeas Corpus. —But Miss Harriet how do you go home?
"I—I dont know" she said starting
"Ha Harriet! —But I will see you to morrow I shall call on O Connor. Good night to you at least."

"And I" again said Hector "will have the honour of escorting you home" At this moment a servant called from the Hall desiring Sdeath to go up directly as his master could not do without him the villian laughed hoarsly at his confidinging[sic] ignorance and preceded the rest from the room

Augusta and Alexander were now left alone, He stood and with clenced hand raised upward cried "Oh my God upon what a course of destruction dost thou drive me!" Lady Percy whom his sudden ghastly and exhausted appearance had shocked into silence burst into tears and throwing her arms around his neck she said.

"O my Love you affright me by your voice and aspect you are indeed dreadfully ill In Heavens name has any irremediable evil happened that you should arrive so unlooked for and so despairing?"

He laughed with a hollow mirth and seating himself with her on a Sopha answered

"Evil, Augusta! Certainly not Ha! why I am First man of my year I have been made Senior Wrangler my love. *Vi et armis* [13] as the saying is I have forced them to grant their highest honours to the man whom most they hated Is not that a sweet comfort. thou at least can appreciate its value I left the Island the week after my examination shaken to peices with nervous exhaustion my soul full of horror and sleepless anxiety threatened by my Creditors detested by my superiors cursed with the brand of Treachery almost outlawry Atheism and destruction I sailed over ruminating on some plan to free myself from my chains

---

[13] "by force of arms."

before circumstances rivetted them upon me The Devil tempted me day and night. and—Now! —I have arrived on landing full into the midst of a vast conclave of Demons[14] I have not cast off the Evil Spirit but I have received seven new ones[15] —My God! they tell me to murder my father! Ere I saw them I was brooding madly on the deed and this night—it has been urged on me by others. —yes THOU tellest me to kill my father!"

"Yes" she answered kindling while she spoke "I tell you to kill your father Percy your studies and exertions have shattered you they have unmanned you[16] do you not see that what I suggest is the only possible means by which you can escape from your difficultys if he lives you continue paying your enormous interests with the certainty of being oblige[d] to refund your principal when perhaps you may have actually paid it and paid it again This day your father met with an accident so severe as to render his life to appearance doubtful though we know it is not so for he is recovering Caversham Simpson and the others who at any other time would not wish you to pay up their principal but rather receive their 20 per cent profit just now want all the money they can command on some scheme or other so I knew they would aid me In R P Sdeath I foresaw a willing Instrument The accident as I said favoured the attempt—and therefore I boldly advised the deed. And Alexander dare I to remind you now of the manner in which you father has treated you have I to relate your wrongs and injuries? do you know of such a word as REVENGE! Yes! he has invidiously insulted me he has opposed my marriage with you determinadly[sic] thwarted it and when he could not prevent it he has striven to embitter it! He hates me as I hate him He hates you from his Soul Believe me the discovery of your Society originated with him! He is a dark a dangerous man! —But—(and she spoke with feirce emphasis) In thwarting me he has found his Match! He has met a deadly an inveterate foe! and you—your latter injuries have been owing to me.! he knew that keenly I should feel your wounds for I love you untill your sorrows and your crimes are mine And Holy Mary! what he has lent me I will repay with his own usurious interest. I will return him per centage and principal Jesus! Is my Alexander dying that he should thus regard this vengeance!"

"My Augusta your voice only attempts to spurr over the precipice a man who is determined to take the leap—I have made up my mind to kill him because if I dont I must make it up to kill myself. At College since August I have been playing—Hazarding desperate stakes in order to recover my tremendous fines and free myself from these human feinds Caversham Simpson and Co I was worried with exertion and anxiety I was only 20 years old and the result of course has terminated in the loss of another HUNDRED THOUSAND POUNDS! I was made Wrangler. the vacation came (My father forbidding my leaving the Island then) But I did come over simply in order to find PAYMENT

---

14 Branwell seems to be echoing Milton's *Paradise Lost*, Book II.
15 Compare Matthew 12:43-45.
16 Compare *Macbeth*, III, iv, 74.

for my victors the attempt was desperate from HIM I could get nothing from Simpson and Co. Bah my soul recoiled at a further entangling I did think once of leaving Africa for ever it was a wild thought. and one thought of Thee chased it never to return. But How am I to pay? my debts are 300000£ when I enter on my fathers property I shall possess. 500000£ —I tell you it is enough My Love, It is finished, the Deed is done!"

"Then I am thine and thou art mine and hope of joy shall never fail us If I can trust in love from thee But that Heart is as Wild as my own and can evil trust evil?"

"I care not I am what I was a year since I know thee and thou knowest how I love thee We will not confess what needs no confession but rather let me live an hour of heaven love in the arms of one with whom I sacrifice all hope of it hereafter—O Augusta with you here I do feel happy. as I or you can feel I know I am Alexander Percy who thinks that years with thee are bought cheaply By Eternity—Where! I know not! you say nowhere. —How I have thought of you Augusta while I was away and you are not one for many to think of others did they love you would take care to search your mind no more than skin deep But I have thought of you till. trust me, I know you! Now dont start because you feel that you are what you would'nt wish me to know remember I do know you! and remember I do love you! While absent, could this form this face these dark Italian eyes be forgotten by such as I and if unforgotten could they fail in their power Oh no this life I forsee affords too little pleasure for me to throw what I possess away The past also is fixing to firm a hold on me and think what thou hast been through the past—the first the brightest the most glorious Star that ever flashed on the eyes of." —"My wild wayward wandering—yes my Divine Alexander Percy!" "Divine! My God is Hell divine?" "THOU art divine for what hath ever kindled my soul or brought tears into my eyes like THEE thine own Music is never so heavenly as thou and what do I care for Hell or Heaven or Death or misery. while I am here with thee Solitary Evenings which in themselves had nothing except a dreary desolate gloom and sounds of wind and rain have wrapt my thoughts like thine not only far away but like Doves (only themselves how un dove like!) they have all flown over the sea and time to their mysterious home in thee!"

To breathing and burning words of which the foregoing are but a meagre shadow the Solemn impassioned looks and melodious voice of the Speaker gave a yet diviner feeling and he to whom they were addressed from his own enthusiastic spirit called up in answer a language of the mind to which I cannot give a name Ideas changing and uncertain but which would gather from all time in a wandering flight a thousand associations of whatever contains the spirit of poetry only in the end to fill that mind full of emotions connected with the Noble Being at his side He took her to a Grand Piano at the Head of the Saloon and after a prelude of full solemn chords accompanied her voice to one of his own rich and melancholy compositions

"Son of heaven In heavenly musing
Gaze beyond the clouds of time

> Future glory rather choosing
>   Than the present world of crime
>
> Thou whose heart that world carressing
>   Bows it Bubbles to adore
> On and hunt each fleeting blessing
>   Still in sight but still before
>
> Christian, worlding, hence and leave me!
>   Here with thee my love alone
> Things to come shall neer deceive me
>   While I hold thee—NOW—my own!
> Fate of bliss can neer bereave me
>   While we two continue one! [17]

"And are we not as one now" said Augusta as they concluded with her most winning smile "Yet why then that sorrow and that wandering eye?"

"It's the thought of how I am repaying My Mother for her years of affection" he replied "I thought I saw her! What would she think if she knew her son! —O my Mother—my Mother!"

Oct 20th
1835
PBB

CHAPTER II^d   Oct 22nd
1835
PBB

With sorrow do I enter upon the detail of those events which marked the morning of January 17th 18 [18] —a wild and stormy morning it was and well fitted for the work it was destined to perform

Mr Percy lay on [the] Bed with Dr Duncan and Lady Helen seated beside him But from time to time through pauses of exhausted silence he would articulate curses and imprecations upon the event which had brought him to his helpless condition and doom to destruction every thing which he fancied had joined to cause it though the symptoms were not dangerous yet his fall had been very severe one arm was broken and he had received several violent concussions on the head copious bleeding had not allayed the fever of his restless mind and no intreaty availed in imposing silence or softening his soured spirit

---

[17]   See Branwell's 1837 revised version in vol. III.
[18]   Branwell left the date blank.

"Helen" said he "By G—d if you disobey me in this manner when I cannot force obedience depend upon it that I will make you repent when I recover Ill have the Horse shot this instant—stumbling D—l! and as to the Insolent farmer who stopped me on my soul he shall fall as low as I did Thank heaven he lives on my land and I can make him smart for it—Steaton Sirrah there! —"

"My Dear sir you may rupture a blood vessel by calling in that manner Shall I—"

"Keep your cursed advice for your own lying quackeries—Ho Steaton By Heaven Doesnt the Dog hear."

Mr Steaton came hurrying in "Are you too determined to disobey me—But Ill have my revenge—Go and set to work with George Hawksworth this moment. turn him out of his farm—out with him into the snow and By G—d I'm glad there is snow eject him Sirrah and set about it! —Ho stop and go down to Montmorency—no desire him to come up to me. he shall proceed legally against the slave for killing my Game—But not till I [have] shorn him of his money. First one blow and then another—He shall see what stunning means! —Begone!"

Mr Steaton gladly left the apartment and Mr Percy then lay for some time still But bending his black brows alternately at his wife and the Doctor after a while with a groan he recommenced

"I suppose now when he hears of it your D—ned son Madam will be ready to cut his throat with joy But Ill cheat him yet which ever way it turns with me Neither he or you shall juggle me out of my life and property! —Call up Sdeath this moment.!"

"Awm here Master" answered the feindish old man entering as he spoke Lady Helen and Dr Duncan both starting as if at the a[d]vent of an Evil Spirit

"Now turn em out Sdeath Go out Helen—begone Dr a word with ye Robert—"

"Eees. but Me Leddy Aw càm up to say that theres Caversham and Vernon and some more's doan below and want to speak to ye uncommon partiklar."

Lady Helen and the Doctor rose to depart but just as she was leaving the room Mr Percys eyes assumed a ghastly fixedness he called her back and taking her hand seemed about to speak but after a silent shudder he only said. "Its gone! God bless you Helen!" Lady Percy afterwards remembered Sdeaths ghastly sneer when she closed the door in leaving the room

In a drawing room below she found Lord Caversham Lord Vernon Mr O Connor young Montmorency and Colonel Wildwood waiting as if to make a call upon their freind Mr Percy. after the usual salutation and enquiry after his health the Earl said.

"My principal Object in coming here this morning is not to see Edward for I suppose he is not fit for conversation—but to acquaint your Ladyship with a peice of news more safely than I could do by letter—Mr Alexander arrived at the Segovia palace last night from the Island after having taken the degree of Senior Wrangler there—of course he dare not let his father know of the fact but

he most earnestly desires to see you and entreated me to persuade you to come
down this morning and my Dear Lady you need not be agitated at his appearance
for his studies have superinduced a nervous anxiety which a row or two with us
will soon wear away"

"Then you will excuse me My Lord." said Lady Percy and without
further remark she drove of with her usual promptitude to Town

"Gad she's gone" said Montmorency when they saw her carriage drive down the
avenue "Now then HE must go too—wheres Patrick"

"Hush" said Caversham "this is no buisness for talking let us call Sdeath in—
But stop what was that—"

"Some clamjamfry with the servants I suppose. Ha Ha Ha —"

"Ha Ha well conscience does make—you know the rest[19] but I had thought
different of old veteran Caversham he's had a touch of this sort before now eh?"

"Hush Vernon never with such inconsiderate confidants. its time to
commence wheres Sdeath. why tarry the wheels of his chariot

While they were sneering and talking thus a noise was heard without
the Door flew open and Sdeath entered abruptly

"What here Old Boy—now up and to your work!"
with a sardonic laugh the Old man answered. standing before them.

"ITS OWER'D SIRS!"

And directly left them. running through the house crying noisily for the
Doctor The "party in the parlour" stood petrified gazing on each other as if
doubting wether all was not a dream That DEED. done ere they thought it
entered on—themselves <ere> they were aware. all—MURDERERS!

Dr Duncan alarmed by the cries for assistance hurried up stairs with Sdeath
clamouring before and the Gentlemen from Town after him. On Entering the
chamber they found Mr Percy lying a corpse with discoloured face clenched hands
and glasslike eyes The Doctor since told me that from that moment he suspected
Foul work in secret, Sdeath said.

"He wor threeping[20] me ower Alexander and swearing he suldnt have a
ha penny o' his brass So thinkin no wrong ower't I just up and told him as haw
he had comed into taan nobbut last neight and the Measter at that starts bolt
upreight with and Oath and a "What Sir" So Aw sez "Alexanders comed hoam"
and then making a tear at me his arm flang out o' joint agean and he fell back
ward wi a gasp and nivver spak more. Aw seed it wor Apoplexy by t' bluid
rushing intull's face and soa Aw banged me daan stairs to fetch ye up to cure
him, Lord—safe us he's like as he war dead!"

"Goodness" cried Caversham "I fear its something serious!"

"We must lose no time in seeing My Lord" answered Duncan who has
told me that it was all he could say for he fancied himself among Demons
Bleeding and every other means were promptly had recourse to [to] restore

---

19   Compare Shakespeare's *Hamlet*, III, i, 83.

20   The word means to rebuke, reprove, chide, assert or affirm vehemently.

animation But all was in vain the Murderers grasp had too effectually done its office and those withered hands which had deprived their master of his life were now hypocritically buisied in the office of attempted but as Sdeath well knew useless endeavours to restore it. Lord Caversham Vernon Montmorency (that very man who is now the Mouthpeice of Reform) and Wildwood with Mr Steaton the Steward and one or two principal Domestics stood round the Apartment till Dr Duncan declared that Mr Percy was certainly DEAD!

Then without a single tear being shed on the anouncement each man seemed eager to make what he could out of the event The servants hurried about in full liberty The Steward drove down to pay his respects to the heir All the vis[i]tors hurried away to acquaint their confederates with the event except The Earl who remained behind To break it to Lady Helen on her return This Satanic Nobleman whose years only increased his crimes walked alone through the Drawing room not in sorrow over the loss of his companion and fellow worker but seeking every possible method of defrauding his Son. as he beheld Lady Percys carriage coming up the lawn he assumed a look of concern and when she entered the room he said with his accustomed statly ease

"I am sorry Madam to have to meet you with intelligence not so agreeable as my last—But you are agitated be seated I pray you"

"No My Lord no—how is Edward? worse?"

"My Dear Lady Percy—" and he hesitated as if unwilling [to] break the news so abruptly But she said suddenly with a fixed look.

"He is Dead Sir!"

"There may be hope madam—But I fear—"

"My Lord" she replied repressing her feeling with her wonted firmess "My Lord I shall judge for myself." and went up supported by Caversham to the Room where Mr Percy lay when she beheld the ghastly corpse she trembled but recovered herself looked long and earnestly upon it and on a sudden turned to the Earl with a gaze which even his hardened conscience could hardly withstand

My Lord you will excuse me I desire to remain alone" "Certainly it is most proper" he answered and as he departed she closed the Door within

That Day Lord Caversham spent cheifly at the Segovia Palace But what passed there I know not In town the report was soon spread that the well known Mr Percy of Percy Hall had died suddenly from an Apoplectic Seizure while lying disabled by a fall received in hunting A mystery hung over particulars but in general people were glad at the removal of so dangerous and turbulent a man. I was myself in the country at the time and when I returned home 3 days after I was thunderstruck on opening a Note from Mr Steaton of invitation to Mr Percys funeral I had not heard a word of his illness and could hardly trust my eyes I hurried out for information but all save the mere fact was a varying mystery Young Mr Percy I found was in the City but had not once been up to the Hall and I knew he would not go up so long as his father lay there—But January the 25th arrived and this was the day for the funeral Full of strange thoughts and old recollections I proceeded toward the Hall all round were the loneliness of Desolation for when the Masters hav[e] departed a Domain will seem strangly drear Yet within the Noble Old Seat. though every room was hung with black and every Inhabitant clothed in mourning there sounded the joyless bustle of the preparations for the last dark journey the Hall was filled with the various relatives of the Deceased and many persons were there of the highes[t] rank and title not only the Earl of Caversham Lord Vernon & etc but the Earl of Elrington Lord Beresford and Lady Hume (Lady Helens cousins) with the youthful Earl of Jordan and many others whom it would be vain to name. At the appointed time a long solemn procession among which how few were mourners! set forth from the park gates the titled or wealthy leading the van with the Body. Servants behind and in the rear a file of the Deceased's hard worked oppressed Tenantry. When all had gathered round the opened tomb and while the solemn service was reading over the coffin I looked up to view the aspect of those who were called Cheif Mourners there Lady Helen leant on the arm of her Son and though it would have shewn a folly very unlike herself to have then felt extreme affliction. she yet looked pale and sad and deeply thoughtful for perhaps Mr Percy was not so completly bad as to depart for ever and with such mystery without exciting some bitter pangs in the mind of his wife the partner of 20 eventful years. Faces well known to me and whom I knew could shew no greif. His relatives and principal servants pressed nearest the grave the first looking coldly and solemnly on the last with flippant callousness But Robert Sdeath struck me by his withering feindish sneer I have long known its real meaning but then I thought it caused by the religious service for He had not put on the horrid cloak of Hypocrisy which for the last few years had clothed his coversation he was then blasphemously impious (and his[sic] is not less so now) Miss O Connor I saw seemed very pale and at this I wondered—but Her conscience was not a seared one and the scene awaked its warnings I neither saw Lady Augusta there or expected to do it But Her Husband I did see and on him my gaze was cheifly fixed I had never seen him since more than a year before when he first set out for the Philosophers Isle But I had thought and heard of him and now I looked on him with the most intense interest But I was indeed startled at the change that time had made How different was he from my former pupil. Much taller and nobler in figure but thin worn and haggard with wasted cheeks and restless hollow eyes his forehead furrowed with anxiety and his lips curled in hardened scorn His arm supported his Mother and upon the recital of the words "Our Dear Brother departed" he smiled derisivly but the words "Earth to Earth Ashes to Ashes Dust to Dust" he seemed inwardly to repeat with bitter emphasis And when the earth first rattled on the coffin lid he looked upward with a desperate triumph that passed into anxious thought and as his eye met Cavershams a mysterious intelligence when The Burial Service was finished and as all prepared to leave the Tomb. that Nobleman came up to him took his hand and said "I congratulate you my Good Fellow on a return to the home of your fathers By Jove a years abscence would wear out my patience!" "Caversham" was the answer "Here is the home of my Father and By G—d I wish he had entered it sooner it would have saved me something Second Cousin to ruin Curse him! nor do I care who hears me However I do go up to the Hall as the demon has left it

come and Hear *your* will read! " "Ha Ha Nay not mine but thy will be done[21]—
You know one must be Devious on the Occasion Gad wheres [that] Jackall
Sdeath?"

"Awm here Measter and naw <   >[22] into the cold earth for By
Gom just as the coffin war covered Aw see the Arth hotch and it whamled away
daant to t' fur spot where just naw he's as het as ony coil in th range"

"D—n the Old villian Ill hear no more about him" said Percy and they
walked away leaving the workmen alone about the vault. I turned back myself as
I left the place and thought had a tear yet wetted that earth or would it ever be
gazed on with a sorrowful eye

The Hall that Night exhibited all the pomp and more than the irreligion
of a great mans funeral. the will was read before all the titled and untitled
relatives of course as the property was entailed all being left to Alexander Percy
with Jointures to Lady Helen &c &c the whole amounting to little short of
500000£ and in condition to yeild interest of 25000£ a year. The New Mr and
Lady Percy were both present to receive their vast patrimony which they knew
would vast as it was dissolve like snow in summer

And now I have concluded the detail of this Bloody Tradgedy this first
step in a long career of crime and woe where Alexander Percy shewed himself the
half maddenned conseller to the designs of a company of the most diabolicaly
wicked Men which Africa held in her bosom with his whole mind inflamed with
hatred of his fathers injustice and all his feelings harrassed [by] a dreadful weight
of embarrassment he in order to free himself from the vast debts he had encurred
and to revenge himself for injuries he would not forget Became the desperate
accomplice in the Murder of his father which his wife an Italian who comprised
every bad and all the few good qualities of her Nation had first designed Which
His Infernal Creditors. Freinds of his father (save the mark!) and of himself but
who nevertheless hated both or what is a[s] bad determined to get every thing
they could from both. being now in want of their principal for present
speculations. directly <carried> on and which Robert Sdeath an Old man whose
name is synonymous with degraded villiany. who had brought up the victim and
been his servant from almost his very birth. with a feindish gladness executed.
All now was over The Victim was gone buried in the heyday of his crimes
without a tear His Guilty Son had entered upon his Estate and though many
spoke of Mr Percys mysterious death and a few suspected the cause of it yet none
felt the interest in the decease sufficient to probe it to discovery Lady Helen
Percy alone being excepted who dared [to] indulge the horrid idea of that parricide
and if the thought flashed on her Mind Affection for her son which nothing could
abate. suppressed all desire of enquiry

---

[21] Compare Luke 22:42.

[22] The top line of the manuscript page has been obscured as a result of the
page having been set in.

Such being the position of affairs on the termination of this horrible transaction I find it my painful duty to enter upon the description of another <deed> scarcly less dreadful but which almost total want of information prevents me from giving with any thing like the fullness of the last Time which has discovered so much of the past Has not yet fully unravelled this event but I have no doubt that what I relate is truth so far as it goes and I must remark it is the first in a long series of expiations for blood of awful punishment for crime where the wicked were brought to die by the snares they had used for others and where in this Great Scene of of Sinners in such lofty stations they one by one fell by each others hands or by the hand of the Arch Sinner whom they had fostered for their own temporary purposes into such a lasting Power I write this with sincerity when I look back and retrace the events which have chequ[e]red the last twenty years for so long back fell the first blow of punishment and then I look round me gazing on some who yet survive and whose actions tell me that the last blow has not yet fallen but that as certainly it will sometime fall What may be the fate of the Principal Actor in this mighty Drama I cannot forsee he has done mighty and dreadful deeds doubtless his end will answer with his life in importance but will it be like it in sorrow and sin?

Ere I proceed with this Life I must remark that I have forgot to say any thing of a person whose name I have often mentioned Mr Simpson. anything definite I cannot say for he was and is a mystery But I will say of his[sic] what I can. Mr Jeremiah Simpson though moving in circles so Aristocratic was nothing more in rank than an Extensive and Fashionable Dealer in Linen Drapery &c in Wellingtons town whose splendid shop attracted a mob of titled purchasers nothing more than this he would have been had he not by his own qualitys made himself a companion of peers and almost princes Where he came from no one knew But on first settling at Wellingtons town which he did shortly before Old Mr Percy arrived there he set up a dashing buisness and appeared possessed of property He was without family and all thought him a person wrapt up in the aim of making money As Wellingtons town by degrees encreased it assumed that singular character of mingled Abilitys and proligacy which it has since maintained and the multitude of of Dark and daring spirits who found settlement there congenial erelong raised it to an importance and elevation of society considerably beyond the other Capitals of the Union Of course in its whirl of dissipation many fortunes were lost while their once possessor still whished to appear great. To this class of men Jeremiah the Draper held forth the only hand for help Money to any amount lent freely upon easy terms and for indefinate periods made his back parlour the resort of a host of Desperate "Westerns" while some titled head[s] bowed beneath his threshold he took care to shew of all his shrewdness sagacity and mental power to engratiate himself by admirable advice on the means of escape from ruin and capital schemes for accomplishing the ruin of others By those means he soon became noted over the City as Gentle Jerry and the "Westerns" spread his fame to their favourite Verdopolis He extended his establisment to the Mother Metropolis entered into wider connections and he was one who only wanted to be known to be appreciated his Mind was so masculine his keenness so penetrating his judgement so clear and his conscience so callous That his Clients found him of infinite use in assisting them on their course to ruin Men who themselves needed no advice but whose years of crime rather qualified them to give it and whose successful villainy had placed them beyond the Usurers gentle mercys still found in Simpson a most able coadjutor in all difficult and dangerous undertakings Sin in the past often assumed a sanguinary as well as splendid aspect and undoubtedly the hands of this Shopkeeper have more than once participated in its stain Foremost in their powerful class Lord Caversham and Edward Percy Esq[r] discovered the merits of this worker of evil Soon he became their confidant and along with them did his utmost to embroil the Politics and injure the Members of the West His keen eyes were continually bent on them but yet though he repressed and discomfited them they went on sowing to surely the seed which the Subject of this Memoir has since n[o]urished into such bitter fruit Simpson never entered parliament but his work lay under hand and though a Seat was offered to him by his Noble Freinds he declined acceptance saying that his eyes could not bear the daylight nor his deeds neither he added laughing with his accustomed suddenness—As he gained ground on the City he encreased his interests and erelong stood the most savage Usurer among a most savage race of them Indeed I may say that he seemed destitute of every kindly sympathy or generous feeling his cheerfulness itself was taunts and sneers his malice was like a dagger and his wrath—why he—never shewed it—not on any occasion was Jeremiah Simpson seen in a passion nothing could raise him beyond scornful jesting and he despised any other state in the minds of others Robert Sdeath the Valet of Mr Percy he took into greater confidence than perhaps any other man certainly these two knew more of each other than any one else did and seemed on a better understanding often they would sit opposite before the fire of the little counting house enveloped in clouds of tobbacco smoke shut up till long past midnight and coversing with each other in low nasal tones while a hollow laugh rising suddenly and as abruptly silent alone broke the montonous murmuring to those without. Simpsons bodily prescence answered well to the Spirit within when I first saw him I was struck by his looks whose repulsive demonism made ones blood run cold on ones heart He was a great bony man with a greisly[sic] black head and long Herculean Arms His countenance was dark heavey and ironlike with distorted eyes and muscles moulded into a coarse habitual sneer his attire was generally rusty black and his harsh voice on whatever subject he spoke had always a tone of solemn scorn. Such a Man as this one would think could never gain the confidence of a Noble and Beautiful Lady yet so it was and Jeremiah Simpson was the prime Minister to the Italian Queen Augusta Di Segovia "By gom" he would swear "If all the women on earth were like this one my spots of work would yeild me more profit than they do. Gad! my old Chum[23] could never find room for them all. One might make a spot in the

---

[23] i.e., Satan.

collieries for S'blood the price of coals would rise!" and he swore when Augusta and Alexander were married "may I be cursed if such a glorious event will happen again till the Old one has 'em all roasting together Heres Sin and Satan with a vengeance upon us[24] and if such a conjunction doesnt forbode all thats heavenly to Africa may I—" But it is needless to give the concluding imprecation all his conversation was blighted with the most blasphemous Oaths and Curses.

Well such a Man it was who had wound round the very vitals of Alexander Percy. To him he had lent 200000£ along with the coldblooded Caversham and a few others like him and now to recover the sum he had stood almost first in the murder of his freind Edward Percy But his keen sagacity foresaw that yet they had not received their principal and his diabolical spirit suggested the means for ensuring it The night after Mr Percys funeral he called upon the Earl of Caversham and remained alone with him for several hours when Robert Sdeath joined them from the Hall—That day Lady Augusta with her usual impetouosity of character had passionatly besought her Husband to refuse payment of the 200000£ loan They dared not institute legal proceedings she averred for such would only implicate them in the buisness of the Society whose members had received such punishment They all [as] heads of the party would receive an irrecoverable shock in politics. it would ruin them and as to their hatred it could never be worse than their pretended freindship Sdeath overheard this conversation and posted down to Mr Simpsons shop with an exact account of it Simpson knew that Percy was remarkable for improving on a hint like this and that he possessed desperate resolution enough to brave its consequences he consulted Caversham Sdeath followed and the deliberations of the trio in sin must have ended in a scheme for the destruction of her who had just before suggested the destruction of another a plan for the death of Lady Augusta Percy!

It was a week after this Dreadful meeting late at night on the 1st of February 18 .[25] When Alexander set forth on horsback for Percy Hall from a Great Party at Lord Ravenworths composed of the Elite of the Metropolitan Aristocracy. as he rode on through the wind and darkness rendered yet more desolate from having so suddenly quitted the Splendid Saloons of Gambia Square his Ardent and Ambitious Mind engaging itself in some vast dream of future greatness some shadow perhaps of those events whose coming yet lay in the future his eye was arrested by a light which seemed approaching before him The wind and rain beating his face rendered him uncertain of what it was but it neared in the darkness and he soon knew it to be the front light of some carriage driving townward. As he rode forward that carriage approached open driven by four horses and containing two persons on the seat notwithstanding the speed with which it came up was it the storm which drowned the sound of its wheels? —but he could not be uncertain whom it contained for as it drove by him the single coach

---

[24] In book two of Milton's *Paradise Lost* Satan couples incestuously with Sin, conceiving Death, thus precipitating the twin blight upon the world.

[25] Branwell left the date blank.

lanthorn cast its light back upon the figure of his own Lady Augusta seated beside a dark form like Jeremiah Simpson's "Augusta" he would have called out as he rose on his stirrups but a nervous emotion of the heart checked his utterance the carriage glided into the road leading up to Jordan Hall and he turned desperatly to follow it but his horse with a start dashed forward on its road home and he gallopped on with a convulsive shudder of awe his Porter long remembered the ghastly oath which he swore when he was opening the park gates for his enterance "As your Lady driven out in the carriage to night?" "She has not Sir" "Then to H—l with both soul and body!" he replied and dashed furiously up the path. He sprung from the trembling Beast and as he met his mother in the Hall asked "Where is Augusta" "In her dressing room I believe Alexander" he heard no further but hastened up thither opened the door and behelde[sic] Lady Percy reclined on a sopha near the fire springing Joyfully forward he exclaimed "Oh My dear Augusta" and clasped her in his arms Hers returned not the embrace they fell cold and rigid he started back. —And—There She lay Her black tresses dishevelled on her marble like shoulders! Her Face white and ghastly! Her Eyes fixed upon him not with inspired emotion—But— in the Blank stare of DEATH! —"Oh my God!" he groaned pressing his hand to his burning brow. and thus stood as he had started almost stunned by that dreadful shock. —It was then that the hardened Murderer entered as if to speak to his Master on his return but [at] the first croak of his voice Percy grasped a pistol and fired it straight in his face with a howl the villain fled forth his blood trickling as he ran[26] but His Master dashed the door to and shut himself in the Room of Death. that act had not sprung from suspicion it was the outbreak of a maddened mind.

　　All night Percy remained there alone with his Ladys corpse. I shall not give [the] Interjections exclamations and broken sentences Because I beleive he uttered none Nor can I analyse the feelings of a mind which was far too much stunned to feel As when one shot by a musket bullet finds at first faintness only and when he recovers his senses Pain, so exactly here that mind wounded as suddenly as if by any any[sic] bullet felt as it were stunned and bewildered till agony came upon it such as its thrilling nerves were often doomed to feel. perhaps through those dark and lonely hours the frightful truth which would press itself on him was often repulsed with horror till in the unreplying silence its voice peirced his ear to acutly to be withstood and perhaps also as the daylight slowly revisited the room its beams would bring a suspicion which became clearer to the inward sight as visible objects become so to the outer but I cannot tell wether from the chaos of that head could yet be created any thought so definate as this. I only know that near the breakfast hour Mr Percy entered an apartment where Lady Helen was sitting and when he spoke the words "Augusta is dead!" She started as if it was a voice heard in a dream but almost before she

---

[26] S'death can be wounded but not killed since he has a form of demonic immortality.

could mark the agonized look of his face he had turned and left the room "Where is Sdeath?" he said to the Steward who encountered him in an ante room "Sir he left the Hall last night running down stairs bleeding and badly hurt after the explos—" "Enough Sir" interrupted his Master who directly Departed on Horsback toward the Hills of Jordan Castle

Lady Helen hardly trusting her hearing went up the Great Stair case thinking of the Beautiful Lady whom she had left the evening before in all the enthusiasm of an unconquerable mind but soon indeed the corpse on the sopha took the place of this picture with an impression which there can be none other to alter again It lay there splendidly attired in an Evening dress with the dark satin and velvet mournfully contrasted to its cold and clayey whitness and the Jewels still flashing amid their black curls over the pallid lifeless brow twice now in the same house and so soon after each other Lady Helen had beheld Death in its most sudden and unlooked for form Her husband and her Daughter in law both cut off in the pride of their life and spirit with all their Sins full blown[27] and without a thought of repentance The strange and yet undiscovered mystery which hung over both these Deaths could not but arrest the attention of one who[se] observation was more than usually clear, Suspicions had already entered her mind regarding the first case But in the last who was there to attempt a life which all who dared attempt were in league with If this event had not happened in the course of nature surely the Diabolical Circle in the City would not murder their Divine ally the Mean Sdeath unaided dared not effect what would be sure to ruin him—And Augustas Husband—no it could not be her Husband—yet horrible as the idea was it peirced through the heart of his Mother because too well she knew what he had done and how unsettled was his mind But in a little while an idea so remote from the truth cleared off and the cloud of Just suspicion gathered on the heads of the guilty alone

During the day while engaged in such appalling thoughts Lady Helen in the utmost anxiety awaited the return of Alexander and an Agitation amounting to pain seized her when at Night she heard his footsteps in the Hall She thought him at first approaching her apartment but he strode hurriedly up to where Augusta lay and Lady Helen who had repressed her feelings when she thought him coming now sitting down again burst into tears of sorrow for her unhappy son

To him after his wild and lonely ride reentering into that house where any Day before he had rejoicingly hurried to his Noble Lady the rooms the objects bursting upon him where but a few hours before she would have been and now hurrying up to meet—Her Dead and stiffened corpse—was a trial whose anguish his Soul could not possibly bear. As he opened the door of the state room where they had laid her out the frightful change so flashed upon him that he stopped and fell not fainting but in a dreadful consciousness to which fainting would have been a blessed releif. He spoke not no tears could burst from his

---

[27] Compare *Hamlet*, III, iii, 81.

burning eyes his heart beat with an intenseness of agony that NOTHING could. releive for

"She was gone his loved and lovely one
What was his being she had ceased to be!" *Byron* [28]

It was more than impressive it was awful to see the voiceless tearless silence of this—your Earl of Northangerland—the face he gazed on was not more corpselike than his its features not more fixed but far did its still unconsciousness differ from the hopeless Agony of his tortured mind a wild and dream like chaos of thoughts rose when he thought "Oh wither art thou gone" but in the (to him) uncertainties of Revelation and vastness of Eternity and horrors of Atheistic annihilation he only found a burning addition of Despair not an object around but added to it and not a thought within!

Knowing so well his strange spirit no person dared to think of speaking to him and therefore all the solemn pomp of the funeral was arranged by Lady Helen and those to whose lot its execution fell the Noble Relatives of the Segovia House those of the Percy family with those Bloodstained beings whose names I have to often mentioned though of course conferring upon the event with the Mother of Mr Percy did not think of seeing or addressing him. in fact he would not have listened to a word on any subject from any living soul his Own Mother spoke not to him though gladly indeed would she have striven to comfort him but it was impossible. upon something being hinted about the mode usual in all great familys of the Deceased lying in state Relatives and others being admitted Percy burst into terrific Oaths and he cried "The first person who enters that room till the hour of burial shall go from it to H—L! His Agony and its cause this terrible Spirit kept to himself. and watching over the Decaying form like a Wild Lion over his slaughtered mate Once was he heard to groan "Oh it is Dreadful to <   >[29] and the Hour at last approached when he should watch no more[30]

As the Day of Burial arrived Lady Helen felt the utmost anxiety in going to mention it to Mr Percy But He heard her calmly and embracing the corpse he looked that last long look which seemed as it would indelibly fix on his mind the features that he should never behold again "Let it be done as you wish Mother—I have beheld now what through all Eternity I shall behold no more—O might there be another world! O might we meet again!" and[31] then there fell from his eye the first burning tear—it was only one—and when All the procession was marshalled he joined it with a rigid and unnatural calm with out speaking to any one he signed all to depart and the Gloomy hearse with its long

---

[28] Compare *Childe Harold's Pilgrimage*, II, xcv, 891-95.
[29] The line at the bottom of the manuscript page has been obscured by the page being set in.
[30] Compare John 9: 4.
[31] In the margin opposite these lines appear the words "I saw it."

train of Noble Mourners left the Hall for His Vault in Woodchurch. without the Park.

All Gathered round the tomb with the Music rolling from the Organ above and the Dark and Narrow house yawning open below I again beheld this Man of Sorrows but far more haggard and ghastly than when I saw him last before His eminently Beautiful features were deeply marked with suffering and as the Service drew to its close His face grew paler till he heard the words "In sure and certain hope of a blessed resurrection to eternal life"[32] and then for a moment he lifted his eyes while his cheeks coloured till the thought these were but a mans words repeated according to custom darkened the momentary radiance and when the first clod of earth struck the Coffin lid His lips whitened and his limbs trembled as if the "Burden were to heavey for him to bear!"[33] At last all was over yet no one dared to speak to him But it was with Dimming eyes that many turned round to see the Tall and Noble Mourner So young yet so smitten and with a face whose paleness looked awful when contrasted with his Deep funereal Black. All left him alone but the last who turned at the Door saw him burst suddenly into a flood of tears and throwing himself on the covered grave he knelt weeping bitterly!

Lady Augusta Percy was now dead and buried! murdered by those whom she had instigated to murder having just entered upon the enjoyment of the fruits of her crime and in the very flower of her Age She died aged 26. 6 years older than her Husband Alexander and she had a far greater controul over and influence with him than any one has ever had since, That character of kindred passion the Duke of Zamorna alone being excepted. I certainly believe that had she lived much longer her influcnce would have passed off for she gained it because Alexander was very young loving her ardently and possesing a strange depth of feeling regarding such as she was that amounted sometimes to an indefinable awe In the opening of his youth she had crossed him as a bright and leading star and the overpowering effect of her Majestic beauty and Italian passion when he was 17 or 18. burnt as strongly when he was 19 and 20 but leaving out of the question this preoccupation of his soul Percys mind when matured and fixed in character was and is so tenacious and unyeilding his opinions so strong and peculiar that However he loves nothing on earth or in heaven can guide him for a moment out of his own way. often he seems led and some times some worthless artful creature like the M⸺s of W⸺y or L⸺y L⸺a V⸺n[34] apparently for a time has ruled him but this is superficial and where they lead him he has resolved to go—I except one person and I own that the extent or character of the influence which the wonderful Monarch of Angria possesses over him is as much a secret to me as to others

---

[32] From the Anglican service for the Burial of the Dead.

[33] Compare Psalm 38:4.

[34] Marchioness of Wellesly and Lady Louisa Vernon.

Augusta was dead and those who had murdered her determined to press their advantage. while Mr Percys mind was yet utterly hopeless and desperate they deputed Mr Simpson to press him for the money he owed them and this Satanic personage choose[sic] his proper period for his cruel demand He waited till Percy had paid off his 100000£ dept of honour due on his gambling transactions in the Philosophers Isle and then his sagacious mind feeling that Alexander having commenced a headlong career of payment and seeing its certain termination would take a mad unconscious delight as it were in throwing his property from off him and in his bitter greif would almost trample to the dust the faithless gold then and not till then he made his demands for so much caution was required to approach the chafed Lion to the first requests for payment Mr Percy would neither listen or answer They became affrighted but Simpson knew it was groundless fear This was only an impulse of despair for he had lost far too great a Jewel to struggle for possession of the poor tinsel chasing "Gom " said the Draper "I should be a poor tool if I killed Lady A— and ran the hazard for nothing Be Gor! had she lived He high in hope and spirits—heartened on by such a soul as hers would I am certain have refused us but Gad it is different now He is broken desperate cares for nothing has begun to lose. the 100000 has given him a shove down hill and the 200000 will encrease the speed!" So for 200000£ he demanded and with an Oath of hatred it was given—fearful of losing so admirable a leader the faction had Authorized Jeremiah to tell him that they would readvance him half the sum upon reasonable Mortgages Percy at first did not seem to hear it was pressed more intelligibly and he answered "No I will free myself from the net if I do leave Skin behind me" "It were better" insinuated Simpson "to lose half than all" "Better" was the reply "to lose all and be free than all and be a slave" and then impatient of farther conference with the man he said with bitter emotion "Mr Simpson a Man struck as I have been will remember as well as feel the stroke if he discovers the striker he will return it and by G—d Sir I Know my Enimies to well to mistake my blow!" with this unpleasant hint Simpson departed but he received the monies and Mr Percy saw at once three fifths of his Estates torn away from him!

In this situation oppressed with a tempest of miseries without a single soul (save his Mother) to look too for consolation or assistance aware of the horrible truth that his freinds and companions were the very persons who were ruining him that it was his closest confidants who had murdered his Lady that it was his own servant the watcher over his childhood who had done the deed that the Nation looked on him with distrust and however that his own heart accused him of a terrible crime—it was in this state and by these events falling at once on so youthful a head that the foundation was laid of the Cruelty Coldness Atheism and utter Melancholy of Rougue Elrington and Northangerland Before this he was full of passions and feeling as troublous as the roughest sea but they raved themselves to rest on shores of unutterable Delight and joy—Now that same wild Ocean of passions raged louder than ever but it beat on bleak and

barren rocks and though one single fair Isle arose once on the waters its <
>[35] without a shore!

The spring of 1813 was to him a dreary winter he wandered about silent and solitary but his mind filled with those thoughts then but arising which have since deepened into such portentous gloominess There actually was not One soul alive to whom he could look for assistance or sympathy I have said so before but I have [to] repeat it There was not one to guide him and I cannot wonder at the manner in which he has gone astray for this was an important period of his life when whatever Ideas he held would be likely to colour his future existence All must know that the Earl of Northangerland is a perfect Atheist but he was not one during the Life of Lady Augusta In his childhood the Bible was his intense delight and in Boyhood the Dim and glorious   [36] of that childhood filled its pages with associations of unutterable delight Then to the Awful glimpses it gave him into Eternity the sublime insight it gave him into far off long ago times the Grand simplicity of its diction all enchained him to Religion I feel reader that I am quite getting out of my depth when I speak of the ESSENCES OF TRUE POETRY. that filled his mind regarding Christmas Nights and Mornings and Divine Summer. Sundays past away visions mingled with all the joys and sorrows of childhood and his Mothers anxious Affection and the freshness of an opening world and Dim indefinable theories of God and Heaven Dreams of the Begginning of the World the Patriarchs Days the Mighty Deluge Abraham beneath his tent shade with the Angels staying on their path of vengeance Jacob the shepheard with his life of changes Israel wandering through the wildnerness and amid so many vicissitudes guided to Jordan and the promised land the Mighty Deeds of Canaans conquerors Davids wars and sorrows and the Voice of that Harps so solemnly swept by the shepherd and Poet King Judah beneath her palm tree weeping over her Zion destroyed the shepherds watching their flocks by night-but here he would think of the Christmas music and sacred winter morn and thus each of these associations and a hundred a thousand more all joined and revolving in a visionary chorus would fill his opening mind with thoughts of the Spiritual World

All this may sound foolish to the wooden headed but his head was not such an one for then it rather beamed with the very light of heaven It was NOW after the terrible sorrows I have spoken of that the clouds began to gather [in] that stainless blue NOW it was that Percys mind shut from all other consolation began to look into Religion with a keenness all its own and as it was without any guidance it ran into fatal and enduring error as he thought with all his intenseness and depth the countless creeds of Men all clashing one with another their sickening follies and cant and hypocrisy the many way[s] in which each read the Bible the many way[s] it seemed capable of being read its (superficially viewed) contradictions in itself the mercy given and vengeance denounced the

---

[35] Again the top line of the manuscript page has been obscured.
[36] Branwell has omitted a word.

Jewish History where a chosen people slaying by command all the nations round them were allowed to retain all the light themselves and yet proved the vilest of sinners though favoured so beyond a world which for a thousand years was purposly darkened and condemned the Grand Failure of Creation itself A thousand arguments which I will not and ought not to mention All entered into by a spirit chafed to madness a mind naturally now extraordinarilly trustless and moral feelings (Bear witness My unhappy Country) miserably Deadened in a very short period made Alexander Percy the firmest and most miserable of Atheists he believes that there is nothing except in this life and he shudders at its hopeless woe "O" he once said "If there were a God a heaven an hereafter I could feel some peace and have some room for Divine imaginings But there is not there is not! and I am condemned to suffer here without the glorious thought that there is one above who knows what I suffer and who if I serve him will repay me in a life beyond my death no none can tell what I suffer and wether I act well or ill at death I must perish for ever in the horrible annihilation of the GRAVE!"

There are a few stanzas the first which have [been] found by him which mark strongly the state of his mind in the year 1813

Life is a passing sleep
Its Deeds a troubled dream
And Death the dread awakening
TO Daylights Dawning beam
We sleep without a thought
Of what is past and oer
Without one glimpse of consciousness
Of aught that lies before
We Dream and on our sight
A thousand visions rise
Some dark as Hell some heavenly bright
But all are phantasies
We wake and O how fast
Our mortal visions fly
Forgot amid the wonders vast
Of immortality
In visionary joys
Or dreams of greif and gloom
We start to hear the thunders voice
Arouse us from the tomb
And <oerborn> we arise
With wildered gaze to see
The aspect of those morning skys
Where shall that waking be?
How will that future seem?
What is Eternity?

> Is Death the Sleep? Is Heaven the Dream?
> Life the reality?[37]

From a long and solitary wandering as far as Elimbos and the borders of Sneachies land where he had travelled from place to place with a restlessness which shewed not a mind flying from sorrow but torn and tortured with it not even seeking an escape from it for it had become a portion of his being and He knew that he could only lose it with his life—from this long joyless journey he returned in July But Percy Hall and the Segovia Palace recalled every hour so many agonizing reflections that he found it impossible to remain in them any longer Each moment there reminded him that a leaf had been turned over in his life that the past was quite departed and that all around him even his own self was the commencement of a new and Iron road He looked so utterly worn down and harrassed that his Aquaintances could hardly know him again the man as well as the mind seemed new

So heart sick of Africa and Hating every person he saw He made up his mind to leave His Country behind him and embark on some long endless voyage over the SEA But while his affairs were winding up and all things arranging for the Departure he plunged himself to kill time and memory into a heartless dissipation in the Capital flying from scene to scene at every Opened Mansion the blighted and despairing visitor. At this time
> "When all around grew drear and dark
> And Reason half withheld her ray" *Byron* [38]

In the wilderness of Wellingtonian dissipation first arose the Star of hope whose brightness for yet a few years longer dashed back the darkness that was fast closing him round On a grand Gala night at the Fete made in the Ducal Palace on the presentation to the Westerns of the Infant Prince of the West where Percy in a whirl of pleasure and magnificence was asking his wretched spirit what buisness had it there His eyes fell on the figure of MARY HENRIETTA WHARTON And a light first rose on his soul.

She was the only Daughter of Lord George Wharton of Alnwick in the Verdopolitan country and had grown up from infancy to youth half in the seclusion of an ancient country seat half in the Magnificence of Metropolitan Aristocracy Her father being a widower and an invalid felt towards his Daughter as too the sole stay and brightner of his life and had taken care that hers should pass without many of the misfortunes that too often wait on our existence She was brought up in indulgence but like an Exotic in an hot house only rendered more beautiful by it—The two Ladies of whom I have cheifly spoken hitherto if they had many splendid qualities had at least counterbalancing Defects Augusta with her Majestic Beauty of person and impassioned loftiness of soul was guilty of more crimes than I can mention Harriet with more cheerfulness and good

---

[37] See the1837 revised version, **The Doubter's Hymn,** in vol. III.
[38] Compare "Stanzas to Augusta," ll. 1-2.

nature more mind and talents than I have often known united in one woman had
made herself completely miserable and from her extreme feebleness of principles
was sure so long as she lived to continue so—But Here I wish Reader that I had
words to express the Heavenly beauty both in person and mind of Mary Henrietta
Wharton She was not one of those unnatural (for I will not call them
supernatural) beings which disfigure the already worthless pages of sentimental
Novels with their amazing ignorance and inanity beings who if they had lived
with their "purities" and perfections ought to be left withering like a sapless leaf
in winter. —She was a human being and a woman and had all the feelings of one
as they ought to be though she had <u>not</u> some as they are Marys mind shone in
all her feelings and actions it was as warm and as bright as a summer sunset and
like it it had a shade of Heavenly pensiveness which only made it the more
lovely, when, putting back the the curls from her ivory forehead she turned
toward you with her musical laugh and the cheerful sunshine of her hazel eyes
you might see the heartfelt freindliness of her spirit brightning all her lovely
countenance Pride she possessed not nor selfishness any farther than must fall to
the lot of every human being But—she had a silent inward feeling—she had that
feeling to which I can give no name but which when alone and with nothing
visible to touch the string will yet sound in a chord which shall make a whole
life seem but its echo and feel in hours of <struggle> emotion[s] that are never
destined to fade from the mind I know that here I have ill explained myself but
this feeling is not to be explained my fault lies not in my failure but in my
attempt to suceed. it was that feeling to whose voice every nerve quivered in the
Man whose life I am writing it was that which first spoke his name to Mary and
in it that she saw him and all his life it was it which seemed to fill her Dark
eyes with tears not only while wandering alone in the Green groves and fertile
feilds of Alnwick but while moving one among a thousand in the Magnificent
Halls of the Palace of the West
     That Night there was presented to the Nobility in His Graces Palace
The Very MAN whose name now sounds through Africa and whose Life has
been as wonderful whose spirit has been as intense as Northangerlands own. I
was there and the memory of that Night has never left my mind but what was
that man like then 23 years ago—I think I see him yet—Held forth to our loyal
gaze in his nurses arms a little helpless speechless beautiful child the cross of
Baptism yet glittering as it were like Dew on his infantine forehead and with
large eyes whose gaze was attracted by nothing on whose orbs nothing was
impressed the impetous burning spirit then a blank and that Organ voice a faint
childish cry. His Majesty of Angria may smile but these lines are a true picture
of what was
     That man who in the wonderful future of time was to become the father
in law and confederate of this Prince of Wellingtons Land then unknowing of
what fate had written in its mysterious volumn cast scarce a single look at the
hero of the night and closed his heart to the bright and dazzling Saloons The gay
and noble crowd and the festive whirl of the gorgeous picture around him At the
repeated and anxious intreaty of many voices whose bidding he at another time

would have obeyed most willingly but whose soft tones now fell hollow and unechoed in his Mind He had seated himself before a Grand piano And the Noble and Beautiful Forms thronged around in eager expectation of the tones to be awaked by that Master hand His surpassing and unequalled skill in music with the impassioned fervour of his Genius and execution was known to every one and at many a Grand Night in the Capital one half hour of Mr Percys playing was a thing to be listened to and remembered as the most delicious morceau' of the evening

O how I wish that I could transfer to paper the actual tones which those hands called forth as they ran along the keys or alltogether struck long chords of tumultous Harmony He bowed to some one to take away the books and saying with a forced smile "My feelings are my own and my music shall be my own" entered into a full rich melody whose solemn sustained tones heard in distant saloons made the hearer unconsciously stop and listen The worn and exhausted expression of his face gave way to an unearthly rapture and while his melodious voice accompanied the music he smiled one smile of bitter triumph that seemed to say "I have shaken off misery if but for a moment" It was but a moment for when the memory of that scene similar to the one before him the one which took place at that very piano before his marriage with Lady Augusta flashed on his mind the smile vanished and his sudden change to anguish forced bitter tears from his eyes this may seem strange to those who only know "The Earl" but he bent his head and the curls fell over his shining brow with his spirit his music changed and became a mourning song

Thou art gone but I am here
Left behind and mourning on
Doomed in dreams to deem thee near
But to awake and find thee gone
Ever parted Broken hearted
Weary wandering all alone

Looks and smiles that once were thine
Rise before me night and day
Telling me that thou wert mine
But art dead and past away
No returning—Nought but mourning
Oer thy cold and coffined clay
Beauty Banished Feelings vanished
From thy Dark and dull decay

It was but a fragment both in poetry and music yet that music filled the hearts of all round and their eyes too—He sung the last word and the chords rung changing upon another key

Frozen fast is my heart at last
And unmoved by thy beams divine
Wild oer the waste and wintery blast
Has withered and weakened thy shine

The pulse that once beat to each look and each word
Is congealed by the frosts of care
Thine eyes are ungazed on they voice is unheard
For Love ever flies from despair

Farewell then farewell then for parted forever
The blooming and blighted should be
Soon shall the ocean eternally sever
My heart from my country and thee [39]

And ending in that wild melody he turned to his Auditors with a look which shewed it was themselves he addressed and that it was their beauty which Sorrow had darkened [in] his mind The Music had not ceased he was gazing on them with a wandering eye they on him with eyes almost in tears but the full tones on the Instrument sounded on in sucesions of thrilling melody stealing insensibly on the hearts of the listeners as it was struck from the trembling hands of the Musician He again seemed wrapt in his inspiration and gave measure after measure of some grand Ancient Requiem whose swelling strains seemed bearing his thoughts from the world they rose and deepened and he relapsed into higher feelings so that it was not untill he had struck the last long chord that he looked Around and seemed aware of the effect of his performance But when he did seem to notice the countenances of his Auditors the Emotion he had kindled in their eyes the looks of earnestness they were bending on him their entranced and unbroken silence—He felt a flush of excitement which belied the words of his song and shewed him to be Alexander Percy still many were the Beautiful Faces that regarded him with admiration but one young Lady who stood beside the piano he looked at with a flash of lightning keeness the tears sparkled on her cheek and the glistening of her large eyes was unshadowed even by the curls that fell above them with clasped hands she had listened till her soul was carried away with the Music her lovely face beamed with a sympathy which she did not think to hide and there she stood knowing that in the man before her she beheld the Founder of a Society whose principles she regarded with horror and whose punishment she knew to be just. a man of whose profligacy few were ignorant and on whose head tonight as it was rested the dark shadow of a suspected parricide She knew this and she was thinking of it but the unconcealed agony of his tormented spirit roused all her sympathy and the Magnificent stature and aspect the beautiful though ghastly face the power the splendour of that wonderful mind had infused all their influence into a heart which felt to exquisitly soon to loose the impression Mary knew not herself that power which since others have often owned untill in after solitariness when there could be nothing around to sustain it

---

[39] See the revised 1837 versions of both songs in vol. III.

But Percy knew the impression and saw in her face the Spirit that had received it and as he looked at the Beautiful Girl with her tearful Hazel eyes and bright curling hair and gentle sylphlike form a light did burst on him that shewed not the Dark Waters of the Atlantic but the once more shining woods of Wellingtons land The Star had risen whose rays for yet a few years were to delay the terrible Night of misery That Star whose setting brought a darkness which has never passed away

P B Brontë
November. 17th
1835

[Volume III]

But however this was Time wore fast on to the end That Beautiful creature whose Life had been hitherto so happy that heaven might be thought shining through the veil that parted it from the other world—As winter approached wasted with a decay that progressed even faster than the fading of the flowers around her She so long as her strength held out would often desire to be placed on a Sopha at a great open window and in the Glorious sunshine of Wellingtons land would gaze with a smile upon the vast expanse of foliaged vegetation which as she said were to accompany her to the grave "Alexander" she said once "you need not cause flowers to be placed round my head when I am laid in mny coffin for all the flowers that I have known and delighted in will then have gone before me or will be going with me both returning to the hand that gave us they parted for ever from their supporting stems and I parting—But not I do trust for ever—from my own earthly supporter—THEE And now my Alexander ought I not to thank God who as made my death so easy for what is there in this strange and dreamy decline to the tormented death beds of those cursed with some horrid plague or the bloody and succorless anguish of thousands on the feild of battle—Here I can feel this divine light of nature I can feel my heart expanding and my spirit rising with it and in every air that <fans> itself on my face there seems something to me breathed from the glorious world so far away from this I am on but yet so very near to me! You say my love that in childhood the old book Bunyans pilgrims progress[1] delighted you so that I need only mention the Time when Angels appeared with tokens to the pilgrims in the Land of Beulah—which were signs that they should now prepare to cross the river into the City of the king—and so I regard the thoughts which seem brought with these breezes into my mind which tell me that beyond us there is a world which will repay all the horrors and Oh they are indeed horrors of sepearation[sic] and death and the grave!"

These Horrors in the days of dreary sickness and the dark restless hours of the night fell upon Marys heart with an agony that might have counterbalanced a life of happiness then the Farwell which she shuddered at—and thoughts upon her Husband over came her His distressing and hopeless agony now which he scorned to conceal and which day after day was preying upon his heart till he had become savage and dark almost to madness and she thought what would he be when the last hour came and when she was gone forever she shuddered and started to picture Her strange wild wonderful Husband then to her Mother in law she said "He is far past my sight for I have never seen the depth of his character Oh I do not think that in the world there lives or has ever lived a man of so mighty a spirit and so utterly unrestrained and unrestrainable a mind— No he never can be bent or taught I see it—but I do not see what his course shall

---

[1]   Charlotte had read *Pilgrim's Progress* by the age of six—see Alexander EW 19.

be or where it must end Is he to live on years on years in his Dark and Dreadful melancholy which I have seen darker than I dare tell the thought is so horrible that a thousand times I have prayed he may not—yet I do not see its end!" —And at other times she would waste herself in tears of bitterness over Her children whom she should never see again and who in all the storms and dangers of life would be tossed and threatned without a Mother or any knowledge of one—without a father or with one worse than the bitterness for she pictured them in distress and sickness but there was none to help them and the heart of this Dying Mother yearned in vain toward those who thought not of her and who she felt would if they lived look upon her grave as if no Mother lay buried there

Thus the time passed till her frame wasted to the image of death and her eyes glittering with an unnatural lustre and her voice weakned to a whisper shewed that her death was indeed close at hand—We must pass over the Glooming Autumn days of its approach till we come upon the last and Darkest day!

All her affairs as it regards this life had been set in order and all her connections with it unbound save that which only the last breath would sever It was Night in a room softly lighted where she lay on her death bed in a Dizzy dying faintness—Her freinds and relatives had bid adeiu, To Her servants she had spoken a farewell which brought her cheerful kindness to their minds till they had left her each one weeping she had given a parting embrace to that Noble woman who had watched over her with all the affection of a Mother—she had kissed and wept over her unconscious child till as it was born away after her last heart given blessing—she fell into a sudden swoon. —But there was ONE still there bending over here—toward whom was directed every every thought and feeling of her mind Percy's face was as pale and his head as drooped as her own but there was the clenched teeth and hands the glistning forehead and the desperate defying eye which shewed a strife and convulsion of spirit—an agony whose effects nothing has ever washed away She kept her glazed eyes fixed upon him and said"

"Now I know that I am dying for this world with all its concerns is giving place to another and Oh Alexander it now seems far away! while that wither I am hastning though unseen is indeed awfully near—But there is something which still chains me where I am something beside which even Heaven fluctuates in the balance you are here and I cannot bear to leave you—Alexander were it not a selfish seeming wish My only prayer would be that where I am going thou now mightest accompany me—even now and to the grave—looking at it only [as if] it is a Dreary resting place But I look to that House of which it is the threshhold and I would Die in happiness if I thought that you will join me there—I know now Alexander that you Do not and cannot Believe in what I am certain is true—that you think me about to decay and perish for ever But in spite of this you have far too Mighty a spirit and feelings far too divine for God after laying a dreadful burden on you in this Life—to doom you to eternal misery in that which is to come—This is no usual mode of thinking But I believe it true. You have had given to you such a mind that you could not Fail under any circumstances to drink to its dregs the cup of sorrow But why after such a life of sorrow should you so far far above those round you enter into a new Eternity of unnuterable woe! —It cannot be unless one thing prevent it—crimes—a life of crime O Alexander I dread to think of the deeds into which I seem to see you entering From them we may be parted for ever! —Only from them—and strive that they may never be? —My near approach to another world emboldens me so much beneath you to speak thus too you—and likewise that terrible doubt which torments me so in dying!"

This she said faintly and by effort but with an earnestness which seemed the light of Heaven brightning the clouds from her spirit ere she should rise in the morning of an undeclining day But what was all this to her Husband why unmixed torment He was certain that what she said was a <bright> delusion that an hour perhaps would reduce her to corpse without life or spirit or hereafter He felt certain that under any circumstances they <u>must</u> directly part for ever That Heart was filling with black feircness toward Men and defiance the as he thought visionary heaven—could make no promise of a life without condemning sin— But He could not speak these thoughts to Mary he could not attempt to destroy the alleviator of death the Glorious prospect which he would have given worlds to know was not—He was silent in utter despair—and she saw it But <sinking> Natures[sic] was past the power of holding out Hope and Love stronger than Death could only feel kindred agony To herself she murmered "such a farewell is Dreadfull!" —and said with a voice Death was fast weakening—"Heaven bless you my Guardian and Protector But oh the happy happy days of my love to thee crowd round me—I see—what I must never see again! My Alexander I know not how to leave thee! —And "Mary Mary" he in a hollow voice replied "How! How! can I part from thee—Oh where <u>is</u> there hope—there is none" and he looked as one who sees no escape from instant Death "Yes" "were her words the last she could utter "In God—for I see what lies open—I—my Alexander—my Beloved Alexander fare well—" His arms were round her Her head on his shoulder and all he could say was with the parting embrace "Oh Mary Mary a long long farewell!—"

Mary was DEAD[2] and Death would have been welcome to Percy His situation was hopeless beyond care and I never felt till just now the utter impossibility of pen to describe it He seemed completly withered and silent from Dreadful torment All the days that had been the being that was gone the thoughts the voices the scenes that were as if they had never been All rushed back on his mind with overpowering distinctness And he leant over the chill white wasted corpse till benumbed with torture his eyes and his mind seemed to receive no impression

I saw Mary Henrietta in her coffin on the morning of Burial—An awfully impressive sight which seemed to bring the eye near to the land beyond

---

[2]   Mary dies on September 19, 1836—see p. 622. For Charlotte's rection in October to the death of her heroine, see Alexander EW, 153-56.

the grave The Angel like look of the lovely but sunken features the strange look of bitter but enraptured death was such as I have never seen in death beside and I have seen the end of thousands—When I saw the corpse Her Grace the Duchess of Wellington was beside it for those two kindred spirits were companions on earth a[n]d in Heaven But Percy was not there Nor did I see him till the funeral where he spoke to no one but stood apparently in intense thought never raising his eyes but wearing a dark gloomy expression worn and pale but never dropping a single tear A Magnificent Horse stood near ready for mounting he was attired in a Travelling cloak of Mourning Black And long after all by him unnoticed had left the grave he continued <there> without turning from the fresh closed Tomb

"Now then" he said "Now then thou art Gone Mary! —I have seen thee Die with these eyes—I have seen thee laid in thy coffin and laid in thy grave It is covered above thee—its marble presses on thee—and here at last it is that I can feel what it is to DIE

There is a long journey of Life before me and before I die I must face weary sorrows yet through all the wild turmoil that I shall pass through through all the Deeds and Sufferings that I <can> see I shall encounter—However long I live—However Mighty I may be—There shall be no look or voice of thine to lighten me But the great certainty that This stone in this West of Africa Here covers and presses over thee

Till now whatever was my Misery however Black my prospects—Thou Mary wert the star that seemed to rise upon me to light me on and guide me through Hadst thou never been alive I should not now be alive and while thou lookedst always to me for Guidance I know it was myself which leaned on thee—But—Here is the end of these feelings—of all save one feeling—Here I feel that the willd[sic] visions of Heaven and an Hereafter must be laid aside— And such a veil withdrawn what is there—Real Death! —Nothing but the Body Hidden in the coffin Dead—buried Here beneath me—fast festering in Decay! —There is an Eternity I know as there has been—There may be a Life for me But through all I know Mary that I have lost thee—and How can I feel a <breeze> of Joy when 10-20 years to come I shall have to say But—Thou art Dust Mary now—gone long before—And I while memory is fading and the past is sinking into nothing shall know as I do know that I SHALL NEVER NEVER SEE THEE MORE

The Horse was mounted and with firery[sic] speed its Rider urged it far from these agonising remembrances and away from Percy Hall Affairs were. settled there and he stopped scarce an hour till he reached the Metropolitan VERDOPOLIS Here he procured a comission in the Army and Captain Percy plunged straight way into a course of Dissipation which he has never been able to exceed thought and feeling were extinguished in a Madness which I have not space or power to detail For this reason I can not describe his Gross conspiracy against Lord St Clair a work read by every one has before me fully detailed it[3]

---

3   See Charlotte Brontë, "The Green Dwarf," Alexander CB II, part i. The Lady in question is Lady Emily Charlesworth.

While with the Army in a Campaign against the Ashantees on the north frontiers of Wellingtons land he had organized a demonaical Conspiracy against the life and Honour on that Nobleman on account of a Lady of high birth and beauty whom (now) Colonel

An Hours Musing::
Written by Alexander Percy
On the North Atlantic Sea   **By PB Brontë**
In A D 1818
295 lines.[1]

Blow ye wild winds wilder blow
Flow ye waters faster flow
Spread around my weary eye
One wide waving sea and sky

> Aloft the breezes fill my sail
> And bend its canvass to the gale
> Mid their own etherial dwelling
> Oer the Ocean proudly swelling
> See the billows round me now
> Dash against my cleaving prow
> Far and wide they sweep away
> Oer the rough and roaring see
>   By Heaven! my heart beats high to day
> Lord of such a realm to be
>   Monarch of the feirce and free

But I'll turn my eyes toward the skies
        And view the prospect their
Where broad and bright the noonday light
        Sheds glory round the air
I see yon mighty dome of heaven
        In deep cerulean hue
The white clouds oer its concave driven
        Till lost amid the blue
Then I'll turn my forehead to the blast
        And think upon the sea
That chainless boundless restless waste
        Which shines so gloriously

---

1   The fifth of five poems in BPM: BS 117-5—see vol. I, p. 203, n. 1. A
revised version appears in the 1837 notebook in volume III. Branwell's dating at
the end of the poem and in the table of contents following is problematical; the
"1818" date, the content, and the repetition of wording strongly suggest that the
poem is part of or closely related to the preceding prose fragment, probably
written in late 1835. Branwell's total of 295 lines seems to include one canceled
line.

Thou only Lethe[2] for the past
   Sole Freedom for the free

The winds are whistling in my hair
   As I gaze upon the main
And view the Atlantic from his lair
   Aroused to rage again
And view the horizon stretched afar
Wide around the ambient air
One mighty water weltring there
   Where I gaze and gaze again

Waves of the Ocean how nobly ye roll
Endless and aimless nor pathway nor goal
Proudly ye thunder your white crests on high
Shaking their foam to the spray beaten sky
Winds of the Ocean your voices arise
Shreik in my canvass and storm to the sky
Ye tell me that life is an ocean of woe
Where the feirce blasts of passion eternally blow
Mans bark may be shattered or ride through the storm
To rot on its anchor a feast for the worm
   Yes Battle may peal in its glorious thunder
     Oer the young Warriors closing day
   Yet if he lie the wet sod under
     Age must rot by dull decay

Well! —Here I am and Afric's shore
Hath sunk beneath Old Oceans roar
It seems as if but first even now
Had set Leone's[3] azure brow
That <u>hardly</u> yet yon bounding line
Conceals fair Gambias shores divine
Not so! —a thousand leagues away
I ride upon the raging sea
And long long leagues of Ocean roar
Between me and my native shore
Oh all the scenes of lifetime past
   Far far behind me lie
There tossing oer a stormy waste

---

2   In Greek and Roman mythology the river of forgetfulness, whose water produced loss of memory in those who drank of it.
3   Sierra Leone.

Who so lone as I
I heard that wind it sighed to me
Like memory of feelings gone
Black blast! my heart responds to thee
With mourning bitter as thine own
And my own voice with hoarser tone
Now strikes upon my startled ear
It seems mid these wild waves unknown
A thing I should not hear
Tis the very voice of my Infancy
The voice of my morning[4] young & free
But whats that voice to do with me
A wasted wanderer here

Oh Afric Afric where art thou
Even I can sorrow oer thee now
Though ere I left thy smiling shore
I knew my joy in life was oer
Yes I had seen my Evening sun
Set in a sullen sea of tears
Had seen his course of daylight gone
Gone lights and shadows hopes and fears
Yes I had seen my day decline
Never again to rise and shine
It was not pleasure blighted
It was not hope destroyed
It was not for love slighted
That made that dreary void
And yet my pleasures all had flown
All my hopes were dashed and gone
And though none scorned the love I gave
Yet Thou—the loved—wert in thy grave[5]
Yes—Yet all these formed but the storm
Which blackens oer even mornings sky
My Misery was of darker form
Of deadlier deeper dye
These were the various streams that flow
Into my deep deep sea of woe
The shreiking blast the pelting[6] rain
May strike the shattered oak in vain

---

4   Originally "manhood," then changed to "Infancy."
5   His wife, Mary.
6   Originally "Howling," then changed to "pelting."

Storm can <u>yon</u> scathed trunk yeild the victory
Go spend thy fury on the yong green tree

Oh when I was a little child
        Upon my Mothers knee
With what a burst of pleasure wild
        I gazed upon the sea
I stretched my arms toward its face
And wept to meet its proud embrace
And when amid youths earliest day
        I paced the foamwhite shore
I smiled to see the wildwaves play
        And joyed to hear them roar
But now! —where am I—? on that sea
Where I so often longed to be
Now! —But away this bitter pain
Shall Percy's heart so oft complain

The waves around my vessel sweep
        And cover her with foam
Yet though they shake the shattered ship
        They still shall bear her home
The sleep which shuts the watchful eye
        Mid dangers threatning near
Though helplessly the sleeper lie
        Still quiets all his care
The Night which darknes[sic] oer the earth
        Mid daylights deep decline
Shall give a glorious morrow birth
        In mornings light divine
But thou Stern Midnight of my soul
        With thy dread darkness closing round
Ye storms of strife which oer me roll
        Where have you hope or rest or bound
Well! —Roll ye waves of ocean roll
Close clouds of sorrow oer my soul
I care not[7] if your fatal blight
Shall shade this mind in lasting night
Yet while one streak of sunshine[8] lies
Behind the far dun twilight skies
Permit the wanderers lingering gaze

---

7   Originally "that."
8   Originally "daylight."

To fix upon its fading rays
The wretch whom naught from death can save
Still grasps the grass around his grave
The lion mid the Hunters toils
      Glares madness from his eye
Nets and dogs and lances foils
      Though lost to liberty
Ever through life when we look back
We see some sunshine oer our track
They falsly speak who say we spy
Naught but joys before our eye
No all the future path to me
Seems beat by storms of misery
And scenes alone long past away
Can struggle through with distant ray
Through his short and hurried span
Pleasure only <u>follows</u> man
Yet still when weariedly he dies
He dreams before him in the skys
He sees its happy Paradise

Oh what is man?[9] a wretched being
      Tossed upon the tide of time
All its rocks and whirlpools seeing
      Yet denied the power of fleeing
Waves and gulphs of woe and crime
Doomed from lifes first bitter breath
To launch upon a sea of death
Without a hope without a stay
To guide him on his dreary way
See that wrecked and shattered bark
      Drifting through the storm
Oer the ocean drear and dark
      Drives its shattered form
Where those sails which late on high
Swelled amid the shining sky
Where those masts which braved the gale
Towering oer the swelling sail
Where the glasslike deck below
Where the guilt[10] and glorious prow
How that vessel lately shone

---

9   Compare Shakespeare's *Hamlet*, IV, iv, 33.
10   "gilt" obviously intended.

Heaven and ocean all its own

Where are they sunk in the surging sea
Shivered and shattered and vanished away
Where are they sawst thou the shreiking gale
Tear from the yardarms the swelling sail
Sawst the Mast in the strife of the storm
Bend to the billows its statly form
Hark to that crash as the foam and the spray
Force oer the deck in a boiling sea
Deep in the waters the curling prow
Bursts on rocks that lurk treacherous below
And There then! its glory all vanished & gone
There then it drifts mid the tempest alone
And now as they cling to the shivring mast
As sickning they shrink from the shrill screaming blast
How do the hearts of the mariners brave
The Heaven and the Ocean the wind and the wave
      Aye! How have the hopes & the sunshine of life
Stood gainst its darkness & dangers and strife
What thinks fond man when—these dangers all oer
Stranded he lies on deaths desolate shore
View him thus sickned palsied and lone
Where is his strength and his beauty gone

            I am a MAN—yes I have seen
            Each change upon lifes changing sea
            I launched upon lifes mighty sea
            As free as fair as proud as thee
            And I am on the track which thou
            And thine and mine are drifting now
                Well when I first launched from eternity
            Upon this undiscovered sea
            Hope shone forth with glorious ray
            Blazing round my dawning day
            Expectations eager gale
            Swelled and sounded in my sail
            Ambitions ever rousing power
            Urged me on in mornings hour
            And Love thy wide and welcome light
            Ever shone before my sight
            Beauty strength and youth divine
            All the heaven of mind was mine
            When I saw the expanse before me
            When I saw the glory oer me

Oh how little did I dream
Heaven and glory all a dream
Life alone with its midnight sea
Howled on in stern reality

Sleeper awake thy dream that[sic] gone
Now thou art on Ocean all alone
I did awake and round the sky
Wild I cast my frighted eye
Where is the love and hope and light
Vanished—vanished from my sight
And now I am on the wild wild sea
Not a hope to shine on me
The winds arise and the stormy skys
Snatch my daylight from my eyes
Ambitions sails which bore me on
Shiver in the blast they seemed to have won
And Glory! —Aye thou welcome wave
Dash that illusion to its grave!
But save oh ruthless ocean save
Save love alone that only power
Which can amid this gloomy hour
Like one mild star amid the sky
Beam comfort on my misery
No—life though all its oceans roll
Can never part thee from my soul
Thou quenchless in this heart shalt lie
With this heart alone to die
Well be it so—the pealing blast
Howls wilder gainst the quivering mast
With what a sweep the surge and spray
Thunder oer the billowy sea
A gloomier tempest darknes down
Love survives—but the loved is gone!
Gone—One hopeless endless sea
Oer me beats unceasingly
Severed cordage masts and sail
I drive before the slackning gale
The storm has past but the shattered oak
Has fallen before the storm
Trunk and branches cracked and broke
<While beneath> the lightnings stroke
A black and blasted form

O Mary! when I closed thy eye

When I beheld the[e] slowly die
When thou before me silent lay
A loveless lifeless form of clay
When I saw thy coffined form
Decked to feast the gnawing worm
When the dull sod oer thee thrown
    Hid thee from my tearless eye
When they laid the marble stone
    Above where thou must ever lie
Twas then my Mary then alone
    I felt what 'twas to—Die!

Oh long long years may lie before me
A thousand woes may darken oer me
And ere I lay me down to die
Old age may strike this anguished eye
Yet through this wide wide waste of years
This channelled gulph of burning tears
Aye if I live till earths decay
Is crumbling in its latest day
If thousand winters wintriest snow
Fall blighted oer my stricken brow
Still through yon vast eternity
I know that *Thou canst never be*
Lost for ever lost to me
That all thy woes and joys are oer
That thou art Dead gone long before
And I shall _never_ _never_ *see Thee more!*

                Alexander Percy. <u>1818</u>.

P B Bronte
November 10th 1834.
Finis[11]

---

[11] The poem is followed by a table of contents for the notebook:

Contents

          P B Bronte. Nov 10
              1834

[Angria and the Angrians]
I(a)[1]

ll.   ZAMORNA.[2] 170 miles long 112 miles broad.
Capital the City of Zamorna. Lord Lieutenant.
Lord Viscount Castlereagh
Population..1986000
lll   ANGRIA. 80 miles long, 180 broad
Capital the City of Angria
Lord lieutenant. W H Warner Esq[r]
Population..1492000
VI   ARUNDEL 165 miles long 90 broad
Capital the City of Seaton
Lord lieutenant the Earl of Arundel
Population...971000
V.   NORTHANGERLAND. 200 miles long 270 broad
Capital the City of Pequena
Lord lieutenant the Earl of Northangerland
Population...376000
VI.   DOURO 130 miles long 100 broad
Capital the city of Douro
Lord lieutenant the Earl of Jordan
Population...71000
VII   CALABAR Length 190 miles breadth 130 miles
Capital the City of Gazemba
Lord lieutenant Wilkin Thornton Esq[r]
Population...59000.

---

[1]   A manuscript fragment of 12 pages, 11.2x18.5 cm, in the Brotherton
Collection. The manuscript originally consisted of sheets folded once and laid
inside each other but not stitched. At least one sheet (4 pages—two at the
beginning and two at the end) is missing. The fragment is unsigned and undated,
but p. 4 of the manuscript contains an internal date of June 2, 1834, and the
final page of September 1, 1834. Also, on the 1837 revisions of the two poems
it contains (see vol. III), Branwell indicates the original date of composition as
Spring 1834. The manuscript, therefore, was likely begun in May of 1834,
about the same time as **The Life of Alexander Percy**. For the title, see p.
278.
[2]   This is a list of the various provinces that constitute the new kindom of
Angria. The missing item at the beginning of the list is probably Adrianopolis,
the capital of the new kingdom. However, it seems that at one time there was
also to be a province named Gordon—see **The Wool is Rising**, and
Alexander CB II, part ii, p. 362, n. 173.

ETREI. length 120 miles breadth 95 miles
Capital the City of Dongola
Lord Lieutenant Henri Fernando Di Enara.
Population..__4000__
          Total population of Angria   4959000

I have just returned to my own Study from wittnessing the Coronation of the King of Angria[3] and certainly I may say that I have seen a spectacle which. employed all the senses of eye and ear and thought nay of tongue and nose and stomach to mark learn and inwardly digest it with that degree of rumination which its overwhelming importance so overwhelmingly demands The vast area of St Michaels its huge dome hung with a blaze of light the gorgeous pomp which swept among its roofed columns the the echo of voices among their capitals and the waving of plumes, <amid> their bases the kings and nobles and grandeur of 7 kingdoms the whole force and enthusiasm and <multitude> of 7 Nations all congregated in one mighty building to hail the Advent of the rising sun. I am not going to give you reader any account of the proceedings of this memorable day I am not about to tell you of the rank and order and number of the processions of the trappings and ornaments and banners of the ceremony of the solemnity of the coronation and costliness of the crown These things have all been and will yet be told and retold by every tongue of thousand voiced fame and ere this moment along every path in Africa will be flying on the wings of Mercury the "Coronation of the King of Angria"
          In this chapter reader you must only expect to meet with a few scattered and desultory hints and observations the nature and tendencies the aspect and consequences of this gorgeous ceremony
          This morning I remember on turning round the bend of Thornton Place dawn fell on the whole wide sweep of the great street leading to the cathedral I was instantaneously struck by the blaze the perfect flash of gold and scarlet which met my eye over the whole heads of the densely packed multitude The air was filled with one vast flutter of the Angrian banners huge sheets of silken scarlet flung themselves abroad in the breeze. and blazed out in their rustling folds the broad bright sun rising in burnished. gold I felt <instantly> the effect this show produced on me and I well knew the transient enthusiasm which roused me as I beheld. the wind and the marching unroll to the sight on scarlet after scarlet the one single word "ARISE" It seemed to me as if a Genius had spoken that command and its emphatic letters seemed the fittest motto for this rising and stirring empire. But in my ride to St Michaels not the show but the feeling of the Angrians most filled me with suprise and astonishment. on entering this full tide of population a long long file of the Angrian Army swept

---

[3]   i.e., the Duke of Zamorna as King Adrian.

by me There might pass 5 or 6 rejiments of Infantry their new scarlet uniforms
and gilded bells and the caps with their Sun starred from the swagger of the
plumed head and the <   > note of the fife and the long thundering roll of the
drums Did shew forth in its brightest light this scene of dashing and military
gaiety. These soldiers I was greived to observe each looked and acted as if not
only all round him but the kingdom whose ensigns he <was   > for its
glory and safty on his particular and individual shoulders such an air of unmixed
arrogance and pretension such a look of scorn and defiance pervaded every motion
and word of that unmanageable soldiery and when they came opposite to a deep
rank of Sneachis Guards who stretched in their bright <wine> uniform far down
the square to St Michaels these insolent Angrians drew up before them and up
with their caps and standards "Zamorna and Angria—Hurra for its Army" It
grrieved[sic] me as the loud laugh of the multitude passed of to see the deep stern
look of defiance cast back by the dull ranks of the Northern Home guards I
confess I then felt some fears for the safety of the day

In my route toward the cathedral what struck me in the feelings of the
enormous crowds round me was the perfect enthusiasm with which every
individual seemed [to] look upon the Advent of this rising nation and the spirit
of insolence which its upholders seemed to delight in displaying toward every
being about them and in every action they committed If a man happened to fall
in the crowd you might know if he was An Angrian by the brazen effrontery
with which he would rise and clear both the mud and the disgrace from his
clothes and countenance

I pass over the mighty multitudes the glorious spectacles the scarlet and
gold of Angria the gloom over the respectable persons whom I saw the insults
offered to the Aristocrats the defiance of the opposite partys the halloaing and
cheerings and fightings and mummery round every carriage where blazed the arms
of Angria I pass over my passage to St Michaels and the glory round the scene
of [the] Coronation.

When I assumed my station amid the minions of the Glasstown
Government just behind the throne and on the long range of seats fronting the
grand Altar I took my "eye" with an effort from the scene of inconceivable
splendour far above and behind and around and wide and high before me

I had arrived late all the Kings and functionarys were seated The trains
of officers marshalled themselves in great arms <directing> round the Altar Anon
from the direction of the Robing Chapel the whole Nave of the cathedral seemed
to sway and bend the loud voices of the Trumpets rung sharp among the arches
the crowds opened and two files of the Angrian Foot guards lined the lane with
their gilden[sic] and scarlet uniform The standards bowed toward each other
formed a long long canopy above and anon the full tide of Angrian royalty swept
up the living aisle and instant[ly] covered platform and steps and area of the
Noble Altar Lo there stood himself the King and lord of All his envied hair
uncovered and his glorious form enveloped in the ample and magnificent robe of
coronation His Queen stood beside him and I smiled when I knew that I beheld
in that fairest flower of <Angria> that bright and heavenly sharer of Zamornas

crown the erewhile Mary Percy the haughty and capricious little daughter of the great gallant <master> of Percy Hall

But to behold and wonder and admire see those thick. lines of men who gather round the Altar and gaze so stiffly on the <tossing> and blazing beneath them see decked in all the pride in all the splendour of official regalia Montmorenci and Warner and Percy and Arundel and Castlereagh and Stannidge and Thornton and Lindsay and Morley and Roslin and Seymours and Lascelles and Elringtons and Howards and Agars. and Sydenhams and all the power and insolence and innocence and ability and indefatigability of the Great Angrian faction

Northangerland stood alone near the Duke attired in plain solemn black without a star or an order looking pale and <distracted> and excited. around him.

The Queen of Angria was supported by a train of the highest rank and fashion and <station> in Verdopolis I was greived to see such numbers of our citizens range themselves in the Angrian fashion and place themselves [among] the dieties of An Angrian Court. but so it was in spite of her.

When after a long train of ceremonys His Highness W Gravi the Arch Primate of Verdopolis advanced at the Head of the Glasstown prelacy and prepared with a benidiction to place the crown of Angria on the Head of its Sovereign that Sovereign augustly waved him sideway and seizing a flashing steel Helmet he fixed it on his forehead then turning to the Earl of Northangerland asked for the Angrian Sceptre His lordship without more ado snatched his own sword from its rest and giving it to His Majesty said sneeringly Theres the sceptre which alone can be swayed over Angria. Zamornas fingers closed on the bright weapon with emphasis He cast his great Robe from his Person and advanced in full armour of steel Erect and blazing as if in Achilles own heavenly mail[4] "Here" said he with a loud thrilling voice. "Here Angrian eyes see your Monarch not dressed out and decorated with the baubles and trumpery of an unnatural office but attired in those Garments wherein alone he can ever prove himself worthy of being a Ruler over you Yes my subjects behold in my hand the pledge of your Liberty and your safety of my rights and my glory from this time forward through prosperity and Adversity as Man and as Monarch I swear to you my Subjects and people of Angria that I devote myself in these arms and from this moment to guide you direct you from the path we have just entered on to wherever it shall lead. and through whatever dangers it may oppose. To devote this head and this arm yes and this heart and these feelings alone to Angria and to her fame and to the spread and the extension of her dominion while life and being last in me the Enimy of an Angrian to be the Enimy of her King, and to any subject who calls for assistance. shall this sword this my sceptre be held out and weilded this heart and bosom exposed to defend

---

4   Thetis asks Hephaestus to make a new set of armour for Achilles when his original set is lost after he had given it to Patroclus and he is killed. It is called the "brilliant gear, the god of fire's gift"—*Illiad* 18, 720.

this life hazarded to raise. Now for the rest. while I pray Providence to watch over and shine above you while I ask only your own good hearts and arms to second me while I give my soul and body to <lead you on> "Long live the King of Angria" cried <   > the Angrians <   >[5] and Long live the Noble Zamorna echoed every column and rafter and stone through the mighty cathedral. The Monarch took the Crown and Sceptre which Gravi had held and placing them on the head and in the Hand of his wife he said again in a voice which forced attention "Now you Mary Henrietta Wellesly I alone crown as the partner of my life. the partner of my crown take you these costly emblems of peace and prosperity for your forehead they are fitted and you reverence them and respect them as the insignia of the Lofty Station you must hold remember that you are the wife of a King that you are yourself a Queen and the Mother of a mighty people Resolve now upon rendering yourself worthy of the office in which I create you as I alone can do the Queen of the Kingdome of Angria." "Little could I ever think. Replied the Queen "of the office which I now must hold and whatever incapacity and unfitness for this station that <ignorance> of my dealing could have entailed upon me It shall now be my buisness as it will be my glory to wipe away all error which can arise from such a suprise to devote my whole life to the service and happiness of my country and in so doing to the happiness of you My Husband and King." The cheeks of the beautiful Sovereign glowed with the heartfelt sentiment and gracefully bearing her gorgeous elevation she bowed with a winning smile of sweetness to her people beneath her and then turn[ed] to gaze and rest with <   > undoubtingness on the Glory of Her Lord and King to him she yeilded the glorious insignia of Her royalty as to one whom she knew could accept and could employ the whole He. with a flash of firelight from his eyes. raised sword and sceptre in one hand and crown and helmet in another "Now my people In peace and war by these united Insignia shall you find suport and a Leader And that your Sky shall never be clouded your Land shall never be invaded your sun shall never set and your reign shall never end will be and shall be the determination and care of your King Arthur Wellesly and your Queen Mary Henrietta Arise My People and I will lead you to glory. all this do I swear and by this I will abide so help me God."

The Earl of Northangerland stepped darkly forward and stretching forth his hands he cried in his loudest and most warlike voice. God save the King" as he stepped back sneering at the final word in his sentence a hundred Heralds shouted at the full pitch of their stentor Lungs God save the King of Angria and all the huge multitude from within and without from cathedral and altar and street and house top. sent up the sudden roar of God save the King of Angria Long live the King and Queen of the Angrians The shouting and trumpets and swelling and tossing had not half died off when just at the time when it was expected. that the primate and the Four Kings should arise from their thrones to pour their blessings on the new crowned Monarch Lo all at once up rises and[sic] vast

---

5   Branwell's interlinear emendations are undecipherable.

Orchestra in the great Oratorio gallery the Organ rolled out a thundering note of
preparation and deep trumpet bass voices and instruments burst forth with a peal
of stormy music.

Sound the loud Trumpet oer Africs bright sea
Zamorna hath triumphed the Angrians are free
Sound for our day Star hath risen in glory
Sound that Loud Trumpet unequalled in story
Sing for the sunbeams have <gleamed out> to brighten
A Reign which hath neare through age or through time
The past page of History burst out to enlighten
Alone in its dark glory and proud in its clime
Never to darken and never to decline
Tempests may threaten and storms may assail us
Afric may tremble and fortune may fail us
Yet with thee our Zamorna alone to avail us
Angria thy full sun unshadowed shall shine

Sing for the power of our foemen hath gone
Quenched in the Sunbeams that smiles[sic] round thy throne
Raise higher and louder your voices to sing
Angria our country and Arthur our King
River whose waves through the wide desart winding
Bearest thy streams toward the Home of thy pride
Each weary waste of thy glory reminding
Play and spread round thee thy Life giving tide

Oh All ye proud mountains which high from afar
Crown your blue brows with the wandering star
Tell you each cliff and each vale and each plain
Zamorna hath triumphed oer Angria to reign
Aye tell ye the North with its storms and its snow
Tell ye the South where the Ocean gales blow
Tell ye the East where the suns ever glow
Angria and Arthur are shining again
Mid night and tempest may darken in vain
Foes may arise
And fate may suprise
Dust on the Mountain and drops in the main

Sing for the Sun hath arisen on creation
Sound ye the Trumpet to herald this dawn
Rise Man and Monarch and city and Nation
Away with your darkness and hail to your dawn
Sound the Loud Trumpet oer land and oer sea
Join tongues hearts and voices rejoicing to sing

Afric arising hath sworn to be free
Glory to Angria and GOD SAVE OUR KING[6]

Scarcly had the Loud voice of Trombone and Trumpet rolled out the last chord of
the symphony when up rose the united cathedral and in full thundering chorus
King and Court and people all joined to repeat at the full stretch of lungs and
voices the concluding stanza of the insupportable ode. a loud Hurra echoed along
the Aisles as it concluded and as a young Nobleman shouted out
Again encore
Lets hear it once more
An universal laugh rattled without the slightest regard to dignity and sanctity
amid the assembly Long live the King. of Angria shouted a. voice and. even I
laughed at the odd puzzled "aye to be sure let em" which the one throated mass
drawled out in answer "Hey for the Noblemen of Africa." "Haw—Oh. m m.
Faugh scraw maw hang em skin em flesh em bone em fire fury smoke and
confusion. —" The Monarchs and their Courts now began to leave the cathedral
it was evident that on consulting their dignity their stay here could not be longer
the legal ceremony was completed and now. the building and its communications
seemed about to be inflamed with the fever of insolent hilarity and
undistinguishing madness as the respective suites and attendants of the Courts
swept out of the vast arena the <suprised> ears of the various obnoxious
individuals were saluted with a shower of exclamations upon their different
peculiaritys and their various public characters Earl St Clairs suite passed
underneath the grand platform and Lord Roslyn that noblemans disgraceful son
and heir leaped on to the back of one of his comrades chucked a halfpenny above
his head and roaring
Mustard to sell
I guess she's well
Instantly ducked again amid the applauding and caressing multitude The more
disgraceful the insults and the more meritorious their objects this day was there
the more merriment and the greater mirth. Also all along the great ai[s]les and far
sweeping archway I beheld hundreds in a string playing at leap frog 2 or 3000
persons had gathered round a Frenchman just under the great Organ Gallery who
was exhibiting the new and suprising entertainment of the "Sun of Angria" The
play is on the feats of 2 or 3 sucessive "enfants" on whose skulls he clapped a
lighted pitch cap.[7] when the pain instantly caused them to spring a yard or two
into the air moreover in the nave French horns and Trumpets were wailing out
the dreary Elrington March in the ai[s]le bugles and clarionets were bursting
forth with the Zamorna Grand March in the transcepts Drum and fife were

---

6   For other versions of this song see p. 8 and the 1837 version in vol. III.

7   A cap lined with pitch which was placed on the head and set alight, used as
an instrument of torture during the Irish Rebellion of 1798. See also vol. I, p.
13, n. 4.

flourishing away on Thorntons jig and up rose in the Great Cathedral orchestra
Trombones and voices and the huge deep roll of the organ Diapasons the
Anthem of the Coronation

Shine on us God of Afric shine
Oh round us shower thy light divine
Sailing across a stormy sea
Mid life and death we trust in thee
That Life and death shall find us free
Thou with all thy might power
Cast our foemen down
Mid the Battles darkest hour
Blast them with thy frown
Mid that hour of bloody strife
Thou preserve each Angrian life
Save us if we die
Nerve our arm with iron blow
Lay our foemen cold and low
God and Angria on that foe
Be our battle cry
Death to every emimy
Death to all who yeild us hate
Down to Dust with adverse fate
Angrian vengeance lags not late
Let the Traitors die

But God save our King
Joy to him we sing
Tongues and hearts and voices shout
God save the King
Zamorna thou alone
Canst sit on Angrias throne
Swear while thou her sword shall weild
It shall not be overthrown
Then thy fame with untired wing
Still to thee shall laurels bring
Then around the world shall sound
GOD SAVE OUR KING[8]

That night while I rested from the turmoil of the day I sat in my own arm chair
by my own fireside and in my own dear secluded study The blaze crackled up the

---

8   For other versions of this anthem, see p. 650 and the 1837 version in vol.
III.

roaring chimney and the candles shed their soften[ing] sheen over the closed and ghost like window curtains I sat leaning back on my chair drowsy enough from the days fatigue to shun the task of reading and to enjoy the pleasures of Idleness but not drowsy enough to flee the charms of imagination and hide fancy in the <down> of Somnus[9] No varied and diversified visions fleeted over my mind. I looked at the warm fire and behold the red coals only displayed "Towers Halls and Steeples" as Cowper says[10] I gazed round the reddened and flickering wall but directly the papering disposed itself into the figure of a new and rising city I shut my eyes fast in darkness but Alas up rose a tall man blazing in scarlet and crowned with the rising sun. he dissapeared and fragments of streets heads and tails of cavalcades bits of processions banners and military or an arch of a roof of some vast cathedral took his place and as soon went. hurried forward to fill the profound of vacuity. my ears too rung with the wild mournful wail of a bugle or the religious thunder of an Organ and short detached sentences or long screeds of sounding Athems struck them with the sudden vigour of absolute reality

Now all this wandering and all the phantasms I considered at last in the light of the undigested fragments the crude and nightmare morsels of the days so ample meal the returning cud of that just ended astounding ceremony There was not a house or a voice or a round of "music" which I could not distinctly recollect having heard or seen that very day. and I smiled when I saw on every vision in every vacuity when I heard in every voice and at every pause of a sound. "Angria" "Zamorna" "The Angrians" Aye this birth of a Nation this Nativity of a Kingdom this revolution in the world this seed of a beginning this might well justify this confusion and well tell forth this dream

I leant my head on my hand and wandered again into a chaos of reflection What I asked myself. can all this beginning end in I saw to day a young man of Royal birth and immense. splendour of intellect. give up all his power bodily and mental use all his influence and venture all his fortune. into one grand stake of victory or death. I saw him take upon himself the lawful Government of a portion of the Verdopolitan Empire. and while he promised to that portion nothing but despotic government continual war. the tyranny of Military Government and the prospect of grim deathlike taxation while he showed the dim outline of foes around a frontier and enimys amid his freinds I yet beheld that people over whom this ruler was placed and to whom this prospect was shown I beheld them all and united with one heart and mind throw themselves on the fate of Zamorna and adore this inauspicious King

I saw a faction in itself. composed of a few men without character or station or principle. men only of dazzling and almost unequalled abilitys obtain from the government of their country. from the men whom they had endeavoured to ruin and overthrow—a large and important district of the great Glasstown

---

9   The Roman God of Sleep.

10   While all three structures are mentioned in Cowper's poetry, especially in *The Task*, this phrase seems to be Branwell's invention.

country given into the hands of one among them without condition or proviso. I beheld these men and this faction seize upon their prize unsparingly appropriate it and then—deliberatly turn round revile their benefactors insult their donor and while they held a whole people in their grasp declare that they only meant to use them as a stepping stone a well in the desert a path to their object one stage toward their goal And oh to see that victim thus given and thus to be appropriated to behold it lick the hand upheld to slay adore the faction by whom it was bestriden and trot gaily on the road where it was to be urged to the very death

Oh the infatuation the blindness which some time we have seen to pervade a nation and dash them into a rapid and unsparing ruin

Well Angria is now under the Rule of the Duke of Zamorna and what is to become of a Nation whose King is Arthur Wellesly and whose cheif ruler is Alexander Percy

Yes but what is to become of a Nation who sees arrayed against its summit against its steeples its Nobles and Kings and Mighty men their own children and their eternal enimys. What is to become of the Glasstown countrys when they must calculate on a struggle with their own sons leagued with their hated DEMOCRATS. See Angria ruled And governed by the sons of the Verdopolitan Nobility and all the highblooded and daring portion of its citizens. —having the hearty good wishes and the enthusiastic adoration of its own people and also of all the peasantry of Verdopolis see it turn round and laugh at. its <gov> insult the Verdopolitan Kings and Government take that National Ceremony the Coronation into its own hands and in every moment on every occasion shewe to ward that Mother Country many of whose subjects so admire it such insult and arrogance and contempt and reckless determination. Verily a high heart is the beginning of destruction and pride cometh before a fall[11] —O Zamorna when I look at you what a cloud comes over my minds eye O Angria you are launched on a desperate voyage you have a JONAH on board you[12] and a wild and angry heaven above you, Verdopolis you have infatuation in your councels and. desertion in your children. —!

Just as my thoughts had arrived to this pitch and as I was picturing to myself the probable events of this very year I was awakened from my reverie by the violent smash on the window and the shock of some soft body hurled on my head. a horrid din of shouting and laughter rushed in straightway through the shattered panes. I had all along in my musings had my ears filled with the stun of distant sounds and voices and cries of wild confusion but I amid my many imaginations either did not at all regard them or thought them almost only the mere impressions and remnants of the bygone uproar of the day.

Lo now as I started from my chair a huge heap of flannel rolled on the rug and. when I rushed to the window the cries of. "A Blanket for Richton"

---

[11] Compare Proverbs 16:18.
[12] See Jonah, chapter I.

"Knock up the Apothecary" "Toss up the halfpenny" "Angria for ever"
"Ipecacuhana to sell" "O vomit for Flower"[13] "Long live Zamorna" burst upon
my ears in rapid and chaotic confusion Behold a huge Mob of men were
sweeping through the street beneath and amid banners and soldiers and Music and
Angrians nothing reigned below but unthinking madness and mischeif. All the
city seemed in the pleasant state I beheld my quarter and I darred[sic] say that
many a window had received a visitation besides mine. Chagrined as I was I
could not help laughing when as I looked down on the gaslighted street beneath I
beheld its vast uproar of hilarious heads the storm of fighting amid the multitude
and the glorious the invincible Arrogance and. insolence of the thousand scarlet
Ribbonned Angrians. The mob had dressed up that infamous Old wretch R P
Sdeath. in scarlet and tinsel. he was borne forward upon a gaunt grey nag and
without any sense of the monstrous comparison was most inimitably
personating a mad and drunken Zamorna As he at once. when the band burst out.
raised up his testimony

Hark from the tombs a doleful sound

Mine ears attend the cry[14]

I. appalled at the voice and action ran from the window and retired to my room[15]

Well—I am now in the beginning of a situation which promises scenes and
adventures both intirely to my taste and holding a harvest of amusement to my
readers While I sat at breakfast the morning after the coronation day. a Servant
entered. bearing a Note. whose official character might be winded a mile off. I
hastily broke the envelope and read as follows.

Home Office.

June. 2. —34

Dear Richton
          I deem it expedient to inform you by this early and perhaps too
unceremonious opportunity that. in a cabinet counsel held. at the Treasury Office
last night all the then present members of the Government I should almost say
unanimously. elected you as the most fit and proper person (under existing
circumstances) to fill the certainly ardous and distinguished post of Ambasador
Plenipotentiary from the Ministry of the Verdopolitan Junction. to the Court of.
as I hope I may with decorum term it the New Born Kingdom of Angria The

---

[13] Ipecacuanha was an emetic obtained in Branwell's day from an apothecary.

[14] These lines are preceded by two canceled lines:
    Aull yee that dwell bee-loww thee dumb
    Aye heere a dole-full crie.
Compare Isaac Watts, *Hymns and Spiritual Songs*, Bk, II, no. 63.

[15] The space following would seem to indicate a chapter division—see pp. 234
and 313.

time of your set out and. the other contingencies of your situation are I believe at your own disposal. And my dear Flow. I must proceed so far as too caution you in the present. crisis against too hastily refusing the acceptance of this truely important situation Apoligising sincerely for the I fear undue abscence of proper official formalitys in this I believe too hasty and needlessly unimportant scrawl I remain. Dear Richton. Yrs &c.

R Pelham.

I did smile I own at this characteristic letter.
However I. thought seriously of the matter it contained. —directly after I had laid down my friends note. I had to open another. just arrived.

Angrian Directory
VERDOPOLIS =

Well. Now—Flower what think you of our birthday. eh. Oh we began bravely Carry on thus and Angria is made however they should have had. a. little more bullying the ducking of Clair and Sydney and you would have done wonders. well however we'll bully enow soon and Volo if we once start. out. I promise there's one. now writing to you who'll soon find himself in the glory of it

Now let this fly stick. Ive sat down to scribble this notice t'ye. by the command of. <u>the child</u>.! Why and for that matter under orders too from the thing who wears on its Baby brow the round and top of soverignty.! eh Flower wise men like you and I. may afford to hold up our unburnt fingers at the silly little puppets above us. pooh they think themselves superior to ourselves because we have chucked them over our head that the crowd may pay and gaze. eh. well never mind—dont we hold the string wont out little finger chuck em down too eh Flower?

Well heres a screed of morality for you Im amazed how I wrote it Im in the thick of buisness this morn and can write myself. Dear Dear Flower yours for our co eternal and co existent welfare.

H M M MONTMORENCY.
Foreign Secretary for Angria.

Post-script. (hastily scratched in)

Oh bless me Bacchus[16] will be the death of me. I had been in such a good way ever since that night that. in talking to you of our eternal welfare I had quite forgot to write of earthly concerns. Now Flower my sole intent amid all this rubbish (I feel my brain in a calm line) amid all this rubbish my sole intent sir was to inform this Honorable House. that. the Government of Angria had accepted the. the. —Lord Richton as Ambassador to its Court et cetera.

Nay Ive done. 500 letters have arrived.

Good < > what o'clock. ist?

MONT'.

---

[16] i.e., wine.

And was not this letter too characteristic as the other Honl. the Minister for foreign affairs too the New born Kingdom Fairly excursive in the streams of the taptub.

It was at 3 o clock. in the morning of the first of July that I appeared alone in front of the General Coach Office in Verdopolis. There amid the hundred vehicles either resting stationary on their wheels or every moment harnessed and tossed whirling round the yard like Heavenly ministers on their terrestrial errandry I speedily recognised the Newly established Verdopolitan Morning Mail the "Royal Angrian" towering in the broad lacquered pride of glossy green and scarlet the Back in the other coaches plain here. blazed in the gilded glory of a great many rayed rising sun and the horses fine active animals were just putting too by the scarlet jerkined drivers This coach was established with three others for the other stages of the day by the immediate Angrian Government And in it this morning I took my seat on the outside for a ride to my official mansion in Adrianopolis I had of course sent my family and effects by widely different conveyance. but for myself. nothing—nothing—have I ever liked better than a free unobstructed ride on the mail coach in a fine summer day I like the very scene every aspect even of the great coach yards and now when I swung up with light and almost youthful feeling on to the coach box and took my seat till all should be prepared for starting. a gaze round. my neighbourhood I. well wonder and delight to see. the various vehicles all starting or about to start. off from this great nucleus of Nations all along the various feeders of the world. when I saw. the Mail to Grenvilles Wharf. saw resting on its wheels and just beside it the. exactly similar coach. lettered the. Highlander Freetown. Sneachies City. Fidena. Denard North City. —and the. Green Erin." Alnwick. Silsden Rossestown Parrystown Ravenshill. Nevada. Ardrah Keswick. Wellingtonstown. When I reflected that ere two or three hours longer these very carriages laden with mortality would have set out. for these long varied journeys would soon be <watched> by the great brows of. Grey garach or Nevada. would sweep along the banks of the red River or Gambia. and would rattle along the streets of. a far distant and remote metropolis. it produced much the same feeling in me as when I have looked on a large family of sturdy little boys and thought of them at 10 or 15 years hence. now all gathered together playing and fighting perhaps. on one parlour hearthrug. then. maybe one a soldier fighting with the Angrians amid the Desarts of Africa. another. a sailor tossing amid the tempests of a stormy tide. then a Rector. enjoying himself in a fox hunt over his parish. the last. a politician consuming in the turmoil of parliamentary opposition

Well however from reveries such as this I was soon awakened while I employed myself in buttoning tight Mr Bellinghams great coat. (an excellent invention by the by) and protecting myself against all the attacks of a cold dark. breezy morning. Lo the whole tide of passengers smacking their arms and adjusting their neck cloths. swilling a comforter of the creature.[17] and swearing

---

[17] i. e., alcoholic spirits of some sort.

vociferously at the drivers all appeared beneath me around the Mail. "Hillo driver What the diedums. have ye got. such an Animal as the left hander under your reins for Why it'll curse. any wheel its tyed too." "Our cattle is just as their[sic] made under heaven. theer isnt a nobleer horse. in all. the city." "Aye they are what theyre made for Volo its not you who have improved them " "I say gemmen move you from that. seat there Im an Angrian and dont intend to take the feet of such a English smelling varmint as you" "In with your legs fellow. dye think Im going to—" "Oh mercy do I care what youre going to. Ill tell you where we are all going to—to Heaven. and so. Hey driver hand me a glass to the sucess of—" "Now Tom you are always for drinking Why. what did you mount [the] coach for since you aim at swimming your journey" "Room for my dogs and place for an Angrian ?" Pooh! were all Angrians here. and in that light --" "Now Gentlemen all ready. Dick out with your Bugle. Ned I say your guns cocked isnt it. now Ill give you a taste of our cattle. Gee. who—oop. Stop Ned I say what were you were saying of me this night inth[sic] stable." "Blood and blunderbuss if you speak to me Ill" "I say Ned you'd better tell me or." "Why Ill let sense out at your ears if it wont come by your mouth." "Was that it" "Go look." "Now Ned Ive the reins in my hand. and. were like to go down my mind isnt peaceable." "Now one fig for your mind and that—for your body." Well this is not such usage as Ive been used to Gee whup. oh oh" —While the arms of the two worthys Driver and guard were darted over the coach top in mutual hatred. twenty hands clutched on them and twenty voices roared death and thunder to stop. meanwhile two very well dressed young Gentlemen with red. ribbons round their necks had each seized the reins with intent to drive forward but no. "William. yeild me the reins." "Clary. take em if you dare." "Sir is this the language." "Sir is this the gesture." a deadly conflict raged on the summit of the coach and a not inferior one on the front box meantime all the nags <heads> had laid their ears together and were coming to a determination The vehicle seemed to spring beneath me I leaned back onto my seat Up struck a rattle. and whirled round the corner tearing allong the street the Royal Angrian swept past with its load of jarring elements.

The lofty houses and long lines of streets swept past us in dark and twilight chilliness. now and then some. huge august Public Building reared itself. in double blackness and. fourfold exclusiveness. and as we passed under neath its vast columns and long vistas. a louder and deeper echo seemed to spring from our thundering wheels few passengers but crowds of coaches burst against us with vying rattle and from the coach office yard to Waterloo Place. there was not a moment amid all this stern early twilight when ceased this eternal roar

I have said however favourable the time for silence. that Godess could not. prevail over the scene round us And truely she was also very weak on the coach top among. us. My readers must know that Insides and outsides together there was not a soul above the wheel. who did not sport the scarlet Ribbon & who did not write himself. an Angrian official. to find yourself. plunged reader into the company of a shoal of. any Government understrappers. is fearful enough to chill the coldest heart. But Oh. to. barely imagine. the chaotic union of. 13 Angrian placemen is to bring on your mind the recollection. of toes bruised to a jelly legs jammed by unyeild[ing] side fellows tongue stopt by overbearing Bullying ears dinned by oaths and clamouring and senses horrified with arrogance and lies and blackguard insolence. Just below me on the coach box sat the coachman resplendent in an immense scarlet cloak and glor[y]ing in the post of distinction on each side of this Phoebus sat or figeted a Phaeton.[18] each looking wishfully toward the reins and striving to insinuate themselves into the good graces of their holder. These two godships excessivly annoyed me. with their vociferous telling upon every subject of conversation and that annoyance they took care to increase by the plague of their two spaniels which kennelled themselves at my feet incommoding my shoes by their eternal endeavours to bite the fleas from their backs and when I saw them devouring an unhappy straggler I heartily wished that so could I treat their masters. who their curled and scented locks tossing above their velvet coat collars raised their white gloved hands in token of the forthcoming of each respective lie.

Beside me on one side had deposited themselves two young Angrian RECTORS. clergymen of an aspect which certainly did no discredit to the condescension and humility of their order. Their whole discourse turned upon the merits and demerits of the nags before them the character for rare sport of the ground over which we travelled. and a vehement controversy with the Phaetons on the pretensions of the winner "At Billys Main last night" varied certainly by the more clerical interlude of a wail over the dissapointment of "Henrys primacy"[19]

Pararell to these Apostolical missionarys and just above thcm Bella Horrida Velle et Angrian spumantem sanguiene cerne[20] Terrific sight over us on the sumit of the coach were ranged in one red line. four military officers from "The Kings own Rejiment." Oh how often "Our Royal yong scoundrel of a colonel" was brought upon the carpet and truely it had been better for his Majestys character. had. either his name been more respected or <   > his supporters been more respectable These four crowned the coach and as ornaments they well became it—they were cavalry officers Two captains a Lieutenant and an Ensign. Their chests were expanded in one blaze of gold. Their strong arms encased in scarlet. their pantaloons shining white and the black helmet the starlike "sun" and the great mourning plume overshadowed faces of no ordinary ferocity. They were certainly to look up on fine warlike figures and when I

---

[18]   Phoebus is the sun; Phaeton was the son of Helios who borrowed his father's sun chariot and , through careless driving, would have set the world on fire had not Zeus struck him down with a thunderbolt.

[19]   "Billys Main" likely refers to a cock fight—see p. 284. "Henry's Primacy" refers to Charles Stanhope winning the election as Primate of Angria over Henry Warner—see p. 424 and Alexander CB, II, ii, 71.

[20]   Branwell's somewhat awkward Latin translates roughly as "Wishing for terrifying wars and seeing Angria frothing with blood."

reflected that these 4 were members of an Army which is soon destined to plunge into the most unlimited perils of warfare either too perish unspared or to go on the terror and destruction of Nations. I could not help feeling a certain sensation of respect and enthusiasm.

Of the Gentlemen who occupied the hinder part of the coach I could see little but hear much The occasional glimpse of the scarlet Ribbon the constant. lying and desperadoing and threats and execrations gave me disagreeable intimations of 2 policemen 3 custom house officers and a Treasury clerk.

As to the Inside of my vehicle I could make nothing of it at last so outrageous did rise the scream of incessant Argumentation there that I turned in fright to the coach man. "In heavens name who have you got below us." "Oh never fear. 3 architects a sculptor and 2 painters!" I sat down in silence.

While we rattled over the streets of Verdopolis—the morning seemed yet to frown cold and rawly in the heavens and the prospect was hardly exhilarating when we turned round the square and burst full on the wide stony ground and cold shrubbery like landscape of Waterloo Place. That huge. dark Palace. stood sternly up and its columned and Granite front looked in one. sombre shadow as if it had never known a ray of sunshine.

Yet in spite of such a desolate aspect the morning was arising and the clouds were dispersing Oh I shall not soon forget the moment when just upon the Boundarys of the Newborn Kingdom Our coach gained the eminence that looks over the feilds of Zamorna. and the plain of the Olympian A few Trees waved over the road. yet. dark with twilight But streight Before over the level flat of. Angria. the wide unclouded Horizon kindled up with. the just rising Sun, directly his bright beams seemed to consume the whole eastern landscape. the shadow of our coach streamed behind us over the stony road and. all down the course of the just now scarcly seen Olympian a flash of silver seemed to break over its surface. That instant of sunrise was delightful—the Horses snuffed the breeze and dashed merrily down the road. while. one hearty shout of "Hey for the sun of Angria" burst from the stentor lungs of our united company

One minute since all before us was grey dead and monotonous now with a feeling like incredulity I. glanced at the bright yellow lawns and the deep dark. woods and the little shadow casting hedges where the wild birds were singing with joy. the. New City of Zamorna lay just before us a mile or two distant The rapidly erecting buildings seemed almost white from their own newness and the sudden sunlight. Beyond its capital the province. stretched out far and fertile toward the almost sun eaten Sydenham hills and oh how unlike hot Africa seemed all the watered and glittering expanse Before me and the fresh bright heaven above.

Now just to the left hand of the road as we rattled down the swell. a great shaven. park. swept up from the little village of Edwardston to the. thick clustering Trees and dark green Avenues of a New and Noble Hall That statly mansion with these grounds around it seemed to preside over and command the whole extensive scenery And its wide deer spotted pasture claiming so broad a glow of sunshine its well trimmed hedges and its heavy foliaged woodland. led the eye up nobly to the red rose trees above in the shrubbery and the white portico and glittering windows and the stacks of Grecian chimneys smoking to heaven. over. all. "Whose residence" said I eagerly to the Driver "Is that noble mansion up there." "What yon just on we're[sic] left. hand there Thats Edwardston Hall the place. of. Young Rogue who's the very head of the country a real Angrian he is soul and carcase" "What Is that the seat of. Edward Percy Esqr M P. for Verdopolis and. M P. for Zamorna. Commercial Secretary of Angria Brother to the Queen of the Kingdom Son of Northangerland and Husband of the Princess of Sneachisland. Ah. then I dont wonder at the pride and magnificence of what I see. But whose seat is that. which I see. beyond this of E Percy's and 3 or 4 miles from us. that Old. dark mansion with its enormous and densly wooded park. there" "That Oh its the Generals place Girnington hall the house of the General Thornton the Commander in Cheif and the best lad that ever planted Bayonet. And dont you see straight afore you full under the sunshine over the Olympian there. we shall drive straight past it enow its 9 or 10 miles in yon long stretch of planting thats the seat of young Rattler. our Lieutenant. thats Lord Castlereagh—Aye Angrian he to the Blood and bone."

Well here their lay before me the mansions of three of the most powerful Rulers of. the Rising Kingdom. First the seat of the Commercial Secretary to [the] Government and M P for the province. then the park of a Kings son the Commander in Cheif of the Angrian Army then the grounds of a peer of their Parliament and the Lord. Lieutenant of Zamorna. no wonder that the Capital before me should. be so filled with new and handsome buildings. Zamorna is a small town yet but it must quickly rise.

After gliding past the Hedges of Edwardston Hall and gazing with raised hands to the. Advancing Sun of Angria we soon found ourselves rattling at a quick pace over the pavement of the little half built capital. a large Bridge is built across the wide stream of the Olympian here. broad and deep and Navigable. over this we thundered and beheld the road turning under a long new line of Mills just building by the proprietor of Edwardston every thing in the little streets about us showed that a new era. was <commencing> the. dozens of small craft crowding with their mast poles along the open river. the. large Brick and lime kilns smoking over the dewy feilds the crowds of stout Athletic Builders yellow as their own freestone. and the multitiude of Timber yards yellow indeed between their planks and beams and the morning sunshine. on. one wide ready cleared space I was told that. a Noble Cathedral is about directly to be Erected. on another the stones are even now piled up for the raising of a vast Hall of Commerce. we passed under the framwork of a great brick Hotel. and. turned by a large church where we saw men bearing in great metal pipes and heard the random notes of an Organ Diapason here they were erecting a new instrument. all <   >21

---

21 Branwell's interlinear emendations are undecipherable.

Deeply did this last circumstance strike into the heart of a fellow passenger who sat on my right hand. on the coach top. He was a tall well proportioned Gentlemen about middle. age but of a fair complexion His features good in themselves lacked that Angrian effrontery which however was made up for by the astonishing breadth of his Scarlet Ribbon, Hitherto since we had left the City he had sat although not dificient in apparant health and stoutness both silent and sickly. But when we entered into the Babel of Zamorna he brightened up and began to look around him and. upon his ear catching the Notes of the erecting organ his feelings lightened up and. he slapped his hands on his knee. "Tremendous! Why Sir this beats England. —Oh Zamorna! There is not so improving a place in Africa. I can see the people are quite Geniuses Now I had promised to open an Organ at Falla. upon the northern Calabar. quite a musical place. —Fala—but oh dear this spot is Tremendously superior. I never heard the tone like that of the Instrument they are building—Oh I must dismount Fala may open its own Organ I must procure the situation for this place its a decided opening I can see. that. ah—a—a. really Mr—your name Sir? —a—a are you fond of muisic[sic]?" I believe returned I "that I have the pleasure of addressing Mr Greenwood.[22] the Gentleman from whose skill I have so often imbibed such exquisite delight in St Michaels Cathedral But I fear Sir from your intimation that you have an intention of debarring us that pleasure I hope I misunderstood you?" "Oh not at all. Sir you have a genius do you—play." "No Sir I fear that I should make but an indifferent proficient and. music admits no mediocrity." "Oh. quite mistaken you should practise the violin you a—a—said—you—told me— you feared. I was about to leave your—your what do you call it. —? and really Sir I—I. confess I have intentions—why in fact Zamorna—I cant get it out of my thought that Organ I heard is infinitly superior to Michaels. and besides. I mean to settle down. I must give over wandering or it'll give over me I assure you that City is my situation for Life Why I have been so weakened by my voyage to Stumps Isle. that I have not yet recovered any thing like my usual spirits In landing on the wharf. there. my knees quite knocked together as I walked. and on the voyage I was indeed tremendously ill. I felt myself sick. after I had been striving to close my ear. against some of the most frivolous tunes you could imagine The ships band was playing them they were quite frivolous a—a—a—nd I called for a tumbler and a bottle of brandy. I poured the spirits into it. neat Brandy you know a neat it was and so I drank it Oh but it made [me] the sicker and so I ordered in a a bowl and. some meal and some water I put them onto the fire and. made a tremendous large bowl of stirabout.[23] it was a tremendous basin I. took it. but oh it only made [me] the sicker Oh I vomited I

---

[22]   At the celebration of the installation of an organ in Mr. Brontë's church, March 1834, the guest organist was John Greenwood, former Keighley organist, who had gone to live in London; see Barker Brontë, 210-211. Compare Alexander CB II, part ii, 109-112; 251-52.

[23]   A porridge of oatmeal or cornmeal stirred in boiling water or milk.

vomited Sir a—a why a—just as I did when I took the mixture yon evening—
well Ill never see Stumps Island again. I say they should have pedal pipes to this
Organ at Zamorna.[24] Stop heres an Inn. Ill just take a glass of mixture and. then
Ill back to that church Ill settle down and I can see theres an opening there."

As this Genius. who although a prodigy for musical talent. is the most
wandering and easy minded being extant. —as he ceased speaking the coach
entered into the only little street of a small village which straggled for some
distance in front of the road.

It was a rough spot and the street I have named. seemed blocked up
before us with a. wild mob. of riotous peasantry They wedged in a dense crowd
more particularly round the door of the public house which spread the Sun of
Angria in ensign above their heads. I observed besides the usual chaos of Rare
apes. dressed in shirtless and red Ribboned dishabille a knot of ragged urchins
holding about a score of. well conditioned and handsome horses. half a dozen
carriages stationed neath the coach roof. and all the signs about the building of.
something of consequence proceeding within. Gentlemen aye and Gentlemen
whom I knew too I saw riding up along the road at a rapid rate They uniformly
dismounted at this Inn and entered it with the most violent eagerness. Its landlord
stood in the midst of the hubbub wiping his bald forehead from the perspiration
dealing out the goes of whisky to the crowds and pocketting the reckoning with
wearyed exhaustion every moment his minions bolted from the interior of the
Edifice and in he bustled with officious haste. In this state of affairs the Angrian
Mail thundered through the crowd and drew up amid the hubbub From my fellow
passengers I only heard the exclamation "Its come on has it? 10 to 1 on the old
one" They percipitated themselves into the whirlpool and rushed into the
"public" I entered also but oh can I forget the astounding confusion which
seemed to reign within that rest for the weary Three Gigantic "rare ones" and as
many fierce soldiers occupied the passage With an Argument like thunder 12 red
Ribboned Angrians crammed the Taproom with measures of liquor and in the
kitchin or "House" the settle was crowded hats and heads rose over the Oaken
partition voices were heard "2 to 1. on Eta. 3 to 2 on Zeta—a plumper to the old
one 90 to 9 on the Old one. Zeta's the go death to. the cold ones." There was a
smacking of whips a clash of pewter a jingle of <glasses> and a chinking of
money which almost drowned these obstreperous voices. "Oh these Angrians" I
sighed. and pressed through the crowd towards the better rooms. Lo at the first I
was stopped by 2 servants in Green and scarlet—!!! who swords drawn stood at
the closed door. The royal ensign of the country was stamped on their arms.
"Sufficient for the day is the evil thereof."[25] said I. as I loitered on down the
stairs From the upper rooms hurried a host of Gentlemens servants and waiters
in slippers bearing salvers and coffee and Brandy and refreshment and whole
Dozens of wine. many of these servants astounded me by their badges of Noblity

---

[24] A separate set of brass toned pipes worked by a foot pedal.
[25] Compare Matthew 6:34.

aye and higher than Nobility. I. walked up Jacobs ladder[26] The large apartment was open before me. a long table or two was spread out not with eatables but with gold. Crowds of well dressed gentlemen surrounded it loud was the conversation and direful the swaggering amid them. I thought I knew several— on sudden a young Gentleman middle height light complexioned and strong made walked forth and came across me. "General"—cried I in astonishment. Thornton laughed loudly and dissapeared. I was about to enter the room but a menial stopped me. "Do you bets Sir." "No" said I. he turned me back. he was a servant of Royalty well. I walked toward another apartment where the chinking of cash was prodigious. At this moment the awful voice "Coach ready" roared. over the tumult from below. As I passed hurriedly to reach it I beheld Mr Greenwood seated amid a crowd of listners his violin in his hand and the music issuing in a "glitter" of sound. well I sprung on to the coach the other pasengers did the same and we moved slowly toward the middle of the street while there they were harnessing the leader the Landlord appeared at the portal of the Inn he shouted "They've started by the back door" and directly with a horrid shout of Zamorna for ever the whole enormous crowd rushed together round the street it was clear directly Our coachman cried to us. "We go by the new road it turns on to their path. just quarter of a mile <ahead> and we shall at em then." He lashed his steeds with fury they flew off on their road. as we hurried like lightning through the dust I saw crowds of "Angrians" leaping over the hedges toward the old path. I was struck dumb my companions were hoarse with <betting> Zeta and Eta and Sigma. were roared from their stentor lungs. The road swept round an Angle and a dense mass of Humanity appeared blocking up all [the] path before us "drive over them" cried the Officers and I verily believe the coachman obeyed. In a minute our vehicle was reined up before the old road to Angria and I saw sweeping away on either side and to east and west almost to infinity a dense line of human beings Far and wide on either hand the <feilds> flew with a thousand runners flinging themselves along the outskirts like the sharp shooters in an Army a tumult of motions but a silence of voices pervaded the whole vast multitude—I looked hurriedly down toward the west. or beginning of the smooth vacant road. all eyes were turned there

Lo forward moving with quick descisive step two PEDESTRIANS. two very. Tall and finelooking young Men dressed in close fitting white jacket and pantaloons and girt about the waist with a simple scarlet sash on their heads they wore each a light foraging cap and forward the[y] walked like two haughty red deer. behind them came another Pedestrian a very Ancient and withered scare crow of mean proportions. habited in a respectable and veteran snuff coloured coat and unmentionable unmentionables This strange old scoundrel however instead of striving to keep on with his more splendid rivals just stopped in the middle of the road as he said with a discordant laugh to "Buckle his breeks tight" The other two advanced—. I have said they were very tall and must add they were

---

[26] See Genesis 28:12.

very handsome. The tallest. to an Appollo like form which his close white dress so noble[sic] set off. added a countenance whose rich curls marble forehead and an eye. which spurned creation heugh!. that face. struck my blood to my heart The second if not by perhaps an. inch so tall as the first was equally formed and in face though of a lighter complexion almost as haughty [in] his eager aspect. Oh those two faces those two faces—that walk. that aspect. the intense the adoring looks of the multitude chilled—terrified me

Hah when as they two the rival pedestrians. passed by the coach. side by side with august and arrogant step. I with violence smothered a rising Oath. (aye an oath from me) ZAMORNA and E PERCY. passed before me. —did not my flesh creep.

Aye reader the Newly crowned Monarch of Angria His Majesty Arthur Adrian Duke of Zamorna and Edward Percy the allied to Royalty the ruler of a countrys Commerce. —both strode along the road among a crowd of excited thousands on a PEDESTRIAN MATCH of 100 miles (!) to be performed from Edwardston and Adrianopolis [f]or a stake. of SIXPENCE—and. in one. journey

My head was bewildered one huge question of what will the world say for ever sounded in my ears and a cry answered it What will History say Just after these Princes of effrontery passed by me. their mutual contender R P Sdeath. walked across the stage. he stopped with an air of scorn "Aw think" said he "A ull gie thi young uns a start a ull just stepp back and hae a sup o drink an's be up wi em in a VARRY FAEW DAYS." amid the roar and clapping of the united myriads this August Hero returned blowing his nose toward the inn.

Now I saw the two pedestrians stopping with feirce looks a hundred yards in front. a vast host collected clamouring round them and 6 Gentlemen on horseback. gallopped up from the starting place. —Our coach was whipped forward toward them it drew up and we gazed as if on death "Well Arthur you are a villain I will have us weighed you may exculpate yourself as you please youre a blackguard." "Say so again Edward and our match becomes a boxing one. Why fool what matters it if—" "What matters you swindler what matters if I bear 3 stone weight and you one." "Stop your sophistry or take care of a sound kicking" —The Earl of Arundel Zamornas backer and General Thornton Edwards backer interposed at the same time. "What in the name of earth is all this Zamorna." "Just what are you bickering over now Percy" "Why this Born scoundrel carrys no <catch>. and I have carried one thinking he did the same is he to go unburdened and I. <laden> —? Fair! —we shall go back and begin again" Zamorna laughed loudly his supreme and unforgettable laugh. Edward Percy inflamed almost to the whole height of his passionate character seemed about to make a rush at him the seconds and Backers were nigh bursting with merriment the huge multitudes wrangling over their favorites At this instant a strange Old fashioned or rather utterly (incomprehensible) Equipage with six horses maned and <lasted> —wheeled up from no one knew where. The quizzical outriders in curious livery Breeches powder and knee buckles hurried to the open door it burst sidewayes and outstepped a tall Gentleman of about <50> years of age 2 long swords stuck under his arm cocked hat in hand a vast redundant pomatumed 3 tailed wig on his pate—his garments a mulberry long tailed coat. a <massive> seven barred waistcoat. all Mechlin. in his Ruffles and half Potosi in his knee buckles.[27]

Ere he had with inexpressible ludicrousity advanced 3 paces toward the disputants he returned to the coach took therefrom 2 more swords and stowing them all under the left arm he again made his leg toward the group. They parted aghast The apparition with a smile of self complacency walked on he took the hand of the petrified Zamorna in one ruffled paw that of the incensed Edward in the other. Then clearing his voice with a smiling <tongue>

"Permit me my lord Duke and you Sir too express my pleasure at this meeting Really Gentlemen will you allow your countenances to be so changed from your Makers image your feelings so <raught> from the politeness of the mode as to indulge in this altercation—I have naturally had a proud an[d] passionate disposition and I have checked it conscious of the respect. I owed myself. for the memory of. a father of spirit and fashion My Birth and fortune and Oh for you was—hardly wise to act as you do now. look not so my dear freinds I am your deliverer. —I confess my heart is naturally good and my temper to sensitive of affecting incidents my feelings are too tender for my peace of mind and I have striven to soothe them by the exertion [of] every <beautiful> sentiment by acting as the greatest and best of men I. permit me to retire for a moment this scene too much affects me."

This astounding figure. turned toward the carriage. Zamorna and Percy looked at each other with a mutual stare of astonishment. Then they burst simultaneously into a loud laugh The figure turned round with what he doubtless in the simplicity of his head thought a look of winning and. easy serenity he stepped up and saying "My education has taught me a trick peculiar to those who understand the art of defence" he made an adroit clutch at the sash of the disputants meaning I should suppose a rush a[t] the pocket. —Lo an astounding kick and a horrid oath from the two pedestrian[s] hurled him on his weapons prostrate on the earth Somehow he and his <elaborate> equipage dissapeared amid the crowd Eta and Zeta with a loud laugh flung away the offending watch. They started on their journey and the hugh crowd closed behind them

The coach rushed forth in pursuance of the Royal and Lofty PEDESTRIANS OF ANGRIA

"All is for the best" muttered I to myself as with my eyes fixed to my feet I pondered deeply over the scenes I had seen. and laughed as the words struck my ear. Well Richton thought I going as Ambassador to the Court of Angria, Angria whose peasants are princes and whose kings are the runners of a race the 6 penny match makers truely the delight <because> the amusement of their

---

[27] "Mechlin" refers to a fine lace made in that Belgian city, with the design clearly outlined by a thread; also called "malines." "Potosi" is a town in Bolivia, well known in the nineteenth century for its production of silver.

.subjects go and prosper thy course will be wonderfully easy[28] Aye but where is this strange course to end I know that now I see a King degrading himself to the least of his common subjects scarce a week after his Coronation and since his course is certainly so downward and so rapid to what depth will he have sunk a year after that awful ceremony. Angria seems to admire him and to proceed in his own plan of action and if so where to shall it have sunk—where shall we all shortly sink. Truly this New Kingdom may appear brilliant in its foundation and may seem to open new paths to those who are weary of the old Rejime But let all those sanguine hearts beware I fancy myself a tolerable prophesier of our future and truely I foresee nothing from that gift of an Empire But a cloud which shall rise on Angria and shall fall on Adrianopolis Aye. Reader I almost fear that Henceforward the pen which now writes these lines to you must act as the miserable recorder of the Decline and Fall of Africa.[29] These splittings these partitions from the mainbody these unhappy divisions in everybody have allways been the sure forerunners of disolution and Decay Who does not see the so strongly marked and so seperate parties which which[sic] the Glasstowners are divided into now those differences are becoming more apparent every day. Who can see when or how they can unite Then who cannot see to what and where they must tend.

I was awakened from a reverie on the horrors of civil war by. the thundering sound of our coach as if passing a bridge I looked up and around me. we were passing over a bridge a line of noble arches spanning the broad and brilliant Olympian. Just on our left hand. northward that River in a sheet of lake like silver opened and expanded itself to receive the Tributary Wave. and they two then united flowed calm underneath the roadway all down the rich country toward the South till lost amid its blue feilds and trees and villiages round the distant sea. Just before us the fine handsome town of Hartford[30] rose above the left bank of the Olympian and the new lines of building stretched up its banks toward the rich park like or corn waving scenery so often met with in this delightful province.

It was now high Noon and. we drew up at the Scarlet Banner whose. imposing front of glittering windows reared over one side of the principal street of Hartford.

Now the whole of the aforsaid principal street was thoroughly choked with a crowd of uproarious Angrians. all gazing eagerly in expectation of their *rising Sun* The Babel like chaos of cries and confusion which struck my ear as our coach turned whirling round the street corner seemed to prove the good. people of the place. to be excited above all ordinary limits "Here they come."

---

28   Compare I Kings 22:12 and 15.
29   Clearly an allusion to Gibbon's *The History of the Decline and Fall of the Roman Empire*.
30   Towns of this name are located in both Cambridgeshire and Cheshire.

"No there not out yet" "listen its a wheel match" <"Its> the Angrian coach" "No it[s] the very men." "90 to 1. <20> on Adrian "The men! The Matches! The cock of the walk." "Whoa its the coach." "Ho Hang em burn em drown em away with em— "Any News Any News Wheres the Walkers have you met em Out with your budget How far off are they—" —Such and such like were the exclamations which rose round our vehicle like the smoke of incense as it drew up before the Inn The annoyance was overpowering I jumped of the coach pressed through the mass of expectation and ran into a little opened parlour which invited me from the passage. A sombre cloud. filled the little room as I entered Humph thought I the Rooms[sic] smokes—no the Narcotic vapour parted and lo six and thirty sparks disposed round the apartment smoking sigars and vociferating prophecies "Ho Sir passenger. Whats the news—Have you seen them—which is formost Arthur. go to—Percy—you viper. Stopp. you ass tell us—stop—" I did not stop cursing the two pedestrians most audibly I rushed forth toward another harbour. and in steering through the vaulted passage. ran stern formost full against the scarlet coachmen of our vehicle "Sir" he said upon recovering from the shock with a doggedness from which I argued no good. "Sir the company our Fare have come to the tarmination as how it'll be more convenienter for them to rest a few hours till midnight. like at this place. —its a comfortable spot. Sir—and wait till the cocks comes up. sir and. as how our Masters would If they knew the reasons agree to our stopping a few minutes and so we have put up the nags. Sir & as good beasts as ever stepped they are. and. we've made bold to exasperate your worship upon the subject it ll be a great hurt to us to stop and"—"Aye you have made bold to exasperate me I think. dont lie man look at your waistcoat pocket what is the amount of your bribery. a years wages eh?. and am I to stop 8 hours for two rascally Gamesters a curse to—" I had gone too far The crowd looked dangerous I made a halt completed the curse in my heart and edging through the multitude. I turned down a lane to the riverside stepped over a stile entered a delightful meadow and determined to take a walk to the residence of my old friend Col Hartford of Hartford House. I knew near this town he lived but of the locality of the spot I was not so certain— "Ho" I cried to a fellow who was hurrying down the feilds toward the town "which is the road to Hartford House." "What Lad are they come do you say?" was the stentorian answer "Are you mad" I retorted. "point me the path to Hartford House" The Gentleman had now stept up he was a stout rare ape his eyes directed full on to the high road from Edwardston "The path to the hall dye want Why youll just turn down this feild and then cross just ower the cornings by the river and go up by the bankside keeping straight forrard to your reight hond till you get to the upper laithe where youll just turn to the left hond ower the Rareheys till you cross the bridge at the Burn foot. then youll turn up the valley just above yon trees there and go straight through the feild path toward the Hills till you get to the four lanes ends where youll just turn to the park gates and go up by the old Hall old Hartford Hall they call it you can see it my rare ape just ower the feilds up bye there well when you pass beyond the Old Hall you get to the 3 mile stone on the road straight to the Hill you cross ower a feild nearest way and then turn down back lane side toward your left hond. till you reach Sixlane top where you turn to your right just <swinging> toward your left to Little Hartford and there theyll show you the streight road to Hartford Hall. —Have they come on yet my rare—" "Now Fool have mercy upon me why you ass do you fancy I. find my path in such a <cretan> labyrinth as you describe There must be a clearer road to Hartford or if not the place must be desolate?"— "Why my Rare ape theres the High road just by us which runs streight by the Old Hall and so on to the park." "In the name of reason why did not you point that out to me first" "Haw why as how tother is the clean nearer gate.[31] Are the cocks getten to the town yet?" without waiting for an answer to this all absorbing question the fellow cleared the Hedge at a leap and dash[e]d. down the feild whistling "Sound the loud Trumpet" as he ran to meet his sovereign laughing at the idiocy with which our peasantry cling to a road. one inch shorter than another. if it should even lead through fire and water. I pursued my way to the Colonels residence

    A quiet and secluded walk through the meadows and up a Hawthorn lane brought me to the shattered and dilapidated gateway of what seemed once to have been some extensive park but which was now converted into extensive feilds and pastures but the luxuriant cultivation they exhibited and the Huge statly trees which here and there stood up amid the grass gave sufficient token amid all this neglect of what here had once surrounded that tall dark pile of Balls and Gables which underneath its ancient rookery overlooked the expanse from the bare swell of ground above—toward this old Edifice I bent my steps and as I approached its front the—total abscence of a garden the doors of different appearance. the tubs and mops which graced their portals the poultry and the pigs all warned me that this Hall had shared amply in the changes of a sublunary life had sunk in grandeur as its park had decayed and like it was now divided and changed from its original destination. The Afternoon was so serene and warm that passing beyond the inhabited parts of the Building I halted in the shadow of a large projecting and ruined Gable and. there underneath the boughs of an old elm tree sat down to gaze on the wide prospect before me and to ruminate over the strange fortunes of Angria and Africa. At this hour the sun was approaching toward the horizon and. over my head the deep blue sky was only chequered by the black boughs and foliage of the great hanging Elms What clouds the day had produced all seemed to have collected in the west where their airy mass of red and golden light had put on their brightest adorning to welcome their approaching sovereign the Sun. Before me beyond the desolate clumps of park trees which rose like ruins above the feilds stretched out in fair luxuriance the whole rich plains of Southern Zamorna. and the white buildings of. Hartford with [the] flashing sheet of the Olympian gave to this wide scene below the same softened brilliancy which the Italian clouds of Afternoon did to the blue heaven above. As I sat. marking the ground with my cane and beating down the weeds from a little neglected rose tree

---

[31] "Gate" is used here in the Scottish sense of "way."

beside me. the warm genial sunshine glowed on my face [and] spread my shadow darkly behind me. Now amid all this repose of Nature. how will Mans mind turn toward himself and his own repulsive ongoings ere 10 minutes had elapsed from the time I sat down I caught myself. a politician and. Ambassador to an Empire. deeply and busily engaged in running over the aspect of this adopted country and moaning over the wretched instability of my maternal Ministry Sundry mere gross political machinations I had engaged in were engrossing the whole of my attention when. a tap over the shoulder awakened me to consciousness of my present more delightful situation I started up and beheld standing behind me my Old freind Col Hartford—on Horseback and turned toward Hartford. after mutual recognitions and all the et cetera of meeting freindship mingled with the everlasting "Have they arrived yet?" I entered into conversation with him upon this Old Hall under which we stood "Colonel" said I "This ancient and neglected House with its perhaps once noble park now turned into pasture as an Old Hunter is turned to the cart. interests me much. Does it Belong to yourself. —For it bears your name. How did it slide into this venerable decay" "What this old Building Richton just Behind us. Well come come on to Hartford House with me I suppose the Cocks wont enter Hartford till Evening we can then go back together—Ha this old place could unfold a tale if it dared to speak. I know little comparitively of the causes of its decline and fall and can only give a mere sketch of things which might be swelled into a novel—It never either belonged to me or my family for we The Hartfords of Hartford House are only distant Branches of the Hartfords which lived at the Hall All that I know about it may be summed up in a very few words indeed—About 17 or 18 years ago when I was only a Lad Sir Edward Hartford. resided there. the head of that family and a very wealthy Baronet in these parts. an active improving man more likely to get into a speculation than out of one You know at that time Hartford was the very centre of. the whole wide and luxuriant grazing district of Zamorna. and its yearly cattle fair was the most celebrated and best frequented in all the east side of Verdopolis I distinctly recollect in the year before I went to the Philosophers Island. what a week of preparation there was before that fair Folk said that it would that season prove quite as large as ever It had done before. The principal Inn was forestalled for some Great Grazier from the west country who had sent to appropriate lodgings stands and pasture for no body could tell how many head of cattle. I being an active country Lad then was down every evening at the Inn for it may be a whole week before the opening day and. that time I did look out for this New Dealer whom men talked so much on During 5 or 6 days the cattle had been arriving from all parts but it was not till Friday evening that I heard them say those great stocks which we looked for were at. Zamorna and shortly would come in on Saturday Evening I was standing on the steps of the Hartford Arms. with the ostlers looking at the different beasts entering when we saw coming up the street 6 or 7. Gentlemen on Horseback. talking and laughing loudly to each other the beasts they rode were as exquisite animals as I had ever beheld and the riders most of them looked very unlike graziers and cattle dealers there was one to be sure a little scrappy old cheif. in a long brown coat and drovers boots with

a hat such as tops many a potato feild who by the way he bestrode his gaunt
grey nag and his hoarse. laugh and discordant voice might be as much underneath
a decent Drover as the rest looked above it. However they all alighted at this
cheif Inn. and. one of them without speaking strode up the steps and into the
passage. he passed me. and [I] saw him. a very tall Gentlemanly figure. in deep
mourning black. with a walking cane and white kid gloves gathered in one hand I
looked up at his face as he strode by. It was laughing or just fininshing a laugh
with such a distorted glance of the eye and such a sneering lip that I had fifty
times rather seen him swear as I did do than have witnessed such a laugh again
"Marry come up" said the second gentleman to the ostler as he with his
companions rattled up the steps after the first. "why volo. If you dont lug your
wits out at your mouth we will out at your brain. Death!. man. we have
<entered> your public here and when Rougues bent his annointed head under
your threshold Dye think. you are to stand idle for an instant—No not if you
were on your death bed. 3 dozen of Claret and a gallon of Brandy your Roads are.
infernally dusty" "Yes" cried a third among them a reckless looking scamp "Yes
And who was it I wonder to day when the drove raised such a cloud on the tramp.
who shook in his skin fancying it was the Bottomless pit opening all its smoke
before him and when the red Bull No 390 tossed up its horns in the air my faith!
who roared so that we couldnt hear a beast whisper for an hour after Volo he
made me look behind me" "Aye" answered the other a very grim sour scoundrel.
"And. what said you O Connor when you looked behind you and only saw the
tail of the white heifer for the beast" "Why I roared. Im caught by the Old One.
and now I think. Ive caught tail and horns and hooves too not of. a white heifer
but a black Gordon"[32] "Na <behave> yourseln. or Ill call one amang ye wholl
clap ye all six and tail and hooves and wings and fire and brimstone o top on
em" thus grated the harsh voice of. the scarecrow as they all entered storming in
to the Hotel.

      Well here were the Western Drovers sure enough and my faith! the town
knew it eer long the place was every night in such an uproar as never was heard
before Rougues set were All Night long laughing and swearing and playing
jokes but jokes of such a bloodthirsty nature as set all In arms against them and
then out comes Rougue himself and bangs his pistols among the crowd with an
oath that fairly drowned the report of two great Double shotted Duellers[33] Aye
that fair was a memorable one and the Rougue transacted such buisness and
brought by his fame such a myriad. of. buyers that folk fancied Hartford was

---

[32] A play on the name of Rougue's associate; Gordan was Byron's family name
and the name of Douro's first wife.

[33] Double-barreled flint lock duelling pistols, with the barrels side by side or
over and under. Lord Castlereagh fought a duel with Mr. Canning, the Foreign
Secretary, in 1809 over the ill fated Wacheren expedition, in which Canning was
hit in the thigh. Castlereagh was also hit, but the shot bounced off a button on
his coat.

becoming a city in the twinkling of an Eye. As for Rougue he never spoke to a Hartfordian without swearing him down for an < > blackguard. One night of the fair the people set on him in a dark street but he so handled a set of them that no body dared look at him afterward. and then there was one man who had brought an action against him at the Justices Aye that man he was so handled in riding home to Wareham that he died in 3 months after

Well Im straying rather from my story If it can be called one. This Rougue. being of most astonishingly fine aspect and. conversation wheedled himself directly into the highest place among the highest circles at Hartford. Why it was considered a great honour when one day he alighted from his splendid. Horse. at the Door of Hartford House my fathers place you know he was so up to every thing that after the mishap which befell. young Lord Cartington that week. nobody dare bet a sixpence with him and then his countenance was so refined and his voice so musical. (Oh I thought him a scoundrelly hypocrite) that Drover or no Drover he directly engaged all the Ladies of the Halls in his behalf. They sounded for ever the praises of his melancholy and Deeply meaning smile but for my part I saw nought melancholy about him I recollect he beat my father one night by. 2 bottles of claret. and then he. got up and went out of the house swearing and black balling himself as he strode quickly but. coolly along He seemed to consider himself quite above everyone. and. when among the cattle he paid no attention to the wonder with which all saw him handle the most ferocious beast on the fair He would take a rampant Horse grasp it firmly by the nose and talked and laughed as at nothing while the mad animal sweated and trempled[sic] in his grasp. Aye I never saw a man so subdue the fury of a beast only his cruelty was brutish.

Well this Rougue sold. Sir Edward Hartford a thousand pounds worth of first raters and visited while he staid at Hartford. that Hall down there every day it was not the place it is now Richton he. pretended to affect a mighty regard for the Baronet and soon entered into some deep gambling transaction with him. I can[t] tell you by what atrocious peice of acting he brought the Baronet in a fortnights time head over ears in difficultys then he humbugged him into some intricate juggle in cattle trading affected to put him again into fair water gave him a note of hand to an unlimited time laughed at the thoughts of Sir Edward paying him his due and swore he should directly be worth twice the sum he owed him. Now Sir Edward had a son. young squire. a freind of mine. Rougue had infatuated him I think. for he almost talked of going as one of Rougues Riders only the Arch Feind one night so swore and sneered him down that I think it cured him of the thought Hartford had. a daughter too. the Honourable Miss Amelia Hartford. She was then 19 Aye she was. an Angel. to look at. she was as beautiful as a lily. the very pride and boast of the country and so. tall and graceful and so Aristocratically Accomplished that one could scarce call her lower than a princess. her pride and haughtiness seemed a robe. over her own sunny spirit—I saw Rougue when he was first introduced to the Hall. he bent on her such a look with his strange blue eyes a long calm unobstrusive look and a singular faint smile I thought his conversation that Night (for I was there) was most astonishingly brilliant. I could scarce leave listening to it. —Aye Richton often then on such a sweet Afternoon as this is I met him and Amelia Hartford walking together in this very spot it was then a thickly wooded park. He looked like a Nobleman and spoke to no one who passed save her. Well. she felt his character and appearance I believe he told her more of himself than. he did anyone else there. Her mind was not of that character to lose the impression which he knew it had received. However Rougue soon left Hartford with his gang. carrying with him all the brains I believe and power over all the property of. Sir Edward Hartford he had humbugged the Baronet effectually. I have since heard that one of his strange sallies was as he turned. down the Avenue to those about him by exclaiming that Hartford Hall was falling and he said to his gang as they passed down the park. "Have I not fine grounds here you moles"

Well many months passed on. after all this I think it was in the winter of the year. that Amelia Hartford Left the Hall on a visit to the residence. [of] Col. St John Streighton at Pequena. (I have since known. that this St. John was a deep colleague of Rougues) He was a branch of the Hartford family As she left. the Hall I heard she looked back with a very sorrowful eye. She knew what others did not. But Amelia Hartford was more splendid than good. yet she was as near an angel as anyone could be. However that was a weary day at the Hall when St John himself came riding like fury to Hartford he was a dark treacherous looking man. He brought news that. Miss Amelia had. been carried off by the Africans while returning from a ride on the banks of Guadima. Well I heard those say who should know that men were seen on that day it was a wild stormy evening who though black as smoke. were not much like Africans. —But however that be amid the distress at the Hall I then left Hartford House for the Philosophers Island.

Here I remained 3 years at my studies and during that time the fame of Rougue had fled far and wide. —I am firmly assured that as I during a short vacation was walking through a Dark. dense wood in Stumphs land I saw walking up a long secluded alley of trees. the very figures of. Alexander Percy as Rougues real name was now known to be. and Amelia Hartford. I could not be mistaken for neither of the two once seen could be forgotten nor could any two be found like them. Now when 14 years ago I returned to Hartford. from the Island I hurried up the river side eager to reach Hartford House. Very soon I got to the park gates of the Old Hall. I just looked almost inclined to call. —where was the porters lodge. it was gone. the Day was very misty and rainy I thought I was deceived in the place. I ran inside the gate. There I saw stone walls running across the shaven verdure. corn and grass springing up where the deer fed before. Huge piles of unbarked timber laid on the ground the remnants of once glorious forest monarchs the road up [to] the house was turned into a common hedge path I ran up the walk to the Hall. lo it stood before me in the rain shut up. almost windowless the knockers stripped from the Doors the flight of steps torn from their places and the shattered windows shaking in their frames. —When I gained home I learnt the mystery of all this 2 years ago. Officers arrived at the Hall arrested. Sir Edward for a vast amount of Depts[sic] due to A Percy. Esqr. and.

conveyed him in a carriage to Verdopolis the Baronet a sanguine man broke down under the blight on his family he died in a fever in jail and. the Hated Percy soon arrived in a coach and 4 at Hartford. with lawyers and so forth to seize upon the Estate Young Hartford who had been absent on the frontiers in the Army upon hearing the astounding intelligence. of his familys ruin hurried to Hartford like lightning he met Percy standing upon his fathers door stones. sternly and heartlessly commanding the demolition of the park. Few words did Hartford bestow on him and the other. calmly smiling beckoned him into the woods Nothing more was heard of young Hartford. The grounds were laid in ruins Percy let the Hall in cottages and. soon after left the place. Hartford Hall he has never since visited. The rents are received by his steward Steaton and this is all I know about. the ruin of an ancient house—". And is this" I said. "Another Act. of the Earl of Northangerland. of the Premier of Angria! "Sir" answered the Colonel. "The Nation hates him. He will hardly keep his place over the first session of our parliament" "Probably not" I answered drily. I could hardly tell what to think of. a speech like this

    After a few pleasant hours spent at Hartford House the residence of my hospitable freind and entertainer who is a very wealthy and influential Gentleman member for Hartford and owner of many of the Olympian Hills I prepared again to return to the town lest the coach after its prolonged stay should set of without me. My host too was restless to the last degree. to be at the scene of action the entry of the pedestrians proceeding on foot we arrived at. the Old Hall just as the very last sunbeam slanted over the country and here I stopped to take one look at the venerable Gables and windows of the dilapidated mansion my feeling regarding it heightened by my knowledge of its melancholy history—when the colonel caught my arm and cried "Listen" He clapt his ear toward the town from whence the gale was blowing I did ditto and heard the stray soft notes of. a Band of Music floating through the air. "Richton" said my companion agonizedly "Theyve got into the town." He rushed down the lane and I followed. as we approached the scene of. action the. rising bursts of the "Angrian ONWARD"[34] swelled more audibly from the fronting rows of building. How suddenly after crossing the Bridge did we emerge from the still quiet country to the stir and rattle of the town. clattering shoals of humanity swept huzzaing through the thoroughfares and in the principal street just before the scarlet Bedizened Hotel two Military Bands from the Angrian foot guards were rousing and inspiring the tumult. "Brandy to the drunken" I muttered while the Colonel gasped out. "Have they passed." to the nearest ongoer. "No your honour But theyll be here presently" was the releiving Answer hearing this. while Hartford joined a crowd of Noblemen and Gentlemen. under the Exchange portal. I stepped on to the flags round my hotel door. If I had flags under my feet. I had certainly flags above my head. for out over almost all the Numerous windows of the Inn front before me a Scarlet Banner or a scarlet ribbon—fluttered in the gale. The Entry

---

[34] Probably a reference to **Sound the Loud Trumpet**—see p. 204 above.

of the House was so choked with people that it was with the utmost difficulty I could force my way to the nearest room door and there on gazing down the long line of close Atmosphere and great lighted gas lamps. I only saw a waving tossing ocean of heads and Hats and uplifted arms I despairingly attacked one door <but> it was fast locked and its front bore in chalked letters. "For Lord Cartingtons Suite." another I attempted a servant tripped up "This Sir is marked down for the Earl [of] Arundel." "Then" said I "where is the public room "Oh its just laid out for. his Grace and Mr Edward with their seconds" "Are any of the upper rooms empty" No they are bespoke or occupied for Lord Danceton. the Warners the Primate of Angria. young Grenville and. various Noblemen and Gentlemen in the country" "Lord! why Im a nobleman too" I cried in misery amid the jambling and beating of the passengers. "In that case" said the servant scraping "would your honour accept of a seat in the great Travellers Room its the only one open there are many Noblemen in it we <u>really</u> are so full to day that we cannot tell how to shift" So saying I followed the menial through a dense mass of. confusion. to where. just under that vast height of ceiling up which ran the great <soaring> stairs a bright <blaze> of Gaslight. flared from a wide opened door. alas what. comfort could I expect from an Apartment however large into which I saw streaming compactly and steadily in a thick line of motley existence as I have beheld. enter some great place of meeting on an important day And out of which I heard proceeding such a wild torrent of voices as you hear roaring from a rough Ocean on a rocky shore I could not tell when I had got into this room for still I formed the centre of the same dense passage. however when I beheld the red vivid firelight flashing through the chinks in the fronting wall of shoulders and glinting amid the pillars which upheld them then I made the grand advance attacked the battlements and fairly carried the place by storm. dire was the push which I made over an overthrown form and table ere I reached the broad blazing fireplace where ranged round the hearth on their long groaning settles sat a black ridge of Angrians shouting swearing and betting to the running accompaniment of a jingling and clashing and clattering of pints and pence and glass and crockery "Well" shouted at the top of his very powerful voice a thin Gentleman in black. with a shattered aspect and hair and eyes and neckerchief all dashed awry. "Well Volo what I say is as clear as a quart and by the same token Ill stick to it as Id stick to a quart. D'ye think you thrice hanged villain that Im to be beaten out of a theory by you Why Sir Id have you to know Ive been on the seas Sir on the high seas and on the high ways for that matter. Ive heard the music of the waves and the music of the gales and the music of the airs and the music of the spheres and when I know the practice of such harmonies as yon am I not. I say a fit fellow for finding the theory of the music of the earth Music of the earth Indeed Why Volo so long as its created by such a scoundrel as you. pretty music its like to be Aye! the mans not such a man as you who plays the organs in the moon—Volo why I in a manner when we were in Norway. it was a cold night oh an abominable Night. I had you see just taken a cordial or I should have heard the music of a frying pan instead of such a tune as I did hear— Well I was just walking over the Ice same as I might be doing now over the floor and all of a sudden on turning a corner to avoid a—a why to—to—Death! because I couldnt go straight on—. I weakened with the intense frost. My brain reeled and down I came ower my heels upon my head which gave just 30 bumps upon the knotty Iron Ice. I lay like a pine log and hadnt time to get up ere a Buzz Buzz Birled through my ears I feared my Brains were concushioned. Cushioned they were I know—But ere I could find out what con-should have to do with the matter Volo the Buzz changed to such a jig jig and whistle that I intended to clap my hand to my face to see wether my eye[s] were dancing a reel with my nose over my forehead. But. my Hands were chained as fast as Gullivers[35] that night he took. the Brandy (Ive a theory on those ligatures) and so I turned the whites of my eyes toward the Heavens Thought I O Connor its like youve drunk a drop to much and the can is dry youll want a glass where youre going to or Im much misgiven and its fitter for you to go down with a prayer in your mouth than a song in your ears—<even> and so I began to pray but for the life of me I couldnt put up a single petition but. "A taste of the creature Tom". "Bob a kiss of the Cleary". Oh Ned—carry I say. just one other rond before we reef the mainsail."[36] and the like profane words and sentences well just as I was singing out in this fashion—I hears the noise of which I just spoke increasing like a cannon Just out about my head and ears I thought—Now something like a carriage coming without wheels it was plain was coming up behind me and roaring out lest it should roll over me I. turned my eye to the back of my head like a spider. There was a famous fat round pot bellied fellow sitting at my head grinding away upon a large round yellow Ball that he held on his knee. it was as big as a hogshead and shone like a Jack O lanthorn a handle stuck out of the side and this he twirled round as folk do a barrel organ "Says I to he—"My man this is a cold Night to be playing in that way now Ive not a rap about me or we would adjourn to an Alehouse—better a jig there than a psalm tune anywhere else. My—Volo that is an organ youve got. my man" Says the little fat man to me <heckling> all the while and his little beady eyes glittering in their deep sockets. "Its much you know my friend either of me or my instrument. I say just look up into the sky its full moon to night." Well I dared not refuse to do as he bid me he spoke as up to command as Rougue himself could do Says I. "I see no moon hereabouts Why theres only a round black hole in the sky just between those clouds there" "Humpha" says he "Now my friend do you know who I am" he looked at me so as he said these words. that for the life of me I could not help roaring like a bull "Oh Im going my sins have gotten me hes come to take me. Oh—" "Hold your tongue" he cried snappishly and gave me a kick with his foot just as Rougue might have done. "Hold your tongue my freind its very like I should be taking you I think. you[re] as moonstruck as anybody Ive laid hands on yet but as you know I never take a lunatic till they are ripe of the stroke I give them theres brag for you now. Now

---

[35] For Branwell's reading of *Gulliver's Travels*, see vol. I, p. 217, n. 7.

[36] Common tavern expressions for one more round of drinks.

dye guess who I am." As he spoke he reared himself up added a fresh light to his little eyes and fresh fatness to his round potbelly—Aye. he struck me all of a heap as the saying is—Said he again screwing up a tune on his instument "A pretty go they talk about the moon and the reap hook sticking out at its side My friend youve. heard I take it of the music of the spheres now isnt the moon a sphere. and if so should it not have music like the rest the darling" and he kissed the ugly ball like a bairn "and if so must it not be an instument to play a tune and what is so good an instrument as a barrel organ well the Moon is a barrel organ the reap hook. is the handle and I my friend I have the honour to be the MAN who grinds it the MAN IN THE MOON I guess youve heard of me ere now you see that black hole in the sky it is the place my Moon holds when Im up there. but Im not always so much there as some folk think I am Oh manys the time I just leave my candle up to satisfy the fools down here and come and take a walk over the earth with my sweet moon for my own dear pleasuring when we meet a goose like you staring about on the middle of our path why I just heave my foot up so my freind." and he kicked me like a horse "And he is moonstruck with a witness. there my freind theres the theory of the moon and its music and the man and your madness" Thus spoke the frightful old sinner heaving up his great yellow globe and screwing over his head a din like 12 feinds on the bag pipes. I cried. oh how I did cry nay he whirled the ball round his head to heave it at me so I made no more ado but just jumped on my feet in a perfect ecstasy lo the man in the Moon was vanished it was broad morning and there was Rougue full above [me] his gun in his hand HIS smile on his lips and he had kicked me up from the ground for an Idle drunken scoundrel. —Now Greenwood theres both theory and practise for thee man Volo a hand of the quart pot there" O Connor leant back on his seat and with a wild reckless laugh emptied at a draught an whole large modicum of neat brandy punch. "Oh frivolous" muttered the whilolm Organist of St Michaels as he too tossed down no mean tumbler of the same refreshing liquid but. a thin withered lad who sat next to Mr Greenwood stared with his eyes at the storyteller as if he had thought him the man in the moon and had just swallowed the instrument. O Connor saw this gullible fellow. and instantly cast his countenance into its strange compound of. dark restless prolifigacy and arch drunken waggery. "Oh my young Gentleman but this is nothing to the tale I'm going to tell you" The youth shuffled himself forward almost of his seat O Connor twisted a quid in his swarthy cheek and what unutterable piece of madness would have come next I know not for like a flash of lightning—No like. a clap of thunder up burst. the music in the street without and in a moment above the Drums and trumpets and trombones and bugles one vast rattling uproar threw all the town into confusion. but confusion worse confounded echoed through the Hotel within. here. every Angrian in my apartment and their names were legion dashed down his drink. and burst into one strong tide to the opened door in a moment I heard. nothing from without for the tempest which raged within and when all the tides of population from every room in the house met with the shock of an earthquake in the great outward passage. Dozens must have been smothered and trodden underfoot. It was

well for me I gained the street almost the foremost. and then as I stood in front
of the deep swaying host of humanity the roar of applause and the flashing of the
firelights through the crushed and crowded street made me almost fancy myself in
charge of calvary at the battle of Zamorna Up a long lane made between the
surrounding thousands a lane fairly lined with standing bands of Music—
advanced pride in their port defiance in their eye[37] side by side the two Angrian
pedestrians It was only for a moment that I beheld the two splendid apparitions
striding forward with footsteps which sprung elastic from the earth their close
white jackets and pantaloons with the scarlet scarfs and. the tight travelling caps
set of their Heroic figures to admirable advantage and realy to gaze upon them
both so young so tall and possessed of such Herculean Symmetry it was
impossible for me to judge with accuracy which of the two would most likely
gain the victory they had now walked 46 miles yet I could not see any
symptoms of fatigue in either except that flush of the cheek and flash of the eye
which might be ascribed to twenty reasons other than the exertion of the
journey. I said I saw them but for a moment Just as they passed me amid
deafning peals of applause. from the mighty concourse. around. their seconds and
backers rode up on high pace. when all together entered the Inn.

The crowds now pressed so closely together that I stood half an hour
incapable of moving and when the coach on which I was to proceed. rose over
the countless heads I had some fears lest I should imprisoned here be totaly
unable to make my way toward it at length however I did climb the vehicle and
after waiting a full hour to see the two pedestrians set off again we whirled
through the street toward Adrianopolis and left the vast outcries behind us

It was a bright and early morning when I woke on the coach top after a
profound sleep which had buried me in comfortable oblivion ever since I left
Hartford. I shall never forget the sense of majical Illusion with which I gazed
wide awake raising my head from the comfortable cravat to view Where was I
how did I come here—? Behold. straight before me beyond the wide open space
of freestone strewn ground rose up into the clouds above. that vast. broad lofty
screen of white and column[ed]. building that huge portal those enormous arches
netted and tangled in the mastlike scaffolding had it sprung at once from the
ground to intercept the prospect of the wide sweet Olympian No I was 70 miles
from the Olympian and then we wheeled round a corner of pillars and there burst
on us the. endless line of street running between those two long long arcades of
yellow roofless houses up toward another monster—to another huge mountain of
marble. when I saw a file of 5000 masons marching before us and heard the
rumble of 200 lime carts behind us when I saw those vast lofty columns
standing to heaven beside us and the New but fast finishing walls towering all
around us then it flashed across my startled imagination now I am In
Adrianopolis now I have entered the Newborn Capital. of Zamorna doomed
perhaps as the seat of Arts and sciences and. riches and Arms. What I saw seemed

---

37   Compare Goldsmith's "The Traveller," ll. 327-28.

like the beginning of a city destined to rule the World. Both Myself and my companions were to much occupied with what we saw to spend much time in making many remarks or observations We rolled swiftly through the unfinished portion of the city and soon entered under a vast Gateway of three Noble Arches into the great inhabited street of Calabar whose finished buildings all resembling rather Palaces than houses. and the Noble shops blazing on each hand of us with the thickly peopled state of the promenade and the air of life and bustle which seemed to reign through this thoroughfare of an almost unborn city all conspired to fill fill me with sensations of unmixed astonishment and admiration As we neared the top of this very long and fully finished street which swept and curved most grandly before us the Majestic colonnades and royal entrances of the Palace of Adrian the First rose up and unfolded its splendour before and beyond the Ministerial Square. This square of. vast size and surrounded by just roofed houses of Regal Magnificence is to be devoted intirely to the residences of the Ministers of the Angrian Parliament above it stretches the entrance of the Palace. on one side the street sweeps on to the vast roofs of Northangerland House and on the other side it makes an opening down toward the wide bright Oceanlike Calabar. it was a lovely site[sic] as we passed this majical scene to view the quays stretching along below us the long forest line of vessels laden with materials for the erection of the city the gay morning waves all dancing in the light and miles of over the blue bounding water the yellow burning sands of the desart region of Africa

The Mansion at which I halted and which is devoted to the residence of the Minister Plenipotentiary from the Government of Verdopolis forms the cheif of a long line of Noble residences which front the water and look over the most magnificent portion of the City they are intended as the mansions of all the Ambassadors from the different Kingdoms and this situation I understand was fixed upon by his Majesty himself as one which would fully impress their minds with the glory of his capital The <Idea> is like him.

When I entered that apartment of my hotel which looks towards the river I stept to the Noble window and gazed enchanted on the glorious scene before me. Oh when I saw the busy active antlike bustle of erection going on in the distance the vast amplitude of people spotted pavement in the foreground the ship covered river before me that mighty stream whose source is 2000 miles away far on in yon burning and desolate and hostile Africa. and the New white enormous palace of the King towering over its grounds and courts on one hand and the roof only the great towering roof of the Palace of the Prime Minister rising bluely on the other. when I knew that here I beheld the Capital of the Kingdom of Angria Adrianopolis the creation of the strangest faction which ever rose in the world nay the creation of the strongest man of a young man of 22 years old son of a King of Africa. heir to £20000000 whose genius and ability and Ambition was a boundless as his power who was Monarch of all the country I had been passing through on this journey AND—whom I with my own eyes had seen walking on foot with one of his Ministers on a pedestrian match of 100 miles for sixpence through the principal province of his dominions—then when

this last thought flashed over me I held up my hands and stood struck aghast
with wonder. Oh Arthur Wellesly and oh Angria what are you destined for verily
when I strive to look into futurity a cloud comes over my minds eye.

I concluded the last chapter with an expression of astonishment at the
state and prospects of Angria Now since I wrote those words I have lived a
month in Adrianopolis I have seen its buildings rising and its streets filling its
King and its Nobles and. Statesmen settling into their Palaces and now at last
Adrianopolis is wound up. all its public movements are at work it acts as the
head of a kingdom. and. HOW DOES THE WATCH GO.!.
Listen and you shall hear I can of all men best tell you.
A week ago on Monday the first of. September. 1834. I received a letter
from the Treasury Office. in the following terms.
My Lord as the Ambassador Plenipotentiary from the parent
Government (parent was erased 3 several times) of. Verdopolis you are entitled to
a seat in the Cabinet Council to be holden at the great Room in the Treasury
Office. at 10 o clock this Night precisely

W H Warner Home Secretary.
Knowing that my Duty to my Government demanded my presence. at
the Cabinet this Night I prepared to go. My readers must know that the Minister
from Verdopolis can sit in the Council of any Nation though he has neither vote
nor word. in it. all the expressions in the papers for a week back the excited state
of the public mind in the city and my own insight into the conduct of the
Ministry of Angria convinced me that all was scarcly right about the head of the
body politic. Waiting with heightened pulse. till the hour of retiring I ordered
my carriage after dinner and drove of to the Grand building devoted to the routine
of Ministerial avocations On alighting at the portal I was shewn through a great
Domed vestibule. full into the Hall of Deliberation. a long lofty spacious
Apartment hung with scarlet velvet and blazoned everywhere with the Gilded
Sun. truely the effect produced by this room in the softer lustre of the great
chandeliers above me was of a character almost Royal. in magnificence in the
Palace of his Majesty however the "Angrian Hall" eclipses this into darkness as I
entered the room the great Throne at the upper end. under a huge Mirror denoted
the active part taken by the Monarch here in his Nations ongoings but the King
of Angria is the literal head of his Ministers
As a matter of course one long Mahogany table. of green cloth. loaded
piled with a sheaf of red taped papers ran down the whole length of the room and
a couple of scores of chairs flanked each side of that table. I however took my
seat on a sopha my own dear post of observation. in the room at that moment
were none but about half a dozen clerks sitting at a side table mending their pens
with industry and a slight. slender gentleman in black. whose pale light features
and restless eye hurried over the choatic heap of material. at the upper end of the
table. while his small lady fingers busied themselve[s] in emphatic movements

of the heavy printed parcels. After a few sentences to me. accompanied by the usual salutation he. the Home Secretary Warner Howard Warner returned to his rewelcomed employment with bent brow and resolved. lips ere long the door again was thrown open and. 3 other Gentlemen entered The foremost. with a dashing air strode up to the fire. adjusted his hair in an instant and after. a most adroit expectoration into the element. paced down the carpet. like the King of the Dandies the second apparent. wiped his feet at the Door. and instantly plumped down to a chair at the table. as instantly with his sandy head bent over his work and his broad lips compressed. and his wide. eyes. fixed he sat to the papers as to work congenial and not hateful. The third laughing with a grand bass echo. and without taking his hat from his head strode up toward me. "Ha Richton you here Why to spy the Nakedness of the land are ye come" "Well no Montmorency If I am to judge from outward appearances my report will be different from that of the Isrealites"[38] "Phoo since. judge of the Tree by its fruits[39] I know my bible better than you. What you see now is the tree for the fruit anon. anon." As the Herculean Foreign Secretary spoke. thus he took a pinch of snuff. and seated himself

[38] See Numbers, chapters 13 and 14.
[39] Compare Matthew 7:16-20.

[Angria and the Angrians]
I(b)[1]

Are these the latter days of Africa. and must this question be asked in the Infancy of Angria

Strange and omninous as this question may sound I fear that it must. for the lights and shadows on the objects around us are too strong and too frequent to be cast from a noonday sky. When I beheld the Council of Adrianopolis and saw the sudden and unaccountable division in its members and when I beheld the Council of Verdopolis and saw the hate and the factions it had split into when I saw a Prime Minister of a country causlessly cast himself from that Country his King and his Fellow Ministers turning feircely against him I saw the Prime Minister of another Country as causlessly resign the helm at a period when storms from every quarter threatned the vessel and how his Ministry distracted and divided had seperated itself into a hundred parties each swimmer had struck out for his own safty and amid the endless slaughter of every private character where was the country who saw her gasping who if she sunk could save her if she died would bewail her

Such were a few of my reflections as I pondered over at my breakfast table in Verdopolis the morning papers of the City and Kingdom. as I felt the beatings of that pulse whose strength or weakness is a sure indication of the health of the Body Politic and after perusing the Leaders of all the Verdopolitan prints and noticing their indignant language upon the retirement of Earl Clair and the retiring of office on the part of Mr Sydney I turned to the Angrian Prints and opened the HEART OF ANGRIA published in Adrianopolis only the evening before. I glanced my eye down the first page the Advertisements had vanished. thick. columns of letterpress occupied their place and I read at the top in large capitals

ADDRESS TO THE ANGRIANS BY HIS GRACE THE
DUKE OF ZAMORNA.[2]

What was there here a document of first rate importance a phisic indeed but would it cool or fire the blood I well know how it treated me as I hurried[ly] glanced down this long and astonishing epistle I could at first hardly gather its plain and descicive meaning so confused was I at the. character of the document so occupied in asking of its effects. What effect said I will this Address produce in Angria and what sensation will it cause in Verdopolis will it not be felt even among the Moors of Sneachies land and the woods of. "My Fathers Vassals"[3] will it not rouse up universal Africa and wither the <accursed> Northangerland.

---

1   A manuscript fragment of 6 pages, 11.2x18.6 cm. Pages 1-4 are in the Brotherton Collection; pages 5-6 are in BPM: BS 120 (leaf 3).

2   For the full text of the letter, see Alexander CB II, part ii, 296.

3   I have been unable to locate the origin of this phrase.

This letter to the Angrians addressed to them by their youthful Monarch seemes to me a just and striking delineation of the character of the Duke of Zamorna. It commences with that flow of language that exuberance of expression those undue flowers of compostion which stamp it as the pro[d]uction of a scarcly experienced youth. and anon there centeres in the page. the. unbending haughtiness and the threatning passions and the impetous eloquence of a fiery Manhood.

"In the time of my proudest elevation" thus he speaks to them "in the moment of hard earned and triumphant sucess as I stood with my then coadjutor Lord Northangerland before assembled Angria and heard and felt her warm fervent enthusiastic congratulation—at that dazzling moment I was shaken by the sudden conviction that my triumph cannot last that to compensate for it and to restore the balance of human enjoyment to its just equipoise Futurity had black moments in store Yes I was shaken by anticipation of evil but fulfilment binds me firm as a rock."

In this vigorous tone of composition the Duke proceeds after the opening and rather tawdry paragraph and here there is no need I <fear> of my remarking upon the truth of the observation I have above quoted but what a King confesses he has felt in his most royal hour sur[e]ly a common mortal may bear in his time of trouble, Zamorna proceeds to say with a bitter sneer that. "Underminers have been among you from whence sent it requires no oracle to reveal Lord Northangerland though far distant in the flesh loves his adopted country too well to leave her <without> the solace of his spirit The bowells of that great and good man yearn affectionatly toward you he would fain <rekindle> the embers of Rebellion in your hearts with his own noble hand and watch the progress of the conflagration with his own brilliant eyes and encourage that progress with his own persausive tongue. But since that may not for the present be ill health blessed martyr preventing it—He hires men for the purpose." And then the Duke exposes his "Coadjutors" pestilential temper shews the effect it had in his ministry and speaks in strong language of his own detestation of the Prem[i]ers double dealing insanity. Ah Zamorna. had you seen and know[n] all this but 6 months ago had you been then as much aware of the character of the worst man in Africa had you taken the advice of. wise and reflecting men cut yourself off from him forbidden his insidious advances then my Lord you would not have beheld yourself placed above a distracted Country Board and an insulted Kingdom you would not then have to dissarange the whole tackling to cut away the fallen mast to adress a letter of threatning to an infant nation

In truth there runs a strange dash of Menace through this extraordinary epistle. but yet I think it gives it a tint which will make the Angrians still prouder of their King the Nation loves a fearless. man and. like a tygger would pounce on a trembling Keeper Of his language respecting the rediculous and I fear. "hired." resentment expressed respecting his choice of French freinds I think leniently for I. believe few could bear the. idea of a restriction of their choice of society but. no doubt. without any excuse and beyond all bounds of decency lies the sentence "Angrians I scorn to stand any longer on the defensive and to your teeth I tell you that a hundred of the grand chevaliers (Murat's) followers shall ere long honour your shores by their prescence how dare you accuse me of unjust partiality to Foreigners" How dare they my lord verily that sentence should shew them and you also how they ought to dare. And when the duke. says he will stake his life and honour on the chances of war when he holds out as a sign of goodwill the consecration of the heir of Angria to blood and massacre and the spread of human misery then not only his people but all people should stop ere they call him King

But they should stop too ere they do not call him King I say there are a hundred things in this letter to counter balance the impertinences I have just spoken of. And Zamornas free fiery language his Nobel disregard of all subterfuge and flattery either in hate or freindship his scorn of weakhearted conduct his determination not to be browbeaten or quelled by an unprincipled and dissipated Nobleman his eagerness to do everything firmly and lead his country with desicion all this marks his character shews him a fit King for Angria and counterpoises the Tyranny haughtiness and ridiculous heat of his headstrong temper counterpoises these at least under proper guidance and in favorable circumstances The letter I am speaking of concludes with a postscript addressed to the Earl of Northangerland and if ever human wrighting shewed forth with clearness the heartless and aimless prolifigacy the utter and dissolute want of principle the uncertain half insane and unaccountable raving of the Earl of Northangerland this letter must be classed at the head of all such most usefull publications it blasts him with a well merited indignation and though speckled with some rash and foolish expressions peculiar to the writer this postscript contains not one word which ought not to be fully and constantly pondered and digested both by the people of Angria and the man it is addressed. to

This Letter the moment it appeared in Verdopolis excited the most intense and unbounded attention all eyes were upon it. and all heads about it. ere the conclusion of the day following news arrived of how the Address would be received in Angria.

Men of. Zamorna
present yourselves early on the morning of September 15. on the County Feild of the City of Zamorna One and all of you. all who can walk. speak or see. who have hearts or heads or understanding

At the Great Provincial Meeting
There to be holden. for the purpose of voting an Address from the People of Zamorna in answer to the Letter of your King for the purpose of deciding whether you will Applaud Treachery Support a Traitor Despise gratitude and insult a Savior OR. defend your Country crush the Enimy Uphold your Constitution and rally around your King.
The time for descision is breif and your determination must brand you as brutes
Or proclaim you as Angrians
ON the 15 of September make your province a desart and. your City.
one of A MILLION men.

And do not make me blush to sign my self.
Your Lord Lieutenant
CASLREAGH

To the people of ANGRIA
On the Morning of September 16 A D 1834. a Grand provincial Meeting will be
held.
In the County Feild near Angria.
When. I request every Man who calls Angria his country to appear
For the purpose of passing an address in answer to the Letter of his Majesty
The Duke of Zamorna our King
I shall never call those freemen who do not stand. that day before me.
And if you desire Slavery remain at home. where your chains shall be bound
round you
Remember these words and. know
That. I will receive no excuse for nonappearance. on the ground but that. of.
"I am a Slave and therefore cannot come"
And the only greeting I ask from the MEN. whom I shall see around me shall be
"I am an Angrian and I stand here
TO RALLY ROUND MY
Country   and   King.
Signed W H WARNER
Lord Lieutenant of Angria.

To the people of = =
Northangerland and Douro
Angrians you have long known me and I do not consider a new introduction
necessary
Deeply greiving for that humiliating condition in which you are placed
A state by which you cannot legally have called a general County meeting
In which to declare wether you like Tyranny or Liberty
I declare the only means by which you can remedy this degredation
MEET Me. Northangerlandians
On the Heath above Pequena. 4 o clock. p m. Sept 16.
And you Douronians
On the Ings near. Falla 12 p m. Sept 17.
In a voluntary constitutional Meeting for the purpose of voting an Address
In answer to the Letter of His Majesty the King of Angria
And to tell me will you submit to the rule of a broken down Tyrant or
The Government of your CONSTITUTION.
Till I know your descisions I remain
Your Freind and country man
W H WARNER.

TO THE MEN OF.
ADRIANOPOLIS
A Great Crisis appears this day in the aspect of Affairs in Angria and
It remains for your descision. the question. Shall the Country of Angria
Be a laughing stock to the foe or a Monument of its glory
Who is to decide such a question and when is it to be decided.
The Men of Adrianopolis are to decide it.
And in the Grand Square of your City
And on September. 16. 1834
It is to be decided.
You boast of your selves as the directors of Angrian energy
Come now and. show us where and how youll guide it
Wether like Phaeton or Phebus
And Mark that in guiding it you will guide yourselves
H M M Montmorency.
From the Committee for the City Meeting Sept. 14

These are a few of the huge Handbills which lay in a vast pile on my table on
the evening of Sept 14. This is the manner in which Angria receives the Letter
of her Sovereign. I believe that the Meetings above mentioned as about to take
place will show the world in a manner never. seen before the true force decision
and energy of the Angrians their horror of degradation their enthusiatic devotion
to Zamorna and their hot hearty hate of the Earl of Northangerland.

Verily Percy has sowed a wind only to reap a whirlwind[4]

The morning after the appearance of as they were called in Verdopolis
"THE Angrian Handbills." for on account of the dashing character of the people
all its affairs have a decided name. I left Verdopolis again for My Ambassadorial
Station Adrianopolis Between the week which had elapsed since my last
departure from that City what an age of Political Revolution had taken place
what a rapid Revolution of the wheel of fate.[5]

Upon this occasion I rolled in my own carriage along the road from
Verdopolis to Zamorna. Every coach car or other vehicle. had been taken up and
appropriated to those proceeding that day to the great Meeting at Zamorna. and as
we passed along the country. every road and hedge and. footpath teemed with the
thousands pouring to the great rendezvous the crowds which I beheld at
Edwardston on the day of the "Footmatch" were as nothing compared to the
<hege> of Mortality which blocked that village now. and the streaming flags of
scarlet and the glittering bands of music flowed forward without end toward the

---

4   Compare Hosea 8:7.
5   Compare vol. I, p. 80, n. 7.

excited provincial Capital. We entered Zamorna at about 1 o clock in two hours after the meeting would commence and now all the streets as we passed them presented one thick black steady pavement of heads raised over the original flagstones like the fall[e]n ashes over pompeii[6] the grand dashing carriages of the various Nobility and Gentry to be present that day could hardly force themselves through the shouting and huzziing multitude. The bells clashed and peal[e]d from every steeple in the City and. their loud. vigorous reverberation sung lustily in the bright sky above us. The day indeed was a glorious sight of sunshine for the sun with unusual generosity had lent the free use of his rays to these. dazzling blazes which flaring on the front of every banner seemed emulous to outshine their ascot original.[7]

While we <u>checked</u> slowly through the vast tide of mortality which flowed toward the County feild down the principal street of Zamorna. the immense bustle and vigorous roars of shouting behind us told a tale of some oncoming favorite. the Bands of music raising their brazen throats or the clamour poured their loud martial strains in full stream against my ear and as looking back I saw the Trumpets and trombones and bugles edging forward. out of the thickening throng and the fiery heads of the scarlet ribboned horses snorting above it beyond them and the. waving host of red lightning banners which popped up in long vista down the street I. knew that the Lord Lieutenant was proceeding here toward the scene of meeting My noble freind Castleregh. throned in his dashing carriage. prodigious in curled locks gold eye glass and waistcoats flying wide over his shoulders and force[d] into a thread at his waist. and. my Lady. Castlereagh. sparkling in the first fashion of the day and. with those bright illumined eyes which so far outshone the diamonds in her hair

The lord Lieutenants carriage upon its appearance was greeted with that hearty and simultaneous shout which so clearly testified the fair feeling entertained by the dashing Zamornans for their as dashing ruler But I heard the shouts swell yet higher and heartyer when just after this chariot and as near abreast of it as due decorum would permit the splendid green open coach bearing the Brother in law of the King Brother of the Queen Member for the Province and cheif man of the City. appeared the coach of the real principal and originator of the meeting Edward Percy Esq[r] M P. and his Lady the Princes of Sneachies Land. She was dressed in scarlet satin and her tall perfect form and haughty goddesslike beauty of countenance with that half unconcious half sarcastic smile which adorned it gave her more magnificence of aspect than could have done [a] world of rank and honours and diadems and royalty. "Mr Edward's" youthful and Athletic person and handsome and energetic countenance seemed more than usually proud and impetous. This day his eye glanced with a look which I could

---

6   The city near Naples buried in ash after the eruption of Mt. Vesuvius in 79 A.D.

7   That is, an original creation designed for the famous racing meet held at Ascot every June.

ill have loved to contradict and he evidently survey[ed] the vast crowd around him with the look of a man who gazes on the satisfactory work of his own hands

Behind the carriages of the Lord Lieutenant and the M P. crushed a host of equipages of all the Nobility and gentry in the Province and this tide of cavalry and infantry and drums and music hurried my vehicle. rapidly along to the great ocean of the country feild. turning round the street full on to its entrance a sight flashed on me equal to any I have ever seen before it was truely sublime to view the immense unshadowed square blocked up as firm as possible with an ocean of human heads far far back. beyond the tossing waste the hustings[8] rising before the city hall. and beneath that grand focus of attraction the wild waste of banners tossing and fluttering to the Angrian winds all the river side and the entering streets and the colonnades and the house tops were crowded with people I should think that at the lowest estimate I saw before me not less than 180 000 men. and it was an hour ere my carriage could clear itself of the crowds and processions and sounding bands of music.

Rapidly leaving this huge focus of humanity for the wide open country my carriage bowled smoothly along the grand open road to Adrianopolis and as the Afternoon sun shone pleasantly on my face I passed the time in meditations on the tremendous <rising> about to be made manifest in the whole country the enthusiasm for Zamorna and the detestation of Northangerland I passed not a single villiage or Alehouse where Huge placards for provincial meetings and county meetings and town meetings and villiage meetings were not <shaking> like snow along the walls The words address[ed] in Answer to the Kings Letter seemed to have roused the whole Nation into excitement every little print and local paper which I took up was filled with devotion to the King and Ministry and with the most loud and vigourous execrations of the Treacherous Northangerland

I reached Adrianopolis at Midnight and. retired exhausted to rest that night I dreamt I saw Angria devouring Percy.

From the GLORY OF AFRICA. Verdopolis Sept. 16th.
LETTER.
TO THE MEN OF ANGRIA.

> Palm. Grove House
> Stumpz Isle. — .
> Sept. 12. 1834

Countrymen.

When I left. Africa for this Island I promised in the farewell I took of the people of Verdopolis that if I could controul my own mind I would still keep

---

[8]   The temporary platform from which candidates in parliamentary elections addressed the voters.

it fixed upon their state and welfare. and as the sea parted me from the Land of which I had been cheif minister I also resolved that I would. think too of your prospects and your welfare it is now a week since I landed on this Island and though my shattered constitution and departed spirits refuse me either vigour or inclination I yet. have memory left me and cannot soon forget. you. Do not men of Angria believe that when I write thus too you I wish to cast a false veil over my feelings and that I vainly wish to parade a sentimental tenderness for my dear adopted country No I wish no such. falshood. I after my life and my feelings cannot entertain such a feeling but in a frame of mind when any object. any pursuit was happiness compared to its own chaotic vacancy I did fix my thoughts upon your country and now though perhaps all thought is useless they remain fixed there still. I know that there are few things which I can now think on or strive for but those few I shall think on till I die. And if I am cast again upon my self alone I have received a repulse from a City of Refuge.[9] and if those whom I assisted to power profit. now would assist me to nothing But disgrace and desolation Yet those people are not the country of Angria are not of the country of Angria and though I will cease to care or think of them it shall not follow that I refuse to think of you. My intellects I still preserve and so long as I have them you too shall have them. and Angrians do not ask me why my heartless feelings have any intrest in you rest assured they have and then rest satisfied with seeking there wherefore. I cannot give a reason for what at times I feel.

Upon retiring to the solitary spot from which I date this letter I still bent my eyes to the land I came from and. employed all the means in my power to obtain information and intelligence from Africa. but during the long hours in which nothing could reach my ears from without and where I must sleep in vacancy unless the mind employs itself within I. meditated. the subject nearest my heart and your own the state of Angria and its probable prospect for the future. in such a subject of contemplation there was enough to occupy the most expansive mind and as I do not often seek my consolation in the wild dreams of supersitition and the hot phantasys of a code of. miracles. [I] employed Angrians all My Intellect on this subject I have spoken of it and when I say all I trust you will hearken to my opinion.

In what an astonishing manner is a century often crowded into a life time and a life time into an hour This [h]as often been the case during the period of my existence and seems no[w] about to be the case with this age of the world. I hope that though the main fact tallys with me and you yet the inferred effects may never never coincide. I have lived through an age of great misery you are living through an age of great events but Angrians are they miserable or glorious. it rests with you to make them either and if you attended to my letter I should say it rested with ME.

---

9   See Numbers 35 and Deuteronomy 19.

The morning of Angria rose amid strife and carnage it was war and confusion with the attendant consequences of a divided nation and excited factions which produced that. portentous birth the Kingdom of Angria and when. the saviour army of Verdopolis with its conquering Generals and their united people. demanded the wages of their hazardous and hard won VICTORY. Then the Nation would not and the Government could not refuse them the boon they wished for. I then was placed by circumstances in a commanding position in the politics of your country and I had determined to give them a direction which would tend to revive the Aged and Aristocratic Verdopolis Men accuse me of having spent a life time of inconsistency and traitorous tergiversation they say I left a party proffessing principles of Hatred to Aristocracy and love of Liberty for that very Aristocracy and government which I had so long spoke against and fought against.

These men either condemn me through ignorance or they lie through malice. I have sins enough on my head without being crushed under the weight of deserted principles

Know then Angrians that when just before the breaking out of the late war. all the Elections had. been decided against the Democrats after the Government had put into execution various oppressive measures against them after the treachery among several of their members and the fear of them which pervaded the well intentioned Nation I then saw that to push forward my principle of Dethronement of Tyrannical Government reforming of corrupted Institutions and above all giving the worn out world a new youth of liberty I could not any longer <risk> its wisdom due to the carrying of so mighty a plan. continue on this old baffled. bugbear of the faction of the Democrats. I am accustomed Angrians to decision and I decided to destroy it I broke up the Jacobin Club[10] dispersed the affliliated unions called in my detached resources and after hurrying on by my foreign machinations a war which sooner or later I knew must break out threw myself into the party of the All Destroying Aristocracy took a commission in the Government Army and associated myself with a young man a Minister a high Aristocrat a proffessor of those pernicious principles which have been ruining the world for a thousand years and which it had been and was yet be my DETERMINATION TO DESTROY or <u>die</u> I. associated myself. with the Son of a King the MARQUIS OF DOURO to him my daughter was shortly married and with him I entered my rejiment on the breaking out of the War of Aggression[11] Angrians I knew that this young man possessed Genius Ability and Mental energy of the highest order that he had passions for comprehending and acting upon those immense principles of liberty upon which I acted and that only his Education had wrapt round him the

---

[10] i.e., his political radicals. Historically, the Jacobins were a society of revolutionary democrats in France during the Revolution of 1789. See vol. I, p. 333, n. 2.

[11] See vol. I.

Artificial coat of Aristocracy. Mind my feelings during this war were only disguised Still they went on surely to work their end. In the middle of the war I. for the purpose of Rousing the country to an affection and adherence to the Army my intend[ed] INSTRUMENT OF FREEDOM instigated and encouraged a mutiny among the principle Rejiments. when upon the Government attempting in vain to coerce those Rejiments the people as I saw as eagerly took their side and espoused their feelings Now Angrians the train was on fire circumstances delayed the War yet longer Aristocratic Principles opened up their hideous insanity and your Twelve and your Kings and your Government had by their base malevolent weak heartedness. almost brought Africa into eternal Ruin but such a proceeding would have ruined freedom and VITALITY. [f]or that is my meaning. it is deep but in a while you will feel it. I then and the Marquis of Duoro and the Army roused ourselves up and bore our Africa from its danger and hurled the French into the sea. Now the war being over Verdopolis gazed on her Saviour Army with gratitude for her deliverance. and here I. determined to put into practice that great intention for which I had destroyed Democracy. I determined to GIVE AFRICA A SOMETHING WHICH WHILE IT DELIGHTED HER AND WHILE SHE FOSTERED IT SHOULD BRING ABOUT UNDER MY GUIDANCE THAT LIBERTY AND THAT VITALITY WHICH SHOULD REVIVIFY AND GIVE YOUTH TO THE WORLD. You know Angrians when a child receives physic it receives it as a sweetmeat and that its first principles of Learning are often imbibed through Games. I grasped at first with eager hand on everything which could strengthen the Army my instrument and could weaken the Aristocracy my foe. —THEN I proposed to Verdopolis that TO the Marquis of Duoro now Duke of Zamorna should be given the Kingdom of Angria in due and rightful sovereignty for the immense service conferred by him in Africa as while he acted as her Saviour. Angrians I know that Arthur Wellesly poss[ess]ed an Intellect far farther above that of ordinary men than any I before had known his eager Alexander like Ambition his noble unveiled. energy and decision of character that youthful generous love of glory and. himself. and so free from cant and weakness that even my recoiled feelings were inspired when I gazed on your King. He though he knew not the meaning of my action seized like a lion on the opening of glory he appeared for himself and for himself the Duke of Zamorna demanded his Kingdom. It was given to him and Aristocracy withered before him But I felt a new youth when I thought of him and I exerted all my powers to AID him to add new glory to his crown and to stand [at] the right hand of my Noble King I cannot Angrians say God bless the Duke of Zamorna but I can say May all my wishes be crowned in him May that Elisha[12] on whom I have cast the mantle of Liberty properly and labour till he sees the reward of his labour Ha. Angrian[s] I would die this moment were I sure that my King Zamorna would with his own Noble hand give that VITALITY to the world which he is so gloriously qualified to give. But I will live Angrians for I do not feel sure that

---

[12] The successor to Elijah; see I Kings 19 and II Kings 2.

he will do it[13] a circumstance has occured which I had never calculated upon to cloud this scheme which I had exerted all my mind to frame and all my power to carry on.

ANGRIANS the moment your country became a Kingdom the moment its existence was made sure by a King whose victory must follow that instant a cloud of Locusts settled up on the Land[14] yes a host of men without feelings without principle without virtue or courage or even common decency men who bloodsucker like made the one object of sex aggrandizement their only subject of study fixed themselves upon the Monarch and seized all the government of Angria. Aye took upon THEM to direct my bark of vitality and freedom.

I HAD INTENDED Angrians that the Kingdom of Angria governed and directed by a young soldier of magnificent person GLORIOUS INTELLECT of a mind fitted to grasp the highest and most abstract feelings of passions and determination to go on unwearied and unwatching on one glorious path of Ambitious existence. whose Noble spirit veiwed the world as his only feild of labour and that world as his only wage of reward I say that I had intended Angria governed by the Duke of Zamorna to act as a grand beacon to the whole world. now liberty could proceed on its path to heaven I knew Angria <whether it> could yet know vitality or not. yet hated Aristocracy and I determined it should crush it Then Aristocracy crushed and Angria spread over Africa should communicate that vital force. which it shall readily catch and should soon catch from me. I had intended—but it is useless to inform you now what I intended a cloud came over the sun and hid his light from my eyes Ha is it that sun which has sunk and do I see the shadows of midnight before me

You know Angrians that I was installed as the Prime Minister of Angria and any other post I neither wished nor strove for But I had rather have acted with my King alone than with the men whose Labour had fallen in the vineyard with mine[15] with my King I had common feelings with your Minsters I had NONE. They hated me and they thwarted me did I not also thwart them. I spoke against them and wrote against them both in public and in private

But you will tell me I also spoke and wrote against my King

I Did—Angrians I determined to keep him before Verdopolis I knew human character and therefore knew that He who is spoken against the world if he be a high adventurer will uphold and defend. The weak hearted will leave him but the strong souls would gather rond him. You know that the seaweed clings closer in a storm. For myself. I should gain the temporary hate of. himself and the country. But I can endure privation I can bear a shade and this is not the first cloud which has overcast my lifetime

---

13　For Zamorna's reaction to the concept of vitality, see Alexander CB II, part ii, pp. 305-306.

14　See Exodus, chapter 10.

15　See Isaiah 5:1-7 and Matthew 21:33-46.

Now my Country men I have opened up to you the whole secret of my tortouous[sic] acting in the recent vast movements of Africa I have shown you a glimpse of the vast end which all these maneuvers had in view but you do not perhaps yet know my reason of vacating the office of Prime Minister and leaving Africa for exile on a foreign shore

I have told you that My Fellow Ministers hated me that I hated them that they are men without principles or morality that they regard only themselves But they are some of them possessed of shallow yet glaring accquirements They are Men many of them of accquired property and over all they are persons who have gained a footing and station in the country

I know they hate the Aristocrats but I know them to be as blind as they Well Angrians I saw that these persons were firmly rooted in the country I saw that they stood in the confidence of my King and in the respect and consequence of the country I saw this and determined to overthrow them to do this my course was short indeed

I set their schemes in confusion threw up my office of Premiership and immediatly left the country I determined to appeal at once to Africa to show my King and country my scheme for their welfare my actions for their glory and then left the Ministers of Angria [to] drift with the Tempest I shall raise.

Angrians[16] I do not expect that upon reading this my letter you will at once agree with my feeling and aid me on my path I know that those accursed Ministers have for the present fixed too firm an hold upon your interests but I will pass over the present I will let time and your Reason decide. From this forest where I now write I shall shortly despatch you a second letter and that letter shall be devoted to an exposure of the characters of your Ministry and an explanation of. my Ideas on LIBERTY AND VITALITY. till then Angrian[s] reflect upon what I have here said too you reflect if you like with <detestation> If you choose with curses I can bear thee one and in the other there is nothing to bear but here you cannot injure me and if I live from hence I will Advantage you

So far I had written in this Letter when the refusal of my strength to act with my mind compelled me to desist writing for a while and as I sat. thinking upon that Monarch whose noble heart I have alienated but which I know I shall regain. I received from Verdopolis the "ADDRESS to the Angrians by His Grace the Duke of Zamorna" I read over this letter with an animation I do not often experience. and as I finished I thought I saw his Noble figure his Animated Countenance and heard his own energetic language his own heart rousing voice. Read this letter Angrians as I have done think of it as I have thought and Vital light is already about to dawn is even now on the horizon to say that I passed over without unpleasant feeling the conluding paragraphs to this Letter would be to act a part in earnest which I would rather leave to your present government did I say I gloried in the postscript you might say I lied. No Angrians I greived at that postscript but I greived not for my self but for my Noble King I cursed

---

[16] The portion of manuscript in BPM: BS 120 begins here.

those <vultures> who had gathered round him I. longed indeed for the light again to dawn on him Zamorna tells me I. have been bent on working misery to the world. Ha.! I have perhaps been bent on working misery to myself I may never have known one single hour of happiness I may often have hated myself. and hated life and <felt a> sick heart sick of all connected with my existence I may have turned my eyes round me and have seen nothing I could share in and above me and known nothing I could hope from and within me and felt nothing I could recoil in. I may have. seen. all that I could love taken away and taken away for EVER. and knowing that bitter truth I may have sometimes turned [my] back on life with bitterness and acted. in error and have. done deeds which I cannot defend—But Angrians know now and you My King let your own heart feel the truth of this one. assertion I never did. seek. to stain human life with one spot which it fears to show I never wished from one human eye one tear to fall from one human heart one sigh or sorrow to arise My own eye has long been dried and my own heart is deadened now. but. May your Souls Angrians. long exist. in happiness may your eyes for ever brighten and your hearts all ways beat high with joy

AND Now My King Zamorna. I will turn a single look to you I see you now. placed on a noble eminence. I see you the pride and glory of your country but I know you are not your own glory I know your eye is turned on a still loftier hieght[sic] and you will never call yourself Monarch till to that long looked at summit you can attain permit then a Man who has fought with you and spoke with you who alike has born and inflicted with you permit Alexander Percy to address one word of caution and advice. I do not boast my abilitys to you you know them though you know not their direction. Zamorna the Nation of Angria are firmly and enthusiastically devoted to you this I know as well as if the breeze which cools my apartment wafted their blessings to this shore they love you and they will die with you. But you are surrounded by a circle of persons widely different indeed from the people of Angria you govern by men whom you KNOW Do not love you who say so and believe so and can you think that such men can act for your interest do you believe that that interest lies along with theirs do you think that if it dies no[w] they will give up their own benifits to serve yours will it suit your extended plans to give up your interest to serve theirs and if none of the expedients will answer tell me can you accomodate can you temporise and conciliate and concede. Can you follow for a while the £.s.d. pursued by the Breifless Morley or can you quaff rum and Burgundy with the Traitor Morley[17] or obey like a Dutiful subject the Monarch Warner or add a few rays of glory to the Apollo Castlereagh nay will you bow down your head for just one champaign to the superiour Exploits of the Martial Castlereagh can you tame all your Horses that they may not outshine the charger of a Murat. Away Zamorna away with all these frantic drone[s] of agreement drive of the thought that Wellesly can herd with these rather would I see you stripped of your

---

[17] Branwell likely meant "Montmorency."

crown robbed of your sceptre. and spoiled of all your riches and reduced to the title of A MAN. Yes Zamorna and far rather would I see your crown press your royal Brow and the deserting peoples again placed in your hands see you governing your people of Angria and govern them without a MINISTER.

People of Angria I know that when you see your Kings Adress you will assemble to show your concurrence in his noble feelings and assemble by thousands and by thousands upon thousands aye meet Angrians Meet all over the land astonish Africa by your vigourous enthusiasm declare yourselves ready to follow your King Zamorna to follow him through life and death through ruin and to glory though heaven and earth shall oppose you Rally round your Noble King. But My Adopted Countrymen. I sorrow for you when I veiw the mean semi slavery in which you lie you are free subjects of a Monarch but chained slaves of A Ministry away with that basest of factions hurle your tyrants to the earth. do you not see the evill they already have done you they have left you an open and unprotected frontier they have allowed the African to commit his unrepulsed depredations They have not dared to call for vengeance on too often insulted Angria they have forced from your shore a man who would guide you to safety they are burdening you with taxes though you are scarcly yet a new born Kingdom and amid themselves the[y] make a profit of your blood they lay their own intrest on your <loins> Aye Angrians and they have suffered suffered with[out] remonstrance without resistance a vessel of War from the Navy of the King of Parrys land. a vessel commanded by your eternal and bitterest enimy to ride even before your own rising City to scorn you and dare you. on your hearth stones and homes

Angrians you are about to vote an Advice an answer to the letter of your King I ask you for yourselves to show your own scorn of his Ministers Cling to your Monarch my countrymen and guard him as your only saviour for your government. down with it down with it even to the very ground

Now with in the conclusion of this letter permit me to speak one word respecting myself. I am here now suffering an exile in Stumpz land that you may awaken to your welfare I regard my self as <indeed> a temporary Martyr to your cause but how my Countrymen do you regard me.

Angrians be silent respecting me think of me and read what I write to you but speak not I intreat you one word of me. amid all your conversations and speeches and meetings let me lie as one dead and let my name be passed over without praise and without censure it is unmanly Angrians to rage against the dead and absent Well. untill again I appear among [you] and. on the opening day of the First Parliament of the Angrian Kingdom upon the First of October 1834 then when I shall appear before [you] on my seat in the house of peers then. I will wish every man in the Kingdom to speak what he likes and. to act as he will. Till then Angrians let me rest in your tongues as the Earl of Northangerland

in your hearts as
Alexander Percy.

I must calmy[sic] my feelings ere I speak or comment upon this letter I have just extracted[18] And to allow these feelings to subside in their excitement let me. speak of the events of my stay in Adrianopolis. up to the appearance of this astonishing letter.

I need hardly to relate the fact so well known that during the week after the publication of the King of Angrias letter all the country arose in one vast. chain of meetings to declare their confidence in their Monarchs proceedings The meetings in Zamorna. Angria. Seaton. Pequena Fall[a] Gazemba Dongola and Adrianopolis were enormous and. overwhelming in enthusiasm. all Africa will ring of the Angrians from the Gambia to the Etrei!

I am just now returned from a visit on public buisness which I have made to Gazemba the residence of. Henri Fernando Enara the Lord Lieutenant of. the Etrei and as this visit showed me an insight into the state of the frontiers I shall breifly relate it

Gazemba lies over the east bank of the Calabar and about 60 miles southeast of Adrianopolis it is far from the nominal frontiers of the country but the reader shall judge how near the real.

Upon the morning of the 17th of September I crossed the Calabar with a Guard of 50 men landing among the wild rushes on a flat sand which forms the bank of the mighty River. The morning was yet unrisen and the sky and landscape was cold raw and darkned. Under such circumstances we rode briskly along over a vast unwatered plain of Arid sand. without a single elevation the slightest cultivation or one mark of movement to diversify the drear desolate scene. as the sun arose in the cloudless heaven and his beams began to warm the soft yellow sand the bright light of the whole landscape the motes dancing in the air the dry. hazy horizon and the intense oven like heat of the atmosphere told us we had got fairly into the desarts of Africa We looked into the sky but its strong blazing glare forced us directly to turn toward the earth again and then the reflect[ed] heat of the sands and their unvaried brightness forced us to shut those eyes. harassed by all around them My brain was in a ferment toward evening and I thought I should have dropt with torture I. asked myself What will the Angrians say to a champaign in these desarts towards sunset our Escort began to be on the alert and to keep watch round the Horizon. We were upon dangerous ground and Africans swept often over this desart Their savage and relentless cruelty was to well known to need much dwelling upon. In these circumstances my delight was intense when just on the. S E horizon. a long line of copper haze announced the vicinity of the Etrei and soon a few roofs and inequalities upon the Horizon in a black evening shadow showed us the far off towers of Gazemba we reached it at dead Night and I was guided through the rough little streets of the infant and islolated city to the Lord Lieutenants residence. the seat of the powerful Italian reputed to be possessed of property worth £100 000 a

---

[18] See Zamorna's and Mary's reactions to the letter in Alexander CB II, part ii, 269-72.

year. Fort Enara is a long low extended wall of compact stone work and the extreme strength and the determined courage of the vassals have long preserved it from the assaults of the vindictive Quashia. Yet to the eye of the entering stranger the totally unpeaceful unornamented character of the building the wild half banditti like air of the citizens and the huge yellow Ocean of Desart expand[ing] far and wide around you save where the vast silver Etreii glides along from the north past the east wall of the City all conspire to fill your mind with no pleasing or soothing ideas. We passed through several long arched entrances guarded by strong piquets of heavy armed soldiers till we were ushered into a long spacious Apartment which burst upon us in a blaze of splendour almost dazzling after the just witnessed Sahara like desolation Mr Morley Mr Howard and myself took our seats on a luxurious ottoman. and awaited the entrance of our host. I was strongly reminded of a similar scene which ocurred to me on my first introduction to the Northern Enara Warner. The door opened and there did not enter certainly 8 or 9 staghounds but 3 little girls of. 5. 6 or 7. years old small and yellow in countenance. with wild black eyes and raven hair and faces of the most. strange elfish animation The necks and arms of the little savages were sunburnt to the last degree and they ran frightened round the room with the speed of 3 wild Rabbits. For a long while their shyness was untameable till at last the eldest dare approach me and <stare> for a moment with her peircing optics into my countenance it was only for a moment She then burst off with an elfin shreik the other two emboldened by this example approached but only approached Morley and Howard when Again the portals unfolded and their father. Henry Fernando Enara entered we stood up to receive him.

A man stood before us about 5 9 inches high straight well formed and his whole frame one. strength of iron nervous sinew. his square turned shoulder. his long arm and his straight. limb with its arched instep pronounced him one of herculean strength and endurance and that broad white forehead those sallow moustachoed cheeks the wild black tyger eye and. the thin expanded nostril. formed an <u>indelible</u> countenance. shaded as it was with the close short curls of his neglected raven hair his firm compressed lips and their grim sardonic smile ensured him the truth of his title Enara. the Scourge of the Africans[19]

---

[19] The text is followed by a sketch of a head in the bottom right-hand corner, labeled "truth."

[Angria and the Angrians]
I(c)[1]

THE ANGRIAN WELCOME[2]

───────────

Welcome Heroes to the war
   Welcome to you glory
Will you seize your swords and dare
   To be renowned in story
What though Fame be distant far
Flashing from her upper air
Though the path which leads you there
   Be long and rough and gory
Still that path is straight and wide
Opened to receive the tide
Youths[3] first flush and manhoods pride
   Age all old[4] and hoary
     Sire and son may enter in
     Son and sire alike may win
     Rouse ye then, and all begin
   To seek the glory oer ye

Angrians when your morning rose
   Before your Monarchs eye
He swore that ere its evenings close
   All your foes should die
He saw the brightest star of fame
   Was flashing forth on high
He knew that Angrias very name
   Should force those foes to fly
And down from heaven. ZAMORNA came
   To guide you to the sky

───────────

1   A manuscript section of 10 pages, 11.2x18.5 cm, in the Brotherton Collection, consisting of folded sheets laid inside each other but not stitched. The first page is blank; the beginning of the poem is dropped on page 2, suggesting Branwell is beginning a new chapter.
2   In the 1837 revised version in vol. III, Branwell dates this version "October 1834."
3   "Childhoods" changed to "Youths."
4   "Stiff" changed to "old."

He shook his sword of quenchless flame
        And shouted VICTORY!

Angrians if your Noble King
        Rides foremost to the fight
Up in glorious gathering
        Around that helmet bright

Angrians if you weild you sword
        Every stroke shall be
Fixed as one undying word
        In your History

Angrians if in fight you die
        The clouds which oer you rise
Shall waft your spirits to the sky
        Of everlasting joys

Angrians when that fight is oer
        Heaven and earth and sea
Shall echo in the Cannons roar
        Your shouts of Victory

And now if all your bosoms beat
        To reach your native star
Shake the shackles from your feet
        WELCOME TO THE WAR.

See there the host of Quashia
        Along the Etrei lies
Then round the Flag of Angria
        ARISE ARISE ARISE

    Such were the strains with which voices and instuments joined to greet
my ears as I took my seat on the Ambassadors bench in the house of peers on
[the] occasion of the FIRST opening of the PARLIAMENT OF ANGRIA. I
will not detail to my readers in cold inanimate prose the stir and splendour of
this eventful day He very probably knows already that. All the City of
Adrianopolis rose in a wild ferment of excitement and that the spirit which
reigned through it was instantanously dispersed through the whole kingdom. that
the Angrian Ministry by a vast display of Armed Rejiments processions Banners
and music and. huge crowds of applauding subjects had given such a character of
dazzling magnificence to this important. day. as all who saw it will long
remember and remember with astonishment The King—Adrian the First. headed
the House of Peers in grand cavalry procession and the Ministers the House of

Commons to the great general Hall of Parliament where with the Monarchs opening speech the first session was to commence

Well just as the bands of 5 rejiments aided by the voices of 50000 men had ceased pealing forth the rousing Anthem I have quoted I turned my face from the great window whence I had been gazing on the huge host of people which choked up Parliament Square and sat down to look round on the Hall which blazed out in gold and scarlet above beneath and around me. This vast room is circular and rises up on all sides above the galleries to the gilded cornices and vast Dome.[5] whose simple unadorned immensity casts back like thunder the voices from below. Then beneath, those galleries this day all lined and hung with scarlet. run round the whole building placed upon double rows of rich Corinthian pillars and. appropriated to the visitor and general Attenders of the house. beneath them the. circular rows of cushioned benches. descend to the pavement and sloping from the pillars on the two sides of the building downward to the centre and appropriated to the two assembled houses of Parliament But at the head of the hall and just opposite where I sat. a vast scarlet canopy fringed with gold and. hung with Banners its front shining in the Rays of an immense gilded sun and. presenting the Talismanic motto ARISE rises in Genii magnificence. over the golden throne of Angria. the Seat appropriated to Her Monarch Zamorna

The Peers and. Commons of the Parliament began fast to enter and strode up to their seats enveloped in their rich robes of scarlet velvet. detached groups of from 2 to twenty had gathered round various public men and for aught I know were receiving from them their instructions for the champaign. This day was secured from being for the present commonplace by the astounding magnificence of its proceedings and secured too from neglect in history by the expected importance of its events. Here Zamorna was to declare to his people the outline of his measures thenceforward and to place his fiat on the rejection or admission of a Premeir and a ministry Here the Earl—but no Northangerland had not arrived that day in the capital nor could any tidings of his approach be gathered from all the innumerable channels of Intelligence

Tallyrand[6] said I to my freind the Ambassador from France. to Verdopolis who was on a visit to me "I cannot think the Earl afraid. Such a feeling would be unlike him he never turns from his path but when his interests bid him" "And you think. they do not bid him here then" "Yes I do" aye but dont you see the expressions on the faces of those senators dont you see how they gather round Warner and Percy and Thornton and Castlereagh as if just now offering life and fortune. in their support. look at that group of gentlemen

---

[5]   Branwell was familiar with the description of St. Paul's Cathederal from his reading of *A Description of London; containing a Sketch of its History and Present State, and of all the most celebrated Public Buildings* (London: 1824), which he was given at the age of ten; his copy is at the BPM.

[6]   See vol. I, p. 242, n. 6.

gathered round the tall handsome man. there that stout. athletic person" "What Mr Kirkwall" "aye Monseiur Kirvall I understand Richton he is an oracle of the Angrians the mirror they dress from the glass of fashion and the mould of form dont you see the darkned countenance. his doubting forehead and eyes cast to the ground as he speaks." "Yes Monseiur but. that very doubting convinces me that the Earl has not much to fear from Angria. a week ago this Mr Kirkwall would have been as far from doubt as he is now from certainty he would have sent the Earl to Tartarus[7] along with all his supporters But now alas." "The fickleness of human principles you would say." "Nay Tally I accuit My Lord Richton of such an insult to you" remarked the silent observant Fouche.[8] "Mr Fouche silence. Snuff. Fouche. eh? bah.!. Now Richton do observe the. horror all these Commons there seem to entertain to the benches destined for the use of the Opposition" "Aye Baron but. that horror arises from the fear of temptation" "Temptation ha eh Bien!. Vat temptation does the Earl hold out. a cloudy temperament and an acid imagination eh. Richton—But see great scarlet groups of Noblemen isolated into two masses round Castlereagh and Cartington There at least we see no signs of temptation no marks of doubting in those faces at least. appear determination and steadfastness." "Aye Tallyrand but these dont form a nation these are comparitively isolated but the Commons The Gentlemen on the other side are part and parcel of the people they represent are the Commons doubting? Angria is so too are the resolute? so is she! Whatever they think Angria thinks and the actions are impelled by her" "Very good but my dear freind vat do you think of the Ministry themselves look at them gathered at the table under the throne that Gentleman de son I think of the Exile ha ha. does he not seem in the predicament of many a hopeful youth who is heir and only heir to some fathers property does he not curl his lip and knit his forehead as he speaks so loudly to the. —that long lean fellow de man with whom I had a combat last night. bah. I left him hors de combat"[9] "and he you ditto" "Bah. not so Few leave me there. —not the conqueror of the world not Napoleon himself has ever so left me." "Aye.!" "Aye Fouche aye. but to make amends he has beaten yourself. eh. Well Richton I am convinced this Ministry will hold together. till. it corrodes with poison these peers till they separate homewards this Commons till—Northangerland comes—but not longer. No If he appears this Night if the King speaks at all ambiguously or seems in any way to regard him with respect if he only makes a speech like his letter. If the Earl makes one only like his then will Angria be shaken then will. it part and let Northangerland catch that which falls to his share. Till then Richton I do think these men whom you see dislike

---

7   In Greek mythology, the infernal abyss below Hades, where Zeus hurled the rebel Titans; more generally Hades or Hell.
8   Joseph Fouché (1763-1820) was Minister of the police under Napoleon, and later first minister of the provisional government that negotiated with Wellington for the return to Paris of Louis XVIII.
9   Out of action; disabled.

the Earl I do think that they determine to oppose him but allons!." "But suppose" said Fouche. "the Earl does not appear to night." "Mon Dieu the Earl is not mad he is not insane he may lose his title and his fortune and his life rather than not appear no If he have to cross the seas on foot he will appear" "In that case Talley I wont stand to abide him"

These two <reverend> Worthies stopped speaking for. a loud flourish of trumpets announced the Approach of Royalty to speak in the Angrian vein "the whole Hall rose on its legs" and every one stood to await the entrance of his Monarch. The lines of the foot guards filled the central arch and filed off with <lowerd> arms upon each side. The parliamentary officers ushers and Heralds advanced and proclaimed The King. every head was uncovered as for the first time his mourning thrown by.[10] Adrian the First. ascended the steps clothed in a gorgeous military attire of scarlet and gold and. with his thick curls unpressed by a crown his white hands uncumbered by sceptre. he turned round in front of the Throne. and stood proudly erect till the wild roar of Enthusiasm had swelled and subsided while the great dome yet sent down a voice of thunder Zamorna. with a glance of triumph round his adoring Parliament addressed all present in his first speech from the throne.

My lords and Gentlemen I now for the first time feel assured that Angria is a Kingdom I see her parliament the elected representatives of her provinces and counties and cities all gathered round me and the external aspect of manliness and vigour visible in every face gives me cheering promise of what I ought to expect from their coming descisions[11]

Here my own eyes bore testimony to the Dukes words every face was turned toward the Monarch with such an exulting determined and. roused expression that. it was evident the prime feeling among the auditors was "Who is like unto us" Zamorna telling them that as the rest of Angria was without paralell so ought the conduct of her King to be uncopied. and hence he refused to divide his words into the heads My Lords and gentlemen My Lords Gentlemen and again My lords and gentlemen but entered alone upon the subject which he knew was nearest to the heart of Every Angrian. Northangerland his letter and the aspect of affairs relating to him. He said that he had read that Noblemans letter that he had carefully considered his motives for its publication and that he knew the duty was dangerous and difficult which called upon him to be Arbiter in a question which could involve the writer of so extraordinary a composition He showed the consequences which might follow a rash judgement in this matter of a deffering of any judgement longer he He told the House that the Address from Stumphs land was like poison in the hands of a charlatan but in those of wisdom

---

10 After the death of his wife, Marian.Hume.

11 Compare with the full text of Zamorna's speech in Alexander CB II, part ii, pp. 304-09. The reference to this speech and to Zamorna's address to the Angrians on p. 236 above suggests a close collaboration between Branwell and Charlotte in the early development of the Angrian saga.

like a healing medicine he described its sad solemn tone of feeling as often a mere cloak over dark treacherous villainy but said the Duke when he spoke of VITALITY I pondered over it I comprehended it Vitality is the errrant light the wandering sun the <celestial> flame which in turn has glowed and vanished on every empire that War has founded and Science polished The pyramids o[f] Egypt beheld it smile it shone upon the cities of Assyria it gilded the Courts of Judahs temple Persia felt it and spread her boundless dominion then like fire it ran along the hills of Greece and Athens and Sparta and Macedon brought forth their mighty men Romulus saw his eagles fly in the light of its first approach like a beacon it burst on the Coliseum and warred the wild goths to carnage Mecca and Medina <sought> it[s] advent it fled thence Mahomet rose Abu bekir flourished and the seven Saracenic Usurpations were founded under its influence Tartary and Tamerlane swarmed from their eastern hive and scourged all Asia Italy Spain and France and England felt its beams centurys past and extinguished in Europe it was rekindled in Africa[12] There now Verdopolis sees it flicker and fade Angria smiles in its earliest dawn And Percy has formed in his Titanic mind a scheme for making that dawn Immortal

Thus in words like these flowing energetic and filled with eloquence. went on the King of Angria and oh Reader if you[r] recollections of this Night are strengthened by the breif sketch I am giving you how vividly will flash on your mind the Majestic form and godlike voice of the Royal speaker. Zamorna proceeded to reprobate the serpent <policy> disclosed in Northangerlands vast machinations he bitterly condemned. that Noblemans attempt to cast jealousy between him and his ministers and then he gave his fixed opinion of the ex premier he called him a man of gigantic Intellect and creative genius that that mind and all his energies he could devote to spread cherish and eternize through the world his discovered Vitality while at the same time his own more personal feelings his peculiar and morbid passions the whole under current of his soul would madly rush against the barriers of reason and right and social happiness would destroy all he had built up and would raise what his great spirit had taught him to destroy He said he was a freind to Angria as a country but a bitter foe to it as Individuals and then the Duke asked the house would they look at Northangerlands vast ideas and take a mighty light into their kingdom or look at his pernicious principles and take a burning fire would they do both would they burn to shine.

My lords said his Grace. to you I leave the option of your choice. Yes after deep thought long consideration I have resolved to place my prerogative in

---

[12] Romulus, with his twin brother Remus, was the legendary founder of Rome. The Goths represent the Barbarian invasions at the collapse of the Roman Empire. Mecca and Medina are the two holy cities of the Mohammedans. Abu Bakr was the first of the Mohammedan caliphs. Under Tamerlane (1336-1405) the Tartars conquered most of Persia and India, Georgia and other parts of the Caucasus.

the hands of my Kingdom[s] delegates and let them through their medium re
elect or finally and for ever cast off Lord Northangerland as Premeir of this realm

Then the Duke of Zamorna. addressed the Earl in a strain of sublime
eloquence upon his own Character his Melancholy miserable notions on the
future his erroneus and dreadful actions in the past and that present strange
aimless bitterness which dashed his whole life with care. My readers may smile
to hear of Zamornas remenstrating with any one on erroneus conduct. He whose
whole short existence has been if as bright certainly as erratic as lightning But
when I heard him speak. I <am sure> I did not smile his countenance was
animated into an expression so far above mere Regal dignity his voice fell on
our ears in that immense vaulted hall with a tone of such rich full melody and
when we knew that it was a Monarch of[sic] that cast of all customary forms of
etiquette who was—in the House of Parliament—opening to his greatest subject
the darkness and crimes of a life of vast public engagements when I looked
forward in to the probable future ongoings of the God <like> being before me
and pictured in my mind the effects on the world hearafter of that splendid spirit
and passionate animation and boundless ambition which in every sentence which
fell like music on my ears I heard so strongly displayed then I confess that my
mind was strongly excited when as the <   > Duke of Zamorna had said

Angrians when I meet you again it will be to give you the signal of
dismissal on my departure with my army eastward"
He looked proudly round the Hall and seated himself on his august throne and all
the thousands who had stood so long so breathless so deeply and strongly excited
raised all their true Angrian voices in one long loud thundering cheer. of warm
enthusiastic adoration.

Just as Zamorna had arisen to speak the faces of the Members and
audience gave on[e]. eager glance to the entrance for the Earl of Northangerland
entered the house and walking through the long gallery or corridor he descended
to the upper row of the left hand benches or those which are intended for
members dissafected to the ministry and there alone with no one near him took
his seat the single mighty Opposition

Certainly if during the Kings speech a single look was directed from
their Monarch by those present it was to that scarlet bench and its solitary
occupant. and many a keen grey eye did I behold glance hurriedly from Zamorna
to Percy and back again to the Ministry

Northangerland himself while the King was speaking sat with his
elbow resting on the back of the sopha and his head leant on his hand fixing one
calm unchanging look upon Zamorna he was dressed in deep mourning and his
face seemed even paler than when he left. Angria a month since. and how
different was this Earl of Northangerland from that Alexander Rougue whom 6
years ago I saw seated on the bench at the Verdopolitan parliament when
Chrashey made his famous speech before the opening of the great insurrection.[13]

---

[13] See vol. I, pp. 181-82.

<u>That</u> man was as tall as this he was dressed in black he was seated almost alone but his firm excited eye. his black Satanic sneer the tumultous change of passions which crossed his features and the restless agony of his expression associated well with the idea[s] which were firing in that mind on that eventful eve ideas of men and carnage of kingdoms overthrown and citys drenched in blood Now the man whom I beheld was so still so calm so statue like. his face so pale and. that high aristocratic forehead haloed with. such golden hair—Such a deep utter sadness of the mind had fixed the eye and. given anxiety to the brow and. all his thoughts seemed so inward fixed upon some matter of mediation[sic] which no one could save himself. develop the vast beginnings character and end that. if. Alexander Rougue looked like Satan the prince of darkness Lord Northangerland looked like Lucifer Star of the Morning[14] —And the sneer was here before me too but it was changed from what I had seen it before it was a sneer of calm contempt at. himself and nature not of feirce hatred of his enimies and mankind I acquit this man of any feeling whatsoever for Man or Nation of the welfair of any state or kingdom I aquit him of kindly affection to society and. happiness But when I saw the moments of convulsed expression which as Zamorna spoke cast a deadly shadow over his features I could not call him cold and Icy and stoical. Say rather. Hot as flame.

When the loud enthusiasm of applause which followed the Kings speech had sunk into silence save in the deep reverberations of the vaulted dome. the Earl of Northangerland. rose and advanced a few steps from his seat. without waiting for further mark of attention or theatrical effect he proceeded to address the house.

Angrians I am here in fullfillment of. the determination I expressed 2 weeks ago. But I crossed the sea once more for Andrianopolis without any feeling of hope or exultation. and when I entered your city this Afternoon the idea that on this night was to be opened the first sessions of the Angrian parliament failed most miserably in producing that activity in me which the passing of THE BILL or the Coronation of your King did not a year before I suppose you will smile when you look back on the very minute degree of spirit which then on those occasions you did observe in my appearance. but do not judge of my mind by my looks and weary feelings. nay men judge of me by action by action and when the news was carried through Verdopolis that Angria had ceased to be a province was now enrolled among independent Nations that the Aristocrats were vanquished lay. toothless and impotent—when you saw Zamorna crowned in St Michaels as sovereign of a sovereign country when you opened the pages of your "Laws and Constitution" when you looked round every day on Adrianopolis and dreamed every night of Africa and India. Then did you not believe that energy might exist without peacefulness did not you gaze upon the path I had opened to you and regard me as the premeir of your government

---

[14] Compare Isaiah 14:12; *Paradise Lost*, X, 383, V, 708-10 and VII, 131-35. Compare also with the poem on p. 556 and the revised version in vol. III.

and. turning your eyes from halls and castles which had stood over their woods for a century. without shedding down on you one poor single ray of happier existence. did not you turn to a man who had never stepped before into your country and ask of yourselves when you thought of me is not a stranger now and then much more welcome than a Neighbour. There are certain fellows who talk mightily of the glory of Angria and act as if they did not know the name of glory while one other man. never speaks of the bright vision but is every[sic] seeking to give it a habitation and a name.

It is only a few minutes since your King concluded his first speech to his countrys Parliament Those sounds yet ring in my ears which rose when you heard the last word that your Monarch spoke but far above all your applause far above any sound I have heard of late above everything my memory retains save my own imaginings far above all recollections which could move me to enterprise. sounds now the voice the thoughts the spirit of Zamornas speech. Then there. men you heard the speech of a king and never. during after life never till death forces memory from your heart should you forget one sentence one word of. what you have just so deeply attended too No my heart will always retain with a feeling of pleasure the voice of my Sovereign and. —I— Angrians—I—know—"

Northangerland whose voice had been evidently raised with an artificial emphasis in the sentences I have above given. ceased speaking not suddenly but somehow left his words to escape without connection and let them stop only for want of Ideas he sat down but. not as if "stuck" he reclined back on the sopha and closed his eyes without making an effort to regain himself. he was not ill that was evident for his face never changed. nor asleep neither. his "declining to have any thing to do with thinking" his seeming disgust at all exertion. produced a strange effect on me the House was confused. every man cast an impatient glance as if expecting an explanation of such conduct. I saw the ministry underneath the throne bending their heads toward each other with scowls of exultation Warner hurriedly spoke to Morley who shrugged his shoulders and sat still then to young Percy who seemed in such a heaven of scorn that he couldnt hearken but after deep consultation between Bramham and Montmorency that latter arose.

"Well! Lucifer Star of the morning how art thou—"
Northangerland waked by that well known voice started up stood again before the house and turning to the thick crowds beneath him recommenced

"Ha! I wanted an impulse an. outward excitement to rouse me my own ideas the speech from the throne made me think but they hindred me from speaking Now Sirs now I have recovered my cause for exertion and now I could speak till death.

Aye Angrians I was thinking when I sat down upon what his Grace has just been saying to myself. I was thinking off. his words and feelings upon my character and Intellect. and. while my voice lost itself in false expressions of an unfelt enthusiasm my mind was wrapt. in deep and anxious thought upon Zamorna or itself. Am I going to *Lie* that I have caught myself of late so often running from present buisness to ideas alien to my situation this very afternoon while on my way to your Capital I lost my consciousness of your existence in dreams and visions most contrary to my intentions I did however enter this house resolved to rouse myself but the words o[f] his Majesty sunk me in deeper abstration and all the time I was speaking to you I was thinking to myself—But a minute ago one word one voice broke the spell of my enchantment one sentence roused me in to existence I am risen from the dead. and have become myself again.

<u>What</u> was that fellow saying who spoke to you just now How did he Dare to break in upon one word which. I might have been <using> is he among you then and if he is here so here are his coadjutors his associates I see them and I know them and this night let it be my duty to cause you to know them to hold the lamp toward them and if it choose let it burn them! Oh men men do not be so blind to your own. constant welfare. when I wrote my late Address to you from Stumps land when I looked from those windows on a bigoted and slaved Island. when I embarked again for a country from which I had so lately exiled myself my thoughts and feeling were turned toward Angria and Zamorna.

And last night as I neared your coasts over the Atlantic and saw the dark outline of land with the full moon rising beyond the hills of Zamorna. the long waves too all hurrying forward to the shore. I did only think of that. light not of freedom not of peace nor of plenty but of life and glory that strange soul which can only animate an uncorrupting country that spirit which I was determining should soon shine on Angria, of the whole world too drifting yet fast[er] than those waves to their great ascendant orb of in itself eternal vitality aye that mighty moon whose wax and wane. causes all the ebb and flow in the ceaseless tide of time

And this night—I sat down and heard the Duke of Zamorna dash at onc[e] into that matter which he knew could now alone interest and excite his auditors I heard him tell you he feared the duty of judgement upon the Earl of Northangerland when a false judgement would plunge himself and you into the punishment. He says my letters are hemlock[15] and healing good and evil. Aye and so they are hemlock to my enimies but medicine to my—. (Friends? Editor)[16] to—Angria. He tells you he can understand my principle of Vitality ha I knew he could I trusted in him for full comprehension and if I die this next moment I bequeath my mantle of Inspiration to my Royal Elisha[17] Then he does openly explain to you the grand outline of this Vitality he shows you in succession the Nile reflecting its columned and palaced Egypt and Palestine bowing at the shrine of its mysterious temple and Greece glowing with the

---

[15] A poison made from the leaves of weeds of the carrot famly, drunk by Socrates.

[16] The parentheses are Branwell's.

[17] See p. 246, n. 12.

lustre of her Pericles her Themistocles her Pleiades.[18] Rome eager. for conquest as one of her own eagles for their prey the Goths dark and mighty as their own Northern forests and. then he showed you Vitalitys that spring from whence sprung the torrent of Mahometism ursurpation and Tartar conquest he told you the light had set on Europe but had risen in Africa that if it was declining over Verdopolis It would fain secure its beams to Angria. He told you all this And he told you well. I never passed a more glorious moment in public than when I saw my King thus unfolding all my own ideas and gilding them with the haloe of his own sovereign soul.

What human joys are there without bitter sorrows you see I drunk this cup up with haste and I found black dregs at the bottom of it Your King goes on to mention the terms in which I described his Ministry your tyrants Theyre there and let them contradict my assertion. your bloody tyrants. he says I have attempt[ed] to fix a jealousy on his soul of these his worthy servants that I have given them demon characters and hurled upon them all the weight of my bitterest curses he says well and so I have. I have tried to make him jealous of them to make you jealous of them to blast them and theirs for ever to over throw all their power and name and existence. but I tell them here before this assembled parliament that what I have done is nothing nothing to what I will hereafter and shortly do. My King shall never again express the feeling he has done this night and his people shall not wither under the load of their gathered iniquities. Your King asks you after this paragraph of miserable blindness such as I am will you take me or leave me. crown me or destroy do not you answer him till I have proven wether I am worthy of death or of dominion. But I rejoice he has left the descision to you. I could scarcly be pleased to hear my doom pronounced by a fool of an Arundel a Murat and a Warner And now he again indulges the feelings of his own heart again he speaks to myself and. the native generosity of his spirit breaks from under the dictation of a few worthless court favorites. I shall not speak to you of my opinions of those words to me. Zamorna only half knows me you not in the tenth degree. My sorrows my melancholy my crimes and my treacheries let all these rest on my head for all these I know are mine. Come I am cheerful enough under the weight and all the reputations I have ruined the fortunes I have withered the throats I have cut and the souls I have sent to perdition they stand up day and night before me and day and night I laugh at and despise them Aye a fellow now stands before me naked. but with a most ragged garment in his hand. he points to one little hole and. howls that in excavating that rent I have turned him blasted on the world and beside this one a fellow destitute. pulls his long visage. at the landscape. and while he himself was born in the parish workhouse and brought up at the parish board he complains that I have seized his parks his seat his heritage. and to back him a

---

18 The seven daughters of Atlas and Pleione who were placed by Zeus among the stars. They appeared in the sky in the middle of May and thus announced the return of the good weather.

gory wretch lifts his unwrung locks from the salt water and. affirms. that it is a black crime in me—when he by his own confession was bound on a voyage to death that I showed him the nearest track to port and stilled the ravings of a mind probably worn with care and avarice. But if I sit down to light my fire in the desart. the very stones rise up from beneath me and. the base inanimate dust around me. cries out that I have driven it into the pit of punishment and have cast it into eternal fire. poor soul it once had life but. all the life it now has fertilized a churchyard or lies crashed in the jaws of a hungry dog—or forms the spoon you eat your porridge withal

Now Angrians I have run through the greater part of your Kings first speech and I believe that you possess the greater part of my opinions on it it is a speech worthy of your King and your country both its excellencies and imperfections are like you I believe if you degrade yourselves that man will degrade himself. but if you rise he too will rise above you My endeavour shall be hereafter to exalt you both. Oh If I could see Angria a country of a strong determined. and active population governed by a King of fire Ambition and energy if I could see her. maybe at arms with every on[e] at enmity with all. men hated by surrounding nations yes detested by freinds and enimies—yet. if she returned this distrust these arms this hatred with corresponding and well founded contempt. if she knew and had that spring within her which could bear her up against allies and foes. If she went on. on her own foundations and attempted nothing without herself and attempted every thing with herself and suceeded in all things by herself. If each man answered his fellow with the word his fellow spoke to him if. not an eye was turned save to conquest and. victory If you determined to do as you wished and. would wish rightly what to do if. you made it you[r] constant office to spread your empire without and consolidate it within. to found laws which should endure for ages and not pass away like the visions of a night aye and to walk in those laws and to go hand in hand with their makers to go hand in hand with your King to follow no one. to take no one as your guide. but to set your shoulder to the wheel. aye to set your foot upon the desart. and say here is a path for my ongoings and I will proceed upon it I will go as far as I can and. as fast as I can with me shall no one walk and without my nod not a soul shall move

Now men if you could do as I have pointed out and act like men with reasons and imaginations I could not. I know promise you peace in this world oh no nor happiness in that which is to come I could not say a life of pleasure awaits you now and a crown of glory hereafter. But Angrians I could promise to you. a country firm as a rock and glowing like fire with Intellect. with mind. I could say Angria shall be a great empire the greatest this world has born it shall spread itself. the very tide of glory the future only track of fame I will build it as the Only Altar of VITALITY. and there there shall burn that eternal flame shall burn shall brighten and revivify sunken mortals and a sinking world

O Thou great divinity thou only GOD. whom my mind ever could stoop to worship. whom I have long long worshipped and whom I will for ever adore Omnipotent and Almighty Creator I stand here before Thee thy only enlightened worshipper amid. a thousand millions of men. yet I am a Man and have the passions and feeling of a man. I can love I can hate I can feel Affection I can nourish vengeance I can do all that these can do save feel freindship and the ties of blood I know that the men who are this night listening to what I say stand looking at me as if they would fain peirce that veil of darkness which thou hast drawn round me but they cannot they cannot yet. they too are Men. they too have the passions and the feelings of men. I can love them as a body though I have not done so though I cannot do so to Individuals. and I now turn to Thee and ask Thee to enlighten them even as Thou has enlightened me.[19]

Oh why do I feel so tied and shackled in my powers of speech. At this moment just now I can see before me and. my mind can fully comprehend things and thoughts and undertakings which have never before been disclosed to man which I know not wether man has ever before had a glimmering of I can see all the causes of the rise decline and fall of empires where that rise exists what has been their summit what their end I know when. the world was at its zenith and where it is now. I can comprehend every law and principle of events and changes aye and I behold the future I see something of times to come. —And why Oh Thou O God when I see and know all this why cannot I tell it these people would willingly know too and grant to me than the power to shew it them. There are they looking at me as if they waited for the fire to descend from heaven here am I that fire within me and around me yet. I cannot flash it forth. to the gaze of their purblind eyes. I may see and think and loose[sic] myself in great imaginings yet where is the utility of my own soul knowing what will. prove unavailable unless 10000 others know.

Then God cast this veil from me cast it too from Thyself. cause all round me to view it and. their immorality is half gained. aye if men could see Thee VITALITY if they could know thee and thy power what thou hast accomplished and whatever thou canst do. Ha! then they would leave all their own vain superstitions their Eternals their Redeemers their Saints and their Angels they would turn and would cleave to thee the only living and true God.
Northangerland apparently exhausted with his speech sat down on the sopha and there reclining with one arm flung over the back of the seat the other sometimes stretched to the House he proceeded in a strange conversational tone of the utmost familiarity yet <flashing> sentences and feelings of the most unevery day order to address his hearers passing his hand over his pale white forehead he said smiling slightly

Now do you know the quality of my mind you dont certainly know what that mind is but. you can perhaps tell what it is not it is not one of your own it looks to higher views than yours. and all that I have done of a public character through a life of wild viscisitude however strange and bloody and unlawful has yet had one grand principle and has been done for the promotion of

---

[19] In the right hand margin Branwell has sketched the profile of a man—see Alexander and Sellars, p. 313.

one grand end. I told you in my address men. what I had done to create Angria what actions of mine bore upon that creation how they have suceeded and where they have been dissapointed aye. where they have been dissapointed! and where they shall yet. succed. I have told you too to night more than ever I told a man before I have guided you to the ou[t]ward porch of my mind and let him enter the temple who dare but stop men a little of my usual spirit is coming over me and I begin to shrink from speaking to a human being I must muse again or I shall freeze directly and oh what subject shall I rouse where is the wind to awaken this sullen sea where are the rocks on which it may dash its foam Oh there they are I see them but by the bones of Sylla.[20] neither you nor I shall see them long

Now Angrians I asked you some time since. wether or not do you understand what I mean when I speak to you and I have answered my own question by saying that though you do not understand me now the time shall come when you may but. here at this point I must enter upon [a] subject which I think all of you will know and feel and feel strongly <   > aye and act strongly too. I say men If you enter upon a path wether upward or downward. you the great flock of the people must have a shepherds leaders[sic] to direct you and guide you may stop when you will you may go on when you will but while you do go on you must go under the superintendence of men elected no doubt. by yourselves or you may at once clap on your chains. now if you wish to seek the road to heaven you always hire a preist and if you. want to find the road to Tartarus you hire a preist too who if he can seldom shew the path upward always manages to do so downwards. Well men if you are desirous of entering on the road to vital. life and glory as I have no doubt you are so—the first thing you will seek after my just mentioned doctrine being established will be leaders and directors on this vast path and undertaking at once you will look to your King. nay men Nay dont shew your ignorance your slavery. A king will act as a shepherds dog on a leash <or a ram> but never never as a shepherd. while you consider him as your bodyguard your stout foremost father of the flock pressing on with his broad forehead and curling horns to oppose the first and boldest front to every aggressor or as the sharp vigilant active dog who. runs unceasingly round you restrains you onto your path warns you by his cry of enimies attacks your foes and if you act unwarrantedly attacks yourselves—But the shepherds have a different course to take Your shepherds what[sic] make your laws must controul your motions you[r] on goings your down lying and your uprising without their order neither dog or Ram [21] <the> flock must move or stay and all these powers you assuredly will not confide in a king No Angrians to doom you throw your selves at once into the arms of despotism into the chains of slavery no your shepherds you must seek in your Ministry and wether your shepherds be good or evil depends on wether your ministry be. worthy or worthless there are your shepherds there they are and now that you are about to set out on a mighty

---

[20] See vol. I, p. 338, n. 7.
[21] Compare I Samuel, 29:6; II Samuel, 3:25.

journey let me shew you wether these men can guide you wether they shall be displaced and others appointed in their room.

Angrians your Minsters are.   22 in number and here are their names and orders there are their crimes and their persons

Charles Stanhope	primate of the Kingdom
Frederic Lofty	Lord high Chamberlain
Frederic Stuart.	Master General of Ordnance.
Wilkin Thornton	Commander in Cheif
Henry Linsay	High Chancellor of the laws
Warner Warner	Secretary of the home department
Hector Montmorenci	Foreign Secretary
Thomas Morley	Colonial Secretary
Jean Murat.	Master of the horse.

All These. men direct the energies of Angria rule her councils and consult with her King

O Thou most Reverend Father in God thou venerable and holy man experienced and saintlike teacher of thy Gospel unquenched beacon in a dark and guilty world What shall I say to thee then great and good man whose long and patriarchal life hath passed in a broad flow of good works and good will toward men whose tongue hast never been employed but to teach mortals the road to heaven and whose heart ever beat responsive in thy Creators praise. what shall I say to thee Oh Elijah[23] unwearied teacher of thine Ahabs wilful blindness. Isaih[sic] whose prophetic numbers hath often roused a land to repentance Jeremiah whose saddened notes have buried a land in mourning Great expounder and teacher of the Christian doctrine I honour thee and I love thee Oh then what shall I say to thee.

I say go on in the course thou hast taken may the beams of heaven smile round the hoariness of thy stupendous age. go on fight the good fight of faith put on whole Armour of righteousness and finish thy course with joy[24] Ha! thou scoundrelly Hypocrite thou base fawning serpent who hast insinuated thyself into Kings houses and princes dwellings who hast whispered into the ears of the unwary and the light and vain minded whose eyes burst with the fulness and whose nose windest the wind and lovest the wine when it is red and the cup <widely> is overflowing thou servant of sin and villainy with righteousness in thy mouth and black crime in thy mind. mind did I say thou a mind oh oh! who only possesst instinctive crouching to to the great and fawning on the powerful that drivelling hypocritical easiness which hast curved they back from thy birth and will squint in thine eyes to thy grave.

O Heavenly <u>Stanhope</u>. who dares speak thus of thee.

---

22 Left blank in the manuscript.

23 See I Kings 21 and 22.

24 Compare Ephesians 6:13.

Stupendous Intellect spirit overflowing with Immortal Genius why hast thou come across me. I shall break the first Commandment.[25] but courage. For truely thou possessest no likeness to aught either in heaven or in earth or in the waters under the earth.[26] Then let me <waken> it in thee. that presiding and overruling genius who hast for 6 months past directed every word and look and action of our mighty and worshipping King thou vast soul and presiding genius of Zamorna all his ongoings have. followed the pointing of thy finger. O thou prodigious Imagination whose whole thoughts are occupied upon purification and sweating and. making whole. What sayest thou to this rebellious and stiff-necked people.[27] "Wash you wash you make you clean cleanse your filth from of you and your abominations from your shirts. for I. will smooth you as a garment and as a vesture will I fold you by hand ye shall be mangled but I am the same and my years shall not fail" Mighty <u>Lofty</u> we obey thee. and when Angria wants her cloth[e]s washing she shall send them to thee

"Who is this who cometh from Zamorna with <u>died garments</u> from Stuartville this that is <u>glorious in his apparel</u> travelling in the greatness of his strength Not a minute ago spake I of cloth[e]s and here ye have cloth[e]s in plenty and fine cloth[e]s too and Nothing but Cloth[e]s either. I see no head no heart no mind no brain nothing but—Whisht those are the priests clothing the vesture of the sanctuary the very linen ephod and holiest robes of <Aaron>[28] Castlereagh thou presides over the artillery roar at thy loudest then or we will cut thee small into banner cloths

But tremble Nations for the destroyer appeareth the avenger of blood is nigh. "O wherefore art thou red in thine apparel and thy garments like his that treadeth in the wine-vat" I have trodden the wine press alone and of the people there were none with me. fore I will tread them in myn anger and will trample them in my fury and their blood shall stain all my raiment."[29] Now Thornton of Girnington was in height ten cubits and a span and his spear was a weavers beam. he was a lionlike man and a man of war from his youth.[30] Quashia ruddy and of fair complexion comely. and a stripling who took stones from the brook. Ha! the comparison ends here Thornton your champion laughs at stones He will flay David alive and eat him to his breakfast.

Hurrah for Thornton the warlike the champion of Angria

---

[25] Thou shalt have no other gods before me.

[26] Compare Exodus 20:4.

[27] See Deuteronomy, chapter 9.

[28] See Exodus, chapter 28.

[29] Compare Isaiah 63:2-3.

[30] Compare with the description of Goliath in I Samuel, chapter 17, and in I Chronicles 11:22-23.

"Who are these who come riding upon clouds flying on the wings of the wind.[31] Why they are Warner and Lindsay and Montmorenci and Morley. —Here then Scripture refuses to do honour to such worthies and. Percy in his own disgust and detestation shall grasp his stone from the brook and crush the serpents to dust beneath it. your Ministry Your Shepherds your. leaders!. your Tyrants your. wolves your blood-suckers! aye if every[sic] leeches fastened on earth earthly country here how they hang thick and fast round Angria and is every drop of that Noble blood which mounts in heart and pulses with all the full fiery vigour of immortality. which rushes through the veins of Angria and warms her sons to love and liberty Is this precious life current I say now and henceforward to be drained by the voracious maws of those human leeches who are crawling in slime and blackness round her noble breast. Oh forbid it. Angria. They say they are there for your health that they are healing you and bringing you into a state of health and vigour again. you prove your belief in this doctrine. tear. the reptiles from the wound dash them to the earth and crush out of them that gore on which they now fatten and thrive Warner and Lindsay and Montmorency and. Morley ha Angrians I know them all and you shall know them all.

Warner is a man. of. long standing and great family influence in Angria by the death of his father he was in early life brought conspicuously to the view of your people. and his cursed and blasted appearance. that withered stunted form which Nature has bestowed upon him as the mark to single out his Cain like spirit. only made him more noticed among a nation remarkable for manly strength and symmetry his mind corresponded with his form and his wretched depraved ambition that morbid diseased irritability of his temperament. his disgusting arrogance and impertinent self sufficiency had cast such a blackness about him that I must feel suprised how man or woman could approach save with a rifle the unwholesome carrion. but the wretch possesses abundance of money and by means of that he has worked himself into a high station in your country and wormed himself into the full confidence of your King Oh I bitterly greive to see Zamorna cherish such a serpent as yon. crawling wretch Arthur he is trying to undermine your throne.

Lindsay is a Grim gaunt ghastly Scotchman bred to the bar and. born to the brandy when unhappily his brain is free from the effects of his regular potions his whole soul is bent upon self aggrandisement and the blasting of everything round him he would not scruple to do any possibly conceivable word or action by which he thought he could gain a momentary a temporary good False and treacherous by Nature lying and unprincipled by proffession you see all his mind stamped in indelible characters on his hideous and deathlike countenance.

I think Angrians I know Montmorency several years accquaintance and united transactions has given me a deep insight into the basest heart that ever corrupted in a human breast. I know his corrupted tastes and debased imagination

---

[31] Compare Psalm 18:10.

his unstaying prolifigacy and his mean dishonesty think not I am scattering these words at random No I could substantiate every expression I have used respecting him by proofs which would make your blood run cold with horror Aye and. shortly I will do so I see the wretch tremble. Tremble then still. tremble till I crush thee into the dust of eternal degredation.

I think I need not speak of Morley he is a slow worm of the <Oelumulvaie> of serpents.[32] a poor fangless viper who can only scare with his hideous shape and never hurt by his lolling tongue pass him over I will directly shake him from my hand in to the fire.

Here then men I have given you your ministry I have shewn you your shepherds the sole guides and guardians of your earthly welfare. and is there a single man here who after he has heard this discription can say these men are worthy to be placed over me they know more than I do and better than I do their actions are infallibly righteous and by these actions I will abide.

Oh Zamorna Zamorna. three times I was about to speak to you this evening but on every occasion other matters forced my attention to be diverted from their first Noble object. But at length I. give scope to my desire and speak face to face with my King. I have come this day from a retreat 500 miles distant in the woods and forests of Stumps Isle. I have roused up a mind to exertion which every day sinks more and more and still further recoils from buisness I have stood up this night and have. unflinchingly laid bare that corrupted ulcer the Angrian Ministry and I have offered without drawback. all my soul and Intellect to the promotion of your Kingdom. power and glory. My great public reason for all these unwonted employments was to revive Vitality and to enlighten the world but my private wish and that on which my heart dwelt continually was to direct you right to point you to the true path of fortune to add a new laurel to the brow a new glory to the Name of my King and sovereign the Duke of Zamorna. I believe you to be Sire the Greatest human being except myself which this world now supports and in comparing you with myself when I oppose your fire to my ashes your spendid qualitys blazing in youthful Grandeur to my wornout <character> withering in the decline of. evening I can no more compare myself with you than I can November with June Yet however time and tide destroy bloom the[y] cannot destroy wisdom. and my Lord Duke I. know more than you I see much farther than you my eyes penetrate far far forward and my mind. looks back to the earliest time. I can point you paths and guide to temples which none

---

32 Branwell seems to have invented this classification. Timothy Tickler, Esq. writes in *Blackwood's Magazine*, XIV (1823), 81: "The qualities of these gentlemen are admitted by all parties; and the smartness of Jeffrey, the buffoonery of the parson, the Billingsgate of Brougham, serve to float the lumber of the stottery of Macculloch, and filth of Hazlitt. We now look on it as a sort of fangless viper, which we allow to crawl about, permitting ourselves to smile now and then, if any of its slimy contortions please the fancy of the moment, knowing that it can do no hurt."

yet ever knew in a vision save me. Then hear me Zamorna and receive me remember I have never before asked any man but you I did not thus ask. the. Magnates of Verdopolis when I threw their City into blood and anarchy I did not so supplicate the King of Sneachis land. when I raised the standard of rebellion on every mountain in his kingdom[33] No These were. dust low grovelling dust beings whom I despised whom I determined to trample on and whom I will yet destroy But you are a different being from these. The celestial fire has in truth descended upon you and ere long it must purify your mind. let the scales fall from your eyes Arthur and behold the things I have shown you You know that. you are at the beck of your insolent Ministers but their minds are as rotten as themselves break them and rise in the strength of your native soul. I know you Zamorna better than you know yourself. 1 year since when you would have shrunk to think of your present mind I saw seeds from which I knew this plant would arise and Now Sir Now I see blossoms from which I do well know what fruit must spring. Well. Zamorna a little while will ripen thee though thou art green even now a few strong vigorous sunbeams will bring the red upon thy cheek and that sun I will take care shall be unclouded shall. shower down on thee its whole flame of VITALITY.

Now then Angrians In conclusion I must tell you that the sun which shines on Zamorna will like wise shine on you the effects it produces in him making allowance for the different soil it will produce in you. and the same seed too is rising in you all if. weeds choke Zamorna they will overrun Angria too if a cypress. darkens over your Sovereign Angria partakes the shade. and If. His brows are crowned with myrtle. his people. share in his laurels

Well. farewel. to you men of Angria farewell for a little while. I have pointed you the enimies of your welfare I have shewn you the characters and intentions of your ministry. I have told you and now again I tell you cast them from you and trample them under your feet. Receive me as the director of your council because I know more than you and have taught you more than any other could teach you. I must be Prime Minister of Angria again and I must mount upon the ruins of my foes mount with my Angrians and let our Sovereign lead us on does the sailor care for the angry ocean when it bears him towards his shore does the labourer shrink from toil when it gives him life and sustenance does the scholar avoid learning does the soldier flee from battle. and shall Angria not rouse herself to her salvation. does the Bird. neglect its nest. does the wild lion starve its young does the mother frown on her child and shall Zamorna. neglect his Angria. Aye sooner may the Nestlings feed the Hawk. the wild welps be torn by the wolves the child. be cast into its grave sooner may Angria. turn from Zamorna and Zamorna hate his Angria. Sooner far sooner than Percy forget them both or in forgetting them forget VITALITY and the interests of three thousand years to come. I hear that wind sighing over the waves of the Calabar and. howling down. the streets of your rising city. its voice is mournful and the

---

[33] See **Letters From An Englishman**, vols. IV-VI, in vol. I.

rain which it drives with it beats heavily over the dome of this silent building
To me in any other mood of mind than the present these sounds would suggest
only feelings of melancholy images of sorrow and slavery and decay. But Not
Now Angrians Not. Now. No. I hear that wind and it tells me a tale which
makes my blood thrill through my vales[34] in a tide which they have not felt for
20 years gone by it tells me men that it has swept over a land. Awakning from
sleep and rousing to the energy of a glorious morning its[sic] speaks of eyes
opened to the light which is to dawn upon them of ears willing to hearken and of
souls able to understand.
O heads hearts and hands of Angria. Men of Andrianopolis Representatives of
your country titled and untitled peers and commoners all all here present all
whom I see not and hear not every soul who bears the Name of Angrian Awake
Awake to your Morning. away with yon hidious Nightmare. away with vain
midnight superstition away with all your uncertain aimless moonlight. it is day
now and a day which must decide your future a day on which you must conquer
or die. Where are your fathers men your Ancestors who have gone long before.
They are dead lying in their graves dust to dust ashes to ashes they have no life
no souls no being now. they know no heaven and they feel. no hell. Their life
on earth was it one of pleasure or one of pain if it was either it was all they can
ever know. I know their[sic] is an Eternity I know that time shall never have an
end but it is an eternity of seperate existences an Eternity which one man must
never see. On then you have only a short life to exist in and you must say at its
conclusion I have never smiled or I have never sighed The first you shrink to say
the last you in your present state will never be able to say then seize the
opportunity I have pointed to you. Down with the Ministry receive your
Northangerland receive his Vitality and all the heaven[ly] things he promises you
shall be yours. To morrow I. set out for. Pequena where I shall convene a great
meeting of all its people. I shall likewise appear on succeeding days at all the
principle cities in Angria there I shall disclose all my opinions to you. and to
gain all that I wish you to gain to Make yourselves the Glory of Creation I
merely ask you Now. through your country attend to my bidding &. up and
ARISE!"

As the Earl of Northangerland had proceeding[sic] in his speech his
voice first melancholy and saddend in its tones had gradually increased in
bitterness and emphasis of expression the sneer had falln blacker and his eyes
glanced with a glassier glaze. When he sat down on the sopha. he had assumed a
tone of mere conversation [with] which he can with such felicity throw out his
strongest and loftiest views and feelings and to see such a tall statly figure like a
Monarch addressing a parliament sitting and throwing out with the ease of after
dinner conversation sentences which other men would have had to work hard and
solicit mighty inspiration ever to scintillate after 10 hours polishing—all
produced that effect which in that assembly the speaker wished it to do. Then as

---

[34] "veins" probably intended.

soon as he. got upon the topic of the Ministry he started up again curled his lips with inimitable scorn and. sneered out his texts of scripture and. cut down their characters with his matchless abuse in a manner which shewed forth the whole bitter deamon and exulting feind to read that abuse printed on plain white paper in the comfortable warm study. is to do nothing but to hear it poured forth with a thrilling voice in a vast crowded hall. leveled with lightning glance and withering scowl. from a countenance pale as death and bitter. as the grave. spoken by a being who seemed only to exist for the purpose of vengeance. listened to by a huge audience of silent figures motionless heads. anxious faces and contracted brows. some men present blackning like charcoal beneath the fire they were subjected to others. catching every moment a renewed glow as the speaker. rose in his periods of malediction was to see and hear a sight which you would never forget while you lived and moved and had your being.

The Earl as he concluded. with loud. clear awful voice. and aspect like a prophet of Judaea pronouncing judgement and. condemnation or. repentance and resurrection—resumed his seat amid deep unbroken silence he smiled most grimly when he saw that everyone was to deeply pondering his words to dream of applause and then passing his handkercheif over his forehead and satisfied with the immpression he had made he arose and walked slowly along the gallery to the great open door which led down to the entrance hall There he left the Hall and drove off again from the Assembly.

When the Earl had concluded his speech I gazed hastily round to note the countenances of all around me. a vast number of the commoners and some among the peers looked Deeply thoughtful. pondering over his speech and exhibiting expression by no means unfavorable to the views of the Ambitious Satan. Zamorna—I cant tell how Zamorna. [felt] he had followed him keenly through the whole of his speech but. the Dukes appearance when much ex[c]ited is always so much the same that it is doubtful to decide upon his joy or sorrow enthusiasm or Indignation. The same flushed forhead and excited <mien> the same tinge of gloom and sternness always burns in his lofty countenance and. dark. flashing eye.

Mr Warner sat as pale as a ghost. and. I am certain at that moment filled with the most horrid bitterness of hatred that any feind could be capable of feeling Edward Percy whose name his father had never even. mentioned seemed sometimes with a glance which ought to have fixed him to stone and then to hardly restrain himself from bursting in to laughter (bitter I know) at his unhappy colleagues Arundel I saw looked at the King knowing his Monarchs unhappy disposition and dreading the effects of Northangerlands insidious inferences. Lindsay and Montmorency seemed to confide in their own great Abilitys and to be feeding on a respectable love for the speaker who had just sat down the amiable expressions of those lovely countenances will haunt me even unto the death. Thornton looked really and deeply offended but Morley bore the castigation with as much <stoicism> as any body seated with his hands spread out on his knees his sandy hair streaked over his well bronzed and corrugated forehead. he seemed busy in concocting some really enlightened liberal and. and conciliatory speech. filled with the mark of intellect if not with that commodity itself. But of all the listeners to Northangerlands speech none struck me so much as one member who sat just below me. up on the Treasury side of the house. He was a Gentleman dressed in black and bettween 40 and 50 years of age. tall well proportioned and once evidently of great strength and vigour. In his countenance there were marks of his having once been very handsome. and the thin and dark brown hair yet curled on the temples with his lighter whisker in his light grey eye there. lurked all the laughing deamon. of dissipation and. his finely cut nose and full underlip. still gave his face an appearance which at some moments neutralized. its aspect of threatning passion. a yellow tinge had overspread his face and. <devious> health seemed to struggle with a perhaps once iron constitution. Yet still there was a goodly enough structure left to promise. an aid of consequence to what party he should declare for this Gentleman by name William Sydenham Esqr of Southwood hall. M P for Southwood rose up and spoke raising the arm now and then. in emphasis.

"My lords and Gentlemen I dont doubt you have heard the speech just concluded. I can tell you I have and marked it too. The Earl of Northangerland I believe to be a man of abilities quite sufficient guide to power any helm he lays hands on or sink to the bottom most vessels that he considers his foes. No man can care less than I do wether he be of good character or of bad. whether he. be. an Angrian or a self seeker. And indeed what have we to do with his soul that is nothing to us its his power Gentlemen his power and abilitys which only could be of service to us and I know that to answer his own ends he would make them of service to us. Many among the Ministery are my freinds but I tell them Ill sacrifice them all to morrow if I can gain over Northangerland to that elevation which he desires to attain to I am an Angrian myself. and what in the world should I stick at in order to give my country the means of increasing the power and fortune of Angria. Why———"

Mr Sydenham concluding his words with a short ejaculation which I decline to repeat took his hat and cane and strode over the house to the empty opposition benches followed by five or 6 of the members of his own connections—a great deal of confusion followed this decisive step. but nobody seemed yet wound up to that pitch that they would follow the prompter member for Southwood. yet as for a hundred or two among them it was evident that a speech or two at Pequena or Seaton would. confirm their wavering and bring them over to Northangerland however as it was the confusion rapidly increased till Warner Howard Warner strode hurriedly and lifted his high rapid voice in unrepressed anger and. hatred.

"Mr Sydenham you have always opposed me you have thwarted me and have done your utmost to overthrow me but I shall mark you for this (here the exasperated home Secretary almost choked with irritation he glanced as feircely as a Roman tyrant) Your last stroke sir has. placed you in the ranks. of not only. mine but Angrias emimies Angrias worst emimies an. enemy and a son. You are too sanguine Sir you are too sanguine when you so readily turn to a falling house. do you think does any one here think. that. —(hugh hu—)—that the Earl of Northangerland can find a freind in Angria when he has so basely deserted

herself so infamously attacked [and] lost the most valued freinds no let him
wander on his pilgrimage through the country let him beg for votes from door to
door let him beseech and fawn at the feet of the meanest inhabiter of the country
they will spurn him they will spurn him and. hunt him from city to villiage. I
am ashamed of you all when I see you so patiently sit under. —"

   While Mr Warner was speaking Mr Morley had been in his own heart
winding up his harangue to its conclusion and now having concocted primed and
charged his artillery he rose in deep abstraction totally unconscious that. any
person was speaking at the time "Gentlemen" he said. in [a] loud brazen voice

   "My Lords and Gentlemen you are aware that the march of
Improvement which has characterized this age has yet met with sundry
obstructions even in this age and those obstructions may readily be divided into
38 heads of the which 8 are practical and cannot be obviated in the ordinary
course of events 10 are conditional and depend upon peculiar circumstances 10
are temporary. and if roused ought to be suffered to pass rather than attempted to
be removed. 10 are. resting places and their use is greater than their
usellessness[sic] and 10 are ornamental or. are fitted to point a moral or adorn a
tale. —he—he—hem—Well as I was saying these obstructions the liberal mind
will regard as no obstructions and rather than destroy by brute force <we> will
conciliate and concede—not that I mean the antiliberal and besotted spirit of
Aristocracy from whence arises so many of these obstructions should at all be
conceded too but that. Reform and Retrenchment and civil and political
economy. should go forward in an enlightened course and should concede to the
spirit of the Age. now I myself stand here a free and independent member of
Parliament brought in by a free and independent constituency I hunt for no place
and seek for no pension and though I possess not the beauty of a Henrietta
Wellesly or a Maria Percy or a Edith Lofty though to be certainly inferior to
these titled beauties in personal accomplishments I have a mind an <intellect>
and a free and enlightened understanding I am above all earthly hope and beyond
all earthly fear I—"

   "Order Mr Morley" shreiked the exasperated Warner. but the hopeless
Scot stubbornly went on "I am in no disorder. My apparel is decent such as
becomes the citizen of a free state to wear and. —my conduct—"

   The laughter which greeted the Honorable Members lucubrations was
almost stunning. roar followed roar partly I believe sincere laughter partly the
effect of <controlled> and intense thinking now bursting out in unconfined
schoolboyism Mr Sydenham swore at them for a parcel of fools and children
scowling and threatning and compressing his lips in anger. Henri F Enara was
standing before the throne engaged in deep earnest and apparently highly
amicable intercourse with the King Warner fretted himself. to fritters Lindsay and
Montmorency were conversing with my freinds Fouche and Tallyrand Morley
stood in his place. looking sullen and malcontent the whole of the house in
general was out of order and out of decency at once The Duke of Zamorna in his
customary fashion started as if to life to attention to the summit mounted the
throne and dismissed the houses.

My[35] last scene was laid in the opening of the Adrianopolitan Parliament this must be laid in the opening of that of Verdopolis I had been called to the great city in a hurry from Adrianopolis and entered the house some time after the Ministers had read the patriarchs speech The hall as I advanced to my place stretched blazing in countless gas lights. and the thick black rows of members and Noblemen blocked up the whole spacious Interior In front of the Ministerial Bench the Duke of Morena. was opening in the first champaign of his frail ministry behind him Mr Sydney sat collapsed in reveries Sir R Pelham smart and prim as ever Mr Goat as bilious and shattered as usual Sir J Bud the picture of perplexed and ill placed good nature Col Grenville clouded with thought And old Gifford blackned with meditation. with these I as a fellow minister joined myself and near us but on a different bench were gathered the Sodom and Gormorrah clique of our party[36] the men who seemed destined to send us to perdition. There was Harlaw dark and sullen clapped on to his seat there Grazier <   > and Musselburgh fidjetting upon his with restless anxiety and Lord Lofty squinting forth his blasted glances and above all the great leader the tall thin light haired sinister eyed sailor Marquis of Ardrah There is something about this Noblemans look a feirceness. a ferocity of disposition which alienates me the more from him the more I see him but who was that person seated close beside the Marquis of Ardrah—that Nobleman in black still taller than him with golden hair and high forhead the one whose countenance as he passes his delicate hand over his face sets my very blood curdling in my veins Now reader this was a dreadful an ominous conjunction The Earl of Northangerland was seated by the Prince of Parrisland They were in deep conversation and their looks were dreadful as the glances of demons Mind I am only sketching this chapter in an historical manner and must pass over every thing with as much brevity and as little comment as the 4 evangelists.[37] —As soon as the Duke of Morena had concluded his speech. up rose the Marquis of Ardrah and entered at once upon his subject he began by warmly applauding liberal sentiments by advocating the cause of liberty and justice—then he defined what Liberty was and characterized it as the offspring of an enlightened age and the bearer of peace economy and Reform Then he shewed that Adrianopolis had less of this Liberty than it ought to have and he said he would point out the means by which she whould have more. Setting his teeth and putting on a feirce smile of <Ardrahism> he went on to inveigh against the monstrous anomalies of our Constitution he exposed its various deficiencies he said the kingly power was perhaps accuratly adjusted the power of the Nobility was to local that of the Ministry should depend entirely on that of the people that of the people must be greatly augmented he cast the darkest innuendoes upon the present Ministry even involving with bitter

---

35 There is a gap between this sentence and the previous one, indicating a "chapter" division—see p. 209, n. 15.

36 See Genesis, chapters 18 & 19.

37 i.e., Matthew, Mark, Luke, and John.

malignancy the Duke of Fidena. he extolled the efforts made heretofore by his Noble Friend the Earl of Northangerland in defence of liberty and of striving to attain a just and equitable Reform he after a while concluded a long speech of. great ability of. infamous treacherous barefaced and disgusting Turncoatism one marked by the blackest <rags> of Ingratitude and Selfishness. by informing the House that he would very early this Session bring forward a bill for the Reform of the Constitution of the Verdopolitan Union

Ardrah had no sooner sat down with a scowl and a blackness on his countenance than up rose the EARL. and commenced with a more agreeable smile than I have ever observed him wear before to come out with a farrago of ridiculous humbug high sounding sentences black bitter sarcasm mean dishonest inferences and calls upon the country and people to join the efforts of the. Prince of Parrisland and exert themselves to break the chains of slavery from their hands. The instant that this Arch Demon reseated himself.

Lord Macara Lofty rose and moved that this house do now adjourn. Ardrah had taken full measures to pack the house A host of the most rascally of the lowland Scotch Parrislandians and Rossites rose and in obedience to his nod they voted that the house do now ajdourn.

Reader whats the meaning of this Ardrah and Percy have formed a coalition and what will they do no man can tell. all Verdopolis is bitterly opposed to them they have left the ministry (I mean the Marquis and <his tale>) The Duke of Fidena made a glorious speech last night against all such base selfish innovators. The country is determined to back the Duke. What will ensue we know not. Of the issue we shall hear more anon at present I am forced to leave for my station on the Calabar

Oct. 14. I this night reached Adrianopolis and in rattling toward my own residence I was forced to halt in front of The House of Parliament Immense crowds of people thousands upon thousands blocked up the streets and squares Some great scene was going on in the interior. My carriage halted before an open space where stood a table with a chair on the top of it. a young man dashed out of the House of Peers ran through the crowd and mounting the table aforsaid he raised his hand to the people

It was Henry Hastings the Poet of Angria the author of Sound the loud Trumpets Welcome heroes Shine on us God and Hurra for the Gemini[38] I knew him by his dark hair and broad forehead and bright black eye. Now said he to the people Now my lads Northangerlands won hes made a speech of glory a majority of 6 and 30. —Mont and Morley and Lindsay have resigned Percy is Premier. Hurra for Angria listen to my new song

History stood by her pillar of fame[39]
A shade on her brow and a tear in her eye

---

[38] See pp. 204-06. "Hurra for the Gemini" is by Charlotte—see Alexander CB II, part ii, 288-89.

[39] To the right of this line appear the words "lay lay lay."

Oh must I blot my Northangerlands name
        From his own glorious chapter of victory
She held oer that chapter the pencil of fate
        But her white arm drew back from the page as it lay
In sorrow and silence she mournfully sate
        And she bitterly thought of Her Angrias decay
She raised her dark eye and she gazed on the sea
        Where all its black billows were whitened with foam
And she thought of her pirate ship gallant and free
        Her Noble Northangerlands empire and home
Oh for the hours of that ocean to come
        When shall I write of such sunshine and storm
When will a pirate so gloriously roam
        As fair and as noble in feature and form
She looked to the south and she looked to the north
        And she looked to the west where the twilights decline
Had. flown from the Morn who exultin[g]ly forth
        Was rising in glory oer Angria to shine
She thought of that Empire. so bright and divine
        She thought of its Monarch its ruler in war
Angria two Monarchs and rulers like thine
        Hath fate then refused to one empires share
And must thou whose bidding hast roused up [a] land
        From. midnight to morning to life from the tomb
Oh must thy great name now be traced by my hand
        In pages of darkness and letters of gloom.
She paused and she pondered. But Angria is nigh
With pride in her port and with fire in her eye[40]
She looks to the shore and she looks to the sea.
And she vows that eternal his history shall be.
Through all my wide empire in ages to come
From palace to cottage from cradle to tomb
Shall the name of my Savior through ages endure
Vast as the ocean and firm as the shore
History seizes her pencil of light
And again in rejoicing she bends to indite
High on the top of her column of fame
She blends with her Angria[41] Northangerlands name

---

[40] See p. 232, n. 37.

[41] "her Angria" written above "Zamorna"; neither is canceled. In his 1837 revision of this poem in vol. III, Branwell dates this version November 1834, yet the rest of the manuscript was clearly composed in October.

[Angria and the Angrians]
I(d)[1]

One word to my Readers—I think no apology [is] needed for the step I have taken and it is sufficient for me to accuaint you with the fact that being now released from my duties as Ambassorder to the Court of Angria I must attend to the buisness of an ardous post in Verdopolis yet though neither on the scenes of action or near the City whence those actions spring it is still my intention to continue that work. which has so long received the public approbation under the title of "Angria and the Angrians."[2]

I said that I am now no longer a inhabitant of that country nor a spectator of its ongoings but there are eyes who are both which can see full as well as mine and of a pair of those optics I here gladly avail my self in the person of Henry Hastings the Poet of Angria farther note or comment upon the chapters ensuing will be useless there own merits will bring them into notice and I will only wish my readers to mark my own generosity in thus bringing into my house a stranger. who will prove so much stronger than I. mark it I say and imitate the conduct of your dear freind and servant

RICHTON.

Flower House-   A NARRATIVE OF THE   Verdopolis Dec. 17. 1834.
                     First War. with Quashia undertaken
                     For the purpose of. clearing his Ashantees
                     From the rightful Territory of Angria.
                          By the Duke of Zamorna
                          In the year A D 1834.
                               The first of his
                               glorious Reign..

                     Compiled from the personal experience
                          of HENRY HASTINGS'S.
                          and written by himself!!

I will not trouple[sic] the readers of this work. with either a long account of the birth and parentage of its writer or an abstruse explanation of the rise causes and ramifications of this subject I am merely going to tell him the things which I

---

[1]   A forty-two page section of manuscript, 11.2x18.5 cm, scattered over four libraries. The initial section consists of the first four pages of a manuscript at the HRC, catalogued as "A Narrative of the First War with Quashia." The leaves are folded and laid inside each other, but not stitched. "Henry Hastings" appears in the top left-hand corner of this page.

[2]   See also pp. 328 and 379.

have seen and the deeds which I have borne a part in during the first Champaign undertaken by My Noble Sovereign. and as I think him the perfection of Mortality I will imitate his qualitys and like himself dash at once into the middle of my subject

The Morning of December the 3^d. 1834 and a brighter never rose over the Calabar found **Me**. attired in the Rejimentals of an Angrian Ensign. and journ[ey]ing gaily on Horseback over the wide wastes of sandy desart which stretch[ed] eastward 60 or 70 miles from the river opposite Adrianapolis to the Etrei before the city of Gazemba. That Proclamation which issued from the War Office on the first instant. and with its call upon the vanguard of the assembling Army to repair forwith to Gazemba. sounded all over Angria like the first note of an inspiring Bugle. included myself in the number of those commanded to obey its voice. And here I rode alone. in my glory to enter upon a new scene of life a new prospect for the future. One Adventurer among 40000. in the grand lottery of "Death or victory."

Behind my Back. along the Horizon down the course of the Calabar the long brown mists of morning lay like. a dim formless monster over the city of Adrianopolis and the scenes of my native home I had ridden so far on my way that the metropolis itself. was ritired back into the haze and Fort Adrian on this Bank of the River only rose like a dark spot over the monotonous horizen in the West. I looked for the gleaming of the river but it lay below the light and the Adrianopolitan hills themselves were hidden by the unenlightened robe of moveless vapour All the sky arched over head in a vault of pale stainless blue till before me in the East its colour was lost. in the bright yellow glow of the rising sun and Here under the light of my countrys luminary I could see little or nothing of all the expanse which stretched before me <little> background for slight swells of sandheaps rose not far off. to break the ocean like smoothness of the desart and no Horizon for here the yellow lusture <cast up> in sight the straight flat sky line of the far off. Etreian marshes. I never before had seen so immense so solemn a landscape. I had never under my present circumstances before seen any landscape. and all t[h]ough at. 4 o clock I had set out fresh and fiery high in hopes in anticipation and nerved with strength for all that should happen though I had looked for this very morning with all impatience all the eagerness that a school boy looks forward to his annual holidays though the breeze was fresh and the pathway unbroken. the steed in spirits and his Rider in youth. still my reader must forgive me if I tell him that in 2 hours from my setout I. had settled down into deeper and more thoughtful musing than ever my mind had known before. Where I thought was my country my home and birthplace where were the scenes of civilization and of. human life.? Behind me all lay Behind me. I had left my parents my acquaintance. my very life and feelings for a new father a new companion a new existence and new actions. These all lay before me. and what was there before me? a wide sandy desart. a faroff unknown River. Burning wastes which I knew nothing off and where I must plunge without knowing how I might return or wether I might ever return and the limits of this days journey must be. a huge iron bound fort. the encampment of 6000 soldiers the gathering place of a great Army. and with this army I was enlisted with it I must go and to what service what actions?. aye here lay the thoughts which if they made my cheek paler and my forehead darker. made too my Heart beat higher and my blood boil within me I was Now a SOLDIER. and I was going to WAR. war had always [given] to me a glorious and mighty feeling I cannot tell you what I felt when I thought of. Armies and Battles and Standards and Cannonry they were not romantic ideas nor false ones but overpowering from their tone and character. The roar of a hundred peices of artillery is not so terrific as the single true idea. of. one scene in war. This was no common walk of life this was not going to college or entering the lawyers court or the merchants counting house. This looked nothing like a life at home and the days of. happy childhood No one month hence and I might be placed the leader of. a thousand soldiers. one week hence and I might be lying shattered amid the thunder of. a raging battle every chance of promotion and ambition was just open[ing] upon me and so was every chance of fatigue and heat and hunger and thirst and fever and starvation and a glorious death on the feild of honour or a horrible death at the stake of the Ashantee

If you feel as I felt reader you will excuse when I say that. I noticed nothing of the scenes about me for miles and hours of my way. I neither was frightened or melancholy but I was excited to a pitch which Nature felt too high for happiness. I could not do any thing but think of what lay before me. and at last I had wrought my feelings up to such a pitch of delusion that I raised up my eyes to see to the firing of a fancied battery But it was no engagement which sounded in my scarce conscious ears when I looked up like one awaking from a dream all was desolate about me the warm breeze whistled in a group of gigantic thistles a few lizards were running over the path and before my sight stretched one vast unbroken sea of sand. The sun was all most in his meridian the sky seemed on fire and I could not have imagined a cloud in the bright arid vault of heaven. I. began to see motes dancing whenever I moved my eyes my steed felt the exhaustion as strongly as I did and I saw that the heat and journey had made their first impression upon such a raw recruit of the "Army" it was not time for joking however The few miles that we crept over seemed long and wearisome the declining afternoon burnt my cheek brown with its rays and my attempts to whistle a song were stopped by my choaking knotty throat Under such circumstances it behooved me indeed to look out for the tower of "Fort Enara" the midway halting place of my journey and as I ran my eye around the horizon with all the impatience of an exhausted traveller. I caught sight of something long and black lying in the southward distance. it moved nearer and as soon as it got below the horizon a new object as low and more irregular than itself arose in the same direction as soon as long looking had accustomed me to the scene I could notice. other and numerous lines of blackness. still keeping the same direction and moving over the extreme of the desart from the West to the point of my own journey they sometimes seemed broken and sometimes united evidently encroaching nearer and thickening instead of lessening. My Horse seemed to know more of the matter than myself for he pricked up his ears neighed cheerfully and carried me over the waste toward them with a swiftness unstayed by the light or heat or drought of the Desart. half an hours brisk trotting soon showed me the nature of those moving objects and I beheld before me. a dozen gallant lines of well armed soldiers advancing nobly along, their col[umns] changing and closing before me and their long trains of. cannon horses and baggage waggons sweeping over the sands from the direction of. Adrianopolis. and the Calabar Before I could enter their passing files the. strong square tower and broad rearing banner of. Fort Enara rose up on its low fortified hillock. straight in advance of us. all seemed bending their march toward it and I smiled to notice how the Desart had risen into the life and bustle of a full tide of humanity

When I reached Fort Enara there might be about 900 or 1000 soldiers gathered about its broad glaring freestone wall and as many more seemed fading away in the forward distance and as many more advancing up from behind. This chain of armed men inspired me with double enthusiasm I thought to myself are not these the men to win glory and what against them can Quashia do. I could hardly fancy a host in the desarts before me which should be able at all to discomfit them and when I knew that the troops which I saw were not a tenth part of the Army of Etrei I believe I rose up in my saddle with pride of the Angrian Kingdom

Fort Enara is a strong solid octagonal mass of freestone standing quite alone amid the waste 30 miles distant from the Calabar and 40 from the Etrei it was built about a dozen years ago by the Verdopolitan Government to command and keep open the road from Moughton to Gazemba. a Colonel and 2 or 3 companys form its garrison and till the foundation of the Angrian Kingdom the African fires were every night seen far off from its walls. Since Adrianapolis arose in its glory. these savages have nearly abandoned the tract. between the River and this frontier the increased communication and the stronger number of military have let in the daylight upon their haunts and in a few dozen cases let it in upon their throats As I rode in under the arch of the gateway I beheld 9 Blackened Negroes dangling on gibbets over the parapet a stern spectacle and calculated to strike due terror on the prowlers of the desart. I confess they struck terror into me too and I felt that the Inhabitants of Verdopolis. and the cultivated provinces of Angria. removed from all chance of invasion and never beholding the face of an enimy know nothing of the stern desolate desart the wild. bloody <savages> and the Rough Military Government which cast such a frightful horror over lands only 100 or 50 or 40 miles from their own homes as little indeed do the Glasstowners or Zamornans or Angrians know of all this as. the Londoners in 1700 did of the state of the Scotch Highlands[3] and here the difference is much greater. and the contiguity much less remote

---

3   Possibly a reference to the events surrounding the massacre of Glencoe, 1692, which Branwell would have read about in Scott's *Tales of a Grandfather*, vol. 2. In 1773, in his *Journey to the Western Islands of Scotland*, Samuel

When I entered the fort all the cattle cannon and baggage of the marching troops were drawn crowded round its walls soldiers and camp followers mixed with them and especially thronged through the inner court of the Building the detachment which I saw belonged to Col Seymours Division and was posting in all haste toward the Grand Rendezvous of Gazemba. For myself I after looking after my horse retired with all due haste to rest from the fatigues of the day

I laid upon a mattress in a little darkened room with a window whose light appeared at the end of an alley sunk 10 feet into the mighty wall. The constant sound of troops arriving or setting off. surging dully round this solid apartment Horses trampling Men shouting cattle bellowing arms ringing and the grating heavey grinding of the cannon wheels. never stayed a minute all night for as soon as one set off sounds began to die away another and often a much louder rose in its place. The perfect novelty of my feelings kept me awake for 2 or three hours but at last tired nature gave in to sleep and I felt and heard nothing more till. the sunlight woke me at morning

Then when I started up from sleep and hurried out to the stables I found all clear round the Fort neither man nor beast to be seen and nothing upon the ground but the litter of last nights arrivals behold the visisitudes of war I said and felt like a man who goes to bed with the ground covered knee deep in snow and rises with all creation robed in the fresh hue of a dewy thaw. I harrnessed my steed and reappeared in the open air but alas all was changing again over the westward horizon a fresh host appeared and. the desart looked alive once more. But for me it was time to depart. ere evening I must arrive at Gazemba 40 miles of Desart lay before me and the duty of a soldier I knew was to disregard all ease when he had orders to act I will not "Tautologize" by relating much of this days scenery in no respect did it differ from the aspect of the day before ere 10 miles had been overpast Fort Enara had set in the west a sea of sand lay all round me no object no landmark to arrest my attention or to point me on my way the sun glaring through all the sky and the heat whitning every yard of the desart my freinds the Lizards were the inhabitants of the land and the huge brown Nettles its only productions I never amid this uniformity was at all in danger of losing my path because the passage of the troops before me had made a distinct road over the sands which in this still weather no whirlwind had swept off them it was the winter season too and therefore the heat. (hardly short of that in a moderate oven) was not so great as absolutly to burn my soul out of its tenement. Under such easy circumstances I moved along miles seeming at first like furlongs. While my spirits were wrapt in enthusiastic meditations and then like leagues when the fatigue of the body had superseded all the wild vagaries of the soul At last the sun flashed out his last beams on the far off Calabar I looked

---

Johnson could still state "yet as Scotland is little known to the greater part of those who may read these observations," and "to the southern inhabitants of Scotland, the state of the mountains and the islands is equally unknown with that of Borneo or Sumatra."

with some envey when I beheld him sinking his glorious light toward the regions of my home and country And then I turned again to my journey I thought once more of the future-How mild how calm seemed all the sky and earth before me twilight was shadowing over the clear gray <ground> and cooling all the solemn silent horizon no hill no tower no tree rose against the pearly light but just straight before me the full pale Moon rested its cold round orb upon the very extremity of the desart this was the aspect of the eastern view and strongly did it contrast with its moral character there under that very moon upon that very Ocean like line armies are just about to assemble and dreadful battles to be fought we are all tending onward to make yon the seat of war and to shake it with the sound of cannonry. —But we meet things every days more contrary than this in their seeming and reality. —There was enough of beauty in the twilight but==Their was more far more in the night. Never shall I forget the state of glory and elevation to which my feelings had roused me when I found myself travelling alone as a soldier to gain the seat of WAR. With the Dark Ebon Vault of Heaven raised far over my head not a speck not a cloud to spot its deepness But the broad bright MOON sailing majestically alone in the black blue Sky a star or two trembled far away from the mighty light Venus itself. twinkled over Angria and I smiled to think that my love was with it there-and wide around me the still solemn desart was whitened by the unbroken sheet of light from heaven objects there were few to distinguish colours w[h]ere only <a sober> grey uniformity pervailed over all the landscape But Never. Amid the storm of a troubled ocean over the glory of a midnight Victory on the domes of an Ancient Babylon or the stir of a modern Verdopolis Never in any scene or season could such a sublimity overpress the spirit as now did mine when looking round on that clear Moonlight Night I felt neither melancholy or awestruck but it seemed as if I was not the being I had been during the day I seemed formed anew to breath[e] this unearthly Atmosphere. I thought that it must have been quite such a night as this when the Shepherds watched their flocks and the Angels came down to announce peace on earth and goodwill toward men—These very words were yet lingering like music on my mind and I was looking at my horses shadow cast forward in the broad moonshine and travelling as silently as we ourselves moved on when one distant heavey sound boomed suddenly upon my ear. This was no loud note and its deep thunder had passed directly over the desart but it worked an instant revulsion in all my feelings for I knew it to be the Evening Gun fired from the ramparts of GAZEMBA—Onward cried I slapping my Horses neck. Here is at last war and its openings before me peace and goodwill where were they now and the Moonlight?—it shone on uncared for by me I gazed intently forward as with a cheek which all the night breezes could not cool I strained my eyes to discern the so long looked for towers and forts of this famous city but here the vapours from the River stretching allong the horizon shrouded everything in dimness before me. and I urged my steed with burning impatience to reach those scenes of strange and darkened story. "There is the ETREI." I cried again "a bright speck of water flashed up in the moonlight on the horizon "And there is GAZEMBA" as I at length saw the low black buildings which rose on its hither bank when I. cleared a long sand hill which swelled at[sic] little before me. a sense of overpowering emotion compelled me to rein my horse to a moments halt. I have spoken of the clear and splendid night before and here all this glory shone over the vast reach of water which faded in mist far northward. and a thousand fires <glanced> and twinkled like terrestial starlight. over all the expanse round the stern walls of the celebrated city a Bugle had struck up in the silence. and its melancholy notes swelled and died upon the night like the wail of that wastes departing Genius—I galoped down the slope over the plain in[sic] and in a few minutes had entered a huge throng of armed Angrian soldiers and next. the wild gloomy street of the tumultous little city After that days passage over the solemn solitary desart the confused roar of voices and the well known tongues of Angrians the moving of waggons and trampling of Horses the living stir and confusion round the great crackling fires broke upon my senses like the beings of a fresh existence. I could Hardly fancy that moon was the same which I saw now smiling wanly through the reddened reek of flame and smoke and over uproar and tumult of a camp of. 9 or 10000 soldiers The town itself looked like nothing save a rabble of wild black houses gathered confusedly for shelter in the night round the immense walls which rose sloping inward above and amid them the stern bulwark of Angrian empire and the proud roof of her warlike Son. I felt as I passed up the main street a sensation of comfort which I did not expect to feel when I heard at every instant the strong voices of my stalwart countrymen and the calling of names which I had so often heard before "Hello Tom Bring up. His Lordships Horses now when he arives" "Castlereagh wont be here till tomorrow" "Theres Thornton come this morning I saw his suite enter under the gateway" "Aye I guess the General will be at the ordering of us" "Yons Hartford that riding up the street there to the castle" "Ah Seymour you here already and hows your Nag that you boasted could carry you across the desart like a camel." "Ring Ring there[s] a turn up ower the Rivers atween Tom o' Mouthon and Searjent Snaps of this place." Etrei for ever" "Gazemba against a dozen" "Theres a main of Cocks throwing[4] down at Williams quarters there" "Where where lets off to it." —Such were the well known cries which saluted me as I passed on to my destined quarters in my Rejiment the 21st foot Colonel. Hartford commander—.

For 3 days after my arrival at Gazemba I remained unoccupied by any duty and a Soldier only in name The Rejiment to which I belonged was stationed in quarters in the city untill the main body of the Army should arrive under its General Enara. and with Zamorna himself at its head as we neither watched guarded garrisoned or fought our men had all their time at leisure and did almost what they liked with it time the moralists say is a precious commidity and knowing the truth of this assertion feeling too that my stay on the Banks of this famous river would probably be limited to a few days I employed what space was left me

---

[4]   i.e., a cock fight. Compare Alexander CB II, part ii, p. 335, n. 126.

in wandering along its Banks sailing over its stream and thinking and feeling and looking my fill of delightful poetic dreaming early in the morning I was roused up by the beat of drums to attend on Parade for our pro-temp-Commander General Thornton would admit no relaxation in this duty after our companys had left the ground I took a stroll through the streets to wonder at the new aspect of things and feed my national pride on the splendid aspect of our troops. however as soon as I turned down the little straggling street from the fort. that wide breezless sheet of water which lay so gloriously before me and the appearance of the mysterious and hostile shores beyond its bank. so completly fired my feelings that it was hardly a moment ere I found myself. skimming in a little shallow bark over its waveless surface. A Spirit of exploration has alway[s] animibted[sic] me when I look at scenery and now as I saw the great Bend which the Etrei made sweeping from the north and beheld all the almost unknown stretch of desart which bounded and closed it in beyond I could not refrain from sailing upwards and onwards till the Drums of the Rejiments from the city sounded up even to my anchorage with their rolling summons to evening parade

It was on the Evening of December 5th at the conclusion of one of these delightful wanderings that I was gliding down the stream from a voyage of 10 or 15 miles up the course of the Etrei my two rowers a couple of stout Angrian soldiers in my Captains Company were almost resting upon their oars for the current was in itself strong enough to impell us down I sat in the boats stern with my arms folded and thinking of sights and adventure[s] and schemes of ambition and all the probable stir and glory of my future. as the river changed its bending and expanded to a sheet of water almost two miles across I could not help looking up at the splendid sight it presented The sun was setting westward over the Desart and underneath its burning beams Gazemba lay like a rugged masse of cottages a mile or two below us. The huge stern walls of the fort rising above it and stretching along the riverside in grand military boldness. But while we were looking at this isolated spot of civilization and thinking of the thousand soldiers assembled in its rugged shelter a white curl of smoke bursting from the western parapets caught our eyesight and directly after the loud heavey boom of cannonry came thundering up the water we all started and the question rose to our lips "What in the world is that" all three of us fixed an eager gaze at the walls of the smoking fort again the white cloud expanded with majic swiftness and a second heavey rattle of sound struck our attentive ears. "Push on my lads" said I "lets see the meaning of this." We swept down toward Gazemba with the speed of an arrow "Hillo" cried one of the rowers "look yonder look at yon long black lines moved[sic] from the west over the sand into the town Ill be hanged if it isnt the Duke and theyre saluting him from the battery" ere he had concluded the smoke and firing was repeated and louder than ever. we had now no doubt but that the Grand Army was entering for we saw their pigmy masses creep over the distant waste and streaming toward the Black. roofs of Gazemba As we plied our oars with zealous industry and made the silent water flash in bubbles around us we heard faint softened strains of Music floating from the western shore. as we neared it those sounds rose and thrilled in heaven[sic] I almost wished the oars at

Jericho[5] they so disturbed the glorious feeling of the scene. but in a while it did not matter how they ploshed and splattered for the clear notes of Trumpet and bugle rose far above their dashed noisiness We ran ashore on the little quay of the city and then I saw the vast masses of soldiers and heard the huge uproar of voices and the loud strains of 20 different Bands of music the rattle of Cavalry and rolling of kettle drums to full and overwhelming advantage I was directly pushing amid the thickest of the press and flinging up my cap in the general shout of "Zamorna Angria for ever" all the large square in front of the castle wall was surrounded with treble and quadruple files of armed soldiery ranged in deep and compacted masses under their officers with arms presented and heads erect in order I never saw a more magnificent spectacle the dress of an Angrian soldier is well known to be most splendid in effect and here the vast lines of bright scarlet and blazing gold the noble plumes and glancing muskets all waving and streaming in even rows almost till lost to sight amid the confusion with the long unceasing lines of marching troops filing on between and entering the city with drums beating and colours flying the cavalry trumpets blasting up their clamour and the Horses prancing proudly on between the steady rows which flanked them all made my teeth chatter with excitement and made my heart flutter with pride Here were before behind and around me perhaps 40000 warriors forming that Noble Army which is destined to crush our eternal enimy and exterminate him from our native country. and all our cheifest Generals the guides of Angrian welfare. Enara Arundel Thornton Kirkwall Castlereagh Moray all I knew were now in the vicinity of me Some of them I saw But at this time I hardly gave 2 looks upon them for my mind and heart and eyes were far too eagerly employed in searching out and endeavouring to fix themselves upon Zamorna himself upon my King I asked every body around me had he passed some said he had not but was yet behind others affirmed he was passing whenever a gallant cavalier dashed up the living lane but the most authentic number declared that they had seen him that he came in first at the head of his men and galloped in front of all his staff up to the fort where Enara alighted from his horse and received him in state to his Temporary Palace it was then that the Battery fired off the treble salute which first gave me notice of the Armys arrival. farther than this amid the uproar and rejoicing arround[sic] me I could not learn but it marks the odd similarity yet vast difference between the highest and the lowest when though a sovereign may enter a city at the head of all his Army and no one knows for certain wether he has appeared where he is or any thing about him could a beggars incoming be marked with less certainty and more carelessness but the causes are different however similar the effect Zamorna the instant it was heard he was coming had set every mans mind in such an uproar and his head in such intoxification and hurried all things so much out of the usual line and so startled the order and disposition of Nature that while there was not one in the army whose whole thoughts and senses were not eagerly striving

---

5   A colloquial phrase, meaning a place far distant or out of the way.

to see the king there were few in comparison who could say at midnight that they had seen him

The night of the 5th of December will long be remembered by the survivors of the Army as one of high and glorious exhiliration it is the character of An Angrian when he has reason for hope to be triumphant yes even if as in our case. an afflicted country be behind his back and probable death be before his eyes such neighbours only make him more glorious for they tell him it will look like Angria. to poke his fist into the ribs of Death and laugh and rejoice when care cometh. I dont know wheter[sic] this night one man out of the 40000 in the city retired to rest. —But I forget for when I took a walk. down to the river bank so near the music at the fort I passed by long lines of. hundreds of gallant fellows wearied with that days long march from Fort Enara. lying stretched out in a dead sound slumber There was no need of the warmth of a fire here for under this still moonlight sky the air lay as mild and balmy as if it were paradise a <gentle><breeze> fanned the face of the river and the glorious notes of the Military Bands rising and thrilling from the fort now the Ducal palace. infused a feeling through the scene whose remembrance shall never leave me I stood on the quay sometimes looking at the moon reflected in the Etrei then at the immense building whose broad walls stretched along behind me then listning to the sound of the Army surging in the distance and noting the roll of Drums and the long drawn wailing of the Bugles as they played under Zamorna's apartments the "Sound the loud Trumpet oer Afric's dark sea"[6] Oh how I wished the words had been more worthy of that music.

> Morn comes and with it all the stir of morn
> New life new light upon its sunbeams born
> The Majic dreams of Midnight fade away
> And Iron labour rouses with the day.
>
> He who has seen before his sleeping eye
> The times and smiles of childhood wandering by
> The Memory of years gone long ago
> And sunk and vanished now in clouds of woe
> He who still young in dreams of days to come
> Has lost all memory of his native home
> Whose untracked future opening wide before
> Shews him a smiling heaven and happy shore
> While things that are frown dark and drearily
> And sunshine only beams on things to be.
>
> To such as these night is not all a night
> For one in eve beholds his morning bright
> The other basking in his earliest morn
> Feels noontide summer oer his spirit dawn
> But that worn wretch who tosses night away

---

[6]   See p. 204.

And counts each moment to returning day
Whose only hope is dull and dreamless sleep
Whose only choice to wake and watch and weep
Whose present pains of body or of mind
Shut out all glimpse of happiness behind
Whose present darkness hides the faintest light
Which yet might struggle through a milder night.
And he like me whom active cares engage
Without the glare of youth or gloom of age
Who must not sleep upon his idle oar
Lest lifes wild tempests dash him to the shore
Whom High Ambition calls aloud to awake
Glory his goal and death or life his stake
And long and rugged his rough race to run
Ere he can rest to enjoy his laurels won
To these the night is weariness and pain
And blest the hour when day shall rise again
Mid visions of the future or the past
Others may wish the shades of night to last
Round these alone the present ever lies
And these will first awake when Morning calls Arise![7]

There reader is a screed of poetry for you as innocent and as aimless of meaning as the mind of a newborn babe I scribbled it that morning I speak of and it is quite different from what when I began I meant it to be

To turn However to the more immediate narrative of my "Days labour"[8] After Dissmal from Parade. which to innure the army to discipline was punctually ordered twice a day. I bent my steps toward the Great Fort or Palace or House of Enara in whose vastly varied and endlessly crowded apartments at this time was Held the Military Court of Our Sovereign and where or in the different lines of building connected with it abode for the time the Commander in Cheif and suite. Lord Arundel General Kirkwall General Moray and of course the owner H F Enara with all their attendants and Horses amounting together exclusive of the soldiers in garrison to many Hundreds of men. My intention was to deliver in person to Colonel Hartford my commander the payment for my ensigney and to speak with him upon many matters of importance to myself the colonel as General Thorntons Principal Aid de camp and as quartered in the same range of apartments with eager footsteps I paced along the great courts within the outer <area> and felt fully impressed with the grandeur of the building when I saw the wall within wall the great rounded towers and huge stone block houses and magazines which all seemed on a scale of the vastest extent and the most

---

7   See the revised 1837 version in volume III.
8   Compare with Milton's "When I consider how my light is spent," l. 7.

iron strength possible passing under the principal gate and nearing the holy of
Holys the habitations of the King and Generals I was made sensible of the
Aristocracy of the spot by the prospect of scores of liveried grooms rubbing
down as many beautiful war horses the <shiny> steeds all snorting and neighing
and prancing as if conscious of the Nobility they were accustomed to bear then
farther on than these and nearer to the sanctum sanctorum's I entered a confusion
of postillions and outriders bustling about in striped jackets and spurred boots,
smart coxcombical Gentlemen in black the immediate servants of the Salt of
Angria and Captains Officers of the Army entering or coming forth from the
different Generals levees My mind was now sufficiently excited and my feelings
awed by the neighbourhood in which I was I stepped with beating Heart to a
smart foreign looking lad of seventeen who held the bridle of a magnificent
brown charger near by. and regardless of the Ducal coronet impressed upon his
collar I asked "Could you point out to me Sir the Apartments of Colonel
Hartford?" The young page with a look of roguery returned. "Not I But. that
fellow is as likely to tell you as any one" I bowed and being in too much
confusion to mark the malicious laugh with which he disssmised me stumbled
rather than stepped by to the person he mentioned. a middle sized Dark
complexioned man in a chequered cotton shirt white pantaloons and black cap
who stood quite alone looking over the open court with a keen glance of
undoubted authority supposing him the overlooker of the parts adjacent for his
very questionable dishabbile[sic] suggested no military distinction I came up
with more confidence. and repeated the questions before given. this person bent
his keen dark eye full upon me for a moment and said in a deep toned voice.
"you mistake me freind. pass on." and never a second time looking at me he
turned to the young fellow who had led me thus wrong and guessing from the
manner in which he stood laughing with contempt at me. the reason of my
blundering he called to him sternly "Sir rein in your mirth there" and commanded
him to conduct me at his peril happily ere I had time to make a second mistake I
met with a freind of my own Capt Seaton who engaged to conduct me through
the labyrinth of the fort to the haven I wished to anchor in the rascal[9] obeyed and
we passed between two lines of windowless buildings and stopped at a small
postern in the huge wall of the main erection two sentinels stood there with
arms shouldered but they gave way to my conductor and we entered a long dark
unfurnished passage vaulted and plastered with stone coloured stucco I remarked
that the plenishing of the fort seemed on a scale of quite military economy but
my companion only answered "Here we are and judge for yourself." he opened a
little portal in the side of the wall and stepping forwards (I could not see where
for I stood down the passage.) announced my name within a murmur of speaking
followed. and he again appeared with a Military servant in scarlet livery "Good
Morning to you and you may march on yourself now" he said leaving me for his
own buisness. and the Menial Beckoned me forward into the room I stepped over

---

[9]   Branwell seems confused about who is conducting the narrator.

the threshold and stared with incredulous astonishment I had been just threading the windings of a dark narrow entry and now at once stood on the carpet of a vast saloon of Noble height and dazzling magnificence its rich hangings glittering mirrors and dark splendid furniture with the Lofty Arched windows which opened their statly lights upon the garden of exotic luxuriance without. all bursting upon an eyesight <dazed> with groping through the darkness so overwhelmed me that had anyone been in the saloon I should inevitably have made him laugh at my ridiculous confusion But it was empty the servant said "you will be attended to directly" and shut the door a little private one very unlike the huge gilt and rosewood folding portal which expanded at the other end of the Room There is something exceedingly awful and impressive to a simple person left alone in a mighty and gorgeous Apartment like this when the servant leaves you and you stand about beneath the Noble ceiling and look round on the Silent and solemn majesty it seems as if you were intruding on the palace of some being of superior order that a king a Genius will appear through the Hangings and punish you for your presumptous temerity nothing present seems made for yourself and you dare hardly step even on the rich turkey carpet beneath you I felt this sensation in full force and a still more unpleasant one along with it I knew that Colonel Hartford whom I came to see was a very wealthy man and would be lodged in hansome[sic] apartments but that in Gazemba where there were so many men far above him in station and w[h]ere accomoddations[sic] were just the reverse of plentiful. that here he should occupy of[sic] a saloon like this was quite out of the question the page had left me with a smile that looked like the essence of roguery he seemed inclined to revenge himself when the stern man in the chequer shirt reprimanded him and I now began to entertain a rather unpleasant notion that he had ushered into the rooms of some Officer of great note in the army Moray or Kirkwall or Castlereagh. I trod as if over hot coals to the great middle window and looked out upon the wilderness of gorgeous vegetation bounded by a range of Olives and the lower works of the battery here there was nothing to comfort me and again I turned to survey the apartment which so awed me a velvet sopha had been drawn toward the fire a great Rosewood Table stood near it covered with a confusion of volumns and overspread by an enormous chart of the Calabar and a great folding map of Angria. a Map of the Etrei lay on the floor with a compass and gold pencil case. I looked eagerly at this Map. mind I was now somewhere in head quarters and here was a descisive index to the operations of the army there were pencil marks on the sheet extending from Gazemba eastward into the heart of the Province of Etrei and south to the marshes of the Calabar another pencil mark lay over the course of the Benguela but my want of self possession prevented me noticing nothing long I was in a restless anxiety and laid next hold on a volumn which lay opened beneath the chart. it was "the Bible" bound in Morrocco and gilt I turned to another it was "Barrows Sermons" a third. "Military Tactics" a fourth. "the Itinerary of the East of Angria." a fifth "the Art of fortification explained". a sixth "the Stastistics[sic] of Africa" a[nd] the last "Facts and Observations upon the State of the Aborigines"[10] This said I looks like the reading of a steady experienced Officer at any rate. every thing seemed of too general a character for any inference to be drawn. from them all was statly and splendid but farther I knew nothing I sat down and awaited in silence the entry of Colonel Hartford. if he was any where in the purlieus of this Noble room no sound could I hear no voice or footsteps all was utter solemn silence about me All things seemed too high too regal to be moved by the ordinary course of Human existence I looked on with eagerness for something like what I had been used to see and the name "Sydney Hall" engraven in the corner of the chart seemed to me to be that of an old acquaintance and I felt quite relieved at the report of a musket sounding from some quarter of the fort without. but when my attentive ear caught the murmur of voices without the great Rosewood folding Door opposite me and heard footsteps advancing toward it you may judge of my agony of suspense about to be ended the voices encreased with various tones unknown alas to me and laughter not hearty and negligent but short and soon ended the Door was touched its folds slid apart and two Bedizened menials stood bowing at the entrance those beyond I could not at all discern nor where they were save that I just caught the gilding of a great picture frame in some place beyond one of the voices said. "He is not here lets on after him" and the speakers passed on and the great[11] folds closed again. I had arisen while this went forward and stood my hand on my seat and heart in my mouth but as it died away in silence I reseated myself in the same suspence as before half an hour past by and yet no other sound was heard. Then. some outer doors seemed to be thrown open somewhere. I heard a dreadfuly deepmouth barking and baying of some huge Dogs. and the voice of a man as if silencing them This thought I is the voice of some of Enaras blood Hounds but nothing further came of it. after a still longer interval of dead solemnity open flew the folding Doors without noise and there entered. Not the

---

10 Isaac Barrow, 1630-1777, was professor of Greek and of mathematics at Cambridge after the restoration, but resigned in 1669 in favour of his famous pupil, Isaac Newton. He was chaplain to Charles II, and by 1675 vice chancellor of Trinity College, Cambridge. His sermons were first edited by John Tillotson, 4v., London, 1683-87 and frequently reissued.

"Military Tactics" may refer to *Rules and Regulations for the Field Exercise and Manoeuvres of the French Army. Being the Ordinance of 1er Aout, 1791). London, 1806,* which became the basis for the tactics of the wars of the French Revolution and of Napoleon.

"the Art of fortification explained" may refer to George Bickham's *The Art of fortification delineated: with rules for designing, drawing, washing, and colouring, in the most elegant taste, particular works and buildings. . . in civil and military architecture. . . A work absolutely necessary for the gentleman, officer and architect,* London, 1748.

11 The following section consists of the first eight pages of a manuscript in the Brotherton Collection, catalogued as "The Massacre of Dongola."

King of the Genii or a crowned Emperor But a very tall grandly dressed young Officer rubbing his hands and laughing with boyish glee as he said to himself. "Ive outwitted them have given the rogues the slip and they shall have a good run ere they catch me" Thus speaking with a tone of self complacent gaity he ran to the windows and looked cautiously out to see if the gardens were clear of intruders and then snatching up Barrows Sermons he leaned against an Ionic column from which one of the curtains depended and soon seemed occupied in an eager perusal of it. I myself after noticing him a moment fairly dared not speak. he bent his head so that the profile stood dark against the window light and the boldly curled hair the peculiarly fine Roman Nose his extreme height and noble dress of scarlet and white made him an object quite worthy of the room and for aught I knew a Genii King in earnest or at least the flash of his joyous looking eye and the delightful tone of his voice gave him the imprint and aspect of one of the cheif among the sons of men[12] while I was making up my mind to address him he turned round walked to the fire and laid himself on the sopha smiling sardonically at the heap of univiting literature on the table I coughed and prepared to speak. "Hey" he cried half starting on to his feet "Who the—have we here?"

"Henry Hastings Sir. Ensign in—" "Henry—.! Sir and are you placed a spy upon me"

"I request to know Sir what right you have to address me with these expletives?"

"The —! Why the right of sovereignty"

The expression of his magnificent features was such a mixture of boyish apprehension and real temporary good humour that I thought twice ere I answered him sourly again besides my heart was sickish with the ominous prognostications of his identity I replied

"I am Henry Hastings Sir Ensign in the 29 Rejiment. Infantry and was shown into this room as the apartment of my commander Colonel Hartford with whom I had buisness"

"What are you Henry Hastings the poet of Angria?"

"I have in jest been called so"

"The Author of Sound the loud Trumpets" "Welcome Heroes" "Hurrah for the Gemini" "Shine on us God" and the like

"I am so sir"

"Then Im more indebted to you than my poor fortune can bear sit you down Henry Hastings and let me hear how you being as you say an Ensign in the 29 Foot could compose the aforesaid godly prelocutions.

"I hope sir you think there is nothing in my profession alien to the delights of composition"
"Why I cant tell Ive donned the scarlet and am just now fleeing from the presence of John Balfour of Burley simply because if he catches me I shall have to write

---

[12] Compare Isaiah 52:14.

and read too.[13] Besides Ensigns as far as I can see into the gentry are more enclined to decompose than compose"

"To rot in Idleness sir?"

"Stuff man Im not so plain spoken my education has been too much laid on the shelves of divinity to admit of my entering so point blank on to the illustration of my text Dont we go near to Decomposing a man when we cut his head of and is it not written. "To Decompose to dissolve to separate" There sir."

"You have the Advantage sir it is certainly the Duty of an Ensign to cut and cleave"

"Oh I have often thought it a strange thing Hastings now that you mention it that. "Cleave to cut asunder" and "Cleave to join to assimilate" should prove exactly the same word though so different in meaning can your philosophy adduce any reason for it. and there was another word which. —what was it? I have forgotten I met with it in the Old Testament this morning where is the book."

"Here sir I was looking at the Edition"

"Were you Hastings? what have you any knowledge of Divine things?"

"I should hope sir I have enough to raise me above the savages I fight against"

"Very true I hope so or you should have your coat stripped from your shoulders but to say so Henry Hastings is not to say I am religious it is not to say I really feel and think and act like one who has a soul to be saved or punished a hope of the future and a knowledge of the immensity of Eternity

"But sir I some times feel as if every moment was spent in vanity which was not occupied in the pondering on that mighty and glorious subject"

"How do you know its glorious Hastings?"

The Bible tells me so"

"Oh but you must not understand the Bible literally in what it speaks of things after this life I am not clear" Seating himself again as he spoke and turning of the Bible he held with the air of a great D D.[14] "I am not clear wether any writer any thinker on the subject of Eternity be at all gifted with a single ray of truth or one word of just reasoning" Here he Began opening the Sacred volumn at 20 different places quoting sometimes from its prints but much oftener from memory and arguing and speculating with most incomprehensible earnestness and much originality and fluency of language upon that state of being which none can look on without anxiety and which I think on with aweful astonishment. He concluded shutting the work with an air of triumph. "Now from all this language and these expressions I have founded and have perfected a system Yes Henry you may start a whole and Noble System of Divinity and eternity which I trust will prove its own enduring righteousness on the last and

---

13 Leader of the Covenanters in Scot's *The Tale of Old Mortality*. See also vol. I, p. 283, n. 28.
14 i.e., Doctor of Divinity.

avenging day I am a Member of the Church of Africa because I think it the best church in the Universe but poor is the best compared with the loftiness of the truth. And though I think that to seperate from my church because many of its Doctrines and much of its government is and are eroneous would be to do more injury to religion than to uphold even its faults yet I will never cease to advocate the Doctrines I have founded and too endeavour to spread them as wide as my name may extend." With this he gave me a full and remarkably finely worded explanation of a series of opinions upon this and a future life. The condition of the soul after death its degrees and states of punishment what that punishment consists in who will be punished and what souls must remain in the grave unanimated a long review of the whole system of Eternity that I felt corresponded with my feelings and awakened me to a consciousness of its truth. I said

"Sir if you had spoken from inspiration you might have made me cry I am certain [of] this no man otherwise than inspired could on such a subject do but rest assured that though you seem [as] a person the last to impress religious doctrines you have made me say that I Believe what you say to be true."—

"Do you say so Hastings" he said warmly and seemed overjoyed and enthusiastic in my conversation we spoke long on the subject and I was amazed at his imagination eloquence and most extraordinary acquaintance not only with the Scriptures but with the whole range of Biblical Literature He quoted Jerome Augustine Thos Aquinas Tertullian Luther Henry VIIIth Jowett Calvin Erasmus Tillotson read from the Barrow on the table and ran over the views of <Evans> Chillcot. Stanhope Flower Porteous Kirkwall Halmers and all the living pillars of our church.[15] his delighful language uncommon enthusiasm the grand ideas he entertained and the flashing of his eye the fire of his features which accompanied their expression would I think have silenced and confounded even the most able opponent. However I did not try the fight with him my knowledge <was> dual to his my feeling agreed with his and a chilling awe at my heart stayed all tendency to dispute when I looked at him And then as he concluded his Noble figure youthful apearance grandly beautiful countenance and dashing military dress formed such a glaring contrast to religion in its robes of humility that my wonder was anything but moderated by his aspect ere I could tell him flatly what I thought of him or ask him who in the world he was (but alack my own thoughts told me this) He himself. broke the silence.

---

[15] Jerome, Augustine and Tertullian were third and fourth-century Churchfathers; Aquinas and Erasmus were thirteenth and fifteenth-century scholars; Luther and Calvin were leaders of the Protestant reformation; Tillotson and Barrow were seventeenth-century Anglican churchmen (see note 10 above); Jowett may refer to William Jowett (1787-1855), a student and Fellow of St. John's, Cambridge, Secretary of the Church Missionary Society 1832-40. The others are all Glass Town and Angrian churchmen who have no obvious historical counterparts (but see p. 140, n. 65 on Chillcot).

"Hastings you said you came here to seek Colonel Hartford! Who the-- (heres piety Reader) "was such a—fool as to send you here on the errand"

"Ahem! <no Relig—. piet—hem.> Why sir a young foreign looking page was ordered by a Ruffian looking fellow in a chequer shirt to escort me to Colonel Hartfords lodgings"

"Oh" returned the young officer laughing, "Eugene Ill bet anything[16] —why you ass.

"Ill not be called an Ass or so cursed by any one Sir"

"What now firebrand some of my Angrians cursed loyal—hem their cursed insolence to a superior I see could you not see that the fellow had rascal written on his forehead and as for the Ruffian you speak of if he heard you call him so he would send you aloft presently"—

I summoned a little courage. "Sir favor me with your address for I have not the advantage of knowing you."

"Col Howard. —But Hush Hastings the—! here they are" he half laughing half. serious sprung from the sopha and bent his head to listen. "They'll pin me yet if I dont mind but here goes and d— the scoundrels" Ere he concluded the nearest window was flung up Flying up to its arch and laying a hand on the sill he vaulted into the garden with all the spring and vigour of a youthful tyger He was gone directly but the renewed voices revisited the great folding door Steps again neared it and as it flew open a young Officer. middle height ably built and light complexioned stepped in looked round with his quick grey eye and turned to 5 or 6 companions. saying, "He's gone again" They all entered and went talking together to the window Here they were at last! The one who first spoke I recognised as the Commander in Cheif Thornton the tall slender handsome officer who stood laughing at the slipperiness of the prey was the Calvary General Arundel. The Amazingly dashing fellow behind whose active countenance belied his fantastic fashionableness I knew to be General Viscount Castlereagh There were several more whose names I being a country Angrian did not know. but of these first I was sure for I had seen them every day reviewing the forces threre[sic] There they stood and half a dozen as fine fellows as could be met with in a days walk but what commanders what leaders of a countrys glory! Not one among them 30 years old yet but if there was not age there was station one of them a Kings son another married to a princess even the slight thin hypocritical creature who stood laughing when the others laughed and prepared to sigh as they sighed. even that slender. pale scion of Aristocracy was an Earl. The Lord Elrington

General Thornton moved to the fire and brandished the poker with all the grace of practice

"And who are you young man" he asked as he noticed me standing confused in the prescence of such lofty personages "What are ye here for eh" surveying me with a keenness more like the look of his Grace of Wellington

---

[16]   Eugene Rosier, the Duke's page.

than any thing I had seen for many a day "Hey what its the Duke the others cried running from the window to the fire.

"No my Lords" I answered "I am an Ensign in the 29th my name is Hastings and I entered this saloon mistaking it for the apartments of Col Hartford"

"Ha ha! and who bummed you so cleverly" asked the Dashing Castlereagh

"The mistake lies in my conductor a page in the yard"

"Varry like. my lad" said General Thornton but I waddnt have you to be trusting every raw hand as you see about such a place as this I guess youre only young in your buisness"

"I have only entered sir a fortnight."

"Varry well. varry well." was the <Doric> answer and then (they had spoken enough to the likes of me) all turned to the table and rummaged over the books laughing as they read the titles "We shall have a sermon to morrow Frederic I think look here is the bible" "Aye Castle. and a varry good light that hes taken to it you might read it more and not heed it less yourseln" "Nay Now Lofty my cousuin[sic] isnt likely to give us a honest sermon anyhow hell plagiarise from Barrow theres the leaf turned down "Honour thy Father and thy Mother"[17] hey Thornton thats a text for you"

Hold your Nonsense Seymour didnt I tell thee to remember thy Creator" Well done thats right you have it between you Eccles Chap xii. v 1st. as the Duke would say" "Whisht lads After all it isnt reight to be daffin it this way. I say where the—is the duke. cant ye tell"

"Sir" I answered to the General "I have never had the honour of being acquainted with his Grace but I believe I saw him here only 5 minutes since and he sprung from that window as you entered."

"Did he then we'll have him" cried one among them and they were making for the window themselves but a man entered the saloon the very same with him of the chequered shirt I had seen in the morning but that distinction was now superseded by undress vest. or jacket of the Blue chintz. and his black short curls unpressed by the black. foraging cap. of the courtyard his dark eye and sallow cheek and black whiskers gave him an appearance of ferocity more allied to the Bandit than the soldier. I wondered to see him here.

"Hey" he cried much after the stern style of a farmer to a set of trespassing football players "Hey whats all this about Thornton! all of you! what are you after?"

He noticed then and said. "Why are you here young man did you not want to speak with Colonel Hartford"

"Yes sir" and then I detailed the roguery of the page. "So" he interrupted "send for Eugene Rosier the Dukes page" a footstep hurried away from the

---

[17] See Deuteronomy 5:16. Thornton, it should be recalled, was disowned by his family.

passage for the servant was not in sight. and in a while. ere which the Noble
Officers had all scampered out after their Royal Master. a soldier entered with the
young Rascal who had misled me among these grand Folks Him of the Blue
chintz vest alias cotton shirt turned with a look like a Bengal Tyger

"If you dare disobey my order here again you shall repent the day" said
he grimly

"I am his Majestys servant" rejoined the coxcomb with a smart tongue
and a brow like brass. but the lightning blow which felled him to the very earth
gave him a stunning conviction of the untimeliness of that announcement The
Inflictor as he turned to leave the room only said "John Campbell. shew that
young man to Col Hartfords Apartment" The soldier conducted me out of the
saloon and to the Officer mentioned. myself all the while wondering at the peep I
had taken into the sanctum sanctorum of Aristocracy and the conversation I had
had with him who I knew to be my Glorious Monarch ZAMORNA.

For a week after the conclusion of the incident above related
If incident it might be called which incident had none[18]
There was little done in Gazemba of which I had any share my time was taken
up on parade at the reviews on rejimental duty or in delightful excursions up and
down the Etrei But meanwhile the operations of the Army were proceeding under
its admirable leaders and glorious Generalissimo in a manner silent shure and
speedy. We understood the primary disposition of the forces to be that General
Moray should with 8000 men march back over the desart and take up a position
on the Cumano to keep open the communication between the Army and
Verdopolis that8 000 more should be sent up the River to hunt along its banks
and rid them of all the sable vermin and the moment an opening offered to
pounce upon a good flock of Negroes The main army should hurry on the scent
of their prey. leaving however a reserve behind at Gazemba to replenish gaps and
garrison this most important rallying point. Nothing further was publicly
known of our position. but things were evidently tending every day to the
ardently longed for ONWARD.

On the 17th of December myself and a dozen Officers of our Rejiment
were seated in the mess room. talking eagerly on the remarkable event which had
occured that evening

A soldier. mounted on horseback gashed terribly in the face mudd
splashed and covered with blood had ridden furiously into Gazemba from the
south alighted at the Fort and after a shortt interview with his Majesty he was
ushered to a large meeting of the great generals of the Army at the temporary
palace nothing further was yet known of the issue of this incident but there was

---

[18] Compare with Milton's *Paradise Lost*, Book II, l. 667. See vol. I, p. 217,
n. 5.

room enough for abundant speculation over all the City At midnight Colonel Hartford just arrived from the fort came into the mess room and read the following paper

Fort Gazemba. 17th inst

Soldiers of Angria.

The Fort and City of Dongola 30 miles distant on the east bank of the mouth of the Etrei and containing 1100 inhabitants with a garrison of 1000 soldiers was stormed by a body of 10 or 15000 Ashantees who burnt every house in the place and massacred every man woman and child it contained. The intelligence of this event has just reached his Grace the Duke of Zamorna conveyed by Richard Hazard the only living being who has escaped the slaughter. —To morrow morning the 18th inst the Main body of the Army will march to Dongola. for Tenfold

REVENGE

Hartford had hardly read this proclamation to us ere we started up in a transport of rage and horror one loud shout of vengeance arose from our lips and we would have rushed through fire swords and millions of Demons to seize one African Body and destroy one African scout.

"My lads" said Colonel Hartford "Im glad that you feel thus. it raises my blood like lightning but you'll have wild work on it to morrow So go all of you directly to rest" We obeyed and retired at once. but sleep was long of visiting us. I felt stunned and sooner fell asleep than I thought I should and my slumber was dead and dreamless. till I entered full onto a vision of the Judgement Day The roaring of a thousand fires bursting from the earth made me start up in bed in a paroxism of horror my cracking ears caught the indentical sound of my dream shaking the very bed beneath me I cried out "Save me" and jumped on to the floor My senses were quite confused and feverish and I could not distinguish anything till the words "Up Hastings are you dead we are going directly" followed by a rapid succession of knocks at my chamber door startled me at once into reality like the charm of a talisman. "Coming" I shouted and ran to the window to see the reason of this sound which had caused the hallucination of my Nightmare looking out I saw a whole <park> of flying artillery galloped by trains of Horses rapidly down the street under the window The terrific rattle of their metal carriages made the house shake as if it was about to grind them to dust. This was no time for staying to see the sight so I hurried on my cloth[e]s and took my arms to go down as I was about to leave the room (the cannon had some minutes ago passed by) up again rose such a Thunder and beating of Drums without that there was not a pane in the windows which did not shake and quiver to its centre. Oh how they rolled and rattled and rose in such a storm of sound as I had never heard eaqueled before directly the shrill exhilirating thrilling of fifes joined in on this Terrific reveillé "My God" I cried "This is glorious this was warlike." The drums of the rejiment were thundering an Alarm over the town and the street beneath was choked with soldiers rushing to the rendezvous. I plunged rather than ran downstairs into the hall where my Brother Officers were gathered and with flushed faces and glittering glances we greeted each other on the glory before us. My Nerves tortured me with exctasy when even doors and rafters trembled to the tremendous rolls of Thunder now beating before the very House But we sprung and dashed into a tumult of Men and Horses and Drums and Trumpets and worked our way to the rendezvous at Castle Square. There there was a Noble sight to see Oh Reader that I could communicate to you the Enthusiasm which I felt and all round me burned with when we saw the long heavey masses of blazing soldiery the great scarlet flags fluttering above them folding and unfolding in the breeze that one gilt glorious word "ARISE." Foremost and most conspicuous in the scene ranged the "Enaras Bloodhounds" a Rejiment of Infantry all dressed in white with the black helmet and the scarlet sash. Stern iron war harden[ed] fellows bred to the fighting of the frontiers Enara's own favorite pets over whom he is the Colonel and who will fight with none but him such a host of Dark whiskered and bearded warriors such looks of savage and relentless ferocity I never beheld before they made me shudder with thoughts of the work before me Their great Raven Banner bore in silver Blazonry the single emphatic syllable. "DEATH" at their head beside a huge iron sinewed. bony horse and accompanied by 8 vast liver colored dew lapped. red eyed Bloodhounds held in leashes stood the second commander of the Army their Colonel Henry Fernando Enara. the very man of the chequer shirt. attired in close white vest and pantaloons scarlet sash and black helmet like themselves he was examining his horses bridle and held a sharp dagger meanwhile between his clenched ivory teeth and the wild ferocity of his look. the yellow wasted face the narrow sinewy frame gave terrible annunciation of the vengeance due upon his everlasting foe. I hurried into my Rejiment grasped my colors and swore never to desert them till death. The scarlet silk. flung itself out over my head and I waited in a transport of enthusaism the moment when I should start in the "Death or Glory" The Duke of Zamorna had before I was risen left the city at the head of his noble calvary The main body was on the instant about to follow Enara. sprung on to his steed reined it back upon its haunches and exclaiming with deed[sic] determined voice.

"Now my lads your King has led you out upon an errand the sweetest that ever called me to my native desart he has led you on to an errand of Vengeance. a fight of Revenge. Mind the man among you who thinks for one moment of stopping till life deserts his body or the body of his Enimy the fellow here who will dream for a moment of fainting in a march from Morn till Nightfall a scoundrel who dare even believe the possibiblity that a Negro can ever receive quarter from a Man. that fool that Idiot if I hear it shall die by this very hand. No we go out to slay and we will make too an ample sacrifice I will never return unless I have slain my own hundred and say you the same with me Dont Arise only but Arise and Kill curse every hour that passes over in which an Ashantee doesnt lie shreaking[sic] beneath your feet. This night you will enter Dongola and then you will see what they have done. Then I will see what you have done and Our Monarch will tell you what to Do Onward soldiers and Remember the Massacre of Dongola."

As Enara spoke thus in a voice as terrible as that of a Lion he galloped down to the path on the River side all the Bands burst up in music the cannon roared terrifically above us from the Citidal[sic] and of we all marched on our road to the Revenge of Dongola.

Oh That days marching I shall never forget it neither the thoughts which came thick upon my mind as I pressed still forward with my Rejiment grasping in my hand the Standard of my countrys glory I had before seen Armies and marching and I had considered myself entered upon the champaign before me but Now I felt that this minute only this moment was the eve of my real Military Life all was now new to me as the vast Fort of Gazemba lessened behind us as its saluting Artillery thundered fainter in the Distance I saw that Civilization and Home and peace and idleness were all vanished as though they had never been. We were 9000 men in number all marching nearly together along the Banks of the Etrei under the immediate supreintendence of Enara and Thornton. I never saw those commanders again during the Day for they kept ahead with the "Bloodhounds" to pioneer us The Noble Zamorna with Murat and Arundel and 3000 cavalry was miles in the advance of us and Castlereagh with the rear of 2000 was yet at Gazemba but just going to start with the cannon and Baggage of the expedition Miles round us over the desart partys of Horsemen were flung out scouring the level plain and galloping and hurrying before us. at the mouth of the Etrei 10 leagues below. a flotilla of gunboats lay waiting to take the forces over to the wretched and martyred Dongola. Ere day had risen far up in the Heaven the heat and drou[g]ht began to make impression upon our ranks and to exhaust the spirits of our hurried soldiers The cooling Etrei had dissapeared for we were tracking the waste considerable to the west of it to escape the reeds and marshes of its banks the sands and levels were wearisome to the foot the heat and sunshine almost blinding to the eye By noon those about me I saw hung their heads and the Dust was pasted over their faces but the Hearts of Angrians still burned within us and we cried from rank to rank Comrades remember Dongola. The sun set at Evening burning and flashing on the western horizon A cry rose in the foremost ranks which rose and swelled with a hoarse and varying murmur. The Rejiments were almost thrown into confusion with eagerness to ascertain the cause of it we listened, and struggled like maniacs to get at the meaning of [the] uproar at length the glorious shout of "The sea. The sea." rung round us like tidings from heaven and we felt that we had endured nothing and could go miles and hours again. The sea! There it lay broad and beaming on the south horizon but Reeds and rushes and marshes and water and lagoons and a horrible extent of allmost impassible canebreak stretched between us and the mouth of the Etrei. The rejiments being stopped all blocked up the approach to the track. the Darkness was fast hurrying on and. what I had never seen in my stay in this country before a great wild mass of Dark. stormy clouds was rising just over the ocean and rapidly encroaching in the clear grey sky. Onward however was the word we pressed like heroes on our track and not a man but felt as if on his exertions only lay the safty and salvation of his country Our Rejiment was soon surrounded by the thickest of the canebreak we could see nothing around us for the Bamboos and the twilight all under our feet was dark but we felt the water every step oozing into our boots and shoes the shouts and cries of encouragement alone broke in on the silence and no man could pay attention to the scene of wildness about him The ranks of soldiers before me suddenly came to a dead halt I heard a hoarse unintermitted murmur and rushing on to see the cause of it a sight broke on me which I shall not forget till my dying day. Three steps in advance—and the canebreak ended at once. One vast wide weltering water stretched out to the far opposite shore. The waves of the tide below were bursting in with the true ocean freedom and resistless majesty far up the River gleamed in the twilight till the haze and darkness obscured the Horizon from view Black tempestous clouds were hurrying over the sky. and the long low wailing gusts of wind from the water told all men that this was the first night of Rainy season in Angria "Rainy Season" Oh what thoughts did that word call up. What feeling of the future. The Flotilla of gunboats was coming up with the tide and the Army pressed onward to Embark. As I with my company stepped into the Boat which was to convey us over. Enara himself rode to where we were. "Stand you back" he said "Stand back all of you this Rejiment and that and you. remain here all night for the flotilla is too small for them to pass till morning Stand back sirs" We fell back on to the marshes as we were ordered the Iron decrees could not be confuted but what in the world were we to do. Night was falling down with extreme rapidity a Dark and moonless night all the footing was wet muddy water around us the <towring> mighty canebrake I for my part after long standing to witness the passage lay down perfectly exhausted here was no warm bed no comfortable dwelling none of the blessings of a calm country life. my resting place was water and rushes my companion a sword and musket the the turmoil of the <passing> army before me and a wild intermitted burst of wind sighing and howling all around me. Dead midnight came on and I fell into a fevered sleep I could not further note the state of the army or the Brave fellows commanded to the same rest as me. all was soon oblivion and my rest was like that of the dead in their graves anon I <shot> up for my eyes seemed scared by a terrific flash of lightning it was broadly and resistlessly bright I glared into the Night wildly and in <dreamy> agony of apprehension Listen what a roar. Hideously broken and rattling and Deep and trembling It thundered and bellowed out in a long protracted roll. it was gone I closed my eyes fast in horror I had never heard any thing of the army the strange impression was on me that I was alone and a hundred of miles from any one but I was so confused between sleep and cold and horror that I never felt the agony of solitude. all was like a nightmare. I said my eyes I kept closed but all would not do a second resistless light burst through my brain and with a crack as if heaven itself was shattered the Thunder again broke forth in its stunning and awful roar I got up The rain was pouring in impetous torrents all was dark and stormy where cried I where are the Army. I was almost amongst them I stared till my recollection and memory returned which my misery had stunned for a while. The stir and turmoil and confusion was as loud and. rough as ever. 2 or 3000 men yet crowded the waterside. and lamps and lights innumerable twinkled and flickered among them. I too soon passed among them solitude was hideous in this Terrific Night. All were standing round like spectres of drowned soldiers arisen from the ocean but who was that very tall statly Officer so young and Noble standing with us and encouraging us all with that lightning glance and rich organ voice. It was Our King the Duke of Zamorna his noble spirit had led him again to cross the Etrei and he swore that he would be the last man to take the passage. when I beheld him he was standing wrapt. in his cloak. heedless of all the weather and Midnight and animated to perfect enthusiasm by the scene. The Tremendous Enara stood by him surveying with cool keen look the whole storm and confusion speaking with that deep entrepid voice that calm unaltered countenance but all his heart in one flame of real southern exitement Zamorna cried. "Let the first company of the 29th pass over." I was one to obey this heavenly command in we [s]tepped and the long low vessel pushed into the darkness and billows and foam as we passed over 3 long miles of water the wind and Thunder and lightning mixed with torrents of rain exceeded anything I had ever seen before we were often in imminent danger and I was glad to leap on to the marshes and join the passed over on the skirts of the Ruined Dongola. surely said I as I looked on the Dark howling night and heard the lashing of the impetous waves and saw the long lights twinkling far on the other side surely none would have attempted this passage but Alexander the Great or Arthur Augustus Adrian Wellesly. none would follow the attempt but the Macedonian phalanx or the Army of Angria."

I was asleep in spite of myself directly among a whole rejiment of comrades when I awoke in [the] morning Zamorna was just riding by on horseback and all the Forces had passed over the River Now amid the Dying Tempest with the clouds breaking up and the morning struggling out we entered the martyred Dongola

"Stand fast" said our Colonel "and look about you my lads here is something to fight for." and as Hartford spoke the muffled drums beat up and the Bands burst out in a solemn funeral march while all the different Rejiments with arms reversed and colours furled passed on in sucessive files among the great Black heaps of smoky stones and the shattered walls of the Fort threatning every minute to crumble to the earth All was a complete dismantled ruin not a roof left standing or a dog or a cat alive the streets black with soot and rendered impassable by the charred and reddened piles of masonry But when the foremost ranks of the army entered what had a week since been the market place of Dongola a stern stifled murmur ran from man to man as each looked upon the spectacle before him I myself was so pressed in by a set of tall Grenadiers who hid everything by their stout brawny shoulders that I could not tell what it was that created such horror before me. but as I held up my face to the sky to catch a breath of air in the crowd I saw something which made me shut my eyes and turn my head down that moment. From a pole which had been an inn sign and which stuck out of the Gable of a House beside me. Hung suspended almost over my head a raw and bloody corpse. the skin flayed off. the gore blackened over the carcase and the throat severed with a ghastly gash stretching from ear to ear. The men before me were marched forward and I could now see all the market place around us. and There Nailed upon close rows of wooden crosses reared up along the sides of the fort and houses I beheld more than 200 Dead Bodies of men with the scalps torn from their heads their mouths skewered up with knives and the dried gore hanging in black lines from their livid sides In the midst of the area. a heap of several hundred carcases their heads chopped of and piled at random among them and all burnt and blacked by a fire which had been kindled round them. diffused through the air a dreadfully singed and putrid smell

Here the Duke of Zamorna dismounted from Horseback. stood beside the horrid heap and stretching over it his unsheathed sword he cried.

"Angrians these frightful carcasses which you see lying or hanging around you 2 days ago were living men. Yes these were Angrians. My own soldiers my own servants and I was their master and King!! —What are they now look at them and tell me shall these things be? this is the work of the Ashantees. Quashia has thus treated your. fellow soldiers and companions. You have hearts in your bodies and you have weapons in your hands. you behold what is around you and now then will you eat or drink or sleep or smile will you heed. rain or cold or wind or heat or the desart or the sea or the marshes or the rivers or fear of exhausting fatigue or prospect of a horrible death till for every single drop of blood shed by this city for every single wound gashed on these bodies for every life departed for every murder done a river of the Blood of the Ashantees a thousand of their gaping bodies as many lives as an Angrians sword can annihilate as many slaughters as his tongue can name shall spread over all this mighty desart and send up their reek to heaven as a sacrifice to an offended God Angrians I despise myself to think that I have laughed and rejoiced and slept. on the very day the very hour when this hideous deed was done that I was within 10 leagues of this martyred city that I had come here for the sole purpose of exterminating the Africans And yet that. there is this sight for you all to see! —Oh soldiers I need not speak to you of the fate of these your fellow countrymen of the torments they have suffered or the deaths they have died you know all this as well as I can do. And Angrians since you feel like me I only ask you to see like me. we have talked about vengeance hitherto but let us talk about it no more All the world is injured is wounded and nature itself must cry out for vengeance the God of Nature himself must avenge. he sees you how he has destined this army as the sword of his power and His sword must have an edge which can never dull. By Heaven soldiers and by him who rules there. by the spirits of my soldiers who have been martyred for my country by the very shade of this ruined city I swear to you that I will not sheath this sword till I sheath it in the heart of an Ashantee that I will not lay it by till from the Calabar to the Benguela there is not one Accursed savage left alive. you must spare nothing Angrians slay them whenever wherever however you can find them slay the men slay the women slay the children give no quarter But exterminate from the Earth the whole d—d race of Ashantees" When our Monarch concluded these words his flushed cheek and excited eye showed that he felt all the fervour of the enthusiasm wich his voice expressed we his soldiers cried out aloud to be led to instant battle "But not yet" said General Enara "Not yet you have plenty more to see" We marched forward and—But hang it reader hang it its no use for me to go on doling out to you the sights that we saw and the feeling which oppressed us Hang it Ill stop for my own blood boils too hotly at the recollection to admit of my hand with any coolness inditing Lets have no more of the corpses flayed alive the Burnt Bodies and half eaten flesh and gnawed and scattered bones or the Horror or indignation or the overpowering emotions of that most unpleasant day. I tell you that if you are an African you will need none of my laboured scribbling to bring with force to your mind Marks and relics of the Ashantees. Enough of it to Bed to Bed let us all retire and wait the rising of to morrows labour.

For more than a week after the day I have above described the Main Army lay inactive at Dongola And I notice it as a perfect peculiarity of African warfare shewn in such frequent and complete pauses of idleness amid the most energetic and effective action The reason is that we are in general accustomed to carry every thing at first burst so impetously that ere long as occurs when a man [h]as taken a strong glass of Brandy we find our selves spent out and incapable of further warfare till energy be restored by rest and all our plans relaid in calmness here the Duke of Zamorna dashed into Dongola but here he stopped for nothing was prepared for a further ongoing We knew not where the Ashantees were nor were we so ordered as to be able to come at them But after all their imperfections Africans are not like other men and though they be for a moment thrown out of breath by haste they are not bewildered in uncertainty or plunged into a chaos of rashness The spring and vigour of Zamornas intellect supported by the vigilant industry of Thornton and the unwearied sagacity and consummate knowledge of this kind of fighting displayed by the terrible Enara. were all exerted during the last week of December in the two grand endeavours of seeking out the Africans and preparing to come at them in a few days the Scouts cavalry and detachments of the Bloodhounds which had penetrated with their brute namesakes all through the marshes of the Etrei and the desart beyond it brought us certain intelligence that a large portion perhaps 6 or 7000 of that Body of Ashantees who had massacred and destroyed Dongola were now lying entrenched in the almost inaccessible marshes of the River Benguela. "Inaccessible" said the Duke when he heard this "Nonsense—But now for vengeance."

The marshes of the Benguela are the low flat swampy grounds which lye round the mouth of that almost unknown desart River 15 miles South East of Dongola. and constantly overflowed either by Tide or by River water they are nearly impassable to all but the native Aborigines and except to them Dreadfully pestilential and destructive to human life. All the Rivers of Angria East of the Calabar empty themselves into the sea in this manner and among these Dreadful wildernesses of canes and reeds and lakes and mudd and water there are the Marshes of the Calabar the Marshes of the Etrei the marshes of the Benguela and the marshes of the Cameroons[19] lying along in a regular line and each uniting with the other as a fit bar to their inward burning and inhospitable desarts. Here sheltered from the Attacks of our military the Aborigines have always been accustomed in any emergency to hide themselves and they have for years past proved perfect nests of ferocious savages All attempts to oust them have been in vain even Enaras untired Bloodhounds can do little in such a Ground of disease and death.

It was reserved however for the Genius and daring of the Duke of Zamorna to drive out from their fortress of refuge the plagues and torments of Angria it was for this purpose that he set out with his Noble Army and this end once accomplished we shall hear little more of the Ashantee invasion of Africa. all the Desarts are to naked to devoid of hiding places to be defensible against the Intrepid soldiers of our country Here and Here only Quashia could keep his ground and flee from the hand of the Angrian or rush forth to overrun a country

On the 30 of December the following Proclamation Appeared in the Army and copies of it were immediately despatched to Adrianopolis for instant circulation over Angria

"Soldiers 6000 Ashantees have been discovered by 6 Bloodhounds in the Marshes on the East bank of the Benguela. Twice 6000 Angrians must instantly march with me to destroy them and on the first of January 1835 I hope to present my kingdom with a more glorious New Years gift than any she has yet seen or dreamt of. The Barbarians are congregated for safty in all the Marshes of the Angrian rivers and I command Major General Sir S Kirkwall the instant this news reaches him to turn back from the North course of the Etrei to its mouth where on the South Western side and adjoining on the marshes of the Calabar he must operate so as to ensure the extermination of every savage that wilderness contains and I believe they are almost as numerous as the canes in its brakes. Should the weather prove dry and the wind blowing in from the north east I direct him to set fire to the reeds and bamboos on the marsh that the flame may drive the Ashantees either on to the sea shore in which case I have ordered the Angrian Gun boats to coast along and destroy them or onto Dry Desarts extending North to Fort Enara in which case I have commanded General Moray to despatch several Rejiments from the Cumana to ensure their radical

---

[19] Branwell's geography here is somewhat fanciful. It seems to be generally based on the map accompanying "Geography of Central Africa: Denham and Clapperton's Journals," *Blackwoods Magazine*, XIX, June 1826, 687-709. Although there is a town named Benguela in what is now Angola, their is no river by that name. The other rivers mentioned (all of which have different names to day, although they appear in the *Blackwood's* map—the Etrei as the Rio Elrei) lie south of the Niger delta, well away from traditional Ashanti country, which is north of the Niger delta. The article does note that "From Lagos eastward to Old Calabar and Rio de Elrei inclusive, above twenty rivers enter the sea"(703).

extermination Arise soldiers! For I must distinguish this sacred season by an offering worthy of a Christian Christmas.

Angrians Remember Dongola and obey
ZAMORNA.

Now Reader! theres a glorious proclamation That day it appeared all the Army was in a state of glorification we had been tied up for almost a fortnight and now at last we were to be let loose on our prey To morrow! that word made many a heart beat under its Gilded breast plate and many an eye lighten under its Iron Helmet For myself I should have felt perhaps more enthusiasticly than any other in the army but the severe and constant duties I was engaged in on the last day on 1834. almost drove from my mind every idea but a sense of exhiliration and rousing activity

Night closed down with a black vault of heaven and a countless host of stars the bivouace[sic] fire at which I was stationed sent constantly up a stream of sparks to imitate the "glowing sapphires" above us and I lay down in the red glow to dream of yet brighter flashes and yet redder glowing the armed and scarlet ranks of Angrians in the full blaze of glorious battle But in a while my sleep fell dead and dreamless Nor did I at all wake untill the Bugles at dawning sounded the Arise! —Then as was my wont I started up and looked about me—
All the Rejiments were up and stirring and a long rank of calvary was drawn up beside the place where I stood with several great officers on horseback. at its head clustered together round a tall dashing cavalier spendidly attired and mounted on a grand black charger that seemed snuffing fire from its nostrils. All the folk about him nay all the folk about me too were shouting their very souls out and it was a minute or two ere I heard the hurrah in articulate words of "Zamorna Zamorna." there he was and I joined my voice in the general uproar but his Grace. as he "put on his bonnet" began to speak and we were silenced like clockwork.

"Now my Lads we must march directly you'll have a hard march before you and a stiff. struggle at the end of it but mind you will have your suppers ready roasted at night time Though I apprehend the kitchen in which they will be cooked is a step or two underground and as hot as the bravest among you dare venture to step into. I dare say that some of you will go down with the dishes to the oven but. as I much fear wether any will get back time enough I'll just hand you round a drop of something meanwhile to stay your stomach with." As the wicked young scoundrel spoke he grasped toper[20] like a brimming goblet of Brandy. put it to his lips and handed it to the austere but half smiling Enara. taking a reasonable draught of the creature this cheif of the Bloodhounds delivered his bottle to General Thornton who shook his head spoke something reprovingly and ended by a taste quite sufficient to ascertain the quality of the liquor Castlereagh next tried it and materially diminished its quantity and by the time that it had gone the round of the Lofty circle it had assumed the aspect of a pure clear christal goblet again. meanwhile jugs of excellent spirits were handed round

---

[20]   One who topes or drinks a great deal.

to every man in every Rejiment Dire was the clutching of the creature and intense the smacking of the lips accompanying the touch when the long long draughts had concluded and the gustos were dying away in heaven Our Monarch (ought he not to be called a merry one) again addressed us.

"Now lads look there at Dongola and all I ask of you is to keep firm in your minds till Nightfall the memory of those shattered towers and smoky walls before you."

Then Zamorna clapt spurs to his Horse and galloped away through the red ranks of soldiers his staff clattering After him and his own Rejiment the Royal Angrian Horseguards turning round in great moving masses followed at a sharp trot making the ground quiver as their dashing Lieut Colonel Arundel. led them through the opening lines. General Enara leaped on to his strong sinewy racer and snatching the reins from a groom he beckoned with his hand to his swarthy crew and rode forwards also attended by 8 great grim liver colored Bloodhounds his almost constant companions and the horror of the Ashantees His Lieutenant the long celebrated Thomas Scroven a Gigantic and Heavy headed Ruffian with a face like bronze an eye almost as tigerish as his masters and his stern mouth half severed by the terrible scar of a sabre wound—led the Rejiment of Bloodhounds (human). These grim fellows filed past me and when I saw their swarthy faces black whiskers and keen cutting Broadswords I felt a sort of novice like qualm for the bloody work in which I was to join them

The Bands of music struck up and all the Army were directly afoot Our Muskets on our shoulders and our faces turned to war

Their[sic] is something in Zamornas character which pre eminently qualifies him for the Leader of an Angrian Army His strange impetous triumphing and wildly merry behavior that morning on the opening of a day which was by his orders to close in floods of blood. was received by all of us with unmingled feelings of fitness and rejoicing all that he did or said seemed fit for the King of Angria and as the soldiers moved along over the plain their conversation was now of the aspect of the champaign and now of the merits of the various leaders above them but always and cheifly of the unconquerable victoriousness of Zamorna our King.

As for my own part I had plenty to do in thinking of myself. All my soul was so wrapt up in speculating upon what I should do this day to make myself known in screwing up my courage to a point of Enara like daring.[21] in thinking upon the stern scene I was soon to be engaged in mingled with Awful glimpses of Danger and frightful wounds and probable Death. Death itself. that I had not room for many other feelings that otherwise would have intruded and this being the case my readers can hardly expect any very elaborate account of our march to the Banks of the Benguela

I have said before that the weather for it was now the rainy season was extremly wild and broken one hour burning heat and a humid heaven the next

---

[21] Compare Shakespeare's *Macbeth*, I, vii, 60.

Black clouds and thunder and torrents of tropical rain to day about 1 o clock in the Afternoon the clouds were seen coming up over the sea red like copper. and piled in towering walls of dull threatning vapour the sea at a distance for our path lay only 3 miles from the shore lay perfectly still and as black as ink. all the desart was oppressivly hot the flags could not be unfurled for there was no breath of air to wave them and in a while man and horse all began to shew evident signs of thirst and exhaustion the foam appeared at the horses bits and would soon have specked the soldiers lips but almost ere we were aware we all had plunged into the thick and <slimiest> of the great Benguelan marshes. And here. my Rejiment was drawn up and I looked round me after taking a long and plentiful draught of the green slimy but as I thought refreshing and delightful water there were many Rejiments. all ranged in thick ranks like the one in which I was stationed. I could see on the uneven and open space of solid ground rows of scarlet jackets and white feathers and glittering Bayonets without number. I knew nothing of the ground hardly any thing of where we were or what was going to be done But I knew that my heart beat as thick as fast as if I was in a raging fever there was something so strange so indescribably awful in the solemn formal scene of preparing war that I felt sick with an uncontrollable agitation nay I cannot tell what I felt as the huge heavy peices of Artillery tugged along by many horses rumbled grating past and dissapeared in the lane of soldiers. all things seemed passing forward but what was forward the masses of military the thick dark canebreaks intirely prevented me from seeing The soldiers in my company and all about me only spoke in whispered mutterings. and they were all to much taken up with their own thoughts and observations to observe me now red now pale my teeth chattering and my frame trembling like an aspen leaf.

"Unfurl your flag sir" said an officer tapping me on the shoulder. I started almost like a man "taken in the fact" but mechanically obeying though only half understanding up went the ashen pole and out flew the Blazoned scarlet to the wind. This lead me to take some notice of the change of weather and I was astonished at the difference it presented. There had risen a most suspicious moaning and sighing and creaking amongst the clustering canes a dead shadow lay all around us and the sky was piled up with terrific clouds blackning and reddning from zenith to Horizon Sometimes the Banner over my head fell down hanging languidly about my cap and feather. then it spread out. and directly was fluttering so rapidly that I had some difficulty in holding it firm in my hand drops of rain began to patter on the ground about us a low murmuring noise was heard from the direction of the sea—stop a bit—and then shuch a sweeping drive of dense blowing pelting drenching rain as I thought was never felt from the day of the Deluge[22] till now Alas there was no running to shelter no uplifting of umbrellas All the compacted Rejiments (hardly seen through the rain at times) stood erect and steady as firm—nay far firmer than the canes about them for these bent and whistled and waved in the force of the pitiless storm—Well thus we

---

[22] i.e., at the time of Noah.

stood for a couple of hours I didnt know where nor for what with cannon passing and ranks of troops filing past among us all eastward through the chaos of ground and reeds and men and flagstaffs. After a while a Peal of Thunder rose up amid the tempest This I thought was a peal indeed. It rattled and bellowed with such a horrible roll of sound that my ears ached as if they were ready to burst with the roar. as it subsided I saw a great sensation it had produced in every body round me. "Yon is Thunder I think" said I to my nearest Neighbour "Thunder!" he cried with a short laugh. "Why their at it man! its the CANNON!". Hillo! I was struck dumb. They were at it. and we must be in the middle of it that sound was to loud for anything further than a few hundred yards off. I looked bewildered on my hands they trembled so that had I had to take a musket if my life depended upon steadiness my life must have departed and no wondrous thing either for my life seemed only in a sort of jeopardy Oh. Boulshill and the green lovly valley of Pendleton[23] with the little villiage and the old rambling farm house! where were ye then!

"I say Harry" cried one of my wildest associates round me. "it looks coming on thicker weather and if I should chance the fate of a drowned rat you'll remember to acquaint the Old folk at Romalla—were in for it now at last. I heard one say that Enaras giving it into em right and left but we cant hear them for the storm! Hang it! I wish they'd march us on out of this drenching torrent here" and he began to sing "Welcome Heroes" to give vent to his rousing feelings. But Hush. For the Horrid roar rose up again short broken and loud as if the world was rending around us. The white smoke came drifting over our heads and I turned cold at the nearness of death. and its horrors. The musketry began to roll and rattle to our right but the Tempest was so violent that we could hear nothing distinctly all was a confused jumble of sounds and thundering but if we could not hear we could feel for the intoxication began to spread among us a convulsed <gulp> of the face and a short toss of the hat into the air betokened the rising enthusiasm of many a brave Angrian around us and anon feet began to pat on the ground and stamp and dance in fitful uncontrollableness. a short snatch of a song passed from the mouth into the wind and when a Man on Horseback followed by a train of mounted Officers dashed up to us from the right. the loud sudden shout which burst instinctivly from our mouths was the safty valve of pent up and boiling impatience of idleness. This man a firm strong built young Infantry Officer dismounted from his steed and screwing on his Bayonet. took off his hat and turned round to us.

"Gentlemen we are thrang[24] at them And. the 1st 9th and 19th Rejiments have orders to march under me to a charge with the Bayonet 1st 9th 19th. up and away lads." It was GENERAL THORNTON. he clapped his hand

---

[23] Boulshill is near Haworth. The village of Pendleton is in Lancashire, just south of Clitheroe. See also vol. I, p. 179, n. 13 and p. 377, n. 25.

[24] Busily employed or hard at them (Scots dialect).

on his thigh on sprang the Rejiments he mentioned. Mine was one Hartford
came forward "Come my lads" he said "onwards" Oh what were my feelings as
Thornton placed himself at our head and I. —I. march[ed] quickly through the
confusion to a bloody charge of the bayonet! I had just recollection enough to
say to myself Now Hastings earn your glory or die." when all made a spring and
I shut my eyes with a gulp. How astonished was I who thought we were almost
in the middle of battle to see brakes and pools before us. and the cannon and
fighting nearly a mile distant! if it was so far off what would the scene be amid
it—however there was no time for meditation our gallant general led us onward
at a brisk pace my brain was a whirl of excitement. I was in a dream we stopped.
I glared round and there we stood on the banks of a still stream the clouds of
smoke and raining flying about us a dreadful smell of Gunpowder and a double
rank of calvary drawn up with a glittering staff and a spendid warrior at their
Head I could not but know Zamorna. his eye seemed on fire he just said "Noble
Thornton you are earning you honours Now Angrians remember Dongola We
hurried huzzaing past his Grace and the General waving his hat round his head
dashed into the river a wild splash of water was in my ears and shouting and
hurr[y]ing when the bank oppossed itself and we—up on to dry land I was not
sensible of much sight noise or danger but on a sudden my nearest companion
splashed back into the stream and a gush of blood burst from his mouth into the
water I gasped for breath—another reeled and tumbled at a little distance. but Our
Thornton gave small time for seeing the sights we were streaming in terrible
<cries> along the marsh and made a sight sufficient to have shaken an enimys
soul Men in white I saw hurrying wildly about before me and bursts of smoke
rolled over head as from a conflagration the white men parted Thornton gave
another Huzza we roared out remember Dongola and all Dashed into [the] noise
and aspect of hell. I saw nothing till my Bayonet clashed loudly with a brilliant
steel opposed to it and with a second gasp I ran it wildly through what seemed in
front of me my mouth was agape. and a salt splash splatted into it and covered
my hand with crimson The man I had stabbed fell a great Black wild beast of an
Ashantee. My blood was now up here they were around us and All the cracking
of firearms and clashing of bayonets and shreiks and howls and shouting only
made [me] lay on like a tiger and dash my weapon into the Heart of him who
stood next to me.

Meanwhile the Heavy Artillery were thundering it seemed behind us
Enara had forced his way among the Savages on one side and though I felt—
rather than saw three sucessive outbursts upon our own lines by the infuriated
barbarians yet we made good our ground and under our Gallant General Bore
everything[25] down before us. I dont [k]now how or when it was that I found my
self resting on my musket crowds of the Rej[i]ment standing round me and a

---

[25] The following section consists of pages 5-8 (one sheet folded) of the HRC
manuscript described in note 1 above.

horrible a hideous heap of carnage stretched and piled behind and about our very feet. my forehead was dripping with perspiration but my hand trembled no more.

Now the Duke of Zamorna with the Earl of Arundel and Joachim Murat. dashed furiously up from the river bank their Chargers snorting dashed with foam and a whole range of Cavalry thundering at their heads Zamorna reined up opposite to Thornton who stood wiping his forehead with his Handkercheif "Which way Wilkin are they thickest" "Yonder" answered the General and the Duke bending his plumed head in acknowledgement burst onward with his own native impetousity A long rows[sic] of White clothed Bloodhounds now streamed past us Enara himself at their head and Thornton then started to action we all fell into rank and raced on over piles of dying in pursuit of the fugitive Africans On a sudden something struck my skull I howled out and down on my back in the quagmire alls a blank. alls a vacuity that musket bullet finished my first furious Battle.

When I awoke from my stupor the blow (a spent musket ball) had so severly stunned me that I had some difficulty in recalling the memory of what had been passing "Ill get up soon" said I "But it isnt time yet for Parade" And then I opened my eyes to see what time of night it was. I stared round all was dark and stormy the wind and rain sweeping by in dreary melancholy gusts as if over an old churchyard I couldnt tell where I was and in searching round for my hat with my hand it fell on something soft and cold. I jumped up and the motion brought all my memory like lightning back again I knew that I was on my first battle feild so soon as custom had enabled me to see something I discovered my locality to be [a] little swell of dry ground surrounded by Brakes of reeds and pools of water three dead bodies lay beside me with a great white horse stretched at my head and a horrible carcase beneath me with its head quite taken away by a cannon shot such a scene suddenly bursting on my eyes at a tempestous midnight was no very composing or pleasant circumstance and I walked forward to remove from the vicinity of so forbidding a touch of warfare while pushing through the reeds a deep great roar at my feet and a shapeless being beneath me "Help lad Im smothered" I knew the tone of my native mountains "Whos you" I asked "George Warren of the 49th" this was the young Blade whose words I quoted not long since "Well George and hows gone the day with you" was my question as I helped him onto the dryer ground and laid him over a forsaken napsack. "Oh Badly Henry Im afraid but were like to meet with such risks. —its gone fair through my shoulder and I dont think of surviving it However Hartford promised. —Ba this is blood spilling—promised to let the Old Folks know himself you understand and youll call if you survive it. —I say its only poor work this for me. but we've beaten em. an thats the main I guessed as much when I saw the Duke he rode primly—I saw you fall but I fell soon after and many of us are just about here. call Harry and see if there alive" I cried out "any of the 49th alive" but all was quite silent "Well done and I saw 4 go down are they every one gone. its hard too our Rejiment has suffered sorely. —its 2 hours since I heard a musket go off. d'ye see anything Hastings" "No George its quite dark. and rains violently" "Well now I feel nothing at all. Im afraid I am going fast. listen what is yon look at it—" "What—I see nothing George—George what did you mean?" It was all over with the poor lad he was dead and what he did see he only could tell. well however I didnt exhilarate me in. acquaintance of my own dead at my feet and knowing that 9 or 10 of our men where lying about all dead like him when I thought of this and look[ed] up at the dark stormy heaven and round at the wet horizon with the little streak of light over the <edge> of the sea such a weight of melancholy came over me that I leant on my musket and fell a musing like a parson The wind was howling and the rain beating and the distant sea roaring so loudly and monotonously that other sounds if there were any could hardly be heard till after half an hours thinking I was roused by the trampling of cavalry and the clash of their weapons as the sound neared me I could see the steel caps shimmering among the reeds and hoarse voices talking but they all were dispersed in the storm soon however a long train of Horsemen passed by file trooping past after file till I thought they never would have done all seemed knocked up and many of them led Horses without riders As they at length came fewer and with spaces between a quicker and more rattling trot was heard and 50 or 60 cavaliers came in with arms glancing and all speaking warmly together 3 of them drew up near me and I could soon tell who they were

"Well a more glorious beginning to the champaign I never could have wished for but my good Philip is tired I dare say" said lord Arundel patting his charger as he spoke "And now Arthur how do you like a touch with the dirty dogs"

"Why Frederic I've been in Heaven if I may never be there again I am glad there are cool old hands with us for my own blood boils so in a chase after the brutes that I have no thought but to kill all before me Dongola has received a foretaste of its revenge the first reck of the sacrifice Enara I admired your conduct and must also right well reward it"

"And I did too how capitally he took the <   > round about them and cleverly drove them into the water without spending a shot."

"I dont like this killing to many of our men so needlessly I study to do the most work with the least outlay but your grace will not have lost more than you have gained"

"Enara if the Army are at all serviceable we must off to morrow we must pursue them and find out the main body"

"Ha by for the best part of this days work is a word which I overheard one of the brutes say. one in among the reeds below said to his fellow "lets fly to Quashia at Loango." Loango is an old fort ruined when I first entered this service many years ago. it lies 30 miles further up the Benguela there I know the main body are"

Zamorna sat silent for a minute looking as if in deep thought "Quashia is at Loango 30 miles of you say" "yes." "Then I will be there too Enara we must start directly." "My men are ready even now" Why let them rest. 12 hours" "12! Arundel. 6. I never will harrass my soldiers but tell them this truth and see

if they will not wish to start. No we must go Sirs and directly. Remember
Dongola and—Quashia"

So they all rode past out of sight and now the foot streamed in my own
regiment passed and I joined it Col Hartford came up and told me that my
Behaviour that day had proved such as could not be passed over." I was glad of
the night for fearing that I had played the coward in the confusion but I was set
at ease by his saying "But you must not be too forward lad keep in your ranks I
hope they will all be so far in as need be." I held my tongue and spake nothing
for I saw that I had done more than I thought on

We all marched forward through the marshes a mile or two to the spot
where the main body of the Army were gathered and beside the great roaring
biavovac's fires there was much stirring and vast confusion but little speaking or
recognising of individuals. It was a fit finish to a rough Battle.

It seems rather odd to me to have to begin a new chapter on affairs which
followed almost a minute after the close of the old one—but so it must be I have
finished the description of my experience of the Battle of Benguela and in place
of explanations which my confusion prevented my making I will just before
entering our other operations give the Short Bulletin of the Army

Encampment
West Bank of
the Benguela. Jan 24.

Angrians   1835

I have redeemed my promise and herewith. Present you with
your expected New years gift. the Heads of 3000 Ashantees The moment that I
arrived at the marshes round the Benguela in pursuit of the enimy whom I had
found lay hid there I halted all the forces on the Banks and drawn up in order of
battle to prevent a surprise. the River lay before us the sea southward North and
east formed retiring points in case of necessity and the men whom I rested on for
the completion of my undertaking were the main Body of the Army of the
Calabar numbering 11000 foot and 3000 cavalry. with 30 peices of artillery It
was the opening day of 1835 and my soldiers called loudly for a present to their
country Pushing onto the very edges of the water with 2 Rejiments of
Horseguards I stationed General the Earl of Arundel to act as a second blow in
my operations then General H F Enara with the 1st or Guardian Rejiment of
Infantry pushed through the water found the enemy opposite and in 5 minutes
had engaged them with the point of the bayonet 10 feild peices were directed onto
a portion of their position uncovered by the canebrakes and at 4 p m I
commanded General Thornton to close renewedly with 3000 men full in their
front which he did in Angrian style in the face of. a murderous fire of musketry
from the savages concealed behind the reeds So soon as he aided by Enara had
driven almost to one point by the exertion of all their Gallantry I passed the Ford
with my own Rejiment of Horseguards charged upon that point and drove the

whole Horde of 6000 Barbarians out into the open plain 6 squadrons of Horse which I had stationed so as to comand the desart now joined in on the pursuit and after a chase of above 10 miles I succeded in ensuring a destruction of the Enimy amounting to

900 killed

1160 wounded

840 prisoners who were all hanged round the river

Total ——

2900 Ashantees destroyed!

The force these Aborigines had in the feild I compute at 7000 most strongly entrenched and thouroughly provided with arms of the best french manufacture Of my own troops about 6000 were engaged in the course of the day of whom the loss runs.

360 killed

<u>540</u> wounded who were despatched to Dongola

Total   900

The deaths of these brave fellows I purpose to Avenge tomorrow evening when at Loango 30 miles up the Benguela the arrears due upon the massacre of Dongola together with the long outstanding dept[sic] upon the fortress I have just mentioned will all Be paid up into my hand interest and principal.

The first Rejiment of Horseguards and the 1st or Bloodhound. of Infantry have done their duty to Angria. General Enara & General Thornton I must single out as having gained the battle. But all must regard what they have done as nothing this battle itself as nothing while an Ashantee remains breathing through All the Calabar or Etrei Dongola is in my memory and 3000 victims are but a 10th of the number I had destined to its ashes. with this morsel to stay your stomachs

I remain your Leader.

ZAMORNA

Oh Reader all the Army were in extacy at this bulletin its wording is so Angrian. and we laughed at the Dukes flexibility in taking up the plain dealing Arithmetical tone of the whole Bulletin.

However we hadnt much time either to laugh or cry the moment that the paper was despatched for Gazemba the moment that accounts had been made out sleep and refreshment taken. and the rejiments were righted in due order Up to the flagstaffs to the shoulders with the muskets and the drums and bugles sound[ed] out the call to march! It was the morning of Jan 2d. the sky was yet threatning from yesterdays tempests but the desart under foot was easier to walk through the waters were all swollen to a height which made a passage hazardous indeed the cavalry and scouts were flung out very far to the right and left and the main bodies of troops pressed forward far very like keeping the windings of the Benguela as near as the branches and pools would let them Enara was far in front Arundel and Murat protected our flank and why—for the rest I knew little for I was to busy with myself to attend to other concerns Through all the day the firing of small Arms was never still for every prisoner brought into the ranks and they were numerous was shot the moment he was seen. I only saw the Great officers for moments during that march the[y] were generally round the king who was far in advance of our Rejiment

About sunset the River began to take a broad bend toward the direct North. and we knew from hence we were nearing the scene of operations It was a glorious sight to look at the gleaming waters widning on toward the foreground the immense track. of plain country some what broken on the horizon and all spotted with the masses of cavalry sweeping across like the whirlwind long regular rows of Battalions were stretching forward in detached and compacted lines whith[sic] the Trains of Artillery and the backward squadrons of Baggage waggons and amunition, The Songs of. "Welcome Heroes" "Shine on us God" Sound the Loud Trumpet" and so forth not the less disagreeable to me who knew so well their author where[sic] pealed forth by voices and music to exhilerate the weary and soothe the impatient. I often stopped my rare base[sic] voice to listen to the shrill cadences of the Trumpets all round or the far off echo of the cavalry Horns in front as they prolonged through the silent wilderness the strains of my Native land.

And now too I had engaged in a battle I had survived it and though sad were the gaps in the battalions round me wo[e]ful the vacancys heretofore filled by my freinds and companions yet the delightful thought of promotion and the memory of Colonel Hartfords expressions dwelt in my spirit like the taste of wine to a parched and weary traveller the long 30 mile march passed over with little feeling of fatigue or exhaustion by any one.

As the Sun Set underneath a terrific canopy of wild dark red clouds our forces wheeled downward toward the Benguela and here all received orders to halt. The Duke of Zamorna by spies sent out last night had received information of the Enimys position and he seemed now determined to take his measure from what he knew of their maneuvres all I could hear of the Ashantees was that their forces might amount to nearly 28000 that they had cannon with them and that they were commanded by Quashia Quamina in person. this was what the Angrian Army longed to hear. where they were and what we were going to do I did not know.

Well we drew up I said on the Banks of the Benguela there was no sign of Africans about us but I heard that General Castlereagh was drafted off with 3000 men to somewhere in the north of this spot and that he was to pass the Benguela clear above the position of the Enimy as for us. an encampment was formed fires lighted and the baggage brought in as if this spot was to be a regular Bivouvac for us. the men all busied themselves in preparing refreshments lighting fires cleaning horses and so on till I could neither see nor think amid such a whirl of bustling excitement A Battle why it looked like anything rather than the order and arrangement of a battle—But any way I was mortal and wanted my rest sorely so I <soon> lay down by a watchfire looking at the scene and filled with proper feelings of its character.

In this Tropical climate darkness soon settles down after sunset so that it wasnt long ere the flashes of light on the upward reaches of the River began to give place to the dreadful shadows of the clouds which coming up over head from the ocean seemed all to settle there for a rendezvous every thing the inconstant blasts which whitened the river with foam or blackned it with the increasing scud The distant growlings of thunder on the horizon the building and mingling of the clouds above us persaged[sic] a rapidly approaching rainy season storm and in proper finishing it so happened that by midnight we were in the thick of as rough and pitiless a tempest as ever I fortuned to be out in It almost beat the Deluge at the Battle of the Benguela. The watchfires all flung their smoke and sparks over the bystanders and all the powder was forced to be most carefully covered from the rain but while all were engaged in this and enobling avocations the merry sound of fifes and the rolling of Drums broke upon our ears and then there troops in to the very middle of the encampment such thick and quickly suceeding masses of well drenched infantry as I neither expected to see or knew where they could come from they were Angrians[sic] Soldiers that I knew but neither Castlereaghs nor Thorntons nor Enaras nor any other of our Generals. but they came in on all points flocking to the river side and shouting as they moved the name of our monarch Zamorna. I was at once busily enquiring who these were and learnt for my trouble what gave me a proper idea of Zamorna's abilitys as a commander

The Reserve of the Angrian Army was stationed at Gazemba. under General Lord Wareham and numbered 7000 foot and 2000 cavalry those it was understood were to act as a bank from which when exhausted the Duke was to draw for reinforcements and so His Grace intended but when he heard that 8000 Ashantees were collected at the mouth of the Benguela he concluded that this would be a spot where many more might be found and that in short their main body for he saw they would keep the marshes like a stronghold would be somewher[e] near the vicinity. Now his Graces temper is impetous and he wanted to make a dashing champaign out of the war and so knowing that one bold stroke struck now would be worth 10 a month hence be[sic] He unknown to every body but the Great Officers despatched messengers to Gazemba on the morning before his setout for Benguela. commanding Lord Wareham instantly to cross the Desart for the south with all his force and marching over about 40 miles of wilderness meet him on the banks of the Benguela. the junction must take place on the 2^d of January and Zamorna knew that ere that he must fight a battle with the Africans so that this sucoour[sic] (quite unlooked for by Quashia) would come in the exact knick of time either as as irresistable blow after a victory or a noble strenghener after a repulse on the evening of Jan 1$^{st.}$ when his Grace heard that Quashias main forces were at Loango he promptly despatched counter messengers to Wareham then on his road to join him at the mouth of the river to alter his course so as to be at Loango on the north bend of the Benguela on Jan 2^d at. 10 or 11 o clock. at night thus the Duke would put in to decisive practice Napoleons grand tactic of concentration of forces on a given point.[26] and all this quite unknown to Quashia. so much resolved Zamorna pushed all forward to be at the meeting place.

Well here they were all come 9000 in number and now when the Army was aware of the Dukes Tactics the highest confidence in his brilliant genius difused itself through every troop in the encampments. We now altogether mustered 17000 foot and 5000 horse. 50 peices of Artillery and all in capital condition The blows[sic] was just about to fall and all were in eager anxiety for the signal to rush on.

About 3 o clock in the morning I was just composing myself to sleep by my watchfire. The Duke of Zamorna rode up with all his staff about him he was laughing has[sic] he reined in by the bank of the Benguela. but stopped and turning to Enara said "Now then Henri—take care dont drown but it does not matter only the change after drowning will be too sudden a shock for your weak constitution" "Why hes burning already" said Castlereagh "and for that matter so am I." But Enara interrupted "Now Zamorna?" a Nod confirmed the Dukes decision "Then Gentlemen prepare Warehams Brigade and you Thomas off for the Bloodhounds let me see is this arm of the Benguela passable here" Enara coolly as he spoke spurred his steed into the water and struggled through the rushing waves almost to the shoulders in the weeds and Bubbles he got into the clear stream where it shot rapidly by swollen with the storm and here had to exert all his own powerful strength and the activity of his sinewy steed to preserve himself from being swept down the torrent having gained smoother water on the other side he turned round and dashed boldly through again till he landed among us dripping with wet but cool & calm as ever "No he said "I would hardly trust infantry in general to pass here My Bloodhounds shall do it and join the rest beyond. they are used to things of this character" "Castlereagh has passed at the ford above the Enimy" said Zamorna. and Wareham must pass in the face of them Ill call him on" the Duke clapt spurrs to his horse and all of them rode into the thicker confusion of Biavouacing

As the Dawning struggled through the Darkness the extreme violence of the storm abated And in a little while I could rationally stay to listen to what might be heard far off many of the troops were sunk in sleep and silence reigned all about where I myself. lay. as I turned my eyes to the northern bend of the Benguela to look at the solemn silver streak which was gradually assuming a first faint blush of crimson I saw something flash just on the horizon in a long brilliant tremble over the river. in a few seconds a sound like distant thunder fell on my ear heavey deep and short but repeated with those flashes again and again a rolling protracted roar followed which I knew to be the running fire of musketry Castlereaghs Division was then now engaged with the Barbarians and the Battle of LOANGO had begun

---

[26]   See vol. I, p. 367, n. 10.

Still by orders from head quarters the troops here were kept quiet till in half an hour more the thunder of the Engagement was taken up and with a nearer note on the south of the first position it seemed 4 or 5 miles off and the smoke might be seen passing along the Horizon till it mingled with a shower of rain which swept past and encroached with threatning drops upon the silent waters of the Benguela as the sounds rolled deeper and louder and more frequently our encampment arose gradually into a bustle Thorntons Brigade was called out I rose up to join my company The General soon made his appearance mounted upon his fine <soul> bay Nap and surrounded by several officers of his Division He smiled to see our own complete behaviour and said in his accustomed kindly tone of voice. "Now my lads theres a bit of real rough work before us and we must just make it rougher than it is theres nought for us but peg it into them like so many d—s. and that I'll see's you a do Come on my lads keep steady and just remember Dongola. aye and remember the Benguela too" We moved on after the General with a loud shout about 5000 of us all real Angrian Infantry and impatient to begin the conflict after a miles advance along the Banks to the north we came to the ford which Wareham had passed it burst full on our view as we turned round a long range of Hillocks the morning was rising and the passage was guarded on this side by long lines of infantry and a grim row of gaping cannon on the other side troops of cavalry were stationed awaiting our coming up I could see Zamorna among them with his sword impatiently beckoning us over—Thornton and the rest off us streamed in to the water holding our muskets over our heads and shouting long live the Duke of Zamorna And as soon as the First Rejiment (Hartfords) had all formed on the Bank. we hurried up the swell before us the cavalry with his Grace at their head rattling on our front waving their sabres and gallopping in long rows over the brow Thornton took down his peice well examined the lock and grasped it in his hands as a sportsman would his Gun if birds were near all of us did the same I saw the foremost files moving slowly to the top what was on the other side I knew not But I heard a most astounding roar of Artillery which thundered without ceasing beyond. However I had my eye on the General and the. first files who advanced spread out in a broad front extending along the whole face of the slope they gained the top and with a strong renewal of yesterdays feelings I saw all make a step in advance clap their peices to their shoulders and off went the Guns with such a deafning rattle as made my ears sing and my heart leap into my mouth with the din. the second rank up—and did the same—Now was my turn now I planted every step with deliberation I could see them fast falling at the top And as I topped my head over the Eminence I cant say but I winked to avoid the Iron hail with a pulse beating 120 I clapt My musket to my shoulder all strode forward bang went the musketry and as the smoke cleared off I saw all below filled with fighting men cavalry charging cannons firing and deep red or black ranks wedged seemingly one into the other as if engaged in the most desperate mortal combat beyond the old black wall of Loango arose but a dense white cloud of smoke soon hid it from sight for an African Battery was there firing full upon a mass of our forces who were advancing under Castlereagh to storm it Arundel was galloping over the plain at the head of his noble rejiment and—but I didnt wait till he joined for Thornton led us calmly down the slope we ranged quietly in front of the uproar and as I saw all our Rejiment so pleasantly and < > forming around me I thought that here we were safe from the storm of shot <among> the dozens which dropped—dropped groaning or struggling about me the frequent gaps that were made in the lines before me gave dreadful token of the insecurity of my situation two men fell close by me but it was a little while ere I marked from whence our destruction came. All Thorntons Brigade was now assembled and their red wedged masses of soldiers gathering closer behind and on each side of me shut out much of the rest of the scene but the wild chaos of deafning sound and the dense rolling volumns of smoke which came flying over our heads told very intelligibly of the wild havoc going on beyond. before us my eyes needed much courage to abstain from winking when they gazed on the Black stern steady front of Bayonet bristling Ashantees who stretched till lost in the thickest confusion with their hideous ingines of death all belching upon us their mortal fire till shattered by ghastly and mighty wounds my companions fell onto the gory ground beside me and I felt a strange disagreeable feeling as if I could willingly gather all my limbs into nothing when I looked down and knew that next instant my legs might be dashed to atoms my heart blown out of my carcase by some lightning flying 20 pounder or my brain peirced by a keen musket bullet. and then to think of the pikes 15 feet long the vast scythe shaped weapons and the terrible jagged sabre headed lances which awaited to receive us not 200 yards distant was as horrible as Anticipation or torturing death could be. but I was bouyed up and kept in enthusiastic glory by the awful unintermitted roar of the Artillery and the very immensity of that danger which threatened me. I knew that I was engaged in what if I lived I should never never forget that I was looking at what History would allways remember the first great conflict of the Sovereign of Angria the Battle of LOANGO and promotion the thought of fame and glory made me resolve to do anything and dare all the disgusting demons the black beastly feinds before me.

But now an Aid decamp from His Grace rode up to the General Thornton I heard with acute distinctness the word "you will charge sir" and then the Officer fell with his head blown into fragments from his shoulders Thornton turned round "on Lads Victory and Zamorna for ever" he waved his hat round we fired a volley grasped our Bayonets and forward like a whirlwind—I defy any one save the consumate bloodhounds to charge with the bayonet without their hair standing on end the sight is hideous. we closed with steel points and hideous weapons flashing and dashed into eyes and faces and bosoms and more hideous black countenances glaring fury behind them and still behind muskets levelled and torrents of shot bursting on us till we fell man on man and gasped and struggled in a frenzy of desperate obstinacy we were closely wedged into each other neither side would give back I soon lost all thought but to slaughter the feind like beings about me and instinctivly warding of more weapons than in calmer moments I could even have looked at I struggled to peirce to the heart a vast dark brawny fellow who held hold of my peice with one hand and uplifted an immense hatchet with the other I cant tell how it would have fared with me but he fell back struck by a ball and another started on to supply his place Darkness even seemed to come over my sight and my ears allmost lost the power of distinguishing sound we drew back and then poising our peice impelled all our strength forward to the blow soon the piles of bleeding wretches rose under our feet in the forced encumbrance of all exertion in fighting we trampled remorselessly upon freind an[d] enimy I never stayed to see on whose face wether Angrian or African Alive or dead I planted my feet so firmly when I Dashed my Bayonet into the man before me. —Nay in a bit the sport seemed so glorious so active so Manly and so filled with wild excitement that I could have stopped the mouth of him who called us away from it we set to in earnest stock or point it didnt matter so long as our Arms drove the weapon and we had a fellow to[27] knock at Our general fought himself like a lion in front of us his fine bay Nag had fallen struck by a hundered stabs so up he jumped seized his Bayonet and dashed like Wilkin Thornton Sneachi into the very thickest of the fray. As we were pegging at it as tough as tygers Thornton fell back a bullet had struck his knee and he rolled over a gasping African into a pool of blood I was (and I glory in it) the first who sprung before him a score followed and making a ring round our favorite General we all with heart and hand kept of and hurled back the masses of savages who impelled themselves franticly upon us to seize him and bear him into the middle of their ranks Thorton only cried "Aye this is what I expected—but mind dont trample on me lads—and now do your utmost remember Dongola." we obeyed him in earnest. and many was the victim who fell before that often shouted word

However though we could see nothing but glory in the matter a cool impartial spectator would indeed have gaped to see the really perilous nature of our situation we were about 3000 Infantry in a desperate conflict with twice as many Ashantees who assailed us on every hand and as well poured in upon us a most deadly fire from the grim battery on the height of Loango. Zamorna knew our situation and he determined to relieve us though he was so fiercly engaged himself that it was long ere he could find respite to despatch us aid At length as we were fainting with the desperate contest. in dashed a Active fellow in white and scarlet a loud shout announced his indentity "ENARA to the rescue"—and it filled our hearts with glory to see the stern sinewy bloodhounds bursting in mixing among us and exerting every iota of their terrible power and ferocity to bear back our frantic opponents like oil flung upon fire their prescence infused a double light into the eyes and madness into the expression of the combating Ashantees they hate each other as intensly as Mortals can hate and Never neverr[sic] I think was death grapple so fell and remorseless as when the bloodhounds closed in first on the Black ranks of Ashantee I saw Enara his Cap dashed off his yellow face as dark as his hair and his sinewy arm bared up to the

---

[27] The following section consists of pp. 11-12 of the Brotherton manuscript described in note 11 above.

elbow as with a knife as long as a sword he dealt deadly gashes between the ribs of his nearest opponents it was frightful to see that broad flashing sheet of steel grasped by so iron an hand and sheathed in a moment—stuck—into the heart or bowels of a sable tyger He drove them back like an Achilles pressed them on[e] over the other We were close at his heels and soon we left our General with his protecting guard behind us—

And now for Castlereagh after a struggle like ours [he] had gained the height the Ashantees own cannon were turned to play upon themselves. The Thunder which had been somewhile silent burst out with redoubled fury and nearer and nearer on my ears rolled out its terrible rattle of Death. All the long long lines which were flung out as the main body of the Africans began to waver and when a loud shout and the shaking of a real charge of calvary brought Arundel and Murat straight upon their middle ranks they fairly bent like a billow and rolled back onto their farthest rear. A wide lane was now made covered with heaps of carnage but it was filled in a moment for up comes the reserve of the Angrian Horseguards and Led by Zamorna. in person to the Attack. I saw him and I shall never forget him nothing could stand his attack. and nothing could stay him from his prey but there was a tall black fellow mounted on a black charger and dressed in a suit of unmilitary sable. who broke from the middle of the Africans brandished aloft a brilliant scyimetar[sic] and rushed like thunder upon the impetous Zamorna. Folk gave over fighting to see the result. they closed together I thought both were overthrown they fell fair back almost to the ground Adrian was clean taken by suprise but he knew his man in an instant they said that he just cried "Ha Quashia by G—d and so linked on like a trooper sure enough it was Quashia—I had never seen him till then and a wild brown terrible looking young blade he was Enara was standing near me I saw every muscle of his face quiver as he looked at him twice was his hand on his sabre but he restrained himself with difficulty Zamorna and the African prince. dealt blows. upon blows as fast as lightning one couldnt tell how they managed to do it both closed in and grappled by their necks while their eyes might have scorched with their infernal glowing their chargers snowy white and raven black were both down on their foreknees when Zamorna dealt such a blow onto the head of Quashia that he brought him flat on his back on the earth and himself leaped from his saddle above him the African Traitor snatched a pistol from his pocket and blew it straight at the Dukes breast he fell back but not a mine of gunpowder could have blown up so suddenly as did Enara spring to horse beside me and he and Arundel and Murat and a score of Calvary were round the Duke the moment that flash burst from the tube. He had given Quashia his licks however for he was flying streaming with blood to his troops with as many shot fired at him as ever a Target on a fair day Zamorna sprung on his knee aimed his pistol at him and the scoundrels horse fell to the earth. He disentangled himself his men closed round him and as he dissapeared amid them Arundel burst after the route with a whole host of his noble calvary Murat followed with the Horseguards and all scoured pell mell over the wide reeking plain of Battle. Zamorna was helped onto his steed covered with blood and his left Arm broken by the pistol shot a little above the elbow The desperate exertion and the excitement of the fight had made his Noble feature[s] pale as death he just lightened when he saw the Africans flying across the plain and then sank back into the Arms of Lieut Percy exhausted and insensible.

Without waiting a moment Enara seized the command of Battle. "William" he said to the Dukes brotherinlaw[sic]. "look you After his Grace. Hartford up to you the eminence of Loango Keep guard there over the plain and direct the Artillery upon the flying D—S. What the—are we in a hospital whose that they are watching so there over those carcasses.?" "General Thornton wounded in the leg" "What? well. and now Castlereagh quarter your troops Here upon the feild Thomas Scroven tell my men to roll up their sleeves and take out their Butchers Knives lead them all into that open space their and draw them up effectivly Now you Gentlemen scour after Murat and Arundel Bring in prisoners as many of the Black D—s as you can catch. lead them up to yon spot where my Bloodhounds are drawing up they'll do the rest for you. Oh Wareham here my lord let your men take a little rest and refreshment for this is not work to be hurried by—. I know that D—l Quashia is taking as near as he can the way Northward up th[e] river then in an hour Sir up with all your men in Close Battalion march cautiously make a short cut Behind that Hillock of Loango and so on to the little Bend of the Benguela where you will meet him take him in the flank. and kill and cut up as many as you can For the rest what the D—l now." Wareham had nobly concealed till then a musket Bullet which had lodged in his side but the pain now overcame him and he fell from his Horse as Enara was speaking "Ha" said the Tyger "A mishap! attend to his Lordship! By G—d! I see I must take this matter myself My Lord Abercorn do as I told him. get his Brigade in readiness 9000 I think they range their—stop Stop—his Lordship is dying! take him up Sirs. By G—d a new retribution for this. Ha! Abercorn tell them their Generals dead and see to [them] the fellows will need refreshment then! Tell them I will lead them to revenge him in five minutes! Saddle my Horse Thomas. Arise all of you and to your work men Ho Scroven the prisoners are coming in go up to my lads and tell them to do it with one stab we shall have so much work. Here give me my sword—Now off.!" "Hem" thought I as I marched off under Hartford to the Fort. "they talk of scourges this is a cat of Nine tails." Our Rejiment paced quietly now over the feild of combat I looked round to view the aspect of the scene All the ground was broken and mashed into mire where ever a horseshoe had made a dint upon it there was sure to settle a pool of diluted blood long ranks of men fallen where they had stood marked the spots where a charge with the Bayonet was contested an acre or two scattered with a wild confusion of Arms saddles Horses and warriors shewed the path of the Cavalry charges but when we passed those spots on which the Cannon from the Batteries or lines had played there the most wholesale Butchery and the most mangled carnage of all affrighted the eyes and feelings. piles and scatterings and ranks of smashed and hideously wounded objects told grimly the effect of 9 12 and 20 pounders flying for hours together from their jets of smoke and flame. We passed by our own place of fighting and here I saw had lighted all the fury of the Battle I think nearly 1000 men lay in a single acre dead or wounded and uttering the most agonising groans for a Bayonet stab is more sharp and painful than a musket wound Well we climbed the hill of Fort Loango where dying soldiers were flung round its skirts and rows of captured cannon blackened the brow above. with the mournful shattered walls which told a story of scenes like the present but now long passed away ranged in due file on this gentle eminence we looked abroad on the Battle feild of Loango on the opposite side of the plain and near to the river the encampment of the Army was formed here 3 or 4000 men were spread and here lay our Noble Monarch wounded indeed but guarded by hearts who would shed every drop of their blood ere one other of his own should fall we saw them bearing over to this quarter too our own Gallant General Thornton who had gained all the army to favour by his conduct on this dreadful day The smoke of the firing still hovered in mist above the grounds but a deep dark mass of clouds was coming heavily on and threatned with their far of streaming to clear the air with a deluge of rain away northward over the waste and up the Benguela the Thunder of Battle still surged deep and distant for here Murat and Arundel with the Calvary were pursuing without mercy the route of flying and disordered Africans and Enara himself like a fowler at his snare or a tyger on his prey was stealing cautiously along the waste with 8000 men to pounce upon the enimy either in flank or rear On a clear spot not far distant from ourselves the Rejiment of Bloodhounds with sleeves tucked up and arms elbow deep in blood were busy extinguishing the existence of the hordes of wretched prisoners who were constantly being trooped in and who allmost all met their fate unmoved and silent save the matter of course groan of struggling Nature At this however the weakness of a novice made me shudder and shrink and shut my eyes

Evening came on us amid a violent storm of rain and thunder as we the Rejiment of Hartford rested on our station refreshing our exhausted frames with rations of Bread Beef and beer hunger proved a mighty sauce though the slices of cake and the sides of the jugs might be dabbed and marked with a stripe of two of blood. But the excitement of the Battle had made my hands so shake that I distributed onto the ground about me almost as much of the refreshing ale as I poured down my own parched and thirsty throat and I smiled to see a troop of Bloodhounds who stood by (despatched in the pleasant task of destroying all the wounded Ashantees scattered under the fort) all tossing off their horns of Brandy without turning a hair But the rolling of Kettle drums and the warlike Blasts of the Calvary horns rising from the plain below anounced the news of the return of the pursuing calvary in a while Messengers were sent up from Enara to our fort to the Detachment of Bloodhounds I mentioned saying that "they were wanted directly" and and Aide de camp came allso to releive Col Hartford with the 30 Rejiment. So we sounded to Arms and again proceeded down the hill But all the sights were quite different now from what they were when we ascended at Noon Night had rested over the landscape Wild Gusts of rain swept by with long Drear howling Blasts of Wind which at times rent open the clouds and showed the Soft Silver Moon looking calmly down on the stern wreck of nature beneath How different I thought was this Night from that when I last saw that full round orb of light hanging over the Fort of Gazemba and shining on me yet unknown to war on that army then complete and on stout active men now in one short month dead or helpless with grim and ghastly war yes one month since and I was simple Henry Hastings of Pendle Farm at the foot of the Warner hills and now I was Ensign Hastings a Soldier Standard bearer of the Army and a charger at two pitched battles a slayer of my fellow men. I was now out on a wild ocean of life and home and childhood had flitted from my eyes Well. —this moon which gave me such moonstruck feelings shewed the heaps of Bodies among which we passed with such a solemn misterious whitness that they impressed even more than when I passed them a few hours ago those who lay on the ground were now dead the wounded Ashantees all having been despatched with the knife and troops of men were now moving slowly about conveying in their Arms the bleeding and ghastly wounded into the camp with a few Army surgeons men whose hearts had never pitied striding along the heaps of carnage and gazing keenly over their mangled contents with a "humph he'll never look up again" "that leg is a compound fracture its useless to set it" "Through the bowels no hope here" "His spine his[sic] broken put him out of pain" "Take this one up its a curious case. Lancelot. was talking to me about such a one this morning he told me if I could get one to be sure let him know where is he?" "Attending Col St John who has lost the shoulder and collar bone" "Hem. No my man this wont do we must attend where our attention will benifit we cant put your Jaw on again. put him out of the way." I passed next where Zamorna had charged in person here the horses lay in vast heaps but they had all been shot a little while ago only a few huge animals flew about foaming with pain till a grim bloodhound levelled his unerring peice and ended its frantic agony. these gentry indeed were the principal orderers of all the wreck for their cool experience taught them what should be done in one spot they were digging a long deep black trench into whose uneven depth the moon beams glimmered on the mud and water where were soon to lie. the last remains of the slaughtered heroes of Angria the Africans were to be left in all right to rot on the plain they had polluted as we neared the quarters of the Army the long trains of lamp light and the rows behind rows of brilliant fires constantly darkened by masses of black and passing objects announced the presence of the troops sooner than I saw their form or aspect their numbers I found when I entered the confusion were far greater than when I left them and new bodies were constantly arriving with troops of prisoners who were all marched into the rear to be butchered by the Bloodhounds as soon as we all took up our quarters amid the rows of glowing blazes an Aide de camp came to demand the attendance of Col Hartford at the Dukes Bivouack. and in about 10 minutes again returned for Ensign Hastings of the 19 Rejiment. Up I sprung and with beating heart followed the Military Aristocrat through the drawn up rows of soldiers to a great open space in the midst of which rose a statly tent and round which were drawn long files of guards their arms shouldered and all as silent as clock work. at the opening of the tents many horsemen were constantly alighting mounting and riding away in all directions sentries were stationed who stopped us till my conductor gave the pass word and then both dismounting I followed him between a double rank of statly horses held by grooms under the canopy and into the interior here I stayed obediently behind a crowd of Gentlemen in superfine Scarlet and white bareheaded and conversing with an animation suited to the scenes of the day I could see nothing forward of these their crowd was so thick but over us the grand cloth draperys reared to an apex from which depended a splendid bronze chandelier the place was very spacious and opened into another at the further end In a while an Officer with double epaulettes calls out from the crowd "Ensign Hastings here sir." I pushed through[28] regardless of the station of the hindrances and making my way with both shoulders stepped on to the soft matted floor of a simple Aristocratical room with a bright fire in the <front> at one end and a tall pale dark haired young man wrapt in a great military cloak. reclined on cushions at one side of it whom by his fine forehead and awfuly grand eyes I at once knew to be our sovereign the Duke himself. he seemed very much exhausted and his Arm was in the hands of a couple of Black dressed civilians with military cloaks and iron features. probing the wound and setting the bone. another Invalid was stretched on the opposite side of the fire a stout fair complexioned young man whose white pantaloons were covered with blood and whose naturally cheerful face was puckered with agony as two servants were drawing of the boot from one severly shattered limb our Noble General Thornton could not be mistaken even though so sadly different from his usual active heartiness. Two young Officers one tall and shadowed by a calvary helmet the other slender and more slightly made watched over the Duke as they were dressing his arm. Colonel Hartford was standing by Thornton and a black whiskered feirce eyed fellow in white with his lips compressed with thinking sat at a table covered with papers writing or giving orders to the Officers about him The same French page whom I mentioned as misleading me into such high company at Gazemba I saw here supporting Zamorna's arm and giving to me a rascally smile of recognition with another French Calvary Officer 6 feet high and blazing with orders completed the group of Augusts among whom I so suddenly found myself. General Thornton first spoke

"Well young man I see its you who stepped over me first when I was down in the fight this morning I noticed you lad—Oh dont pull so hard—and I never noticed a body who did me a good turn without doing them another—Now thats it put the boot side ways and Brodie look here. now there see you its what I expected. so as I'll neve[r] get well on't. —well lad there's one on the other side and end who'll do more for you than I can do but I do what I can" The Duke as <u>our</u> General concluded beckoned me nearer he had had his peculiar look fixed on me since I came in"

---

28   The following section consists of pages 19 & 20, then 1-16 of a manuscript at the PML, catalogued as "relating to the battle of Loango," bound in green morocco.

"Well" he said "I have seen you before freind and noticed your conduct more than once what do you think of the day"

"I wish that to morrow may be like it."

"Not for my left arm I hope.

"Yes your Grace and for Our Generals right leg too"

"You are Angrian Hastings I see you will let nothing stand before your gratification—But I dont wish to morrow to be like to day—if it was not for this cursed arm I would have made this morning worth the slaughter but it refused to aid me when I could—but it doesnt—Enara! is he off?"

As the Duke spoke he clenched his teeth with vexation the Black complexioned Italian at the table taking his pen from his mouth. said

"You'll hurt yourself we shall find ere long be calmer the—I could greive too."

"Well Hastings you're an Able bodied Angrian and your shoulders seem crying out for their ornaments You shall have two epaulettes for them a Captain in your Colonels Rejiment has fallen Hartford let Henry Hastings take his place. and now Captain Hastings I have an errand for you servants of mine will find labor with promotion you must carry the Despatches to the Home Secretary prepare to set out for Adrianopolis to morrow dont let the heat or dry up or the rain <wash> out your Angrianism. its a pity to spoil you youre almost perfect—w[h]ere were you born in Adrianopolis?—"

"No your Grace in Pendleton"

"Hem thats well. —the D—l."

muttering the last word to himself. King Adrian reclined his head back on the cushions and I bowed with a real gesture of what I felt. as I turned round Enara called

"Henry Hastings be at my tent. to morrow 10 o clock precisely"

I bowed again and with a "I will so" was conducted out of the room

Throughout the whole of this interview I thought that our Monarch Zamorna looked gloomy and I did not like the peculiar way in which he mentioned "Angria and "Adrianopolis" he seemed to almost dislike their names or qualitys. I heard since that with his strange mental turn he had been all the evening brooding over the sudden snatching from his grasp of Quashia whom he would have given any thing to slay and that this had disposed him to rec[e]ive the news of the unfortunate fate of the election of Adrianopolis where his steward was defeated by a Northangerland<olt>. and which was brought shortly before I came in as a personal insult and mark of disaffection to himself which his Graces mind cannot brook after (as in the case of this Battle) he had confered a splendid favour on the persons he thought ungratful.

Next morning after an interview of 3 minutes with General Enara I found myself Captain Hastings of the 19th. Infantry on full trot accompanied by a guard of calvary over the Desolate wilderness to Gazemba intrusted with the Despatches to Government of the Battle and Champaign just staying to change Horses after a ride of 50 miles at this City I started straight over the other Desart to Adrianopolis crossed the Calabar on the 6th of January and on that evening entered the capital and laid my important charge on the table of the Treasury Office before the eyes of W H Warner M P. Home Secretary. As the conclusion to my first champaign I give this as a summary of the proceedings in Zamornas first Champaign against the Ashantee's

"Angrians I believe I have satisfied you at last in my labours yesterday I fought the Battle of Loango. for on Jan 2^d having heard that Quashia with an army of 30000 D—s was encamped at that place on the Banks of the Benguela I marched up my whole forces and halted within 3 miles of his position till at midnight I was joined by Lord Wareham with the reserve from Gazemba of 9000 men. now mustering 17000 foot and 5000 horse I determine[d] to attack him immediately having first learnt. his position I pressed Castl[e]reagh with 3000 troops suddenly against his north flank Enara with the same number on his south flank brought forward Wareham with the same number on his front and when they had joined battle brought on Thornton with a fresh force of 5000 to charge them with the Bayonet and prepare them for my onset with 4000 cavalry which I made as a last movement and which drove them altogether from every position in one route across the plain had not a pistol shot broken my arm at the conclusion of the fight I should have conducted the pursuit in person but as it wa[s] Gen Enara promptly assumed command harassed them front and rear [what] were left of them into the river and brought in a whole hoard of prisoners. ere evening I found that my movement had proved perfectly sucessful and that of Quashias force of 30000 men the following account may be ascertained

                    2800 killed.
          <3750> wounded <   >
          5000 <prisoners> <   >29
          Total. 11550 in all.
On my part I have to report the loss of
                    1100 killed
                    2200 wounded
with General Lord Wareham slain and General Thornton wounded.
                    Total
                    3300 in all

by this stroke the savages I have driven quite of the Benguela. Kirkwall has cleared the Calabar Moray the Etrei. Dongola has been revenged and this Champaign is ended. I have received Intelligence from which so soon as my wound permits me I must hasten to Verdopolis and meanwhile the Army is to remain in cantonments along the rivers and positions the Despatch following will tell you the rest

                                                        Zamorna
reader Angria must greive for His Graces wound and feelings but rejoice in the glory he has gained for her I could say more but the press yawns for my works

---

29 These two lines are badly blotted, with several words obliterated in each.

Here I too redeemed my promise to you you have my experience of the war. take it for I must back to my post at Gazemba.

Henry Hastings.

Since my excellent young freind has so admirably executed the work allotted to him since he has intirely pleased myself and seems to have accomplished the more difficult task of pleasing my readers also I conceive that I cannot do a wiser action than suffer the forthcoming story of Angria and the Angrians to be built by the hand which erected that most handsome apartment the War with the Ashantees. In truth the public seem very unwilling to hear of my resigning the work which I commenced a year ago and since the pressure of buisness in these tremendous times totally prevents my carr[y]ing it on with my own hand I can think of no other course to please my Readers but resigning for a while at least the duty to an able and competent Lieutentant. such an one I have found in Henry Hastings and all Africa has applauded my choice.

With this short explanation of the course I have adopted an explanation due both to yourself and myself I remain my Readers your constant freind and servant.

RICHTON and Flower
Flower House, Verdopolis. 1835

I think it *my* duty before I commence my picture of the politics of 1835 to do for once what an Angrian seldom chuses to do I mean to take a short retrospect to look back on my former life and conversation and bring out again a few scenes and figures whose colours may have faded in your recollection though you only turned from looking at the painting about a month before the period of this present writing

I suppose you all know that on January the 3^d A D 1835 was fought upon the banks of the Benguela the ever glorious and memorable Battle of LOANGO you know that there were. engaged upon that feild. 22000 Angrians under our Monarch Zamorna and 30000 Ashantees under their Butcher Quashia you know too something of the immediate results of this Battle. in the total defeat of the Savages with a loss on their part of killed and captive—12000. on ours 3000. But what were the permanent consequences of this slaughter of 15000 men Let us look round us a little. At the beginning of the champaign Quashias forces were much stronger in anticipation than in reality his own immediate Hordes of Barbarians were composed of unreasoning and ferocious brutes who could not be brought into the feild save under hope of conquest and plunder the numerous aids which he looked for among the Negro tribes about him of course could only think of lending their support to him if he should prove victorious and with right barbarian cunning they had delayed their quotas of men untill they should see how the wind would set Quashias more civilized allies the court of the Thuilleries[30] and it is supposed another palace whose name I am lo[a]the to mention—had the forethought of their superior knowledge and knew that without strength their Black tools could not begin to work. they supplied them in the present sense with both arms and money but it was on the condition that they should pay for the gift By that heavey price immediate victory. They did not give their aid for generosity or for mere revenge their reasons for meddling in the matter were not love for Quashias black vizonomy or desire of his vain statements in the rights of sovereignty—And Quashia well knew all this he was possessed of no little Barbarian cunning and being filled with duplicity himself he allways suspects it in others. He knew that he could calculate on the Hope of aid from the Negro tribes of further supplies from France and N——d H—— ge[31] on the union and existence of his own forces by immediate victory which could not be achieved but by immediate battle. therefore casting aside I dare say with many a draught and execration his own rational plans of protracting the war making it a guerilla affair leading the enimy in[to] wild burning inhospitable desarts and when their paths were lost their provision gone their strength broken and their cavalry annihilated <   > upon them and murdering them by wholesale casting this plan of operations aside he determined to have recourse to the opposite one of taking up a strong position in the marshes violently insulting the Angrians by some hideous act of brutality and provoking that onset which he was determined to confront All know how this plan suceeded Dongola was destroyed. Zamorna <   > to revenge it the Battle of Benguela followed where Quashia lost 6000 men slain or dispatched through the wilderness Zamorna without one moments delay having discovered the totality of his Adversaries main body pushed his conquering army up the course of the river and uniting at the ruin of Loango with a large reinforcement under Lord Wareham assaulted at the head of this combined body of 22000 Angrians the strongly intrenched 30000 Ashantees after a course of simultaneous and impetous attacks gallantly directed and couragiously withstood he threw the Barbarians into disorder and routed them from the feild nor did his vehemence relax untill the whole body of them was either cut to peices or effectually dispersed beyond hope of all present rallying meanwhile as these decisive events were proceeding on the Benguela. the 6000 men under Sir J Kirkwall were clearing the whole marshes of the Calabar and 6000 under Sir W Moray the upward line of the Etrei acting in compact and energetic masses the[y] drove their prey from cover to cover from marsh to marsh out in to the open country and then full chase over the desart away into the "east countrie." So that when the last Gun of Loango thundered over the desart the seat of war had been completly cleared of the enimy On the 6th of January the Duke of Zamorna published a bulletin address[ed] to the Nation in which he stated that this champaign was virtually ended by the total

---

30 i.e., France.

31 Northangerland and ?? —the second name is undecipherable.

discomforture of the hordes of the Barbarians that pernicious nest of plunderers the great marsh country where the Calabar the Etrei and the Benguela empty themselves through their countless channels into the sea had been rid of its occupants as sulpher might purify a bed of Bugs that coast which had always hitherto shewed only like a weak point in the fortification a wide chink in our armour the vulnerable heel of Achilles <a coast> where vermin might lodge secure and Frenchmen land unopposed was now fumigated combed and made as clean as a running brook. —when the Negro tribes heard of the disasters of their sable freind Quashia when his own hordes saw him beaten and flying when his white Allies heard of him as a useless unfortunate lying on their hands all shrunk back drew in their horns and left him to mend his cloven cockscomb alone in his glory—Zamorna saw the helpless condition of his adversary and. knowing that now would prove the time for resting his Army and trying new forces through the country. while his wound also claimed a little rest for himself and the black lookout of Verdopolis called for a short visit to its distant streets He issued an order commanding that the forces comprehending Enaras Thorntons and Arundels Brigades 10000 in number should be cantoned along the line of the Benguela placing it as a defence between them and the desarts, And their headquarters and rallying point. and magazines at Dongola in their rear. that Castlereaghs Morays and Warehams Brigades. 10000—should be cantoned along the line of the Etrei for about 50 miles upward from its mouth with Gazemba for their headquarters and rallying point. that Kirkwalls Falas and Dances Brigades be cantoned along the marshes of the Calabar with Fort Enara as their Head and rallying point and that finally the Royal Angrian foot and horsequards 5000 in number should be cantoned along the Cumana with Fort Adrian in [the] rear as their headquarters and rallying point. This admirable arrangement every Judge of the Art military has admired it shews that Zamorna possesses the calculation as well as the energy of a great General. by this plan. each of the great rivers forms a <kind of> fosse a bulwark. to the forces placed before it against the threatned attacks and legions of the east and should the division of the Benguela be beaten from its positions it has only to retire on the Etrei where uniting with that division and stationed [at] a position stronger than ever it would be next to impossible that it should fail in making good its ground and every line also would prove a reserve to the one before it while if Quashia made an assault from the north he would find himself so soon as he came to blows with the marsh army. flanked eastward by the Gazemban troops and his rear occupied by the Guards on the Cumana—Nor could he coming from the N East attempt to stop the communication with Adrianopolis by seizing upon Fort Enara and the great road to Gazemba for then he would find the March troops on one flank the Cumanys on the other and the Gazembans themselves in his rear with a reserve behind them of 10000 on the Benguela. His only chance of sucess would be in assaulting an overwhelming force of 80 or 100000 men storming a dozen points at once and holding all the other positions in check while he bent his main strength against some single one. This however both himself and Zamorna knew that he could not do. having just fled in disastrous rout his own men dispersed his wily allies alienated and his white freinds frozen by the cold blast of misfortune. It would take several months to bring his soldiers again into any viable aspect of organization

Thus having so judiciously cantoned his 35000 Angrians upon the ground which they had won with their arms and energy the Duke of Zamorna appointed Gazemba as the grand head quarters Enara as the Generalissimo and Sir W Moray as his Lieutenant along the whole line of cantonments Thus on the 19th of January his Grace left Gazemba for his country palace at Hawkscliffe in the north of the province of Zamorna where he arrived on the 22d having purposly lengthened his journey to avoid Adrianopolis which lay under his displeasure for having ejected his Nominee in the then raging Election. At Hawkscliffe he lay in quiet and retirement recovering from his wound and exhaustion with a rapidity which speaks well of his fine springy constitution

But Now having given you a slight sketch of the position of the Army at the expiration of this short but glorious campaign I must return from the wide feild of view that we have been exploring to a certainly much more confined but to my thinking a much more pleasant prospect. Myself and my own concernment. "Ego" to An Angrian is the finest word <in> <an> Virgil or Horace. and as I profess to be one of the most Angrian of all Angrians I will hasten with all due speed to construe or decline it.32

I Believe Reader you left me at the conclusion of my last Volumn. at Adrianopolis after my interview with Mr Warner on the 5th of January 1835 I was now Captain Henry Hastings of the 19th Rejiment of Infantry Author of the just published work on the Champaign of the Etrei A soldier who knew the smell of Gunpowder and one who heard his name mentioned in every street and saw it printed in every shop window—I promise you all this was by no means unpleasant to me I was a[s] merry as a prig and looked at my clean tight leg and figure with no little exultation on viewing it all free from the tap of bullet or dint of cannon ball But though a tried soldier I was only a young one. Home was yet the great rallying point of my thoughts the world was a new freind and companion and I felt that praise had hardly its due relish till I should hear it from those I knew and cared for So seeing that my services were not likly to be particularly wanted on the Stern Banks of the Etrei I applied to the War Office for a furlough of such time as they should think proper In answer to my request I received the following note.

Fort Fernando. Gazemba January 19th.

Since Mr Hastings has served his country not only with sword but with pen also and in a manner creditable both to himself and itself. it is but just that if the former service be rewarded with promotion the latter should with peace. By which is meant that if war give warlike honour the Muses must give meditative

---

32 To analyze so as to show its grammatical construction and meaning, to translate.

ones. therefore I have the Honour to inform him that his furlough is granted till
the 19th of Febreuary[sic]. after which day. he must stand in read[i]ness for
immediate recall to his Rejiment unless orders be sent him to the contrary

signed J. CHA'S WARNER. under Secretary.

much elated by this testimony to my services from no less a man than the "only
Gentleman of the House of Warner" I straight way. mounted the coach and
whirled away for my Native Villiage of Pendleton. what were my thoughts while
perched on the vehicle how I felt on exchanging the waste howling wilderness of
the Calabar for the fair fertile plains of Zamorna and the dear native hills of
Angria How I started at the rattle of the Horses hoofs as if they were the tramp
of Murats or Arundels cavalry how I looked round when the Guard blew his horn
as if I had heard the Trumpets sound the charge to battle How all this fleating
visions[sic] dissipated when we rolled up the road over the arch which bridges the
waters of the well known brook Romilly and rattled over the stones and whirled
by the crowds of Old familiar faces and finally drew up at the Warner Arms of
my native villiage of Pendleton and then how on alighting I almost ran down the
street turned into the feilds up the "Water Side" threaded the "Thorney Lane"
jumped over the "Mistal gate" and ended my race by bursting into the kitchen
and stopping at the fireside of my fathers house my own dear home—I say reader
how I did these things and how I felt these thoughts I will spare you the trouble
of hearing they only belong to myself and no body else can feel them But Home
however I had returned and though I had not been absent half a year I found that
that time had passed like an age to me It had changed me as much as half a
century by my own hearthside I had left home and Pendleton "Young Hastings of
Pendle farm" I returned Captain Hastings of the 19th Infantry" under the first
name I had been the pest and trouble of my father mother Brothers and sisters
now I was after a fashion their pride and glory and then with my Neighbours at
the "town" in the Newsroom Inn. market every where I was a great man I was
spoken to at church by Sir George Hillton I dined at Squire Howards and was in
company at the Rectors with Sir Markham himself. where my book. was quoted
praised and commented upon in a way calculated to set its Author on end with
vanity A few repetitions of such scenes made me think that I was not made to
spend my furlough in the country. I received a Note from Lord Richtons own
hand written in the highest terms of compliment and desiring almost
commanding me the moment I entered town to call at his residence and visit
him. After this there was no more to be said to town I was determined to go and
the more firmly because Verdopolis was the word in every bodys mouth about
me. All Pendl[e]ton all Angria yes and all Africa too was in one universal uproar
of excitement as too the result of the Grand Federal Election it had just concluded
the various members chosen were preparing for their set out for the metropolis
Sir M Howard Sir F. <Fala> Sir G Hillton Sir T Marshton Mr Sydenham and
above all The WARNER. with all the rest of the Warners. had all either gone to
Verdopolis or where[sic] now about to set out.

Whats the state of parties whats the strength of Ministers will Fidena
stand till February will Zamorna attend the parliament Wheres the Earl of

Northangerland Whats the Marquis about. what Reforms on foot. such were the
questions which every morning and evening cried out to be satisfied by
Newspapers or Mail Indeed to speak seriously I know not when Africa was in
such intense political excitement as now in the commencement of 1835 and
when a man seriously looked about him first at the tremendous strength and
balance of all parties. wether Fidenans or Zamornans or Ardrahians and
Northangerlandians at their direct opposition and furious hatred to each other at
the lengths each faction was determined to go at all in power and crush its
adversaries at the frightfully unconstitutionall spirits displayed by the Reformers
and the mys[t]erious uncertain aim of their actual leader at the dangerous position
of the Duke of Fidena the interests risked by his overthrow and the consequences
which would result from confusion I say when a man looked at all this he had
need of firmness to keep from trembling I confess for myself my hair many
at[sic] time seemed to stand on end with amazement and I know that the
prospect. affrighted many far older heads than mine

In such state of Affairs with Parliament rapidly drawing on and such
principles to support such struggles to be fought such power to be overthrown
and such a faction to strive for victory all in Verdopolis all in the cheif of citys
no wonder that every man who could think of it turned his head toward the south
and prepared for a flight to the mouth of the Niger. when day after day I saw the
carriages and horses and outriders sweeping from the north for the mighty
Verdopolis I set my house in order and on the 18th of February. mounted the
coach and away for the Capital of Africa.

And here then Reader I am in Verdopolis. in verite. I shall not trouble
you with any account of my 24 hours journey but land myself fairly and at once
in the Travellers room of the Angrian Hotel Seaton Street. Verdopolis I am
sitting writing at the blazing fire tea is laid out on the long table Newspapers
piled on a short one the Gas lights shining from the chandelier and a score of
customers gathered in knots about the room in hot and fiery debate upon what
will be the event of this nights <opening> this is the 19th of February to Day
the Parliament meets to Night the kings (in the plural) speech will be read by
the Prime Minister and in a couple of hours I am going to look upon for the
first time in my life All the <politically> worthiest greatest and most famous
men in Africa or the world I must desist from writing I am in such a flutter
every minute I hear something calculated to set me in the tiptoe of excitement
Just now every body in the room were running to the windows on the cry being
raised without of "The Earl is coming" and a roar of execration was just rising
on our lips when the approaching carriage was discovered to be that of the
Gallant Arundel. but every instant a crowd of Equipages are rattling past the
windows on their way to the House though the wind is howling and the rain
beating in torrents while I write a tall yellow black complexioned Ardrahian has
come into the room vapouring and boasting about the triumphant sucess which

his party are to gain to night all my neighbours are at him and if they dont mind we shall be at blows directly. But Stop—the waiter has just popped his head inside the door with the words "There coming past Gentlemen" just listen what a rattle of wheels without. every one is straight for the windows. —Ha I saw the Scarlet.!. away with my writing and "Huzzah for Zamorna"!

Well the moment that last Night I left of writing I ran to the window and crushed among the gazers just in time to see the last outrider of the Angrian cortege dissapearing amidst the dense crowd which blocked up the streets without As I did not intend to be put off with the lack of a footman I turned from my station and bolted like a madman out of the room through a back passage into another street and joined a shoal of humanity which was speeding away on the shortcut to the parliament house. To make the street fly faster we all joined in a harmonious call every man as he flew along roaring out as he felt the spirit within him "Zamorna" or "Ardrah" or "Fidena" or "Northangerland" I knew nothing about the road I was going but just looked to the end and looked up in flying past at the vast and splendid buildings or glorious touches of perspective around me with very little feeling other than an unconscious elation which swelled the already ungovernable excitement into which things in general had plunged me However before long the van of the Herring shoal or wild goose flight rather came to a sudden stop before me. being now a veteran warrior one glance warned me how matters were going to turn fists in plenty were already on the whirl in the advance so I pulled of my white military gloves and stepped up to the scene of action the intent of our operations was simply to make our way out of the storm of rain into the shelter of the vast porticos which instinct rather than eyesight informed me were standing on high over the multitudes and make our way we did in a fashion though I suspect that when once got through several of our peepers were in [no] condition to benifit by the spectacle about us. I account myself as having been supremly fortunate for in a few moments I found myself stationed on a vast flight of steps But I cant say that I had the advantage of an understanding with them for the crowd above round and beneath me was such as to lift me and keep me fairly off my legs among them. it was all in vain that I drummed like a fury on the shoulders of these immovable Glasstowners— stationed in this pleasant condition I began to breath[e] more freely and collect my ideas sufficiently to know what sort of sight I was looking at—

But Reader the misery of the matter is that I cannot in the slightest degree hope to collect your ideas and make you aware of the scene I was looking at. —that is unless you were there and then why you will laugh at all my vain daubery—However here goes—In the first place the eye seemed bounded by an immense square of dark wet pillared buildings which stretched in front down a triple row of noble streets till lost in the steely shower of rain. or upward till the advancing bases and down descending steps of the "House of Parliament." cut out all things from sight but their own masses of well wetted Grantite[sic] it was glorious to look back and see just behind you and high high above your head these tremendous columns and the dark vault of their mighty pediments whence upon your unhappy pate was incessantly streaming rather <the chilly> drenching deluge of the rain of I suppose an almost <acre> like roof. and—then all the steps beneath you on each side was an hillside of human hats and heads sloping into the midst of a huge <roaring> crowd below that Ocean of Christianity swelled and surged away till it beat against the sides of the distant but still gigantic buildings of parliament square and then to see that fast deepening twilight. for the lamps were already lighted in the streets and the wild sombre heavens with the doleful gusts of wind and the drenching sheets of rain which flew howling along over the heads of the people and made hats and roofs and walls <shimmer> in the shades of evening there amid peals of shouts or execrations to see the grand carriages and Barouches which dashed through the crowd blocked up the space beneath the portico and reined in till the magnificent horses backed against each other in wild confusion as the various inmates alighted and strode up the steps where a lane was kept clear by the almost over awed spectators it was strange and exciting indeed for me to view these rulers of Africa step up past me and I not knowing but that in each I saw Northangerland or Ardrah or Fidena or Montmorency Lindsay Richton Pelham Percy nay its endless to mention who these magnates might be who stalked or crowded under the Huge Doorway into the Gas lighted terra incognita[33] within my conjectures were roused and wakened by each from the Grand six foot military looking Aristocrat to the mean shriveled little man—aye and an Aristocrat too However when I saw a Peer or member with one inch of scarlet about him I was not the last to raise my voice in applause or if showing an ell of yellow the last to raise it in testimony But it was with bitter regret that as I first mounted among the spectators I saw the score of splendid scarlet carriages which stood empty but flashing before all the rest at the foot of the flight of steps tokens that the magnates of Angria had already entered and thus I had been deprived of an opportunity to exerting[sic] all the powers of my lungs in tribute to my countrys glory. —Well Here I stood gazing entranced by the space of half an hour totally heedless of the drenching rain or the night which darkened down with heavy and storm threatning the gas lamps were flashing thicker in the distance and the heads were becoming more blended about the Mansions but the arrivals and roaring and tumult had not been the slightest abated when a deep heavey rattle broke on our ears heard even above the lung splitting outcry of an excited Verdopolitan populace that note of Thunder Oh how it brought in a rush of tremendous associations to my mind well well did I catch the unforgotten voice of <u>cannonnry</u> and the memory of sounds far more awful than those I now heard began to rise in my spirit and shake my nerves as if I was yet among them But my thinking was broken by the sound of Bells deep incessant and booming as I well knew from the distant Dome of St Michaels. and here was a second thing to rouse me for who could hear without emotion the toll "swinging slow" from the capital tower of his countrys mighty cathedral. The great bells rung out louder and more awfully and soon a shrill sound of Trumpets peirced the air from

---

[33] Unknown, unexplored territory.

far off For many minutes I could hear this "voice of victory repeated at short intervals yet never seeming to advance and as to all accompaniment the uproar of the crowds and the moaning of the wind effectually stifled it. if it existed so that as I stood thinking that the music was yet half a mile off. the spectacle came upon me with the strange suddeness of a dream a grand phalanx of cavalry moving through the throng a Broad serried mass of soldiers mounted and armed with their colours flying and the forest of swords glittering over their heads in the rain and gas light on and on they advanced yet the crowd never seemed to crush one and the effect was in the highest degree peculiar to view the vast masses of soldiery trooping forward till all the square seemed crowded with them and still none of the concourses which had occupied that space could be seen to retire. verily it looked like the famed pavilion of Prince Ahmed which could < > a mouse or an army[34] But as I stood comparing it to this wonder of my childhood A clear harmonious Halloo ringing obstreperously through the air and raised again and again in trebly repeated roar warned me that there was something else to see and think of than the scenes of an ancient fairy tale St Michaels Bells were ringing louder and faster the mighty mass of cavalry were all stationary with presented arms and through a wide space lined with Officers of War and Royalty advanced up toward the steps of the Parliament House Six huge carriages Blazing with gold and surrounded by Attendants each carriage surmounted by a golden crown and drawn by six magnificent white Horses there was the first chariot with all its postillions and outriders all blazing in green and gold. the second Blue and gold the third yellow and gold the fourth Orange and gold the fifth and six last and abreast pink or Buff and gold Of course directly cognisant as I was I knew that these were the carriages of State which bore the Monarchs of Africa the Royal Kings of creation and Angrian as I was I stood hat in hand overawed in to silent veneration Ere these Equipages reached the steps a seventh appeared between the line of silent military it with its Horses and attendants was covered with crimson and silver muddled as I was with amazement I could not tell who this should contain then next rolled forward an 8th purple with a mitre above it then two others with Ducal coronets Here at any rate thought I are the 12's. and so directly I struggled to obtain a sight of them dismounting But the Officers and attendants of state crowded all the stepps and area in such overpowering numbers that it was vain indeed to struggle for one single look. I saw Banners and Military and I heard music and shouting But I only knew that the kings were passing within a few yards of me by what I certainly never dreamed of a perfect storm of roars hisses curses and execrations drowned directly by an over powering volley of tumultous cheers I say once again Angrian as I was I had not dared to think of opening my voice before the kings However the rest seemed not so bashful as me for in awhile the tumult became deafning nothing could be heard but a tempest of contrary shouting and It

---

[34] See "Prince Ahmed and the Fairy Peri-Banou" in the *Arabian Nights*; for the Brontës' reading of the *Arabian Nights* , see Alexander EW, 18, 30, 52, 106.

had risen to a pitch of demonaical fury when on a sudden the man beside me fell and I pitched on my face into the open space under the portal there was a slender little gentleman in black with a <scarlet> ribbon round his neck stepping outward as if to see the cause of the tumult. I ran upto him crying "I intreat sir permission for admittance" Mr Warner turned to a soldier saying "Allow Mr Hastings entrance to the General Hall and bowing to My Lofty Landlord with a rapture of gratitude I. found myself.streaming with a crowd of priveliged persons through an immense arch doorway into a great bare place hung with lamps and so out of sight of the open air and following the living torrent up up up a great winding staircase where I left the lamps some below me and on the opposite hand another grand flight of soaring human beings each staircase tending a different way till ere I was aware I popped suddenly into the Gallery of the General Hall of the African Parliament My introduction into this noble Hall had the effect of majic and I sat down gazing in amazement first upto the vast circular dome over head with its one unequalled lustre sheding down it[s] pure flood of light and then round a[t] the grand girdling gallery filling with people and all the front row of which nearest to the outer and lower front was adorned with such a bright continuous and dazzling line of "Rank and beauty" such a glorious circle of plumes and Tresses and Diadems and jewels and velvet & satins as till then I had never seen or formed idea of. But to[sic] opposite to me Beneath a mighty canopy of crimson velvet emblazoned with the Arms of Africa. I saw the Thrones of the Earth first in the midst and highest a mighty golden seat which I at once knew as the seat of a bygone Humbug then on each side of this one. 3 other thrones in a line six in all the seats of the kings then parrralell to these but lower still six other tribunals the seats of the other 12s. and next in the middle but lower than all a rostrum for the premeir of Africa and last beneath this a long crimson sopha for the ministers of the Confederation then on a line with this all round the building under the pillars of the Great Gallery and sloping downwards towards the centre of the hall the amphitheatrical velvet covered benches of the peers of Africa and like a sink at bottom of all the centre itself was filled with the Benches to hold the commons of Africa. I have said that the whole front of the circular Gallery was lined with the peeresses and ladies of rank. in full dress and that the Back of the gallery was filled with priveleged male spectators add to this that the awful Dome spanned overall above us and poured down on every thing it[s] flood of golden radiance and you will perhaps have a dim conception of the sight which greeted my first entrance. to the Opening of the Verdopolitan Parliament

Well Reader I have lingered to long on the outskirts of my subject it is high time to alter my course and bring you at least a little nearer the termination of your journey I must proceed directly and you pray that the power may have been given me of seeing with both my eyes and what is far more difficult of describing as if I saw with a couple more I will not tell over to you what you must know I experienced my suprise and astonishment at the scene before, while I sat in my seat wiping my forehead and anxiously awaiting what was yet to come on when I leaned forward to view the seats and spaces below I found that they were as yet all empty for the commons members were engaged in their own Hall in the act of choosing a Speaker and the Lords were voting in the grand chamber appropriated to that purpose so I <een> turned my eyes from the desolate vacancy beneath to the glorious galaxy around which far eclipsed all the dazzling <lustre> above and as I gazed on the celestial (and I speak not this coldly or formally) the Heavenly forms and countenances which lined the front row of the Gallery I could not help liking myself "Hastings what are you that you should be here" I felt that I was not fit to remain in the presence of these and it was only a violent struggle of arguement to the effect that I was quite as good as many of the Aristocrats whom some of these called Lord and Master. that I had stood the fires of Battle and had dedicated myself to war that I was Henry Hastings and above all Captain Henry Hastings I say it was only after this amount of reasoning that I could remove some particle of the oppression of inferiority which tormented me as I looked round the splendid front of the Gallery and even then my self confidence was so small that I had steadily and much against my will to fix for a while my eyes on 3 grim gash[35] old Ladies in redundant Blue yellow and orange draperies who occupied the most distinguished place in the circle—lest I should fall back into my self depressing notion. But Alas when I did turn from these purse proud old. (as I shrewdly guessed) not less than Majestys—and saw the scarlet shining division in the midst of which sat the golden haired fair complexioned girl with the slender circlet of Diamonds round her clustered curls. and the Bright beaming beauty near her whose sparkling eye and rosy cheek so nobly suited with her dashing crimson robe and then the pale hansome young lady whose extravagant drapery sought to eclipse that of the above mentioned. or the tall Noble Dark complexioned peeress in the trim crimson velvet and raven plume who sat at the right of the golden haired girl or the younger slenderer but quite as dark eyed woman who sat on her left. I say when I did look on these my whole soul and spirit rose in the cry "When Hastings When shall you be worthy to win a single smile from one of these when man shall your deeds and the glory entitle you to a look of notice from them!" —Oh How did I long and burn for the day to come (If come it will) in which I might attend on the floor of that house looked at and listened to by these! How I envied the lot of the men whom I should soon see appear who would many of them be seen and heard with interest and admiration or hatred (for hatred seemed pleasant here by those Angels before me while I—! But off with the thought for the voice rose in my heart "Courage Henry If thou art a man what is impossible to thee?" But Now reader Oh for the power of a looking glass to shew to thee the things which came across the stage I saw a thick gathering of Official staves without the <large> open Door then. the first Senator stepped on the area of the House oh how I hated him when I saw all the curled and plumed heads bend down from the front of the gallerys to gaze on him but courage again a Most Ancient and venerable octogenarian habited in a black gown and

---

[35] Dismal in appearance (obsolete).

redundant flowing wig stepped up to the feet of the thrones looked over the Hall with his sharp antiquarian eye and giving a most tender ogle to the well stuffed woolsack on the one hand of him he turned round and dissapeared again. this I thought is the lord Chancellor Gifford and his buisness is to see that all is right the moment he vanished the bustle without increased in confusion the officials lined both sides of the portal. And then with a sound as of innumerable footsteps the endless file of men habited in grand flowing Robes of all the National colours coronets on their brows and swords by their sides streamed steadily through the <assigned> portal and ranged themselves on either side from its opening up to the foot of the thrones Here they were the peers of Africa but Alas my recollection had failed me the hour of trial had come but my brain had clean evaporated. Half unconsciously I saw a long rank of white robed full wigged personages ascend together to a row of Benches which occupied one side a tall old man at their head with a golden mitre on his own. The "Right Reved Bench" was all I could mutter. But a new sight roused me in to a little more consciousness I had momentarily turned my eyes from the door to look at the persons but a glance of Brightness which I caught with the corner of them made me turned[sic] hastily round again when I saw all the space round the portals crowded with a glorious gathering of scarlet Oh how my heart warmed to that colour for there came on the peers of Angria And at their head like the very sun itself the Monarch the Leader of my Countrys glory. Robed in a magnificent Persian Robe of scarlet velvet with scarlet sashes knotted to this[sic] shoulders and the opened folds in front showing a golden sun glittering on his white satin vest The Duke of Zamorna advanced through the Hall at the head of his troop of immortals This face at least was not unknown to me amid the whole great crowd of stranger countenances. No I had seen it before and once seen it could never be forgot His princly head was unencumbered by crown or coronet and his own dark brown curls clustered freely above his Lofty forehead A more majestic figure than the Dukes could not be conceived and his as I may fairly call it immense Robe and dazzling decorations very well beseemed his air and person he stood for a moment beside one row of Benches with all his scarlet attired peers about him among whom I could recognize the handsome heads of Murat. Castlereagh and Arundel. But as they were all talking together Zamorna moved to the upper line of seats not far from the level of the bottom of the gallery front and there he stood speaking to the Galaxy of Angrian rank and beauty or walking along the line and dispensing his favour to each of the delighted Angels. I saw their eyes sparkle and marked the brightening of their countenances as the Sun shone upon each in sucesssion with his own omnipotent beam In half a minute all they[sic] younger portion of the Angrian peerage had clustered under the gallery and by words and nods and <wreathed> smiles were paying their devotion to the Goddesses it contained For my part I confess that I found my attention absorbed in looking on His Grace and as I had never seen Zamorna since that night when he lay wearied and wounded in his tent at Loango I was both suprised and elated to see how speedily he had recovered his health strength and personall vigour. His elasticity of step was distinguished even under the cumberous and costly robe which he wore and never could he have displayed more nobly than now that lustrous eye and rich racy smile which when in bold spirits form one of his graces most striking characteristics. —But Now while thus I gazed and wondered a blast of Trumpets suddenly rung through the hall and Their Majestys the KINGS entered attended by the other surviving 12[s] and—but I had not time to see who else. There were the Monarchs of Africa and how could I look at inferior personages not an eye in the Hall but was directed toward them as they mounted the steps and took their seats on the thrones—Of a truth they did not look unlike the 12. The three first. tall Erect Iron looking men whom from the colours of their robes I had no difficulty in recognizing there was first a very lofty man with a spare lathy figure and a pale determined countenance. his keen grey eye and bony eagle nose shewed him at once Arthur Duke of Wellington And Next him sat. His Majesty Alexander Sneachi as tall as himself older by half a score years and really dignified in the aspect of his high forehead white haffetts and Aristocratic figure His Majesty William Edward of Parrisland was I think even the sparest of the three and his look expressed terrible coldness and unmitigable severity But King John of Rossesland compensated by a shorter stouter and every way more frank and open person. The two Lords of the Isles I thought shewed a singularly <vain> insincerity His Highness the Arch Primate was very like his Majesty of Parrysland. His Highness of Morena was the most soldierly and what struck me most in Duke Bravi was his vast gigantic person But what was the impression which on the whole the first sight of the 12 produced in my mind.?. Verily I could not have wished to encounter those hardened sinewy frames in war. or have met those Iron calculating visages in peace. they seemed like my Idea of them keen and cold and rusty as those swords which once with such effect they weilded Their Majesties had hardly seated themselves and the peers all seated in ranks on their places when when the Domes[sic] was awaked to echoing by a most desperate sound of scuffling and murmuring beneath the Gallery where I sat I could not tell what was the matter when I saw all the peers turn at once to that <   > and the ladies bend their eyes at once. in the same direction I heard such a banging of folding doors such growing clatter and confusion that I was fearful some popular commotion had forced its way into the sacred precincts of the Senate House but anon the cries "Speaker Speaker. Order Order Chair Speaker Order Order" told me that the "House" was advancing that the peoples men were coming. Alack Alack. that instant the idea dawned upon me all those fiery political anxietys these hot ungovernable party feelings which the grand scene about me and the Hemisphere of the Aristocratic peers had hushed within me all at once they now rose into a <flame> "Who is the New Speaker" that was the question which *looked* from every face I could see before me. who, who, is he!. Oh how I wished they would come in sight from under me. and when they did when that unutterable mob of divers coloured gentlemen in dress coats long swords boots and shoes and pantaloons and unmentionables crushing one against the other hurrying pell mell forward beating upon each others legs and drumming upon their shoulders When they all crowded in from under the gallery into the area. of the Hall I felt as if all my 100 senses were fastened upon the unhappy being at their head. The speaker vain Sir ever to hope to keep in subjection such schoolboys as you. —But Oh dear oh dear!! that long lean consumptive being that poor wigged gowned rascall—was That Sir Charles Hutton Flower. was that weak. cracked voice the famous orgonic organ my fainting Heart told me No. and the confused sneer from so many of the peers answered in hollow accents NO. —Well this peice of Intelligence did sober me for an instant or rather roused me into tenfold fury Had the Liberals the Reformers the Ardrahians the Northangerlands the Anarchists the bloodthirsters. had they then Triumphed.?— with what a feeling of rage and hope. I turned my eyes to the Ministers seats beneath the thrones. —There was a dead pause of silence after all had assumed their places. and I well recollect how startling the feeling came over me as I cast my eye wildly around the Hall and thought. "Is the Earl of Northangerland here?"

A tall man in a crimson robe. arose. calmly from the prime ministers tribune and uncovering his head bowed first to the kings and then with a loud manly voice thus addressed the excited assembly.

"My Lords and Gentlemen

Their Majestys the kings of Africa having in compliance with the usage. of the Constitution Dissolved the last parliament of these kingdoms on the first of January in the present year they now after 2 months given to the necessary forms of the General Elections and sufficient time afforded wherein the people might choose calmly and deliberately fit and proper persons to represent their opinions Have determined this day to re[o]pen for the despatch of public buisness the Houses of Lords and Commons of the Verdopolitan Union And furthermore their Majestys from the same feeling of their Duty to Africa which dictated the justice of the late appeal to the sense of their people Have on the 30th of November 1834. deemed it right to remove their late official servants and to appoint as their secretaries in the various branches of Government John Earl Gifford Edward Earl of Lofty John Earl of Richton Sir Robert W Pelham Sir Charles H Flower Sir John W Bud Sir John Tuckett Barts. Thomas Grenville James Bellingham John H Hooker Esq^{rs} with myself as the Nominal Head of the Government in the office of First Lord of the Treasury along with many minor offices <remodelled> which it would be here unnecessary to name

Appearing before you as I do this night in obedience to their Majesties commands and entrusted with the declaration of their Majesties sentiments It would not become me to stoop to any excuse for my assumption of an important office or any affirmation of any inability to sustain its duties I obey dictates which I trust I shall never have cause to disobey and it is sufficient to clear myself from all aspertion that I should strive to render my obedience of avail

My Lords and Gentlemen I would with rejoicing have come before you to speak pleasing truths but since I greive to say that this cannot be let me at least speak truths and leave their quailtys for you to deliberate upon It is now more than a year since the glorious victory of Zamorna concluded a bloody and dangerous war causlessly carried on against us and met on our part by in that great end at least a noble and triumphant resistance but though the first of January 1834 saw Africa (which 2 weeks before had bowed beneath 240000 Invaders) rising without a single foreign foot upon her soil or cause to dread the musket of one hostile soldier Still that man would have been shortsighted indeed who could not perceive that though war and our enimies had passed away their operations and struggles had left tremendous marks upon us Victory had indeed given to our country a splendid Robe of triumph but it had wrapt it round a shattered and shaken form I do not intend my lords and gentlemen to indulge you with a speech <glaring> in metaphors and ornament. but the one figure which I have just used I cannot refuse admittance since it brings to my own mind so forcibly the condition of my outwardly conqueror[sic] Africa. When the first body of French Invaders under Massena landed on the eastern coast of Angria the Verdopolitan confederation was in a state of peace and prosperity never attained to before since the conclusion of the Insurrection in 1830.[36] The Elections had concluded prosperously for the cause of our constitution the proceedings of a ferocious faction had been opened up in a light of enormity which had crushed and confounded their efforts the Government of our Confederation was united and the Governed were contented—But a cause for vigorous exertions now arose and the energy <demanded> from the kingdoms proved to violent for the infant Bond of union whose fibres were as yet only <beginning> to grow around them—I will pass over for it is painful to dwell on the mistakes and <events> of our first campaign against the French in November 1833[37] and I know that now I do my duty in passing over them since I was very principally engaged in it any attention upon the topic would appear like an assumption of egotism and in this hour self must be of as little importance in the subjects we shall treat upon as any single man can be whose interests pretend to stand forward before those of 50000000 of men On any other occasion than the present I shall be quite willing to explain my conduct in the winter of 33. to any person who may be intitled to ask an explanation you all know how by a train of almost unexampled misfortune our Federal Army was in less than a month defeated routed and almost annihilated you know how misfortune tends to seperate freinds and heap the ashes of hatred you saw an instance of its terrible effects when the Armys of the East assembled their scattered forces under the walls of their threatened metropolis when the Government and parliament which should have been unanimous in arising to defend their countries spent weeks of threatning engaged in the wildest discord among themselves you remember the debates the strife the confusion in these very houses of parliament I remember the divisions and heart burnings in our Government and All Africa remembers the rebellion and anarchy in our general country It was not till Our Army was dispersed our constitution destroyed our Government annihilated our metropolis taken and 230000 foemen had devastated our undefended country it was not till then when hope lingered on

---

[36] Branwell presumably meant 1831—See vol. I, pp. 179ff.

[37] See vol. I, **An Historical Narrative.**

the very verge of Despair that this very desperation made us all gather together as
sheep in a thunderstorm and opposing at last to our ill fortune something like
the heads and hearts and hands of Africans we drove our mutual Enimies back
onto their native shores—But my Lords and Gentlemen though we had beaten
back.from our homes the French and Ashantee Invaders we could not suppress in
our hearts factions strife and political hatred that Infant Union which the
struggles of war had so dreadfully shattered among us and the prospect of
destruction had only for a moment rallied again now when the emergency was
removed seemed to break in peices and leave us all seperate and contending A
faction which the exposé of the autumn of 1833 had caused to hide its head in
shame now again rose up in renewed vigour strong minded men who thought
that the constitution had not protected them from almost destruction joined a
plausible outcry for Liberty in the beginning of 1834. the question of the
Angrian kingdom was agitated and in a month after I took part in dismembering
the confederation of Africa I did this my Lords and Gentlemen because I saw that
if Angria was not given to the army Verdopolis would directly be given up to
rebellion I strongly disapproved of the principle of that measure but I felt that we
had better <   > a breech in our constitution than that fabrics total destruction
Had Angria not been created a kingdom in February 1834 Verdopolis so far as
Human forsight can stretch would have been destroyed perhaps forever before
February 1835 That measure as I knew well <done> no good but it has prevented
the commision of mighty harm Now still though an outlet was made for some
of the discontent of Africa the aspect of politics appeared not brighter than before
the newly risen feature in our social organization. the kingdom of Angria at this
time materially changed the current of politics men with that disposition to
extremes which seems inherent in our nature. ranged themselves unhesitatingly
in two ranks one the unconditional opponents the other of the Determined
supporters of Angria and the Angrians but there were still remaining in Africa a
number of men who could not consent to blindly Idolize or invidiously hate any
single member of our general federation these men considered our constitution as
our rallying point and determined by it to abide among them I enrolled myself.
but so did not all the Government to which I belonged violent divisions broke
out in the Ministry The Premier the Right Hon the Earl St Clair determined to
resign his office and in August 1834 their Majesties appointed his Highness
John Duke of Morena to fill the vacant station which he did for several months
though with a divided cabinet and a Nation fermenting in the conflict of parties
But when in the Autumn of that year commotions in the cabinet of Angria had
spread over the country the opinions of unprincipled and reckless men and on the
opening of our parliamentary sessions a portion of our own party a section even
of our own Cabinet. came forward with a loud outcry for Reform of the
constitution. a Reform which no power could fix on as anywhere tangible but
which as is often the case a great multitude of men espoused from its very
obscurity Then His Highness the Premier saw that oppositon seemed to strong
for his divided ministry and upon his resignation their Majesties on the 30 of
November 1834 thought proper to dissmiss the whole ministry and select

another and if possible a more unified one in its place—The task of this selection their Majesties thought proper to confide in myself and when made aware of their resolution though I knew the Divided State of Africa the unprecedented complications of her Politics the alienation of many of our freinds the difficulty even of knowing freinds from enimies yet when I saw the need my country stood in of immediate and unhesitating assistance of agreeing and rational councils of the aid of those who loved their land and laws when I knew that my Monarchs desired my acceptance of its premiership. as a Subject of the confederation of Africa I could not for a moment hesitate to accept it. And when I was enstalled premier I gathered beside me a cabinet of Colleagues such as my judgement and reason told me were fit for the guidance of their Nations interests. In order to be possessed of the full sense of their subjects or the extraordinary character of my present position their Majesties on the first of January 1835 Dissolved parliament by public proclamation and after a month of universal electioneering they have again been pleased to convene it for Deliberation upon the interests of our general confederacy.

My Lords and Gentlemen It is upon this occasion that I come before you to declare their Majesties intentions I cannot ask your pardon for the review I have just taken of the history of Africa since the Autumn of 1833 nor shall I excuse myself before you for any opinions of mine upon the events which I have been detailing I know that I felt unwilling indeed to touch upon them at all for in so doing I had to allude to errors and transgressions among my freinds and to uphold the proceeding[s] at times even of my opponents But I felt when I rose that It was my duty to shew to you your situation and I knew that you could not know what you are till I told of what you have been But My Lords and Gentlemen the past is over now It is the present and the future that you must hereafter think of and act for you see or at least I have done my utmost to cause you to see the condition of your Native Country You are here assembled by your Monarchs orders Not to advance your own private emolument Not to carry forward your individual schemes of Ambition Not to foment the frenzy of factions opposition Not to indulge in the Atrocitys of Hatred and Revenge No My Lords and Gentlemen cast off from your hearts all such vicious and degrading passions Remember what you Are and where you are and what you need here to execute Remember that you are the Noblemen and Gentlemen of Africa met together in this Ancient Hall of your National Assemblies and underneath the eyes of your lawful Sovereigns to listen to the voice of the people to legislate for their glory and happiness Remember too whose All seeing eye looks upon you and whose word you are to make the foundation of all your deliberations It is God himself Africans who calls you together it is by his will alone that you are here All your lives and welfare are in his all powerful hands and you must all obey or suffer beneath his Almighty will your country may be troubled and distracted but <that> you trust in God and he will Restore it to peace and prosperity. It may Be glorious and fortunate but unless you put your trust in him it will wither like the upstart gourd of Jonah[38] In this Age and Generation I know too well that what I am saying will be averse to the feelings of many But I speak what I know to be truth and my truth is immutable and eternal

My Lords and Gentlemen I believe that a struggle is about now to commence between Laws and Justice on the one hand and violence and anarchy on the other it is you who are placed as the supporters of the first and the determined opponents of the last I have told you what Guide star you are to take into the storms and tempests which may assail you Let your Bible be your great director your God your only protector and then if only firm and united among yourselves what force what foe is that which you ought for one moment to fear.

My Lords and Gentlemen for my own part I know that My Sovereigns have placed me in the Office of Premier of Africa to stand the formost amid what ever light or shadow which shall hereafter fall upon us. I believe myself not worthy of the place I occupy I think that there are others that would prove more fit than me. but since I have taken this station By it I will swear to abide In obedience to Our Laws My country my freinds and every supporter of our constitution must consider me as their Nominal Leader And let all of you then mark the Standard I am bound to raise and the conduct I am determined to adopt In those six Sovereigns above me I recognize my only superiors and in these my colleagues around me my immediate fellow workers and assistants During the course of the present sessions of parliament I shall bring before you several measures for the reparation and consolidation of our immortal constitution and others for the effectual operation of its principals in the various machinery of our confederation Whatever other Reforms may be brought forward in this sessions[sic] by other hands than mine I shall at once if they prove reforms for the better support them with all my influence If Injurious to Our country oppose them with all my power And in all events under all circumstances I swear never except at my sovereigns bidding will I desert my post and office never at any ones bidding my word and principles And if my country approves of my conduct if Africa thinks as I do It will be your duty My Lords and Gentlemen as her only representatives. To take your Bible for your first Director your God for your only protector and with my self as your commander and justice as your Armour know that it is your Constitution you are called to defend That it is Those Thrones you must look up to Its Noblest Bulwark and your only Thermopylae."[39]

Thus concluding His Grace the Most Noble JOHN Duke of Fidena Bowed proudly to the Thrones he had appealed to and resumed his seat upon the Prime Ministers Tribune

While he spoke you might have indeed heard a pin drop I never saw an assembly so still and silent and I really do not recollect hearing any other noise than two or three coughs from a man in black seated on the peers opposition benches Every one seemed listening devotedly to the Deep Manly Voice of the

---

[38] See Jonah, chapter 4.
[39] See p. 10 above.

Prince of Sneachis land I could not take my eyes from off him That statly
Athletic figure that Arm now and then stretched out which seemed itself
competent to defend the cause of his country His aspect of calm superiority to
the degrading passions of faction His words so distinct so emphatic and his
whole speech so majestically expressing the feelings of Africas darling Defender
When the Lord Chancellor rose to signify their Majestys pleasure that the House
adjourn. I thought that John was the man for Africa and when I took another
look at his proud reserved countenance his light northern hair and calm
commanding brow I thought and he is the man for me too More I could hardly
mark for while John spoke my whole soul and senses were absorbed in what he
was speaking after he had finished my mind was in such a state of excitement
that I could make few further observations And the Aristocratic reserve of the
peers in general prohibited much inference being drawn from the expression of
their faces as to the Commons—why I almost forgot the Commons their base
and dirty conduct in choosing such a lemon peel of a speaker as they had done so
disgusted me that I was fain to turn my eyes away from them

A minute after the Prime Minister had resumed his seat the Lord
Chancellor rose to adjourn the Houses but I could not catch his exact words for a
disturbance which broke out among the commons just under my part of the
gallery a Member in rusty black seemed struggling toward Lord Gifford but
wether it was only to obtain fresh air in the closed up room I cannot tell save
that I saw him laid hold on by several beside him and at that Instant the
Commons made a move for departure I lost sight of him and saw him no more.
But up I rose Red in the face with excitement of this never to be forgotten scene
and when the crowds streaming from the gallery bore me along with them into
the Open Night among the Darkness storm gaslights and soldiers I cannot tell
with what emotion I looked upon the city even now I might be on the eve of
convulsion and ruin.

March   40 1835 on the Night after the one whose proceedings I have been
delineating found me seated in the Gallery of the House of Commons awaiting
the arrival of the Speaker and commencement of proceedings Meanwhile that day
had passed over in a manner calculated to give me the amplest materials for
reflection and anticipation—when I awoke in the morning my first impulse was
to desire to see the Newspapers and on descending to the great Breakfast Room of
the Hotel I beheld a crowd or rather several seperate crowds of Gentlemen
gathered round their nuclei! Men reading aloud with violent emphasis and
gesture[s] the opinions of the various prints upon the state of the country the
opening of parliament the Premeirs speech and the choice of speaker I beheld
before me a striking specimen of the Nation of Glasstowners every face was

---

40   Branwell left the date blank.

agitated with the fury of politics and the knots of Gentlemen going to set out for the country with the morning coaches were busy gathering like Bees the marrow from every paper in the room Here was the great Broadsheet the Himes.[41] levelling its thunders against the men of the reformers and the choice of the Commons The Banner sounding with all its eloquence in praise of the prime ministers speech. The World exulting in the "Triumph of Reform by a majority of 10" the Beacon taking Duke Johns words to peices with mean and venomed carping. and to all these various opinions the different Readers and listeners added each his own commentary and observations The Verdopolitans are seldom at a loss for a word when triumphing or vituperating and as there was plenty of both here we had enough of tumult and confusion and I am much mistaken if something more serious did not occur for when an Athletic Military looking Verdopolitan denounced the Marquis of Ardrah as a rascally traitor to his principles a tall dark complexioned Reformer desired those who were rascals themselves not to be profuse in throwing their rascality around them wereupon both in about 5 minutes left the room But wether fists or <bistols[sic]> decided the dispute I cannot tell—when I left the Breakfast room to walk through the town I found all the streets in the same state of tumult. each Newspaper office was beseiged with applicants the public places were crowded with politicians and each man seemed agitated with hate to his opponents and triumph in his part. Once or twice during the day the Mob of Reformers seemed disposed to attack the Residences of the Duke of Fidena and Zamorna but a party of cavalry was stationed in the square before the first and a livly demonstration from a few scores of stalwart Angrians detterred the visitors from further insolence against the palace of the second—when the evening papers came out the excitement in the capital was again roused to fury and as I passed through the streets on my way to the House of Commons I met several patroles of soldiers ordered out for the security of the City

And Now while I sat in my place in the Gallery of the House of Commons my mind felt fevered with the idea that now I was in the very focus to which were directed the eyes of 50000000s of people. that I was in that very house where during the late war such mighty deeds were done the house where the freinds of the Army Deposed the Ministers and the Army itself deposed the Government Here Warner and Montmorency and Pelham and Sydney and all those well known names had spoken and here they were now about to speak again the men whom from my childhood I had heard so much about who had produced such a mighty effect on the world I was about to here[sic] again debate and again weild all their <wonted> power

While the spectators who crowded the Gallery looked on in anxious expectation the officials trimmed the lamps and lustre the Black Rod[42] moved awfully round to keep the requisite order and in the reporters gallery these

---

41   Obviously the *Times* thinly disguised.
42   The chief usher to the Order of the Garter and the House of Lords.

Minions of hundred tongued fame brandished their pens and Notebooks to supply the craving of an anxious and eager Public In a short time the Members Benches began to fill with incoming Senators and I opened my eyes to see though from want of knowledge only ill able to comprehend However I knew the different positions the Speakers Chair the Ministerial Benches the cross benches and the opposition Benches The Speaker had not himself yet appeared but the Ministry I saw were determined to have their forces alert on the ground Before 7 o clock their places were almost filled with Members But at that hour the Reformers began to troop in quick and fast faugh I could hardly help spitting at them there had been that day a grand dinner of Members at the Marquis of Harlaws and of Peers at the Marquis of Ardrahs from the gluttonous feast the Opposition came wiping their lips and chewing the cud of greivance in church and state I longed most bitterly to know who the different Individuals were and which were the men who I had so often heard about In every one I fancied a Montmorency Lindsay Sydney Lofty or Harlaw and at last so strong grew my desire that I addressed a Gentleman Beside me apologizing for no acquaintance and desiring to know a few of the principls characters in the House "Who" said I "Is that very tall handsome looking man on the cross bench near the table" "Oh Lieut Jones of the 11th" said my Cicerone "Humph" I answered "well who is that very genteel looking well dressed man in blue dress coat with black velvet collar—him with the light hair so finly arranged and the fancy stock set with such an air of ease and elegance." "Mr Shaver the Earls valet." "Nay Sir Ill give it in If I can ask only the names of subalterns and servants point out the magnates yourself." So my Obliging Neighbour who by the by himself looked the perfection of Gentility smilingly directed me to look at a short Heavey looking sandy haired person in Blue who stood one hand in breeches pocket the other fixed on the Button of a thin pale middle sized man whom he seemed stultifying with his coarse jokes and conversation "That Sir is a Nobleman a Prince a Senator one of the heads of the Reforming faction the Right Hon the Marquis of Harlaw and his pale spindly Neighbour is the Honourable Viscount Macara Lofty and again Note that sorry looking ill dressed grey complexion[ed] person with the Blanched face and corrugated forehead there is the Right Hon E G S Sydney. so you see sir all is not gold which glitters and many things that dont glitter are— "Dust and Dirt" I replied But as I spoke the speaker J J Goat Esqr M P. entered looking as yellow and meagre as a withered leaf. after him with looks of derision poured forward a lot of Angrians onto the Ministerial Benches at whose head my heart warmed to see the Tight Active General par excellence with his Blue coat military black and white pantaloons when I saw his red hair and keen grey eye with the not uninteresting lameness of his right knee in walking I felt roused to thoughts of war and Benguela and Loango. "Ha" I could not help saying "Theres our Gallant General theres Thornton" "then" remarked my Cicerone "you have served under him have you in what war." "The Campaign of the Etrei" "Ah. may I request your name Sir" "Henry Hastings" "Indeed—But soft here rises the Giant of the "West." As he spoke a great Black. Broad chested man with fiery whiskers and scanty dark brown hair got up from the opposition Benches and turned to the speaker with a Demonaical twinkle in his malignant eye the moment he rose All the Reporters brandished their weapons and every member changed his aspect of Anxiety for one of deep attention My Now freind had only time to say. "Hector Montmorency" Ere the member on his legs stretched out an brawny black gloved arm and began in a voice of articulate thunder

"Mister Speaker I am right glad you have taken your place so soon for I faith I could not have held myself for 10 minutes longer so a pretty affair is this we have on [h]and and a bonny hand we are likly to make of it I did think when I came to Verdopolis a week ago that I came to exert my facultys in aid of my country to act as a Senator should act to Defend and attack to create and reform But not 24 hours since I was undeceived of this nonsensical notion undeceived with a vengeance, 2000 years since the Old Emperor Titus cried out I have lost a day[43] But this morning Sir I cried out I have lost a night (hear hear from the opposition) I tell you that yesterday I went to attend my place on the opening of Parliament in the expectation of having a hearing on my duties of being taught the way I should go—"

At this instant a servant in livery entered the gallery and stepped up to my Neighbour and Cicerone After a minutes conference with the man my new freind said to me "I am requested to proceed to the other House the Duke and the Earl are both up will you go with me" In fair trepidation I answered "I will sir" and forgot every thing present in the Idea of the Earl of Northangerland As my Acquaintance rose and left the gallery I followed him quite confused for the excitement which the House of Commons had thrown me into carried me past all thought and I had no clear Idea of where I was going to or what I was doing As we entered into the lofty passage which communicated between the two houses a tremendous cheer followed by a torrent of hisses followed us from the Hall we had left the attendance upon the speech of Montmorency. Ere the cheer had died from my ears we were both on the threshhold of another and more statly hall the Aristocratic house of peers here so soon as we came into the light of the chandeliers my obliging Cicerone commanded his servant to show me into the gallery. while (a thing which almost petrified me) he walked coolly into the body of its August assembly.

When after mounting the staircase I seated myself in a seat on my elevated station with the lights above me the crowds of Aristocracy beneath my eyes were taken instantly from people ministers thrones and prim[e] minister to the two men who stood opposite to each other at the table and on whom every eye was rivited with an aspect of intense anxiety

At once I recognized the Duke of Zamorna Erect and Majestic all his soul thrown into the subject he was speaking on and what was that subject—The Dissmissal of His Mighty Premeir. Even Zamorna himself could not prevent my eye from fixing on that Convicted Lucifer that Arch feind and Traitor the Right

---

[43] Titus Flavius Vespasianus, Emperor of Rome AD 79-81, once remarked, observing that he had benefited no one all day: "Friends, I have lost a day."

Honourable Alexander Earl of Northangerland & Viscount Elrington my head felt
dizzy when I looked at that Renowned and Mighty Man How awfully appalling
was the expression of Northangerlands features What a convulsed and withered
aspect what a fell stricken eye His white hand trembled violently as he removed a
pile of papers from before him while His sovereign stood and smote his very
heart with his impetous fire breathing words

As Zamorna concluded[44] He grasped the Earls hand in both his own and while
his countenance darkened with a flush of excitement and his eyes glittered with
feirce determination he told his Apostate Premier that 5 minutes more must
determine his fate and prospects that what he had threatened he would perform
were eternal death the consequence He told him to speak and determine the fate of
all he loved in the world.

As Alexander Rougue turned round from him to the house His
countenance grew deathly pale and his lip curled with a cold withering derision I
trembled to hear the voice of him whose name I had so often heard Satan himself
could not appear more [a]terrible <sight> what Zamorna had just now spoken in
words of breathing flame In a hollow broken voice Northangerland cried

"Whom do I love in the world and what reason have I to love any one I
swear that I never stood before in the situation in which I do stand here now I
feel as if the Earth had <collapsed> from under me and truely this world has left
me desolate But I care nothing about the world I say (raising his voice till the
Dome shook) I say D—n the world and D—n all the fools that live within it Do
you think Duke that I Have lived on till this night as I have done to cry like a
child when I know that I am forsaken By any such as those whom I must now
be taken from No not so. I care so little for you all that even now while I speak
to you I feel that every word I utter will be as much lost on you as on the rocks
and hills of the Jibbel Kumri and far more for they used to echo to my voice
while you no more do it than the Benches you sit on I tell you that unless this
man stood there to here[sic] no I would not open my mouth before you were it
to save you from the torments to which you believe yourself hastning" laughing
wildly as he spoke Northangerland stopped for an instant and then said turning
round to Zamorna and almost gnashing his teeth when he began

"And who the D—l sent you here to pester me now with your D—d
nonsense now when I was just about to open up the schemes of laborious life
now when I was about to accomplish that blow at which I have toiled for twenty
eventful years Now when I was about to crush that power which has so long
thwarted and oppressed me Now when I was on the point of receiving that reward
which either fate or chance or Heaven or hell has so long and so <fraudfully>
withheld from me. Now you have dashed from my hands the hope of my life the

---

[44]   Zamorna's speech is recorded in Alexander CB II, part ii, 369-77.

crown of my glory all the aims on which I had fixed as a recompense for at least one thousandth part of what I have suffered the fullfillment of at least a millionth of that for which I have longed—I say young man you do not know what you have done You think that you have only been giving vent to your own store of bitterness that you have only been punishing me for the faults I have committed against you that you only threaten me with the loss or disgrace of my Daughter a mere plaything for a Political Agitator if you do think so never were even yourself before so wretchedly mistaken By G—d Man you have ruined me Destroyed me for ever What in heavens Name could prompt you to speak as you have done before all these what in the Name of H—l."

Here the Duke of Fidena rose and said "language like this cannot with impunity be permitted here blaspheme not the power which you have so long pretended to despise"

"What do you speak for you fool" retorted Rougue with frantic vehemence "for what do you push in your saintly tongue Silence you D—l silence while I speak to some body different from you—Arthur Wellesly—Do you know what I am do you know what I can feel. —If you did you would not do that which just now you have done you would not ask of me to decide between the ruin of my Only child the eternal severation from your schemes and ongoings and the ruin of my Only hopes the eternal severance from my own schemes and ongoings You know what conversations I have had with you you know how often I have striven to make you understand what are my intentions how they will work and how they will affect you Oh Arthur Remember what were the hopes I held out to you remember the conditions on which I held them Do you not recollect the flashings which burst on your spirit when I spoke to you Do you not recollect how though you cried Humbug and Nonsense you left me thinking of things which you would never relinquish the thoughts of. I say Remember Ellrington House and the War of Angria Northangerland House and the Palace of Zamorna Do not you feel now that miserable ruin you have wrought by your impatient rashness what wretched destruction you have brought down by your restlessness under seeming opposition Do you not know what once I promised to effect with you and for you what a pledge I gave you for the fullfillment of my promise Did I not tell you that for the Advancement of my aim It would be necessary for me at times to act as if against you seemingly to oppose you. To rouse up But stop. theres no speaking Here—Arthur cannot you understand me. Do you not Hear me—By God I will speak out and D—n them— what care I who heres[sic]. —Well Did I not tell you that it would be necessary to rouse up your country by the fire of a Barbarian Invasion to give you not only an army but an active and conquering one that it would be necessary to remove from you a power which would thwart you at home By removing that. froward willful and pedantic Angrian ministry that it would be absolutly necessary to remove from you a mighty power which would thwart you abroad by removing the worthless and contemptible old Aristocracy the intractable and Antiquated Constitution of Africa Have these not always opposed you when when did they befreind you and if you think what opposed you must be removed why do you turn restive when I strive to remove them why cannot you see my only way to remove them What Arthur could I do but strive to ingratiate myself with the people of Africa and place myself as the premier of Africa and how could I effect this end but by over throwing those people who stood in my way and affixing to my cause those who would aid me in my ascent. Where is your reason for refusing me the road which I have taken since I have told you and told you again that it will end in the Accomplishment of all that your heart would wish for. And Arthur cannot you see this cannot you see. that when Angria had become inurred to war and trained to victory when I had driven from your hands those Domestic shackles which would so miserably bind you the pedantic and scrupulous Warners and and D—ls and Demons when I had crushed forever those foreign powers which would have at every turn risen up to oppose you the Kings and the Constitutionalist[s] and the Reformers when I had given in to your power all Angria and Verdopolis and Sneachisland and Parrysland and Wellingtons land and Rosses land aye and Stumpz lands and Monkeys lands too could you not see that Nothing then would have prevented you from turning your head and hand and heart to the Eastward and gone one[sic] conquering and to conquer till All the World had felt your prowess till all the world was called your own And How Arthur could you effect this how could you become such a mighty one with A Nation innert and sluggish at your feet Barbarians threatning and smouldering beside you Tutors and Advisors preaching and pestering within you Enimies watching and opposing without you your right hand helpless and nerveless a Broken Down dissipated Nobleman yourself an insignificant and tormented King Oh God—do you not see what you have done. There lies the hope of your heart the very being of mine there lies with it your <peace> and happiness here and my very life and light and being—You Have ruined me I say you have ruined me I have not a hope or a trust to look to. And Do not you get up and answer to what I have spoken with your contemptible trash about Justice and Religion and your conscience and your Rectitude Your Justice your Religion your conscience your Rectitude where are they I ask where are they Dare you after the life you have spent after the Deeds you have done after the speech you have just now spoken though that to your actions is like smoke to lightning Dare you speak any thing about Religion or talk any thing about your conscience Faugh. freind away with such trash and give it to those who need it. —But My God! what does all this matter now—Had you told me to give up to you the seals of Angria had you commanded me to give up al[l] my titles and orders and appointments I have I would have done it directly and done it without heeding it I could deprive my self of your countenance for a while and go on on my own path advancing my own ends and perfecting and ripening yours I would have made my self Premier of Africa and I would Have come before you with a power which should be all your own But. you Ask me Arthur to do all this and something else beside you command me to look at the Ruin of my Daughter the

Disgrace the Death of my Daughter[45]—D—d fools around me do they gape with astonishement that I should care for this that I should put this into competition with omnipotence. that this should occupy one instant of my thoughts or weigh even one feather in my scale. Oh Arthur Do you feel like them Do you think as they Do. —No—No this weighs down all that can rise before it you Arthur know what—What. the D—l what she is you know what she is to me. I look back—this moment!—life flashes across my mind. the memory of a time gone by Oh If ever I could weep I could weep now Before thee Arthur but not Before these I can remember what I have felt and seen I can" Northangerland stopped an instant in agony—"I—"—"I can remember—can remember this your Duchess childhood her Mother and by Heaven she was not to be cast away to the revenge of one of my angry moments—I can remember what I shall never never feel again And if your wife if my Daughter died as die she would if you acted as you say you will—If she died where would these rembrances be then where should I be—what should I be—A Blank A frightful Blank. without a gleam of Happiness to look back on without a ray of comfort around me without a thought of hope in the future. All one wide Hell in the times past times present and times to come. —Death and Furies and what are you and why do you listen to me you D—ls Reformers Ardrahians. Ha away at le[a]st with you I have ruined myself the man whom I would raise has ruined me has forced me to the acknowledgement of schemes such as you cannot penetrate. you will forsake me your followers will he has done so my allies now that I am powerless will he will—you Aye you Arthur you will cut off from me the last—the—D—n it away with the thought and for what Because I would aid you in a manner that roused your scanty patience Oh Arthur Arthur take your seal of office take back this miserable Bauble Look at it and Remember the Giver. you have ruined me Arthur Rejoice in your power you have ruined one whom the world could not ruin Rejoice in your fortune Arthur I cannot help you because I am far to overwhelmed with misery Ah young Monarch you do not know Despair and I trust you never will. Arthur Wellesly. I leave you and I fear for ever But Do not I intreat I implore Do not tear from my heart the last hope of my life. If I Die If I perish at least let me know that though a frightful gulph of annihilation receive me into its bosom. there may still remain behind my Only Daughter Mary Henrietta my King my Monarch Zamorna Dont you see what you have Done look no farther Act No more Heres my Lasting Hatred to all of you and now Farewell to you Arthur see if Fidena and Warner can do for you what I could Do. let me take your hand for once fare well Noble Duke of Zamorna"

The ghastly agitation of Northangerlands Countenance was terrible his Eyes glared with the wildest light of Insanity as he seized His Monarchs hand Zamorna started at the icy coldness of his own He turned then to the Opposition or Reform peers and with a horrible oath at them staggered rather than walked from the table and seemed to bewildered to proceed he stood for a moment his

---

[45] i.e., if Zamorna rejects his wife, Mary Percy, it will kill her.

frame convulsed with Despair and then turning round left the Hall with a glance which revealed in all its horrors a mighty mind destroyed by its own satanic machinations and by its own evil deed overturn[ed] and Deprived of every ray of reason.

At the present moment the two Houses of Parliament like the Loadstone mountain in the Arabian Tale[46] attract toward them every heart and foot in the city of Verdopolis while the city acts to ass[sic] a magnetic pole to every quarter of the country and the various newspapers—and other organs of intelligence—everywhere present their mirror face of attraction to whosoever enters within the range of their omnipotent influence that vast hurricane politics has blown a perfect tempest over the ocean of African existence. and many a gallant vessel are the waves even now swallowing in their troubled vortex. the Night before last I myself beheld One great Double Decker go down But Alas No freindly Sail hove in sight to the sea monsters rescue for every Bark scudded far away from the sight of that mighty Pirate so terrible to them even in its sunken and shattered ship wreck.

When After the Adjournment of the House of Lords on March. [47] the night of "Zamornas demand" I again mixed with the people of the city and entered the crowded shops and coffeehouses. I saw from the whole tone and language of Verdopolis that Northangerlands downfall had been utter! —terrible! Not a hope that he could cling to not a single thing to save him His king had demanded from him imperativly either to make an end of his treacherous double dealing to put a stop to all his left handed and seditious machinations to cut himself lose[sic] from all connection with the Reformers and all hope of advancement in Verdopolis. and to unite himself again with Angria again act as her premeir and director of her rising energies Or—to continue in the course he was pursuing But severed from all association with his King deprived of present office and ground to stand on inveratly to be oppposed by the "Duke of Zamorna and witness the Destruction of all peace and happiness in the ruin of his Daughter and her children the heirs to a crown Northangerland knew at once that between these two alternatives there was no third expedient to hold to keep out at he knew the fiery impetous spirit he had to do with he saw that Zamorna would keep to his word. But for the last dreadful vengeance of which none But Zamorna had the power to take Northangerland would very readily and unconcernedly have cast aside all hold on Angria thrown up his seats engaged in contest with Zamorna and trusted to his own surprising Ability and powers of delusion to regain with him the ground which for a time he must evacuate such an event would only rouse his mind by its complicated difficulty But—there was

---

[46] See "The Third Calendar" in *The Arabian Nights.*

[47] Branwell left the date blank.

the final one tremendous punishment of his perfidy the ruin which could not avert the ruin of the Queen of Angria and of course in that case the everlasting and never again to be humbugged hatred of its king Northangerlands feelings where they are at all are intensly powerful. Soberly moral Ambitious men like Ardrah or Pelham or more reckless desperadoes like Montmorency or Lin[d]say would with out hesitation have left this consideration alone nor have felt it press against "Their duty to their country." But Northangerlands heart recoiled from the idea he could not bear a moment to crush the memory of a life which however melancholy he clings to and looks back on with an unshaken tenacity. on the other hand he could not bear to cast of forever all hope of Ambition Victory in the crooked paths he had chosen he could not bear to expose to the world the miserable duplicity of his political conduct and so though he did in desperation do this latter he saw his ruin and fairly sunk under it

I have allways felt myself powerfully impressed upon beholding though hitherto from afar off the ruin of a great public man partly perhaps I took the immidiate[sic] interest in their career which the Adventurer takes on the percursor in the reigon[sic] he himself was bound to when I saw a ruin made in the path [on] which all my energys were concentered to walk on I could not help feeling deeply and uncomfortably But independantly of this there is something interesting indeed in looking upon a man of great and active intellect who for years perhaps has shone the brightest star in all that heaven to which you were so often gazing whose word was power and whose will was law To see that man for a while heading and triumphing over difficultys and dangers till the wind changes he turns round lies at once exposed to a treble weight of opposition drifts lose of all consideration party or people dashes upon the most flinty rocks of hatered[sic] and defeat and either drifts away onto the sea of life an unregarded and soon to be forgotten wreck or sinks at once to the bottom in a whirlpool of confusion and astonishment

Now to me viewing as I did the most terrible of these downfalls for the first time with my own eyes and hearing that ruin with my own ears to me just arrived at the age of 21 to have a first peep into the hitherto far removed and mighty mysteries of the worlds affairs to me this scene I had just witnessed was awfull and impressive above every thing which my mind could conceive and when upon the immediate adjournment of the House I left it to return to my Hotel I thought with peculiar emphasis through those street[s] who was it that passed but scarce an Hour ago and did He mark the Buildings their architecture the Dawn or the twilight—No Northangerlands mind was so miserably shaken that wonderous indeed must be that sight which could force him for one instant to turn his eyes from the gazing into his own sunk and shattered spirit.

While engaged in such thoughts as these I passed along before the Doors of the Warning Beacon office where crowds of people were waiting for the delivery of the papers with gestures of feirce dismay they were cheifly Reformers and Ardrahians and stood talking and arguing upon the disastrous event of the night. while I remained for a moment stationary among the crowd with my lip curled in contempt of the parcel of rascals. A mounted Horseman dashed furiously past his shining steed snorting with the torment of the unpit[y]ing spurr. But the Rider with his mourning dress and pale ghastly countenance. the blasted eye fixed in weary vacancy the wildness with which he galloped along the street heedless of what lay before him it was that which made my blood thrill so coldly from my heart that <one> glance at the Earl of Northangerland a smouldering murmur among the crowd of Ardrahians was drowned directly in a sudden howl of hate and dissapointment a number of the most worthless desperadoes rushed round the Horseman and yelled into his ears the cries of Traitor Scoundrel Turncoat Satan Demon D—l Rougue. and a hunderd plebian insults But it was humiliating to behold the fallen Nobleman. here no mightier than the commonest slave rein up his horse for an instant in the bitterest agony. to be assailed with such a wretched multitude at that moment was to his chafed spirit as the little rock. hardly even above the water is to the vast wave which has roiled over 3000 miles of the Atlantic to be broken in foam over its miserable points of grantite. The Earls features became a dead white and every muscle quivered with anguish he evidently could not speak. and when the Brutal Mob of Reformers crowded around him and seized the reins of his frighted charger He involuntarily removed his hat from his forehead and showed such a collapsed and corpselike countenance. while fire rolled in his despairing eye. —that even that base mob recoiled from the ruined <person> he. did not swear or pull out his pistol But with a withered glance on the people again stuck his spurrs to the rowel heads and galloped headlong along the street. I think I gazed a minute upon the spot where he reined in before I hastened forward to reach my Hotel and there on the Breakfast table I took up the morning papers and opened them at their Leaders cursing and thundering at the Double traitor Northangerland "Well" said the Himes "this wretched traitor has gone out from among us we trust with all the sins of the faction he has created upon his head and we are certain with all his thousand own. Well Africa will reap the benifit of his miserable downfall and will not forget a due gratitude to the Duke of Zamorna for the effectual manner in which he has removed the veil from this new prophet of Khorassan[48] and let him to go let him seek in his own heart that peace and security of which he has so long deprived his unhappy country."

I longed with the utmost eagerness for night to come that I might see the manner in which this event would be taken by the Great Heads of Parties in parliament and all Day I was in [a] Dream hearing the conflicting curses and exclamations on Northangerland fall But all was cursing for no heart no hand no voice was exerted to speak one word for him the Lost Leader of the Reforming faction And all Day I too thought about him till as the lamps began to beam in the streets and the crowds of Equipages to thicken through the thoroughfares the increasing darkness within Doors and the encreasing tumult without told me it was time to prepare for another <sortie> to the House of Commons And to that

---

[48] "The Veiled Prophet of Khorassan" is one of the verse tales in Thomas Moore's *Lalla Rookh*, 1817.

cynosure of neighbouring eyes I instantly set out joining a stream of people who filed down the streets increasing in number as they moved along when we entered parliament square the numbers became so dense that it was impossible for many minutes to proceed so I stopped to hearken the various peals of shouts or groaning which welcomed on their enterance the various popular or unpopular members and as a a carriage burst through the crowd beside me I rushed into the lane it made and followed its Rattle till it drew up at the foot of the steps here again there was another obstacle for those steps rose in one broad uninterrupted slope of human hats and heads my hope of further promotion lay in the influence of the member I had followed he stepped from his chariot a Tall portly man pleasant to set eyes on and to a lane [that] was made up for him alike by Reformers and constitutuionalists so he stepped up and I followed with a host of other expectants the murmer was "Thats the General theres Crosus Grenville" and I knew I was in the train of the great first magistrate of Verdopolis—It seems however that the atmosphere of the Commons is one whose demands are turbulence and uproar for the instant that we stepped under the portal all thought of decency was lost in one universal and <uproarous> rush to the gallery I stormed a staircase at the head of one detachment and planted myself at a seat in the front gallery as joyful as if I had gained a town my first look was upon the arena below me The Speakers chair and the Ministrial cross and opposition benches The sight was <exciting> enough 3 or 400 members collected in two or 3 great ranges or scattered in little knots or seated alone apart and far retired but almost all of them wearing that look of anxious thought with which men little or great generally enter upon buisness of high importance—But there was one thing which exceedingly tantalized and mortified—But never mind at this moment there occured another thing which exceedingly tantalized and motified me and that was—just as I had taken up my coat tails sat down and snuffed up a pinch of real Blackguard[49] just as I had directed the orb of my eye glass full upon the centre of a constellation of the brightest stars in the political heavens just in fact as I was settling in my mind to what system and universe belonged a knot of swarthy or sallow Gentlemen with sharp shirt collars and guady waistcoats and cabbage watch seals and sandy whiskers I felt all on a sudden a yawp gash feeling as if I suddenly recollected that I was to be hanged to morrow and as I turned hastily to see if "His Majesty" was standing behind my shoulder I caught a glimpse of a white feather rising above the floor of the Gallery and as the owner of that feather mounted the stepps till his whole person appeared I kept staring [at] that rise with a wild and stricken gaze and a mind in a maze of bewilderment On came the apparition through the Gallery Aisle down between the rows of seats stalking with horrid solemnity plumed hatted and blazing in scarlet and gold

As he came nigher still and nigher

---

49 A kind of snuff, also called "Irish Blackguard."

Sunk quenched and quailed my spirits fire[50]
That brightened uniform that breadth of chest that methodical gait But the face
the features my eyes had not strength or sight to view them and as the visitor
stepped full in front of me drew from his pocket with an air a large white letter
and presented to me its blank face and Broad red seal I rose with opened mouth
and took it with trembling hand I broke open the envelope and unfold[ed] the
letter a short but fearsome scrawl of black was spread right across.

Gazemba. March 20th. 1835

Sir your furlough expired upon the 19th But you have not appeared
according to my orders. You are required to present yourself. at the
Court Martial in the fort upon the 22[d] instant

Enara.

"This is a D—d Bad buisness Searjent" said I. as I pushed passed[sic]
him and hurried out of the House he followed and I found my way with him to
the Hotel. in as great a mental mist as Ever Eneas[51] walking in a Bodily one. a
quarter of an hour from that moment beheld me at dead of night stuck upon the
top of the coach and whirling away for the Banks of the Etrei!!!

Well Good times and Bad times and all times get over and after diverse
fashions did that time which intervened between March 21st and April 8th pass
over I hurried as if on wings of fire to Gazemba when there sought the favour of
high places and strove to avoid the anger of the relentless Commander of the
Army Having implored Col Hastings[52] and through him another high quarter to
aid me. I found my non obedience of furlough passed pretty decently over and got
off with a stern intimation from the Tyger General to attend above all things to
my duties and keep my future furloughs in my memory

The Evening of April 9th found me after a fortnight spent in agitation
exertion and the Bustle of Military duties Again rattling through the streets of
that Verdopolis whose vast scenes and individuals I had after so short a glimpse
been so suddenly snatched from And here now I am reseated in the public room
of that very Hotel. which 3 days since I was 200 miles away from But during
my 14 days absence from the metropolis what strange what overwhelming
changes have taken place in this excited and tumultous Political Arena I had
thought the Astonishing fall of the Great Earl of Northangerland had been
strange enough for one while But now Behold the ruins of another fall almost as
strange and we may be yet doomed to see falls and rises stranger still

---

[50] The lines would seem to be Branwell's.

[51] When participating in the fighting around Troy, Aeneas was wounded by
Diomedes, and when Aphrodite tried to save him, she was also wounded. Apollo
then hid Aeneas in a cloud and spirited him away from the battlefield.

[52] "Hartford" obviously intended.

I while once more on the banks of the Etrei heard the accounts of the violent debates on the 25 and 6 upon the Downfall of Northangerland. Montmorencys sneering rejoicing and Harlaws vulgar insinuations then the anything rather than Debates upon the Navy bill which Sir R Pelham attempted to bring forward in the lower House but which so soon as he began with all his cool keen sagacity to open up the veil of the hideous abuses and disgraceful management of that branch of service. excited such a storm of opposition and unprecedented abuse from the guilty and interested heads of the Reformers that after 3 nights spent in tumultous excitement the Reform party threw out this measure of Reform by 320 to 290. and following up their victory by a vote of censure against the Duke of Fidena on the following Night and a successful motion for bringing in a bill to enquire into the connection possessed by Angria with Adrianopolis directly after compelled the Duke of Fidena to announce to the House of Lords the Resignation of his Ministry in that Assembly[53] this information was received with the most bitter regret and anxiety for the Peers of Africa were aware that for a time at any rate the best defence was removed which could guard the Constitution from its assailers But the Majority in the Commons hailed the event with a shouts[sic] of triumph echoed among lanes and streets from the mouths of a miserably deluded populace Sorry I am to state that there are some among our monarchs who regar[d]ed the Downfall of Fidena with but slender sorrow and shed only crocodile tears over his fate The Marquis of Ardrah cheif Leader of the Reformers (Alas shade of Northangerland!) well knew that he enjoyed the full confidence of his Royal father who possessed the full power over His Majesty of Rosses Land and likewise over the Kings of the Islands so that 4 Kings arrayed against Wellington and Sneachi of course carried the Day at the Royal Councils and these news was[sic] only what all expected which announced in the Gazzete World Messenger and Beacon that His Royal Highness the Most Noble Arthur of Ardrah had been appointed to form a Ministry After a few days of confusion and Bargaining and chicanery the following list was <flashed> upon the Delighted gaze of Verdopolis

Arthur Marquis of Ardrah-------Prime Minister and as before Lord High Admiral
John the Marquis of Harlaw------Sec.y for the Home Department
Richard Marquis of Wellesly-----President of the Council
Edward Viscount Strafford-----Commissioner of Crownlands woods and forests
Lord Macarra Lofty-------Chancellor of the Exchequer
Lord John Musselburgh------Paymaster of the Forces
Sir Alexander Elphinstone------Secretary to the Board of Admiralty
Sir Andrew Douglas------Secretary to the Maritime Department. or Colonial Affairs
Colonel John Luckyman-------President of the Board of Trade

---

[53] Fidena's appointment (see p. 344) and subsequent resignation closely parallels Sir Robert Peel's appointment and resignation—see Barker Brontës, 221.

Hector M M Montmorency-------Secretary for Foreign Affairs
John J Goat-------Speaker of the House of Commons
The Right Hon Thomas Tree Esqr M P-------Ambassador Plenipotentiary to the
Court of Angria

with a profusion of hungry Sawnies[54] to fill the minor offices And this was the
Ministry to bring in which the Duke of Fidena had been expelled from office
why there is not one among them which has ever proved capable of a single
good action not one who can shew forth as his own one single shred of character
Pah! their very scent poisons the imagination But it avails nothing to execrate
them their Harpy talons[55] are fixed in the vitals of the country and when that
country feels the pangs it will rouse and I hope not too late. shake them
abbhorrently[sic] off.

On the Evening of April 9th 1835. I reentered Verdopolis by Waterloo
Square wedged upon the Coach top amid a thick mass of humanity towering
above the wheels till it seemed like a living Car of juggernath[56] So soon as our
vehicle the Phoebus of Angria had whirled past the Dark and statly environs of
Royalty rearing their great grey Roofs and porticos all along our way and had
whirled into the commencement of the town or city Area the first thing that
struck my eyes was the Desolation and quietness of the streets we passed through
Then when the endless ramifications of building had closed far and dense around
us when people and Inhabitants did appear the[y] seemed each man retreating
from us and driving away for the very Heart of Verdopolis The coach still rolled
on like eternity of which it is no bad emblem since it carries with it so hasting
such numbers of our fellow creatures And when the farther course of the streets
began to open upon us the thickened and blackened crowds of men with crimson
and yellow cards or Ribbons in their hats the Hasty flight of Horses and carriages
before us the Distant Bursts of music down at the ends of long crowded streets
the walls windows and lamp post[s] pasted all over with crimson and orange
Handbills the Inns and Hotels shewing a Double Ensign in the vast flags of
yellow or crimson which streamed over the streets from their windows and above
everything the endless recurrence of the Names Grenville or Goat Goat or
Grenville flashed into our eyes by card and placard and sign and Ensign dinned
into our ears by shouts and roars the bravadoing Hurrahs All soon and loudly
informed us that April the 9th was the Nomination day for the Great and

---

54 "Sawney" is a derisive nickname for a Scotsman (colloq).

55 Any of several hideous, filthy, winged monsters with the head and trunk of a
woman and the tail legs and talons of a bird; they carried off the souls of the
dead, etc.

56 An incarnation of the Hindu god Vishnu whose idol, it is said, so excited
his worshippers when it was hauled along on a large car during religious rites
that they threw themselves under the wheels and were crushed; also any terrible
irresistible force.

Important Election for Verdopolis South Division where a great struggle between J J Goat Speaker of the House of Commons and the Hon Thos Grenville son of the Great City Cresus Grenville was to decide in its termination the relative power of Reformers and Constitutionalists in Verdopolis and to hurl down or seat in security the odious Ardrahian ministry

An Election I think comes as natural to a Mans heart as eating or sleeping or swearing and shew me a fellow in Africa who can avoid the excitement of its influence shew one who is not a Dab in its maneuvres the moment he puts a colour in his <hat> or Button hole All its proceedings moreover not only agree so well with the feelings of humanity. but so admirably well with the feelings of African humanity in the constant turmoil and Bustle the endless racing and running the shouting opposition and exertion the noble play for lying threatning and humbugging and the grand display of shew and glitter and ostentation that every one affirms A Contested Election is the only feild in which you can see an African in all his Glory—And this evening I saw enough of Africans in all their glory and if I did not see them in a feild I saw them in streets squares lanes and Housetops which was pretty nearly the same thing Ere we on the coach top had entered far into the Bustle of the City and as soon as the colours upon the Hats about us began to warm our hearts there was an universal fumbling in the pockets among us little folded papers were opened Ribbons were unveiled and after a stay at a Haberdashers shop to to supply the fire or fix Angrians unprepared with favours we again rattled off Heads and Hearts of men and Horses showing the Glorious Nationalist Hue of Grenville and Verdopolis—The results of such an Exhibition However appeared when upon turning down Lofty street we thundered streight into the middle of a vast crowd of Brimstone Ardrahians A Hoarse and Horrid roar burst from the yellow multitude it swayed on both sides vengefully toward our vehicle. the coach man drew his steeds backward and we all elevated our Hats to the shout of Grenville for ever the sentence must have possessed the power of Enchantment for it straight way conjured up a hail storm of stones which broke the carriage windows seriously injured a fat old Gentleman inside and brought the Nations colour streaming from the Gums of my next Neighour beside me the whip was applied in vain to the Horses the[y] backed heedless of its smart and its crack which I think. is the cheif terror to a horse was quite drowned in the hideous bursts of clamorous discord Our Angrians spirits however would not let us give in I am sorry to say that I set an example of rashness by standing up on my seat All did the same and we again joined in a hearty shout of "Down with the yellows" the ill fated coach must have looked a pathetic sight standing still foundered with its elevated crop of crimson Angrians amid the mighty mob who roared so Brutally around it and thickened so densly from the Neighbouring streets with such threats of its instant destruction there was No Help around us and like a little rock surrounded by a furious sea we kept in compact station above the tumult never ceasing to shout our party cry of Grenville for ever Hatted brows and Broad orange cards pressed up to the wheel of the vehicle Infernal scowls from hating eyes were bent upon us open mouths roared and strong arms were stretched for our destruction No event in life could exceeding[sic] in sublimnity the crash with which the Phoebus of Angria broke down the Burst of the horses from their traces the suddenness with which the mob forced them to recoil onto the shattered coach and the Hoarse Halloo with which the <venammous> Host of scoundrels rushed upon the Heroic Heap of of Crimsons How I escaped as I did is to this moment a source of wonder But I know that with High drawn breath and fists impetously hurled about me I Dashed forward trusting to the powers of my own right hand and my <holy> arm It was almost suffocating to press with such fighting through so vast a mass of enimies But I Dealt my fists like lighting till stopped by a shout of "what the D—l mad as a ma[r]ch Hare" and opened my eyes (they were nearly bunged up) to the ridiculous sight of my blood lighting sans ceremonie upon the persons of a dense crowd of crimsons joining with the rest in laughter I calmed down as well as my bloody nose would let me and asked what was there doing But the singing in my ears drowned the answer given to my question I could perceive here was a body of Real Tories but how large or where we were was quite hidden from my intellects so I grasped hold of a rope and swerved up into the top of a waggon laden high with Wool which stood wedged among the thick crowds of people standing here aloft and casting my eyes below me a mighty spectacle Burst upon my sight One Huge Ocean of men filling most densly the whole of a vast square of Houses and spreading with equal density down every street that led into it Thousands of crimson hats thronged around my waggon and Hundreds of Broad Crimson Banners or splendid sheets of silk intermixed with crimson and Blue The Great Gilded Letters "Grenville and the Constitution Africa for ever Grenville the freind of Fidena opened and closed to the delighted eyes this blessed sight of Gallant fellows with carriages innumerable Rejiments of Cavalry Noble Bands of music stretched in a crescent onto one side. But Alas tens of thousands of Gaudy Oranges an Enormous multitude of infatuated wretches spread their monstrous myriads over every other portion of the scene and a forest of yellow flags inscribed "Goat and Reform Ardrah and Reform Goat for ever and &c. waved over their heads till lost in the confusion of streets and Houses Just opposite to me and under the Grand pile of Columned Buildings a prodigous Hustings reared itself! Divided into equal proportions of Crimson and Orange and is of course crowded with all the wealth and power in the mighty city of Verdopolis I looked with interest enough on the Gentlemen who stood in front but with my accustomed misfortune could not divine who they were However the one Athletic Honourable in Black with the Broad orange rosette on his breast and the Hat doffed from his scowling Bull like Brow who stood in front elevating his iron arm and sending forth over the surging tumult a voice of such thundering impetousity—that One Gentleman could not be mistaken for though I had only once seen him before I knew Directly Hector Matthias Mirabeau Montmorency[57]

---

[57] Branwell witnessed first hand the election campaigns in April 1835 that led

"Well Gentlemen" He cried after standing sternly smiling till a hoarse shout of applause had died away "Well—How Doth the city sit solitary that was full of people! How did she become as a widow! she that was great among the nations and princes among the provinces How is she become tributary Judah is gone into captivity because of affliction and because of a great servitude she dwelleth among the Heathen she findeth no rest all her persecutors overtook her between the streights[58] Alas Alas Poor Judah and are not thy seventy years of captivity now at least expired verily thou[g]hest been in Bondage a long time. yes and for really 70 years have thy 12 tyrants of the 12 tribes with such an iron rod ruled over thee. —But I Do think that now thy chains are fallen off thee I do think that now thou shalt become free! 1765—1835 exactly 70 years—The punishment of thine iniquity is accomplished O Daughter of Zion He will no more carry thee away into captivity But He will visit *thine* iniquity O Daughter of <Amon> He will Discover thy sins! —Howl O Heshbon for all is spoiled Cry ye Daughters of Rabbath gird you with sackcloth lament and run to and fro by the Hedges for their KING shall go into captivity and His PREISTS! and His PRINCES! together!"[59] —Here as the greatest of Demagogues exerted all the energy of his voice in that last emphatic quotation another loud shout of applause roared in terrific chorus to his song I cannot give the vivid feeling of that pause in his speech or the glance of triumph which he shot round the crowd when He again raised his arm and voice to renew his blasting thunder

"Well Gentlemen Here is scripture read to purpose and is not this sermon worth a hundred of the soporofic[s] you Doze under on every Seventh Day of every week in every year of your all and several lives I. will give the to opponent a screed of Doctrine to the Righteous a word of comfort to the Wicked a word of Doom! *I* will point out to your Kings prepared for the pit of Tophet your princes sleeping in fat and wantoness your priests the Blind leaders of the Blind I will point out to you the Daughters of Edom with their tinkling feet and their mincing step and their <neck> swollen with pride!"[60] —A loud burst of Groans and Hisses here rose from the crimsons ranks and Hustings But the yellows took up the note in a triumphant yell of applause. —"Howl" cried Montmorency "Howl now ye RICH MEN weep howl for the miseries that are come upon you your Riches are corrupt and your garments are motheaten! your Gold and silver is cankered and the rust of them shall be a witness against you and shall eat into your flesh as it were fire YE! at least have heaped treasure for the last Days—Behold the Hire of the labourers who have reaped your feilds which by you is fraudulently kept back crieth and the cries of them which have

---

leading the Tory opposition—see Barker Brontës, 221-32.

58 Compare Lamentations 1:1-3.

59 Compare Jeremiah 49:2-3.

60 Compare Isaiah 3:16.

reaped enter the ears of the Lord Sabaoth"[61] Here an universal shout of shame! shame! broke from the crimsons and the Hoarse roar of the yellows directly <strove> to drown the expression of indignation However the speakers Doubly pitched voice over came every other in <erruption> and he cried anew "Be patient my Bretheren unto the coming of the Lord Be patient stablish your Hearts for the coming of the Lord draweth nigh! And I should like to ask who is better able than I am to discern the beam of his dawning I have now lived eight and forty years in this world and I have trafficed for thirty years in all the politics of this Nation I have acted in all its actions through a whole Generation It wont pass with you may be should I mention the name" (a Deep murmer of indignation almost drowned the Demagogues voice)—the name. (here the voice swelled higher and sterner) the name of the M—"—I could hear nothing further for some time so woeful a shadow had this name before its coming on the minds of the hooting crowd beneath me Montmorency stood laughing with a feindish grin upon the Hustings And when he recommenced his eyes flashed with a light of triumph and exultation He turned toward the west stretched forth his arms and cried with a trumpet voice. —"O Lucifer! Star of the morning how art thou fallen! —Now is thy glory wasted! —How is thy power and thy might destroyed![62] —Well Be it so or rather so has it been He whom I have known for 40 years and acted with for 20 years He whom I thought the Redeemer the 12 Apostles the champion of Liberty and Reformation and Regeneration has been— Aye Gentlemen! the Redeemer has suffered on the cross the Apostles have been martyered the champion has just spent his last life blood in the defence of his most Righteous cause Oh, John Huss! and Jerome of Prague! Oh Peter Waldens[63] and Oh Preacher Percy. (Groans of Disapprobation on the name being mentioned) Well—He is Gone out from among us Achan Scapegoat Leper[64] as he is gone with all his crimes and cruelties upon his Head The Traitor the paracide the prodigal the pirate the Robber the <Gow> Jobber the Bankrupt the Rebel the Gambler the Drunkard the father in law of the king the Prime Minister of the Court of the Kingdom of Angria. Oh unfortunate Angrians did you but know your own misfortunes!"—(Here a stout craven looking man who had been laughing for the last 2 minutes cried out. "Dont kick a Dead Ass. Hear ye")— Dont kick a dead Ass did my right Hon freind say I say. Kick it in earnest to get it out of your path But why do we talk of Asses when our speech should be of Angels I was not thinking of a dead ass I was moaning over a dying Angel For never more bright more benificent did any sacred spirit waft wings over the world

---

61   Compare James 5:1-4.

62   Compare Isaiah 14:12.

63   Huss (1369-1415), Jerome (1379?-1416), and Waldens (dates unknown) were all early Protestant reformers and preachers, the first two in Prague, both strongly influenced by the writings of Wycliff; Waldens in France.

64   Compare Joshua, chapter 7.

than did my ruined freinds great intellect watch and hover over the destinies of Sire and Son His Sire His Son his House his country His—His Oh my Heart my Heart Break not in greif for the fall of Northan—(Horrid roars of scorn prevented the completion of his name being heard Montmorency stood with his hands clasped together his eyes raised upward—How are the mighty fallen how are the weapons of war perished! Tell it not in Gath publish it not in Askalon lest the Daughters of the philistines rejoice lest the Daughters of the uncircumcised triumph[65] —ye Daughters of Africa weep over Percy who clothed you in scarlet—with other Delights who put ornaments of Gold about your necks—How are the mighty fallen in the midst of the battle O Percy thou wast slain in thy high places—I am distressed for thee my Brother Percy Very pleasant hast thou been to me thy love to me was wonderful passing the love of woman—How are the mighty fallen how are the weapons of war laid low[66] (loud cheers and laughter)—Well Gentlemen I have been running on too far In laughing at that poor creature of his own wickedness whose heaped and contradictory crimes have crushed him underneath their portentous weight and when the poor christian floundering in the Slough of Despond Daubed over with the mire of unrighteousness lifted up his hands for help from his punishment the fellow standing near of whom he besought help just put his foot out heaved his toes at him and sent him sprawling backwards way into the Bathes of everlasting oblivion[67] —I can see nothing of him you can see nothing of him But we all of us at one time have both seen and heard to much we all remember I believe his empty claptraps his discordant apostrophes to liberty his blustering hate of the tyrants we have seen what shadowy unreal blessings he held out to us and when he drew us after him to catch his rainbow we have all felt into what a puddle of blood we were shure to slip by the way Who I wonder pays any regard to the private Affections of a man who has slain his own father and who would slay his own Son who cares a whiff about the Remembrance of the jail Bird whose past has lain among theft and imprisonment whose every action has begun in dissipation and ended in murder who wishes to hear of his trafficing with his Dupe. of a son in law Humbugging his vanity mystifying his fear and ending up by roaring on his knees for mercy mercy. —Poltroon and Renegade His warmest freinds he had before cast off from him and How could he dream that yon shallow pated fop would ever have strength to stick by him! (loud groans from the Crimsons in which I heartily joined here prevented the speaker from continuing his Adress He stood apparently cursing and swearing at us while the crowd of yellows swayed and undulated as if tossed with the winds of Hatred

---

65 Compare II Samuel 1:20.

66 Compare II Samuel 1:27.

6 7 The Brontë children read Bunyan's *Pilgrim's Progress* at an early age—see Alexander EW, p. 19.

A tall well made young Gentleman with light fierce features pushed into the front of the Hustings and made his voice heard over all the tumult

"Mr Montmorency!" he said vehemently extending his strong arm toward him "I say how the D—l dare you use such language as that I say What the D—l could induce you to speak in this insolent manner of a—a Gentle—a—D—n it an Elector! upon our side of the Hustings! I tell you Sir that if you use any further language of this Sort By Heaven But you may speak to our eyes for our ears shant hear you! I ask what in Heavens name have you been running on at this rate about a man whom no body here be he blue or yellow cares one whit more for than I do for you"— Further speech from this orator was also here stopped by a Dreadful storm of Groans and loud cries of "The Rot" "Stinking Wool" "2^S—6 a week." and other undistinguishable expression[s] this let me into a notion of who he was whom they were interrupting and with Double interest I beheld Mr Edward Percy standing forced to keep hard rein over his stormy temper lest it should drive him upon the crowd like a flash of lightning—Mr Montmorency (and he was evidently enfuriated at Mr Percy) again raised his Arm and voice over the tempest of conflicting opinions.

"And so it seems I am to suffer unnoticed such dictation as that and I am to be told and at this time of day what I am to speak and what I am to think.! I who knew the world this people the Earl of Northangerland before that young Gentleman was born who knew the Duke of Zamorna before either Mr Percy or the Duke him self could know either themselves or me that young Gentleman perhaps fancies that he is acquainted with the institutions of his country does he know that their[sic] is a law which declares the punishment for swearing to be not whipping or the stocks or the pillory for these he cares no more for than I do for him but A scorn which far closlier[sic] touches the character the honour the invaluable character of a man that worst of all punishements! a fine!—a fine amounting to the united sum of 2 weeks of out of[sic] the Hon Gents combers wages—a fine of 5 shillings I tell him to reflect upon what I have said and to beware for ruin stands as his door—The Hon Gentlemen desired me to speak to you no more upon the uninteresting and worthless character of Northangerland. Now If the father is not fit to be brought before the eyes of the public The Son ought certainly not to arrogate more notice or a higher Destiny If I am Not to trouble your ears with Details A O H'[68] about the life of Alexander Percy so neither will I weary you with Discourse about the world of Edward Percy (Hear Hear and laughter)—I was Interrupted Gentlemen in this Needless and insolent manner Because I called His Grace the Most Noble Arthur Duke of Zamorna Marquis of Douro King of Angria et cetera et ceterum a—what was it—Oh a—a shallow pated fop. now I did not come here to defend my speech but to make my speech and therefore I will leave the Reasons for that offensive appellation to be detailed by the one at my right hand who is far more able and far better qualified to do it than I can possibly consider my self to be—(Here Montmorency

---

[68] See vol I, p. 30, n. 25.

encreased his voice to Double Volumne and emphasis. as he took of his Hat and shewed [his] broad forehead to the multitude)—Gentlemen! —I have now concluded my speech—I have now finished what I had to say! And if the River of my oratory did not flow onward so smoothly as you could have wished Remember that it did not bring down in its own course the rocks and stones which have chafed its waters but that they were hurled into its channel But men who would right willingly see that channel parched dry with Drought and those waters all vanished away—you have Now Heard expressed as well as I could express them my opinions upon the scenes and the events which are so constantly changing and thickening round us you have heard me tell you that in this crisis of National excitement whatsoever means you use whatsoever remedies you resolve on must Decisivly determine either as they shall prove in effect the extinction of your Life or the cure of your Disease That vast crowd which I see beneath and around me that Immense multitude whose glorious display of orange [and] yellow seems to me to cast the beams of sunshine over them though the sun itself [h]as so long since sunk down—that mighty concourse of Africans has told me and told me with no feeble voice that Now at last is all Africa conscious of her Dreadful situation of her wasting Disease you have told me that the evils which have through all this last Night of ignorance surrounded and grown upon our country are at last fully seen and since the sun of knowledge has only just risen they are yet both strange and new to your eyes But men like myself who have walked through the midnight with a lamp in our hands have long since seen what the monsterous Incubus was which lay upon you we have long told you that The Constitution of Africa is parlarous[sic] that its materials are. heterogeneous that your Rulers are Tyrants from the Nature of their Office that your laws are oppressive from their inherent qualitys oppressive when withheld from you and oppressive when exercised upon you A weight of the rod is laid over your shoulders and a smart when it is laid on your back. We have told you all this and now when you see it you believe it. You know the Nature of your disease and you want to know the character of your physicians It is to determine this important point to fix upon who are the men who can cure you that we have all met in this place upon this present day Many Aspirants to the Office have presented themselves before you but you have rejected the Quack Northangerland with his Elixer of vitality you have rejected the Quack Fidena with his alter[n]atives and corrosives and now you have only remaining to choose between the keen steady knife of Ardrah and the harsh edgless hatchet of Zamorna. Here my Freinds here is the Bright Golden Cordial of Reform and there is the Red Bloody Draught of Tyranny Thomas Grenville stands before you dyed in the Gore of your own Land of Africa But John James Goat I present to you Radiant with the Bright Yellow light of the New Risen Sun of Reformation!" (loud and long protracted thunders of Applause")

It is not very easy to express the effect this portion of Montmorencys speech had on me nor is it easy to shew in print where its effect cheifly lay My Reader should have felt as I did not accustomed as he perhaps has been to seeing and hearing the Demogogue every day perhaps privatly accquainted with him and often passing him in the street or meeting him in all the mixed ramifications of Verdopolis buisiness[sic]—No I had heard of him certainly during all that portion of my life in which I took notice of anything and I had thought of him too thought of him as the Tremendous Coadjutor of the Mighty and terrible Northangerland the almost instructor of His erratic youth and often the servant of his bidding in his tempestous middle age I knew him as a Man Who had assisted more than save one any other man in all Africa to bring about the restless and fatal political spirit the endless and not yet determined Revolutions. of the present day and latterly too his planet had appeared to me redder than ever in the ominous instance of Dark treachery and reckless profligacy I mean when he so cold bloodedly tore himself from communion with the falling Northangerland and turned upon him determined to accelerate to the utmost his coming Destruction—And now to See this man to See and to hear Hector Matthias Mirabeau Montmorency. to see that Great Strong Herculean figure to note the every change and variation in the features the actual features of the real countenance of Montmorency not to see a shadowy image in my minds eye but a very Substantial one with my bodily eye that towering ferocious ill nature was just what I had thought would be the expression of his features now when Hated and distrusted by all parties and forced to exert all his powers to keep on the surface of our wild political ocean But it was what I heard which the most vividly impressed me when I stood before him first the torrents of Scripture Quotations so sternly given and with such emphasis as they were diverted at the different objects of his sarcasm and malignity the qualified pause while the people roared out their applause of his language the savage Delight with which he gloated over their weathercock hate of Northangerland And then at last when He stopped uncovered his head and faced the Multitude throwing open his surtout to give free play to his powerful lungs stroking the thin brown hair from his massy forehead and Loud and thunderingly pound[ed] forth the unchecked volumne of his last concluding words Oh How He felt the power he had over the thousands of hearts around him how he gloried in his triumph and how delightedly came over his spirit the thought of the hate and rage with which his enimies were then hearkening to him

As Montmorency concluded Amid the most tremendous shouts of applause I ever heard mingled too with a deep and emphatic groan of indignation from all the true freinds of Africa and her Institutions He bowed to the "ocean of yellow" and clapping his hat over his eyes stood side way for the advent of Mr Goats seconder—I had had pointed out to me before in the House of Commons the Right Hon. or rather his Royal Highness Edward Marquis of Harlaw therefore I was at no loss to know who might be this great craven clumsy looking fellow in the white beaver hat. Bright yellow waistcoat and maritime slops who edged roughly forward to the front of the Hustings set his castor[69] with sullen defiance on his brow plunged his <mitten> fists into his Great Coat pocket and

---

69   A hat of beaver or rabbit fur.

commenced his speech amid vast clapping of hands and shouts of derisive laughter with a real mast head halloo which told us that the Marquis had good lungs if he had nothing else good about him

"Talk of shallow pated fops" he said squirting a quid[70] on to the gentry immediatly beneath him "Talk of shallow pated fops Why I wonder what they mean!—I was Born and Bred to the Navvy—" Roars of laughter here prevented for some time the Noble Marquis from proceeding But he stood with stoical solidity till the noise had subsided. "I was born and Bred to the Navvy.—" the roar was again revived and as the Marquis with winning openness joined in in a loud hoarse grin the mirth became universal for all saw that he stood in blessed ignorance of what they were laughing about. this surmise was seen to be well founded when he again commenced "I dont know what ye are laughing about I say. —What the D—l is there odd in a mans telling what hes been brought up to! —But Howsomever I (said with a louder twang than ever) I was born and bred to the Navvy! and that (snapping his fingers) is none of your drum beating fife squeaking and coated flummery "Hearts of Oak are our ships hearts of oak are our men" as the song says[71] —But Howsomever—They want me to talk of shallow pated fops as If I knew anything about them when Haw—Hum—when All my life as one may say I have been born among Hon—(the Noble Marquis declaration of having been born all his life excited much mirth among the Crimsons) the D—l I say among Honest and upright seamen it fits ye land lub—I mean landsmen to talk of fops for ye have seen more of 'em than I have but Hows'oever when I am speaking the truth I don't care a D—n either for them or ye or us or all put together!" (again the Worthy Marquis snapped his Digits and an overwhelming burst of applause followed the promulgation of that last most manly magnanimous sentence—) Now I wonder whats the hae of you skirlling and clapping down there I want none of your applause and none of your sensure[sic] the approbation of a Honest heart and a good conscience alone satisfies me (thunders of approval and howlings of contempt the Marquis rescusitated his cheek with another quid and rested a little after this extraordinary effort of Genius. with a maritime twinkle in his eyes he began again) "When I was a lad I entered on shipboard and began at the beggining and sat myself down to the mast like any other midshipman but then my s[t]ation was higher nor theirs and so I kept my due distance from them I warrant you I knew what was due to me as the Heair[sic] to the throne of a country one of the thrones of Africa (a voice from the crimsons "O Happy Ross's land") they dare not oppen their maaths to tak in their meat but as I upped with my little finger. —Im none of your Revolutionists and your Anarchists and your D—nd levellers I want to see all things as they should be not as they are I want to see things on a level to know that is each on its proper level I want a king always to keep on the level

---

[70] i.e., tobacco juice

[71] A patriotic song from the pantomime, *Harlequin's Invasion*, written by Garrick in 1759.

of a king and a clown on that of a man!!! (shouts of applause) they talk about levels but howsoever the best level that I know of is the level of a ship board and the best elevation is the mast head <Beating> the Gallows—and there I was (No you will be there ere long) And there I was and there I will be. (till you are cut down and your body given to disection) Naw thats not fair By G—d it isnt. when Im talking o' mast heads that fellow is talking of Tyburn trees[72] But Howsever they want me to talk of fops what the Henker![73] should I know of fops! Im none of that gear my self and by the lord Harry Ill have none of any men fops ither!. I say I call a great fat Rolling porpoise of a Parson a fop. who gets into his pulpit of a Sunday Afternoon after the prayers are read Trims his band sets his wig opens his Book dons his spectacles and Deals out to a staring congregation some 10 minutes of his confounded written trash about repentance regeneration and a cleansing from sins and then goes home to his sleep and feeding and draws a 1000 or 2 a year for a two or 3 Sundays in they year of such sham[e]ful idleness as you and I call that Man a fop and a real fop who goes about priming and mincing with his pale face and his lordly airs pluming himself on the fact of his having spent his estate and murdered his father and runned away with a score of poor innocent females (bursts of applause) Hah Hah—Ive hit him there! and at last married for her brass a D—d trucculent Jade—(tremendous cries of shame! disgusting! in which I heartily joined)—who claps her thumb upon him and forces him to do as she wishes and as for Herself. —(Roars of Dissaprobation from the crimsons and cries of shame! shame! from several even of the yellows) And I call that man a fop (Here the anticipation of the orange party rose so delightedly that they stopped the Marquis speech with three sucessive bursts of Applause) Hah—Hah—Hah D—n you take me—! Howsiver Ive nought to say against never a man breathing But I do call him a fop—Him who stands on his pins only just escaped from school Gets up in a Morning curls his hair paints his face put rings on his fingers and brass on his Nose Cloth[e]s himself like a merry Andrew[74] goes into his study writes a screed of trash about his life and action tells how He cheated his father wheedled his mother Ran from his Home told his Munchausen stories about killing tigers and <Rattens>[75] and the like Deluded and betrayed a—(Groans and hootings of contempt and derision)—a—(renewed uproar.) D—n you what will you be after. there I say Howsever! and married in a hedge priest way[76] a mere Roman a D—

---

[72] The former place of execution by hanging in London.

[73] Old Scottish for "What the devil."

[74] A buffoon, a clown.

[75] The German Baron, adventurer, and soldier (1720-97) known for his exaggerated tales of his exploits. Rattens are rats—see Alexander CB II, part ii, 133, n. 114.

[76] i.e., by an illiterate or uneducated clergyman. "Hedge" as a prefix generally signifies contempt or something clandestinely done.

d—(renewed groans) and killed his preserver more fool he was to save him! and got into company not quite as ill sure as himself and got out by another 50th marriage and half frightened his silly wife to death and killed her the other half. and married a 51st silly creat——(Dreadful ferment of indignation with loud cries of fetch the soldiers!) Aye let the soldiers come I dont give a farthing about them the tom fools of a Rascally Tyranny—(here the Marquis freinds about him attempted to appease and draw him from the front of the Hustings But his Noble Nature was now aroused He turned his shoulder gracfully toward them and bawled out) To H—l with the soldiers and all such like as them my blood boils in my knuckles to see them with there[sic] Bloody Angrian livery. —And this Tom O Rascal Im talking about is a soldier too and sports his cockade and his sword and And speaking o that hes been a parson likewise and I know something of whats what and Ive heard from quarters he little knows of how he got through his parsonship and all. over the Ducking stool are the Synod and the like. a Ducking stool is not a punishment for nothing no nor for all things either Does he know—(loud hooting which lasted several minutes Does he know the name—(tremendous groans from the crimsons) the Name—the fact. —(Here it became impossible for the Marquis to proceed the tumult had increased to such a formidable pitch During the whole of his speech it was next to impossible for him to have been heard but for his loud and well exerted voice and now at last the Crimsons kept up such a steady Huzzah for Grenville and the yellows roared shuch[sic] howlings of execration that the Right Hon Marquis standing fixed on one leg then on another chewing his quid swearing and speaking unheard—at last motioned to Mr Goat as if to say he seconded him and was pushed by his own freinds into the crowd of yellow magnates.

The Duke of Zamorna then came forward upon the Blue Hustings and was well received with a Glorious Burst of Enthusiasm from every true Man among the thousands even the yellows with the exception of the Brimstone Squadron the Hustings dare not at first raise a head against the pride of his county. His Grace looked magnificent in his full Crimson sash and Gold Sun of Angria uncovering his Royal head he began with a voice which yeilds not to Harlaws in power and immeasureably surpasses it in deep toned sweetness. the Gross attacks which had just before been made upon him produced on his features no other effect than a slight glow of just indignation encreased to real crimson flush by the glorious cheer his party greeted him with

"Gentlemen you have heard quoted to day by one person several passages from Scripture to serve the purpose of blinding misrepresentation Now here[sic] a few from another to serve the purpose for which scripture was intended the purpose of information and guidance to your souls. —Woe to the land shadowing with wings which is beyond the rivers of <u>Ethiopia</u>! that sendeth Ambassadors by the sea even in vessels of bullrushes upon the waters saying go ye swift messengers to a Nation scattered and peeled. (cries of Stumpz land Monkeys land) a Nation meted out (loud applause) and trodden down, whose land the waters have spoiled!—[77] And again on another subject. Woe to the multitude of many people which make a noise like the noise of the seas and to the rushing of Nations that make a rushing like the rushing of mighty waters The Nations shall rush like the rushing of many waters but God shall rebuke them and they shall flee far off and shall be chased like the chaff of the mountains before the wind. and like a rolling thing before the whirlwind!"[78] (loud applause from the crimsons followed this apposite quotation from the Erudite preacher. But the yellows at last mustered courage to take off their hats by degrees as if in shame and first hardly daring to hear their own voices the[y] took up a murmur from the roar of the <Gentlemen> on the Hustings and gradually swelled it up to Howling and hooting indeed like the rushing of many waters I myself saw a Tall light headed disagreeable looking man whom I shortly found was the Heir presumptive to the throne of Parrysland whisper to 5 or 6 fellows who immediatly descended and stationed themselves among the crowd it was then and near where they planted themselves that the opposition first begun The Duke of Zamorna turned to his own freinds and addressed them for some time but to my great misfortune the Howling of the yellows prevented my hearing one word of what he said He continued by introducing the Hon Thos Grenville amid the loudest shouts of applause. Mr Warner my landlord then stood forward and seconded the motion but I could not hear him more than before I however saw enough in the pallid cheek compressed lip and quivering fingers to know that willingly at that moment would his Majesty of the Warner Hills consign all the thousands of yellows to the pit of Tophet[79] —Then the yellow candidate Goat appeared Attired in a brown surtout Greyhead sallow faced hideous and wretched loathing and scorn filled my heart to view the new Speaker of our Parliament the fit candidate of Reform

"Stop a bit" interjected Mr Edward Percy with stern resolution addressing the Hon J J Goat. "Unless you Sir give us your partys promise for a quiet hearing of our candidate we cannot consent to a quiet hearing for you.!"

"I am perfectly willing to give you my promise that I will give the Gentleman no interruption on my part." croaked the Speaker—

"Very likly. Sir but you are only one in a 10000.! will your followers here follow you"

"I feel convinced that they will"

"But this will not do" broke in Mr Warner "Gentlemen of the Yellow Hustings will you hear us if we hear you?" the unmannerly rabble cawed and hooted.

Much talking and shuffling ensued among the yellows

---

[77] Compare Isaiah 18:1-2.

[78] Compare Isaiah 17:12-13.

[79] Compare Jeremiah 7:31-33.

"Gentlemain!" cried Goat. "Time wears late our proceedings are drawing to an end I come before you the chosen candidate of your hearts and voices and if my en—

"Oh is that your cane" cried Mr Edward Parry "then By God! if you will not hear us we will not hear you follow me Gentlemen—Huzzah for Grenville— the crimson men beginning to Roar But the Duke of Zamorna signed them to desist.

"Once more you of the other side" he said "will you promise to Hear Mr Grenville?"

The Hustings of the oranges continued in Division some cried yes others were silent Mr Goat stood sullenly and opened his mouth to commence But the Marquis of Ardrah white as death and quivering with rage. pushed forward glared ghastily at Zamorna and cried

"Mr Goat proceed.!"

"Gentlemain the present aspect of politics is Both glorious and encouraging I—".

Here the crimsons raised a second Halloo. Zamorna. like a peacemaker called out "Sir answer my question will your party hear Mr Grenville.?"

"I will go on no one shall interrupt me Jantlemayn. We are called—"

The Duke turned to the Crimsons waved his Hat toward them and up rose another. Huzzah for Grenville the Yellows were already raging with excitement when the Marquis of Ardrah foaming at the mouth with rage white as a sheet with malice raised his cane waved it toward the crimson Hustings and cried (I heard him myself.) Pull them down pull them Down." —Lord Macarra Lofty in terror at the look of the scene placed his Hand on the Marquis Arm as if cautioning him to desist. He fiercely repulsed him and now the heaven was rent with tumult the yellow mob swayed over toward the Crimsons I closed my fists for an Encounter. and an appalling spectacle of the forced union of the two parties began we pressed forward upon each other struck hand over head and tore their opponents down under their feet to the ground ere long the closeness with which they were pressed. prevented further fighting in spite of the Ghastly Marquis encouragement But when Mr Goat came forward to speak. Not one syllable of what he bawled could be distinguished by those the nearest to him He cried and declaimed his short hour and retired exhausted with vexation. Mr Grenville as fine a young fellow as ever stepped then came forward and greived was I that I could not possibly hear him All Afterward was to me a dumb show But I saw when amid the wild cries and clamour after both candidates had ceased pantomiming it on their hustings. the High Sheriff Mr Searggent Bud Arose and demanded a shew of Hands for Goat. a "forest of hands" was immediatly held up. then one for Grenville. a shew if smaller certainly far cleaner more aristocratic and every way more honourable. But Alas honour has no weight in an Election. the Sheriff. Declared Mr Goat Elected amid a howl of Delight from his party Mr Percy Demanded a poll for Grenville Mr Haynes of Freeport Hermes a poll for Goat. while matters were in this last stage and the concourse cheering for their respective candidates. My attention was directed to. an. Immense MAN. who

strode through the parting myriads mounted a high pedestal. in the throng of the
Numbers. and while those who had occupied it jumped from. it in instant
obedience. He erected their[sic] his Gigantic Height. Uncovered his Stern Iron
Brow and Bald Head. rising like a mighty summit crowned with his silver haffets
as white as snow. RICHARD NAUGHTY. the Champion of Africa. Bent his
lionlike scowl on the mingled multitudes who all turned in silence toward him
and stretching forth an Hand immense wasted and sinewy as that of an
antediluv[i]an patriarch—He cried in a voice whose tone of tremendous
distinctness so far suprassed[sic] the loudest voice of any who had gone before
him.

"My lads what is this that you have been doing and what do I see here?.
For what are all these Colours of yellow and crimson! I never before knew them
and you never before have worn them! I say what has entered into your hearts
that you should so forget what you have so long ago learnt. and run in to
conduct as vain and ridiculous as that you are now pursuing. you Have Come
Here to Here[sic] these men talk whom I see upon those two Stages you Have
Heard them and What Have they talked to you?. I know now you can not tell me
be cause you dont know what there has been to tell! —My Lads you have
behaved foolishly you do not know your own interests you are serving like
slaves the men who though they seem to court you will never in one instance
hereafter serve you I know these people on those Hustings I have now lived
Eighty years in this world and I knew what this world is long before Any on
those stages were born I have known their fathers and I have known them When
did these people who carry their crimson colours do you any good is not their
ensign the one you have for so many years fought against and as to the other
colour the yellows are not they your bitterest enimies. did you ever expect
benifit from Parry or Ross.? —My Lads the world never changed during eighty
years past of my life and I do not believe that it has turned topsy tur[v]y in one.
But My lads I[t] is getting fast toward Night. I must speak to you more upon the
point I came for for 20 years Has Alexander Percy. (Here the scoundrel cheifs on
the yellow Hustings attempted to raise a hiss but the people did not join and
Naughty raising his tones went on) Silence there I say or I will streight my Rare
lads upon you—for more than twenty years has Alexander ROUGUE spoke for
you and wrote for you and fought for you. and ad[v]ocated your interest where
there was no other to speak and conquered in your cause when there was none
other to fight. I said My lads that the world has not changed ex[c]ept that you
seem to have lost your sense and since the world has not changed I tell you that
Alexander Rougue has not changed. he still is as he always was he still is
willing and determined to live for you and to die for you. for some years past I
have been estranged from him and have had nothing to do with him but now
when I see his enimies and our enimies so triumphant and himself our friend so
cast down I determined to forgive and forget all the past and to exert myself to
remedy it in the future I left at once my retreat at the Source of the Niger and
went straight to Alnwick at his express desire. I saw him there and conversed
along[sic] time with him while. I was yet at the place but unable to rouse him

fully from his great agony and anguish of spirit Arthur Wellesly arrived alone at the Hall. (another Hiss was attempted by the yellows and Here Oh the change which I did see many on the crimson rank many on the crimsons hustings joined in a groan of dismay. almost every respectable person shook his head with sorrow) Yes. Howl Tyrants and possessors of the good things Arthur Wellesly arrived at the Hall. Now My Lads I am an old Man and a rough and plain spoken one too but Arthur is a young one and he can shine where I cant be seen He spoke a good deal to ROUGUE and Rougue heard him out but he neither hinted or promised much to us any other than that if we would leave him till evening he would see us both again—we did leave and I walked about the park with Arthur talking about our country and telling him what he should do at Night Old King came and told us his Master wished us to come to him we came and he gave me a letter and Zamorna another Mine he told me to go away with to Verdopolis and Zamornas with himself to H—l! we both left the place neither know each others letter I left Arthur at the town and I have not seen him since till I see him there now But when I got on the road I read through ROUGUES letter and when I finished I saw that I must read it to you. Here My Lads your[sic] are all gathered together here are your enimies likewise. and HERE too is the Word of your countrys Salvation

TO THE PEOPLE OF AFRICA

Once again my country men I address my self to you Upon a Subject which I know must be always nearest to your hearts and which I tell you has always been the Nearest to mine. Once again Men of Africa I will write to you of the present state of your country and of its future prospects of your conduct in relation to its Government and of my opinions in regard All these both <as to> past present and to come—When last I addressed my self to you Africans it was from my House at Palm Grove. in Stumpses Isle[80] and there I had retired in exile from a Government of which I had been the head but which contained members I could not for a moment act with and which brought out opinions in which I could not for one moment concurr Willingly I would have staid in Angria but I neither could or dared and now at this time when I look back upon what I did. though I bitterly grieve for the effects of my departure I know that their cause was necessary to preserve my principles and my character. you all know now unless indeed subsequent events have made you forget both my life and me. —you know that I left Angria in the Autumn of last year because the Ministry of Angria had imposed upon my Sovereign and were proceeding with his consent deluded as he was to act in a manner which if successful would at once have destroyed all my hopes for your further prosperity in this Generation this Country and this world they were <alling> themselves to The kings the Constitutionalsits and the Duke of Fidena when I tell you this you will know that I could not consistently with my past life act with them and that you ought not to have done it whatever in reality you have done. —I left them Africans

---

80 See p. 243.

after addressing a body of you in the Harbour Quay of Verdopolis but when I was removed from Africa your Enimies rose into stronger power My King was yet further predjudiced and He published an Address to his people which when I saw it filled me with greif and roused me to anger. I published an address to my people to the people of Africa and there I explained to you the spring of my Actions Vitality! the conduct of his Ministers and the situation of himself. But before my Letter could reach your shores the people of Angria had risen in meetings to darken their monarchs blindness and to sharpen to their rulers swords. Africans I never was dismayed by opposition though I have been born[e] down by calamity I instantly though weary and dejected in mind and body set sail again for Africa and Landed at Adrianopolis on the Opening of its first Parliament their[sic] I heard My Monarchs speech and I noticed its glorious strength of spirit mingled with its ignorance of right. He seemed to me like the fabled Sampson blinded indeed and chained by a faction but still strong in his spirit and bent to work an awful Destruction Ah the Downfall of the idol temple in Palestine[81] was nothing to the Downfall of the Mighty land of Africa. when he had concluded his speech I made one of mine You Africans have not forgotten that speech unless you have forgotten me I know that then you approved of it and that your rulers sunk under it. But My Country men My King was still against me and before I could convince him fully of my intentions he left me for a champaign against the Ashantees on the River Etrei He had reinstated me I know in the Premiership of Angria but I yet would never stoop to act for a moment with the Angrian Ministry I. felt Harrassed and wearied with the struggle and retired to Alnwick hardly knowing what It would be best for me to do. Meanwhile Africans your Monarchs had imposed on you and weep while you hear it. A Government of. what are called High Constitutionalists men whom you would have fought against and against whom I have led you on these people led by the son of one whose name should call the blood to your cheeks with indignation after throughing[sic] the land into a General Election to strengthen their power Assembled your parliament the mockery of your thoughts and opinions. their[sic] the Prime Ministery[sic] made a speech detailing the History of a war where he had nearly ruined your country and I had with Zamorna saved it only perhaps to still greater ruin He hinted to you that he meant to reform your Laws and called upon his Gods to aid him in the undertaking Africans I would [not] have cared for that man or that speech more than I care for the Bee which is buzzing through my room It was Not Fidena which could affect me It was not him which could injure you. —Now When I my countrymen saw the Exertions which your Enimies were making to overthrow you when I saw the ministry they had formed and the deeds they were about to do. I cast aside all <minor> notions of expediency and right and I determined to save my country or fall in the attempt—I Do own Africans and Now Listen to me I Do own that I initiated Quashia to make war upon Angria to divert my kings attention from

---

[81] See Judges 16:23-31.

unthinkingly injuring you I do own that I entered into alliance with the French Republicans because these advocate my principles because their Country is enslaved and because they themselves are Men—I DO OWN that I entered into instant coalition with a faction of people styling themselves Reformers Men willing to own that Africa lay now in bondage men proffessing themselves willing to raise it from that bondage I Do own that I allied myself with people whom I had ever before detested and fought against men whom I had held up as the greatest enimies of Africa whose existence I had declared was an evil in the the unhappy land the[y] lived in—Nay Africans I do Own that I still hated these men that I still thought that the[y] deserved being Hated I do own that I disbelieved their professions of desire to reform that I knew they me[a]nt only to pull down so much of the old tyrant Castle as would give them a breach to enter that I knew they would next strive to repair all whole again and make it if possible stronger than before But I own also Africans that I Believed that I might use these Ardrahians or Reformers with good effects as weapons and batter the Building and Mark you this I did think that when they wished to rush in I with you should be strong enough to Heed them not to proceed alone with our work to pass over the Bodies of those fallen tyrant[s] whom they themselves had slain and then Africans ther[e] should we have set fire to the Stronghold and sent its flames up to Heaven as a Burnt Sacrifice to that Vitality I worship of the the victims we have slain to her name!. —Africans with you I should have done all this But. an unforseen event occured which crushed me into dust. as nothing. My King Zamorna returned home from his succesful campaign on the Etrei repaired to Verdopolis at the head of his wretched counsellors and ministry entered into active cooperation with the Ministry of Fidena and received their impressions respecting me which led him to form the worst possible opinion of me He appeared before me my countrymen in the House of Peers And there he at once commanded me to leave the prospects I have detailed to you to go on with him and with his Constitutionalist allies and advisers Or—to give up the seals of the premiership of Angria in to his hands that very moment. —This Africans this I would have done and have cared not one instant about it or thought it a speck on the pages of my existence But—My Countrymen—He Told us too. that wether I gave up the seals or not. If I did carry on my coalition with Ardrah if I did carry on my designs against Fidena and his slaves. —He would. —Ruin for ever His Queen My only Daughter and far exert himself to oppose and ruin me. —I Rose up in answer my freinds I cannot bear to think with what feelings the impressions I receive are allways strong and here they were both strong and true I know that my misery had nearly destroyed my reason and I fear that I acted as if my reason was destroyed—I know that I exposed at once and with the utmost abroubtness[sic] the springs of my actions that I did not hardly defend them because I could have longed for Destruction I know that I Told Ardrah and the Reformers I hated them and would wish to destroy them. I shewed my king the unutterable agony he had caused to me and I left them in a frame of mind which I would wish never to feel again. —Now Africans when I spoke that Night I spoke nothing but the truth but I spoke it in so abrupt and startling a manner

that I satisfied his feeling I had done what he thought I had done shewed Ardrah
that I hated him and his collegues and that I saw through their Hipocrisy And as
you were all Reformers when you heard me apparently shew myself a cool
hearted traitor to All of you you cast me off from your Heart and joined yourselfs
with your Enimy Ardrah. —Since that time Africans many events have passed
across the world. Fidena has brought out his measures has been beaten by the
power which I aroused and by that power has been compelled to resign. This was
what I wished him to do and would have striven to have accomplished but
Here[sic]—I intended that you and I should have entered into his power Here lay
the evil of my downfall. I was not near and Ardrah and his legion my tools
whom I would have then flung into the fire with their Enimies—Here they
Rushed into his place and filled His Offices with men just as bad they filled
them with themselves And they possessed now a terrible strength in their union
with you they possessed a power attached to them by me a Promethean fire from
my Altar of Vitality I could have trusted in them now to crush and overthrow the
Constitutionalists but I never could trust them to build another fabric for
themselves—Yet what mattered it Africans what or whom I trusted. you had
forgotten and refused to put trust in me! I continued in my solitude at Alnwick
wretchedly miserable at heart because I saw the objects of my life dashed in
peices and my power and my people devoured before my eyes and I could not
turn to aid them or to save myself for If I did my king had sworn to crush my
only hopes and himself to turn against me. It was that king which had ruined me
but it is that king which was perhaps destined to save me to save you to save
himself and the world He has visited me and he has told me that since [h]is
Enimies are increasing in power he will give me leave to rise and crush them
whatever I may do in the end—Now then Africans I may speak now I may act
without immediate certainty that if I stir this world will be at once to me
changed into a wilderness. And now when I look around me when I see you in
the state in which I Do see you when I know who those are who are placed
above you how you still hope to find from them those benifits which they will
no more give to you than they would give the life blood from their hearts Now
My Countrymen Now I again send out my voice among you Now Africans with
All my voice I warn you to ARise you have shaken from you your foes the
Constitutionalists now shake from you your foes the Reformers one brood of
tyrants you have laid on the ground for your own sakes do not raise up another
in their room—Africans you Received the Reform Leaders into your Ranks only
because I asked you to do it they you knew always had been your Enimies. you
cast me from your ranks because you thought I had betrayed you. Because you
thought that my spirit was to thrive <me> Africans I Intreat you to cast out the
Reform Cabinet Because I bid you to Because I have shewn you what they are
And Receive me again to leave you because I have told you who I am. Africans I
intreat [you] to re place Ardrah in my station and me in [h]is Africans
Countrymen I command you to hear me I command you to obey me If ever I
have led on to battle if ever I have advocated your cause through storm and
sunshine if ever I have acted as your leader and received from you one mark of

your approval one note of your applause. Now or never rally round me Now or never defend and save yourselves A wild wreck has been made upon us a mighty scheme has temporarily failed a dreadful evil has been done But this wreck Africans you will repair this scheme you will render sucessful this evil you will far more than remedy if you listen to the letter I have sent for you recoil from the faction which has led you return to the shadow of the Blood red flag of Liberty to the Guidance of your ancient Leader to the accomplishment of your long wished project to the Salvation of your long oppressed Country—Now is the time to save it Africans now is your victory My Country men Attend to the words I have written to you.

Act up to them   NOW OR NEVER.
                                                           Northangerland.

Alnwick Castle
  May 10th 1835

The manner in which the multitude received his Letter the Effect it produced upon them I will not Detail to my readers for I hardly know it my self. time which is developing mighty things will shortly develop this the mightiest and I wait for the Development prepared to act. for My Country

                                                           H Hastings.

                                                           June 15th82
                                                           1835. P B B

Reader however devoid of general interest may be the publications I have hitherto presented to you I can answer almost for this one that its contents shall come home to the hearts and feelings of you all. and I am sorry to say that I take my pen in haste because I see some clouds fast gathering whose aspect I must sketch and whose effects I must describe

On the first day of this present month I received the following note at my lodgings in the Angrian Hotel

"Flower House. Verdopolis June 1st

The Earl of Richton requests Captain Hastings company at Dinner to morrow evening"

---

82 The following section consists of pages 1-6 of an untitled manuscript in the Symington Collection, Rutgers University, catalogued as "THE HISTORY OF ANGRIA I," bound in red morocco. The leaves are folded and laid inside each other.

Short and sweet thought I This High and Mighty Earl then has not quite forgotten me he remembers that theres[sic] is such an one as I am in Verdopolis and at last has mustered enough <curiousity> to see the man to whom he has confided his "Angria and the Angrians." Oh these Noblemen.! —Well excuse this bit of spleen at the airs of Aristocracy I have sometimes felt it But what is that to you. Reader or to me either provided I abstain from Lingual or fistic demonstration.

However on the Afternoon of the second ins^t [in]spite of my Democraticall scornfulness I began to feel a fluttering at the heart as if I was going to be ushered into the presence—No such mean thing I assure for an Angrian farmers son to be admitted to the company and saloon of the Late Ambassador to Angria the Associate of Wellington Zamorna and Fidena a pillar of the <portico> of the constitution a peer a Millionaire and the Historian of Angria and the Angrians. 5 o clock in the Afternoon came on and the anxious palpitation increased in the Ratio of the Hour I walked about the Room unable to set too any thing I tried a book or a newspaper but the[y] seemed distractful and I could not stoop to make out the letters so I contented myself with crossing and stopping before a mirror to examine my Effigies. Blazing in an Angrian uniform of bright Scarlet and White with the golden Sun rising upon a chest of no contemptible power and expansion then when I had surveyed myself from top to toe I turned to count over on my fingers the names of the illustrissimi whom I might perchance behold or to dilate upon my own consequence and think of how the world has praised my book. Haw Haw! cried I courage you can hold up your head with the highest of 'em yet. Anon the clocks struck 6! there was the hour so on with my hat. up on my horse and I trotted through the Aristocratic streets and squares up to the front of the statly pillared mansion at the head of Rosses place. 2 or three carriages had set down just before I came up and when I ·alighted a servant in blue and orange Livery took the Animal into his care and keeping up the grand flight of steps I marched like a "Stormer" and gave in my Name. whereupon I was wafted under the portal. through a Noble Marble Hall at the head of which an extremly wide flight of steps rose to a magnificent landing in front of a Noble Coloured Window and then branched winding up on either hand with bronze and gilded balustrades and carpets whose softness drowned the slightest sound of footsteps marshalled by a footman I walked briskly up with muffled tread. till he ushered me in[to] a silent Ante Room and here he whisked off leaving me to cool my brains amid the courtly elegance of the Airy apartment. I walked about upon eggs as it were surveying the rich Hangings and luxurious sophas or looking from the (shall I call them windows those large lucid sheets of glass with their slender divisions of Rose wood) then I sat down on a yeilding sopha. but I did not <win> rest and the contrast was too great between its ease and my restlessness. volo I muttered these Noblemen and their servants do the[y] count hours as minutes! But Hush! a sound. the door opens I rise up and in steals a thing in a muslin frock black shoes and <moncy> hair streaked over its eyes and forehead with the fingers of one hand sucked into its mouth and those of the other pulling down its frock from one shoulder it marched hesitatingly forward upon its heels in true Aristocratic nonchalance But when it observed me stand erect to address it the creature gave a well bred stare. and turning round effected a hasty retreat from the room I resumed my seat in about 5 minutes more. the door opened again and the same being loitered in with 3 or 4 sisters and brethern at its tail marching up toward me with a circumgyrating motion and jostling one another with their shoulders and taking keen observations as they took their ground about me "Who are you" asked a gentleman in Blue and white the Heir as I conjectured of the mansion "May I return your question Gentlemen and Ladies by asking who you are." "Does Pa— know 'nt youre he—are" asked one in a frock and sash with a truely fashionable drawl But her Brother cried. "He has'nt told me yet what are you putting out your tongue for" "I am'nt putting out my tongue" "She did" "A! what a lie" "A for shame! a for shame." "Shes told a fib!" "She hasnt" "She has" "She hasnt" "She has" "you tell fibs" "and so do you" but how long this altercation would have risen or in what it would have ended I know not the disputants were getting unco feirce. But a step was heard out side and anon Lord Richton entered the room I have before stated that I had seen a very Agreeable elegant and Lordly Gentleman who after conversing with me most affably in the house of commons calmly walked into the peers benches when we entered the house of Lords. Judge reader of my utter suprise when I beheld here before me and no mistake that very man I stood unable to speak. while His Lordship. advanced with a peculiar smile as if guessing the cause of my astonishment after ordering from the room the clamourous group of elves who ran round him complaining and maligning each other he said to me "I believe Captain Hastings and I are not quite unaquainted at least if my identity is unknown to him his is known to me so that you see Sir your fame has already eclipsed my own but indeed Captain I owe you an apology for not requesting the pleasure of your company much sooner. I must plead as my excuse that the proceedings of the late election and the changes consequent upon the overthrow of the Ministry so entirely swallowed up my time that I had not an hour to spare from the tedious routine of buisness. we shall need no formal introduction since I know you from your works and allow me to say that the manner in which you have taken up my rambling idea has given me the purest pleasure and the most real satisfaction I have only a small party to meet you at dinner to day but you are no stranger to any of them for they have read your works and as I do they admire them" such were the expressions with which his Lordship greeted me and leaving little time for my embarrasment to answer he led me toward the Dining Hall conversing most affably the while upon my literary prospects As we entered the lofty and splendid Room I cast a troubled look to the company seated at table First I saw shining in full and fashionable Dinner costume the Countess of Richton apparently a fine fashionable Lady with large dark eyes and pleasant smile on the left of the Earls seat sat another body whose Richtonian looks convinced me that she must be his sister <Miss> Caroline Flower who report whispers will shortly change her title to Lady Caroline Pelham. To these two personages and to the Gentlemen at table the Earl of Richton introduced me as Captain Hastings of the 19th and first one of the visitors came up to me whom I felt to my hearts core to be my High and Mighty Landlord. W H Warner Esqr M P Home Secretary for Angria &c &c "I tell you" said he with the high and rapid tones which <erst> had bowed my spirit when he visited my fathers farm and without alighting gave his comments at the gate while we stood awed and curious afar off. "I tell you that you have pleased me much by your work. it contains nothing I dissaprove of and you deserve a reward." "And I approve of your work while with me at any rate Captain" said Lord Hartford my commander "I have seen a little of you before Hastings and do not need introduction" "Well I answered "I feel overpowered enough those whom I see here are so much my superiors and I have so long been taught to look up to them that you must excuse me if I fail in self possession my Landlord the cheif ruler of my country my Colonel a peer of Angria My literary employer a leader of the Tories. these other Noblemen. —Gentlemen all such Magnates of Africa and by whom 6 months ago I should not dream of being spoken to! —Excuse me my Lady if I fail in the ease and conduct to be expected from my proffession" "I can almost excuse Mr Hastings any thing after the pleasure he has afforded me." And so with a deep bow to her Ladyship I resumed my place at the table. I could not eat much it was no use trying if nothing else could keep my teeth closed the sight of the "Great Squire's" thin pale face and wild restless eye just opposite would have done it and was I sitting down to eat with him! I looked to see if my legs were longer. The party present was quite private not more than a dozen. But select in conscience. I noticed the famous Sir J W Bud. the Tutor of Northangerland in one seat and Northangerlands as famous son in another As for the Earl at the Head of the table he filled me with admiration at his urbane and cheerful address in keeping up mirth and good humour And my Noble General Thornton and my Awful Commander Enara. there they both were reminding me most strongly of the Etrei and Benguela

"Different quarters these Mr Hastings" said the General with a hearty smile. "and different again to what we got in the latter end of the winter I dar[e]say you havent forgotten what you saw at yon wild land or what you did either I am sure I havnt."

"Why" replied Warner with what was meant for a smile "The young— M—Officer cannot forget that to which he owes his promotion and prospects."

"And I my wound and a bit of the Rheumatize—but hawsiver it wor a glorious time out we hed. and a <decent>"

"Are we not" said Richton "a real mess table now Gentlemen for positivly without intending it I have got together a set of soldiers there are 10 of us. Thornton Enara Hastings Hartford Bud Myself. all militaired Pelham Warner Percy Halford civilians we have 2 of a majority. and Halford and Warner wavering"

"I always thought" interposed Pelham "that Verdopolis was a highly military Nation

And I" said Warner "always thought that it should be so"

"Why Howard I should have classed you with the soldiers here for you are one in earnest."

"I Glory to say that I have seen warlike service." As the Head of the House of Warner said so his bright eye[s] flashed brighter and all the enthusiastic in his nature rose in his excited glance.

"By the cross" said Enara looking keenly at him "and Howard will be soldier yet in earnest"

Edward Percy only interjected. "Then he will be a D—d fool.!"

After Dinner was concluded we All retired into the Earls Library and as I went last I could not help noticing the very walk and bearing of the company I had got into I said when I took my seat.

"I must confess that I feel slightly embarrassed amid persons who call up so many thoughts and ideas to my mind. and you must excuse my diffidence among Founders of an Empire Heads of parties. men intertwined with History Tutors of Northangerland and Masters of Zamorna Really sirs the ideas of the actions you have done the persons you have been connected with the persons whom you are now far to overwhelm the son of an Angrian farmer."

And. added the Earl. "The Author of the Campaign of the Calabar."

"Aye" said Enara "and that thought should bring you Sir into full companionship with us I make no doubt you remember your service for and I have never told you it yet. you have so justly described that service your work Captain Hastings is as good a picture of the operations as you can paint and I am qualified to judge for I saw every scene and perhaps with more coolness than you could do at least my acquaintance with such work has been longer and in that trade few novices shew much coolness"

"Aye its a rough job feighting I know I thought so when I first handled a Bayonet in the buisness It wor at this very city and not mony streets off. I wor then nobbut 19 years old and had just entered the army under my canting knave of a brother and it was in the great insurrection that I first smelled gunpowther I recolleck. our rejiment with the born D—l my brother at the head on us came smashing up Northgate wi myseln as ensign in the varry front of em I thought mony a time Id run just to spite John and then I reckollecked that if I did I sould spite myseln too so I bit my tongue and determined to stand true and besides we had i my company a score or two of young lads that I knew whom it would [not] do to run fro. we were all a horseback as proud as kings and I had as nice a nag as ivver I handled i my life I wor a prince then ye know. a prince of the royal blood. forbye John always wad hev his legs astride o' horse back. but hes nought but conceit. Well we drave forrard we a rattle and aw wore fain to mak a clatter to help me on wi it. there wor sich a serious roaring o guns in the distance and soon it werent ith distence nother for we lap full gallop into a whirry of smoke and fire and sich cracks as no man iver hurd afore. Ive since gotten weel used to fighting by the Northern rebellion and the campaign in Angria and this other onth Etrei but I can nivver see old Sdeath there withaat a grin for there we wor we his hands in his pockets and his pistol in his teeth walking amang th' shot as cool as a cucumber John cut through em but hawsivver it wer nobbut to get into a new hobble"

"We should make said Pelham a complete military history of the last 40 years among us. from Bud to Hastings. —I think. Bud is our veteran."

"Yes" answered the portly and pleasant looking Tutor and Historian. "I think I am the oldest of you it is 43 years since [I] first took musket on my shoulder and thats a long time back for our country I am now 64 years old and the first time I ever handled musket was in the winter of 92. under old Bobbadil[83] against the French Turks and Spaniards Oh dear we had some rough work. I shall not soon forget our storming of Doverham at midnight in a thundershower when the tempest was raging and the lightning flashing above us the cannons roaring and balls flying around us mines exploding under our feet and Bayonets <glanced> before our eyes. But Enara he stands next in the History he has seen something too he beats us all I fancy

"Well Bud but the wars of the settlers were rough spots of work. I entered service. at 14 years old and it is now 26 years since. It was in a campaign against the Ashantees of the North frontier our work lay under His Majesty of the North among the Branni hills and along the Banks of the North river. I have never since then seen that stream and I almost fancy it Dyied now in blood. I recollect the the building of Northfort whose foundations were laid in battle for while we were engaged on it the Ashantees attacked the place. and while the ceremony was performing within the ring of soldiers the Battle was raging around them without—The Savages might well feel affrighted at the erection of that fort for ever since it has proved a noble scourge to them in that farroff quarter I was there 10 years ago quartered as Governor and then I did not catch a dozen in a quarter to ornament the wall Those terrible mountains lessened my height for I was then as tall as I am now but the fatigue of our operations among their moors snows and marshes cut off. 5 or 6 inches for anything I knew of my stature. I promised for 6 feet two or three. and am 5—9 or 10. But Jesu! they did not cut away my power of endurance or infliction—Maria! I got my sinews there!

"Hartford an I." said Richton "come next and we both entered the Army 12 years ago But Garrison duty and suppressions of Robbers (your pupils followers Bud.) with pleasant quarters at the cities of the Empire took up the first 5 years of our employment it was in a row with the French who attempted a landing at Mouthton in 26. that first shewed what pith we had in us

"I Sirs. determined." cried Warner "To act as a soldier for my country first in the Rebellion 6 years ago when I raised a rejiment of volunteers in my native district and laid them at the service of the General Union. I. only led back. 600 out of the 1000 and have not to this day received a thousand pounds for them except the wounded.

---

[83] This campaign is part of the early history of the settlers and is not covered in Branwell's earlier work; the inclusion of Turks and Spaniards would seem to be a bit of Branwellian revisionism. For Bobadill, see vol. I, p. 93, n. 5.

"And Ive told already that I shewed fight when Warner did" added the General.

"Well Gentlemen I come in my act. the last of all for the first foe l have met was on the Banks of the Benguela in the January of this present year."

"Stop Mr Hastings not so fast" interrupted Mr Percy sneeringly "I am the last of all for I have not yet seen the face of [the] enimy and heaven willing I dont mean to do it either

Such a sentence displeased Mr Warner "Not so fast Mr Percy not so fast" he said himself fast enough and spreading his hands over the table "How sir! can you not see that ere long you will have to face more enimies than if (I judged only of your character by your last words) you would ever dare to face I tell you sir that the time is fast approaching when one heart willing to face danger will be worth 10 heads desirous to avoid it. I tell you we are approaching dangerous times Sir and wether hands will be wanted I know not But I do know that hearts will!"

"Well Warner and I suppose that in the expectation of obtaining a sale you are exposing your own hands on that table and your heart on your tongues end."

"Sir do not jest upon this topic I tell you it is too serious for jest when measures are now scheming which if put into practice would render your property and my property and all property not worth a cracked halfpenny even if our lives were thrown into the bargain I say it is neither time nor occasion to jest"

"The D—l Warner and who is it that is bringing on this state of things My own D—d father and my own silly king and when my parent and my monarch lead me on what right have I to stop for fear"

"Sir your king is not silly he is not silly I—I wish—I had rather he were he is wicked Sir blindly and foolishly I allow but yet folly is not the foundation of his conduct it is undisguised and profligate wickedness!" The Home Secretarys features whitened and his eyes flashed. he rose and walking quickly through the Apartment continued rapidly and warmly

"And you have little right to call him silly Sir he is your king and your relative.—" Edward the Woolstapler broke out into a laugh "I repeat he is your brother in law the husband of a sister whom you ought to be proud to call sister—"

"Ought I! By G—d!"—"I say you ought to be proud to call his wife your Sister and himself your Brother for I tell you he is the most ardent spirited has the most lofty views could execute the most daring actions of any man in this our age his views in Church Government are undeniably perfect his spirit I dare you to question he has a noble hatred for much that is hateful Oh this execrable Northangerland could I but get him free of his influence.! he may foam at me and contradict me as he likes but I call it influence. I say the wretched profligate has made him self appear in My Kings eyes other than he really is and—" —"And I say that Warner Howard Warner has made the Duke of Zamorna appear in his eyes other than he really is. why you restless little viper what has introduced all this nonsense into your unappeasable brain and what is all this company gathered together here for not to hatch treason I hope for when the[y] listen to such a lecture as yours I must say I doubt them and the more for listening under the roof of a smooth double faced Janus like Richton the freind of Lofty and Arundel.!"

His Majesty Adrian the first king of Angria disposed of himself quickly among our astonished group. laying hold of the transfixed Warner by the Arm with his long slender fingers and enjoying the suprise of his sudden appearance among us.

"Caught in the fact" he said "And stunned and stupefied too caught in an evil fact. and to be hanged and dissected." All my subjects—except 2 or 3 too bad for subjects all plotting evil against the lords annointed—Well my masters do you know that I have paid a visit to this Arch Rascal and Renegade this very evening and am but now come from thence" Warner flinched from his Graces grasp and writhed as if heart struck. Mr Percy called out.

"And go back again for its the only place youre fit for"

"Nothing of the sort Gentlemen I am fit for any where for any where receives me the Ladies in the Drawing room below the children in the Nursery Ive had my own way in both cases and now for the gentlemen (hem!) in the Library Ill have my own way here!" As he spoke both jewelled hands laid hold on Warner who was about to depart. and fairly pinned him to the sopha. —"I say Halford[84] Do you see the Earl. he is worse again."

"I see him every morning your Grace. He is sadly shattered. and I cannot tell how to recover him whatever remedy I propose is us[e]less. he will not exercise he will not enter company or divert his mind in any manner the only thing which would arouse him I of course as an African will never advise him to adopt.

"But I will Halford. for a beat at the Ardrahians he shall have if I can loose him on them"

"And then he shall cool in jail. with all his abettors D—n him"

"Why Mr Percy he tried that before and it did him little good for any thing I know he may try it again and I fancy with still less effect when I called this morning the Countess only was in the Breakfast parlour And she told me that he was constantly either thinking to himself. or if writing he took raw spirits every 10 minutes to keep himself to the point of labour that <day> Newspapers he never read[s] except when her ladyships herself read to him that his Dejection in the morning was extreme. But toward evening he often rallied that breakfast he never took while tea seemed his principal hold for support after it he conversed more cheerfully and as another thing which Her Ladyship and as I said justly conceived to be the principal reason of his not sinking under his life. He always slept soundly though his sleep was short. indeed. his former life with

---

[84] Sir Henry Halford was physician to Mrs Charles Arbuthnot, a close friend of the Duke of Wellington. See Alexander CB I, 6 and 25.

all its wild vissicisitudes taught him to seize slumber when he could and the accumstomed trouble and monotony of his existence wearied him out ere night. The Countess said that He never dreams but often now changes in expression of countenance. and as Her Ladyship rightfully again conjectured from his use of spirits acting on the nerves Indeed I told Lady Northangerland that she seemed as well qualified to watch his case as myself. No she said He himself was better able than either but Events changed him more than all As to his only actual complaint palpitation of the Heart or Angina pectorus that only appeared in paroxisms after unusually severe Mental and Bodily agitation and she expected it after a short time now I added that as to his total loss of appetite could that be cured much might be done But it cannot your Grace I believe it is only one effect in 20 of a shattered constitution and general decline And it is well that it is so for if [as] strong in corporeal as in mental power the country would have much to fear."

"Well then I say Doctor." cried the manufacturer of Zamorna who had listened with a curl of the lip. "You'll take care not to give him the chance of mischeif you understand. the D—l Africa is not to stand chance of such [a] deplorable event. D—n the fellow"

"Halford." said his Grace. "Recover him if you can for in his recovery the country at present would have nothing to fear. you are mistaken Ardrah and the Reformers might tremble but neither you or. I."

"Sir your Grace. I tell you we all should have all to fear I should feel it no sin to pray for his Death. Hardly a sin for you Doc—"

"Go on Warner" said Enara looking blackly. "But not so. let him meet. me. for I have an account to settle with him.

"But he shall meet me for I have a larger one first. and speaking of accounts. I have some to settle with others too So I'll off Richton to 'change. and good night to 11 12^{ths} of you" So speaking Mr Edward departed and in a while the company broke up his Grace. the Duke only declaring that He would stay with Richton to supper and Richton himself. desiring me to call upon him ere long again

I returned Home for my own part. thinking much of myself and everything else as far as I saw. I had that day been initiated into mighty company and in fact had sat and spoken with my King Whereever Zamorna was matters were sure to pass of with eclat. So that this Dinner at Flower house was secure from being forgotten to memory And after looking back in my own mind the aspect appearance and mind and conversation of the Great men I had. left. I could not help feeling that with these at their head the freinds of our Constitution might hope for triumph over both Ardrah and Northangerland the fragments of their conversation which I have given above is far from the pith of what they said but only a little <discourse> which shewed their temper and the feeling they bore to each other

x x x x x x x x x x x x x x
x x x x x x x x x x x x x x x x x   June 25th
                                          1835 P B B.

Well Reader what shall I say now times are blackning events are thickening
above us and not in the horizon only but in the meridian arch of heaven As my
intention in troubling you at all with these lines of my inditing is to give you
my fresh and vivid impressions of the present history of our Nation had I not
best at once without other circumlocution enter now upon the detail of the
events which have happened and which I have seen this day.

It is now a[sic] ten nights since I before wrote a fortnight since I visited
Flower House and During that fortnight the principal event which has occured
you are by this time no doubt all aware of the 5 penny work called "The Duel"[85]
[which] has made you fully aware of the origin rise and end of that singular and
unhappy quarrel But the constitutions of the two sufferers are made of cast iron
their equality of strength was shewn in the Pedestrian match of Angria and this
fortnight [h]as further shewn that their powers have not since suffered reduction
though the Duke of Zamorna has suffered a broken arm and wounded shoulder.
and Edward Percy received balls in his head and side. still both I believe are now
up and doing almost as active as any of their active people—for my own part
during this fortnight I have employed my time in doing what I have yet through
2 or 3 months had no time or leisure for. I have seen the principal sights of the
city Tower of Nations St Michaels Cathedral Citadel Harbour palaces of the
kings museums picture Galleries Theatres Operas Concerts & all the splendid et
cetera of the most splendid city in the world. Various Great Men I have seen and
great Women too some Reader[s] I have spoken too and that better still indeed I
have been present at assemblies Both in Thornton Hotel Warner Hotel and
Hartford House. There is one person however whom till this Day I have not seen
though him I much desired to see I allude to that melancholy scoundrel the Earl
of Northangerland But of him more Anon.

During the whole of this past fortnight his Lordships Emissaries have
been activly at work throughout the city and country preaching down alike
Constitutionalist[s] and Ardrahians and Angrians. Richard Na[u]ghty M
Berrandotte[sic]. M Dupin M Barras. and others have been making tours and
speeches in aid of the Great Fox who is to come in between the Dear[sic] and
Lion to steal away the prey Several of the Newspapers moved no doubt by
means which need not be mentioned have fulminated away eaten words and held
up a brazen front in favour of the newrisen Demagogue. And as the grand chef D'
oeuvre of the whole Early on the morning of the 12th inst. Great Blood coloured
placards were posted in every possible part of Verdopolis. Bearing the following
words emblazoned on each sanguine front

---

85   There is no evidence of either Branwell or Charlotte having written such a
work.

MEN OF AFRICA
Be present in Elrington Square
Verdopolis.
At 6 o clock on the evening
of Friday June 19th 1835
To—Hear.
The Right Hon The EARL of NORTHANGERLAND
Explain to you
The Character and measures of.
The present Government
of your Country
And bring before the only true parliament
A Bill for the reform of the Verdopolitan
NAVY

Here was the trumpet Note of preparation and during the whole of the following week the populace were plied with incendiary writing and speaking from various satellites and underworkers while the Authorities were kept on the watch for breakers of the peace and the Ministerial prints directing all their venom against Rougue and his Machinations the Constitutionalists in general kept aloof with hands clean from contact with the Traitor But it was more than hinted that among this number was not the Duke of Zamorna his Graces weakness forbad activity but it was said his heart was with the Destroyer of Ardrah whoever this should be Hereupon the Papers and conversations fecund with dark hints of a split in the Angrian Cabinet. those who ought to know best affirmed that all that Ministry at heart whished to have nothing to do with Northangerland or his crew but since Adrian had made up his mind to run in couples with him. Arundel Castlereagh and Enara determined to follow their king while Mr Warner the virtual Premeir who could not think of deserting him or yet of following was trying with all his might to Hold him back. Thornton it was said yet wavered and Mr Percy held back indeed As for the Late Ministry of Verdopolis with all the Great Noblemen and Gentlemen in their interest and the kings wether Whig or Tory They regarded Northangerland as an enimy whom no power on earth should induce them to conciliate. The people why the people surged like a boiling ocean and that is all I can say of them.

On the Evening of. Thursday the 18th when I. returned through Verdopolis from a journey to Freetown and the glorious valley I could see very plain that excitment had risen to 85 in the shade. Now Blood red Placards in hundreds assumed the places of their faded and half destroyed progenitors. and as another feature in the scene broad yellow and orange papers to flared out on every street and shop window with the following announcement.

REFORMERS OF AFRICA.
I pledge Myself.
That the instant that

Renegade Northangerland
Has concluded vociferating
I will Rise—
And in your prescence
Confute every word he says.
Shew up his Blackened Treachery
And adorn the Tree of Reformation
with fresh flowers of. truth and.
Liberty.
signed. H M M Montmorency
June 17th
1835.

I passed that evening through Elrington Square and beheld workmen erecting a spacious Hustings in front of the splendid Elrington Hall while directly opposite another was in progress for the yellows and their speaker Montmorency. A great blood red flag was waving over the portico of the Mighty Mansion but what use was there in further gaze who could tell from that pillared building the state and projects of the stormy mind within it was with some emotion though that my eyes wandered over the rows of windows behind their lofty columns as if unconsciously seeking for the one where the Rebel Lord might be.

Night came on. then morn and with it the fated 19th Day of June what were the feelings of the men in power the Reformers the Maritimes at breakfast that Day wether their ruler the Marquis of Ardrah sat with accustomed relish or looked for ward to evening as a time of pleasure I will not undertake to answer let me speak for my self and I do say that I looked forward with interest The hour of Dinner arrived hastily I swallowed a few mouthsful for past the windows of my Hotel I saw the crowds of people already filing past in shoals and what I particularly noticed above every thing else was the numbers of Rare Apes and men from the country whose strong rough forms mingled so thickly with the more dashing citizens I sallied forth at 1/2 past 5 and repaired to the Square where the crowds were thickening every instant having secured a good place on a sort of hustings not far from the Great one. I resolved to stand and view the sight around me twice before I had seen a Verdopolitan crowd and twice I have said that none other is to be seen like it. here was a third but I need not particularly describe it there were thousands here and thousands upon thousands. Orange Crimson Scarlet and Bloodred favours mingled in the tumultous confusion. at 7 o clock. the yellow Hustings began to fill with the Ministerial grandees and leaders amid the hoarse applause of their partisans. Shortly after 6 or 7 foreign looking persons sallied forth from the portals of the Great Hall and mounted the bloodred Hustings then a Dozen Lawyers and Minions with a huge Old Giant and a scurvy old rascal. the two factotums Naughty and Sdeath. people were all expecting the cheif when there mounted a Gentleman supported by a page and wrapt in a black military cloak and cavalry Helmet What a horrid and universal groan was that which greeted his appearance how haughtily he bore himself advancing to the very front of the Hustings was there none to Applaud him! where were the Angrians to shout long live Zamorna? The Balconies and windows of Elrington Hall were adorned as by exotic flowers with a Brilliant Display of. Aristocratic Beauty. evur[sic] Thought I it is that women stay where men forsake. for these all appeared in honour of the Duke of Zamorna. some great men I did see there who ought to have been round their king but lowering concern for his rashness now clouded brows which erewhile I have know[n] opposed for his sake to the hottest storm of Battle

Ere I was aware. Another Person stood in the full front of the Bloody hustings But the Roars of Hate and Triumph rose in such deafning volleys that I could hardly steady my eyes to see him Amid astounding clamour and waving of hats around. he stood not bowing like a parliamentary candidate. But tall and solemnly with his head uncovered and his high bald forehead. pale features and sunken eye. —My sight almost grew dim while I felt in my mind that I saw before me the immortal Alexander Percy immortal for his greatness and crimes that there stood the curse of Africa the root of all our evils for 20 bygone years And yon was the Man. who drenched this very city in blood. who threw all the North in to civil war. that was the Drover the Pirate the Robber the Bankrupt the Prime Minister the General the subject of such wondrous and mighty changes the causer of such terrible and ceasless change. the scenes of that life which have become scenes of History painting and poetry crowded on me his sunny childhood His troubled youth. His wrecked and wrecking Manhood. I saw the Husband of Augusta, Mary, Zenobia, and where are names more known than that. I looked with intrest to the very wasted hands whose touch had so often awoke such noble music. the form which had wandered through so many climes. the eyes which had seen such scenes of sorrow love or danger. which had looked on persons and events and crimes and terrible Battles. which we all can only see in our imagination and by the eye of our mind certainly these feelings came vividly before me as I this day first beheld Northangerland. —I had never seen him save once on the occasion of that terrible speech from the Man who stood next behind him when all his spirit was withered within him then I thought he could not recover from its effects and yet here he stood again sunk and wasted it is true but ought not this to be expected after <u>his</u> life But yet. again rousing a land to agitation and making one bold throw to gain power in that land again this which I was now to behold was to be but a agitation of all the terrible struggles which have so often placed him on the pinnacle of power and from which he has been so often dashed to the very ground

His Lordship. seemed attired in a black frock coat light waistcoat and the red ribbon round his neck while his profuse orange whiskers and severe lips contrasted strangly with the melancholy of his forehead and his eyes. His <u>servants</u> Mesers Shaver and Steeton <u>MP,s</u>.! stood on each hand of him and the pale Dark. Monarch of Angria with (for the first time and with horror seen by me) the Ancient feind Sdeath. in a rusty coat and greasy breek. side by side the nearest. next. Immense Old Naughty towered above the french Gentlemen and behind ranged a row of Agents of. the Pit

And now for the main act of the Day. the Earl. gave his hat to Shaver—and at once. rose up a hoarse roar of hate and greeting again Oh How I wished it to cease how I wanted to hear that voice.! —He did not bow but turned from the Duke of Zamorna to the people and. —I heard. that solemn voice. the signal of such. ruin past. sound on my ear.

"I. am glad to hear that shout. Because from it were I blind I should know what thousands of Africans are assembled to hear me speak. And since Gentlemen you come here to learn things concerning your own interests and well fare I will at once commence the detail of what I know respecting them—Your own interests and welfare Gentlemen! Why I say where are they? or who regards them now? you thought of your own interests when you followed me 5 years ago to a struggle which was not destined to suceed you thought of your interests when not 2 years ago you rose up in arms to defend a country which the phantom like weakness of its rulers was letting hurry down to destruction Nay you even <u>thought</u> of your own interests when scarc[e] 2 months ago you drove me from among you as a leper or an Achan of your camp. But—Have you thought of your own interests when ever since my departure you have supinly allowed your Enimies to entrench themselves in your very Citadel. To grasp that rod of scorpions whose lash is yet severer than the blow of the Tyrants who have given way yes you tell me—you did think of your interests in allowing those men to ride you and direct you for they swore they would direct you to happiness and peace—Ha well and why have they not set forth on their journey and why delay so the march of prosperity. —My Countrymen! they have bestridden you as a Butcher bestrides a calf. and like him they mean to divert you to the slaughterhouse to kill you and devour your flesh as meat—Here it is where I am come to tell you that you have not attended to your interests. But Africans Another Hour shall shew you that you have Attended to your interests in coming here this day to listen to my speech, Blinded to them you may be now Blinded I fear you are But. I will flash such a light upon your eyes as not all the clouds of ignorance and Despotism can ever darken or cause to fade away. —Africans the error in which you at present lie with regard to your present rulers consists In your Belief that they have assumed place and power for the sole purpose of benifiting the people <afirming> all abuse in Laws and Offices Diminishing Taxation restoring the church to its state of primitive simplicity sixty days have they now been in place and power—Need I repeat again that those 60 days are sixty Nights for all the good they will ever do to you—Sixty days! My Sons! in that time what good would I have worked for you! (tremendous cheers) Give me sixty days of Office my Countrymen and my head and my heart. would work a change for the Better in our Government which not sixty ages could. moulder or sweep away. —But let us not now look to what might be done let us discover what has been or rather has NOT been done. I know that the Reform Ministry has entered the places of the Conform Ministry. That the Marquis of Ardrah has

taken the Premiership that a host of Scotchmen Sailors and Traitors fill every minor disposable office That a regular attendance has been kept up at the Treasury Office but. that there has been attendance on nothing more. And I Dare That Government All or singly to produce one fact in opposition to these which I have asserted I confidently challenge them to prove one assertion a lie—And Now my Countrymen listen to what I say. You All believe that this present Ministry has done you no good will do you none and can do you none you believe that its continuance in Office is prejudicial to your best interests and prosperity—Well you Believe[d] exactly so of the Late Ministry and because you believed you Rose up and ejected them from office. But by what means did you eject them from office. —Why you tryed along[sic] time the Legal course of meeting and petitioning and explaining your miserys and intreating for redress. But to this their flinty hearts would not soften. Next you tried threats and manifestations and displays of phisical force you Demanded your rights and you fought to obtain them. But what cared they for to this their flinty skulls would not break. Then last you bethought you that the best manner for you to work upon their selfish spirits. was to prove to them that their <   > was rotten the citidel decaying their foundations in the air and their superstructure mouldering to the ground. you exposed to them all the weak points in their strong places you shewed them their great corruptions in Church and State and War their contemptible peculation their reverence for rottenness and Death. their care in preserving laws which had rusted and crumbled. or which only continued keen to destroy. And when they saw what a frightful heap of corruption they had ensconced themselves in That Ministry and faction fled frightedly from a power which I hope they will never grasp which I trust never shall be grasped again
Well my freinds when you rushed to that last sucessful attack. you deposed from his trust the General who had so long led you and who was then leading you to victory you gave the command in to the hand of some loud tongued much promising proselytes who boldly led the way before you. ensonced themselves in the Castle and Down with the portculis against you and all their cannon levelled at you once more—So—Africans! —you Believe this Squad of Reformers to be just as rotten just as tyrannical just as Bad. as the set they have expelled and If you believe this if you see that they have taken the same pose and hold it in the same manner Why My Countrymen Arise and eject them and eject them by the same means which ejected the former ones. and if you wish you shall have the same General to lead you on even though he may suffer the same disgrace again My freinds shew up to the present Government the corruptions the[y] hide and the corruptions the[y] feast on and the corruptions they stand on. and. they will quickly fly away to H—l! I it was who shewed you the Evils of the former men. And I will shew you the evils of the present. I know them and they know I know them—Africans! I know them well!! for me to think this night my freinds of. exposing all the Reform Abuses and corruption in all the Ramifications of < > would be absurd because not 10 shuch as I in ten such nights before 10 such meetings could do it fully and openly. But Africans If my arm be strong enough. (stretching forth his. own muscular arm. above them) and it has proved of effect

in your battles. and your cause. if this Arm serves me as well as it has done I will this Night grasp the monstrous serpent and strangle it before your eyes. —There is the Wide Sea Before me. and once again over that wide sea I will sail! —I know and you know Aye and they know too that above every thing else the Management of the Admiralty is what the party now in power have most wholly had in their hands and the point in which they have been most infamously trustless. Gentlemen the Admiralty Board of our country is not like the Admiralty Board of any other country. it does not confine its powers to the surveillance of our vessels of war. it is an engine of vast power and its feild embraces half our confederacy. Let me first explain to you the scope of its influence and next the manner in which that influence is employed.

My Country men! Forty 5 years ago when in 1790 the Land was first divided. the Government first establishd and the constitution arranged in a tangible shape. The Whole economy of the state was divided into 4 great heads the Church the <country> the Army and the Navy. with as their directors. Gravi Sneachi Wellington. and Parry. cum Ross. On the 3 first divisions I could have much to say but I must lay them aside for the present and confine myself to the Monster Mass the Navy under. Parry and Ross this Branch of the Government formed a board called the Board of Admiralty of whom. His Majesty William Edward was director in the office of Lord High Admiral. and John. of Rossesland. Acting Cheif Admiral of the fleet. In the first place. every vessel of war built by the General Government of the Confederacy. was with all of its crews and officers placed in the power of the Admiralty Court and. could only act under their directions Here were the instruments with which to work! Now secondly. these Instruments of the fleet of the Confederation Blockaded every port in the Union without their permission and unsearched by them No Vessel for trading or other purposes could pass out of port. It was their duty to examine wether they were engaged unlawfully in french service. (mind that was the Bugbear then!) The fleet likewise kept up a constant cruise upon the coasts of frenchiland established posts all down the west coast of Africa. and kept in station off Stumpz and Monkays and the Mauns and Wamons Isles. Thirdly. The Admiralty recognized as its peculiar property for the use and convenience of the fleet. Ascension Isle. with its fort and magazines. Parris Isle, Juan Fernandez. the mouth of the Congo of the Camaroones and an Ivory Station on the coast of Angola. from which 9/10th of the Ivory used in Africa is usually exported.[86] Fourthly The Board of Admiralty. and mark the power they possessed here. possessed full controul over all the custom house and Maritime Excise Offices. the Officers were appointed and paid and instructed by them the Houses were under their inspection and all export and import duties passed through their hands to the Treasury.

---

[86] During Branwell's time, Luanda and Benguela were the major shipping points of ivory. In 1832, 3000 lbs. passed through Benguela, by 1834 the figure was 105,000 lbs.

Now I have said that the Admiralty Board. weilded all this power and that its head was the Head of the Fleet of War that. this was the King of Parrysland. But my freinds as the light of knowledge spread among us we saw the evils of kings obtruding themselves into the executive departments of our Government Therefore Wellington was forced to quit hold of the Army. Sneachi of the Trade. (lodged afterwards in a Treasury board) and. oh how reluctantly! Parry and Ross of this Noble Navy Now these kings were too cunning for us yet for though they gave way themselves they took care that their families should not suffer. Wellingtons son was yet at school or somewhere worse. Sneachis office was swept away so Fidena was comfortably lodged in command of the Army. As to the Church that. department is pristine purity cannot change Gravi was and is and shall be there till—But never mind. Parry gave up the office of Lord High Admiral to his son a youth 21. years old and Ross his office of. Acting Cheif Admiral to his son a youth of. 24 Now Against the Constitution of the Navy Board as just now sketched by me I have nothing particular to state it was a good powerful comfortable mass of Duties all very well It. duly performed All very effective. If. not tainted with corruption. But this I have to urge against it and against all its fellow Branches of Government That it was most disgracfully yes and most intentionally liable to corruption And by. this world. its rulers took care to make the best of the liability—10 or 15 years ago My Countrymen when the corruptions of the Navy were spring[ing] up like mushrooms and ripening into alas not Mushroom maturity! I was myself. thrown by events into the most intimate connection with maritime affairs and all the feild of which I have spoken. I know that ere I stepped my foot on a Deck. I saw much to dislike in our Government and Monarchy but when I was initiated by circumstances into the mysteries of the Admiralty. my Dislike arose shortly into incontrollable disgust. I threw aside the shackles of those Atrocious laws and Mounting that flag of Liberty which has so long waved and which even now waves over me. I determined to set aside the power which only acted for evil and devote my energy to my own preservation and the release of my oppressed country. (tremendous cheers and hisses followed this masterpeice of <analysis>)

Well Africans and what was the state of Our Navy. 10 years ago. really I can hardly tell you I know not how to grasp the porcupine its back is so full of prickles Let me first look over it as connected with War. with that with which it should alone be connected. well here. The General Fleet of All the Countries in the confederation amounted to 200 sail of the line and 400 minor vessels manned by by 200000 seamen and marines This vast force ought to have been intended nay was __intended__ to act for the safety of all the kingdoms alike since all alike contributed to its support. But No! The Admiralty with their head. were all Maritime Men and all Scotchmen. I mean by Scotchmen Natives of the Scotchsettled plains of Rosses and Parrisland The 2 kings cheif Directors were Scotch their kingdoms their subjects their favorites the men whom they would flatter and conciliate. the relatives the families whom they would enrich. Or put them in the Navy give them [a] commission on board a ship of war. the consequence was that a Wellingtonian a Glasstowner nay even a Sneakeyan could not possibly obtain entrance in the service except as a common sailor. unless he paid for his commission at a rate which was sure to beggar him and if he did get in as Midshipman. where was his chance of promotion he knew it lay in a thousand pounds so either he must get that or be a Middy still and here so great was the demand for commissions among the the hungry Sawnies themselves that for every 100 pounds offered by an Irish or English descendant <100> was sure to be accepted from a Scot. and consequence was that in order to obtain money for this maritime simony. the minor Officers on board had recource to the meanest and most grinding extortion cabbaging the wages of their crews and peculating among the rummaged Merchantmen. And again from narrow and contemptible Nationality the ports and merchants of Wellington or Verdopolis were neither protected or favoured while those of the two Southern States could command a ship at <any> day. (provided pay were offered in decent acknowledgement)—Then as it regards the second Branch of Admiralty supreintendance[sic] I said that the fleet or a portion of it kept up a constant cruise round the coasts of France this was a rich farm for as we were allways in a state of warfare with that Nation many prizes fell in which were neither fully accounted for to the Government or the <Men>. the two Monarchs took care to engross a full share of these. again the Naval stations on the Coast of Africa from whence Verdopolitan merchants obtain their Gold and Ivory being placed under the surveillance of the vessels on cruise became scenes of the most nefarious jobbing not a pound of either costly article could be exported from shore without the Acting officer dipping his hand most freely into the package and a regular tale was made to merchants of exemptions partial or compleat from extortion but if after paying his price the Merchant thought himself [free] really he was a real greenhorn. for all was useless unless he paid another sum to free him from attempted breaches of the promise. As to the Mauns and Wamons Isles what Oppression what greed what open tyranny was practised there! Never did Islands before groan under a slavery like these the moment that the Dark hulls of Their Majestys Navy appeared hovering on the Horizon that moment was the signal of wealth to be hidden. the rich to seem poor and the poor. why these had no escape for the rich seeming poor could pay the imposts on the Poor. But the Poor in truth. what could they pay they could not seem yet poor[er] and there was no further gradation for them—Now I come upon another Vast Mountain of Corruption the effects of another Enjine of power given into the Management of the Scottish Kings and Admiralty. Like the vessels of the Navy itself. the Customs and Excise offices were filled with Scots. Relatives freinds dependants of the Great Par[r]isians peeraged Houses and Merchants If you examined the list of Officers of Excise or Customs in any town of Wellingtons or the Great Verdopolitan Land you would be certain to find them of Scotch termination so in the Islands and so in the settlements. The consequence of this was first that all Merchants or vessels belonging to the two Southern Nations were forever excepted from search or winked at if guilty The Traders of any other power in the Union were ground with extortion and if condemned had the misery of seeing behind the one legal fine to Government payment on payment to men with whom they had nothing to do all darkening the rear. There was a regular graduated scale and he that had to pay 1000 £ to the Government woe betide him for 10000 would come in for the Navy and the customs and the Kings. —

Such my countrymen and undeniably such was the State of the Naval Department. when the Two Kings resigned their profitable trade in favour of their two youthful sons Youth is sanguine and ardent and generally will strike out a new path instead of the old beaten one of age. But these two youths Lord High Admiral the Marquis of Ardrah and Lord Vice Admiral the Marquis of Harlaw. knew the profit attending on their fathers path and prudently they contented themselves with widning rather than deviating in direction. Also their father[s] though they gave up the Offices would not give up one of the emoluments and the Sons would not take the offices without emolument therefore there was a new demand to be supplied let the money come from where it would. —Two large and Beautiful islands lie in the Atlantic side by side opposite to the Wellingtonian and Parrisian Coasts about 400 miles in distance. These two Islands are Stumpz and Moncays lands members of our confederation each with an active trading population of great worth and buisness amounting to 5 or 6 million souls. These Islands are Governed by 2 Kings who have no children The Monarchy is Disposable by will of the Reigning Kings and the Reigning Kings are dear freinds of the Monarchs of Parrys and Rosslands. Therefore. My Freinds Stumpz and Moncays towns are in[s]tantly to be made the principle out stations of the Navy. The two Cheif Admirals must land there and forthwith ingratiate themselves with the king so in a while I suppose a bargain is struck. whereby the two Island kings agree to leave their Crowns to the Heirs of the Southern Kingdoms. —upon a consideration hardly <a failing > know. at once the Scotch Navy lords it over the Isles the Scotch Admirals Captains &c are every thing the Scotch vessels looked upto as every thing Merchants strive to get their sons in to the Navey to wed their well portioned Daughters to the Officers. at every public Dinner the Officers in port have a distinguished place and honours nothing is thought of but how to please their future Monarchs and Rulers. The Merchants Natives of these Islands have something mean in their nature. their conduct was carried to an extravagant pitch. Meanwhile. the Sagacious young ruler of. All Our Nations Ocean saw what a Noble Trade his countrymen were driving an Idea struck him too good to be cast sideways. There were. several stations of the Navy far more productive than others What was the outward bound cruise the cruise of the Ascension or the Stations off the Mother country too. the cruise off Mauns or Moncays or Stumpzez Isles. What if the stations were Farmed according to their value. (over powering laughter)—Yes! Africans I know it to be a fact that these posts were sold to those Admirals who could pay best for them that they might enjoy their advantages till their time expired. I say I <u>know</u> and can bring proof before you that. in one year and for that year. 3 Noble families of the South clubbed 60000 pounds for the station of Mauns and Wamons Isles and that many a time have the <Dongbases> and Elphinstones and <   > names renewed their leases of. the two great Island shores. From the sums these Admirals had to pay for their farms. extortions were carried on now to a yet greater pitch. the Islands were ground further to make a profit As for the reversionary monarchs these <licked the dust> voluntarily. Compacts were made with person[s] taking commissions whereby they agreed to surrender up so much of their pay to the Admiral in acknowledgement of his obtaining it for them by these means a Captaincy was often mortgaged down to the value of a Lieutenancy and as the Holder (for I must use civil terms to such unwarlike conduct) was still forced to keep up the state and appearance of a Captain he directly. set about trying to replenish himself from his inferiors as his superiors had done for him thus the burdens fell on the Backs of the Seamen whose wages were held back and prizes denied to them these fellows seeing the example set them. pounced upon the people the last unhappy bearers of this intolerable weight of iniquity—But I am wearied with detailing this never ending round of profligacy. I am disgusted with the ulcer which I have opened and I know and I see that you are too. In Parliament My Countrymen in Parliament I will substantiate with the fullest proof every iota of what I have here brought forward Nay I will also crush them with much which yet lies loathingly behind. I will then bring forward a Bill for the REFORM OF THE VERDOPOLITAN NAVY and if any branch of any Government ever needed Reform most assuredly I will say it is THIS The people my freinds the people shall take the matter in to their hands the proffession which was intended for their protection shall be placed under their guidance to act for their good and then we shall see a Navy As powerful and as Noble as the Mighty Ocean it rides over. as open to entrance as its waters as wide in dominion as its shores! (Tremendous rounds of Applause

Now then My Countrymen! I have shewn you the sword with which if you aid me I will mow these your Rulers to the ground is not the Blade a sharp one and do you not think. it well fitted to slay.? I tell you that Never were Men assailed by such a weapon before. for the Navy in all its wide Ramifications of Seas and Lands and peace and war is what the self called Reformers the present Ministry exist by and without it they are not only harmless but their very existence will pass away. The Navy I say is their great scource[sic] of Nourishment. But it is not a scource of strength it is born down by the might of its own wickedness and should a war come on which would call all the Machine into play it would then be found impossible to work and Our coast of 2000 miles would be laid open to our foe. —Africans Not in the last stage of the Roman Empire when that mighty mass falling in the weight of its own immensity lay corrupting over half the world not. in the last stage of the Roman Church when the huge Engine of superstition had laid hold of a continent that shrunk. from its <filthiness>. Not in all the institutions of our own overwhelmed country has there ever been or is there now such a scene of iniquity as this our National Navy. And what then shall we say to its rulers to the Men who have created this state of corruption and who increase the evil where it has any room to expand what shall we say to them—what shall we <u>do</u> to them <u>rather</u>!" —There—stand some of them. and let me Address a word to THEM!.

Mean hearted troublers of a world already vexed with confusion wretched darkners of an existence already like midnight in gloom. Detested enimies to mankind and to your country you have roused my spirit to a pitch from which it never stooped but to seize its prey. I make no vain boast I speak not when I cannot perform when I tell you that from this hour your days are numbered and your safe existence is at an end Tremble! Bloodsuckers Tremble Parricidal murderers of your country. How have you ever dared to oppose my actions who have acted from such different motives from you how have you ever possess[ed] strength to oppose them when your own hung still so heavily around you God if there be a God. Myself if there be none have sworn that not another year shall you sleep in peace with your feet on the neck your talons in the heart of my Native Africa. Alexander Percy tells you that he from this moment Devotes every hour of his time every faculty of his mind every feeling of his mind to the accomplishment of your eternal Destruction I tell you this Tyrants I whom Once you feared whom once you crouched to whom 10 times you strove to ruin. You shall strive no longer My Country has risen around me and swears with all her soul to aid me Here At My Right Hand Stands one whom no power ever yet conquered but who himself has ever beaten down his foes Here stands a Man whom Time or Sorrow or a Life of Passion and dissapointment has not yet shattered but who possesses a body and a soul to which the proudest among you must witheredly give way. And this man has sworn that he will aid me. he has told me that He will Live to Destroy you And with Zamorna[87]

----

[87]At least one half sheet—two pages—is missing between this section and the next.

Angria and the Angrians
I(e)[1]

fitly allied to other forms and scene[s] as grand as she is beautiful

The Duchess of Zamorna is not much like what the Angrians are accustomed to depict her She does not seem exactly that proud capricious sometimes gay sometimes silent being whom I have so often heard them speak of But struck me as appearing possessed of far less pride than she really has in fact she appeared without any perhaps the reports of her caprice rose from the strange mixture of thoughtful sorrow in her large hazel eyes and extreme gentleness of voice and manner as she turned a moment toward the windows where the sun was setting the glisten in those eyes made her seem almost in tears but when she turned from them to me her face lightened with a heartfelt cheering smile and desiring me to be seated she herself. assumed an opposite sopha with her laides[sic] behind or beside her Still I saw no pride for at once she <spoke> of my campaign on the Calabar in terms which pleased more than any praise I had ever heard before "And do not wonder" she said smiling seriously "That I like that work better than any other of your own because remember that it treats of a subject in which my intrest could not fail to be great. and as I of course was not among those scenes my wish to know something of them was strong in proportion to the faintness of my knowledge. I wished to see you Sir. that I might tell you what pleasure I derive from reading your account of the Campaign and victories of my Husband and I owe you some acknowledgement for the manner in which you have described them" As she spoke her cheek flushed and her eye shone with the feeling of her heart and with earnestness she added "I have a right to read with pleasure the account of what I could not look on but which the less I know of the oftener and more intensly I have thought upon I could not reply to such words as these and uttered in such a silver voice But I saw directly that one marked characteristic of the Duchess's mind is the complete earnestness with which every thing she says is spoken because it always expresses the feelings of her mind indeed her voice sounds almost foreign from the expressive emphasis of her tones And in this earnestness I discovered a likeness to her father Northangerland for whenever he speaks it is always as if he wished to convey [to] his hearer all the force of what he was speaking and in his most utter charlatanery you can hardly persuade yourself that he believes nothing of what he advances—But in some other respects the lik[e]ness between father and daughter is not so striking Though her features and hair are the mirrour of his yet in her there is no trace of his heartless sneer or cold and bitter meaning and her eye how different its large thoughtful orb from the fell distorted fire of his—But stop at times he has just her look sometimes his fine eye shines just

---

[1]   A twenty-one page section of manuscript, 11.2x18.5 cm, scattered over four libraries. The initial section consists of a two-page fragment in the Berg Collection.

as thoughtfully as hers. —I think there are <tones> in their minds which respond for Mary Wellesly seems to have a tendency to melancholy and some of that passionateness of feeling which has wrought him such bitter woe—Of course I could not perceive the truth or falshood of those who say that she is spoiled by extreme indulgence But I dare say it is true so far as that she cannot bear to be without all the comfort and pleasure she chooses (and I dare say she is very seldom without them) and when once displeased she needs soothing down again However she has seldom cause for displeasure and all her attendants adore her because she as much wants to see all happy about her as to be happy herself To speak shortly the three cheif characteristics of her mind are extreme acut[e]ness of feeling whence her earnest voice passionate fondness for music and musing and indeed her devoted love to the Duke of Zamorna an hereditary melancholy whence her thoughtful eyes and gentle manners luxuriousness of <habit> resulting from the indulgence of her father in her childhood and Zamorna in her youth then I believe she is very firm in purpose of spirit but quite indisposed to the hair breadth scapes and prodigies of a Heroine

On reading over this portrait of the Duchess of Zamorna I am amazed however so many words can so ill describe her character such tedious iteming is quite at variance with the aspect of the Gentle and beautiful original But I cannot mend it and must let it pass

Ere long another person entered the room the Duke himself the Owner of this Gorgeous Palace and that living gem before me His Grace soon found out the easiest sopha and appropriating it to his own royal person commenced a rattle of volubly[sic] gaiety which I greive it being impossible to remember I was to taken up with it to think of recollecting and the cheerful and animated conversation of the Duchess made time fly fast away Tea.was announced as ready and she said "now Mr Hastings I conferr on you an unusual honour in asking you to tea in my sanctum with myself an[d] his Grace what have you done to deserve it" I answered "If I have by line or letter pleased you[r] Grace I will lay down my reception to my <merit> there. and so the Duke and herself led me forward into a smaller room hung with flowered velvet and lighted by exquisite silver lamps into a scene of beautiful radiance a glittering service of silver stood on the table with waxlights and a glowing fire I felt almost to much excited the honour conferred on me was too much above my thoughts the door opened by the hands of Mr C Peascods himself. and when the Duke and Duchess were seated he stood at her Graces hand to wait on them there seemed something in such a quiet beautiful room and secluded tea party which seemed to touch his Grace for his wild dark eye laughed as he said "Come I should now feel at home if there was not this Gentleman to eat up my goods before my eyes" I did not understand him fully at once and answered "Does your Grace believe that I care much about eating here or now" but then I remembered his odd crotchets about himself and his possessions. However all things—But Hush the Door opened and A Gentleman walked in But such an one. The Duchess only said My Father!" and I had risen in fixed Bewilderment But Northangerland placing his hat on a sideboard stalked to the table and I beheld within three yards of me the Man of Sorrows and Crime

As I stood in amaze he looked on me with such a repulsive sneer of contempt (I suppose at my standing) and then seeming at once to lose thought of me said "Mary Peascod may leave the room" her Grace turned to the Prince of Menials "Go Greenwood[2] and tell Julia that the Earl is here" he vanished at her bidding and the what shall I call him for his life so flashes on me that I know not how to term him Percy Rougue. Elrington Northangerland. —well HE sat down by his Grace and muttered something to which his Grace answered by introducing me as "That clever lad whom I take pleasure in shewing you Captain H Hastings of the 19th infantry" He said it as <intending> to provoke the Earl who hates introductions and who only returned "you need not have said so much" without alluding or speaking to me. I of course could not speak to HIM Lady Julia Sydney now came in to the room saying "Must I take my place as Barmaid nay waiter." and so with enough of a rustle and magnificent display assumed her place as directress at the head of the Table for it seems that Northangerland when he sups at Wellesly House no unusual thing wont have a servant but calls for Lady Sydney to wait on them He evidently thinks that Himself his Daughter and his son in law form by far to high a trinity to be attended by even an extraordinary menial and once the only time he noticed me at tea he looked sternly and contortedly at me as if enquiring what buisness I had to intrude myself there. he need not however have been angry for I felt myself in his and their prescence lower than dust

Having had placed before him by the fair and Noble waiter his cup of Dark strong liquid with about as much milk in its mixture as he had in his disposition he sat silently looking at the Hangings round the room while the Duke was criticising Lady Julia and she either defending herself or again criticising me "When Dye mean to go" was his first unconnected sentence to Zamorna.

"Why when I have finished Tea and loitered as long as my avocations will allow" "Stuff. I mean to the other place" "Nay Percy you must wait for that till I die" "Eastward Sir Eastward" "Nonsense is it treason to depart that you speak so darkly leave off this ridiculous appearance of trustlessness I shall depart in three days from hence to Adrianopolis" "Right and By My. Heart we will raise a flame there!"

```
X X X X X X X X X X X X X X X X
X X X X X X X X X X X X X X X X
X X X X X X X X X X X X X X X X
X X X X X X X X X X X X X X X X
X X X X X X X X X X X X X X X
```

2   Various Greenwoods had played a part in the lives of the Brontë's by this time—see p. 216, n. 22, and Barker Brontës, 87, 103, 143, 218.

X X X X X X X X X X X X X X X
X X X X X X X X X X X X X X X
   X X X X X X X X X X X   July 25 th
        X X X X X   P B B 1835
                                     46

"I rise" said The Hon George Wharton Esqr Member for Ardashir "I rise Not I will allow under feelings of embarrasment in my first parliamentary effort for I do not think it right to let private considerations have a moments place in the consideration of the question I this night wish to lay before you But I rise under feelings of Disgust and indignation when I reflect upon the mass of corruption which it will be my duty this evening to expose and when I know also that this Rotten limb whose amputation I call for is a member of the Body politic of our Constitution I say that I almost lose my pride as a Verdopolitan and my love for my country And it can be expected Gentlemen."—"

Here Mr Haines M P for Freetown called to order "Sir he said it has been a practice in members on the opposite Benches to address the House of late rather than the Chair is this an intentional slight upon the upright and excellent individual who fills it I call to order!'

"Mr Haines" continued Mr Wharton "I neither adress the House or Chair for that I leave to such precisians as you I address the Hearts and Heads of my countrymen and I ask them Can it be expected that after taking up a ripend apple when you cut it open and find decay in the place of sweetness you should still regard it as the same. goodly eatable you did before you examined it. as little should you expect me after having beheld the late exposition of the mortification in our constitution to think it the perfect creation I did before I examined it— Gentlemen I rise—"

"Mr Haines again got on his legs and with pompous voice cried. "I call to Order."

Cries of "Order" "Chair" "Order" echoed through the crowded house mingled with exclamations of "Adjourn Adjourn"

Yet Mr Goat sat still in his seat without attempting to stop the confusion

"Let the discussion proceed" cried the Member for Angria "or let this question be decided Mr Speaker is it or is it not consistent with the rules of this house that the persons occupying the floor should adress the Members instead of the Speaker"

"I believe" said Goat "that—that it—is—not—"

"Belief Sir will not do are you sure"

"Not untill I have consulted the rules"

"I fancy" cried Wharton "that the conscience[s] of some Honourable members sadly prick them and they anticipating the measure I am about to introduce seem willing to interpose in my course every frivolous hindrance they can light on certainly I have said nothing indicating my motion as yet save generally declaring that there is in our constitution a peccant part a member which ought to be cut away now this they must acknowledge or why their cry of

Reform but when they hear of a branch pronounced rotten the cap fits and they know it is the branch on which they have their rest and to which they at present cling Now let me end their fears by saying that I rise Gentlemen—"

"Mr Speaker" again interrupted the indefatigable Member for Freetown "As I opine this custom of the honourable Member for Ardashir to be a breach of rule I feel willing to take the sense of the house upon the subject I move that the House do divide upon the propriety of addressing the Chair in preference to the assembly"

Here the Ministerial Benches rose up in a made up ferment calling out "Divide Divide" while the Constitutional Benches shewed in conversation and murmers their sense of this scandalous interruption The opposition remained silent or laughing

Lord Lofty arose. "Let the question be set at rest" said he. —But the hiss of dissaprobation which greeted his words effectually prevented his being heard further. Mr Goat seemed moved by the scene and his visage elongated but he did not speak

"I second Mr Haines motion" cried Captain Douglas and that party then called out "put it put it"

Mr Goat said. "I question wether it becomes me to put a motion so personally interesting myself." —and pausing ere he uttered the treacherous suggestion—"Would it not be better to adjourn into committee upon it—"

"A storm of dissaprobation rose from the constitutionalists and opposition Members under which the Speaker shrunk into his seat

Mr Wharton continued loudly. "Sir you disgrace yourself—Gentlemen you act shamfully—Mr Haines I shall call for an explanation of your conduct. —Senators of Africa. I rise this Night before you to move for leave to bring forward a bill for the Reform of the Verdopolitan Navy—"

Here the Marquis of Harlaw to create another interruption pretended to believe that Mr Wharton had finished speaking

"Mr Speaker As Aw said once before Being Bred to the Navvy myself"—

—"Hey how is this" cried Wharton keeping his temper wonderfully considering his irascible eyes and the style he was treated—"I had not concluded Sir what was your motive for interrupting me—"

"Aw did not interrupt you Sir Aw thought you had done—"

"Oh Oh" resounded from all decent men in the house at this palpable lie

"Aw did Aw'm sure I did He stopt and made a motion to sit down—But as Aw was saying—"

"Nay this is too bad. —But I had not sat down my lord and I keep my place still mark you. —As I "before observed" You have acted gentlemen of the Ministerial benches as if you shrunk from the discussion of a question which you felt involved so many crimes and corruptions of your own and you have exerted yourselves to the utmost to prevent my laying before you another course of the dish you have just risen from swallowing when the Earl of Northangerland lately crammed it down your throats. But I can almost pardon your stomachs rising against such unpalatable food—though Scripture tells me that the wicked must drink the cup of their abominations to its dregs[3] —Gentlemen this Night—"

Mr Haines again came to the scratch "Sir Since it is highly expedient that the question which has just produced such a sensation in the House should be settled to our satisfaction before the discussion of any other matters of minor importance and since it must be very unpleasant to Hon Members to hear so frequently repeated a mode of addressing the House which there are great doubts of being authorised I beg leave at once to move your own proposition that this House do adjourn into commitee to consult upon the propriety of settling a form of adress from speaking Members or publishing that which I opine is already settled—he—hem—it is customary I believe in 0011 public meetings[4] for the Speaker to <adress> the Chairman or President for the time being and that this is done to secure that order which would be violated most probably by bringing onto the carpet all or part of the general meeting—hem—um—certainly I do suppose that the present House. does not less stand in need of a check upon tumultous and dissorderly proceedings And I think it highly objectionable—hum—to allow our rules to be broken and our Speaker to be insulted by the insolence of a small and malignant faction—"

The Marquis of Harlaw "I rise to approve of the Hollourable[sic] Members motion and I must say that all the malignity displayed to night is o' one side, o' Board ship or o' dry land the motto. of a reasonable Man is to preserve order and decency and I would mysell preserve decency and I would have others to do it and indeed I vow that I have never seen it transgressed as I have to night and move by that token the scandalous motion just laid afore ye." (loud laughter and crys of hear hear—). I mean by the Member of Ardashir (cries of order keep to your subject order) The Henker whats all this rout I am o' my subject what are you pouring your broadsides at me this way for—the Loard Harry tak' ye let me steer on i' my winds eye like a racer. —And as I was saying I—you—Nay were was I Aw lets see. A more scandalous motion than the one just laid before you I have never seed so Ill sit me dawn" (roars of laughter.)

Sir Robert W Pelham—(stroking his chin and simling[sic] a benignant dimple. —"The Tact displayed by the Right Hon and Gallant Member who has just sat dawn. in steering down as if to the assistance of the Hon Member for Freetowns motion and directly upon bringing to. pouring such a terrific broadside into its bows. I hope we cannot to strongly admire and since I have no doubt that the volley must have left it a complete wreck my advice to its Captain would be to make his escape from the vessel as soon as he possibly can—"

---

3   Compare Psalm 75:8.

4   While the question of who is to be addessed demonstrates Branwell's knowledge of parliamentary procedure, the "0011" designation seems to be his invention.

Amid the applause which followed Sir R Pelhams sneer. Lord M Lofty—white with nettled rage at Harlaws stupidity was forced to step over and whisper to him he bolted onto his pins

"Aw didnt I knaw what yarn Sir R Pelham was spinning but I beg to tell him that I meant Mr Whartons motion—" here he sat down onto his seat again[5] Lord Lofty whiter still was forced to say "My Honourable and Gallant freind has forgot to putt his seconding of Mr Haines motion regularly"

"Oah—I second Mr Haines motion"

"And I" said Mr Warner rising quickly and speaking with emphasis—

"I rise to move an amendment for never did [a] motion more need amendment God knows that I do not profess to approve of all the opinions of the Hon Member for Ardashir belonging as he does to the party of a man who has inflicted such curses on my country But this I will say that never did [a] Member of a Verdopolitan Parliament suffer such intentional insult and insolent interruption as he has done this night and never upon slighter grounds unless I take as an excuse for such conduct the fright and horror of a party fearful of the disclousure of the accumulated wickedness. But—Sirs you[r] day of punishment shall come the day of your disgrace must arrive and when it dawns at last on Africa none shall hail its beams more joyfully or with more hope than I. truly it shall be a day of darkness and of gloom to Egypt though Not a cloud shall rest over the land of Goshen[6] —and when all these schemes first born and cherished of your hearts lie prostrate and perished before you great will your howling and weeping be But then Sirs mo[u]rn rather for yourselves than your children for can you escape in the destruction of your principles and your Deeds. Gentlemen what right I ask what right has a wretched faction to palm up on your attention a contemptible question of antiquated formality to the intire hindrance and staying of a Question primarily brought before you and involving great and important interests to your country

"Nonsense called out Mr Montmorency fearful of the feeling Warner might exite It was done because the larger question could not go one[sic] without invol[v]ing breaches of the rule which the smaller question is intended to certify."

"Oh Sir" continued the Member for Angria "Be you silent and what need is there of a rule upon the smaller question at all Why deprive Any Member of this House of the right to speak either to the Speaker or his Audience as he deems it proper Gentlemen I move that the discussion upon Mr Haines motion stand over till the settlement of Mr Whartons motion—"

"And I" said General Thornton "most readily second it"

The cries of Divide Divide now became deafning and upon the House proceeding to the Division it was found

---

5   The following section consists of the remaining three pages of the Rutgers manuscript described on p. 379, n. 82.

6   See Exodus 8:22 and 9:26.

         For Mr Edward Haines Motion----------297-
         For Mr W H Warners Amendment-----<u>239</u>-
         Majority for Mr Haines Motion--------- 58-

The announcement was received by the Ministerialists with loud and repeated cheers

The House immidiatly formed into Committee Andrew Dunbarton Esqr in the Chair But from the excited state the members had been thrown into by this disgraceful juggle it was some time ere any thing like order could be obtained at length

Mr Haines rose. "Sir as it cannot be expected that at this hour and under these circumstances I can trespass upon your attention with any very long disquisition upon the merits or demerits of my arguments I will proceed to read to you the Statutes and sentiments of the legislature upon the subject." —here the Hon Member commenced a series of imterminable qoutations[sic] from all manner of scources out of the books on the table so evidently and disgustingly with the intention of keeping the house in committee till it should be too late to recur to Mr Whartons motion that Mr Warners fiery spirit could endure it no longer. He cried—

"Sir or Gentlemen If you be Gentlemen if you are worthy of the name decide at once upon this despicable subject and allow the blushes of shame to leave your cheeks in discussion of something of more consequence—Mr Haines—Mr Haines! —"

"What is the reason I demand of this interuption?"

Mr Warner "I will divide the House imediatly For Heavens sake settle it— Gentlemen I move that the House enter directly upon their books a permittive for a speaking Member to address himself either to the house or speaker"

Mr Edward Percy rose "And By G—d I second it"

The Constitutionalists and Opposition cried out Divide Divide and Mr Haines called out.

"And I move that the House declare their opinion that it is against the received and written rules and regulations of the African Parliament for a speaking Member to address himself to any other than the Chair"

Sir A Elphinstone "And I second the motion"

Mr Dunbarton put it it the House in huge confusion divided and the result stood

         For Mr Warners Motion------245
         For Mr Haines Motion--------<u>291</u>
         Majority for Mr Haines-------- 46

Here Mr Montmorency muttering sotto voice-"D—n them I'll slick them yet" rose and overbore the clamour with his brazen lungs.

"Sir As it is entirly without precident for this House after resolving itself in commitee again to sit as a house that night—(Deep murmers of anger. Mr Warner jumped up.

"No for because it has been without precedent for this House in the middle of an important discussion to form into a commitee. There. fore till now there has been no reason for forming again into a house!"

Mr Montmorency continued laughing sneeringly.

"And I see no reason now what is there for the night on our books but a bill for—for—what was the Champion of Ardashirs bill for (cries of order order. and confusion from several Members leaving the House in disgust) A bill which shall never be carried with the consent of my country and shall never be read with mine (this was spoken with feirce emphasis) No the rules of this house have been broken too often this night already unless you wish to make them a cipher do not break them again I repeat. (with double energy) I do not wish you to hear another word upon the Bill for the Reform of the Navy because I think time wasted on it would be worse than wasted it would be given to the working of evil—"

Mr Wharton who had kept a most laudable controll over his feelings hitherto through all these scenes of scandalous baseness—could no longer controll himself. He sprung up and shouted

"What is Judas saying? is this House sunk so *far* will it bear such conduct any longer? —"

"Who dared call me Judas I ask.?"

"I Dared and I repeat it false traitor to your master!"

Deafning shouts of "Order" "Chair" and "shameful" stopped for a time further altercation but as soon as he could be Heard Montmorency retorted with offensive bullying

"Let him come on the Slave because he has bound himself for his own damnation to the Man whose company I have long foresworn he dares to think that all others who have not cut of their tails like him are Knaves or fool[s] and Judases and such other Mythologicals.

Mr Wharton struck his hand on the table "Say that again Sir"

"Not at your bidding Nigger!"

Wharton frowned feircly at him saying "I must receive an explanation of this" And the Western Demagogue went on cutting his speech short for fear of decisive interruption "I move in pursuance of the usual forms and proceedings of this house that This House do now adjourn till 8 o clock pm on July the 2<4>[th] instant.[7] And if no one else will second it I will with my own voice."

Col Luckyman "The Hon Member need'nt put himself to the risk. I second it"

All the mob of members cried out "Divide" or "Shame" except 20 or 30 who retired from the house in disgust at such unconstitutional proceedings The result of the Division the third of this night stood as follows.

For Mr Montmorencys Motion————283
Against it———————— 245
Majority for Mr Montmorency———— -38

And now after the disclosure of the result Mr Wharton cried. "Well my countrymen more than one half of you have disgraced yourselfs[sic] but perhaps

---

7   Branwell seems to have first written "5," then changed to "4."

it is from ignorance of the crimes of your leaders If I am spared (emphatically) to morrow night I will again bring forward the motion you have shuffled off this night. There is one among you who demands a heavy reckoning and Mr Montmorency knows where to find me. —"

Thus closed this stormy and ominous deliberation every one leaving the House as if fearful of an earthquake so well all knew that such iniquitous proceedings could never be settled without future and perhaps more terrible struggling how the ministerialists expected to meet the country I know not but fright and fury has often made men blind

Throughout all the next day July 24th and it is on the night of this I with the whole city surged with astonishment and conflicting opinion and every hour seemed to add to the fever of political excitement. About Dusk the two Houses. of Parliament met and first for the House of Peers.

Here when a large Number of Noblemen had collected the Ministers took their places and The Right Hon The Earl of Northangerland also took his the Duke of Zamorna shortly afterwards entered but instead as some thought he would of[sic] taking a seat removed from the Arch Traitor he walked up and sat down by his side—In a while the Right Hon the Marquis of Ardrah entered grasping a roll of paper in his hand on mounting the Prime Ministers tribune he unfolded it and hawing drily and coldly <began> as follows.

My lords Their Majesties the kings of Africa in council assembled have deputed me as their Servant and Secretary to read aloud to your Lordships the following proclamation

"WE By the Grace of God Kings of the united Confederacy of Africa with the Islands thereunto belonging having met in council together have by command from our own will and pleasure that from the 24th day of. July in the year of our Lords redemption Eighteen hundred and thirty five—That Our House of Lords and our House of Commons in deliberation assembled be Prorougued unto the first day of September in the aforsaid year. And we direct that the[y] close their proceedings upon the hearing of this our proclamation.

signed   William Edward Parry   **L**

John Ross

Frederic Stumphz   **S**

James Moncay

Given from our Hands to The Palace of Parry.

This twenty fourth day of July 1835.

God save the Kings

As Ardrah concluded with a cold feirceness of countenance and in deep silence. the Earl of Northangerland Arose and saying loud and solemnly

"I WILL READ THIS PROCLAMATION TO MY COUNTRYMEN!" He turned round and left the Hall alone

Zamorna arose and said "My lord Marquis By this step you have taken you will certainly obtain a great deal of notice but I cannot answer wether that notice shall be of such a nature as to make Africa desire to have the head of that man who could devise this paper you have just read the step you have taken is a hazardous one and you ought best as the prime minister of our country. to know how that country will receive it however Evil men may strive to crush all things save their own domination there still remain in this Land and among Our people. hearts to feel the oppression they suffer heads to divise the means of extricating themselves and hands to execute the measures they devise One person My Lords has just told you that he will read this proclamation to your countrymen and I DECLARE TO YOU THAT I WILL COMMENT UPON WHAT HE READS!"

And thus these two Mighty Spirits having sternly declared Their determination left the House of Parliament to enter upon the course in which they mean to proceed

The Marquis of Ardrah in proud official silence received the defiance of his awful enimies and commanding the Officers to close the Hall doors he with the Other Ministers left the House to communicate the proclamation the the Lower House the Peers all crowding to their carriages with what different feelings they know best themselves

When the Premier appeared before the thunderstruck Commons he found the whole House a scene of confusion Mr Wharton in vain attempting to make himself heard amid the overpowering howls of his opponents and the loud cheering of his freinds But when the Marquis Read the proclamation in his cold high voice. Mister Warners pale face flushed as red as crimson He beckoned to all the Constitutional members and they filed out after him 150 men. George Wharton arose tore his Bill into fragments hurled them before the Premiers rostrum and said "The Curse of my Country upon you" —then the Speaker with a tremulous voice declared the House dissolved and soon all the Hall was left empty save by the Doorkeepers and clerks.

I have only arrived at my Hotel an hour ago from the House of Commons and as yet I cannot tell anything as to the manner in which the country has received this Unheard of measure. My Room in which I sit is closed and lighted without I only hear the Bell of St Michaels striking the hour of 12. all else is in the darkness and silence of Night But My Spirit tells me that this Silence is not destined long to endure such conduct from such a Government at such a moment. will bring upon them a terrible punishment They have taken this step in terror of the disscussions and Disclours[sic] of the Speeches and measures and feelings on the Bill for the Navy Reform. But let them take care lest their determination to avoid this evil does not plunge them into another far more terrible both to them and their country

Their Country! Africa.! what is in store for it. what is rising in its horizon or rather gathering fast over its head have I already heard the first two claps of thunder before the tempest in those Loud Words of Zamorna and Northangerland

We will read and comment upon what we read

In a very short time I shall have to leave Verdopolis for my Rejiment quartered on the remote banks of the Benguela from thence and my Military duties I shall not be able to return till the beginning of winter But then—when I do return what shall I behold. Ere then what will the Nation of Africa have said or thought or done.

Truly there lies a fearful cloud before us and every man who calls himself an African has now cause to tremble for the fate of his Country But what ever may happen however we may be cast. however events may distract us and whatever scenes may divide us still let us look my fellow countrymen up to one Standard to rally round to one Pole Star to guide us.

Let us rally round the Broad Flag of Liberty
And fight under Zamorna and Northangerland

Henry Hastings
July 24th 1835.

P B Brontë   July
Twenty Fifth.
1 8 3 5. A D.

PB Bronte[8]
October 3^d
1835

4 months had elapsed yesterday since I last had seen Gazemba. To day I am there again But it is 8 months since I first saw it and in the interval of time lying between Dec 4th 1834 and Aug 10th 1835. what years what a life time has passed over me! How changed am I what changes have I seen! Since then my thoughts and feelings have gained as great an accession as the Missisipi when it receives the Missouri I am hardly any longer Henry Hastings and like that river I should be called by a new and not my former name Where is the likeness between the new made Ensign just come from college and going for the first time to join his Rejiment and the warlike Captain who has passed through an ardous campaign survived 2 general Engagements been accustomed to Death Blood and Danger seen men dying as thick as grass killed his share himself. and resided Half a year in VERDOPOLIS been initiated into its wonders looked at all its political revolutions known all its Eternal Characters visited with Lords and Dukes written THREE VOLUMNS and heard his name mentioned through the

---

[8]   The following section consists of pages 17-18 of the PML manuscript described on p. 325, n. 28. There are three and one half blank pages between these two sections.

land as the Author of "VERDOPOLIS AND THE VERDOPOLITANS."[9] Ah theres the point when a man hears others speak. of him He begins to think of that about which they speak. it is then he is most changed But—it is not this which has altered me—no my vanity is to great to be puffed up by this we must seek something higher to raise IT. it is the light which has opened on my eyes the insight I have got into this world and this country the way I have bowled on in my Career—the things which I see be fore me on my way. it is these things which make me say I am not now what I was last year.

Some say that a step into public life will cool a mans Ambition I dont say so because it has not cooled mine what I have seen in Verdopolis what I have described in the works I have published has lighted the flame into threefold intensity and with double diligence I set myself to work to open for me a path which may (Oh may it) run along side of ZAMORNA and NORTHANGERLAND. Ah reader these are two mighty names! you may have high ideas of them but your thoughts can only figure a Ben Nevis unless you have seen the Real Cordilleras de los Andes![10] When I behold the vast parks of Alnwick. or Hawkescliff. the Majestic Houses of Elrington or Victorias Squares when I see the Countess or Duchess when I hear of the 3 or 500000 £s. is not that sufficient to fire the spirit of a man. But when I. see. Arthur. or Alexander in person when I hear their living words their sentiments of fire when I know the feeling that actuates their exertions when I know the vast multitudes who follow them The great forces opposed to them. and above all the Awful struggle they seem about to dash themselves into Then does my spirit most long to partake their destiny to receive some portion of their fame! —But perhaps all this is in vain for what am I to them. yet still my present situation looks fair and I have reason to hope for some thing to come.

Reder[sic] if you have any knowledge or observation I have no need to assure you that we stand on the brink of wonderful times that another year is not destined to pass over us without scenes and changes which might fill a century Neither you nor I can guess what these events will be but we can guess that they will be An Earthquake [An earthquake] never occurs without warning or a sea storm without the swell. Outwardly—in its commencement the War of Invasion had nothing to do with intestine convulsions (I say outwardly for if we believe Northangerland underneath it arose from his machinations) But when once it had commenced All our factions were stirred up hatreds and attachments increased insane conduct on the part of the constitutionalists swelled the ranks of a dangerous party Men acted and thought without restraint and the consequence was that though peace left us apparently victorious our victory had cost us terribly dear it was like the conquest of Pyhruus[11] one other such and we should be

---

9   Branwell seems to be confused—see p. 279.

10   Ben Nevis is in Scotland, the highest peak in Great Britain at 1343 metres.

11   A too costly victory, a reference to the victory of Pyrrhus, king of Epirus, over the Romans in 279 B. C.

ruined What followed on it—why before that war All persons inimical to our kings our Religion and Constitution were comprised in one small party led by a man whom every one detested. The Constitutionalists were united and overwhelming in unspotted sovereignty. —After this war Northangerland with high title vast wealth a firm footing in the admiration of the country connected himself with a Prince of Wellingtons land by that princes union with his Daughter that Prince had just come forth crowned with glory surrounded by a host of followers by every gift which fortune could conferr on man they both stood the leaders not of the heretofore abandoned faction of the Democrats but of a vast and noble portion of our Confederation all in opposition to the Constitutionalists (and this was the worst feature in the case) who split into two divisions wrangled with each other and of course could not contend with their general foe. In consequence by an innovation on the Constitution the Duke of Zamorna obtained a noble division of the country for himself in Sovereignty a new interest was created and round the Advocates of new doctrines flocked all the young active Able men in the Union forthwith rose a mighty spirit of inquiry all old things were laughed at The peculiaritys of our Constitution the secret of our Political Religion the force of our Ven—Patriarch (eh?)[12] all things which Rougue and Elrington had laboured in vain to deteriorate—were at once despised and trodden under foot of men meanwhile awakening from their infatuation one portion of the Constitutionalist[s] determined to rally round their banner but they had been quarreling with another and that other determined to separate from their banner In separation the second and four[th] Kings with the Marquis of Ardrah headed another new branch of enimies Here the Land was torrent[sic] three opposite ways But still Fidena held the reins of Government and so long there was hope. —But that Strange Demon or Angel Northangerland had torn himself from his late freinds and came over to the side of the Ardrahians with a Great force of followers straight the Reformers became most powerfull assumed the reins of Government and. all other parties kicked the beam while by a by play in this intricate game Zamorna struck of their New leader and Northangerland fled withered into exile. So far all had been a Game a succession of wild moves and wondrous changes—now it began to assume a more serious aspect The Iniquitous faction that had assumed power began to abuse it—to plan a scale of innovations series of insults to Angria a multitude of base ways for accumulating gains that forced the Zamornans and Constitutionalists once again after a years severance into a necessary union to save not themselves but the Great Vessel they contended on.

Northangerland reappeared rejoining his Son in law and exerting himself as their Second Mighty Leader. a grand assault was planned in parliament on the faction of the Governing Reformers But they had a majority in the Commons and stood firm—What was to be done none could tell—but Lo another move—Fidena and all the Constitutionalists shrunk from Northangerland and either he or they must seperate from Zamorna while the scale hung trembling These our two Mighty

---

[12] The parentheses are Branwells.

Leaders arranged a grand push at the Ministry Northangerland made his never to be forgotten speech on the state of the Navy a new light burst on the Nation they saw the horrible corruptions of the party in power and the[y] rose to demand justice on such wholesale plunderers this Percy and Wellesly determined to give them a bill was brought forward by Mr Wharton for the Reform of the Verdopolitan Navy—But this was striking to far home this was touching a sore spot The Ministry knew that even discussion on this question was victory to the Zamornans and constitutionalists—that victory to them would be ruin irremediable to the Ardrahians and Reformers—the Prime Minister was a feirce fearless man—Ergo by a most flagitious proceeding the reading of the Bill was stopped the Marquis of Ardrah came down and without an instants warning DISSOLVED THE PARLIAMENT.

This was as it were the sun plucked from the sky All was dark and hope of peaceable adjustment of our quarrels was GONE! Men began to look to themselves for the storm was coming and we now beheld it nigh! 4 months were to elapse ere Parliament again met but those four months have been filled up with the incessant agitation of Elections Africa has been kept in a fever and to rouse it to a fury the Earl of Northangerland has made a progress through the North and the Duke of Zamorna through the East Delivering Speeches of Overwhelming and Heartrousing eloguence Then the[y] Both met in the West that Hot bed of convulsion and darkness while the Abandoned Operative of the Reformers Mr Montmorency travelled over their ground in a counter mission of Agitation At this Moment the Elections are all over and there seems a short but perfect Quiet Preparations are made. the Tug is coming and All wait in silence looking at the terrible future! Africa in all its factions is winding up for the ordeal of the things to come.

"What is to come? —nay do not ask In pity from the search forbear" I cannot conceal my belief that the Election has proved far from decisive if [it] had been so there had yet been hope for then might the Reformers have been hurled from power by parliamentary proceedings and with the reins in wise Constitutional hands we might yet go on as we have used to before the last 6 years in prosperity and glory—But of this I fear there can be no hope All parties seem nearly balanced their aims are to one another deadly. and that Execrable that Demoniacal Faction the Reformers and Government are determined to introduce their Bill for the Reform of the Angrian Kingdom—Ardrah is Determined but his ferocity approaches to madness—On his head lie all the trouble[s] which his measures will arouse

But while all these latter events have been transacting in the great world across the Calabar I Henry Hastings have been attending to my Duties as Captain in Lord Hartfords Rejiment stationed on the savage shores of the Etrei yet though far away from Home and Civilization without a single object animated or inanimate around me that my eyes have been accustomed to My stay in this Barbarous Land will through life form an Oasis to be looked back on with delightful remembrances Parades twice a day and severe Garrison Duty is horridly irksome But not so the Dress and pride of a soldier not so the sense of

Command not so the seasoning of Hazard and danger And Oh not so the lonly wanderings along that River side till far away in a drear burning waste while gazing at cloudless sky and Boundless Sand the Great Bright sun sett over the water and the Evening Gun booming on the silence called me back to the warlike town Or when At the head of my 50 gallant followers I set out over that African waste over it[s] pathless surface marching till a new scene of tall palm trees and a stranger Brook whose sourse of course none knew of would stop us scenting like bloodhounds The cindery ring with the half charred Bones around it Then the moonlight search as if we were following our own mysterious seeming shadows the shining of the great orb in the ebon vault the sudden shot and the grim deathly corse or Black ferocious prisoner—pursuits and flights too through the endless stretch of Hot Steaming marches with thousands of tall reeds scorched and withered even among the pools of the swarming tepid water—the sudden burst upon Benguela or Etrei through those reed forests—the solemn glimpses of the shining sea—!

But an end came of these days that are eternal in memory on the 1st of December while I was in the Dongolan Encampment engaged in the protection of the new works building there a letter arrived from Headquarters announcing the expiration of the term of service to the first division of the 19th Rejiment and giving January 1st 1836 as their period for reassembling The night I read it was a sleepless one with me and the morning after an early one I was up and on Horseback hasting ere daylight toward the grim towers of Gazemba—there I received my furlough from the under Secretary of War Chas Warner Esqr and again forward toward Adrianopolis—O glorious Name how my chest felt as if it could not contain my heart when I saw the youthful Giant stretching its buildings along the opposite banks of the Calabar—I could have knelt and adored it. and what a sight for me who knew that 2 years ago that shore only was dotted with a heap of thatched huts and that river spotted with scarce half a dozen fish boats where now—NOW! A City of. 200000 souls palaces churches and streets filled with every effort of civilization reflects itself. in waters that bear vessels from every part of Africa I remained here 10 days after an absence from it of four months and looked back with wonder at the far away horizon of wild burning sands behind which I had so long been working—I almost thought it a dream— However in a few days I lost sight of it and the City gazing from the vessel that was bearing me down the broad basin of the Calabar away for Verdopolis over the wide and open SEA[13] Oh where thus standing on deck with the winds whistling in the sails above you and in advance the glorious main expanding oer the bow.where is the Heart that will not swell with unutterable feelings! mine

---

13 The following section consists of pages 1-14 of an untitled collection of manuscript pages in the Taylor Collection, in a red morocco case, labeled on the spine "THE RISING OF THE AUGRIANS[sic] PATRICK BRANWELL BRONTE 1836." Pages 1-12 consist of three sheets folded and laid inside one another.

did and almost too highly when I knew that I was Bound for Verdopolis the metropolis of Africa and the stage for a mighty mighty Drama there the curtain was drawing up and what part among the Actors shall Henry Hastings fill—He was guessing to himself and thinking about the struggle to come till twilight had almost faded and the cold wind drove him from the open deck. —But in a while impatient to look on the ocean reascended—Lo Night and the Full Moon riding majestically through the drifted clouds! —Our keel snoring through the waters that foamed in sparkles to either hand but before the Billows still— tumbling toward a welking horizon in an hour I went down to the cabin again and remained there till midnight at which time I was roused by sudden voices on Deck so once more I raised my head to "see what I could see"—The moon was yet up the ocean still restless but what attracted the attention of all on board— Why the first thing I saw was—A Mighty SHIP in shadow rolling past its great sails swelling darkly and three grim tiers of CANNON bristling from its bows. in advance a mile or so the sea was peopled with a Squadron of great vessels tossing toward the Horizon but the Appar[i]tion made my head creep with the unexpected suddenness of its Awful show— "And what IS this" said I— "Why its the Island Fleet returning to Verdopolis" And that Huge crowd of swelling canvass thats bearing down upon us" "She's the CALEDONIA[14] G—D—her!" and a nearby response from all on board seconded the wholsome curse—That first rater seemed a tremendous exhibition of naval power and I felt the privelege It had to swell and darken past us with its rustling crowd of sheets and Black bristling bow It was astonishing to see how soon it rolled past us in its majesty till the dark shapless thing in the offing looked like any of its far off line of companions—But that transient vision of the Noblest vessel in the African Navy the flag ship of the Lord High Admiral and Prime Minister the memorable instrument of insult to the Angrian Kingdom in short that vision of the "Caledonia" did not fail to leave us all filled with many and serious reflections I kept mine to myself But thought I There's a squadron of 13 line of Battle Ships Sailing onward to the Harbours of Verdopolis at the rate they dissapear they will be there in less than twenty four Hours anchoring with 8 or 900 Guns and 8 or 9000 men to listen to the progress and fate of that Bill which if passed will annihilate their privileges and disgrace their commanders and eject from Office the Ministry under whose sway they tyrannise over the Seas—viewing it in one light how thoughtless and impolitic was the order which brought a force so interested to the decision of its doom—viewing it in another—nay but I dared not view it in the other—though how could I not know that the Government which gave the order was not a thoughtless one But a feirce and desperate one that its situation was desperate and—but no they <u>could</u> <u>not</u> calculate on the

---

14   Algernon Percy, 4th Duke of Northumberland (1792-1865), entered the Navy in boyhood (1805), was a midshipman on the *Fame* and the *Caledonia*, later acting captain of the *Caledonia*, then the *Cossack* (1814).

employment of their terrible Engines they <u>Dared</u> <u>not</u> intend to overawe and threaten the proceedings of our legislature

Such Thoughts occupied the mind of a young Captain in what His Sovereign was once pleased to term the "fieriest Rejiment out of the Angrian Houseguards" till in the first dawn of light the black coast line appeared under the revolving lights of Rochester[15] and by noon we were dividing with full sails the waves of the Immense mouth of the Niger all round steamers and merchant men were ploughing their path up or down out to the far Islands of the South or up to the distant wharfs of Sneachistown and we held on toward our Mother Metropolis whose far extending smoke hovered like a brown streak of low lying cloud before The wind slackening in this land bound sea arm impeded our progress considerably so that an impatient night was passed on the heaving waters and not untill another Evening set in did we fairly enter between the magnificent forest of masts and street of Hulls that announced the vicinity of VERDOPOLIS where thought I as the count[l]ess shipping revealed itself in front—where is the tremendous Agitation which I have heard and thought so much about Here are vessels and men from every port of the Union all engaged in the fullest tide of prosperous buisness But this was only the surface—The still green water began to swarm with passage Boats small craft and city looking people the lines of Masts to part away right and left. the sweep of waves widen in front like magic and—Lo the Great HARBOUR of Verdopolis! Far round, The diminished crescent of Dim[ly] seen wharehouses beyond the quays that looked swarming with mite like people But all indistinctly seen through the Mass and Cordage of the Gigantic Vessels at anchor with their Broadsides grinning at the City and their immense hulls lying vast and Black like an incubus on the water—Our vessel of course not being allowed to enter the Naval Harbour was moored in the Niger Dock and we after considerable detention from the custom House Officers proceeded in a Boat under the very Bows of the "Thistle" the "Neptune" the "Thunderer" and the "ROYAL CALEDONIA"[16] those mighty Tyrants of the Sea stretched their endless yards above us and when a sail was let fall made a rustling rush that startled me off my position we had got quite entangled among their rows of cannon mouths when our Boat was commanded off. and we pulled out so as to afford a full view of the Crescent. All their canvass had been taken in and nothing but great Bare poles stood up against the Twilight sky But a vast Bustle of joy seemed to enliven their decks and every Mast bore the Parrisian or Rossian yellow beneath the Union Jack and [the] crimson colours of Verdopolis—whats the meaning of it said I when I saw the Reforming Banner floating over the collonnade of the Admiralty and—when we had crossed into the Mercantile Docks—from the Masts of the Merchantmens and the Roof of Col Luckymans Wharehouses "Phoo" was the answer "The

---

[15] The actual Rochester, well-known seaport and naval base, lies on the River Medway in Kent.

[16] All names of ships in the Royal Navy during the early nineteenth century.

Navy Bill has been kicked out on first reading" "When" "Last night Sir—Reform forever" —I hasted aghast out of these strongholds of Government and plunged into the Inland looking streets to gain a clearer notion of the News the song was still the same—"The Navy Bill is kicked out" and I in utter consternation joined the throng moving toward the interior of the City Verdopolis looked crowded But I saw no public display of feeling so that I reached my Hotel in Georges Street without having seen a colour since those displayed in the Seafaring Quarters But when I entered the Great Room of the "Angrian Arms" I found it filled with Gentlemen eagerly discussing the Politics of that day they were cheifly constitutionalists with a strong sprinkling from my native country and they told me

    "We expected this Sir we expected it—the city was prepared for it since the fact was no secret that the Commons are packed to all intents and purposes A Majority of. 19 But its a sure one—"

    "Only think" said a Gentleman "Only think of the conduct of the Chancellor of the Exchequer—" taking the Himes of the morning in his hand "Hon Gents opposite—said the Noble Lord—might thank themselves for the agitation which pervaded the country they had spoken much in reference to that subject during the evening—was it because the things which are uppermost in a mans mind are ever the foremost on his tongue—and he could not but say that a line of conduct had been adopted with regard to the Government of which he felt proud to call himself a member—a line of conduct which more than any other he could mention seemed calculated to keep up the struggle he deplored!" —But undoubtedly the speech which excited the Justest indignation was that made by the Marquis of Harlaw just after the division was announced. "Gentlemen" said the Home Secretary "might rest assured Government would follow up its present path some people had taunted it with desire to shirk the question of Reform But He could tell them that to morrow night would open their eyes to the truth He could not promise them that the sun would shine to shew them their error because it would most probably be midnight But he could aye and he did assure them of a loaf as he might say that would fill their mouths as Hon Gents might have seen the cork of a Bottle do in the pantomime that should fill the mouths of the Hungry expectants and satisfy them that Reform was something which would stay their stomachs thought their[sic] might be a fear that the suddenness of its entry would with some few force a tooth or two down their throats (great uproar through the House) But said the Noble and Gallant secretary as he resumed his seat—what a man loved to hold continually between his jaws he could not complain of if it slipped into his Belly—!!!" Every one present spoke in the strongest terms of the indecency of such language and it appeared that the whole conduct of the Ministerial Benches had been of a character that tended to rouse the feelings of every honest and honourable African But more particularly attention seemed directed toward the proceedings of the present night for all owned that last night was the fullfillment of the last fortnights expectations On the present the Premier himself would bring forward His Bill for the Reform of the Angrian Kingdom—My Blood boiled at the idea—But without delay I hasted to procure the means of admittance to the House of Peers and meeting my Colonel Lord Hartford He procured me a ticket of enterance so that I had nothing to do but push on for the Parliament Hall—this I found no easy matter however for on entering the square my ticket would avail nothing in wedging me through the dense multitude that crammed it to suffocation and having unfortunatly by dint of main Angrianism crushed through a hundred yards or so I found it impossible to turn back into the opening where the carriages were passing up to the Portal and which being kept by the military the crowd could not force in on An hour I was fixed in the mighty mass that stuck or surged without any mark of feeling save a breathless expectation As I began to get exhausted a general sensation struck me as having spread through the Crowds But what it was I had no means of guessing Some said an accident had happened others that there was a tumult in the city and no hesitation was lost in fixing it at Bravis Square most however declared that Parliament had suddenly adjourned and while we were canvassing the reasons for such a proceeding a new report I know not how risen declared the Ministry had resigned this startling intelligence added fire to my temper and I forthwith made a wild push at the centre of the thousands stopped however by a close ring who were surrounding the Reporter of an Evening Paper he was returning it being the hour of publication and could only inform us that the Houses had Just met in conference here was a fresh stimulus I crushed forwards as he vacated outward and straight fell upon the open lane for the carriages so shewing my ticket to the soldiers I hurried on sprung up the grand flight of steps In Beneath the Portal and still up the Gallery staircase of the General Hall. then breathlessly running down from the top of the Gallery I settled into a vacant seat at the bottom of it and in trembling gazed down below the brilliant light first dazing my sight till it settled amid the densely filled Hall upon a table in the midst where two Gentlemen stood opposite one a tall person in black with light hair who stood his back toward us the other in Blue with still lighter locks and rolling up a parchment he held in his hands. Hundreds round stood or sat with intense excitement upon their faces Lords on the raised Bench[e]s each side Commoners in the space between All in the Gallerys leaning over without motion—And through the whole Mighty Assembly—a deep—an awful SILENCE. I cannot tell the startling manner with which it affected me My entrance did not make the eyes nearest to me turn round. —it was evident somebody or something had struck a great blow—I felt my nerves quivering with excitement—the thrilling agitation as the Gentleman holding the parchment broke that silence in a calm buisnesslike voice

"Would it not be preferable if those looked up to by different parties—could draw nearer—?"

Things seemed doing without affectation for no delay being given to ceremony or modesty several persons rose from different parts of the house and while others draw back in clear circle round the table these stept in—it was a moment worth a world—that when I saw The tall beautiful complexioned Military Personage—the thin man with the bald brow in mourning—the slight light haired Gentleman in black—the Herculean man with the Brown frock coat—the vulgar person in white slops—these with many more collecting round that Table indiscriminatingly and divested of all save an expression of intense thought with the Prime Minister again unrolling his parchment before them—and

"My Lord" said the Gentleman who first was standing opposite to him "Will you be pleased again to have read over the preamble of the Bill?"

The Marquis of Ardrah delivered the parchment to one with a wig and gown who began in a clear voice

AND Be it therefore Enacted in order to the maintenance of order and tranquility through the Union

I   1st, That all persons whatsoever upon taking the oaths and their seats for the purpose of qualifying themselves Peers of the Upper House of Parliament for the time being in the Kingdom of Angria—Do by that act and at that moment render null and void any claim they may have had or may then have to sit in or any othewise compose part of be considered a peer of the General Verdopolitan Parliament and that if at any future period they shall seperate themselves or <be> by any others seperated from the House of Peers or any other house of parliament for the Kindom of Angria that though they may be a titular peer of the General Union shall be required to reprove and reenter upon their peerage and reregister it and take new oaths and requirements if they intend to take a seat in the House of Peers in the General Union

II   Secondly Any person or persons or any number of persons intending or assaying in any wise to enter or become a member of the House of Commons or lower House of Parliament for the time being established in Angria shall by such an act even if attempted wether or not suceeding hall thereby forfeit any claim or right they have to be elected a Member of the Verdopolitan House of Commons or to hold the duties of a Citizen or elector in any other part of the Union except by complying with all the forms by law required from Aliens when entering into the privelege of citizenship

III   Thirdly That the king or other head of The kingdom of Angria for the time being shall at the instant he assumes the rank and office of an Angrian Sovereign by that act and from that moment be held in law as in no respect qualified for any station or office in the General Union farther than a frenchman or other legally considered Alien

IV   Fourthly that any any[sic] and every subject owingallegiance to the Monarch of Angria cannot from that moment be in any respect considered as a Subject of the General Union or any portion of it or be legally entitled to the honours and privileges of the same"

The paper was returned to the Prime Minister and the person before him replied upon it

"My Lord Marquis I must express my firm conviction that in justice to the Country the Peers and Commons with the Monarch of Angria must be allowed their own choice of the two alternatives—"

"What alternatives may I ask your Grace?"

"To be Members of the Union without [a] parliament of their own or to accept the Bill which is here offered to them"

"Permit me to state My Lord Duke upon the part of their Majestys Government that any uncertain conduct any leaving of a great question to chance or choice would certainly tend to compromise the Dignity both of the Crown and its Servants they can have no choice themselves for they must act as far as they see it for the benifit of the many under their jurisdiction"

My Own Noble Sovereign whose own crown was so atrociously aimed at with an expression of the justest contempt at such language replied stepping beside the Duke of Fidena

"And permit me to say my Lord Marquis upon the part of the Noble Nation I am head of that the Government must be blind indeed which can mistake the Bill lying before you for a law intended to benifit the many And permit me further to say my Lord Marquis that If I have read the laws arright a blind Government—'from the moment it becomes blind by that act and at that time forfeits any claim it may have or have had to be considered a Government of the Verdopolitan Union'"

The Dukes white teeth shewed themselves as he concluded with a contemptous <twang> And the Premiers hand shook slightly while he replied with guarded calmness

"I congratulate the Noble Duke opposite upon the readiness with which he applys the words from the Bill he has heard but I beg leave to tell him that the Government of Verdopolis has at least sight so sufficient to see the littleness of the sneers of an enemy and a close knowledge some have said begets contempt."

"I agree with the Noble Marquis that in some cases it Does"

"But" said the Duke of Fidena "Am I to understand that the Ministry refuses to assent to my proposition?"

"My Lord" replied the Premeir "They cannot consider it"

"I believe they cannot" retorted Zamorna as he stept back again beside Lord Arundel But Fidena turned to the House and addressed them

"Then My Lords and Gentlemen there is only one course which remains for you to act upon—Yourselves consider it—I mean to make no speech because this conference was not intended for one But I must beg of you to reflect upon the prospects of the Country and so determine that in truth you shall deliberate for the good of the Many—at this critical season I must say that I believe the Kingdom of Angria ought not first to be looked at—On any other occasion I should certainly give it primary consideration—But the peace of Africa is at stake and therefore I cannot now—I Do consider this Bill as in some respects unfair toward that kingdom But reject it and the dishonest dealing will be reversed upon the whole of Africa—Angria seems wishful for independance and this gives it to her—"

"Fidena" interrupted the Duke of Zamorna with warmth. "Fidena you are placing yourself on slippery ground—you stand between two fires and unless you get clear of them both will burn you Angria is part and parcel of Africa and the force which can tear her from it must be sufficient to seperate them shore from shore I should like to know what power is authorized to make mincemeat of our country to please its own hungry appetite for prey none but those of wolfish minds would attempt it and the Lion is stronger than the Wolf.

"Hear Me Zamorna" said Fidena "I entreat the Peers and Commons of Angria this night to encorporate themselves with the General Union"

"My Lord Duke" hastily cried Ardrah "Such a request is unformal it is illegal. —"

I shall not forget the Stern Brow with which the Duke turned toward him

"Unformal" he said "It befitts no one here to speak of formality And learn My Lord not to trifle with ceremonies upon such a night as this is—It may be both unformal and illegal I know not and I care not But it is just my lord and upon such grounds I will press it—My lords and Gentlemen of Angria I must request you to enroll yourselves as members of Our General Union—I myself am one and I know that I shew no stains of disgrace I know that I am no dishonour to my country—" (His <   > manly voice had waked a feeling which declared itself in a thundering cheer)—where I stand without fear or blame I hope that as unspotted you may come—and I know that if you renounce your privelege of seperate parliaments you enter the ranks of defenders both of the East and the West and the North and the South"

"My Lord" said the premier loudly "I will press my question"
Ardrah seemed agitated his whitened face and harsh elivation of tone declared it for a anouncement of seperate privelege and an amalgamation with the Conservatives would seal the death warrant of his ministry and he knew it—So did the whole ministerial party for with out consent they rose up and vociferated "Question! Question!" But the Noble Duke of Fidena stood unmoved save by his kindling courage and with the unconsciousness of a just heart he replied sternly to their roaring

"My lords and Gentlemen I am on the Question and from it no power of yours shall move me Desperate men who gloat of the spoils of anarchy may struggle to shut out an entering pacification they may hate it as Robbers hate the return of Daylight but the world hates not the one and Africa hates not the other You know my lords and Gentlemen of Angria the results of any line of conduct you may adopt—do not hesitate but choose the one which shall end in soothing the land you live in—It needs it and I believe the course I have mentioned will procur it"

Hector Montmorency mounting the Premiers seat exalted his infernal Trumpet—"MEN of AFRICA—attend not to the voice of a faction—Despise the counsels of a place man immersed to the chin in the comforts of office and emmolument a man who has proved himself but the organ of intolerance and the instrument of incapacity a man who—" But Fidena fronting with a magnificent display of manly rectitude the incarnation of traitor insolence just told him "Get down from thence Sir" and the Duke of Zamorna said "On my life if he does not

I'll make him!" The Demagogue got down rather because he saw it was impossible to make himself heard in the confusion and our Glorious Sovereign turned to the House

"Angria takes no part in this Question My country is in Africa and no one can part it from Africa All the Ministrys all the Parliaments of the world could not do it therefore we care not a straw for the result of your deliberations"

"Zamorna" cried Fidena "But the country does—"

"I am sorry for it John for it is not worth caring about and it will not have been the first which has made a great matter out of a trifle Warner call the Commons of to one side My Lords follow me!"

with breathless awe We beheld the Angrian Nobility a hundred men with their magnificent leader mount a long row of upper Benches and seat themselves there while the Angrian Home Secretary led his Commoners—nearly 200 onto the row immediatly beneath they stood their with a look of utter scorn But the Ministerialists were stunned and silent save their Leader who looked terrible from his feirce and ghastly determination he compressed his whitened lips and called out discordantly

"Put the Question"

"Constitutionalists" cried Fidena "Vote neuter!"

In a conference of two Houses on[e] Reading decides the Question. it was put and

For the Bill————————390

Against it————————— 0

"It is Passed" cried Ardrah but the drops burst from his forehead and he wiped them with a shaking hand—A Hollow laugh was heard from the Angrian Peers benches and NORTHANGELAND rose

"Here ye have the much wished for agreement—it is unanimous—But have you heard a saying After a calm comes a STORM"

A Tremendous shout of Assent burst from the Zamornan Benches and as it ceased the Duke of Fidena spoke

"We are all the sons of One Mother Country And Africans Africans let us shelter her from that storm—" a murmered expression of feeling ran throught the assembly and he continued "A law is now passed which excludes Angria from the Verdopolitan legislature—IT IS PAST—and I OBEY IT. —But Country men let us exert ourselves in strengthening our interests let us rally the people round us let us bring forward just and energetic measures and in a short time we shall be able I do trust by the blessing of God—Able LEGALLY to repeal this unjustifiable Law—" Hundreds rose up with the words "Right" on their lips but the Duke of Zamorna spoke

"Oh John you are mistaken! The Bill has never been passed—But—and he rose into an irresistable look of majesty—But to morrow night we will Deliberate further upon the subject"

So saying he headed his party from the Hall the others broke up after But it is a fact that the Prime Minister stood his teeth clenched and the paper grasped in his hands after every body else had gone from the Building

So ended the Night of December
the Nineteenth 1835

P P B---te
Dec. 24th 1835

Sunday December 20th 1835 dawned—The Sunday Papers came out the Church Bells rung for divine service the streets of Verdopolis were crowed with well dressed people. the congregations were numerous as usual—But their countenances bore little of the usual expression and the sermons in cheif part dwelt rather on the futurity close at hand than the one a little farther off. I attended as is my wont the choir of St Augustines and saw the Angrian Court there with Our Monarch in person with a great number of the principal men in the Angrian Party the Right Rev Henry [Stanhope] Prelate of Angria preached a sermon which from its eloquence and power with the bold blows it aimed at the Governing spirit of insane infatuation was evidently the production of Our Right Hon the Home Secretary—This was the morning But the Afternoon did not bear the same aspect there were no great men at the churches there was no listening among the congregations people had been talking and thinking till they began to see the danger Knocking at their doors—Again Evening brought lighted streets and blazing windows with gatherings of the Lofty and splendid but you saw no 'mixture of party feeling' in earnest for good care they took not to come in contact. I had the Honour of an invitation to the Warner Hotel where were all the Warner family [a] <great> part of the Howard and Agar Ones with Sir J Kirkwall Bar^t Mr Percy and many Ladies and Gentlemen of high distinction in Verdopolis the entertainment was splendid the political feeling most fervid and from every lip breathed an encouragement to withstand the law just passed in Parliament the Angrian Secretarys Wife and Sister appeared both in scarlet—with the latter I had the Honour after introduction of some conversation and certainly though very like Her Right Hon Brother she is a beautiful young Lady—when I arrived at my Hotel I found myself in a state of enthusiastic devotion to my cause and country which changed to an intense looking forward of the thought upon the Dawn of—
—Monday the 21st—whose first hours elapsed in an absorption in the Pages of the Himes the Binnacle the Messenger the Warning Beacon the Sun of Angria and every other fresh damped vehicle of Political Intelligence at Noon I took a walk through the principle streets of the Centre Down Georges Street and Twelves Street to the Quays But except in numerous detached groups and eager thoughtful counten[an]ces I saw no public demonstration so returning back I dined with a freind and Hastened to the House of Parliament where in the Great Hall it was understood there would be held a second conference at the instigation of the Duke of Fidena But every one knew that there would be little time for conferring in the Agitating Scene that seemed certain to take place

I sat in the Gallery wrapt up in anxiety and expectation with a Heart whose pulsations rapidly encreased when the Great Doors Leading from the peers and commons were thrown open by the attendant ushers and Members Dropt in to their seats among the first who entered was his Grace the Commander in Cheif who with the Earl of Richton and Lord Hazelton stood for a while in earnest conversation at the central table the Prelates with his Grace the Arch Primate next followed and soon after Ministeria[l]ist and Constitutional Benches were almost filled but the Angrian or Zamornan and Northangeriandian section was completly vacant short sighted persons believed that the Law was bowed to and rejoiced or feared according to their party what the Premier thought I know not for he strode through the Hall to the Robing room without casting his eyes round him and before he returned—Many dark figures flocked in at the Great Door and a sound was heard of the ascending of Benches and a sight of two hundred Gentlemen coolly seating themselves with their faces toward the house fixed in Iron determination—nobody attempted to stop them the Ministerialists looked on as doubting their eyes the Constitutionalists in steadfast expectation Our King in an Hussars uniform stood in the front of his phalanx with just above him the Earl of Northangerland seated silent and reservedly "as a Lamb to the Slaughter and as a sheep before her shearers is dumb so he opened not his mouth"[17] All the Halls was now thickled peopled with Legislaturters[sic] and last nights law was coolly and calmly broken who dared to enforce it and punish the transgressors only one—He reentered followed by Ministers in a Body. His Eyes bent down and abstracted according to custom—But—the Benches which ought to have been vacant were not so—He stopped gave them a fixed and ferocious glance and then striding to his place sat down
"Call the Usher of the Black Rod"
The Constitutional Benches rising simultaneously called out "No No— reconsider the Bill!" and the Reformers shouted "Order Order" But the Premier turned feircly to them and made a motion with his hand for silence However the Duke of Fidena still stood up saying
"My Lord Marquis it must be the conviction of every disspasionate mind that the course you commence will conclude in ruin To do what you meditate will be to declare a Civil War—"
Immovable as a rock the Prime Minister replied
"Youre mistaken!"
And as the officiall appeared before him he continued "Take in to your custody the Duke of Zamorna and the Earl of Northangerland—arrest them and convey them to the Tower"[18] to another usher he said "Bid the Police stepp in—" and the men walked to their duty The Premiers voice evidently shook and he never moved his eyes from the spot where Our Monarch stood But the usher advancing

---

17 Compare Isaiah 53:7.
18 Presumably the Tower of all Nations, the Verdopolitan equivalent of the Tower of London.

respectfully laid his hand upon the Dukes shoulder and then on the Earl at which instant a wild whoop yelled from the back gallery and the Deathlike Silence was turned to a tumult All the Angrian Benches rose as the Duke and Earl rose— some cried defend his Grace others for vengeance but the Duke himself. said

"That insane person believes that a Law is passed which cannot exist I cannot dispute with him now but in a few days the case will be tried at a court from which there is no appeal!"

Ardrah cried with passionate feircness "Take them away!" and the Police escorted them out of the Hall Angrians and Constitutionalists Peers and Commoners rising with a tremendous cheer to the retiring prisoners The Duke turning bowed to them and it was repeated louder than be[fore] Half the Galleries joined and the Ladies standing up waved their Handkercheifs in farewell and sign of succour—The Marquis of Ardrah Glared round the house with eyes like a baited Lion He did not know on whom to fix his fury—so with a forced calmness and an agitated vehemence together He broke silence

"My Lords and Gentlemen I am astonished at the imprudence manifested by a portion of your House—I am astonished at your imprudence—But my Lords and Gentlemen your conduct weighs not a feather with me The Ministry with whom I act possesses so firm a hold on the affections of the people that they are enabled to despise alike empty clamour and insolent disobedience We can tell the opposition of Both Houses that the Affections and confidence of kings and people will ever with us over balance the enmity and Hatred of a falling and bigoted faction—A faction My Lords which the spirit and feelings of the age is as rapidly covering with oblivions as the tide covers the shore with water—But My Lords and Gentlemen this Night our proceedings having been broken in upon by persons who have no legal right to enter among us [we] cannot any longer possess the calmness and harmony necessary to a rational discussion on the present state of Africa I recommend therefore an adjournment of the conference untill to morrow at four o clock of the Afternoon at which time I trust we will again meet with an earnest desire to heal differences and proceed in a steady and rational course of Reform and amelioration—But meanwhile My Lords and Gentlemen I do assure you that proper measures shall be arranged for the prevention [of] such an insolent attempt at a breach of our laws as that which we have this night witnessed And I must assure the persons up on the Benches opposite—I must assure those persons that if the insolence— " A simultaneous hiss of scorn from the Zamornan and Northangerlandian Benches drowned the voice of the speaker who stopped with clenched teeth and as the Hiss subsided recommenced with the most evident appearance of Agitation— I tell you that if your insolence of this night be again repeated" —Several of the Ministry rose as if to entreat silence from their excited Premier— "May I be[g] of you to be seated Gentlemen I have not concluded—I say that in such [a] case I will feel it my Duty the Duty I owe to my Sovereigns and country—To use toward you precisely the same measures as I have been compelled to do to your two Ringleaders—" he seemed to fear a fresh ebullition for he stopped a moment and said "At your peril Sirs!" —and again continuing "under such circumstances

I feel bound to declare my intention and as the law empowers me to do in a case like this when the meeting is not a regular sitting of the Houses I from this moment Adjourn the Conference untill to morrow at four o clock in the Afternoon"—

As he concluded with a voice which agitation made tremulous but a look which announced indomitable feirceness he turned without bowing to any one and left The Hall—Strangers were then ordered to depart and I left the Gallery for the Cold Midnight Air and the lowering crowded streets of Verdopolis

Being decidedly in alarm lest there should be some popular uproar I did not go to rest that night But started at every unusual sound I could hear without the Hotel at intervals shuddering at the prospect so rapidly opening and again fired with the most burning indignation at the detestable Outrage commited on the person of our king the inefasceable[sic] insult offerred to my country an insult which I felt could not but be returned with some terrible revenge—and future events may declare that Henry Hastings though keenly alive to the terrific character of a bloody struggle between fellow countrymen is yet possessed of feelings that can push him forward in the defence of his king and country and every principle of his heart

Tuesday Dec 22^{d} arose and still the buisness of the city whirled round as usual Open shops and crowded marts and brilliant scenes and active people presented to the eye the same "Mighty Heart"[19] as ever But a terrible blow had been struck and no one was ignorant of the fact that the two most powerful men in Africa were now in confinement at the mercy of a Tyrannical Government— What the Cabinet Council or the Great meetings at the Fidena Palace or Warner Hotel planned and thought I shall not speculate upon or describe because I mean only strictly to relate what I have seen and felt and done—or seen others feel or do All I know is that there were meetings at all those places and that a hundred reports were afloat as to the manner of their termination. News and speculations of the overwhelming importance I have mentioned occupied every column of every vehicle of intelligence things were coming too near home to make other matters interesting and steamers and <coaches> were laden with families leaving the city for a quiet harbour from the storm yet it was painfully remarkable to notice the utter silence kept by every one on the almost certain result of this struggle Ones heart failed when the voice attempted to mention WAR—and REVOLUTION—these are fine names when they sound from a distance they possess a musical sublimity then But—only hear them at your ears and—that Crack partakes too strongly of the terrific when a man feels that there must be no more cheerful and unstartled days and nights amid his own <un> protected family when he knows that surety is over for his own House and his. own property and his own Life then and there it is that the voice dare not articulate "War" I know this and I have known what war is but my Readers ere this work

---

[19]   Compare with Wordsworth's "And all that mighty heart is lying still," from *Composed Upon Westminster Bridge, September 3, 1802.*

be published may know it as well as I do and better for I may be laid in a bloody grave

Still though such were the feelings of all men on this day Party spirit and headlong support of Tyranny and a Glorious desire of Revenge for insults and underneath the incessant incitement from Desperate and Demonaical men prevented every one from stopping an instant on his course—and made the certainty before them not a whit less sure—I must except that true Nobleman and firmest freind to Africa the Duke of Fidena with a number of Constitutional Adherents of the Highest Rank and Influence It was currently reported over the city and proved to be strictly correct that His Grace had sent overtures to the Ministry for a meeting to avert our Dangers But the firm conviction of the Gover[n]ment and that He would not abate one jot of his rectitude and principle with a violent negative from Mr Montmorency and others prevented the overture from meeting acceptance—So four o clock came and I hastned to the Parliament Square—there I beheld the result of admirable measures and organization and the silent underworking during the day of the Leaders of Our Noble Blood "Red and Scarlet Legions—A Dense and Magnificent Host of stalwart men filled the whole square and presented at every opening a front that denied all entrance The carriages of various Peers and Members drove up but they were sent back with a stern refusal not a single shew of violence not a knife or pistol appeared the Mob was as orderly as a Rejiment on parade no Ringleaders were visible But I heard that Richard Naughty was there None of the Angrian Parliament or the Northangerlandian Peers and Members appeared for they knew that they were not wanted. But in Due time I saw the carriages of the Ministers Drive up together they halted in front of the iron mass commands and Threats availed nothing they must return—the Prime Minister sent off a Gentlemen (I think Admiral Cockburn) to the War Office for the Military and meanwhile sat determinedly in his carriage it was an uneasy waiting amid those roars of reproach and execration most of the other Ministers seemed excessivly uneasy and Lord Lofty with Lord Strafford proposed a departure But Ardrah was not to be moved and in a while the Duke of Fidena himself on Horseback rode up in person Halting at the Marquis's Barouche He said in his Loud Manly voice

"My Lord Marquis I should Deem it highly improper and inexpedient To endeavour to enter Parliament this evening at a certain and perhaps great loss of Human life—I have therefore refused the assistance of the Military But to morrow I will take care to have matters so arrayed that resistance to the Law shall be impracti[ca]ble—And My Lads I would request you to go home with out any disturbance for this is not the proper way to redress your greivances it is by Parliament alone that your laws can be altered and amended—Go home my Lads and keep the peace—!"

Fidena turned his Horse and rode off But a most Hearty and soulfelt cheer from the multitude told their appreciation of his fearless and open Rectitude But when the Premier's Horses put about before the wind and he drove sourly off followed by his Ministry an astounding thunder of Groans and Curses burst on his guilty head

The Evening papers came forth filled with comments upon this remarkable proceeding and they stated that the Mob after keeping the square till 6 o clock. departed with 3 cheers for the "Duke and His Lordship" but the Ministerial prints concluded in adresses to the people of a most inflammatory character only calculated to stir up new strifes when old ones were already over flowing

Next came Wednesday the 24th and now My Readers the Storm begins to mutter now for the first time the mighty flow of Buisness fluctuated and the day with its events seemed to absorb all attention—what was it which caused this change Why an event which among us would be sure to cause it—now we first saw called forth the instruments of war—without bloodshed certainly but the sight is sufficient in Africa Two complete Rejiments of Cavalry the Verdopolitan Guards from the Citadel crossed Twelves Arthurs and St Michaels Streets filing among prodigious crowds of people till they finally drew up one on each side of Parliament Square—3000 Infantry In six divisions occupied the Streets and Avenues to that place and then The Great Building as its front was thrown open to the meeting of parliament. —I hasted there as usual But there was no crowd before it now save indeed the noble fronts of Scarlet and Sabres and snorting Chargers Two or Three Hundred carriages containing members of all parties occupied the centre and at 4 in the Afternoon the Interrupted conference began—from my station in the Gallery I could perceive the intensly thoughtful looks of the Nobility and Commons But the Ministry seemed harrassed with incessant occupation—Oh no easy birth had then the destroyers of their country—Mr Montmorency alone preserving a hard brutal joy at the scent of confusion and Ruin The Prime Minister looked in particular pale and jaded but His keen sinister Eyes glared with the fury of a Feind Incarnate He had met with marked insults on his way and therefore opened proceeding[s] under a double cloud—He had just risen from his seat to speak when a great Throng of persons entering filled the Vacant Benches in front of him and settled before his eyes in the aspect of the Angrian Parliament. As they first caught his Eye he sat down and remained seated till silence was restored—Then rerising He Broke forth

"What is this? —Do these persons Beard me still? —How dare you Do it! —Mr Warner Mr Percy General Thornton Lord Arundell Lord Castlereagh —you are placed under arrest—Ushers take them away these 5 persons in the front—take them to the tower—The Law shall be obeyed—!"[20]

Mr Warner rising spoke thus

"You are playing a Desperate Game you Hazard all for nothing—But— Remember Evil shall hunt the Violent Man to Destroy him—and know that though for a few short hours you may place us under custody when they have elapsed perhaps before it your own punishment will fall terrible and unalterable!"

"Silence Sir or you shall suffer more! Take them away"

---

[20] Barker suggests that these arrests were inspired by Charles I's arrest of five members of his Parliament in 1642 (Barker Brontës, 248).

"My Lord" said the Duke of Fidena with Indignation in his Looks "—You know not what you do for such contembtible[sic] shortsightedness as this measure indicates—

—Mr Montmorency roared out insultingly—"Have not they broken the Laws—" —"This is the first time I have heard you Defending the Laws But know that a breach of an unjustifiable and hardly dry Enactment weighs nothing against conduct which will end in the destruction of all Law—!"

"Take them OFF I tell you!" discordantly shouted the Premier and The Angrian Ministry calmly and scornfully followed the Officers amid a Cheer that told[sic] from Dome to Pavement But this was adding fuel to the fire which consumed the High Admiral

"At your peril" he cried striking his hand on the table "On your peril I say Silence Do you mean to share the fate of your Leaders for you are all equally guilty?"

"And why not" replied His Grace the Arch Primate rising from His Benches— "Why Not My Lord for you say all deserve the doom alike in which case your conduct seems the effect of party malice—from Hence thou learn the folly of a course which you dare not pursue to its extent Desist members of the ministry and do not call the curses of posterity upon you!"

The Marquis of Harlaw started up. "May We Be D—ned if we do! Aw say what buisness has a proud preist like you to thrust in your oar in a buisness which has so little to do with your Psalm singing knavery!"

A just expression if Indignation burst from every honest lip in hearing this atrocious Brutality His Grace said he repelled the insult with scorn And Lord M Lofty on the part of Ministers arose to soften the disgusting Insolence He said He was very sorry that the warmth of his Noble and Gallant freind had startled him into such indecorous language toward one of the cloth of the Right Rev Speaker yet he could not but say—Here a hearty roar of Groans drowned his Hypocritical voice and then Admiral Sir Alex Elphinstone started up Exclaiming against the disgracful conduct of the Opposition—a vigorous cheer greeted him from his own party and Mr E Haines of Freetown followed

"My Lords and Gentlemen—I do think that if consistently with a due regard to our principles we could discuss the important matter before us in a manner more calm and disspasionate it would redound greatly to our credit as reforming Legislators—"

"We Leave" replied Mr Wharton "we leave calmness here to men whose hearts are too frozen to be ruffled for myself I declare that what I have heard and seen this night has put it quite out of my power to talk in the tones of the Member for Freetown—No I feel enraged at the conduct of his party and the the Ministry nor do I hesitate to express my enmity But every hour of such conduct brings us nearer to a clear pathway where we shall Act and not recriminate!"

A Man while Mr Wharton spoke had come in and passed up to the Premier to whom he communicated some intelligence the Marquis Rose—

"Silence—Silence—A Mob have rescued the prisoners from the Hands of the Officers and the Military have refused to interfere—(loud cheers from the

Angrian Benches)—My Lord Duke of Fidena I call upon you as Commander in Cheif of the forces to step forward and enforce the execution of the law!"

Fidena did come forward and with a loud voice he replied

"NO I WILL NOT!" (Deafning cheers and hisses)

"Will you not?"

"My Lord Marquis you have acted desperately enough already I will not encrease it—The Military so long as I continue Commander in Cheif shall not fire a shot in support of the Law passed on Saturday they shall maintain the peace they shall protect the Parliament But they shall not serve the cause of a measure which must if you wish for peace be directly repealed. —I call upon their Majesty[s] Ministers I call upon the both Houses of Parliament this moment to recall that bill and pass another incorporating Angria with the Verdopolitan Union"

Tremendous Applause showed the feeling which the House entertained of this speech But the Ministerialists and Reformers cried no! no! and the Primier[sic] rising said

"Not while I am first Lord of the Treasury!"

"Then replied the Duke "your Blood be upon your own head!" and turning to his freinds the Constitutionalists "My Lords and Gentlemen—we can do no good here a Factions Ministry and a frantic Majority defeat all our attempts at pacification let us go and strive to give a good direction to the torrent since we can neither stop or delay it!"

"And we" said Sir John Kirkwall to the Angrians "We will meet together this night and swear that rest or mercy shall not visit us till we behold safe among us Our Monarch the Duke of Zamorna!"

As he spoke Mr Warner with the 4 Ministers walked calmly into the Hall and Ardrah starting up in the utmost Agitation cried

"I adjourn the Conference—I adjourn it indefinatly Reformers unite and stand firm for I tell you that Angria shall pay dearly for this!"

And Richard Naughty the Comons Member for Fidena elevating his Big antic Bulk cried in a voice of literal Thunder

"Africa Africa now thou art stript to the Battle Good night to peace But Good morrow to Victory!" —So All under their Different Leaders Broke up and tumultously left the Hall.

Aye Good night to peace indeed! I write this in my room at the Angrian Hotel But I believe I shall not write here long—it is now 6 hours since the scene I have described but so short a time was not destined in these days to pass without events Montmorency has been and I suppose still is addressing in language of the most Bloodthirsty In<bstig>ation addressing an immense mass of people at The Harbour Square with 40 or 50000 Determined Reformers round him and in the Back ground the Great Bulks of the Island fleet at anchor Victoria Square since 8 o clock has been like a sea of human heads save the great space in the center where all the Angrian Parliament with the Leaders of the Bloodred and scarlet Banner from the General Senate—Have in a Body with Heads bared in the face of Heaven sworn an Oath[21] of Adherence to their Constitution and vengeance for their King a Cabinet Council is holding at the Home Office and a meeting of Constitutionalists at Waterloo Palace where are under stood to be present their Majesties of the West and the North while the other 4 kings meet at His Majesties of the South.

Thursday now rose after a sleepless and excited night in the City and so soon as I came to speak with the world from which I had been divided New news broke on me like waves in a tempest Last Night at 11 o clock A great mob after Breaking the carriages of several Lords of the Ministerial Party gathered before Strafford House and would have Burnt it to the Ground but the Commander in cheif despatched the Royal Guards who without bloodshed dispersed the assembly then they met the masses of infuriated Reformers who were returning from Mr Montmorencys speech and here they were required to repress disturbance on the other side—Patroles of Cavalry were ordered to traverse the principal streets throughout the Night—But what did the four kings do why after a conference with the Premier they (being a Majority of the United Monarchy) actually Demanded the Duke of Fidena to resign his appointment of Commander in Cheif alleging that he had refused to obey the laws His Grace gave in the required resignation without comment—such was the Intelligence which burst upon me at Breakfast. I own I was violently excited—Now the Mails from the country were comming in with accounts of the manner in which the Angrian Bill had been received within 200 miles of Verdopolis At Rosses town a Great Meeting was called for to Day whence an Address would be sent up in support of Ministers At Sneachis Town ensued the most violent excitement Both parties were to have meeting[s] so at Freetown But the feeling which accounts brought from Angria suppressed all in ominous nature at Adrianopolis Angria Zamorna and many other places meetings were convened on the moment and resolutions passed expressive of a fixed determination to support their claims and Sovereign by—THE SWORD—yes it seems they first had courage to mention that dreadful word and all their papers called them to Arms—Reports arrived to which stated that Major General Henri Fernando Di Enara was at Hillton concentrating every disposable Regiment there at Zamorna Dancton Wareham up as far as Angria and Seaton upon the centre point of Zamorna—My Hand shook when I read these reports and I fancied that the Guns of Loango were thundering on my ears—A walk through Verdopolis only fired me the more and when I saw whole crowds of people Hurriing up to the Citadel Hill upon report of a general Mutiny of the forces in favour of their Noble Commander I followed till closed Gates and stern sentries denied all entrance then I turned back. and in an hour or two Blue and Crimson Handbills were posted over the city as follows

The Constitution for Ever!
Africans know The 3 Regiments of Royal Verdopolitan
Horse Guards

---

21 The figure "79" appears at this point at the bottom of the manuscript page.

The 2 Regiments of the Northern Greys House Guards
with The 19—28—29—72—75—76—77—89—111th Infantry of the line
in all FOURTEEN
THOUSAND Strong
Determine henceforward to obey no other Command than that
Of Their Only Commander in Cheif the Most Noble
John Duke of Fidena
The Constitution &
Their lawful commanders—

W[m] Harrison
J—Fergusson
H—Mackinnon
D—Bobbadil
R—Dunsandle

To the Whole Army they say go and do likewise!

These were all the troops at present in Verdopolis and with the exception of 7 Regiments of the Parrisian and Rossian House Guards these rose and Declared for the Government and Reform! at 2 o clock in the Afternoon

While the public mind was swelling and surging with these events A Scarlet Paper blazed from every street in the city—breaking out as it were with the force of a fever

Determined at all risks and with all their
whole power to Defend their constit
ution and Rescue their sovereign the
Ministry of the Angrian Nation Have
collected together 9000 troops of the line
At Zamorna Edwardston and Hillton
who will enter Verdopolis to morrow
the 25th of December and orders have
been despatched to the Etrei and Beng
uela upon the receipt of which every
Disposable soldier in Our Kingdom shall
Advance to save our Country and ourselves

Just after this Proclamation appeared the evening papers came forth when Behold—An Order signed W H Warner Home Secretary. and addressed to the Lords Lieutenant of every Province in Angria directing them to raise each a new levy of 10000 men—with information that a Military Commission was forming by the Government for the Government of the Army and in the Ministerial Prints a Direct declaration that the Ministry intended to stop they[sic] pay of every soldier who refused to reenter under their direction—I was in the shop of the Great Publisher Tree when I first saw these above tremendous announcements But while I was engaged in their intense perusal a Gentlemen burst Breathless into the Shop and broke forth

"Hurrah! Ive news to tell you—Zamorna's escaped—long live King Adrian!" I did no[t] move but just tossed my hat to the ceiling with a perfect shout of joy! "He Has and Heres the manner of it That Dog the Home Secretary Hog Harlaw on his own account Had our Noble Young Leader removed in secret from the Tower to the Royal Neptune and there he placed him under Hatches But by G—d Sirs the young Duke kept his eyes about him His Hogship had forgot to insult him with shackles and there was the port Hole for a 24 pounder—well out of it slided His Grace and into the water like a Spaniel Dog They do not know where he is but its said he has set off for Zamorna Heaven bless him! and Heres D—nation to the Infernal Reformers up to the Gallows with their Bodies and down to the D—l with their souls!"

This strapping Gentleman kicked out into the street in first rate style and I after him hurr[y]ing breathless I did not know where But when I got to the General Post Office there was such a dense crowd gathered that I turned into my Hotel and tossed off two Bottles of Sherry at a supper in the Great room then to my apartment in a dream of unbearable sensations

I must have slept soundly But it was Friday Morning December 25th 1835 when I awoke springing from Bed with a wild confusion of ideas which made me feel I did not know how—it was Christmas morning—CHRISTMAS! Oh the days [of] Pendleton—! —However would I could give the sounds of music in words on paper—what did I hear—Deep and thrilling the Trumpets and Trombones of a great Band with the long warlike rolling of the Drums

Welcome Welcome Mighty King

Welcome to our hearts and homes

Hope upon untiring wing

To announce thee onward comes

There was a majestic flood of sounds for ye Then a Symphony of Horns and Hark the Blast of the Chorous[sic]

Welcome Welcome Lord of Glory

Who on earth is like to thee

Shines the light of Triumph oer thee

Beams thy Brow with Victory

And another thundering Reveille of the Drums! —It was too much so up flew the window curtains and My Soul! —All the street was filled in compact columns with my own Noble comrades—My Glorious fellow soldiers the flood of gold and scarlet in sunbright—Banners and at their Head—the Man—the Cheif of Men— "God Save the King"! I roared out and jumped into my clothes dashed down the stair case alighted on my head on the pavement and raised a pair of noble lungs in the incessant shouts of rapture around me—where was mortality for I never felt it I howled for agony of the soaring spirit on and on we moved with the scarlet ranks passing through street after street where each crowd seemed vaster than the other I never saw such prodigious masses of humanity and then when we reached Victoria Square what a sublime sight what a mighty throng of United and unconquered Africans there could not be short of 150000 souls But what was there on the great steps of Wellesly House why the Angrian Ministry and in the midst—ALEXANDER EARL OF NORTHANGERLAND The Tower had been surrounded while I lay asleep the keepers were bribed and the Man of Revolutions was here—Make way for his Majesty was the cry and The Glorious Duke rode through on horseback Bareheaded till dismounting he stood by a Earl and they took each others hands then a wild shout rent the Heavens till it seemed that each mans heart had gone up with the sound The Duke began to speak but I so far off could hear nothing nor could I have attended if I did my heart beat with such incontrollable vehemence—Nine thousand Gallant Troops stretched away from the center of the Square far down the square Ninety thousand pressed on each side of them the mighty folds of scarlet waved over the portico of the palace and under the portal stood the two leaders of their Age—But a wild rumor was flying among the Multitude that no one could make out but at which every one gasped with agitation—groans were heard of mingled agony and glory I shook with emotion—Zamorna was still speaking and when he saw we did not hear he beckoned to Naughty who after hearkening to him raised his voice to a Gigantic tone

"Men and Brethren The Ministry have sent to state that Unless Arthur Wellesly and Alexander Percy are delivered up to them again to be put in the tower they will have recourse to extreme measures immediatly Will you diliver them up or will you not!"

A Horse laugh from every one was the reply and then we roared out "let 'em come and take em if they can!" So the messenger went as he came and the Earl of Northangerland Began to address the Multitude "Well My Countrymen" he was saying "we all smell blood in the wind!" When—suddenly—A Horrible ROAR pealed up like Thunder through the Air—It was vast and stuning—not a sound escaped us till a dreary cry came as it were from afar—Then our voices came to us "The Ships The Ships" was the cry and a burst of tumultous ex[e]cration told the feeling of our minds It was useless—The Terrible Crack Burst up again—and Good God was the cry what will become of our city the whole 150000 were rushing forward to overwhelm the detestable foe. But their Leaders from the Portico cried out "Where are you hasting would you rush before the mouth of a volcano—what can you do before a thousand cannon" and the Soldiers were directly ordered to range themselves before the masses these promptly obeying prevented the rush towards the Harbour which must have ended in placing a hundred thousand souls among the shattered walls in face of a murderous fire the universal Broadsides of the Island Navy—

PROCLAMATION

WE By the Grace of God Monarchs of the Verdopolitan Grand National Union To all our Loving Subjects of Parrisland Rossesland Wellingtons Land

Sneachis land the Verdopolitan territory comprising the Division of Angria. and the Moncays and Stumphs Isles with all our other dependancies whatsoever hereunto belonging

Whereas—A Bill having been on the Nineteenth of December 1835 Brought before our two Houses of Parliament in a conference assembled To the effect that No Persons calling themselves or being called Peers of the Kingdom of Angria and no Persons acting and officiation[sic] as Commons of the Commons House or Parliament of Angria Likewise no person having the title of King of Angria shall not in future from that day forward for ever have or possess any right or title to sit or officiate as a member of the General Parliament or Government of the Union—And this Bill being legally read and passed into a standing law to be placed on the Statutes of the Realm—

—On the Night of the twenty first of December 1835 a body of men terming themselves Members of the Angrian Parliament Did treasonably and illegally in defiance of the Statute law of the Kingdoms—force or attempt to force their enterance into the Grand Hall of Our Peers and Commons in parliament assembled whereupon the proper officers arrested as in duty bound the persons of two of the Rioters—called or commonly known by the names and titles of Arthur Augustus Adrian Wellesly Duke of Zamorna and Alexander Percy Earl of Northangerland and ejected the persons of the other rioters from the House. these men upon the Night of the 23th of December 1835 a second time attempted to force an entrance into the House of Conference of the United Parliament But were again ejected the persons of 5 of Ringleaders being taken into Custody namly Warner Howard Warner Barrister and articled Attorney— Edward Percy Woolstapler and worsted spinner—Wilkin Thornton Sneachi— Major in the 30th Rejiment of Infantry Frederic Lofty Colonel in the 1st Rejiment of Horseguards and Frederic Stuart Colonel of the 30th Rejiment of Infantry—yet those five persons wilfully and feloniously made their escape and absconded from the Legal Officers and Where has[sic] upon the 24 of December these men with others proffessing to be Members of the Angrian Parliament published or caused to be published in their Name a Treasonable Declaration affirming that the law passed to exclude them from Our parliament was null and void and expressing their determination to resist its execution by all means in their power—Also a second Declaration treasonably exciting the People of the Angrian Provinces to Seditious Acts against Our Authority and declaring their intention To defy and Rebel against our Government And whereas on the 25th of December 1835 being Christmas Day a large Body of Men clothed and armed as Soldiers and proffessing themselves subjects of the Angrian Kingdom Did willfully maliciously and feloniously enter and break into the City of Verdopolis with intent to rescue the Duke of Zamorna and the Earl of Northangerland from the Power and whereas these two prisoners did consent to and abet their escape and afterwards did address a mixed multitude of people in false treasonable and Rebellious Language And whereas from that time forwards these persons aforsaid with many other wicked and designing men have gone about the provinces of

Angria inciting the people to a resistance of the Laws and a rebellion to our authority and have in meetings convened by them or their assistants have declared openly their intention to slight and disobey the orders of Our Government and have refused to deliver up the absconded prisoners to the lawful Authoritys

WE. By the Grace of God Monarchs of Africa Ever anxious for the good and prosperity of our Loving Subjects and resolved to maintain firm and inviolate those rights and privileges of our Government which we have received and sworn to watch over on our coronation And as in duty bound as Heads and Guardians of the Statutes laws of our Kingdoms—seeing that in the manner aforsaid sundry designing persons in the Kingdom of Angria have thus falsly traitorously and seditiously arrayed their fellow subjects against our rule and authority Do hereby Declare—
THAT—firstly—The Persons of

1ly—Arthur Augustus Adrian Wellesly -------Wellesly House   Verdopolis
2ly—Alexander Percy ---------------------------- Elrington Hall   Verdopolis
3ly—Warner Howard Warner --------------------Warner Hall   Howard
4ly—Wilkin Thornton Sneachi -----------------Girnington Hall   Zamorna
5ly—Frederic Stuart --------------------------------Stuartville Park   Stuartville
6ly—Frederic Lofty --------------------------------Arundel House   Steaton
7ly—Edward Percy --------------------------------Edwardston Hall Edwardston

Having wilfully and feloniously Broken into the deliberations of parliament Traitorously escaped from the Hands of Legal Officers maliciously and seditiously striven to inflame and incite the people against the just and lawful Authority and wantonly and mishceivously[sic] arrayed an armed force against our Legal Government—ARE—Hereby Declared and We do now declare them to be Outlawed and Excommunicated from the protection of all and every Legal and Social privilege. Deprived of all their Rank titles offices and possessions and money lands rights or other privileges of citizens and subjects of the Verdopolitan Union—That all their Houses Lands monies or properties of any discription and wheresoever situate lying or being are Her[e]by and henceforth confiscate and made over to Officers appointed for the use of the Government shall be adjudged by our several Secretarys of State—That Whosoever after the publication of this proclamation be found Guilty of aiding abetting sheltering or otherwise communicating with the persons aforsaid shall be guilty of High Treason against our authority and punished accordingly And that All our Loving Subjects may unite with our Officers in the furtherance and assistance of a search after and pursuit of the persons afforsaid we hereby [grant]22 that to any one not of their number who shall seize the Body of any of the persons aforsaid and place it in any one of Our Gaols or in the Hands of any of our legal officers the sum of 20000£ pounds sterling current money of the realm for each such Body wether

---

22   Branwell has omitted a word here.

alive or dead. And that if any one of our subjects refuse to join in and abett any search or pursuit or any constable neglect upon proper suspicion to raise the Hue and Cry or any person or persons whatever be found guilty of any attempt to hinder the inforcement of the provisos of this enactment shall be delivered over into custody of Our Officers for this service appointed

That Secondly—We do Hereby declare the Whole of that part of Our Union generally known by the Name of the Kingdom of Angria to be henceforward placed and considered as under Blockade and interdiction So that proper Officers by us to be appointed shall see that no person and no goods or other articles shall enter that kingdome either by land or sea under any name or flag also that no person or goods or any other Articles shall be permitted to pass out of that Country under penalty of Death to the first and confiscation of the latter

That Thirdly—We do Hereby Declare that any vessel Bearing the flag of the Kingdom of Angria found upon the High Seas or in any Port or Harbour whatever shall be considered confiscated to the Government and upon resistance being made its crew shall be liable to Death by Law of Court Martial And any person in our whole Union who declares himself a subject of the Angrian Kingdom shall unless he take proper oaths of submission to our Authority be considered a felon and disposed of accordingly

That Fourthly we do Hereby Declare that in order to the Better carrying into effect these the provision of our Enactment to execute our will and to punish Rebels to our Authority We Now and Straightways Place the Whole Kingdom of Angria under MARTIAL LAW Of a Grand Court Martial General to be appointed in our city of Verdopolis and Court Martial in every Rejiment of [the] National Army with such other courts and officers as they may appoint the whole to placed under Orders from the Commander in Cheif of Our National Forces—Also We Hereby Declare That we place the whole coasts of our kingdoms and the coasts of Angria and the High Seas under corresponding Naval Law to be distributed by Our Admirals Vice Admirals and Captains of Our Fleet under the cognizance and at the Will of Our High Court of Admiralty and the Lord High Admiral of the Fleet

That Fifthly We Hereby Declare

Major General The Honourable Sir Jehoram Henry Jehu De Bruce MacLurin Macterrorglen Baronet M P. Commander in Cheif of Our National Forces—Our Lord Lieutenant of Angria and Cheif Judge of our Courts Martial with full powers to direct our military forces to the furtherance of the Law—Also we Declare—

The Right Honourable Arthur Parry Marquis of Ardrah Lord High Admiral Our Admiral in Cheif for furtherance of Justice on the the High Seas— And moreover that As First Lord of the Treasury He be empowered to direct the operations of both fleet and Army aided and assisted by our several Secretarys of State

And Now Having Declared Our Royal Will and Intention to enforce Obedience to our Laws and Government in every part of the Union But more particularly in Our Division of the Angrian Kingdom We call upon all our loving subjects to rise in aid and assistance of our just endeavours and command them to Devote all the powers w[h]ere they may be required to the quelling of Sedition and Rebellion And in the same act to the advantage and succor of themselves By the Will of Almighty God under whom we hold our authority a Dreadful spirit of Wickedness has been allowed to spread through Angria and lest it should corrupt the sounder portions of our union we have Determined upon the most Energetic measures for its extinction and We must suceed if Our Loving Subjects duly rally round Our Throne

Under all Circumstances Our measures are taken to inflict a terrible punishment on those who refuse obedience to or wilfully oppose our rightful Authority

Given at our Royal Court of St Michaels this Twenty seventh Day of December in the year of our Lord Eighteen Hundred and Thirty Five

By their Majesties Command signed ————————

ARDRAH[23]

God Save the Kings!

To the Lord lieutenants Justices of
The peace or other state officers
In all our provinces and citys
Throughout the Union—

PROCLAMATION

IN The Name of Arthur Augustus Adrian Monarch of Angria and Duke of Zamorna To His Subjects the people of the Kingdom of Angria

Whereas A proclamation Has been <issued> upon the 27th Day of this Month Dated from Verdopolis and signed by the Prime Minister in the Name of the Kings of the Union Declaring

Firstly—That the King and Government of Angria have broken the Laws Resisted their execution and incited the Nation to revolt against their Authority

Secondly that this King and Government are Outlawed Excommunicated and deprived of the right of citizen ship that their titles are annulled and their property confiscated that every man is invited to hunt and seize upon them like wild beasts while a reward of 20000 £ is offered for the Body of any one of them Dead or alive and punishment of Death Denounced on any one found guilty of aiding or concealing them

---

23 A coat of arms is sketched next to the signature.

Thirdly that the whole Kingdom of Angria is declared placed under Blockade and interdiction so that nothing shall pass out of or enter into it under pain of death or confiscation

Fourthly that All vessels carrying the Angrian flag are forfeit to Government and their crew punishable with death in the case of resistance

Fifthly that any person calling himself a Subject of Angria shall unless he renounce his subjection be considered a Traitor and accordingly punished

Sixthly That in order better to carry into effect these declarations—THE KINGDOM OF ANGRIA IS TO BE PLACED UNDER MARTIAL LAW AND ITS SHORES AND WATERS UNDER LAW OF THE ADMIRALTY while Military and Naval Forces are to be raised to enforce its ordinance

Seventhly That The Commander in Cheif Sir Jehoram Henry Jehu De Bruce Maclarrin MacTerrorglen Bart and the Lord High Admiral The Marquis of Ardrah be appointed the first as Lord Lieutenant of Angria the second As Admiral of the Fleet and in capacity of Prime Minister the Cheif Dictator of our Country

Eighthly That All the people of Africa are commanded under pain of terrible punishment to rise and assist Government in carrying into effect those aforementioned Declarations

WE The Lawful Government of the Angrian Nation Do Her[e]by in the sight of Almighty God Declare

That No laws have been broken or resisted by the King and Ministry of our country

That Our King and ourselves in their persons and property are sacred and inviolate

That any Injury to them or arrest of them must be visited with Legal punishment

That Angria is a free member of the Union and resistance to its commerce is illegal

That vessels of Angria are as secure from the laws as those of Verdopolis

That a Subject of Angria is a Member of the Union and sacred from injury

That it is impossible for any Government to place Angria under Martial Law

And That any attempt to do so—The first step of a human being not her own upon Her territory shall unless he can produce a passport from Our Officers on the frontiers in seaports—render him liable to the penalty of Instant DEATH

And In order to secure the maintainance and execution of this our purpose we Hereby—place the Whole Kingdom of Angria Under Law of Court Martial appointing Major General the Right Honourable Wilkin Thornton M P Commander in Cheif the Supreme Head of the Court Under The Ministry of Angria who exist under Our KING

And we call upon every Subject of Angria to rise up in support of His King his Country himself. and the Common rights of every human being for never before in the memory of men Has a Country been so unjustly so impiously assaulted as ours And with the Aid of our Countrymen never shall a Country have been so rightfully and righteously Defended

Angrians Every thing which you can hold dear as men is now threatened with annihilation by The Government of the Union at Verdopolis without the slightest just grounds where on to attack us and without the slightest legal power to assail! They cannot by Law debar us from their Legislature they cannot imprison our King and Ministry They cannot restrain the Commerce of our Country They cannot place Angria under the Tyranny of a Military and Naval Tribunals[sic] They cannot impose as our Emperor the Marquis of Ardrah—And It is Our Duty as your Government to say that

THEY SHALL NOT!—

Angrians We Declare the power which we must exercise against their Attempts. —WE CALL ALL THE KINGDOM TO ARMS. We command every Subject of our King to take what weapons he can find and ARISE to defend his Land Every person not an Angrian and unable to produce his passports must instantly DIE All Sheriffs Mayors Magistrates and Legal Officers through the country must place themselves under the Courts Martial which will be formed in every district and act under. their direction The Lords Lieutenant of every province must bring into imm[e]diate muster their respective Volunteer and militia forces and place them at the Orders of Government ports must instantly shut and frontiers barred Taxes for the struggle must be raised and above all AN ARMY MUST BE RAISED Every soldier and Officer absent from his Regiment must repair instantly to head Quarters passage and quarters for any one in an Angrian Uniform must be given free and and if any injustice is done or injury suffered redress can be obtained only by applieng to a Court Martial.

But above all it is Our Monarchs Desire that Voluntary Bands are to be raised. Guerilla partys as it were Bands uniting by common impulse of what ever nature or number But joined in a fixed determination to Defend their King and Constitution and Country from any invader. and the moment any of these Bands reaches the number of 1000 it is to be placed under the orders of the Government or Court Martial by whom it will be Officered and armed.

Angrians Now forsake your manufactories and shops and callings Devote yourselves henceforth at the Altar of your God to the preservation of your Country and so long as a single hostile foot stands armed upon your shore Bend all your thoughts and actions to the Prosecution of Our Righteous War We your Government under your Glorious Monarch will do our part to push on the measures we have mentioned. But Countrymen Do your part Remember that God himself commands your undertaking And wherever his Vault of Heaven may cover you. By Our Countrys watch word we command you—

ANGRIANS ARISE!

By his Majestys Command Given at the Zamorna Palace Adrianopolis and signed in his name

Warner Howard Warner Secretary of State for the
Home department[24]

Castlereagh	William Sydenham
Arundel	Wilkin Thornton
Dance	William Moray
Henri Fernando Enara	Markham Howard
John George Kirkwall	Frederic Fala
Edward Percy	Charles Warner

God Save Our King!

:

    Appropriatly I conclude My First Volume of My Experience in this[sic] Troubles with these two Manifestos the first of Malignant Tyranny the last of Ennobled and ennobling patriotism—The sensations they each excited through the country I find it impossible to describe and their full effect no one as yet can know But close upon them has just appeared a Magnificent Address from Our King to his people in which all that a majestic mind and glorious feeling can fix upon paper unites to swell the hearts of its readers with an enthusiastic courage which can never die It tells us that The feindlike Ministry of Verdopolis have called in to their assistance the French and the Ashantees our Natural and irreconcileable foes and Right it is that these people should assist in what they have allways assisted—the attempted destruction of our Native Land.

    But this Certain Intelligence that a Great Body of French forces under Marshal Massena either will directly arrive or have actually set foot on the Shores of Angria under cover of the Guns of the Thistle and Nevada and Caroline and their attendant Enjines of Tyranny while forty Regiments are nearly assembled from the south to attack it upon its Western frontier and a Cloud of Locusts from the East[25] even now have crossed the Etrei and this Intelligence Terrific though it be has roused up the Souls of every True African to a pitch of unconquerable resolution All things shew as Our Monarch tells us that the conflict is doomed to be a protracted one that victory cannot crown our first endeavours—nay all things shew that the tempests will ere long spread its[sic] Desolation over Every Part of the Union But This cannot alter the conduct of Angria Our King has been thrown into a Dungeon—Our Government have been brutally insulted A price is put upon their Heads Our country is <altogether> outlawed a Dictator is imposed upon Our Land Feirce Military Law is our only refuge—on that side of the picture—But Our Monarch is The DUKE OF ZAMORNA our Premier is the Earl of Northangerland our Ministry are the

---

24 To the left of the list of names appears a sketch of the Angian coat of arms.

25 See Exodus, chapter 10.

Ablest Men in Africa Our country is the Land of Angria Our selves are the
Apostles of a worlds Redemption

    For myself I look forward with Untameable Excitement to the Life
which is opening out for me—But let me not speak of it It may be finished ere
to morrow and under any circumstances let me remember that

There are Thrones to be shaken
There is vengeance to be taken
Ere this dark and Dreary Midnight shall give place to rising Day!
Ere the cloud of the Eclipse shall give place to lucid day

Henry Hastings
Verdopolis Dec 28th
A D 1835

P B Bronte
January the
Seventh
1836

:

According to his 1837 volume of poems (see vol. III), Branwell composed the first draft of **Lines**—"Now then I am alone"—on December 17, 1835, and of **The Spirit of Poetry** sometime in 1835. No manuscripts have been found.

He rode across the Moor at night[1]
  When starlight only shone
But even their dim beams were bright
  In that woe which weigh[ed] His Spirit down

He galloped onward furiously
  But could not fly from ca[re]
He fearless faced the winter wind
  But could not give His thoughts to air

How fast that Horse rushed thundering by[2]
With Arching neck and flashing eye
So black the Night so loud the Storm
I scarce could know its fleeting form
And yet the those flanks all dashed with mire
Those Nostrils wide which seem to expire
The hot short breath of agony

---

[1] Trial lines for the opening of the earliest version of **Misery** (see next page) on the first page of BPM: BS 118, part of an autograph manuscript notebook, originally bound but now dismembered and scattered among four libraries. Consisting of at least sixty pages, 9.5x15.5 cm, the notebook contained, in addition to the trial lines, fair copies of eight poems (some unfinished), dated December 1835 to May 1838, and a short prose passage.

[2] These lines appear on the back of the final page of Charlotte's "Letter to the right honourable Arthur Marquis of ARDRAH," dated December 6, 1834, in **The Scrap Book** (see Alexander CB II, part ii, 316-24). The lines, undated and unsigned, are however in Branwell's hand and are also trial lines for the opening of the earliest version of **Misery**.

How Fast that Courser Fleeted by[1]
His arched neck backward tossed on high
His snorting nostrils opened wide
His foam flecked chest and gory side
    I saw his Riders darkned form
As on they hurried through the storm
Forward he pressed his plume behind
Flew whistling in the wintery wind
But his clenched teeth and angry eye
Seemed wind and tempest to defy
And eagerly he bent his sight
To peirce the darkness of the night
And oft he gazed and gazed again
Through the rough blast and driving rain
    Look up and see the midnight heaven
Where mass oer mass continual driven
The wild black storm clouds fleet and change
Like formless phantoms vast and strange
That bend their gloomy brows from high
To pass in midnight darkness by
And still they pass and still they come
Without a flash to break the gloom
—I cannot see the foam and spray
That mark that raging torrents way
But well I hear the ceasless roar
Where swollen and chafed its waters pour
There—where yon blackned Oaks on high
Blend wildly with the Midnight sky
Tossing their bare and groaning boughs
Like some dread fight of Giant foes
There—where that glimpse of Moonlight shines
    From the wild wrack of heaven sent down
And spreads it[s] silver trembling lines
    Amid the darkness then is gone—
—There stays the Horsman—wide before
Deep and Dark the waters roar
But down the lone vale far away
Glances one solitary ray
The sound of winds and waters rise
And sweeps the sleet shower oer the skies
While dreariest darkness all around
Makes still more drear each sight or sound

---

[1]   The first draft of Scene I of **Misery**; the lines, in BPM: BS 118, constitute
pp. 2-8 of the notebook described on the previous page.

But heeds not such that Cavalier
Reining his trembling Charger there
He halts upon the rivers brink
Where all its wild waves surge and sink
Shades with his hand his anxious eye
And through the night looks eagerly
—Why smiled he when that far off light
Again broke twinkling on his sight
Why frowned he when it sunk again
Mid the rough wrack of stormy rain
Till brightly flashing forth once more
It streams and twinkles far before.

   "Oh through the tempests of this life
      However loud they sound
However wild their storms and strife
      May burst and thunder round
Though reft and riven each aid or prop
There may be Heaven!—there may be Hope!
I thought just now that Life or Death
      Could never trouble me
That I should draw my future breath
      In silent apathy
That oer the pathway of my fate
      Though steady beat the storm
As I walked alone and desolate
      Ide to that path conform
Affection should not cherish me
      Or Sorrow hold me down
But Despair itself sustain me
      Whom itself had overthrown
I knew that Fame and glory
      Were names for shame and woe
That Lifes deceitful story
      I had finished long ago
That all its novelty was gone
      And that thus to read again
The same dull page in the same sad tone
      Was not even change of pain
Defeat had crushed me into dust
      But only laid my head
Where head and heart and spirit must
      Be soon forever laid
My fearless followers all were slain
      My power and glory gone

My followers met the fate of man
       And Power—! I am NOW alone!
Not so! —I thought it—till that light
       Glanced glittering down the glen
And on my spirits dreary night
       Flashed brighter back again
Yes! I had thought I stood alone
That I need sigh or weep for none
Had quenched my love in apathy
Since none could sigh or weep for me
Yes! But that single silver beam
       Which flashes on my eye
Hath waked me from my dreary dream
       And bade my darkness fly
But pardon that the storms of woe
       Have whelmed me in a drifting sea
With death and dangers struggling so
       That I—a while—forgot even THEE
The moment that I gained the shore
       And clouds began to dissapear
Even steadier brighter than before
       THOU shinest my own—my Guardian Star!
—Oh could I speak the long lost feeling
The inward joy its power revealing
The glimpse of something yet to come
Which yet shall give a happy Home!
       Oh should I speak my thoughts of thee
Whom soon again my eyes shall see
—The Dove that bore the Olive leaf
Could never bring such glad relief
To wanderers oer the shoreless main
As in my weariness and pain
       That single light hath given to me
My Gallant Horse speed swiftly thou
Soon shall a Hand caress thee now
Gratful that thou hast born me on
Through deadliest deeds and dangers gone
A touch thou mayest be proud to own
Though thou so oft hast felt my own!
—Oh that fair hand and faithful heart
From mine what power can ever part?
What power!—Ha! well indeed I know
The very fire that burns me now
The very energy of soul
       That to thine arms impells me on

When once I have gained that heavenly goal
Will—Like a comet from the sun
Hurl me with power that scorns controll
Far from thy beams of Happiness
Into the Expanse of mad distress
Where passions lightnings burst and battles thunders roll!"

Impetous then that Horseman sprung
Down the deep bank—His Armour rung
Mid the wild waters roar
And Dashing through the Old Oak trees
His Coursers hoofs upon the breeze
Their reckless rattle swiftly cease
In that Dark night before!

He[2] that hath felt the feeling wild
Which struck upon the excited mind
When perhaps long since—while yet a child
In awful mystery undefined
Old tales and Legends darkly told,
While winter nights fell long and drear
Have made his hearts blood curdle cold
Their dreary tales to hear
Of Ancient Halls where Destiny
Had brooded with its Raven wing
Of Castles stern whose riotry
Hid not the gloomy crimes within
Of Death beds where the sickman lying
Mid anxious listners standing by
Ere he had told the secret dying
And left a sealed mystery
Of Heirs who to some fearful Doom
Suceeded with their ancient Hall
Of Marriage Feasts where Ghosts would come
The New made Bride to call
—He that Hath still in memory
Kept fast those dreams of childhoods hours
Who these far visions yet may see
Of Castle halls and feudal towers
—To Him I show this stormy Night
That seems to darken on my sight!

Far above their forest trees

---

2   "He" written above "Who"; neither is canceled.

Those dreary turrets rise
And round their walls the midnight breeze
Comes shreiking from the skies
Scarce can I note the central tower
Amid the impetous storm
Till shimmering through the pelting shower
The moonbeams mark its form
Far downward to the raving stream
The woody banks decline
Where waters flashing in the gleam
Through deepest darkness shine
Those Giant Oaks their boughs are tossing
As wild winds wilder moan
Trunks and leaves confus[e]dly crossing
With a ceasless groan
And over all the Castle Walls
Rise blacker than the night
No sign of man around their Halls
Save that lone turret light
The upward path is wild and steep
Yet hear that Horseman come
Not toiling up with cautious creep
But Hotly Hasting Home
The steed is to his stables led
But wheres the Rider gone
Up the high turret staircase sped
With gladdned haste alone
The Ante Room looks hushed and still
With lattice curtains close
That tempests sweeping round the hill
Disturb not its repose
Alls soft and calm a holy balm
Seems sleeping in the air
But what on earth has pow[e]r to charm
A spirit chafed by care
The Warrior hastes to seek that power
He knows the only one
Whose love can sooth his lonly hour
Or hush his rising groan
And where that soft and solemn light
Shines chequreing[sic] oer the floor
He Hastens in with armed tread
Toward the opened door
And entering—Though a sacred stream
Of Radiance round him fell

It could not with its silent beam
    His eager spirit quel
"Maria!" —But the silence round
    Would give him no reply
And straightway did that single sound
    Without an echo die

"Where hath my Gentle Lady gone
    I do not find her here?"
Lo on that statly couch alone
    Reclines thy Lady fair
But—cold and pale is her marble brow
    Dishevelled her sunny hair
Oh! is it in peacful slumber now
    That she lieth so silent there?
"Heaven bless thy Dreams!" Lord Albert cried
    But his heart beat impetously
And as he hasted to her side
    He scarce had power to see
All wildly the scenes of his former life
    Flashed back upon his eyes
And at once a cloud of Despair and strife
    Before him seems to arise!
But as the sailor to his ship
    Clings with more frenzied power
As louder thundering oer the deep
    Fresh billows whelm it oer
So madly on his only prop
    This war worn man reclined
He could not would not deem his hope
    Delivered to the wind!

Yet then why is this start of bewildered fright?
    And whence can arise this fear?
Is it not now the depth of night?
    And sleeps not thy Lady there?
And art not thou on thy castle height
    From wars alarms afar?
See—is that sleep?—
                —With open eyes
Chilly white and cold she lies!
Sunk her cheeks and blanched her lip
    That trembles as with suffering—
She sleeps not till the eternal sleep
    Its dreamless rest shall bring!

Heaven had occupied her mind
To onward hasting Death resigned
But mid those strange uncertainties
     That crowd their ghastly phantoms round
When all our Reasons guiding ties
     Are from the parting soul unbound
She thought when first she heard that tread
     That Death himself was hasting near
The conjured vision of his form
     Obeyed her ready fancies fear
     And to her dim eyes seemed to appear
     Till—that one word—and all was clear!
Then—sinking Reason rose again
Then—joined the links of memorys chain
Then—spite of all her Dying pain
     She felt—she knew her Lord was there!
Oh! when across that dreary sea
The light broke forth so suddenly
What soul can feel what tongue express
The burst of raptured Happiness
          That from her spirit chased its care
          For—She was dying! But—He was near!

AH! surely swiftly art thou gliding
     Over Deaths unfathomed sea
Dark and Dread the waves dividing
     Thee from earth and earth from thee!
Life thy own thy native land
Parting far on either hand
     As the mighty waters widen
          Onward to Eternity!
Shores of Life farewell for ever
     Where thy happiness has lain
Lost for ever! Death must sever
     All thy Hopes and joys and pain!
Yet how blest that sound must be
     Which strikes upon thy dying ear
From off the dim departing shore
     Allt[h]ough its landmarks dissapear
Still sounding oer the eternal roar
     The voice of HIM whou holdst so dear!
     Tis as when the Mariner
Just parted from his native home
     After a night of dread and fear
Whose storms have riven the waves to foam

When Nights dark hours have wrapt away
All save the sounding of the sea
Morn breaks where all looks new and strange
But Hark—! a sweet and sudden change
For on his ear strikes soft from far
In Sabbath chime his Native Bells
He starts and bursts the joyful tear
For things unutterably dear
   That farewell music tells!

Yet stay—why do I wander so
To wile me from that scene of woe?
   There stood that Armed man
The very maddness of Despair
In his red eyeballs stricken glare
   His cheek so ghastly wan!
And on her couch his Lady lying
Still and slow and surely dying
Yet with an enraptured smile
  And glittering of her glassy eye
And her weak arms she would the while
  Have stretched to clasp him standing by
But they would not her will obey
And motionless beside her lay
Then her white lips moved to speak
   But nothing could she say!
This was Deaths triumphant hour
Grasped by his tremendous power
   She must pass away!

"Speak Maria! —speak my love!
  Let me hear thy voice
Nought on earth or Heaven above
  Could make me so rejoice!
Speak O speak and say to me
I am not come too late to thee!
Oh tell me that my arm can save
Thy spirit from the hideous grave!
Maria! O my only love
  Tell me thou wilt not die
And naught below me or above
  Shall feel so blest as I!
Oh would that I were far away
Alone upon a stormy sea
Might I awake on yonder plain

Where I have left my Soldiers slain
So I could wake and rise and know
   That this was but a frightful dream
That thou at least wert living now
   In love and life and beautys beam!
But here's the truth which now I know!
My God My God I cannot bear thy blow!"

All was vain! she moved not spoke not
Speech or sound the silence broke not
But he flung him oer her lying
As he would catch her spirit dying
All was vain! —That spirit flies
To God who gave it in the skys!
That within his arms which lay
Was but a lifeless form of clay
Nought of feeling in that face
No return to his embrace
Not a wish or power to save
Its own cold members from their grave
   Go Lord Albert go again
     Drown thought amid a world of storms
   Go—for thy Despair is vain
     And thy Hope lies food for worms!

Finished Dec. 18th
1835
P B Brontë
Haworth
Yorks

[Angria and the Angrians]
II(a)[1]

P B Bronte
January 7th
1836

This is the first of January 1836 and it is NEW YEARS DAY Truely Readers to you and to me and to All Africa it is a New Year must I alter the word and say a New Eve—The future alone can determine that But the present seems strongly to Indicate it Most Certainly our Native Land was never in so tremendous a Darkness before never with so many Elements of Discord so thouroughly[sic] lighted up—And Wrongs inflicted and Tyranny exercised and Rights maintained and courage roused upon so mighty a scale

But I am writing not a History of my nation but describing my own prospects of and experience in it therefore I may well ask. and what is this new year to me—Why read this Letter

Sir

You are request[ed] without Delay to join your Company in the Twenty Ninth Rejiment encamped at the Town of Wharton

Chas Warner S.W.

War Office Adrianopolis   (To Captain Hastings
December 26th 1835.   Angrian Hotel Verdopolis)

Wharton[2] is within 20 miles of Mouthon and near Mouthton the French will Land This is enough and the moment I mount the Coach A new Era of my Life begins I am writing at the close of New Years day All my affairs are settled and the moment the Sun of Angria gets its Horses put to I Leave Verdopolis and peace and the comforts and prosperity of Social Life—for WAR and fighting with the French and the Defence of my country against the Reform Ministry of the Union!

It was night When I got onto the Coach which wheeled through the streets into the middle of Elrington Square Here a mighty sight presented itself Quite round that great expanse was drawn [up] the Nine thousand Angrian soldiers who had entered December   3 —Inward of these the whole Square was filled with Carriages Coaches Waggons &c filled with Angrian Residents and the

---

1   A ten-page manuscript section, 11.2x18.5 cm, divided between two libraries. The initial portion consists of leaf one of Ashley 187 in the BL.

2   The actual town of Wharton lies between Leominster and Hereford in Hereford and Worcestor.

3   Branwell left the date blank.

Households and Valuables of the Angrian Nobility and Gentry As every thing which belonged to Angria that existed in Verdopolis was legally confiscated and every man legally dead Here while our Troops were yet in the City was the only time when these things could possibly leave it to stay behind those Rejiments would be Madness so everything was going with them All the priceless Riches of Wellesly and Elrington Houses with a hundred other Mansions with all their Establishments were piled in these

It was Night when I got onto the Coach which was to carry me and itself with all its passenger for we knew not how long from the City of Verdopolis The Troops of Angria 9000 in number and all the Angrian Residents had departed during the Day for Zamorna We were almost too late for another hour and we should have been captured But as it was under cover of night through glaringly lighted streets filled with a distrusted and excited population we rattled away till past the Majestic Squares of Waterloo Palace and extricated from the palace like Mansions of the suburbs we gradually advanced onto the Adrianopolitan Road All cloudy and starless was the Winter Night. as I looked back over the coach upon the wide haloed haze of Verdopolis And all its buildings were hidden and all its wonders passed away and nothing but a dream of what was in it remained upon the mind of him who was going to plunge into scenes which came like a mightier vision of the future before his eyes with arms folded and muffled in my cloak I sat back my head declined into the fur collar in an intense thinking upon the buisness I was to launch into. I have seen War before as my readers know and can never forget the wonders of the Etrei and the Benguela But my very initiation only opened to me more fully and freshly the unparralleled scenes of WAR. Now I Do here Declare that I am a courageous young man. I mean one of sound healthy and vigourous nerves moreover my mind is easily and strongly roused into enthusiasm by any thing great and terrible But that very keen sense of every thing most certainly makes me feel keenly dreadful things And those awful volleys of thunder whose Iron hail I had beheld transform powerful heavey men into <sent>ient and tormented masses of flesh the sweeping charges of Iron hoofed Horses over helpless wretches without hope crushed into Death and the frightful sights that I had seen after Bayonet charges gasping and howling and sick with incurable torture—indeed the whole unutterable sight of Battle could not now recalled fail to make a mans nerves quiver within him—But—this I do say that the quivering only excited a flushed and restless excitement that went to form the grand edifice of a stirring and glorious futurity so that it was with feelings which for the world I would not lose that when we drew up at the Hotel in Zamorna I saw the lighted streets crowded to witness the Angrian Rejiments filing through from Edwardston and then rolling over the new Bridge when by the gaslights upon it we could just know that two immense Redoubts were forming on the Ings to protect and command its passage for almost certainly within a few days this spot will be the scene of a contest in civil war and when again we plunged into the dark night beyond I felt my soul brightened with magnificent pictures of future glory— From Zamorna to Danceton in about 9 hours we had passed over 70 miles of the province through many towns and villiages which in spite of those Late and early hours seemed often astir with preparations for war but the night was so dark that I can say no farther. At last about an hour before sun rise beneath a grey uncertain veil of clouds the spire and roofs of Wharton appeared with the mists of the Assonda stretching across the country. and as I knew though I saw it not 10 or 15 miles in advance the Armies of the Invaders and the wide opening of the Calabar—When a Man finds himself so near the seat of war he expects to see manifest signs of it But I did not do so all at once for the land look[ed] like what in any dreary Winter morning it may have looked before But when we entered the town we found houses shut up and streets crowded with soldiers the usual indications of a military Biavouck.[sic] yet there was nothing very striking even here. Wharton is not a large place and I saw no more than 1000 or 1100 men cheifly from the Rejiment to which I belonged. Lord Hartford it seemed held command of it and with him I was to have an interview So I set out straight for the Principal Inn filled with Servants and Orderlys and costly Appointments while in front of it several Grooms held charge of a Travelling Carriage and half a Dozen Noble Horses The place was evidently something more than a Colonels quarters even though the Colonel were a Nobleman. However so soon as my name was announced I obtained free admittance to His Lordship who was seated alone in a little room that opened onto a crowded large one Shaking me very heartily by the hand My Commander pointed to the only chair disencumbered of Luggage and said

"Now Hastings you have written well let us see wether you can fight equal to it for G—d Sir! we are like to sweat for it It is not 2 days since I entered from Verdopolis and such a tangled peice of work as the operations present I never yet beheld Its well for me that I am not so much called on to devise as to execute though as I have the title of a General I expect before long to have the duty of one—"

"Why my Lord I am sorry at what you have told me for I thought to get from you some insight into the machinery of the champaigne I am sure I know nothing of it—"

"Oh Captain If I were aquainted with it I would not scruple to divulge some of it to you for you have deserved it at our hands—Not but you know if I were engaged in the concoction of it I would keep the secret from every one—But thats not been the case for I left Verdopolis the Night before yesterday and haven[sic] not once seen My fellow Ministers at Adrianopolis—But I guess what you ask for is what I need not scruple to tell if I could—the present situation and first movement of our forces and those of the Enemy the last matter I do know middlingly considering my short stay for it has been my employment to collect news for the Commander in Cheif on his Arrival. Yet heres a large Map of Zamorna and a look at it only confuses my facts into nonsense—The truth is Captain we are in a tremendous state and a look beyond our nose nobs will shew us all Africa in the same predicament though the D—ned Proclamation of the Infernal Ministry who would push the whole world into ruin makes ones blood boil till one does not care for any thing beyond Angria—However Here we are

8000 men under my orders at Wharton—half of them down at the River which I am strengthning As well as I can. 20 miles down theres Mouthton with 9000 under Lord Castlereagh both of us muster 17000—Well Massena has landed at Southpoint and he is now with 26000 men between this and that midway. ie. 15 miles looking at himself only in a bad position for Mouthon is directly on his flank and we in his front But mark you he does not reckon without his host for The Caroline Eclipse Thunderer Thistle St Andrew and Ardashir[4] with four frigates Ride just off the fort streng[t]hning his right and Marmont with 19000 men has landed at Fernando Bay is coming up and equally streng[t]hens his left—But again on our side we have the Doverham Militia they say 11000 strong one days march on Marmonts flank—and the famous 9000 from Verdopolis under Moray at Zamorna to support us in our rear two long marches West But still—they have in their front the expected—I dont know how many D——ls from Verdopolis. Our Judge and Jury you know G—d d—n them—Yet Once more we have N E in our rear All Adrianopolis with 12000 troops under Arundel and I dont know how many more manufacturing with as a strengthner on their flank Enaras 30000 veterans Our Comrades of the Benguela Captain just ready to em[b]ark over the Calabar to aid us and when they arrive Our Noble Young King will take command of the whole at the Capital who will reach 50000 strong Enara and recruits included—But stop yet again—on their flank. and if they join us in their rear gather the Hordes of Ashantees thousands of Incarnate Feinds called up to destroy us by a Magician who can never quell them—Now theres a Grand Game of Chess for you Try to make a move if you can and mind be circumspect or it will leave points unsupported and gaps and advantage given which Our Enimies wont be slow to make the most of and as for them—But no they have the advantage it wont deny Numbers. three grand divisions to operate in against us and our one—"

"Aye But your Lordship has forgotten to name one point more move the others as you will there still remains upon the rear of all four noble provinces filled with Gallant Hearts all RISING. Angria Arundel Douro and Northangerland"

"Oh Captain if you say so Heres to oppose it the whole power of the Monarchs and the Government and the cursed Reformers without too wide to give it a locality of flank or front or rear"

"Well My Lord and to follow the Game Ive another Chessman to check that—Wellington and Sneachi and the Noble forces of the Constitution"

"Ha there you have me BUT—But Hastings a move there lifts the Sword not alone on the Calabar and Guadiana but on the Niger and the Red River and the Ardrah and the Gambia—but it matters not—such a move there must be and God grant it may soon be made!"

---

[4]   Except for the Ardashir, these are all names of ships in the British Navy in the early nineteenth century.

I listened with intense interest to Lord Hartfords account of the positions of the forces but the more I looked the less I could make of it And I said so

"Well Captain" Hartford replied there is one entering the Inn who I should think could enlighten you there

"The Commander in Cheif I have been expecting him all the morning"

I looked out of the window But General Thornton must have entered below yet His servant was leading of his Horse and from his livery I knew that All the Equipages and Grooms I had before noticed belonged to his suite arriving before him As I was gazing forth The Room Door opened and an Officer entered briskly whose square turned shoulders and open cheerful countenance I knew at once as those of my Whilom Commander and Leader of the charge at Loango

"Ha How dye do How dye Do Hartford somewhat latish Im afraid but what could a Body do when there were so many things to put to reights up yonder Now Lets have the long and short of it here for theres a deal to do and little time to do it in—What Captain Hastings—Im varry glad to see ye Man Fight as weel as you write and wes get on"[5]

The Hearty manner in which the General held forth his hand admitted of no ceremony I was proud to shake it But when I showed an intention to withdraw

"Nay nay do not go yet why Ive scarce seen ye man Stop and we'll all go down to the Bridge together to see how they get on But to work—Hartford how are the French Thats the point

"Why General Massena is with[in] 20 miles of us at Linwood[6] with 26000 men and he seems bent upon getting straight up to us and breaking our centre Marmont is at Twelveston twenty four miles off What he is going to Do is not so clear"

"Isnt it Stop Ill tell ye—weve made it aat for they've sent fro Kirkwall to tell us—He's aiming fair for thither and in two marches he'll be at Danceton then he's on our backs and Massena on our front—But we'll tent him The Duke is coming down on Danceton Enara stepps into his shoon in Adrianopolis We's be on his flank and Kirkwall at Doverham on his rear"

"Is the Duke coming"

"Aye marry he is"

"Then we shall have hot work of it—when?"

"To Morrow Lad"

"Hey presto! we must be quick!"

"Nay stop have ye a bit of something for a body Ive gone the 40 miles in four hours and Im fair.gaunt Wes like let em see what we're made of enow and as for Death If he take the formost why Deil tak the Hindmost So we're quits like—But How's all wi you Hartford and how did you leave your lady?"

"Oh well enough considering the circumstances of parting and How—"

---

5   The following section consists of leaf two of BPM: BS 120.

6   The actual Linwood is in Lincolnshire, between Lincoln and Market Rasen.

"Now tels here How yeve getten on at the Brig"

"Certainly—and How's—

"How many men say you you've in the town Hartford"

"Really—Why two Regiments—and How's Lady Julia General?"

"How can I tell I havent second seight!"

And the General set himself assidously to taking off his boots with his face averted in a peculiar expression of uneasiness

"Hey what! something wrong surely you did not quarrel and at such a time!"

"Yes but we did Man!" And the Bell was rung violently for the servant

"Really that was too bad General when for anything Her Ladyship knew—"

"She might be married agean in a two month but it doesnt mean! its all reight!"[7]

"Its well it is but I should not think so" But the servants enterance stopt the dialogue And the General gave him directions to Bring him his shoon and get him his dinner—A conversation upon the Awful state of Africa and the Atrocious proceedings of the Ministry was then entered into in which I joined untill the period of my visit

The whole of that evening was employed by me in Regimental <matters> and at night I and a Dozen Brother officers celebrated our meeting at a rattling and hope inspiring mess table It was well int[o] morning before I went to rest and well into day before I woke with a curious feeling to find myself in the thick of my proffession before I knew almost that I had entered it At mess that day nothing was talked of but speculation upon the news and buisness of sundry Aide de Camps and messengers who had kept arriving in hot haste from Adrianopolis to Head quarters But at Night the Coaches came in from the capital and these Brought the Newspapers which contained important news—The Ashantees under their Infernal Cheif Quashia along with a horde of allies under the King Alanna of the Inward tribes had suddenly made an irruption from the N E and Enara was detained on the Cunmana[sic] with all his troops in the buisness of keeping them back. —Five Rejiments of Southern Cavalry had crossed the frontier at Edwardston and Sir Jehoram MacTerrorglen was at Verdopolis with 20000 ready for marching—Moray was falling back upon Hartford Evidently to cover Adrianopolis—and it became evident to the military man that it was the grand point of contest—Of course all saw that the 30000 under Enara failing we must here retrograde upon some point nearer the capital for the smaller the circuit of Defence the stronger it would grow and besides if a large space was left behind the Advance of our enimies the more room the people would have to rise in Guerilla—the truth of these conjectures was made evident at midnight for then after orders sent from the Commander in Cheif the Troops came in from the Bridge having vacated their entrenchments and Orderlys from the same quarter waited upon the Colonels of each Rejiment—In bed I lay awake

---

7   Lady Julia Montmorency eventually marries Castlereagh.

listening for the Trumpets and before dawn their sound broke upon the silence. Up I sprung and hurried out as soon as ready The Rejiments were getting under arms and General Thornton and Lord Hartford with their staff were on horseback in the Market place Lord Molineux first rattled past with his Rejiment of cavalry the troops to which I belonged started next soon 3000 soldiers were clear out on the March for Danceton with a melancholy train behind them leaving their town to the mercies of the ferocious Invader

It was a Dark dreary morning when we set out and the roads were bad and cloggy but with some exertion the Guns were dragged over them and we moved gradually on in two divisions the first under Hartford the second under Molineux but that young spark received orders to lead it off about Noon where the roads bent northward nor did he join the main body again till two to three hours when all were within 8 miles of Danceton Here there seemed indications of something particular But I knew not what being stationed with my company in the rear and employed keeping the ranks clear of the distracted and distracting people It was rumoured through the ranks that General Thronton had received intelligence from Danceton But to what purport was not so certain However the Drums again beat up and we shouldered our Bayonets once more and as the Day was both cold and densly misty I fired my spirit by keep[ing] a steady gaze upon the Banner of my company the one I had erewhile born through the fire and smoke of Benguela and Loango. There it was waving its magnificent folds of Gold and Scarlet above us The "ARISE" opening and closing upon it while flags behind flags in front lessened into distance Two miles farther passed and now in the village of Winston the cry was heard "Halt Halt" and each one stopped Then an order for an opening for the Guns A lane parted and the black Enjines filed sucessivly forward Then our Lieutenant Colonel Howard Led us into a great wet feild Two more foot Rejiments followed and Thornton next rode up accompanied by his staff but I started to hear the Drums beating and to see the other Rejiments hasting on in quick step along the road and the cavalry spurring their horses to a trot ahead of all

"My lads" said the General "We are like to have a spot of work at Danceton—I received news that theres a fight going on there as far back as Noon And now I tell you that you'll have to take part in't. You mun use your Bayonets weel this evening for its them that will decide the difference atween a Regular Bred Angrian and a frog eating Frenchman You'll recollect who it is who sent the Rascals here and for what buisness they came But please God well teach them another song before they turn their backs to straddle homeward I must hurry on myself wi them thats gone on the Road And I expect if I live to meet you to night on the Bridge at Danceton—Hartford you'll head 'em smartly and a Merry New Year to us all!"

We answered with uncovered heads and a mighty shout as the Gallant Thornton turned round and Hartford putting himself at our head we strode at a great speed over the meadows through the steaming vapours

x x x x x x x x x x x x

X X X X X X X X X X X X
X X X X X X X X X X X X
X X X X X X X X X X X X

Storms are waking to inspire us
  Storms upon our morning sky
Wildly wailing Tempests fire us
  With their loud and God given cry
Winds our trumpets shreiking come
Thundering waves our deeper Drum
   Wildwoods oer us
   Swell the chorus
Bursting on the stormy gloom
Whats their Omen Whence the doom

Loud their voices stern their pealing
  Yet what ist their voices say
Well we know when, God revealing
  All his wrath their powers display
  Trembles every child of clay
   Still we know
   That blow on blow
  Oer us Bursting day by day
  Shews that wrath as well as they

Oh tis not a common call
  That wakes such mighty melody
Crowns and Kingdom's rise or fall
  Men and Nations chained or free
  Living death or Liberty
  Such your terrible decree
   And yonder skies
   Whose voices rise
In such unearthly harmony
   Through Angria round
   Shall wake a sound
  A Voice of Victory
  A Thundering oer the Sea
   Whose swelling waves
   And howling caves
Shall hear the prophecy

   Storms are waking
   Earth is shaking

> Banners wave and Bugles wail
>> And beneath the tempest breaking
> Some must quiver some must quail
> Hark the Artillerys Iron hail
>> Rattles through the ranks of war
> Who beneath its force shall fail
> Must the Sun of ANGRIA pale
>> Upon the Calabar
> Or yonder bloody star
>> Oer Afric's main
>> With fiery train
> That wanders from afar

> No O God Our Sun its brightness
>> Draws from thine Eternal Throne
>> And come what will
>> Through good or ill
> We know that thou wilt guard thine own[8]
> Tis not gainst us that Thunders tone
>> But, risen from Hell
>> With radiance fell
> Tis the Wanderer of the West whose power shall be oerthrown

> Tempest blow thy mightiest blast
>> Wildwind sound thy wildest strain
>> From Gods right hand
>> Oer his chosen land
> Your music shall waken its fires again
> And over the earth now and over the ocean
>> And wherever shall shadow these storm covered skies
> The Louder through Battle may burst your commotion
> Twill only sound stronger OH ANGRIA ARISE![9]

These were the sounds which greeted my ears from Our Noble Band of the Royal Guards stationed in the churchyard of Grantley on the Evening of Jan 6th 1836 The church porch was filled with Generals and the Duke himself was within Regiments were drawn out through the feilds and a dreadful thunder sughed on the wind from a distance but lost as the voices of our Army accompanied the Music in that last noble stanza

But My Readers will ask how have you taken such a leap in your narrative and presenting us meanwhile with stars and verses passed at once from

---

[8]   The following section consists of leaf 13 of Ashley 187 in the BL.

[9]   See the revised 1837 version in vol. III.

Jan ^{10} to Jan 6. Where is the Battle of Danceton Bridge and the retrograde of the Army and the reports of the tempests progress through all Angria and Africa—I answer that this Battle of Danceton Bridge glorious as it was to our Army Had like to have proved doleful enough for me I saw nothing of it for as our Regiment was rushing through some feilds toward the Bridge Occupied by the French a storm of shot levelled from thence upon us struck some of our foremost soldiers to the earth and to my honour be it spoken myself among them—when I recovered consciousness I saw myself lying in Bed in a little Inn at Danceton Dizzy sick and bound about as to my head with a linen napkin a Bullet had hit me Obliquely and though it cracked not the skull it stunned my senses it was 1 day ere I woke from my stupor—and in that Day Danceton was won by us and also evacuated I saw not even the relics of the fight for the night on which I awoke I was lifted into a cart and carted to Grantley there for 3 days I lay invalided and ignorant of all outward ongoings but on this Day I again resumed command of my Company and you find me now with swelling heart listening to Our National Music and Looking up to a twilight heaven and round upon rural quiet transformed into every shape of war

The Music ceased and the Duke with his staff came forth but I could not see them owing to the close ranks of soldiers and then I hardly knew my own position or the work I might or might not be called to the parsonage House peeping from its trees formed the Head quarters of his Grace the villiage was filled with General and other commissioned Officers the Gentle hill which rose beyond the villiage and sloped eastward to Grantly-Beck. was one great Bivauock and down the stream at Thurstone Bridge where it meets the Rapid a tributary to the Twelve River—some brisk firing was going on Between Castlereaghs Division and Lannes Brigade

Well I went to my station on the Hill and stood looking at the Gusty skies Images treasured up from childhood when beneath the portraits of Great Commanders I had seen the cannon balls and standards piled and at times in the Background a Gun rolling its smoke over the dying with a flag topping the cloud of Battle sublime enlargements of a long lost little print where a heap of Dead lay underneath just such a gusty sky—still farther back scenes of the Battle of Issus or Arbela[11] colored to suite the taste of a six year old—twenty such Images filled my thoughts and did the wild long blasts of wind did the hollow heavy thundering from the vale did the bright blowing watchfires and the Armed men about me tend to deaden these thoughts divine—never an inch I thought and thought till I began to see with wonderful clearness All Africa now as it were boiling with strife and my own native Land the scene of civil and foreign war—There was no moon and the glare of the flames about me making all beyond

---

10 Branwell left the date blank.
11 Issus is located in southeastern Asia Minor; Alexander defeated Darius there in 333 B. C. Arbela is an ancient Persian city, now Erbil in Iraq.

look doubly dark shut out all prospect of a distance so I sat and dreamed away till the peep of Day at which time I was sent for to the villiage by my Colonel

—But whats the use at such a time as this of my telling you what I did during this day in comparison with the great scenes going on its value would not weigh a feather in that scale But on the 7th of January Our Division was marched to Glenton and on the same night or rather toward dawn next morning still forward to Aunvale with[in] 7 miles of Adrianopolis from that Hill I first beheld the Ministerial fleet in the River full sail and straight for our National Capital 15 sail of the Line 5 frigates and among the first the Royal Caledonia 120 Guns containing the prime Mover of all our troubles the virtual Dictator of Africa our own deadliest Enemy His Hig[h]ness Arthur Marquis of Adrah—It was only today that we knew he had arrived in the River and now we heard along with it another peice of Intelligence Quashia Quamina with King Boy of the Negroes and Abdallah Medina Sheik of the Alannas Arabs were about to Land below Adrianopolis with 45000 D—ls Incarnate Black brown and yellow Massena and Marmont with 30000 were just going to attack Glenton and Sir Jehoram Macterrorglen with 25000 Reform Soldiers had last night occupied Grantley ONE HUNDRED THOUSAND foes of 6 Nations Backed by a Great fleet with 12000 sailors and 1400 cannon—opposed to 60000 troops under Our Noble Sovereign and 4 great forts with 10000 men and 800 guns—Two to one against us But we were Angrians God was on our side and Zamorna was our Leader—Yet Odds like these were terrific and the more so since our Opponents were Ardrah Massena Marmont Quashia Medina the Elphinstone Douglas Ecclesfechan Macterrorglen Caversham Harlaw Lannes Vandamme Endi Begenni King Boy King Jack. —All Detestable men who hate us with the malignity of Demons—Yet still could not Zamorna Northangerland Thornton Castlereagh Dancton Arundel Hartford Warner Moray could not these eternal Name[s] stand up before them?

When I looked from Aunvale Hill upon a wide tract of country still dark and shrouded with twilight. and considered what immense and conflicting forces were gathered here about me and knew that I Henry Hastings Captain in the 29th was one atom of the power a unit in the sum that I should directly be placed in the full front of the tempest I Began to see that I was not what I had been

And to me something particular seemed to hang over the weather itself. at dawn it was Dark and dull but when the clouds began to gather thicker from the sea a wild wind sprung up that first only wailed and whistled about my ears with cold gusts of sleety mist and so increased till at 10 o clock A. M. wild showers of rain were flying over the country and dim seen clouds through the dreary greyness over head and howling mournful blasts that bore them on with strange and hurried swiftness

I am sorry to say that Captain Hastings Narrative must for the present stop here—On the Morning of the 10th he was called to accompany his Regiment to West beach where General Thornton had drawn up 11000 men to oppose the Landing of Quashia and his Allies These came over from the oppo[s]ite shore in a fleet of Government Rafts Boats and Barges while the Caroline 100 guns the Thunderer 100 the Ardashir 90 the Volcano 85 with 2 frigates of 40 each Bore up the River to flank and protect the Land. General Thornton had thrown up several strong redoubts against the landing place with 50 feildpeices and long files of Musquetry a front indeed which would have blown his opponents into Eternity had not this Great Naval force ranged itself just opposite with 250 heavey Cannon all pointed at him and ready to pour in their awful broadside—on such an occurrence to face that Battery would have been infatuation therefore He retrograded on his position falling back to Ludlow[12] where he lay in the flank of the Blacks aided by 3 regiments of Horse under actual command of The Home Secretary himself though nominally under His uncle Sir M Howard—matters being in this state the Africans landed in complete order Quashia first forming with 22000 Blacks in two columns the right headed by Beginni the left by Endi behind ranged 23000 Bedouin Arabs on Horseback. under the Scheik Medina and last 18 Or 20000 Negroes well armed with Verdopolitan weapons under King Jack and King Boy—This great force pushed forward with all haste to join itself with the Army under Massena ranged against Aunvale about thirteen miles distant But ere they had proceded two leagues they were destined to encounter a terrible resistance for at Crossroads[13] near Ludlow General Throntons troops were drawn up in their old order on the hillside with bayonets fixed and muskets loaded tier above tier all topped by the long Redoubts and the 50 peices of Artillery From these a most murderous fire was opened upon the Enimy whose front ranks of Ashantees suffered cruelly and when the fiery Arabs made a charge upward with their lances all on horseback. Thornton himself nobly headed a charge of his Foot with bayonets upon their front and the Home Secretary led on the 3 regiments of cavalry against their flank such dauntless and well sustained opposition was more than they could well bear savage unconcentrated and unsupplied with Artillery The peals of thunder redoubled from the Hill in distinctly measured volleys and the warlike Mr Warner so threw himself upon them no quarter being given that Quashias troops fairly gave way and rolled back in complete disorder—Now had the Angrians possessed force sufficient [it] would have been the moment to complete their ruin. but—they dared not stir from their Redoubts for their number was 13000 against 45000 and the French were hastening to the combat—Warner called his men back and dispatched Aides de camp to Aunvale for aid from the Duke But before they returned he himself had fallen most severly wounded through the right side by an African Bullet This secular warrior was heading a

---

12 There is an actual Ludlow in Shropshire.
13 There is a Crossroads on the road between Haworth and Keighley.

charge upon the Bedouins and Medina had arranged a line of muskets who opened fire upon the cavalry and while the Secretarys pistol was levelled at a Cheiftain the ball took effect under his raised arm he fell directly without a cry and strove to regain his seat but it was useless and so his man dragged him out and conveyed him to the redoubt Quashias troops elated by the supposed death of Mr Warner redoubled their efforts upon the Hill and as to Crossroads it was flaming from twenty roofs through the hasting darkness Boy and Jack were cheifly at Ludlow burning and destroying with feindish barbarity the thunder of the french cannon upon Aunvale was heard too pealing up and rolling terribly upon the wind So Thornton determined upon a retrograde nearer the principal scene of Action Sir M Howard was instructed to keep the savages in play with Hartford and the 19 regiment while The General decamped and marched across the Hills to Aunvale It was while Hartford and Howard were retiring that Captain Hasting[s] received his wound but his Readers will be glad to know that through the whole day he had conducted himself with such heroic courage in the most ardous services that assuredly promotion will follow in no long course of time But I am sorry to state that the wo[u]nd he received a (lance thrust through the thigh) will totally incapacitate him either for war or writing for several weeks to come and it is from this cause only that I take the pen again to recapitulate in a hasty manner the great events which he ought to have described

When Thornton arrived at Aunvale the Attack for the present[14] had been repulsed and His Grace was occupied in ascertaining the condition and losses of his forces during the day. From the returns made out it appeared that at Aunvale where for 3 hours 16000 Angrians had resisted 28000 French the losses stood

```
              Angrians — killed--------------------------580
                         wounded--------------------1856
                         Total---------------------2436
              French   killed--------------------------------------911
                       wounded------------------------------1602
                                                            2513
```

At Ludlow where 13000 Angrians had opposed for 6 hours 45000 savages

```
              Angrians—killed --------------------- 386
                       wounded ----------------1100
                                               1486
              Africans—killed----------------------------------1259
                       wounded-----------------------------2100
                                                           4359[15]
                    Grand Total          3922    6872
```

---

[14] The following section consists of four pages (one sheet folded) in the BPM: Bon 150 (2).

[15] Branwell's addition is in error here, as is the figure of 13000 below.

Forming a Loss from both parties of nearly 13000 thus the 10 of January proved
the real commencement of what I fear will prove a most bloody and terrible war

In Adrianopolis Excitement was most violent and preparation unceasing
every Government office was filled with action evry square presented a review of
new regiments the Arsenals were gutted and filled again But the forts were
silent—All prepared All ready for a mighty display When I passed through the
streets I could not help thinking at times that an Attack was making at the
moment—people looked so wild and things seemed so unhinged then on the
11th long trains of wounded filed through the streets with waggons groaning
under their heaps of suffering mortality Morays Division of 9000 likewise
entered about Noon and Heathfeilds new levy of 12000 left it near the same
time—Music played and Bells rung in token of the victorys of Ludlow and
Aunvale which appeared flaming in the papers and public documents Confidence
filled every heart with sanguine hope save those initiated in the secret who knew
that the Odds were too great against us to be born

The 12th of January shewed us that the victorys had not improved their
position for any man standing in an upper window or in a clear silent place if
there was such might distinctly hear the Artillery firing both at Aunvale
Crossroads Ludlow and Westbeach an Attack seemed threatned in a grand semi
circle and at dark a long line of fires was seen upon the chain of Hernden Hills
and a new line far off northward upon the Zamorna Hills This last was the signal
of the Reserve under Enara 30000 admirable Troops who occupied the road to
Angria and the North keeping it open for the retreat already concerted in secret.
This Night it was rumoured that the Duke would arrive in the city but he did not
enter till the Morning of the 13 when he with a full staff passed through the
square in which I resided on their way to the Zamorna Palace the people in a
mass of 60 or 70000 received him with immense acclamations to which his
Grace answered by uncovering and bowing—I afterwards waited on the Duke at
the Palace where I had an opportunity of more closly observing him—He looked
rather stern and hasty but a fire dwelt in his eye which augurs terrible struggle
ere he would surrender I thought he sometimes looked affected with a sudden
languor the effect of constant exertion and excitement but he chased it off and
gave his shoulders nobly to the wheel

I understood afterwards that his Grace had a long interview with the
Premier but what passed is unknown as they were alone together

On the 14th Hartfords Division of 6000 men entered and Thorntons
now of 20000 men with Castlereaghs of 18000 was understood to be ranged
from Aunvale to West Beach while Enaras of 30000 still kept back on the
Zamorna Hills From these appearances I augured that his Grace would not
attempt any very terrible struggle in the city though I knew the Enimy would
force him to it And this we could tell from the fact that while Massena and
Quashia were facing Thornton Macterrorglen was making Desperate efforts to get
between Enara and the city thus shutting it in as it were to Destruction Indeed
from his ceasless endeavours to do this a Determined contest was sprung upon

Avehill 9 miles off [to] which a column was dispatched from Adrianopolis to support and In a few hours a fresh one was sent after it—All Eyes were now turned to this quarter for mighty results hung upon its descision one way or other Interest in its ongoing became intense every tower in the city was climbed to view it from afar every ear stretched to listen to the Heavy discharges which rolled Deeper from that quarter But still neither the Duke nor any Great General went that way though 3000 wounded had been sent in since morning. At length about ten o clock at night the firing instead of encreasing diminished and the air seemed to abate in its Deep thunders of threatning—I was just retiring to rest when I heard a great noise of voices in the street and presently a Nobleman Lord Lyondale arrived at my door in a hurry saying that the whole Government fleet were bearing up for the Harbour—In that case said I we shall hear them and indeed so we did for while we sat breathless the Boom O Dismal crack burst on us that shook every thing about us almost to peices Lonsdale[sic] jumped up and rushed out to his horse and servants I ran up to the Balcony but ere I reached it a second awful burst as if it were the day of Judgement seemed to bring the Black Heaven in ruins about our heads the Night was intensly dark but Adrianopolis lay in the light of gas and palaces the west Horizon was tracked by a long line of watchfires the Calabar and Harbour lay in impenetrable gloom I saw no boats no ships nothing beyond the street lights in that direction—But anon a far-off flash from the fronts of Fort Adrian and Fort Cumana the whole wide waters gleamed & Mighty Spectres became visible upon them but all went out and a hollow thunder rolled in upon the wind Then the Caledonia unseen as yet hung out signal lights every vessel answered riding up the River Forts Augustus and Calabar at the Mouth of the Harbour. (they it was who made the crack which startled us) presented 3 rows apeice of hundreds of lights marking their terrible tiers of cannon but the lights of the twenty vessels crowded nigher and all the River appeared distinctly with its vast black sea castles ranging opposite to the mighty castles on land I saw the Calabar gliding forward with the sails covering its Stupendous Masts till it furled in and lay under bare poles coolly amid the centre of the expected horrible firing It is said that Her Commander calmly walked the Deck. with his Glass in his hand and a sheathed cutlass at his side for all his preparations were made and he could calculate the chances of what should be Brave hearts must have quivered for fear in the jaws of those terrible forts not a muscle of his Iron countenance shook and not a fibre in his strong heart The Caroline was moved alongside of the Caledonia with Harlaw the base and brutish Admiral the Thunder Ecclesfechan the Thistle Douglas and the St Andrew Elphinstone next in the range A <   > yellow Rocket was shot up from the flagship and straight a sheet of bright red smoke and fire covered all the Harbour rolling with a horrible roar over the fated city and echoed dreadfully from the flaming forts such bursts of sound were terrific and I cannot find words to express them They seemed as if nothing could stand their concussion But their effect was far more horrible His Grace had issued orders that Red hot balls should be thrown from the forts and Ardrah unknown to us had issued the same orders with regard to the fleet thus both sides shewing the same wild vindictiveness of disposition Bombs and shells were likewise hurled from the volcano [of] 90 guns till the Black midnight flashed with trains of arching light and on the opposite side of the river Cumana and Adrian saluted a long line of ships with a hollow protracted roar from far. Listen there were 1400 ministerial cannon and 800 Angrians Belching forth death in the space of four square miles—But as to the affrighted and shaken city the Duke with all the military 22000 men the sick and wounded the principal Inhabitants with a long train of fugitives were leaving it at the north and north west outlets—Thornton was silently retreating from Aunvale and that semi circle all were drawing to ward Enara and the Northern Road In fact resistance would only have been suicide and youthful magnificent Adrianopolis was to be left to its fate I was with its Royal founder as he left the city surrounded by thousands of Brave troops and tens of thousands of Distracted people He looked Darkly and threatningly resolute but though his lip quivered as the wild glare of light shot up from the Ignited Arsenal it was with the Agony of vengeance unattained and a tyger thirst for the thickest of that conflict The stunning cracks of Artillery from its Dear Citadels the Hellish Din in that quarter the knowledge that there triumphed his Deadly foe was too much for the mind of 23 unless supported by a second soul within <itself> which no horrors could subdue

His Premier in a close[d] carriage followed near him But what lay in that heart I could not tell nor can I now unless it might be meditation of another flight to Lady Louisa Vernon! —An old man on horsback who had been riding beside the Duke just as we got clear of the suburbs turned round and coolly trotted back again I thought him distracted till I learned it was Mr Sdeath

The Dreadful firing grew hotter and hotter on the River Red Hot Balls soon fell and in a while after catching fire in many places the Thunderer Blew up with a flood of fire that shewed River and fleet and city and country as beneath a suddenly exploding Moon we saw that mighty sheet and heard its hollow roar which the whole Army answered with a shout of joy—1000 men and the value of 200000 pounds had vanished in a single moment. —The falling fragments did dreadful damage on board the Caledonia dashing down upon her masts yards and bleeding decks but Ardrah cared not he only smiled the more sternly

The fronts of the two Harbour forts were now horribly shattered. but a scheme had been concerted By the Duke—for in the midst of the most astounding fire the Garrison simultaneously left them and hasted after the retreating Army the fire slackened at once from them and in a while their wide spread roofs burst into a raging flame

Thus Arthur Marquis of Ardrah landed on the quays of an almost deserted city with two flaming ruins on each side and a shattered and blood stained fleet behind. Harlaw and all the commanders followed and at Dawn of morning Macterrorglen Massena Marchmont Vandamme Lannes Murat Quashia Medina King Boy and King Jack. Entered at the Head of the vanguard of their Armys—

Zamorna with all his Generals were meanwhile hasting to join each other on the
Hills of Zamorna But tis only

for a short space the great Avenger stays[16]

And a Power is rising in Africa which shall inflict vengeance upon the Tyrants
of Adrianopolis

So[17] spends its hours in thinking on
The dear loved home whence it has flown

But Oh at last a time will come
When heaven is lost and earth is home
When all that fascinates thy sight
The moment seen shall sink in night
This light shall change to lightning then
This love of Heaven to hate of men
For that which from on high is thrown
Will always fall most quickly down
And sinks the deepest so with thee
Thy quick and passionate heart shall be
The further plunged in agony

These spirits round thee oft may find[18]
Earth and its joys to suit their mind
For dust to dust the sons of earth
Will love the land that gave them birth
But never thou or if thou dost
Too quickly thou shalt find it DUST

He sleeps in slumber calm and deep[19]
An Infants blest and balmy sleep
Dreaming of heaven those closed eyes

---

[16] Compare Pope's translation of the *Illiad*, XXII, 419.

[17] The foregoing covers the first three pages of Bon 150 (2); the following
lines appear on the fourth page; they are trial lines for ll. 293-335 of the poem
beginning on p. 588 below.

[18] In the right-hand margin opposite this stanza is a sketch of a human profile,
possibly that of Percy.

[19] In the right-hand margin opposite this stanza appears the name "Henry
Percy."

See glorious visions of the skies
And tremblingly their fingers lie
On the soft cheek of Infancy

The softened curls of golden hair[20]
Just moving with the moonlight air
But his white brow so sweetly still
So free from every shade of ill
Shall it be so for ever NO[21]

Who of this world would wish it so
Tis the forehead of a mighty man
Destined on earth to lead the van
Of Onward minds a man whose soul
Nor Death nor Danger shall control
One whom no mortal power may tame
One who shall set the world on flame

---

[20] Between this stanza and the next appear the names "Thiternell," "Ahia," "Atica," and "<   > of Edward Percy."

[21] Between these stanzas appears the name "Percy."

[Angria and the Angrians]
II (b)[1]

She was right a person whose head touched the door top stepped in and casting off A great scarlet cloak strode on in solemn black with pallid brow

"My dearest Vernon! My Enchantress! why youve drawn me from among them all" he said as Lady Louisa starting up ran to him with an air that might have passsed for fright or joy but the shock past off in an instant and she was soon folded in his arms

"Good heavens Percy how can you have left them

"Why Love the temptation was too strong There was the Marquis Jehoram Massena that worthy young man Quashia—Boy and Jack—all within a hands breadth My heart yearned after them—But the King of the Cats with his green jealous eyes kept watch and ward over my movements Cords of love drew me to my freinds Cords of a Cart Whip Kept me from them I thought I would escape from such a dilemma at any rate and so levanted[2] from the whole pack together freinds and foes!"

"You have done strangly I cannot believe you!"

"Aye thats the fashion when I tell a lie every body gulps it down if I speak truth the greatest rascals boggle at it But never mind I shut all such thoughts out in closing that door dont let them trouble us now Vernon—Why I think I am turn Coward. Ive shrunk from the Gunpowder of Adrianopolis the looks of Arthur the voice of Zenobia and now I feel aghast at the eyes of Louisa—What the D—l are they so black and you so white for.?"

"I'm thinking what you are about Percy—something unaccountable Do you know you'll enrage them by the step you've taken?"

"They? —Who?. The two last and meanest letters in the Alphabet the two Izzards[3] —Zanys—Bombastic breaths of a moment—hectoring vapouring evaporating breaths of a boaster. the Masculine and Feminine personifications of flummery. Ive laughed in my Carriage all the way from Calais at the Idea of how they will flourish when they hear of my decampment Oh Vernon how you will get varnished. He'll murder you by proxy. in the shape of the next African and then come over to take you off bodily—while She poor wretch she'll fasten up on me knocking me down twenty times for the once she did before—What say you Louisa Shall we go out to meet them Innocent Davids against these Goliaths but I forgot you're no David He was fair and ruddy. he was <u>not</u> clothed

---

1   This section consists of one sheet folded (4 pages), 11.2x18.5 cm, at the BPM: Bon 152 (2). The prose on the first two pages is likely a continuation of (a) above with a short intervening section missing; pages 3-4 contain trial lines of verse and seven lines of prose written upside down—see II (c) below.

2   See vol. I, p. 97, n. 14.

3   Zenobia and Zamorna.

in an armour of brass And for my self I like him taller by the head than any of the childern of my people afflicted with the evil spirit only soothed by music— But its dreadful to pursue the parrallel Saul was slain by his armour bear[er]. You happen to be mine. you carry my brass and Iron. on your head and in your heart. He died while fleeing from the Philistines Im doing ditto its evident but as to my death pray recollect the fate of the Amalekite!"[4]

"How long will you go on at this rate? —"

"For ever an it please you—"

"But it does not please me Percy—"

"Well it pleases me then and I came here to be pleased—What not please you when I am sending Zamorna and Zenobia down to the pit of Tophet as fast as their iniquities can hurry them—Take care lest I should throw you in too and the weight of your sins let me tell you would crush you to atoms when you reached the bottom

"Insane man. Know you have by this action alienated your only supporters save one. Would you now alienate that too—"

"Do you fancy Vernon that Ive been vapouring at Ludlow or Aunval[e] or Adrianopolis—that in short this is only a wooden leg[5] and that you mean to demolish the other?"

"This is unlike you it is farcical.! it is Absurd! for Heavens sake be yourself. and take back your Character"

"Why if Ive left it I can reenter for Im sure after such a Tenant it will remain a long while "To Let"—"

"Well my Lord you arrived suddenly and I will go suddenly—Good evening and—"

"Nay" said his Lordship hastily starting up "Nay now Louisa. are you blind that you cannot see through my thin veil of nonsense—Do you not know me? —Is it not from the very bitterness of my heart that I speak so wretchedly and nettlingly—Why Vernon I feel to my hearts core the certain seperation the final severance I have made between myself and those whom I love—As for Zamorna I could kneel to him but it is useless and willingly right willingly now would I bear all the reproach which Zenobia could in justice pour on me I am unworthy of her—but so bright and Noble a being as she is must exert an influence. If. I go up to heaven she is there if I go to Hell she is there if I flee to the uttermost parts of the earth she is there also[6] I tell you that unless now she seemed to my mind present here the room the house would be hateful!"

Lady Louisa stood fixed with indignation

"Weak contemptible driveller" she cried "Just about to speak in earnest and then wafted off again on the wings of the first nonsense that enters your brain" —She stopped looked searchingly at him but it was Northangerland.

---

4   See II Samuel 1:1-16.
5   A figure of speech for a "useless Appendage."
6   Compare Psalm 139:7-9.

—with the fickle changeable look from bitter mirth to bitter greif. and with eyes whose cold distortion looked wildly sad for a moment only to glitter the next with heartless joy at some stinging or sneering thought or sentence—But it <u>was</u> Northangerland And the striking though faded magnificence of that Aristocratic form seemed at length to revive old impressions in the Indignant Gazer—

"Now Louisa come and be calm. —Where's Caroline? —"

Caroline was not there for seeing the Earl took no notice of her though she ran to him in perfect joy. she had slid out of the room and was now found crying alone with vexation

"Well my little Caroline" said Northangerland when she came back "Do you too hate to see me—I'de forgotten thee child or I would'nt have forgotten thee!"

"Forgotten me! Who for?"

Louisa laughed at the pithy question but Caroline turned to her

"Dont you laugh! it was for you, He never spoke to <u>me</u> Why did you come first and only to scold?"

"Well done Caroline the hit was hard" and the Earl laughed in his turn whereupon his Daughter seemed reassured

"Then you are not angry papa you had <u>only</u> forgotten But dont forget any more—where have you come from and what have you been doing and have you seen Zamorna—and—and—I had a hundred things to ask but Ive forgot too—and yet papa I did not forget you! —But is that cloak yours papa its a fine one isnt it."

"No it belongs to the D—l. I stole it from Zamorna."

Caroline was out of his arms like lightning—She ran to the Magnificent mass of drapery spread out its bars of Gold and undid its massive sunshaped clasp then turned it inside out to view the bright satin lining pressed her cheek against the soft Ermine collar and cried in triumph—"Heres his name—A. A. A. W. Arthur Augustus Adrian Wellesly—and was it really his papa and did he really clasp this round his neck—let me see how thick was it. Oh but he wears a coat collar—and did he wear this in battle papa has this been to the Guadima or the Benguela—has he in it lain

Still and stiff and drenched with rain

Wishing the dawn of morn again

Though death should come with day[7]

Is there a stab or shot hole in it—let me see where was he wounded—nay was he ever wounded. Oh yes by that frightful Man Quashia. where is <u>he</u> now papa its long since I saw him is he killed to—But this cloak is so new Zamorna cant have worn it in battle—how fine he would look in it—and as tall as you too. Just put it on and walk like him do now and I'll be Ardrah—"

---

7   These lines were likely composed by Branwell.

"No Carry theres no need on't if I play at Zamorna Furioso[8] Her Ladyship will do excellently for the object—"

"Mamma hates him does he hate her then? What <u>have</u> you done to make him hate you—I'll be him then and you shall be yourself. and I <u>will</u> scold you—lets see how does he put his hair. over his forehead. but mine falls back so—Now then. "You vile kidnapping wretch stealing from me my friends and—"

Louisa dispossessed her of the cloak with some haste—flung it away and turned to the Smiling Earl with Cheeks like crimson

"Where did you get that plague tainted gewgaw—where—"

"Vernon its worth 200£ in gold and diamond clasp alone. I stole it from him The breeze blew coldly from the Calabar he had thrown it off to take an oar for warmth in going over to Fort Adrian. I put it on and never returned it—"

"Mercenary being! Always reckoning up the costs I tell you Percy that your constant practice is to value every thing by its price and your insufferable pride is only satisfied by having a tune laid out in the paltry articles about you—take the red rag out of my sight Caroline and leave off mimicing—Come now my Lord sit down act like yourself—be yourself and I'll be myself In truth I felt irritated at your conduct before—you came. now explain it to me and clear yourself from this wretched doubledealing"

"My dear Louisa Vernon Ill tell you one thing—You shant hear a word from me to night upon any such d—med subjects hither I came to be happy and not as to a confessional

"Yes Percy and if your own mind destroys it not you shall be happy but it is your own mind I fear—Oh if I thought you were earnest in seeking happiness from me I would give it—but I dread the thought that you have come to torment and sneer—What have you done to night has not your whole bearing been most sinister and sneering. what do your eyes show even now. would he whose portrait looks at you here—<u>did</u> he act or speak thus when he was alive for he is dead now—dead or absent. I am the same I feel the same once I never found reason to shew the character I do—to you—but did I not do it to others—it is nothing latly risen it is what was when first I saw you—act. worse—drive me to desperation—it shall be still the same I know that feelings may be diverted from their ancient course but <u>they</u> shall be still the same and that course shall be there too—though perhaps all dried. How ever I hate you I shall remember that I loved you so when the shower of reccollections comes on it must make [a] stream of love once more—You are far away now from those whom I hate Percy you are with one whom you did love—let the abs

---

8   A play on the title of Ariosto's poem, *Orlando Furioso*. Also a musical term signifying "furiously or with vehemnce."

The moon in glory mounts above[9]
The darkness of the distant grove
As if the skies were given to be
The palace of her majesty
A silver grey is round her throne
And far away the clouds are blown
With all the lonly mountains dying
In the pale haze above them lying
   Now shines she silently and still
Over the brow of yonder hill
In golden glory gazing down
On feild and forest tower and town
But the dense trees that around him rise
   Give lonlier prospects to his eyes[10]
To hide such prospects from his eyes
With far off cypresses whose gloom
In Wood church yard oer shade a tomb
And oer the forests waving crest
That mild moon in her heavenly rest

   The moon in glory oer the grove
      Majestic marches on
   With all the vault of heaven above
      To canopy her throne
   And from her own celestial rest
   Upon the darkwoods waving crest
      Serenly she looks down
   Yet beaming still as if she smiled
   Most brightly on the beauteous child

   But what thought he as there he lay
      Beneath the arched foor
   Amid the ever trembling play
      Of Moonshine through the bower
   That unobstructed enternce made
   <As> the breeze moved foliage shade
      In an uncertain shower

---

9   These trial lines for ll. 154-217 of the poem beginning on p. 588 begin at the top of p. 3 of the manuscript, suggesting that at least one sheet folded (4 pages) laid inside this sheet is missing. Sketches of two male profiles appear in the left-hand margin opposite the first stanza.

10   This line was added above the succeeding one; neither is canceled.

But what thought he as there he lay
            Beneath the arched door
Amid the ever trembling play
            Of Moonshine through the bower
Gazing with blue eyes dimmed by tears
To that cast vault of shining spheres
            Till all its heavenly power
Makes the bright pearl drops trembling break
To dewy lustre on his cheek

O how I could wish to fly
Far away through yonder sky
Oer the trees upon the breeze
            To a paradise on high
Why am I so bound below
That I must not cannot go
Lingering here for year on year
            So long before we we[11] die
Now how glorious seems to be
Heavens great arch spread wide oer me
But [12] every star is hung so far
            Away from where I lie
I love to see that Moon arise
It suits so with these silent skies
I love it well but cannot to tell
            How it should make me cry
Is't that it brings before me now
So many things gone long ago
When Angels used from heaven to come
And make this earth their wonderous home
Ist that I think that very moon
Those vanished wonders beamed upon
When Shepherds watched their flocks by night
            All seated on the ground
And Angels of the Lord came down
            And glory shone around
Ist that I think upon the sea
Just now its beaming beauteously

---

[11] "we" is written above "I"; neither is canceled.
[12] "But" is written above "with"; "is hung" above "all placed"; none are canceled.

Where I so oft have longed to be
But never yet have been
Ist that it shines so far away
On lands beyond that oceans spray
Mong lonly Scotlands rocks of grey
Or Englands groves of green!
Or ist that through yon Deep blue Dome
It seems so solemnly to roam
As if across an Ocean wide
Breasting the dark unfathomed tide
Far far away from home

As if upon some unknown Sea
It were A vessels statly form
Over the waters wandering free
Through calm and cloud and storm[13]

He is but a child so all his dreams
Are wanderings of the mind
Where all before with glory teems
And little lies behind
Formless as any childs might be
Yet he who looks in them may see
In glowing light defined
The first fond feelings of a Soul
Destined a nation to control

---

[13] The following are trial lines for ll. 318-35 of the same poem; the two passages are separated by II (c) below.

[Angria and the Angrians]
II (c)[1]

P B B
Feb 10th
1836

The subject whose consideration forms the matter of the following pages is one of so vast an extent and so complicated character that the mere enumeration of its parts the simple table of its contents requires a steadier look and closer thinking than most men are willing to bestow upon the most important volumn and unless its depth and breadth be clearly laid down before the reader he runs a very great chance of plunging into the question with no more knowledge of its magnitude than the mole has of the world it burrows in

---

[1] These lines appear upside down on p. 4 of BPM: Bon 152 (2), between two sets of trial lines as noted for II (b) above, and may be an abandoned beginning for II (b).

[Angria and the Angrians]
II (d)[1]

"Oh Dear Vernon struggle not so to leave me This is a downright contradiction to my language—. But what say you supposing I was to sit down to the organ there and play for you Kents Anthem" Then I said Oh that I had wings like a Dove then I would flee away and be at rest"[2] it seems a wish very proper for your present situation"

Her Ladyship seemed not at all appeased but murmering among tears "She wished She <u>was</u> at rest" still looked determined to escape from the arms of her tormentor But he recurred to his stinging, saying with another short laugh

"Eh. now Louisa the Anthem brings another suggestion to my mind. —Supposing I should send you instead of [to] the Guillotine to the Rocks of Ascension Isle.—!—That would accord with the feelings of my Lovely Exile? Her life has not been so religious as to fit Her for an immediate launch into Eternity—"

Vernon turned round upon him her large black eyes with a look of horror at the Idea of Banishment but fright humbled her pride

"Oh Alexander" she cried with clasped hands. "Dont Banish me! —"

"Yes yes Love. Lady Vernon shall be banished for ever But not the COUNTESS of NORTHANGERLAND.!"

The sentence was desperatly ambiguous but the emphatic tone in which it was uttered gave it the appearance of Honesty Louisas heart palpitated with sudden pride and she hushed the idea of a double meaning though the light wavering eye and curling lip of her Judge. might cast a great doubt upon the earnestness of his Sentence But ere a complete reconciliation had taken place. The Door opened suddenly and a Tremendous swarthy Gentleman with rolling eyes and coal black curls. got himself somehow into the room giving a fiery drunken glance round him and somewhat astounded at the company he lighted on.

"I Didnt expect this! So that's Macara. the little one. and the big one Montmorency. —But hows this the ones as lean as a Ghost and the others a woman. — Oh! —my Lord. I say this is your game and—"

"Quashia. my Lad is it you—I'm glad to see you—My mother Lady Helen—Your Ladyship—Mr Quashia Quamina."

---

1   A manuscript section of four pages, 11.2x18.5 cm, that is a continuation of II (b) above; it may be a straight continuation or there may be a short intervening section missing. The fragment consists of leaf 6 of Ashley 187 in the BL and pp. 21-22 of the Taylor manuscript noted on p. 415, n. 13 above.

2   Probably a reference to James Kent (1700-1776); his anthem "Hear my prayer," based on Psalm 55, was very popular in the nineteenth century.

Louisa half laughed and half cryed. The prince looked most drunkenly amazed.

"I didnt expect this it is too good. your Ladyship. Im happy as the day is long—I mean to see you—and hopes. your well. and is glad to find you keep your youth particularly. he—hem—an —and D—n! Percy you are making a fool of me!

"Not in the least my dear friend!"

"Well. your Ladyship will excuse an old chum holding a little conversation with your friend here. I mean your son. my freind he is—and I hope yours"

The prince bowed as he spoke but in the congee. as he made a most respectfully low one. the Balance was lost and down he came upon the carpet with his nose undermost So Louise ran shocked but laughing from the room and Percy giving an infernal look helped him. up saying under his breath

"So! this is one of Zamornas persecutors! a Wolf against a Lion.!"

But the prince looked as if beginning to be ferocious

"I Say you d—nd infernal villain its all long of your carpets. and—and—now what was I going to say! Oh this—Now listen. Sir. Attend and mark me!"

As the prince spoke with many gestures and oratorical flourishes of the arm He. set himself leaning forward with his Elbows upon the Back of a Regal Easy Chair. and rolling his Moorish eyes about as if to collect and arrange the scattered figments of his brain he strove to pin his weary and slippery listener to an attention which the lanquidly restless face of his Lordship seemed very loath to grant him Quashia waved his Bronze like hand.

"Now listen. —I am come Here. —to Elrington Hall you know Dont you? — Well I am come from the Blood red feild of Edwardston. for you see having Heard at noon that you was—"

"You were—Quashia my Boy!"

"Curse you if you interrupt me Ill fill your bones with gunpowder. Ill Blow your Nose off. by G—d! —D—n you you were tip top quite high. and Ardrah shuffling about like a lousy mangy old tyke ready for drowning whenever you please whereupon you just tossed him and his Beggarly Itch bedaubed crew. into the Deep deep sea! —more fool you were that you did not roast them Why I grilled as many as 200 only the day before yesterday for a less do than that—Yes I have—But. where was I—Lets see. —Oh. We in the stormy Hall of Mars[3]— the very plains of conflict. held a committe meeting where Macterrorglen and Jordan and Massena and I—resolved that it was no manner of use for us to bother with a dead dog like the ministry. in fact that it was just like the trick we copied tother day from old Mezentius.[4] coupling the living to the dead till they harmonized into one peice of rottenness. So as I had (and they knew it) the pleasure of an aquaintance with you. It was sworn I should mount and be D—d.

---

3   i.e., in battle; Mars is the Roman god of war.

4   An Etruscan king; in the *Aeneid* a blood thirsty and impious tyrant, killed by Aeneas.

—yes—no not that but be off. Aye—How the D—l could I call my self. D—d. but you see here I am with a vengeance and them that dont like me Let them leave me—Gad Im as good as any ten!"

"Very good my young freind though if you had said "Those who" instead of "Them that" I should have better liked it— But. my Boy what am I to believe from your lucid statement.? —That when you heard Ardrah was overthrown your freinds held a meeting where they decided to send you after him and thus be rid of you? —Eh. is that the truth Quamina?"

"Now curse em—if it is Ill be bound to cap all the Deal. at Zamorna and bear all their D—ation. Now I will go back this moment and Ill blow up such a whirlwind Ill say. nay. what was it—Percy you theif. what was I saying—Oh Blood. —nay I'M. DONE!"

"I think so. But Quashia you are horribly drunk. where in the name of wonder did you get it?"

As the Earl spoke He burst into a laugh which no one [could] restrain who beheld the wild brown figure in military surtout and snow white tights standing as drunk as he could stand and pressing his Equatorial forehead to collect the thread of Ideas which His volubility had bewildered almost beyond recovery. He would Have very shortly however flown into a terrible storm of fury had not the sneering Earl. helped him out of his difficulty.

"Quash you were sent to me to stipulate for conditions to ensure the safty of the Angrian Army!"

"Thats it my Lad! Thats it. now may I be—"

"Quash—you have had an engagement I see from your speech. What have you done"

"Done—weve done them brown Sir—we have really Dash my fingers. Here we lay. 30000 strong in a couple of lines paralleled to Morena. and your sons place behind us. now come my lad turn your face to me again Im not going to trouble you with details well ever so many thousands of us just like a legion of D—ls covered Girnington and Stuartville with a line down to Zamorna it was a Triangle with Zamorna for the point and by Gad. we hoped to whip the Angrians upon it most purely! Ill be hanged this minute if we wernt 30000 as prettily disposed as the Old One could have wished us and Saturday Night came on particular Sharp and Dark—There was the cavalry of Medina skipping like fleas over Croyland Marsh and thence Spreading up. upon the Olympian Hills They wanted an Airing most horridly we Did not care a D—n for your Olympians and stuff. but we had as much Beef and Brandy as would have served all the Legions in the pit—But Massena and me were at the Edwardston Hall with a Dozen tip top. ones. Deciding a Bet of 50 Angrians which of us could turn down most neat cogniac. —We had not got Half Floated when it came on like midnight and. Massena upped and swore by His Breeches. He would Have Edwardston Church burnt to give us light by it was just opposite the Drawing room windows near a quarter of a mile and somewhere near 200 Angrians wounded and prisoners lay saying their prayers in it. But the D—l we cared for[5] them or their prayers either—in one hour the old Bigging was all of a bright red [g]low with the smoke rolling forward down the stream till the darkness hid it from sight—you cant think however how well the scheme answered our purpose for there wasnt a face in our room but looked as if it was in H—l! and such laughing and swearing and drinking that I know of one man who popped in and out again like a flea roaring that we had the Old One making merry with us for you know I was standing just before the door. preparing to Jump clear over a dozen chairs because Medina had D—ned me to do what he could not but—By Jove I knew what to nick him with! He Jump over one chair! —He be Hanged! —"

    "Thank ye Quash its very likly!"

    "Now hold you your tongue Daddy and you be Hanged. —I say we were in a complete roar of fun when in runs a fellow with an Aid de Camp "Oh curse your Aids de Camp" say Massena "what are you coming here for?" "I'm comed. to tell you were done Sir" them was his very words Uncle"

    "Gad Quash your exile has given you a little rusticity!"

    "Gom how you put me out. "Done!" roars Massena "Why we arent at the third gill yet!" "Ant please ye" says the Aid. "You maynt be but your done for all that look ye not to know what I mean this <way> —we are all blown tight Sir!" Blast his eyes! I got onto a table and made spring for I saw the Aid was done at any rate. made a spring I say fair astride of his shoulders coming across his pate with such a thud as mashed him sick. and away it flies Be gad I dont know where he got such a sea! he vomited a Hogshead My teeth! He <u>was</u> done now—we swore by all thats sacred we would make a night of it after such a joke as that but I nailed Massena. for I had seen him with half an eye doing— now—what was he doing—Oh—no—well Hang it I drew my sword at him thats all and flung a sweet cake besides—I did—"

    "Oh what a climax!"

"Curse your Max we'd enough of it for Massena upset the table and burst his nose over a stone bottle—But. I forgot how we were when up comes a carriage to the Door and in steps Macterrorglen I knew by the driving it was Jehu the son of Nimshi—Captain of the Hose![6] — "D—n your Souls" he roars and we say Amen! "D—n your Souls why whats your game now is it a Drinking match you are contesting with Zamorna?" Bah Uncle the name makes me thirsty its such an infernal one "On my Soul!" He says "the villian's upon us and he'll decide it with a wanion[7] But Be Gow we'll drink it in Hood!" thats my Humor says I but says Jehu "Blast your eyes hold <u>your</u> tongue its drowned in liquor!" so I says "then by Dad Jehu you shall have a taste it" and I squirt a shower of spit direct at his Nose and Jehu whips out his pistols and I defy him on my Damnation But

---

5   Pages 21-22 of the Taylor manuscript noted above begin here.
6   See I Kings 19:16 and II Kings 9:1-3.
7   "With a wanion" means "with a vegeance."

Oh how he did curse and swear "Off to your posts!" was his word "off to H—l" was ours He swore we should go Massena swore we shouldnt I said I wouldnt Fenton cried He'd be D—nd if he would not like to see the Duke that minute and shake hands with him over a bottle Jordan claps a brasspunch bowl over his pate for that and then bursts into a fit of laughing Lannes was sick with drinking an Fenton falls over him and off. sets the carriage and Horses sweating at the Din they heard for there were who thought it was the very pit with the cries of them that was in it coming up to the firmament. "Oh Adrian King of Angria" roared Jehu "H—l <u>is</u> moved to meet thee at thy coming!" But Im thinking the sound thereof was mortally like a pack of hungry spaniels Besides we had the Drums beating to arms through the villiage and a crowd of Cavalry coming up the Grass plot of the park. —How Jehu did shake Massena when he got him by the neck. I never saw [a] mortal in such a tantrum I never felt such swearing I never heard such a press of crushed confusion.

"You were in a Drunken mess and the Enemy upon you thats the short of it Quamina!"

"I know I mounted and was at Castle feild in quarter of an Hour. Jack and Boy were hurrying their lads down Ingle Side and the D—nd Angrians were marching like mad through Elm wood and over the Morvena. Elmwood thinks I. Absalom will be found hanging in a tree there abouts—Bah. Ill be Joab but instead of the Darts I took three oaths and levelled them all into him[8]

A Horse A horse my kingdom for a horse![9]

Stand fast boys! off and away!—That was my word with 'em and hardly a streak of morning yet in the Heavens! I know I began it for there was a fellow standing by the roadside with ever to many Scythes sticking out round him and a Spanish peaked Hat on his head altogether. near three yards high Stop a bit! I hadnt either Bayonet or sword But I took two or three stones from the brook heaved them at him and sprang forward like another David—'Dad Uncle! How I did go down speiling from top to bottom of a deep ravine roaring like any ten and him showering shale and stones as I went. but lying on the broad of my Back in the sludge I swore so that Him and my own scamps all cleared of like lightning till there was nothing but a spruce fir just same size as his self standing within a trifle of his place and the rascals say that he was little better and I was blind drunk. I G—d Ill Blind some of them any how! the Destitute Heathens—"

"A hem Quash my Boy drop the last epithet. stones cast forth fly back now and then—!"

"'D'rot! am I not to use my tongue? —I upped and mounted as miry as a soul. just rising from his grave at the Judgement—It was broad daylight and I'll be hanged if I had been sensless! —

"Aye as sleepy as I am"

---

8 See II Samuel 18:9-17.
9 Compare Shakespeare's *Richard III*, V, iv, 7.

"Sleepy! how could a man sleep with all his bones broken. However I was alone in my glory and a dreadful Thunder rolling up Castle feild vale. So being but 3 miles to Girnington Hall I mounted and gallopped through the woods over the very tree tops in at the North drawing room windows! Two miles farther there was Halton[10] and from this to that. not five and twenty fellows to keep the D—l from the plain of Zamorna. Gad the victory is all owing to me I throw Endii and Begonii and King Jack. all into the gap with 6000 as Beautiful a set of Ivorys as every got smoked in the fires of the pit No sooner done than the feind Arundel comes into Braintree[11] at full trot—So Dod! what could foot do against Horse. my lads ran! yes they ran as if they had fire in their tails and the Horse after them—whooping and hallooing like mad Oh how I did sweat to have em turn and fight em. they say the very walls shook and trembled to hear me swear. and more than that two men rose from the dead but its a secret between you and me!—I turned at one place. same as it might be this carpet and that table Halton Beck. we'll call the organ pipes fire there and Angrians and this Dog here shall be me—now—"

"Oh Dear Quash. I can do without practical illustr—"

"Be quiet now I say. look. Here I go!"

In his furor the Prince grappled a Great Newfoundlander to hurl it at the organ in imitation of the fashion he threw himself. upon his enemies. of course the Beast retorted with grinning teeth and a horrid growl. But the Earl was so shaken with laughter that he could hardly manage to part them and as he held. Quamina at arms length one way and the Dog the other they both set up a chorus so Beastlike that it was difficult to tell the Dogs voice from the Mans!

"Gashes and Slavery! the terrorbitten vermin I'll have thy lifes blood before the day be an hour older. Off you Hog I say and let me tear its Guts into ropes for hanging you!—Whrow! ye theif! Have at your eyes then—But Gad. keep your hands off you Hoary Scoundrel. and the black plague upon you!"

"It is upon me my Boy. a most deadly plague why you theif your as Drunk as you are black!"

"I'm not Drunk. you theif. —Drunk. have I had time to drink when weve been thrashing Zamorna from Nightfall to Nightfall Blast thy trousers I'll take 5 yards at a wallop—"

Suiting the action to the word he gave an Indian whoop and leaped more than his own height toward the ceiling. Lord Northangerland rung a Bell and Shaver made his Appearance

"Oh Lord.! Shew the rest in James I can make nothing of this Gentleman!"

So the M P. ran out and. Mr Montmorency Lord M Lofty Lord Strafford and J J Goat soon after came in while the prince was storming and the Earl laid along the sopha half deafened with his clamour. Montmorenceys Devilish little eyes

---

10   The actual Halton is on the outskirts of Leeds.

11   The actual Braintree is in Essex between Chelmsford and Colchester.

twinkled as he noticed the Sable Hero and then he steadily and unflinchingly fronted the Earl In the first Interview which for 18 months this Man has had with the person whom he has betrayed and abandoned and abused so darkly Northangerland likewise gazing at him arose but with a Desperate Oath at the shouting Quashia—whereupon ensued a long and deep conference of which the particulars are uncertain and its results hard to be under stood.

Wide I hear the wild winds sighing[1]
     Oer the Hills and far away
Heaven in clouds before them flying
     Through the drear December day
     Dull and dark its evening ray
As oer the waste the ceaseless rain
Drives past is gone and then again
Sweeps cold and drenching by in showers of sleety spray
And now the watery mountains rise
All dimly mingling with the skies
At times some black brow darkning forth
Cleared by the tempest from the north
And then as fast the clouds sail on
All its crags and heath knolls gone
The changing vail[sic] of sleet drives oer the waste alone
     Alone I list to hear the sigh
Of the wild Blast passing by
Far away with mournful moan
It Bends the Heath on the old grey stone
Then rising in the Ashtrees bough
Scatters the withered leaves below
Blackens the wall with pelting spray
And wails and wanders far away
     Oh when I hear that wintery sound
     The very vales[sic] of a mountain land
A thousand feelings crowding round
     Start up and rise on every hand
And wake to life as the wild winds wake
     And pass with them away
Sunbeams that oer the spirit break
     Amid the dreariest day
But Hush! —And hark that solemn wail
     Tis past! —and yet—tis on my ear
Shrill peircing through the misty veil
     Like [the] voice of the departing year!
Oh Hush! —Again and yet again
Bursts forth that loud and longdrawn strain
Soldiers! Attend! it calls you back
From the pursuers bloody track
And wildly oer your foemans fall
Resounds your Evening Bugle call

---

[1]   The first draft of Scene II of **Misery**; the lines, in PML: MA 2696 R-V, though separately bound, constitute pp. 9-17 of the notebook described on p. 444, n. 1.

The Battle is done with the setting Sun
The struggle is lost and the victory won
Tis over no sighs no anguished cries
From the wild wreck of conflict rise
The sensless corse on earth reclining
Nor feels defeat nor knows repining
And they who survive in their agony
Now stiff and spent and speechless lie
With dim eyes wandering toward the sky
   Yet seek and see no comfort there
For here upon this storm beat heath
The laboured faintness of the breath
The chill approach of Iron Death
   Demands a sterner care
And well I know that lifes last light
Just bordering on Eternal night
When all these souls shall take their flight
   Must crush those souls with fear

There thy lie and wildly oer them
   Howls the wind with hollow tone
While between its banks before them
   Hear the torrent chafe and groan
   Heavily with sullen tone
   Yet still careering swiftly on
And torn with shot a shattered tree
  Shakes it bare arms in the bitter gale
Oer the blood red eddys that rapidly
  Down the swollen streamlet curling sail
And the blackned stones of a fallen wall
  Dashed down by the Iron hail of war
With their earthy bank above them thrown
  Obstruct the torrents passage there
Till angrily its waters roar
All white with froth and red with gore
And—There! —a shattered carcase lies
Without the power to look or rise
Tis He! —the conquered cheiftan—he
Whose look could once give victory
But sightless now as
The shot has torn his eyes away
And that gashed face is dashed with clay
Cast backward in the eddying flood
That washes of his bursting blood
The stones across his body thrown

Which as he fell drove following down
Oh scarce we know the Human form
In this cheif victim of the storm
 Yet though thus crushed and torn he be
  Though hence he never more shall rise
Though just as now still waves[2] shall wash
  From the crushed bones the wasting flesh
There shall he lie. as there[3] he lies
Yet still! oh still! look down and see
How VAST may mortal misery be
For in that bloody battered cell
Still Life and Soul and Memory dwell!
Never when he was fair and young
Did feeling thrill more fresh and strong
Never the Hell hounds of Despair
Had wilder power to worry there

 "Oh could I untormented die
Without this gnawing agony
That wrings my hearts[sic] so—!
     Heavily and slow
The blood ebbs forth but parts not so the soul
 Hither I came with pain and hence must I go
Still Still in pain! —Is such my changless doom
 God! shall such destiny unroll
Its agonies Beyond the tomb?
 All Dark without All fire within
 Can Hell have mightier hold on sin
 But yet through all my dying mind
 From such a present turns behind
 To—what has been—and then looks oer
 The Dark Dark void of things before
The land of Souls beyond the sable shore!
Oh how my eyes have stretched to see that land
How even when sunk in lifes bewildering roar
 All my strained thoughts have striven to reach its strand
 Have striven its mysteries to understand
Though dark indeed the unreturning sea
That seperates what lies beyond from me
Though those vast waves which bear such thousands thither
Have never brought again one spirit hither

---

2 "Waves" written above "streams"; neither is canceled.
3 "There" written above "Now"; neither is canceled.

If spirits those who pass may truely be
Those fearful passengers whose sightless eyes
    And blanched lips and tongues which cannot move
May either see the expanse which round them lies
    Or tell the scenes which open where they rove
Oh might I send across yon sea that Dove
Which bore the Olive branch[4] Oh might it bear
From hence some token toward me hovering here
Even though it were the fruit of bitterness
So I might cease thiss[sic] doubt and fearfulness
    While I embark to sail—I know not where
I scarce know whence—or how—but such distress
Vain in the Hope that it will end! —and then
How vain the wish to know where lies my pain!
        Oh it lies here—and if my mind
        Survives it will not lag behind
        And if indeed—I truely Die
        Lost—in the abyss of vacancy
        Why THEN. the sum of all will be
        That I on earth have lived to see
        Twice twenty winters beat on me
        Not one whole day of happiness
        And year on year of mad distress!

"They say when on the bed of death
    The wasted sickman lingering lies
His breast scarce heaving with his breath
    And cold his hand and quenched his eyes
    See—how resignedly he. Dies
Aye what a look of peace and love
That glazed eye casts to heaven above
Even those those white lips will scarcly quiver
Though he must leave this world for ever
And though his children round him stand
Tis not for them that outstretched hand
Angels shall press those clay cold fingers
In the unknown void round which he lingers
    Ha! does the victim reason so
When bound beneath that fatal blow?
No! There indeed he lies inert
For deaths cold frost congeals his heart
Yet while that dim and dazing eye
Can wander oer one stander by

---

4   See Genesis 8:6-11.

While those mute lips that silent tongue
Can one short broken gasp prolong
While in that whirled and burning brain
Reasons last spark can wax and wane
So long across that parting soul
Unmixed—unmingled—torments roll!
Ha—look on death with smiling eye
Ha—content and peacful die
Ha—no like fire one burning strife
Convulses each riven string of life
And could those lips be moved to say
Could those stiff hands be clasped to pray
That only voice and prayer would be
       'Oh save me from that fatal sea
Where Hell and death join agony!
       I am dying! and what a rayless gloom
Seems darkning round my dreary tomb
I know no hope—I see no ray
To light me on my heavenly way
       There was a light—but it is gone
There was a Hope but—all is oer
       And freindless sightless left alone
I go where THOU hast gone before
And yet I shall not see thee more
Ha! say not that the dying man
Can only think on present pain
Oh no Oh no it is not so
For where Maria where art THOU!
—O do I seem to see thee now
Thy smiling eyes and shining brow
Thy sunny cheek and golden hair
In all thy Beauty Beaming there!
All through the noontide of my years
How thou di[d]st enter all my fears
And hopes of joy and smiles and tears
How often has thy bright blue eye
       Driven sorrow shrinking from its shine
And banished all my misery
       Before one heavenly look of thine
       How often has that look divine
Roused up this heart from bitterness
Or bowed it in its worst distress
       To kneel before thy shrine
Oh once we thought to pass together
Through stormiest change of wind and weather

And thou wouldst never shrink from me
And I could never part with thee
I clasped within thy arms and thou
Lying on my breast thine ivory brow
Unthought uncared for storm or shine
While I was thine and thou wast mine
    When troubles hastned thickning on
When every hope of rest seemed gone
When mid the blight of hating eyes
    I stood bewildered sick with woe
What was the star which seemed to rise
    To light me on and guide me through
What was that form so heavenly fair
Untouched by time unmarked with care
To whose fond heart I clung to save
My sinking spirit from its grave
Maria! hadst thou never been
    This hour I should not living be
But while I strove with Fate between
    The strife thou camest to set me free
And wildly did I cling to thee
I could not would not dared not part
Lest hell again should seize my heart
    Can I forget how toward thy eye
        Still ever gazed for guidance thine
As if I were thy star on high
        Though well I knew twas thou wert mine
That azure eye that softened smile
That heavenly voice whose tones to me
The weariest winteriest hours could wile
    And make me think that still might be
    Some years of happiness with thee
That thou amid my life to come
Shouldst be my hope my heaven my home
But—we are sundered—thee thy grave
And me this dreary wild will have
Whateer the world to come may be
I must never look on thee
If theres no God no Heaven no Hell
Thou within thy grave must dwell
I here blackning in the storm
Both a Banquet for the worm
If there is a heaven above
    Thou in bliss are shinig[sic] there
At the wondrous throne of love

Angel bright and Angel fair!
From Heaven thou wanderedst like the Dove
   To the wild world of waters here
But never made oer it to rove
   Thou hast left this site of sin and care
Back to thine Ark while I staid where
The rottenest mass of carnage lay
A Raven resting on the prey
And Hells dread night must close my day!
      Oh God my fear lies there
      Without a hope to meet thee then
      But howling in despair!

*   *   *   *   *   *
*   *   *   *   *   *

Why why will the parted return to our heart
   When the sods have grown green on their tomb
Oh why will the twilight refuse to depart
   When it only gives depth to the gloom
Oh why in the snows and storms of December
   When branches lie scattered and strewn
Do we oftest and clearest and brightest remember
   The sunshine and summer of June
Oh why mid the hungry and cottagless waste
   Do we dream of the Goblet filled high
Why will our spirits when famishing taste
   Such visionlike revelry
Moralist speak! —ist in lifes deepest sorrow
   That these gleams of the past which hath vanished away
Though misery and mourning await on the morrow
   May strengthen to bear through the shades of today
   Since we have had our sunshine we must have our storm
   First with an Angel and last with the worm
Christian speak—dost thou point to the sea
And shew me the Mariner drifting away
Behind him the shores of his desolate home
Around him the billows all crested with foam
Yet he casts not a look upon ocean or shore
But fixes his eyes on his haven before
Sayest thou thus should man smile on his joy and his sorrow
And press toward Heaven. his Haven of to morrow
Aye Man! on let him press till that Heaven shall break
     In lightnings and thunders and tempest and gloom
Then let the Spirit in *safty* speak!

Where is the rest beyond the tomb
Where are the joys of his heavenly home
Then let the moralist seek for his strength
And smile on the past in its visionlike form
Then let the Christian anchored at length
See light in the darkness a Sun through the storm
Away with all this false disguise
View midnight truth with noonday eyes
The past has had a single joy
But when that past [h]as long gone by
When cares have driven cares away
When general darkness coulds[sic] the day
That Single Star amid the sky
Will shed a brighter light on high
And in the Horizon only one
Is yet the <u>ALL</u> that can be shewn
Well oer me shining let it be
That thus one glimmering I may see
Fixed far above to shew my gloom
And light my spirit to its Tomb!

Yet How I wander! grasping now
At the glorious dream of a world to come
Then recoiling back I scarce know how
Upon that hideous hopeless gloom
The NOTHINGNESS within the tomb
Thinking on THEE and then again
Shrinking within my present pain
All wide All wandering—This is Death!
And I would calmly meet him now
As stern I'de feel my shortning breath
As I have felt my life blood flow
But for the thought—
Oh whats to come!
God if there be a God look down
Compassionate my Fall
Oh clear away thine awful frown
Oh hearken to my call!
Nay—all is lost—I cannot bear
In mouldering dust to dissapear
And Heaven will not the gloom dispell
Since were there one my home were Hell
No Hope No hope—And Oh fare well
The form so long kept treasured here
Must thou then ever dissapear

Gone long but real in memorys shrine
   Now dying again as memory dies
First passes from earth my star divine
   And now tis passing from the skies
   Thou art alone and Heaven is gone
   And and sights and sounds and all are gone
Oh what a shade is life—I am dying
And HOW LIKE A DREAM IS EXISTENCE FLYING

See through the shadows of the night
   Burst hotly hasting onward here
A wounded Charger vast and white
   All wild with pain and mad with Fear
With hoofs of thunder on he flies
Shaking his white mane to the skies
Till on his huge knees tumbling down
Across the fallen Cheiftan thrown
With a single plunge of dying force
His vast limbs cover Alberts corse

Finished March 2^{d}
1836
P B B.

[Angria and the Angrians]
II (e)[1]

PBB—te
March 23
1836

How dreadful is sickness in the midst of bustle and activity Helpless prostration of strength where the sufferer ought to have been up and doing in one of the mightiest struggles that ever desolated the world. Such [h]as been my situation for six weary weeks laid wounded in a wasting fever among depressing sights and sounds within the wards at the Seaton[2] Military Hospital It is not that I shudder so much at pain and fever. but that I am miserable when I think of so long a time passed in complete inaction when every nerve ought to have been strained to reach my point of ambition when twenty opportunities passed by and so much of youth vanished in pain and deleriums and restlessness—Then how glorious it is for me to take sword in hand once more and mount my horse and dash again into the mighty events which are changing and thickning around us. since the day when. I fell on the feild of Ludlow Jan 10th[3] how awfully has the eruption spread over the face of my country—Then certainly Zamorna was one sore 100 000 enimies covered and overran it and a great fleet blockaded its coasts But Since! —Our capital has been taken our Monarch forced to retreat into Angria Half our Nation in possession of our foes. Verdopolis made one mighty warlike depot Sneachis land and Wellingtonsland sending forth distant muttterings of war all hearts fevered and trade and commerce suspended the Kings devided the Government only preserved from falling to peices directly by the quickness of their descent to destruction and—worst of all the dim uncertain vista of—but I sicken when I mention it—New powers—New Heads—A new state of things—but a yet more dreadful one—Did I say I sickened at this thought—If I did I told a Lie my nature wont let me—I'll be candid for there is in the out look I hint at far too much to excite the feelings and passions and hopes and Ambition to make Henry Hastings sicken. I am well aware of the dreadful nature of this coming change but—However its useless to mention it Heres Hastings up again and let him be seeing who knows whats in store—Blows and blood very true but perhaps likewise—However again lets stop—my Angrian Heart is

---

[1]   The following section consists of one leaf (pp.15-16) in the Taylor manuscript noted in (d) above, and may well follow directly on from that section.

[2]   There are several Seatons. The nearest to Haworth is in Cumberland, near Workington.

[3]   See pp. 465-66.

too high and my Angrian wantoness miserably disposed to toss and trample Old things and Old institutions and old orders of Society

But how strange it is that thousands and thousands of young fellows like me standing foremost in the battle and fighting boldest in the cause of old things against new should yet at heart be laughing at and despising our principles—Nay I say it is not strange we are but following our two Leaders. And when was Northangerland ever known to adore the "Good old cause" while as for Zamorna God bless him well does that noble heart when beating so high as now well does it know that no aged vision of king or constitution inspires it but the work of defending his own dear kingdom the first steps in a plan of glorious dominion the hate to bitter and feindish Enimies and thats where we follow him there it is where Angria is willing to spend her last blood in his cause

Once again I say it is a terrible thought that hints to us Should our Enimies even be annihilated peace would not be gained mighty thoughts and immense Ambition will only then develope themselves in a track of fiery light which all the world will behold as the path of Adrian and Alexander.

Verb Sap[4] this is enough indeed it's speaking too plainly so I must recoil back upon my own more immediate concernments

On the   [5] of March I for the first time reendued myself in Gold and scarlet But my new Regimentals while they enwrapped but half the strength and vigour of Captain Hastings clothed nearly twice his rank. —Major Hastings of the 19 Infantry—That was something but the toy only pleased for an hour or two ere night the word was—and why not Colonel But morning answered. lets see if it shant be so. Now my Majority <gave> me the privilege of a Horse which was most desirable in the case of one who had his leg stuck through by a Bayonet this was the case. but it likewise demanded an immediate trot to Angria this was work. and like Macbeths Ghosts more and more was rising behind it. But the Glorious Bracing feeling of one roused from sleepy yet sleepless confinment in the Steaton Hospital[sic] to such a stirring look out of change and danger as the future presented was enough to rouse up a much less elastic spirit than mine My Appetite for war and trouble and excitement and the glimpses of prodigious Spirits and some movement in their prodigious works and over all some chance of a step in to a nich among them. My Appetite for these daintys was sharpened by a two months fast. recollecting too that I had been snatched from the very middle of a most plenteous feast—by the way how extraordinary dim is my memory of that affair of Ludlow. the intervening haze and vapours of fever and delerium had almost wrapt it from my mind At dinner while they were congratulating me upon my advancement and recovery an express came from Angria to Col Sir Charles Warren with dispatches which as soon as he had

---

4   Verbum sapienti sat est: a word to the wise is enough.
5   Branwell left the date blank.

looked on made him rise from the wine in an unangrian hurry He left us but in a while sent for me—"Major Hastings" said his Honour when I had closed the door

"you know we sit next to the fire here?"

I nodded

"Well so being it is not convenient for us to get roasted and we have orders to decamp"

"What said I and leave all the foot of Arundel open—Impossible!" then I ran my hand on the Map over those parts of the country which our retreat would give up and I said—"And Steaton is the key from Verdopolis to Angria"

"Aye well the door is to be opened and the key left for them to shut it."

"Humph well Colonel it seems the policy at headquarters is to keep out of the fire!"

"Quite contrary its to get into it—why we allow the french. to enter that it may be hand to hand and the weakest to the wall.

"So be it but I only pretend to be an Army man and this I know as such that my comrades wont like it"

"My Good freind heres a paper worth the weight of twenty comrades you see that scrawl. —Z.A.M.O.R.N.A. thats a talisman that must be obeyed.

I had nothing now to do but bow in silence

"Well Major" said Sir Charles "I wish you to carry your submission to head Quarters—a stir after this tedious confinement will do you rare good you know we Angrians live in a stir And by Heaven we have <it>. Some one must bear my despatches to Angria and I think you'll like the job. —6 o clock this evening—"

I Got ready with all possible despatch and waited upon the Baronet at the time appointed. received my orders mounted my horse and left my Prison Steaton at the rapid trot of a freed and ambitious soldier

Sir Richard Warren was the actual commander of about 3000 troops stationed in Steaton and forming the rear guard of the Angrian forces for Zamorna The Hill and the Olympian Plain were all occupied by great bodies of French and Ministerialists. with those human Demons the Blacks wasting all the fair province with fire and sword the constant risings of the country people could make no impression so great was the force arrayed against us. but a terrible spirit of Vengeance was springing up that any blow of our enimies would only bring into more perfect and palpable Shape. all their cruelty being only like the whitesmiths[6] strokes whereby he would shape the strongest and sharpest sword.—

Every hope of the Angrians and of freedom was concentered in the province of Angria whose capital formed the Headquarters of our Monarch and the real seat of Government in the city and through the country were disposed about 80 000 excellent troops filled with a fiery and indomitable spirit burning for revenge upon the destroyers of their Metropolis and the invaders of our Land The Leaders of these men were the best Generals in the world the head of all.

---

6   A worker in iron who does finishing, polishing or galvanizing.

the—BEST MAN—its out now and I'll not retract it—Hither then was I going this was my native Province each town and Hill and stream were familiar to me and how strange did I feel at the thought that—Angria Sydenham Pendleton Howard. Romalla. Pendlebrow Boulshill all those well know[n] scenes were now the encampment of armed men and might soon be a great battle feild. in war— nay would soon for it was evident that Every day and every movement made Angria a more distinct mark for the discision of the question. Is the Land to be subdued or not. Northward there are the Gordon Mountains inaccessible fastnesses to retire to But if they are reached in safty. all the really peopled and actual Land of Angria must be relinquished to destruction

Misery. Scene 1st[1]

How fast that courser fleeted by,
With arched neck backward tossed on high,
And snorting nostrils opened wide,
And foam flecked chest and gory side.
  I saw his riders darkned form
As on they hurried through the storm;
Forward he pressed, his plume behind
Flew whistling in the wintery wind,
But his clenched teeth and angry eye
Seemed wind and tempest to defy;
And eagerly he bent his sight
To peirce the darkness of the night;
And oft he gazed and gazed again
Through rough blast and driving rain.
  Look up, and view the midnight heaven,
Where, mass oer mass continual driven
The wild black storm clouds fleet and change
Like formless phantom's black and strange,
That bend their gloomy brows from high,
And pass in midnight darkness by:
And still they pass, and still they come,
Without a flash to break the gloom.
I cannot see the foam and spray
Which mark that raging torrents way;
But I can hear the ceasless roar,
Where, swollen and chafed, its waters pour.
There—where yon blackned Oaks on high,
Blend wildly with the midnight sky,
Tossing their bare and groaning boughs
Like some dread fight of giant foes;
There—where that glimpse of moonlight shines,
  From the wild wrack of heaven sent down,
And spreads its silver trembling lines

---

[1] Autograph manuscript of nine pages, 18.3x22.7 cm, in the National Library of Scotland: MS 4042. Undated, but sent to *Blackwood's* with an accompanying letter, dated April 8, 1836. For the text of the letter, see Neufeldt PBB, pp. 379-380. In the letter Branwell indicates that he has a third scene in mind— "a Scene after Death—the soul followed to its final misery" —but there is no evidence that he ever attempted it.

Amid the darkness, then is gone,—
There stays the Horseman—, wide before,
Deep and dark, the waters roar:
But, down the lone vale, far away,
Glances one solitary ray.
The sounds of winds and waters, rise,
And sweeps the sleet shower, oer the skys;
While dreariest darkness, all around,
Makes still more drear each sight or sound:
But heeds not such that Cavalier;
Reining his trembling charger there,
He halts upon the rivers brink
Where all its wild waves surge and sink,
Shades with his hand, his anxious eye,
And through the night looks eagerly:
Why smiled he, when that far off light
Again broke twinkling on his sight?
Why frowned he, when it sunk again
Amid the darksome veil of rain?
Till, brightly flashing forth once more,
It streams and twinkles far before!

"Oh, through the tempests of this life,
          However loud they sound,
However wild their storms and strife
          May burst and thunder round,
Though raft and riven each aid and prop,
There may be heaven, there may be hope!
I Thought just now, that life or death
          Could never trouble me,
For That I should draw my future breath
          In silent apathy.
That, oer the pathway of my fate
          Though steady beat the storm,
As I walked alone and desolate,
          I'de to that path conform.
Affection should not chain me,
          Or sorrow hold me down,
But despair itself sustain me,
          Whom itself had over thrown.
I Thought, that Fame and Glory,
          Were names for shame and woe;
That lifes deceitful story
          I had finished long ago:
That all its novelty was gone,

And that thus to read again
The same dull page in the same sad tone
        Was not even change of pain.
Defeat had crushed me into dust,
        But, only laid my head
Where head and heart and spirit must
        Be soon for ever laid.
My fearless followers all were slain,
        My power and glory gone;
My followers met the fate of men;
        And power! —I am *now* alone!
Not so! —I *thought* it, till that light
        Glanced glittering down the glen,
And, on my spirits dreary night
        Flashed brightness back again.
Yes, —I Had thought I stood alone,
That I need sigh or weep for none,
Had quenched my love in apathy,
Since none would weep or sigh for me.
Yes! —But that single silver beam
        Which flashes on my eye,
Hath waked me from my dreary dream
        And made the darkness fly!
Then, Pardon, That the storms of woe
        Have whelmed in a drifting sea;
With death and dangers struggling so,
        That I—awhile, —forgot even thee.
This moment, as I gain the shore,
        And clouds begin to dissapear,
Even steadier, brighter, than before,
        Thou shinest—my own, my guardian Star!
O, could I speak the long lost feeling;
The inward joy, its power revealing;
The glimpse of something yet to come
Which yet may give a happy home!
Oh, could I speak my thoughts of thee,
Whom, soon again, my eyes shall see:
The Dove that bore the olive leaf,[2]
Could never bring such glad relief
To wanderers oer a shoreless main,
As, in weariness and pain,
        That single light has given to me!

---

2   See Genesis 8:7-11.

My Gallant Horse, speed swiftly thou,
Soon shall a Hand caress thee now,
Grateful that thou hast born me on
Through deadliest deeds and dangers gone;
A Touch, thou mayest be proud to own,
Though thou so oft has felt my own.
O, That fair hand, and faithful heart,
From mine, what power shall ever part!
What power! —Ha, well indeed I know
The very fire which burns me now,
The very energy of soul
    Which to thine arms impells me on,
When once I've gained that wished for goal,
    Will—like a comet from the sun,
Hurl me, with power that scorns controul
    Far from thy beams of happiness,
    Into the expanse of wild distress
Where passions lightnings burst and Battles thunders roll!"

Impetous then that Horseman sprung
Down the steep bank—His Armour rung
    Mid the wild waters roar;
And, dashing through the old Oak trees,
His coursers hoofs, upon the breeze
Their reckless rattle swiftly cease,
    In the dark night before.

Who, that hath felt the feeling wild
    Which struck upon the excited mind
When, perhaps long since, while yet a child,
    In awful mystery undefined
Old tales, and legends, often told,
    While winter nights fell long and drear,
Have made his hearts blood curdle cold
    Their dreary fates to hear.
Of Ancient Halls where Destiny
    Has brooded with its raven wing.
Of castles stern, whose riotry
    Hid not the gloomy crimes within.
Of Death Beds, where the sickman lying
    Mid anxious listners standing by,
Ere he had told the secret dying,
    And left a sealed mystery.
Of Heirs, who to some fearful doom
    Suceeded with their ancient Hall.

Of marriage feasts, where Ghosts would come
      The new made Bride to call.
—He, that Hath still in memory
      Kept fast those dreams of childoods hours
Who these far visions yet may see
      Oh Castle Halls and Feudal towers,
—To Him I shew this stormy night
That seems to darken on my sight.

Far above their forest trees
      Those dreary Turrets rise,
And round their walls, the midnight breeze
      Comes shreiking from the skies.
Scarce can I note the central tower
      Amid the impetous storm,
Till, shimmering through the pelting shower
      The moonbeams mark its form.
Far downward to the raving stream
      The woody banks decline,
Where waters, flashing in the beam
      Through deepest darkness shine.
Those Giant Oaks their boughs are tossing
      As wild winds wilder moan,
Trunks and leaves confusedly crossing
      With a ceasless groan.
And, over all, the Castle walls
      Rise Blacker than the night,
No sign of man amid their Halls
      Save that lone turret light.
The upward path is wild and steep,
      Yet, hear that Horseman come,
Not toiling up with cautious creep,
      But hotly hasting home!
The steed is to the stables led,
      But, wheres the Rider gone?
Up that high turret staircase sped
      With gladdened haste alone.
The Ante room looks hushed and still,
      With lattice curtained close,
That tempests, sweeping round the Hill,
      Disturb not its repose.
All's soft and calm, a holy balm
      Seems sleeping in the air,
But, what on earth has power to calm
      A spirit chafed with care?

The Warrior hastes to seek that power,
    He knows the only one
Whose love can sooth his lonly hour
    Or Hush his rising groan:
And, where that soft and solemn light
    Shines through the opened door,
He hastens in with armed tread
    Across the chequered floor
And entering—though a sacred stream
    Of radiance round him fell,
It could not with its silent beam
    His eager spirit quell.

"Maria!" But the silence round
    Would give him no reply,
And straightway did that single sound
    Without an echo die.
"Where hath my gentle Lady gone
    I do not find her here?"
Lo, on that statly couch, alone
    Reclines thy Lady fair.
But—Cold and pale is her marble brow,
    Dishevelled her sunny hair,
Oh! is it in peaceful slumber now
    That she lieth so silent there?
"Heaven bless thy dreams!" Lord Albert cried
    But his heart beat impatiently,
And as he hasted to her side
    He scarce had power to see.
All wildly the scenes of his former life
    Flashed back upon his eyes,
And at once, a shade of despair and strife
    Before him seemed to arise.
But, as the sailor to his ship
    Clings with more frenzied power,
As, louder thundering oer the deep,
    Fresh billows whelm him oer;
So madly, on his only prop
    This war worn man reclined,
He could not, would not, deem his hope
    Delivered to the wind.

Yet then, why is this start of wildered fright
    And whence can arise this fear?
Is it not now in the depth of night?

And sleeps not thy Lady there?
And art not thou on thy castle height,
From wars alarms afar?
See—Is that sleep?
—with opened eyes,
Chilly white and cold she lies,
Sunk her cheeks, and blanched her lip,
That trembles as with suffering:
She sleeps not, till the eternal sleep
Its dreamless rest shall bring!
Heaven had occupied her mind
To onward hasting death resigned,
But, mid those strange uncertainties
Which crowd their ghastly phantoms round
When all our reasons guiding ties
Are from the parting soil unbound,
She thought, when first she heard that tread,
That Death himself was hasting near;
The conjured vision of his form
Obeyed her ready fancies fear,
And to her dim eyes seemed to appear,
Till—that one word—and all was clear!
Then—sinking reason rose again;
Then—joined the links of memorys chain;
Then—spite of all her dying pain
She felt, she knew, Her Lord was there!
Oh! when, across that dreary sea
The light broke forth so suddenly,
What soul can feel, what tongue express
The burst of raptured happiness,
That from her spirit chased its care,
For—She was dying But He was there!

Ah! swiftly, surely, art thou gliding
Over Deaths unfathomed sea,
Dark and deep the waves dividing
Thee from earth and earth from thee
Life—thy own, thy happy land,
Parted far on either hand,
As the mighty waters widen
Onward to Eternity.
Shores of Life, Farewell for ever,
Where thy happiness has lain,
Lost for ever, Death must sever
All thy hopes and joys and pain.

Yet, how blest the sound must be
    Which comes upon thy dying ear,
From off the dim departing shore,
    Although its landmarks dissapear,
Still sounding oer the eternal roar,
    The voice of him thou heldst so dear.
    Tis as when the Mariner
Just parted from his native home,
    After a night of dread and fear
Whose storms have riven the waves to foam
When nights dark hours have swept away
All, save the sounding of the sea,
Morn breaks, where all looks new & strange
But hark, a sweet, a sudden change,
For, on his ear strikes soft from far
    In Sabbath chime—his Native Bells;
He starts—And bursts the joyful tear,
For things unutterably dear
      That farewell music tells!

Yet stay! —Why do I wander so
To wile me from this scene of woe?
      There stood the Armed man;
The very wildness of Despair
In his red eyeballs stricken glare,
      His cheeks so ghastly wan.
And, on her couch his Lady lying,
Still and slow and sur[e]ly dying,
Yet, with an enraptured smile
And glistning of her glassy eye,
As her weak arms she would the while
    Have stretched to clasp him standing by,
But, they would not her will obey
And motionless beside her lay.
    Then her white lips moved to speak,
But nothing could she say.
This was deaths triumphant hour,
Grasped by his tremendous power
      She must pass away!

Speak, Maria! Speak my love!
    Let me hear thy voice;
Naught on earth, or heaven above,
    Could make me so rejoice!
Speak! O, speak! and say to me,

I am not come to late to thee.
O, tell me, that my arm can save
Thy sinking spirit from the grave!
Maria! —oh my only love,
   Tell me thou wilt not die,
And nought below, and naught above
      Shall feel so blest as I!
Oh, would that I were far away,
Alone upon a stormy sea!
Might I awake on yonder plain
Where I have left my soldiers slain;
So I <u>could</u> wake, and rise, and know
      That this was but a fearful dream,
That *thou* at least wert smiling now
      As once in love and beautys beam.
But—Heres the truth which now I know,
My God—My God—I cannot bear thy blow!"

All was vain! She moved not, spoke not,
Speech or sound the silence broke not.
But, He flung him oer her lying
As he would catch her spirit flying.
All was vain! That spirit flies
To God who gave it in the skies.
That within his arms which lay
Was but a lifeless form of clay;
Naught of feeling in that face,
No return of his embrace;
Not a wish or power to save
Its own cold members from their grave
     Go, Lord Albert, go again,
       Drown thought amid a world of storms
    Go—! for thy <u>Despair</u> is vain,
       And thy <u>HOPE</u> lies food for worms

Scene. 2^d

Wild I hear the wild winds sighing
   Oer the hills and far away,
Heaven in clouds before them flying,
   Through the drear December day:
   Dull and dark its evening ray,

As, oer the waste, the ceaseless rain
Drives past, is gone, and then again
Sweeps cold and drenching by in showers of sleety spray.
    And now, the watery mountains rise
All dimly mingling with the skies,
At times, some black brow darkning forth
Cleared by the tempest from the north,
And then, as fast the clouds sail on,
All its crags and heath knolls gone,
The changing veil of sleet drives oer the waste alone.
    Alone I list to hear the sigh
Of the wild blast passing by,
Hark, far away with mournful moan
It bends the heath on the old grey stone,
Then rising in the Ash trees bough
Scatters the withered leaves below;
Blackens the wall with pelting spray,
And wails, and wanders, far away.
    Oh when I hear that wintery sound,
        The very voice of a mountain land,
A thousand feelings crowding round
        Start up and rise on every hand,
And wake to life, as the wild winds wake,
        And pass with them away,
Sunbeams, that oer the spirit break
        Amid the dreariest day.
But, Hush! —And hark that solemn wail;
Tis past! —and yet, tis on my ear;
Shrill piercing through the misty veil,
    Like voice of the departing year.
Oh, Hush! Again, and yet again
Bursts forth that loud and longdrawn strain
Soldiers! Attend! —It calls you back
From the pursuers bloody track.
And wildly oer your foemens fall
Resounds your evening Bugle call.
The Battle is done, with the setting sun;
The struggle is lost, and the victory won.
Tis over. —No sighs, no anguished cries
From the wild wreck of conflict rise.
The sensless corse on earth reclining,
Nor feels defeat, nor knows repining;
And they who survive in their agony
Now stiff and spent and speechless lie,
Their dim eyes wander toward the sky,

Yet seek, and see, no comfort there;
For here, upon this stormy Heath,
The laboured faintness of the breath,
The chill approach of Iron Death,
Demands a sterner care,
And, well I know, that lifes last light
Just bordering on eternal night,
When all these souls shall take their flight,
Must crush those souls with fear.

Then, There they lie, and wildly oer them
Howls the wind with hollow tone,
While, between its banks, before them
Hear the torrent chafe and groan;
Heavily with sullen tone,
Yet still careering swiftly on.
And, torn with shot, a shattered tree
Shakes its bare arms to the bitter gale,
Oer the blood red eddies that rapidly
Down the swolln streamlet curling sail.
And the blackened stones of a fallen wall
Dashed down by the Iron hail of war,
With their earthy bank above them thrown,
Obstructs the torrents passage there;
Till angrily its waters roar,
All white with froth, and red with gore.
And—There—a shattered carcase lies
Without the power to look or rise!
Tis He! —The conquered cheiftan—He
Whose look could once give victory;
But sightless now—
The shot has torn his eyes away,
And his gashed face is dashed with clay
Cast backward in the eddying flood
That washes off his bursting blood,
The stones across his body thrown
That, as he fell, drove following down
Oh! scarce we know the human form
In this cheif victim of the storm!
Yet, though thus crushed and torn he be,
Though hence, he never, more shall rise,
Though just as now, till waves shall wash
From the crushed bones the wasting flesh,
There shall he lie as there he lies;
Yet, still—oh still, look down, and see

How vast may mortal misery be,
For, in that bloody battered cell
Still Life and Soul and Memory dwell.
Never, when he was fair and young,
Did feeling thrill more fresh and strong,
Never the hell hounds of despair
Had wilder power to worry there.

"O, could I untormented die,
Without this gawning agony
Which wrings my heart so! —
                              —Heavily and slow
The blood ebbs forth, —but, parts not so the soul.
Hither, I came with pain! —Hence must I go
Still, still, in pain! —Is such our changless doom?
God!—Shall such destiny unroll
Its agonies beyond the tomb?
                Alls dark without—Alls fire within—!
                Can Hell have mightier hold on sin?
                But yet—through all, my dying mind
                From such a present turns behind
                To what has been, —and then looks oer
                The dark dark void of things before;
The land of souls beyond the sable shore![3]
Oh, how my eyes have stretched to see that land!
How, even when sunk in lifes bewildering roar
        All my strained thoughts have striven to reach its strand,
        Have striven its mysteries to understand,
Though dark indeed the unreturning sea
That separates what lies beyond me.
Though those vast waves which bear such thousands thither
Have never brought again one spirit hither,
        If spirits those who pass may truely be:
Those fearful passengers, Whose sightless eyes
        And blanched lips and tongues which cannot move
May either see the expanse which round them lies,
        Or tell the scenes which open where they rove.
Oh, might I send across yon sea, that dove
        Which bore the Olive branch; Now might it bear
From hence some token toward me hovering here,
Even though it were the fruit of bitterness,

---

[3] Two canceled lines follow:
        Oh how my eyes have striven to reach its strand
        Have striven its mysteries to understand.

So I might cease this doubt and fearful-ness
    When I embark to sail—I know not where—
I scarce know whence, or how, —But such distress,
Vain is the hope that it will end, and then
How vain the wish to know where lies our pain
    Oh it lies here! —and if my mind
    Survives, it will not lag behind!
    And, if indeed, I truely die,
    Lost in the abyss of vacancy,
    Why then—the sum of all will be,
    That I on earth have lived to see
    Twice twenty winters beat on me,
    Not one whole day of happiness,
    And year on year of mad distress!

They say, when on the bed of death
    The wasted sickman lingering lies,
His breast scarce heaving with his breath,
    And cold his brow and quenched his eyes,
'See! How resignedly he dies!"
Aye! What a look of peace and love
That glazed eye casts to heaven above!
Even those white lips will scarcly quiver,
Though he must leave this world forever.
And though his childern round him stand,
Tis not for them—that outstretched hand!
Angels shall press those clay cold fingers
In the unknown void round which he lingers!
    Ha! Does the *victim* reason so,
Thus, bound beneath that fatal blow?
No! There indeed he lies inert,
For death's cold frost congeals his heart;
Yet, while that dim and dazing eye
Can wander oer one stander by,
While those mute lips, that silent tongue,
Can one short broken gasp prolong,
While in that whirled and burning brain
Reasons last spark can wax or wane,
So long, across that parting soul
Unmixed—unmingled—torments roll.
He—look on death with smiling eye!
He—content and peacful die!
He! No, like fire, one burning strife
Convulses each riven string of life,
And, could those lips be moved to say,

Could those stiff hands be clasped to pray
That only voice and prayer would be,
"Oh save me from that fatal sea
Where Hell, and death join agony!'
  I am dying, and what a rayless gloom
Seems darkning round my dreary tomb
I know no light, I see no ray
To guide me on my heavenly way.
There <u>was</u> a light—But it is gone!
   There <u>was</u> a hope—But all is oer!
And, powerless, sightless, left alone,
I go where <u>Thou</u> hast gone before;
And yet, I shall not see thee more!
Ha said I that the dying man
Could only think of present pain?
Oh No! For scenes gone long ago
Make the main torrent of his woe.
I meant, he thinks of pain alone,
It skills not wether come or gone:
All dark alike to him and me
What has been, is, or is to be!
And keen I feel such misery now,
For where, Maria, where art thou?
Lost—Though—I seem to see thee now,
Thy smiling eyes and shining brow
And sunny cheek and golden hair,
In all thy beauty smiling there.
How often has that Bright blue eye
  Driven sorrow shrinking from its shine
And banished all my misery
  Before one heavenly look of thine!
  How often has that look divine
Roused up this heart from bitterness,
And bowed it in its worst distress
  To kneel before thy shrine!
When troubles hastened, thickning on,
When every hope of rest seemed gone;
When, mid the blight of hating eyes
  I stood, bewildered, sick with woe,
What was the star which seemed to rise
  To light me on and guide me through
What was that form so heavenly fair,
Untouched by time, unmarked by care,
To whose fond heart I clung to save
My sinking spirit from its grave?

Maria! —hadst thou never been,
  This hour I should not living be,
But while I strove with fate, between
  The strife thou camest to set me free,
And wildly did I cling to thee!
    I could not, would not, dared not part,
    Lest Hell again should seize my heart!
Can I forget, how toward <u>my</u> eye
  Still ever gazed for guidance thine,
As if I were thy star on high,
  Though well I knew twas thou wert mine
That azure eye, that softened smile,
That heavenly voice whose tones to me
The weariest wintriest hours could wile,
    And make me think that still might be
    Some years of happiness with thee;
That thou, amid my life to come,
Shouldst be my hope my heaven my home
But—we are sundred—thee thy grave,
And me this dreary wild will have.
Whateer the world to come may be
I must never look on thee,
If theres no God, no Heaven, no Hell,
Thou within thy grave must dwell,
I here blackning in the storm,
Both a banquet for the worm.
If—there <u>is</u> a Heaven above,
    Thou, I know, art shining there
At the Almighty throne of love,
    Angel bright and Angel fair
From heaven thou wanderdst like the Dove
    To the wild world of waters here,
But—never made oer it to rove,
    Thou hast left its waves of sin and care
    Back for thine Ark, while I staid where
The rottenest mass of carnage lay,
A Raven resting on his prey.

x x x x x x x x x x x x x

But, Oh why will the parted return to our heart
    When the sods have grown green on their tomb?
Oh, why will the twilight refuse to depart,
    When it only gives depth to the gloom!
Oh why, in the snows and the storms of December,

When branches lie scattered and strewn,
Do we oftest, and clearest, and brightest, remember
The sunshine and summer of June!
Oh why, mid the hungry and cottagless waste
Do we dream of the Goblet filled high,
Why will our spirits, when famishing, taste
Of such visionlike revelry!
Moralist speak—Ist in Lifes deepest sorrow
That these gleams of the past which has vanished
away
Though misery and mourning await on the morrow.
May strengthen to bear through the shades of to day?
Since we have had our sunshine, we must have our
storm,
If Once with an Angel, Then now with a worm.
Christian speak—sayest thou, Cares and annoy
Are probations on earth to a heavenly joy.
Or next, wilt thou point to the desolate sea?
And shew me the Mariner, drifting away,
Behind him the shores of his vanishing home,
Around him the billows all crested with foam,
Yet he casts not a look upon ocean or shore,
But fixes his eyes on his haven before.
Sayest thou, Thus should man smile on his joys and his
sorrow
And press toward Heaven his haven of to morrow.
Aye, Man! —on let him press, till that heaven shall break
In lightnings and thunders and tempests and gloom,
Then, let the spirit, *in safty*, speak,
Where is the rest beyond the tomb?
Where are the joys of his heavenly home?
Then, let the moralist seek for his strength,
And smile on the past in its visionlike form,
Then, let the Christian, anchored at length,
See the Light in the darkness, a Sun through the storm!
Away with all this false disguise,
See midnight truth with noonday eyes.
The past has had a single joy,
But when that past has long gone by,
When cares have driven cares away,
When general darkness clouds the day,
That single star amid the sky
Will shed a brighter light on high;
Is yet the *All* which can be shewn.
And still, as gloomier frowns that night,

Brighter it flashes on the sight,
And still—Oh still—as time flys by,
While other things in shades may die,
Tis but more present to my eye
My own sole star of memory!
        Well, —oer me shining let it be,
That thus one glimmering I may see
Fixed far above to shew my gloom,
And light my spirit to its Tomb!

Yet—How I wander! Grasping now
        At the glorious dream of a world to come—
Then, recoiling back, I scarce know how,
        Upon that hideous hopeless gloom!
        The nothingness within the tomb!
Thinking on Thee, and then again
Shrinking within my present pain.
All wide!—All wandering!—This is Death!
        And I would calmly meet him now,
As stern I'de feel my shortning breath,
        As I have seen my power laid low,
But, for the thought—
                        —O whats to come?
God! —If there be a God—look down,
        Compassionate my fall!
O, clear away thy awful frown,
        And hearken to my call!
Nay—All is lost, —I cannot bear
In mouldering dust to dissapear,
And Heaven will not the gloom dispell,
Since, if theres Heaven, *my* home is—Hell!
No hope! —No hope! —And, Oh, farewell
The form so long kept treasured here!
Must thou then ever dissapear?
Gone long—But kept in memorys shrine,
        Now dying again as memory dies,
First passed from earth my star divine
        And now—Tis passing from the skies!
Then—Thou art gone, and Heaven is gone,
And sights, and sounds, and all are gone!
Oh, what a shade is Life! —I am Dying—
AND HOW LIKE A DREAM IS EXISTENCE FLYING!"

        See, through the Shadows of the night
        Burst hotly hasting onward here,

A wounded Charger vast and white
   All wildly mad with pain and fear,
With hoofs of thunder, on he flies,
Shaking his white mane to the skies,
Till, on his huge knees tumbling down,
Across the fallen cheiftan thrown,
With a single plunge of dying force
His vast limbs hide Lord Albert's corse.

Northangerland.[4]

---

[4] The first time that Branwell uses the pseudonym he used for all but one of the poems he published.

[Angria and the Angrians]
II (f)[1]

more sorrowing over the dreams of a blighted and evanescent world greiving about likes and dislikes in the <dirty> heap of corrupting mortality more marks of your progress on the cursed road of self ignorance when not a joy not a sorrow should enter the heart o[f] a penitent sinner—aye you may start but I only despise you for it—wait and I'll tell you how that should be—Oh my father cries one among you—Oh my Mother. how my feelings cling to you who protected me and guided me through the world oh my Sister my Brother the Companions of my childhood the beings round whom thye[sic] associations hang that sanctify my early years. Oh my friend my friend the object of the natural yearning of my heart to [whom] <thy> sorrows and joys are known with whom they are shared and by whom they are alleviated—Oh my Lover the only celestial vision that ever can be known below Oh my Wife my Husband. the blessed stay of a period when childhood with its fairy dreams is gone and age with its hideous realitys is come the only harbour of blessed repose from the frightful suddenness of that changing heaven and coming storm—Oh all feelings that link me to my fellow creatures and shew me that life has at least some dregs of honey mingled with its draughts of bitter bitter gall!

O world—world—! and oh the vanities and wickedness of the world Little do you know what all these feelings are and to where they tend you Cherish them as the certain but ruined remnants of that state from which you have fallen in our first fathers fall when truely to speak each thought each feeling of Love or tenderness or freindship or any social joy or sorrow is only another mark of the D—l and a stronger link of hell My Brethern it its false and sinful to care in the slightest for any relationship or affection of this Life I tell you to set your affections on things above and not on sins beneath for your Fathers Mothers Wives husbands Brothers Sisters Sons Daughters freinds and Aquaintances what are they poor D—ned souls choked with sins thinking nothing but wickedness doomed if they repent not to no place but Hell I tell you there is not one among [you] that that[sic] is not possessed with Demons So what is your duty toward them? —Why My Bretheren you must shun and hate and despise them as Instruments of Satan wherewith to torment your souls He it is who gives you such ties to bind you down to the dust you grovell in and to turn your eyes more fully from the light which is above—But what says Our Saviour Leave Father and Mother to follow me—My Father is dead—Let the

---

1   A section of manuscript consisting of 10 pages, 11.2x18.5 cm, spread over three libraries. The first section consists of pages 23-24 of the Taylor manuscript noted on p. 415, n. 13. At the same time that Branwell was composing this satirical sermon, Charlotte was composing an equally sardonic portrayal of a Wesleyan Methodist meeting in the Slugg Street Chapel in "Passing Events," begun in April 1836.

Dead bury their dead—you listen to the puling precepts of your Destroyer and you neglect the stern command of you Redeemeer—According to this Life I have had the relations I mention but what do I do? —Why I scorn them and cut them from me Neither Wife nor Mother nor Daughter shall interfere with my Salvation I know their wickedness and I shudder to think of them—Go then and do likewise[2]

My Brethern I have mingled the method of escape with the Sin to be fled from I have told you to Hate the relations and Sympathies of this Life to remove far from you its sorrows and its joys. therefore I have entered upon the means of Salvation which I said must form the second portion of this Nights Sermon—Yet I am premature—Do you now know your Abominations? —You do not—youre as blind as stones you still are weighed down with the world and I see no struggle made to escape from it But my strength will not hold out much longer and on another night I must proceed to fill up the Sketch which to night can only be outlined when I tell you to flee Love and Affection you see a shadow of your sins Now let me tell you to flee Salvation and you will see a ray of your Hope

Start not my Bretheren start not. start not though I shall say that I hate you all I Hate you as filthy and Abominable Sinners—as such I abhor you. but there is a Hope of your Salvation and while that hope lasts I will strive to make it a certainty—So start not when I now tell you to fly from Salvation Such doctrine has not been preached before but I said The whole world has been D— ned till now—the whole world. has been preached to therefore if such insults could follow that preaching such preaching must be very vain—now I am commanded and commissioned from Heaven to save therefore my Doctrine must not be like to that which has ended only in condemnation—I speak as my Creator directs me and I say—Fly from Salvation! —Oh not till you see your sins in so strong a light and such amazing numbers rising up in every action and prompting every feeling. tempting you day and night. still alway[s] leading you astray not till then can you wish such a terrible wish. but till you can see your abominations thus you must not cannot obtain Salvation I know not than[sic] any man yet has prayed to be condemned therefore I know not that any man has yet been saved—But when you know that not only these deeds and designs which every thing tells you are sinful but all deeds and all designs having an or[i]gen or termination here are equally sinful and that while in this state any thought or desire leading to heaven is more presumtous and therefore yet more sinful when these convictions press upon you with gigantic and overwhelming force you will feel that no portion ought to be yours but condemnation and so will you loathe yourselfs that you cannot do otherwise than pray for the punishment of Eternal Woe!—

My Bretheren when God hears such a prayer come from earth there will be joy in heaven over the repentant and regenerate sinner.!

---

2   See Matthew 10:37; Luke 9:59-62; 10:37.

I have not spoken to you about Saving Grace and faith and Hope nor the glorious extacy of a soul set at liberty nor that flight to heaven through paths so divine to such a home of enraptured and eternal Joy—I tell you that you have nothing to do with such thoughts—for who can enter heaven till he has passed through the River of death and none can be saved untill he has endured the fiery trial of Despair And If any word could bring a man at once to Righteousness it would be this— "Lord let me be D—ned" And I will not hold out to my Creator a hope of your Salvation untill I hear you all cry out "Lord Let us Eternaly Die!"— What must I do to be saved[3] is a constant cry—I tell you—Be D—ned—Lord Give me Grace! —Thou fool grace cannot be given to him who yet clings fast to sin and sin cannot be forsaken till the sinner see it so fully as to shrink in abborhence from it and he cannot shrink till he see it in terrific fullness and he cannot see it thus without a Hate of himself the possessor of it and and he cannot Hate himself till he pray for punishment upon himself. and for what punishment must he pray—the greatest—Eternal fire!— Then the Lofty looks of man shall be humbled and the haughtiness of man shall be bowed down and the Lord alone shall be exalted in that day And worldly Love and heartfelt affections and the tears and sorrows attendant on earthly scenes and ancient recollections and divine Imaginings and and all those spurrings of the spirit to glory and power and exertions of the human mind. and a Knowledge of the secrets of Nature on Earth and Her Mighty Misterys in Heaven. All these shall then vanish away and we shall smile that such vanities could ever have settled on our spirits and freed from their weight we shall direct our eyes above and shining with a reflection of that glorious immortality which we behold time shall pass unnoticed till time shall end his passing and who then amid the coming close of Nature when nothing that exists can continue longer when the sun and the stars shall be darkened and the moon shall be turned in to blood[4] who then can hover longer here but All the Redeemed will enter with joy into the New Heaven and the new Earth And God shall wipe away all tears from their eyes and there shall be no more death nor sorrow nor crying neither any more pain for all former things are passed away![5]

I seem to see that vision which St John in Patmos saw[6] but now when I look round me the cloud of your sins covers me and nothing is seen but H—l Go to therefore let ME weep and howl for the misery that is come upon me And Hear my voice perhaps for the last time in tones of warning declare to you Repent Repent ere repentance be snatched away—Jerusalem Jerusalem know thy abominations.[7] My Hearers see and feel your sins they are vast and hideous for

---

3   Compare Acts 16:30.
4   Compare Joel 2:10: 3:15.
5   Compare Revelation 21:1-4.
6   Compare Revelation 1:9-18.
7   Compare Ezekiel 16:2.

every thought is a sin yea it is a sin in you to come here beneath the roof of God bringing Satan and his deeds to pollute the words of Eternal Life and to defile the Sanctuary of the Most High—

But you know not your sins and I must conclude with prayer for knowledge[8]

O Lord God Creator of heaven and Earth who hast in thine Infinite Justice so long chastised man for sin and who hast declared that unless he repent thou wilt punish him eternally look in thy infinite mercy upon these thy creatures kneeling here before thee Thou knowest O Lord that theire[sic] act of kneeling is but filthy and self righteous hypocrisy that their groans and sighs and ejaculations now are either the besotted drivillings of spirits lying to themselves or impious efforts of spirits lying unto Thee thou knowest that all their thoughts and words and deeds are only evil continually thou knowest that they know thee not feel thee not hear thee not that they are ignorant and weak and blind that they have fought against thee are fighting against thee and will fight against thee. Then O Lord why wilt thou keep them thus in filthy darkness. thou has commanded me thy wretched servant to command them to a knowledge of their abominations. I have done what I could but what could I do—nothing—for they would do nothing—and none can open their eyes but thou Then O Lord bid me no more to do what is impossible but do thou arise in thy strength and in the power Make bare thine arm and put on thy armour of strength Gird thy sword upon thy thigh O mighty one and Go thou forth to conquer. I pray for a terrible visitation and a shaking and trembling of the Earth and I tell thee that Nature will revolt unless thou defend thy right with power now when wickedness rules in high places and sin has covered all the earth as the waters cover the sea Now is the time in which to display thy might and to make known thy power Through thy Holy Spirit give unto these wretched sinners a knowledge of their state—a burning blasting and consuming vision of their sin—hunt them into the dust that they may cast ashes upon their heads and in howling and gnashing of teeth behold the frightful life they have dragged on Grant that they so hate and abhor themselves as the instruments of Satan as to wish that they had never never been born and so heartily and truly repent of their transgressions as to shout aloud for VENGEANCE VENGEANCE against their blaspheming and accursed heads Give them that sense of their own hatefulness which shall cast them headlong hopeless of mercy for such Hellish Sin and praying aloud for eternal punishment And howling We are unworthy to see thee Oh shut out Heaven from our eyes! —Yes O Lord Hear me I intreat thee hear me. Crush this roof above our guilty heads and cast us at once into the Lake that burneth with brimstone[9] and the worm wich gnaweth for ever Why wilt thou delay thy vengeance will not I say the very Elements rebel will not the Heavens sin when

---

8   The following section consists of leaves 7 and 11 (4 pages) in BL: Ashley 187.
9   Compare Revelation 19:20.

they see sin spreading thus unpunished over the world Come down O Lord Come down annihilate our Bodies—And cast O cast our souls for ever into hell!—"

The preacher concluded in exhaustion he stood his head bowed and trembling with the exertion. throughout this SERMON His Voice and gesture had been awfully emphatic at length fearfully terrific for his hollow hoarsened voice then rung in cracks of thunder on our ears his brow shone and his eyes flashed while his wasted hand[s] quivered as they were raised in his Blasphemous Impiety No one But Northangerland COULD throw himself into that madness of passion none other could so work upon his own or his hearers feelings for the Dirity[sic] Rascals—I could not for my heart give them another name—seated in the pit and front of the Gallerys [and who] Groaned ejaculated and Amen'ed at every climax of the discourse—unmindful of the preachers constant sallies of bitterness at them they only Groaned the deeper the more he lashed them many were acting the arrant hypocrite more were doing it for the sport and farcicality of the thing but numbers of weak heads there were drawn away by Ashworths[10] divine fury till they did [not] know wether they stood on their heads or their heels "OO Loard" "Come down Loard" "Slay us" "Do take vengeance" was rederverated[11] through the assembly when the preacher stood up and again raised his thrilling voice

"Let us sing to the praise and glory of God. Long metre. four eights[12]

MILTON!

"I   Before Jehovahs awful throne
       Now let us trembling kneel in prayer
    And Justice ask and Justice own
       For we must pray that he may hear

2   And deep O Lord be our despair
       And clear our consciousness of sin
    Lest from thine eyes our outside fair
       Should strive to hide the crimes within

3   We know that we are formed in crime
       And through our lives that crimes we form
    Yet maddly dreaming all the time
       That mercy sheilds us from the storm

4   Or as long since in Shinars plain
       Rebellious men their tower of pride
    Raised up, in hope, by labours vain[13]

---

10 Northangerland has taken this name when playing his role as preacher of the gospel.

11 Presumably Branwell intended "reverberated."

12 For two revised versions, see vol. III. The first line is the first line of a hymn by Isaac Watts, but the rest is Branwell's.

13 See Genesis, chapters 10 and 11.

That thus thy power might be defyed
5   So we by impious moral code
And creeds of ever changing faith
Think we may climb the heavenly road
And shun they power and vanquish death
6   But Oh when once we reach the gate
In hopes the eternal crown to win
Long must we knock and lingering wait
Ere yon bright spirit lets us in
7   "Hast thou repented from thy sin"
And who oh who can answer then!
"Go back. thy path again begin
And weep and watch and wait again"
8   But if returning be denied
By Deaths grim portal closed behind
Where flies our Heaven our hope and pride
Vanished like chaff before the wind
9   Lord may we know our treacherous mind
And feel the feirceness of despair
Since grovelling thus accursed and blind
We must not hope that thou wilt hear"

After he had given out the last stanza and while the congregation were singing it
Mr Ashworth completly exhausted left the pulpit to the Revd Brother
Simpson[14] who was to lead the prayer meeting that Night a few words of godly
purport passed between them at the foot of the stairs and then the preacher
dissapeared among the crowd

CHAPTER   II   P P B—té
May 4th
1836

May day morning rose over the plains of Edwardston with an uninviting and
desolate aspect answering as ill to its accustomed character as the frightened and
desolated country beneath it could do If one stood upon the well known swell of
road that from Verdopolis opens the first clear view of Edwardston and Zamorna
and the Olympian plain no sign would appear to him of the recent prosperity of
this most noble province of Angria Mr E Percys Hall sent up its smoke as of
your[sic] but the young wood in the park was all felled the greensward black
with horse hoof marks the front hashed and cut into a long grim Redoubt with
greenwood sheds behind it and a dismal ditch before Such another mass of earth

---

[14] i e., Jeremiah Simpson

occupied the place of the poplars along the road and Edwardston itself with half its houses down and scarce an Inhabitant to be seen lurking among the ruins shewed that devastation in striking the houses of the great had not forgot the steps between the summit and the base Far off the Tri colour was flying forth on the chimney of [the] great Mill of Zamorna the yellow Ensign on the steeple of the Cathedral and the profaned crimson of our nation on the denuded Roof of Girnington Hall whose park was covered with cavalry horses and each Gate flanked by a couple of 9 pounders

Here was no stirring scene of actual warfare but a far more depressing sight of a gallant country overpowered and crushed to ruins by a tyrannical Enimy of 20 or 30000 men French and Southerns were quartered here free upon the people but few of the people remained to give them quarter for almost every man who could bear arms was either a soldier in his Monarchs ranks at Angria or fled to bear arms for his country as an insurgent on the Olympian Hills. But there was a Hideous spectacle in the great Market place of Zamorna a monstrous Gibbet. and that was looked on as the final rest of these gallant and devoted men

Edwardston this morning was filled with soldiers for there had been in the park a review of some new troops destined to march against Angria The well known Inn at the Entrance of the village was crowded with officers And its common room hidden in clouds of tobbacco smoke from the pipes and segars of servants and soldiers. There before persons could be distinguished a cracked and drunken voice was constantly heard talking incessantly in a strain of maudlin intractability

"Aw say Mester Redcoit. Am em not druffen and Aw darn thee for saying so! —and mon be that Awm as domned thrusty as an old fuzball and Aw cannot stand no more waiting on ye—Be hanged tull ye for a threeping goid for nought D—ned—Aw say what the Hang are ye doing for noan sending in me breakfast there? —Aw'll be hanged for an old lice bitten bug eaten flea poisuned murtherer if e' ha'ent up wi ye for yer manners—Its noan the way i which Aw've been used to be sarved be hang tull ye! By Gums Aw'd sarvants and mate and a soap o'summut to drink of till Aw did know nother which wor me hend nor me fet aw wer so fat—And yaw Mester Captain Cornel yaw'll stop will'nt ye. Am noan so laasy but what yor war so yaw neednt sputter so fast fro an old body— Aw wonder what yaw'd be doing on th— dry land like a freak aat o'watter? —Aw know what o clock it is If yaw do not! —Aw been ont sea and mud ha' been a Captain to but—Aw waddnt! —and scorn it be D—d. Mak way there aw'z go in to th'upper chamber Aw'm as gooid as them Dash me buttons if Aw am'nt

The wretched old fellow who spoke with his pipe in hand and his little feindlike eyes reeling in his head was making headway against the crowd of surrounding soldiers and though drunk almost past standing his tongue went in curses and execrations as fast as a dozen sober christians But two persons who had dismounted at the door were pushing past preceeded by servants and to them each soldier doffed his cap with most ready haste and decorous silence They were both wrapped in military cloaks and seemed officers of distinction returned from the Review the Landlord before them with hat in hand was shewing them up the staircase But Old Mr Sdeath pressed before him and fell full sprawl upon the floor

"Dash me old bones!" he cried with a frightful laugh "Awd as leave be D—ned as shew me monners i'this a way but me owd cocks am as goid as yaw un—" here he was rudly pulled back by the soldiers One of the Officers laughed a short laugh the other and bulkier one morosly seized his arm and they both proceeded up stairs There was something rather wildish in that laugh which struck the excited ears of the old feind He sprung out with a clash of his old clogs and caught hold of his cloak But a sergeant seized him again by the throat and throttled him off so the hoary Drunkard in a transport of rage gaped with his tusked jaws and tore open the cheek of the soldier then turning round with a summary sending of their souls to H—l the slenderer officer caught Mr Sdeath and hurled him back down stairs leaping above him like a tyger the cloak collar flying back discovered a tremendously swarthy face guarded by enormous Black whiskers that encroached on the bony cheeks till they left visible scarce more than two red tyger Eyes. His comp[anion] for the first time speaking said.

"Quashia come back and be D—d.!"

And then Old Sdeath escaping from the prince stared at the speaker with a gaze between drunken fury and th[e] wildest surprise

"Eh my old Lad—Eh! —And are yaw here my boy—There he stopped unable to take in much more

The stairs was now a scene of confusion several feild officers from the upper rooms were hurrying down at the loud voice of the taller person and the soldiers round could hardly tell what to do in the presence of their superiors But a third person in a Drab Great Coat alighted at the street door and walked forward and was proceeding to escape from the bustle the bustle[sic] in to a room upon on[e] side [of] the passage but the Landlord laid hold on the door handle saying

"Your pardon Sir but the Apartment belongs to Major General Maison I really can not accommodate you there "

The stranger who was an uncommonly tall man without heeding placed his hand on the handle So the Bewildered Landlord. Mr Kershaw turned respectfully to the Bulky officer on the staircase

"If your Honour will pardon my forwardness General Maison[s] room is intruded on by a stranger"

"Why who is he Man" was the answer in a coarse tone whereupon General Maison peeped from his den

"Mon Dieu! vat is de matter Vat you vant Sir Soldier take him avay!"

The Frenchman stood frowning the soldier waited for orders from his own General But Mr Sdeath cried

"Aw'll tak him away come alongs wi thee tha old D—d foil who told thee to come—Odd Buttons!" He stopped as if he had burnt his fingers and the shock seemed to sober him first staring at the man in the Drab Surtout. then at the Great Officer in the cloak The stranger turning from him said

"Landlord I seek the Quarters of General Macterrorglen where are they"

"His Honour is here Sir"

The stranger turned a keen grey eye on the crowd which glanced for a moment at Prince Quamina and then furtivly at his companion But Sdeath having done staring pointed mutly from one to the other and would have spoken if fright and drink would let him

"Loard" he broke out "Ha tha'st presarved me—Dod and Rattons[15] but Aw cannot believe it—"

"Come Gentlemen" said the huge Macterrorglen "let us up Kershaw any more confusion and your head answers for it Quashia and Elphinstone up and be D—d"

They were trooping up but Sdeath kept his withered finger at them And the stranger stood confused but being apparently a Desperate Haughty man he flung off his Great Coat and strode forward in a Brown frock and loose white pantaloons not heeding the rush of soldiers to prevent him keeping on his hat and fixing his eyes on the ascending group he cried imperiously

"Quashia Quamina come down you D—l" and the African prince being somewhat flushed with Liquor obeyed with an astonishing alacrity for in turning aghast at the expression his balance wavered and he thundered down the steps[16] in no very seemly fashion gathering himself up he was for aiming a desperate hit at the strangers physiognomy But the voice of Macterrorglen thundred from above

"Guards take him to the Halberts"[17] then said Sdeath

"Noo noo aw say noon Oh Mon thaa'rt the D—l Doesnt ta knaw him be Gum!"

And Quashia likewise roared

"Come here Jehu and be D—d!"

The ruler of Angria was heard muttering sotto voce above and then he reappeared at the stairs top towering with Anger. An Aide de Camp stepped down and requested the stranger to follow him which request being complyed with they both and Quashia dissapeared above and Sdeath after a moments fixed study trooped in strange amazement with the soldiers and servants back to the Kitchen

Macterrorglen took his seat at the head of a large room where were many officers of superior rank Quashia stood rolling his eyes in a noble frenzy! The stranger calmly leant against a cabinet

"Well" said the Mighty man with ineffable sourness "Speak out and be hanged what did you come kicking up a dust here for Sirrah do you know the Halberts?"

---

[15] In northern dialect, "Dod" means to make round or blunt or bare; figuratively to behead, to poll or clip hair as in a tonsure. "Ratton" or ratten is a rat.

[16] The following section consists of four pages, 11.2x18.5 cm, in the Brotherton Collection, catalogued as "Events Preceding the Angrian Revolution."

[17] A frame used for whipping. See vol. I, p. 35, n. 1.

The stranger stood erect dashed from his head both Hat and hair and stood—the Awful form of Alexander Earl of Northangerland!— Not a man kept his seat for those even who recognised the vision felt the transit from muffled darkness to such majestic light But what was the matter with the Lord Lieutenant of Angria His Immense and dusky form seemed unfitted for a suprise But each massy hand clenched an arm of the chair and he could not take his eyes from the vision for his Life a terrific gloom overspread his face

"By Gom" he said "Fetch Medina"

An officer sprung up and left the room soon returning behind the Scheik[sic] in full Turban and robe and slippers this excellent person was lounging into the room but He saw Northangerland and started up as if a wasp had stung him The Earl meanwhile seemed searching through Macterrorglen's countenance yet without the look of suspicion till Sir Jehoram in a smothered fury said

"This imposter must be confined—By Gom!"

Then something struck the Earl HE. started advanced a step and with an earnest glance. till his eyes flashed fire he tottered against the cabinet

"By G—d this is the DEVIL!"

"Seize him ye D—ls" roared. the dreadfully enraged commander but keeping a horrid sneer over his Iron and inflexible countenance. then a shout as heard Below repeated like a cheer Old Sdeath had told the soldiers of the identity of the Earl they were Reformers and thought heaven was come so they set up a shout. Sdeath was heard tumbling up.stairs the men after him and as the[y] threw the lobby into confusion the Earl turned

"JEREMIAH SIMPSON! remember me!" he said and dashed through the Guards felling Medina to the ground where he stood and speiling[18] down stairs at a bound he mounted his steed and was off like a fiery dragon

Sdeath banged down next and coolly marching to the stables he led forth his old hoary Nag putt the saddle on donned his "Old Boits"[19] and leisurly straddled over its back Then he cantered forth getting over the ground in the direction of the Earls flight with that prodigious pace with which he is known to keep up with the most exquisite steeds of King or Noble. His old carcase flew on jogging on the back of the Animal with his Elegant hat sunk between his shoulders and his head beneath the ancient coat cape. till as he reached Northangerlands Magnificent Courser that Nobleman turned round throwing his steed on its haunches "Robert—Zamorna rather than Simpson!"

"If he ll take thee!" was the laconic answer And both gallopped desperatly on

---

[18] To go fast, to run away, to make off.
[19] "Boits" is Yorkshire dialect for "boots."

P B B—tē
May 23
1836

The eyes of every one are now open to the fact that Our country Africa has just entered upon what will probably prove one of the most terrific Intestine wars that have ever desolated the world We know this because we see the Firey and daring character of our people the embroiled and exasperated state of parties their widely different and irreconcilable interests and above all the Bold mighty and remarkable men who at present act as their leaders. Who are these leaders? —Let me Adjoin their names and the names of their factions

1 The—CONSTITUTIONALISTS..John Duke of Fidena

2 The—ANGRIANS. Arthur Augustus Adrian Duke of Zamorna

3 The—REFORMERS. Arthur Marquis of Ardrah

4 The—REPUBLICANS Macara Lord Viscount Lofty and H M M Montmorency

5 The—DESTRUCTIVES Alexander Earl of Northangerland (or REVOLUTIONISTS)

6 The—PEOPLE Richard Naughten (or DESTRUCTIVES)

Fidena. Zamorna Ardrah Lofty Montmorency Northangerland Naughty Six men of whom in point of talent the world is not worthy but save ONE the first and Best. How dark and suspicious are their good and trustworthy qualities Does one of them act for or care about the good of our country Are they bound by any ties moral or political? —I am afraid by none! —Indeed the best of them laughs at and scouts such things the worst swears their[sic] is no such thing Fidena alone holds up the standard of justice and Religion but he is allied to one who I fear cares for none of these things. But we may hope still provided Fidena be the most powerful—is he so? —Not alone and the Angrians can hardly be reckoned as Freinds for every view of their cheif is contrary to ours—Then which of the six singly is the mightiest now—The Reformers. with their four Kings. the possession of Government the Navy and their ALLIES. —these we have not mentioned yet but if possible their entrance on the stage forms the worst feature in our prospects

7 The—FRENCH. Napoleon Buonaparte

8 The—ASHANTEES. Quashia Quamina

9 The—NEGROES. Quacco Camingo. (Alias King Jack)

10 The—BEDOUIN ARABS. John Earl of Jordan

All these Leaders and followers who hate and detest. Africa with an undying hatred have the present Ministry called into our Land to murder its children by this act they have earned the hateful immortality. A countrys parricides And though the deed may give them a little additional power for a time yet in the end it certainly will bring down double and treble ruin over their impious heads If they succeed these faithless and feindish Allies crowned with conquest and flushed with slaughter of their countrymen will be ready and able to turn instantaneously upon themselves—If they fail. Africa will not tamely spare those apostate children who thus horribly designed her Death. I know I write warmly but what true heart can do otherwise when he sees his Land about to be torn to peices by Bloodhounds called in from an alien and Barbarous shore— Where was the accursed head which designed this plan.? —It is yet among us unstruck by lightning and its unabashed though degraded forehead still fronts the world as a freind to Africa—It was the Earl of Northangerland who during his short alliance with Ardrah conceived the atrocious idea of calling in Quashia to Harass Angria and whistling on the French to aid himself. This I see he still keeps up and thus he forms another party

     11 The—FACTION DU MANEGE[20] Jean Prince of Ponte Corvo which completes the host of Clouds that have gathered over our Social Heaven

     And this being the State of Africa no corner of the Land can be found unoccupied by political fury for the objects of each party are known and their efforts are begun The Angrians whish to revenge themselves on those who have wronged them and to seize their possessions The Reformers whish to grasp power and place to oppress Angria and destroy its national existence The Republicans whish to Alter the foundations of our Government and abolish the Kingly Authority but as the Reformers proffess to go a litle way with them in altering and as they really join the Reformers in hate to Angria whilst their Leaders are confessedly needy they appear bent now upon assisting Government in return for wages of place and profit Hate to for Angria likewise draws the French & Ashantees to their Assistance though these equally Hate them and promise of Booty from the desolation of that devoted country brings in along with them the Arabs and Negroes who otherwise care for no one. The views and proceedings of the Revolutionists it is difficult to state for they are hardly formed yet But they remain grovelling and adoring their broken down almost Insane Leader and impatiently waiting for his word to lead them on to a general attack on every law and right and power that pretends to be established on age and justice The Destructives naturally go along with these their only difference consisting in the Fact that these last being composed of low and ignorant men lend their hate indistinguishingly on every thing of any kind above them through malevolent envy—whereas the others do it from profligate Ambition. The CONSTITUTIONALISTS alone refrain from attack and only gather to Defend. They have sworn to preserve inviolate our Ancient Laws and institutions and Monarchy and Country from every assault and every foe. Among the other parties may be found many great men but in this only are collected the good men

     An atrocious attack was made in parliament by the Ministry and through last December upon the very existence of the Angrian Government This Attack the Angrians Resisted whereupon their King Prime Minister and principal Governors were thrown into the Tower But the people of Verdopolis disgusted with such tyranny rose up. and freed them The Ministry directly declared Angria in a State of Rebellion as indeed it was pronounced it part and parcel of the Confederation and therefore placed it under martial law appointed a Governor General pushed over its frontiers a large Body of troops sent a fleet up the

---

20 See vol. I, p. 16, n. 13.

Calabar to Blockade Adrianopolis and accepted the aid and Alliance of the French and Ashantees who simultaneously entered the country from opposite directions

The King of Angria on his part rallied round him his Ministers and people issued proclamations and organised troops negotiated a loan from Verdopolis which our Merchants though aware of his perilous state nobly volunteered him. Then he advanced his forces against the Enemy while his people rose up in arms wherever they could gather together several desperate but indecisive Engagements were fought at Westbeach Ludlow Grantly and Aunvale but the Gallant Duke beaten down by the overwhelming force of Invaders was at length forced to retire on his Capital and from thence being disloged by the terrific fire of the Blockading fleet He found no alternative but to make a hurried retreat from Adrianopolis to Angria thus leaving the whole province of Zamorna in the hands of the Victorious Reform Ministry These used their newly accquired power with terrible effect The Lord Lieutenant is a brutal and bloody man he has exercised the full severity of martial law shooting and hanging all who were found in arms against him imprisoning others on the slightest suspicion and extorting money from every one till the whole land groans under such iniquitous exactions Likewise Quashia with his blacks living upon free quarters and Medinas Arabs scouring the province put numbers to death without cause and in the most excruciating torment so that Zamorna has been and now is the scene of ever changing and never ending cruelty and horror. —Mean while the King with his Army in Angria have fortified and disposed themselves among the Warner Hills their Head quarters Nucleus and present capital being the Ancient Ecclesiastical City of Angria the same which saw the Marquis of Fidenas Army make its memorable halt and retreat in 1833[21] And now it is shaken by the beginnings of perhaps a far more awful war while in addition to the Brigades within it thousands of new recruits are continually arriving to fill up and multiply the ranks of defenders of their country and every movement shews that here Zamorna means to make wether aided or not a grand stand against his foes

But what all will ask as many have done What are the Constitutionalists doing will they see Angria desolated and her foes triumphant without moving tongue or hand to assist them I answer that the Leaders of this party determined not to help till help would be available. They are wise and prudent men they that is the Duke of Wellington and Alexander the First. —before they would talk of assistance organised their forces recruited their Army replenished their funds and assured themselves of their subjects this took 3 months to execute during which time Angria was unavoidably left to its own struggles and as unavoidably defeated. —Then in April a remonstrance was sent from the Courts of the West and North to the Verdopolitan Ministry with proposals for withdrawing Foreign Aid calling home the troops from Angria and submitting the Affairs of that country to a Convocation of the Legislature. The Marquis of Ardrah declined agreeing to these proposals Then Earl. St Clair and myself were despatched on an Embassy to the Courts of the South requesting

---

[21]   See vol, I, p. 386ff.

their Majesties to acquiese in the dismissal of the present Ministry for a majority of the Kings can call or dissolve our Government. And this likewise was refuse[d]. Now a final Embassy waited both on the Premier and his Masters presenting the Alternative of agreement with one of the proposals or a declaration of Hostilitys against Parrys and Rosses Land and a refusal to acknowledge the existence of the Ministry. The Premier remained unmoved and their Majesties adhered to their first resolution—The Die was cast and the North and the West simultaneously published

A DECLARATION OF WAR!

The feeling which this step produced in all thinking minds is awfully impressive We know it has not been done in the heat of passion but warily coolly and after maturest deliberation Therefore it appears a step which could not be avoided but then how dreadful the state of that Land where Civil War is inevitable But all the crime and blood must rest on the head of the Verdopolitan Prime Minister for in him it rested to give peace and hope to Africa but he feircely and stubbornly refused

The very day upon which this declaration was received by the Verdopolitan Government and the Southern Courts that very day the advanced guard of 3000 cavalry from a force of 30000 men under John Duke of Fidena set forth from Sneachies town to take possession of Freetown on the Niger while two divisions of 9000 each moved from Sierra Leone and the head of the Calibar under Generals Hill and Murray direct upon Parrys and Rosses Capitals

The Premier startled perhaps at this energetic demonstration threw himself upon the people publishing an appeal or address to them calling them to rally round him and unite in defence of just laws and reform of Bad ones and ending in a hope that they would yeild if necessary to taxes and levies in support of their rights and Liberties Mr H M M Montmorency likewise issued his manifesto wherein he declared with his accustomed unblushing effrontery that the present demonstration of war was a thing concerted by the Western Northern and Eastern Kingdoms for the purpose of establishing a Grand Despotism over the whole Confederation and he too called upon his countrymen to "Rise and whash their hands in traitor blood!" Next appeared a Proclamation signed by the Duke of Fidena and addressed to the "People of Verdopolitan Territory" and adjuring them as they constituted the grand Nucleus of Africa and belonged not to one Crown but to All To rise up. and assist in protecting their fellow countrymen the Angrians and in crushing the infatuated Ministry that ruled them This paper coolly laid open Ardrah's designs shewed how all his aim was to aggrandise himself and his own country pointed out the intimate connexion between Verdopolis and the West North and East shewed how it had allways leaned towards them and with what justice it had done so declared that one vigorous effort on its part might at once end the war and asked it would it above all things consent to see Frenchmen Ashantees and Savages brought upon its soil to hunt down like bloodhounds its unfortunate countrymen?"

All these things uniting together have produced a terrific sensation in Africa which from the Gambia to the Guadima through 1600 miles of territory is one scene of confusion or dismay The partisans feel inflamed with headstrong and revengeful feeling the Ambitious are starting into activity with a hundred dreams of conquest and glory the vacillating seem drawn from right to left as the torrent hurries them and the peacable and just look agonisedly back on the times and state just departed asking when shall we see them return and fearing never till our country fall exhaused with a bloody protracted struggle

One of these I avow myself to be for I cannot look unconcerned even leaving my own concerns out of the question when I know what bold Bad men now throw the Land into confusion for the purpose of crushing each other and gathering the wrecks of the storm—. But I avow myself a firm Constitutionalist and to that party I shall adhere in defence of my Country and its assaulted institutions We mean not to change or rend away

[Angria and the Angrians]
II (g)[1]

Then shall I perish for ever for doing what I could not avoid say rather that if I obey the dictates of my feelings I fulfill the end of my being I do what I must be and

One truth is clear Whatever is is right—[2]

But this panacea would not do long He might cut his Neighbours throat. it would be predestined it would be from his natural conformation or natural feeling of malice and anger Therefore it would be right. Such philosophy could not Stand the. test for a month and then Paley was unanswerable[3] Christianity must be true if so so must the Bible It teaches widly different doctrines from these therefore these must be wrong—But again who could surmount predestination He must do what he must do—at last he cried with the noble poet

> Well didst thou speak Athene's wisest son
> All that we know is, nothing can be known
> Why should we shrink from what we cannot shun
> Each has his pang but feeble sufferers groan
> With brain born dreams of evil all there own
> Pursue what fate or chance proclaimeth the best
> Peace waits us on the shores of Acheron
> Where no forced banquet claims the sated guest

But silence spreads its couch of ever lasting rest[4]

Following this most mistaken advice Mr Wentworth determined upon a visit to Verdopolis there to see its pleasures and dissipation and wild approaching turmoil the good which fate and chance should hold out to him

He set forth on his journey of 300 miles in his own carriage with servants and plenty of letters of Introduction It was a bright and balmy May morning so throwing himself back on the seat he was shortly wrapt away in a world of thinking the text of his ideas being the uneasy knowledge that all this stirring expedition to the mightiest City of the world where he was to begin real

---

[1] An eighteen-page section of manuscript, 11.2x18.5 cm, spread over three libraries. The first section consists of four pages in the Brotherton Collection, catalogued as "The Adventures of Charles Wentworth."

[2] See Alexander Pope, *Essay on Man*, Epistle I, l. 294. See also Wentworth's comments on pp. 547-48.

[3] William Paley (1743-1805) was a principal exponent of theological utilitarianism—see his *Moral and Political Philosophy*. He found proof of the existence of God in the design apparent in the natural world, especially in the human body.

[4] See Byron, *Childe Harold's Pilgrimage*, II, vii.

life and in a while may be to take a lead in it had not created one half or one quarter the excitement and pleasure he had always fancied in it—Now this—he thought—was always looked to by me as one of my grand fountains of happiness and when I found the stream of pleasure running drier and drier I comforted myself with the idea that as I approached twenty one I was nearing the great spring where all my thirst would be gratified—But what is it which has for a year or two been whispering in my ear—Happiness consists in Anticipation— and again—Anticipation must necessarily be impatient and imperfect pleasure of course the hope and not the possession of pleasure—Therefore as Anticipation is no pleasure and yet the greatest pleasure—there must be no pleasure—This is very fine but if the world is so the sooner I get out of it the better—Next he recollected what his advisers had told him when they saw him in expectation of an ample fortune falling into his arms. give himself up to idleness and go about doing nothing and caring nothing. but building Air castles for the adornment of his far future life—Now they said you can never have real happiness without working for it exertion is the nutshell which holds pleasure crack it and it will be found otherwise never—again the harder the shell the better the nut a walnut is finer than a hazel nut moreover God hath said that man shall eat and drink in the sweat of his brow—[5] that is he shall enjoy that pleasure only after exertion—But now my first Argument leads me to the conclusion that I shall have nothing to reward my exertion then why should I labour—But I am certain I shall have nothing without it so what is to be done there are plenty of paths in this life which shall I take—only they all require walking to get on them—But I have it now—Life is a downward journey all concurr in saying Age carries us down hill now Life being a downward sort of a slope its paths must necessarily all lead downward then dont I know what the downward path ends in—the regions of destruction—therefore as men move on in life they are allways tending there—And I cannot remain on the summit of Chidhood for time comes wafting past seizes my hand and hurries me along wether I will or not—Ill go across life sideways and never down—But No No that will never do there is a curse in the very sound going across in life cutting through the parallel streams of men one after the other treading on the flower beds and running a risk of man traps I must give up that bright thought—But is not the whole of this strain only a bright thought a vain metaphor—?—But there is one thing which I know—Oh how I should like to converse with Zamorna and Northangerland the two greatest men that ever lived they have seen life they have tasted of all its pleasures of some that seem paradisaical ones they have had two or three bitter draughts of pain and sin beyond counting and they have minds that fit them above all for searching to the bottom of things—" This Idea of an interview with Zamorna or Northangerland once flashing on Wentworths mind in his usual manner soon became all in all to him he thought of it daily and dwelt on it till it seemed the sole object of his visit to the capital. It was his disposition when he thought a man truly great to adore him as a God for contradistinguished from the

---

5   Compare Genesis 3:19.

rest of the world that mans character would appear so high so rich so striking and so far from common that it instantly arrested the heart of one who was to much alive to anything fresh and vigourous Yet let me not give the Idea of his being a devoted follower and firm freind. He was to open to ill report. he took too much for granted the first distraction he could lay hold of and if any of these Great men went against his feelings they became instantly dust and ashes For Wentworth [was] most obstinate in his generalised feelings—but as too fixed detail of character he had none. Now the Noble Figure and Magnificent Genius of Zamorna coupled with the fact of his being a Duke and lastly a King—The vast course of life he had contrived to run through in 23 years His three marriages with their gilded and dazzling accompaniments of strange Romantic incidents and feelings so deep and so much above the common world—likewise His Graces free and fiery Independence of Disposition Interesting episodes of Dissipation Natural and Human Errors and remarkable moral philosophy—just implanted him as the Natural Deity of Wentworths Idolatry. But next in the Pantheon came his noble whilom Father in Law who possessing a Main story of Dissipation with Episodes of Degredation united to a Grand but vil[e]lly directed Genius a life widly experienced both in Events changes Characters and Scenes and a Soul bitterly dejected (from its own shameful misconduct) among scenes of Glorious and Aristocratical splendour—shone upon Wentworths mind as something far above humanity. Oh he thought if I could advance myself to an equality with these men should I not be happy If I were like them should I not be happy to be unhappy. and if I were over them if I could kill them or ruin their power by mine—but that is above the chances of this life. that is only in heaven—" Excuse that last sentence from an adorer I before said he was not a very affectionate one—But after all he could almost slay himself in admiration of Zamorna Northangerland Ardrah and Macterrorglen—now admire the liberal mind of him who could at this juncture in the same thought adore those four. But he was fairly of no party Any man of vigourous unshackled and original mind who had gone through a respectable viscissitudes been allied with great or Imaginative things and held a high place in the vision of things to come—any one of this kind met with Wentworths admiration

On the second day of his journey he arrived in the Mighty Capital of Africa and took up his abode at Johnsons Hotel first walking through his room in a pleasant sort of excitement then as that ebbed off longing for supper and lapsed into musing—Several odd unformed thoughts flew through his mind which naturally was what philosophers call an inventive one—and kept his spirits up but he shook his head when he felt that these were anticipations and the realitys would not be so fine as he took them to be—In this way he staid up all night though tired enough with his hasty and lengthened journey

Next morning he first reflected that he had not a relation in the city which to him was a pleasant and delightful reflection then he examined his letters and put them up again thought of his wealth and independence took Breakfast and sallied out into the streets with an outward appearance of most remarkable dejection and something very like broken circumstances but which really arose from constant thinking a dissatisfied mind burthened with its mass of half formed Ideas and a present intentness of. observation—He threaded the dense and bustling crowds of Western Michaels and Twelves Streets till he turned round on the outlet of the Magnificent and memorable thorough fare of Great St Georges Street which leads from the fashionable Quarter of the city to the Government offices and forms in a manner the commencement or termination of the Great Roads to the West and northward here his eyes looked round more animatedly He strayed along in a dream of indefinable—Anticipations—and some stirring recollections when he met every now and then with some such thing as Bravis Hotel stretching forward its seven hundred feet of frontage Trees grand publishing shop the mouth of that torrent of glorious writing which has consecrated Africa York Place and Grenvilles Square—then St Augustines with its Gothic front and towers of prodigious altitude the scene of the coronation of his Noble Deity Hence he passed along Arthurs Street under the collonades of the National Theatre beneath the Opera House and the Hall of Science and Arts A Distant But glorious glimpse of the Southern Palaces. the Square and an odd end of St Michaels—Benin Place Grenvills Wharf. the Harbour and the SEA. —All day Wentworth had been walking about objectless but given up [to] impressions made from passing scenes never staying to eat or drink never calling a coach nor attending to personal appearance but with a wildish disjasked[6] look of poverty stricken abstraction His mind was to restless to stopp and fully examine any thing He was not searching for information or gratifying his taste or curiosity— Here is what he was doing—HE was going about striking sparks from his mind by a contact with the scenes connected with glorious events associations and persons. He felt that want. that restless uneasy feeling with which rest is torment and ease begets stupor. The flashes of feeling which were constantly scintillating thrilled into his soul and he cared and thought of nothing more I said he came upon the harbour. The Afternoon was gloriously bright the mighty bustle of the city was in his ears its wondrous edifices in his eyes. Before him stre[t]ched Docks and shipping and merchandise and the blue boundless SEA.

P B B—te
May 28
1836

While Charles Wentworth leant over a parapet with the sun shining upon him and on one side a great merchantman just come in from Stumpsland. on the other the white dazzling new erection piling up over the ruins of Grenvilles Wharf. (remember the two cracks of canonry on the [7] of December) and before when quit of the boats ships sails and masts—the wide waving main

---

6 "Broken down, dilapidated, decayed" (OED).
7 Branwell left the date blank.

then on a sudden the tears came starting into his eyes and a feeling like a wind seemed to pass across his spirit Because now he felt that not even the flashes of glory which these streets and buildings had struck from his soul not even these feelings which he had reckoned as something to supply years of dul ness[8] could preserve his thoughts from aimless depression. We cannot tell often what impulse it is which changes our mind from one state to another nor could He tell why the sudden sight of the sea made him learn at once "What shadows we are and what shadows we pursue"[9] But somehow the view of the waters assimilating to his native scenes on the opening of the Cirhala being so widly different in their far off summer lonilness[sic] to the stir and Bustle of Verdopolis that it too violently broke his current of thoughts and from his mind being overstrained the relapse was as strong as the spring yet it was long ere he quitted the spot and then he turned passing through many noble streets without hardly turning his eyes to look on them He entered his Hotel stretched himself on a sopha and listlessly dreamed away his time till dark.

Next morning found him bending his way toward the Central Square Shrinking from introductions and letting his letters slumber in his desk and his freinds remain in ignorance of his arrival—Arriving at the vast Expanse he Beheld. St Michaels Cathedral swelling its enormous Dome into the cloudless sky and round but far apart the Great Southern Palaces and two Houses of the Twelves spread their storied and Columned fronts with the walls and Bulwarks of the Citadel above and the "Arches on Arches piled"[10] of the Tower of Nations beyond all forming so sublime an assemplaye[sic] of our National Glory that none beholding it could be other than constitutional—Wentworth wandered in front of the Western Towers long before he dared trust himself to Enter the Mighty Temple but after he had asked himself the reason of his hesitation and found it proceeded from instinctive fear of ending his pleasure by approaching reality. He dashed through the dread. walked up the grand flight of steps and soon found himself with Hat in hand pacing the Marble pavement in the still shadowy coolness beneath the vast expanding roof and glorious Dome—Standing upon the pavement immediatly beneath this enormous concave and gazing upward through a wide uniterrrupted void of four hundred and fifty feet the effect to him was overpowering for the Air itself seemed to dissipate all harshness and left him nothing but the Sublime to Gaze on he looked till to his dimmed eyes it seemed to rise and soar beyond his sight. he lay on the pavement and still looked till he thought it would thunder down in ruins over his head but that was a passing fancy all was utterly still the lonly mountain tops of Sneachies land could not be more sublimly solitary. Men might be in the church but no one noticed another hundreds would not have dissolved the spell and when the stunning crash of the

---

8   Compare with Wordsworth's *Tintern Abbey*, ll. 23ff.

9   Edmund Burke, *Speech at Bristol on Declining the Poll*, September 9, 1780.

10   I have been unable to locate the source of this phrase.

great Bell struck one at noon it did not so much break as yet more express that silence—Wentworth lost the calculation of time while he was here gliding about as sucessively attracted to the Cupola the Nave or the Aisles then he stepped beneath the Organ screen and entered the choir turning back upon the imposing front of gilded pipes above him and thence to the high dark aged mass near the Altar whose gloomy and mysterious form attracted a nearer gaze upon which the warlike sculpture round the base the cannon the standards and the martial Bronze figure above who kneeling on a Dead Barbarian seemed falling backward into the Arms of Victory. All told at once what the Inscription confirmed to him "FREDERIC the FIRST. the King of the 12[11]

Next day found him still Unknown and un visited without participating in the splendours of wealth any more than if he had not a pound in his pocket Nor was he bent studiously on ransacking the great Libraries or studying in the Picture Galleries he was restlessly aimlessly and with the same anxious face feeding his feeling with little squibs of rums as he called them to himself since he was perfectly aware that they would only the more depress. him afterward— But that evening while walking from the eastern Dock he struck into a new line of streets In the fashionable quarter of the city and erelong found himself in a great square fronted by an Enormous Palace surrounded by columns which reached from base to pediment while its grand portico stood out above a broad flight of steps as far as the lofty wings on either side The doors and windows of this statly Edifice were nearly all closed and it seemed to cast a chilly unsocial shade over all the square. as he turned back Wentworth through the long vista of streets opposite caught a glance of the sea—putting this to that as the saying is—an Idea burst on his mind. He asked one passing whose residence was that "Its Ellrington Hall to be sure man"— "I thought so" And forthwith he knelt upon the lowest step of the portico and kissed the stones rising with hat in hand he looked upon the steps which that Great Demagogue had so often trodden. The portico from when[ce] so often he had addressed those famous speeches "wherewith All Afric rings from side to side"[12] He strove to picture the <Tail> with their mighty head trooping up those steps making the midnight silence vocal in the calm moonlight. These windows lighted with the glare of pompous festivity. The "Saloons" the Halls within the huge train of servants each possessing in his memory a History of crime—The August and Noble Lady of the mansion whose whole existence had lain on the summits of Life all whose actions had been interwoven in the consecrating and glorifying pages which hand down Douro and Percy and Augusta. Mary. Victorine. Marian—names which shall be the grand fountain of future poetry and Imagination. Yes He Wentworth was looking in the Lordly dwelling of Her whose everyday life was the paradise

---

[11] Almost certainly modeled on St. Paul's in London. For Frederic the First, see vol. I, pp. 147ff.

[12] Compare with l. 12 of Milton's "Cyriack, this three year's day."

of his inward musings He thought of this and broke out. "Oh when shall I arise to such a circle as that.!"

Turning from Elrington Hall after looking and stopping to take in its soul. he hurried to Johnsons with feelings turned into a new channel by new impulses—Now Wentworth was in a manner a creature of impulses. He hung[e]red and thirsted after impulses through the City he had been going about hunting impulses So now he had got one that impelled him to come nearer to the Glorious Regions one of whose Portals he had been contemplating that day—But at midnight there came upon his mind the word Anticipation! and he remembered all his present feelings were those of anticipation how anxious and impatient and incomplete was his present pleasure and was it all that was to be? For those who possessed what he thought about in reality were they happy Was Percy happy was Zamorna? —Zenobia? —If they were not was there a hope of his being so

At morning he arose cast down and melancholy with these and such like reflections again the world looked futile and he spent that day without an aim until late in the Afternoon when at the East end coffee house He noticed much bustle among those in the great room and found them speculating upon the exact nature of some great news flying through the City which some stated to be the capitulation of the Duke of Zamorna others a great victory gained by him and the rest either a dissolution of the Ministry or some great aim achieved by it. Something in short as likly as the Rattling of Fidena—never mind the monstrous improbability of such reports if they are wonderful that is all which is wanted till certainty comes in to conclude the pleasant amusement of guessing it is enough that what he heard sets the soul agog after something. Wentworth felt the infection around him and his mind was instantly absorbed in the terrific politics of the day But when the Evening papers came out The Banner The Messenger and The Sun of Angria sounded an Alarm to Affrica[sic] exhorted her sons to rally round her constitution and declared that most decisive steps shortly to be divulged had been taken with regard to the monstrous crime of foreign and barbarian aggression concluding with an affirmation of momentous Intelligence tomorrow. The Universe The Lode The Spectator and The Reformer on the other hand fulminated all their thunders against the courts of the West and North repeating assertions of the Ministrys steady resolution and exhorting the people to resist the interference of a tyrannical and corrupt Aristocracy—Both sides declared that St Clair and Richton had had an interview with the premier at the Home Office and thus Night sunk on the suddenly aroused agitation of Verdopolis

Next morning Wentworth found laid upon his Breakfast table the yet Damp Intelligencer and on impatiently opening it beheld in large characters over the leading Article **"WAR!"** and next the Declarations of instant Hostilitys issued by Wellington and Sneachie against the Ministry Parry and Ross afterwards mention of two Cabinet Councils and a great meeting at Waterloo Palace then the military announcement from Fidena of the instant advance of 30000 troops on Freetown and Genl Hills movement in the west lastly a nobly written and heart stirring Article addressed to the Men of Verdopolis in whom lay power to turn the balance for good or evil Wentworth read rose and hurried forth with anxious looking brow and highly excited mind—All the world was excited and mens hearts were blown into a feirce wild flame of civil rage and hatred— Now thought Wentworth what shall I do! He leant against a railing ran over the misfortunes of Zamorna the righteousness of Fidena the cant of Reform and the mysterys of Northangerland— "It shall be the last" said he "It shall be the last— He is a glorious man I do not know what he cannot do and here is every pleasure of excitement Zamorna is my Deity but he is on the black side of the Hedge—I will see Sir John to day—I will see him now! But to think! Africa in the flames of War.! Why should I be suprised? —however farewell peace and welcome glory!"

So saying he hurried through the crowded and troubled streets repaired to his Hotel dressed himself took a coach and drove to Lofty Square[13] In answer to the card which Mr Wentworth sent into the Baronet. Sir John himself came forth welcoming his young freind with a gracful smile and courteous demeanour

"Gad I'm glad to see you more especialy as I was about to sit down to a most comfortless dinner not a soul beside myself. which here at Verdopolis is too bad seeing I did not come here for ritirment[sic] But I vowed I'd make up for it in the evening and you shall assist me—"

Wentworth followed his host to the dining room where they sat down to a quiet pretty dinner in an elegant little room furnished with all the taste or rank and none of its ostentation Sir John himself was a tall bald crowned and silver haffetted man with Iron complexion—gay waistcoat and youthful tights— Not a Bean of the old school with the dress but without the vigour of youth nor a naturaly young looking senior who kept on the outward shew of former days along with a deal of the inward. He was one of a set not unfrequent especially in the west of Africa who though sometimes worn out or broken down in looks and constitution and parted from every generous and openhearted feeling of youth still hold their pride and energy and such passions as they patronise in all the wonted perfection therefore they dress in the fashion and lead the fashion and mingle with the fashion till sudden wreck and dissolution sends them home to their master. Sir John Denard was a prince among these and accounted one who had seen a vast deal of Life and character He has a large fortune heavily laden with mort[g]ages and a spirit so headstrong that if an Election comes across him a few tons weight more is certain to be added to the heap Residing at Fidena and being Uncle to Lady Louisa Vernon He became accquainted with Mr Percy a dozen years ago. The Drover saw Sir John's failing and took advantage of it he lead him into a quarrel with the Marquis of Fidena and from that moment he was sure of him for directly Denard turned a raging revolutionist devoted head and hand to the Insurrection of 1831—plunged again into the Northern Rebellion of 1832 out of which he escaped with the loss in fines &c of *nearly* half his fortune

---

[13] The following section consists of pp. 9-12 of the HRC manuscript described on p. 278 , n. 1.

and the deepest hatred of reigning Authoritys. So rescuscitation being necessary after such a drain he threw himself into Elringtons grand robbery scheme—and it is said got well fleeced at the Elysium.[14] but certainly aleviating his misfortune by the fleecing of others for the Turf the Ring the Hazard Table were always the strong holds of Sir John for 2 years during the war and foundation of the Angrian Kingdom He lost sight of his Noble Associate but when in the Autumn of last year Northangerland repaired to Fidena for the purpose of returning Naughty and Bernadotte. and fell into the toils of Lady L Vernon. Sir John again met him and after disbursments in that affair has since in politics been closely united with him except in his Lordships Elysian repose at St Cloud when the Baronet with Wharton Naughty and "the rest" threatened death and desertion till Mr Ashworth half assured them again

"Now Charles" said Sir John "when came you here to pray—last night or this morning?"

"Neither for its now near a week since"

"No surely! why what can you have been doing with yourself.? —Have you determined not to see me till the wells dry.? muddy water wont do in Vedopolis but it will in the eastern deseret[sic] eh? —Now Zounds Wentworth I cant believe you"

Thats as you please Sir John But I have not till just now seen a soul that I know in the city"

"What the D—l have you been doing then!"
"Walking about chewing the cud of sweet and bitter fancies—nor should I have seen you yet but last night I looked at the papers and Sir John—my blood rose! I could not bear to be Idle!"

"So you came to me for work eh?. well you know who's our Master— the Old Gentleman—and a very Egyptian one of course Long Hours and little pay. for the present though I must say that there are great things for the future"

"Anticipation Sir Anticipation—why every thing looks great in the future!—I dont believe a word about the future we see things in a distorted medium—we are all distorted. for in nature distant things look least and those near at hand greatest but with wretched man the present is nothing and the future is all!"

"Why have you been so far left to yourself this week as enter the H—ls without introduction and so get plucked without civility"—

"No Sir John I have not been near them—But I'll tell you where I have been—In front of Elrington House—"

"And you might have stept ben noboby would have hindred you except perhaps the spiders on the doors—"

"Stuff—I tell you—I want to be introduced to that Great man!"

Sir John expanded his eyebrows in a well bred stare He thought he did not hear aright—

"Introduced to whom?"

---

[14] See vol. I, pp. 289ff.

"The Earl of Northangerland"

"Impossible!"

"Not a bit—I am just what I am a man and little more—"

"If you were a woman you might hope better!"

"Stuff again I have my own mode of thinking and acting my own brains and my own will I have 140000£ and I am 21 years of age—now all of these advantages I am ready to lay at the beck of the first man whom I find great enough to warrant the sacrifice If I go by hearsay Northangerland is such an one. But I know what a liar hearsay is and I want to go by my own feelings and they will only move from impressions received by me and these can only be received from actual observation so I want to observe him!"

"Oh take my observation instead and I observe that your labour will be all thrown away for if you see him you will see nothing but hauteur and insolence if you hear him it will be humbug and blarney. Besides I cant mention such a thing it is unheard of. he would ask if I was mad. Why he'll hardly speak to any one except on his cursed Theology—"

"Confound his Theology it only makes me think him the greater—and I tell you Sir John that sooner than remain unintroduced to him I would leave Verdopolis and never enter it again Why a sight of and speech with THAT Man the greatest in the world except one who is eclipsed just now—that man whom I have heard of ever since I heard of any thing—the Boggard of my Infancy the Wonder of my childhood the Fountain of thoughts for my youth. he of whom such strange things are told who acted in classical and imaginative times who—"

"Heigho the fool is not out of you yet Charles if you go on this way— Why man I know him better than I do you and Gad he cares for none of these things He is a hard cross keensighted but imperious fellow broken up I fancy or nearly and. has been latly D—dly under the government of one worthless She D—l or another

"So be it—and none the worse. either he is Marys father Zamornas Father in Law and associate—yes the associate of one who is above a man of the Real Rising Sun!"

"Why man and he is the associate of John Denard too!"

"And he is the Husband of Zenobia—"

"Aye and of a dozen more—"

"Sir John this wont do what care I if he is he is a Mighty Man and I am determined I'll see him—come now start no more objections they are useless but just give him this letter Ill read it

"My Lord I wish to see you—we are both men—and only think how absurd it is for one man to refuse to speak to another when he knows nothing ill of him and is aware that he would not be inconvenienced by him on the contrary in this case—I may prove of assistance to you at least it is my firm and steadfast purpose to strive after doing it—I speak plain my Lord and grant my request

Charles Wentworth

"Gad Wentworth this is odd! —but since you will have it so I'll try it though I forewarn you of nothing but a torrent of curses or else utter silence in return"

"You will will you Sir John!. Now then I'll take some wine now I feel able to see and hear—Let it be soon—to morrow—

"Aye the day after that of the Judgement![15]"
This matter being settled Sir John and Mr Wentworth entered into earnest conversation [on] the state of Africa.

P B B
June 4
1836

At the Day and Hour appointed for the interview which Sir John informed Wentworth Northangerland had granted. Charles ordered his carriage and Drove to Lofty Square where taking up Sir J Denard they proceeded to D'Aubigne's Hotel

"Well Wentworth" said the Baronet How dye find yourself.?. I'm Deucedly astonished at his Lordships civility but I saw directly that it was merely the effect of caprice and having no doubt been forgotten before I left him stands little chance of being remembered now

"I dont know Sir I dont know—But I have only one way of acting I will be straightforward—"

"Yes But he cares not a fig for that he hates alike honesty and duplicity—indeed I tell you that supposing (which is very unlikly) he grants you an interview at all you are not to reckon upon any conduct or character of yours as either pleasing or displeasing to him if he sees you it will be through caprice—ergo all his other ideas during your stay will be founded on caprice if that can be called foundation which in its essence is devoid of foundation—But he has forgotten the matter Wentworth—Or If he has not he will not speak at all that is most likely—But—Now Wentworth. here we are at DAubigne's—"

They both dismounted from the Barouche at the front of this well known and fashionable Hotel But as they were threading the surrounding crowd of carriages Wentworth could not help remarking the strange whim which could lead the Earl to forsake his own magnificent palace for a public resort like the one before him

"Has he taken the whole Hotel?" he asked of his Introducer. who replied

"Oh dear no far be such pride from our meet and Holy Wesleyan Methodist Missionary. He has simply occupied rooms for himself. a pack of servants and a squadron of cavalry with chariots—its true though that he caused all the furniture to be emptied forth and replaced by his own more valuable Hupholstery that being the only symptom of exclusivness he manifests—See that knot of persons in black turned back with blood colour those are some of

---

[15] i e., the Biblical Day of Judgement—see Revelation 20:11-15.

his Servants. And as for these carriages half. belong to waiters on his Lordships Levee—the rest to Lord Clermont or Sir Joseph Fenton or some other Residents at the Hotel—Now then the levees breaking up. for they are coming down the steps.

"Who" interrupted Wentworth eagerly. because his mind was so excited by the vicinity of the mighty man that he fancied every object must be something memorable

"Oh Us—The Revolutionists—but mum—be silent—"

Among the Dozen or two of. Gentlemen with kid gloves and black canes who seemed descending to their carriages Wentworths excited glance fell on a little shabby person in a snuffy coat with Grizzled hair and Iron frenchified countenance.

"Is that Sdeath?" he asked with a thrill.

"Oh dear no. its—M Barras—![16] Ho wither away friend. glad to see you—wont you turn back for I am on a perilous expidition. M Barras. Mr Wentworth—Mr Wentworth M Barras. There <now goes> Introduction first. but we are just about to face a second one—and you must accompany us with your countenance and support.

"Vat do you mean Denard is de Gentleman about to be introduced. for I can tell him it is useless unless he possess power—I mean something to attract notice. purse tongue or title—. Hah? you will excuse me Sar—But it is the fact. His Lordship is wrapt up just now—puzzled and confounded—for—But I suppose we trust Mr—a—a Ventford. —He seems hatching a plan—But. Good heavens! Chickens wont do. it must come forth. a young Eagle. nay a very Minerva.[17] armed and active—Dis is no day for nursing—eh—?—

The course of. Barras hard and emphaticly uttered sentences. brought all three into a marble Hall where they turned up a broad flight of steps and entered a Long Saloon above where they gave in their names to a Gentlemanly looking servant Afterwards Denard and Barras walked through the apartment talking lowly and earnestly But Wentworth sat silent and excited striving to bring to his mind the requisite piquancy of associations connected with his present neighbourhood. to think himself under the same roof with the Earl of Northangerland and about to stand face to face with his God to picture his own images of that man and recollect his former visions of Rougue and Elrington. with his Midsummers day dreams on the sunny banks of the Cirhala or in the Academic Groves of Philosophers Isle of Mary the Daughter of Percy the Wife of Zamorna (alas wife no more) Zenobia the more than friend of Douro the Wife of Elrington (is she too wife no more) with a hundred similar delightful picturings of the mind which I am a great fool to mention seeing I cannot give them to others but which Wentworth felt to his heart of hearts and which—But STOP its useless these things come on me but they will not come onto my pen. So fancy Wentworth

---

[16] See vol. I, p. 366, n. 9.

[17] The Roman goddess of wisdom, technical skill, and invention.

who adored <wind> sitting silent till in this saloon a long wild blast from without sughed on his ear carrying with it a crowd of other ideas the Angrian War. the foundation of that Empire the struggles in which This was fought shoulder to shoulder with the God of the Sun "Stuff" he exclaimed—"what am I that I should be here unknown and unworthy wretch treading where such as these have stood.! You two are near gazers on the Sun Angels in a manner but I—I do not know how to face him

At that moment the valet (not THE Valet[18]). threw open the door and they all walked forward preceeded by a Menial through a handsome Gallery into a high Airy noble Room whose Mirrored walls struck Wentworths heart till it died within him and where at the lower end of a long table in a flowered gown and with an open snuff box before him sat ONE who rose on their entrance

"My Stars Barras !" he said while Wentworth shrunk aback. flattered at the mighty moment "my stars! how he was enquiring for you!"

"Its very well I have returned But you know theres Sir Johns turn"

"Ah good—yet stay. Sir John—Good morning by the bye!—He has not alluded to your affair. of course there can be no hindrace in your own case but as to that of. Mr—let me see (opening a Ledger like vol before him) Mr a Wentworth. it might possibly be better to hesitate—you perceive I had charges to prohibit Strangers And I fear he has forgotten the assent given to this introduction—you will excuse me of course—"

"D—n him" replied Sir John— "on me be the hazard. Ill warrant he has not forgotten—"

"I pray you may be right Sir John—" answered Him at the table smiling benignly and so arising he advanced and ushered them through the room.

Gad thought Wentworth Im a fool mistaking that infernal puppy for him—But Ill mind next time however—if this fluttering of spirits will let me— Come he is but a man and has he not shewn himself to many have not many seen him even in shuch a place as Salem Chapel is he not Mr Ashworth the Methodist Missionary and am not I Chas Wentworth Esq[r] of Arthurstown Hall?"

While muttering these resolutions Mr Shaver (M P) opened an inner door that admitted them at once into a library round which Wentworth only glanced for a moment for his eye caught that of the High and Mighty Earl. with a feeling unlike what he had ever before felt he precipitatly withdrew his gaze and shrunk behind Sir John not daring to take another look but feeding his soul on the half a one which accident had offered. His companions said something which he did not attend to and the

A voice spoke—

"Denard—is that a milkmaid?"

with a start for he did not expect being taken notice of till he got reassued Wentworth. burst fairly off his guard and while his ears sung and reddened he rapped off a—bruptly

---

[18] i.e., Shaver.

"No Sir I am a man!"

And then having made the leap lifted his eyes hastily as if he was taking poison to the Earl whom he had a moment to observe for He was engaged in talking to Barras

Wentworths first impression led him to imagine a low broad figure seated in an Arm chair. Now He saw—a very "interesting person" of tall stature in a light Brown frock coat standing with his face turned to the frenchman who had gone to the fire and therefore his back to Wentworth one hand placed backward rested with its knuckles on the Desk while on the velvet collar that crowned a pair of Elegantly drooped shoulders a border of Auburn curls lay beneath a serene and baldish crown the little finger of his hand on the desk maintained a gentle piano quiver till removing it gently from thence into the depths of his coat pocket he extracted therefrom a silk handkercheif werewith he smoothered a short but gentle cough and then turning an ear to the french Democrat Wentworth beheld a haloe of orange whiskers relieving against an innocent cheek. and just one glimpse of the famous "Nose." The Hat of the piratical Bankrupt lay on the table—A glossy simple thing narrowing to the crown annihilated in the brim and lined with snowy satin. Beside this Deifyied attribute lay a supple yellow Cane and a pair of white Kid Gloves—in fact all the personals of the bloody tyrant looked elegance innocence and peace— Wentworth longed to see his face and in a while the desire was granted for his Lordship turned round with a neighing laugh and jaunty manner saying with an elevation of the eyebrows

"Well Denard Barras says Ardrah has spat into the tinder box"

"Gad" answered Sir John "Then he has been spitting fire!"

Wentworth glowered to get the Earl into him before he turned again—just as he stood But he threw himself into his seat resting with one elbow on the Back and with one leg flung over the other his eyes drooped sideway to the fair though far from plump hand that displayed its thin fingers and diamond ring on the upper most knee from whence the long tightly cased limb descended to a small neat shining Wellington[19] —those being details [of] what was Wentworths total impression—that of a supercilious fastidious frivelous person who had once been handsome and was yet elegant one against whom it was easy to believe the accusation that Augusta. Mary. Zenobia <Louisa> or Louisa Dance had for a while ruled him with despotic sway till arrant faithlessness and insincerity slipped catlike from their yoke

Extracting a snuffbox from the pocket of his Delicate Buff waistcoat and raising his eyebrows without his eyes He said

"What do you want me for young man?"

Wentworths heart jumped to his lips

"I—I Sir—My Lord I—But D—ni—n its useless—My Lord I have forgotten all that I intended to say I cant make a premeditated speech here. I came to see you because I thought you the greatest man in Verdopolis I whished to

---

19 A boot named after the Duke of Wellington.

tell you that I was ready to espouse your cause to the uttermost wether right or wrong it does not matter a pin—not a fig—knowing what you are and have[20] been I—

"Yes—thats very well—But what is your opinion of Man?"
Wentworth scratched his ear instinctivly

"Man Sir!—my Lord—man is—Why Ill out with it savour as it will of pedantry to broach my doctrine before you. Ill say what I think. —Man is it is evident to me a mere Machine a simple Machine Sir who like a clock or watch can do nothing but what he is wound up for. that for instance If I just now struck you dead I should simply be ticking the minute striking the hour doing in fact what I was made to do if the present confusion results in Civil War it will simply be setting the mill at work to make a lot of Worsted—If I think and reflect and calculate I dont do it of free will but because I am born the <atom> set agoing and the wheels will of course revo[v]le as they are intended to—Now I am not a Philosopher of Chances I think nothing is done by chance True I know not what I shall do but I am so organised as to do my doings in time. as a clock though silent is organised to strike in time all the movements of the world are determined to all eternity and men are simply the Engines to manufacture events with I believe sir that I know nothing feel nothing think nothing and am accountable for nothing though—mind I know not but I may be punished for nothing if punishment is the manufacture of another world—Now this I believe because there must be an Almighty Creator he must know all things—if so every thing must be ordained then Man cannot have free will therefore his whole life must be mechanism and in that case how can he be accoutable he cannot possibly be good or evil so he cannot be a rational existing being—Excuse me my Lord for this lengthy Dogma you asked me a plain question and I have answered it plainly[21]

"Now I wonder will the peice which intended politics are to weare. be black cloth or white—eh? —for Yours is the philosophy of Manufacturers—!"

"My Lord I cannot joke. I know not But—"

But I DO! —I am organised to see farther than you it will be <watered> into black lights and white shadows! Bah Young Man you are raw. you have predilictions for things this philosophy is the adored of your heart and on an opportunity given you will instantly sketch its portrait. no surers[sic] sign of country breeding than this enthusiasm for favorite crotchets—like nothing—whats your opinion of my left leg as distingushed from my right

"What? —Oh—they are jarring elements for they never move together—"

---

20 The following section consists of pages 17-20 of the Taylor manuscript described on p. 415.

21 See also Wentworth's comments on p. 533 above, and the comments.on p. 136, n. 21. It would seem that he may have read the opening chapters of Hobbes' *Leviathan.*

"No they are alike but oh how different—Well do you think it is a pleasure to me to converse with you eh?"
So saying the Earl rose and commenced pacing through the room while Wentworth was so engrossed with viewing the Mighty Personage in this new position that he forgot to answer but recalled to recollection by a grim sidelong glance of impatience he abruptly and without thinking answered

"No"

"No" replied the Questioner stopping with a sneer. "Ah youre a keen observer to be sure! could you not see that my change of position was a decided proof that I liked you!"

"Liked me!"

"Aye Man"

"Impossible!"

"Aye Impossible <u>I Think</u>" returned the Earl with a cruel Squint "What the D—l When I shunned Zamorna and Zenobia and the Marchioness and Louisa By G—d was I to be pleased with your company—you D—d insolent fool Why you cursed puppy you believed that so you will believe any thing to H—l with you!"

"My Lord in my philosophy I should have mentioned that caprice is a symptom of the Machinery being out of order striking anything like a bad clock." This was uttered with an exhibition of spirit

"The fudge family are here I think![22] Whose do you fancy that portrait?

"I should say my Lord the D—l"

"You are wrong but not far if it is not the Master it is the Man. Henri Riguetti Compte De Mireabeau[23] —One who was something and is nothing One who before he had reached his fortieth year suffered imprisonment seventeen times who had deserted his own and run away with other mens wives who had had the most scandalous lawsuits with his own family who had been condemned as a criminal exiled executed in Effigy who had written one of the most depraved of books who had led one of the most dissipated of lives who was known to be a dangerous Enemy to those he hated and an unsure freind to those whom he pretended to love who when his name was first mentioned as elected in the first National Assembly received in acknowledgement of recognition only groans and hooting and reproach—Bye the Bye Earth possesses its persecuted or martyred saints as well as Heaven—But they receive a crown of glory in the present world as those do in the world to come for mark in four short years from that day what was this Monsters funeral—Why it was Rather an Apotheosis than a human Entombment Nearly all paris followed hid body to the Pantheon The melancholy music the Torches and the intermittant cannon producing an effect which has been far better remembered than described by many an Eye wittness while those who feared and hated him with those who had been enchanted by his genius

---

22 Possibly a reference to Thomas Moore's *The Fudge Family in Paris*, 1818.
23 See vol. I, p. 306, n. 14.

Alike saw the Grave close over MIRABEAU with an awe and feelings which can never be described!"

"Oh" cried Wentworth "That I might die the death of mirabeau and that my last end might be like his—you my Lord are a Divinity greater even than him—I only bow before the veil—My Lord! what must I do to be saved? —[24]

"Why fight the Good fight of faith put on the whole armour of Righteous—ness—and win the crown of glory[25] —But an oracle shall speak.

> Then climbed the fugitive an airy height
> And resting, back oer Eden cast his sight,

> Far on the Left to man for ever closed
> That Mount of Paradise in clouds reposed.[26]

crack that nut!"

"I know it my Lord I know what you would say and I feel—"

"Humbug—can I sway you any way? Well then Listen—But stop Denard—Denard—Go away with him Go away. bring him to the Rooms To Morrow—TO MORROW. you shall see something man and now go away!"

His Lordship looked so changed and impatient that Wentworth saw nothing for it but a bow and exit both of which he accordingly made with more amazement than Edification

Northangerland turned to Barras next saying

"To morrow Barras to morrow shall see something go and collect them Do it diligently man and go away!"

"I will My Lord but do not dismiss us thus or you may do as heretofore dismiss your hopes along with us"

"Yes yes Barrass very likely but have done and Tramp—Shog— be off. and to the D—l with ye!—"

with the last word the door was closed on the retreating Statesman to leave his Lordship alone in his glory. where he threw himself on a sopha and rung a small silver bell at whose well known call the valet. M P entered directly

"James close the curtains place brandy with a Glass on the table order the Barouche to be got ready and wake me at four o clock—off.!"

The Door shut after the servant silently and soporifically after which Percy laid down his head and closed his eyes

The closing of the curtains cast over the room a sweet dreamy Afternoonlike shadow. where though the full blaze and warmth of Heaven shone over the world without the most cool and quiet stillness rested within Crowds through the Square might faintly be heard to pour along like a sea mixed with the hum of flies on the window and the tick of a time peice on its pedestal yet

---

[24] Compare Acts 16:30.

[25] Compare Ephesians 6:11,13.

[26] Compare James Montgomery, *The World Before The Flood*, 1813, Canto I, ll. 123-26. The fugitive is a descendant of Cain.

all these sounds were so dim mellow and soothing that with the single stripe of the Afternoon sunbeam through the curtainpartings they only hallowed the scene into a more blissful repose

The longlimbed elegantly shaped figure on the sopha lay motionless with one hand covering the forehead and the other declined to the carpet And perhaps the reader may think that as he seemed inclined to sleep he would as soon as possible chase all ideas from his mind but Not so for he ran directly <over a> hundred varying thoughts and crowding Ideas dreamily indeed but yet vividly—for his spirit wether depressed or excited could never be vacant But was allways overflowing—Then the present. time. coming events. designs and prospects were of so prodigiously momentous a character as to demand imperiously some exertion of the mind

Calm he thought and Beautiful was this Afternoon Bright on the earth and in the Heaven without a frown of threatning and in itself breathing peace and goodwill toward men But he who stood on the summit of affairs knew too well wether such a feeling answered with the Condition of Man

"And can it be" he said "can it be that I lying now on this sopha a sort of atom in a city of 2000000 souls possess just now the power to turn this summer sunshine into little better than the glare of Hell And what a mind is mine when I resolve and determine to do it! —So I do! and Faugh! all this puling is the effect of a conviction its inconceivably[sic] how clear it strikes me that while I lie here HE—ZAMORNA—is struggling with fate fortune and a host of Enimys. within a hundred miles of me. Half ruined now and without a chance but of total ruin. this Afternoon may shine as clear and as bright as it pleases but it wont alter his condition he is done for unless he can be helped—!

Helped! and why should I help him? —he called himself my Son in Law—and in a few months as good as divorced my Daughter. he made me his Prime Minister and then snatched the seals back from me he patronised every man whom I hated and hated every one whom I patronised He detested me and yet was consumed with Jealousy lest I should be inveigled by Ardrah or Quashia He is a D—ned fool a confounded Idiot—I have more occasion to detest him—Hang him and his wife and mine Ill forget them all Something is coming on which will give me plenty to do!"

After this effusion his brow cleared at least outwardly and again he shut his eyes nearly an hour of silence passing away while he lay seemingly peacful and asleep but really retracing a crowd of images and impression[s] that continually illumed or darkned his mind in a manner he lived a life during that hour but his face did not tell what manner of life it was. That face reclined pale placid and insidious with something hovering over the lips between a sneer and a smile once or twice the brows gathered in thought but that only looked like the changes of a dream till gradually a reall[sic] change came on the lips first compressing as forcing firmness and the depressed features contradicting it till beneath the closed Eyelids a light glistned and at last their[sic] rolled down the cheek a solitary Tear. The hand upon which it fell started or shrunk instinctivly its white fingers were dashed across the eyes and the contracting brow made an

endeavour to regain composure—But it would not do those eyes filled again so
He sprung from the sopha and began to pace hastily through the room
    The time he mentioned for sleep having now expired and. Mr Shaver
hearing his Lordships footsteps entered to say that the Barouche was ready
    "D—n it" cried his master "Let it wait!"
"Certainly—but when will your Lordship require it?"
"Never—off scoundrel begone!"
The Parliamentary menial bowed and quitted the room. the Earl flung himself
into the chair by the desk dashed his pen into the Ink and when the black drop
fell from its overcharged <nib> onto the paper he seized and hurled them both
into the fire a few minutes elapsed ere he could calm sufficiently to make another
attempt and then he carefully dipped his quill with a sneer which shewed a most
irritable disposition to hate at the moment even such a poor inanimate object as
that with emphatic vehemence he inscribed the following earnest but not very
coherantent[sic] Letter—(I give his exact phraseology)
    "Oh My Dear Zenobia
                for let me call you dear whom once I did and
whom now as much as ever I feel that I can Since Now when events of which
you can have no Idea and whose consequence I myself can hardly appreciated[sic]
brought into being by me are on the very eve of development and so terrific that
though if I suceed in them my worldly Ambition will be exhausted yet the
prospect of their arising fills my whole mind with startling and ex[c]itement.
Now, at such a time your Name your form every scene connected with you is
present to my feelings with wonderful vividness. And hear why Zenobia. while
in hearing do not mock me—A new era of my life is just bursting forth. nay
perhaps it will attain maturity in a few short nights—If on one hand it ruins me
that ruin will be irretreivable. No body cares for me. those who could love me I
have alienated those whom interest might endear have been shaken off. All. All
in one short year have gone save some who only apparantly stick by me in one
united resolution should this effort fail to foresake me and for ever Therefore if it
does fail I am finally and utterly undone. I have no private rectitude no stoic
firmness no strength of constitution to support me so I shall die in misery.
either at the block or as an exiled beggar I shall die cursing God and defying man
that is certain as that I am now writing to you. On the other hand if I suceed—I
sicken at the idea of the future—I shall be pressed with all the responsibilities of
power and surrounded by a whirlpool of tumult I shall be confused by new
adherants and new faces. But Oh My Zenobia. all Old Scenes all old pursuits all
old faces and voices and affections will be buried in the wreck which must take
place before I rise The glorious Zamorna my Daughter. and your own noble and
lovely self. will have passed from me either dead in the storm or living as
Enemies So what shall I Be. I shall get feirce and savage I shall hate every body
and perish like Herod in the day of his Glory devoured by worms Vermin
Reptiles will devour me for I shall be for trampling on then—Then again if the
strife be protracted if a long doubt intervene between defeat and victory I shall be
so harrassed by Exertions and exhausted from the total abscence of any rest any

thing bright to look to or rely upon that I shall die and so there will be a cursed end of me

You Zenobia now so far off were once with me and through four or five years of very varying fortunes you though perhaps unknown to yourself have been the only tie that kept me from moral (not actual) madness. —stay—even you did not at last for the last year of my life has been almost real insanity— Nay then I cannot defend I cannot accuse I can only confess And what good will that do? —I feel Zenobia that your desertion of me was just so why should I call you back. I know that you could not and ought not to bear my causeless desertion of you that I literaly had not an excuse for my conduct—But do I promise a wiser course in the future? —There is the point! —**NO**! I promise nothing! —By G—d my Soul is my own and if I must hurry to destruction I'll go Neither you nor any one else shall stop me and as for my Daughter—As for her—I could kill myself. —I have ruined her peace of mind and happiness in life perhaps for ever and doomed her to perish as I saw the Marchioness of Douro perish Yes Zenobia I shall never forget my impressions upon that occasion—I shall always keep the astonishment with which I eneetered[sic] into the soul of that most remarkable Man—I saw that there had never appeared one like him in my day and then—THEN I determined to abide by him. But it was impossible— But this is not the point I. saw the bitterness of Marians end.[27] He may say what he likes to his conscience but it was bitter. and am I causing such an end to Mary? —I know instead of being weaker her feelings are stronger than. Marians—I know too that Zamorna is so glorious a being that He'll make if he pleases any woman who has a soul or a heart to adore him and there is another thing its fifty to one wether he adores them at least for four weeks consecutivly. He is but very young But he has seen a grim touch of misery and after that day now five years since—No more on him

The freshness of the heart could fall like dew [28]

But for a glorious buoyancy of spirit which would keep him active energetic and as divine as he is through ten such miserys—Then he is so Deeply Selfish that the sorrow of another will though it many a time touches him—never produce an effect upon him—G—d he is nearly as bad as I am—but a vast deal nobler and[29] being younger by 20 years he has a Generosity and a wild rejoicing of spirit and fresh romance of Intellect which I have as much of as the old D—l Sdeath—In short he is the Only Man in this world whom I would care a fig for and him I have made my Enemy! Oh Noble heart of mine theres another thing for thee thou canst not make him freind again—D—n freindship If he would rush on the same carreer[sic] of dominion with me and direct his attacks at the same

---

27   See Alexander CB II, part i, p. 318, n. 5.

28   Compare Byron's *Don Juan*, I, CCXIV, 1706.

29   The following section consists of pages 13-16 of the HRC manuscript referred to on p. 278, n. 1.

Old Musty Infernal institutions and feelings I could thank him or at least Join with him—But now—well I cannot tell what I am writing about!

Zenobia I am going to enter upon a desperate struggle you are alienated from me Zamorna is my foe Mary is my victim—Your alienation is JUST. and I swe[a]r that By heaven I cannot turn and repent. it is not pride or Obstinacy or any such D—nd humbug you know that I am above that it is the spirit within which wont let me So why do I write Zenobia—Because I Do Love you more than any one else in this world. Your high and Aristocratic Rank your Noble and generous Soul your fiery heart your Lovely and Majestic form they are present to my mind and I cannot bear to have lost them forever from reality—It is horrible to me when I think that the Eyes which once gazed on me with love and adoration are now averted with the determination to forget for ever what they had seen that the Bosom which sometimes once could swell with pride and joy while it pillowed the Head of Lord Elrington will now only fill with scorn and contempt at the Traitor name of Northangerland—High and powerful I may become I may set my foot on the necks of kings and rule over trembling nations but your warm heart will not beat in sympathy with victory gained or give one throb for threatning or existing dangers I can hope no more to share with [you] a pleasure which once would have been great. indeed to me. My aquisitions and glory with My Noble Countess whose Imperial Form and Spirit would so Beautifully become such exaltation—By Heaven I cannot I will not think that you could cooly and uninterestedly look upon my future prospects—It shall not must not be I cannot repent of wrongs past or promise a cessation of them in future I can do nothing but love you as Zenobia Percy deserves to be loved and as Alexander Percy has the power to love—Remember that I am PERCY that neither you nor Zamorna nor any one else that has been or is can fully know my character that I know my self to be greater and more competent in mind than any save ONE of all the Inhabitants of Africa—But it is useless I know neither what I am saying or doing and the prospect of Sucess or Defeat alike hollow and joyless is enough to make me Hate the world—Oh Zenobia Zenobia be mine again!"

"By G—d" exclaimed the Earl as he concluded the letter—"I'll do something terrible. what it is I know not but I'll make Africa quiver to its centre—!"

As he spoke the door opened and R P Sdeath Esqr stumbled forward desperatly drunk and scarcly able to keep upright either his legs or his senses

"Gow this Whost Weather makes a body fair mazy But we's all be off wor fit moderate sharply and some folks off their heads too. —There agean. Aw een not well—so theres noa use talk abaat it—Hillos. Aw see sommut—wi yar favvor Sir—"

"Saying so he laid hold of the Earls untasted glass of Brandy and soon washed down the crimson liquid But his Master was making for the fire Irons So Sdeath gasped eagerly forth

"Stop a bit—just one bit—Aw've—eh dear Aw've—nay nay— Parliaments. called—it is!—"

"Get off you D—d Idiot. Begone—" cried Percy brandishing the poker with a furious look but Robert gesticulated and bawled forth

"Its true aw tell ye—And there Banged up for this wik—This wik—this vary blessed wik—no its t' hoist and hoist but one—noo—noo—no donot strike and aw'll tell ye as meet as aw can—Be Gums their called hawsivver and it is next week But He swears he's have ye and mash ye like turnip tops aw've the paper I me Breeches pocket Here—na—D—n its goan—D—n"

"Cracked Beast. explain your stupid drivel!"

"Yaw will ne let me. and awm so mazy. aw nivver seed sich a day noan sin e war born—nor afore nother—"

"By G—d But you'll see a hotter after you die.

"And yaw afore for yaw'll be called up and have yer mittimuses[30] made aat like smoke—Gow yaw mud a made me a parliament man and yaw'ed a seen how Aw wad rattle em ower—Me uts eaten and druffen of yar. Bread and meat ivver sin e war a two months owd and nivver getten so mich as a Mr clapped to my name Awll bide na langer wi ye Awm as thirsty as a Draw Well i't Dog days Aws goo! —Gums man are ye doited strike up lad and strike weel in theres sommut more nor common o foit aw can tell ye if e could nobbut find me Breeches pocket but e cannot so theres no use int—But dash my shoe tops if they be ent as red as red next time aw walk through Parliament Square—Aw tell thee they have called parliament for next Wednesday. will ye. nill ye. Be Gow!"

A Valet here entered the room mentioning several Gentlemen as waiting in great haste to see the Earl and his Lordship starting for a first time to a consciousness of the truth of Sdeaths statement ordered them to be introduced They came Sir R Summerfeild Mr Wharton Lord Clermont and the Prince of Ponte Corvo with Richard Naughty as a rearguard equal to all the rest put together. But as soon as they began to explain the intelligence they were come to communicate Northangerland saying he should meet them that night glided from the room and dissapeared

He only left them for another room where he stopped as he closed the Door. saying with a look that shewed unusal excitement

"G—d. Then it is begun the first knell has struck. so now for a terrible retribution. All I have done has been undone all I have inflicted I have suffered. but let us see a change at length when—I least can compass it—Zamorna if you joined me you might you could. you should be powerful—but if not with you without you let my will be done!"

He called Shaver and ordering his carriage. stepped in commanding the coachman to draw up at the Countess of Carringtons Mansion in Arthurs Square where with the Countess herself. Lady Castlereagh Miss Montmorenci and Lady Julia Thornton He remained two or three hours conversing with unusual gaity and a less degree of sneering compbrehending[sic] a singular vein of benevolence

---

[30] A mittimus is a warrant or writ for putting into prison a person convicted of a crime.

to the Husbands of Harriet and Julia and the warmliest expressed prospects of peace both to Angria and Africa avowing with many well handled and ivory phrases that to gain peace was now his sole political object

Attired in his delicate snuff frock and primrose waistcoat with his locks prettily curled and his countenance lightened by seeming gaity His Lordship lounged about as aristocratically easy as possible at length unbending even so far as to cast his limber limbs over the music stool place his toe on the pedal and lay his fingers to a solemn chord upon the keys of the piano. so now he was in for it for another hour at least mingling his sweet and expressive melodies with huge handfuls of chords cast from his fingers with the power and prescision of 4 hands instead of two

How little thought these Ladies as they admiringly listened to or sweetly joined in his gracful and easy flow of conversation that the voice which spoke and the fingers which played alike so musically now were in a few short days to rouse and direct the furies of Revolution and Anarchical violence

However His Lordship knew it and as he entered his carriage consoled himself with muttering

"All Humbug All D—d Humbug!"

P B B
June 22
1836

Ashworth[31] after his Interview with the Mighty Earl felt himself at times a new man. an object was given him and the slightest political movement created a fire in his heart that warmed him nobly after his hitherto cold comfortless condition of Doubting and deliberation. But All that Day and night his Soul was filled with northangerland he could neither get his voice or his look or his character out of his mind. and oh more so because on leaving DAugbignes Hotel he had driven through Victoria Square where he snatched off his hat and rode Bare headed devouring with his eyes the Noble Mansion of the God of the Sun. this sight of the temple of his divinity kindled his spirits still higher so that the Erect bright looking Wentworth of the evening was very different from the disjasked pondering person of the morning. Likewise after getting Intelligence of the Order published from the Home Office for the reassembling of parliament next week to provide against the atrocious treason against the union from the West and the North. His Mind was elevated still more Sleep was useless. The terrible situation of Africa seemed present before Her Child and He could not help putting the following lines on paper

---

[31]   Obviously Branwell meant Wentworth.

L U C I F E R[32]

Star of the West whose beams arise
    To brighten up oer Afric's shore
While coming clouds and changing skies
    Bring down the shades of twilights hour

Who as our day sinks fast away
    While flowers of pleasure close their bloom
Sendst down from heaven thy flashing ray
    And shinest to dazzle not to illume

Who as upon our sunken sun
    The storm clouds gather from the sea
So far above goest wandering on
    As if our hopes were nought to thee

And gathering glory while the night
    Comes deeper darker drearier down
And shining still with brighter light
    When every beam save thine is gone

Star of the west we see thee shine
    We know thy glory from afar
But we have seen our Sun decline
    As if it sunk for thee to appear

We have seen our Sun of happiness
    Mid coming clouds of conflict fall
Nor can thy lustre stand in place
    Of that which blessed and brightened all

We know that in our time of pride
    Mid summer suns and noonday skies
Though heaven were cloudless clear and wide
    Such lights as thine dared never rise

We know thou art and[sic] orb divine
    Whithin thine own celestial sphere
But still a storm portending sign
    To us who gaze in wonder here

Star of the West though storm and night

---

[32] For the revised 1837 version, see vol. III.

Gave birth and glory to thy blaze
Still what has kindled up thy light
   May in a moment cloud its blaze

As darker grow the clouds of woe
   As day declines As Empires fall
Brighter and brighter burst thy glow
   Till thou soarest onward Lord of all

But westward clouds are rolling on
   And louder thunders swell the wind
The tempest comes—and Thou art Gone
   Past like the sunshine out of mind

Percy! —amid the coming hour
   When peace and pleasures dissapear
Those storms and strifes that give thee power
   May Darken Africs Western Star!

The morning after. this night gave Wentworth ample scope for reflection or rather for feeding the flame of his fancies. Since now it was first clearly published that Fidena was descending Upon Verdopolis and had occupied Freetown with 20000 Northerns so that the City was wound up to an intense pitch of excitement—At noon the report was spread and confirmed in the Evening prints that the Island fleet was coming up from the Stumps Land Station where they had been on their six months cruise ever since the memorable December 1835—At night Whentworth with throbbing Heart beheld Sir John Denard arrive to take him again to Daubigne's Hotel

"Now" said Sir John "I must tell you Mr Charles that you are on dangerous ground I have the Earls command to introduce you to an important but strictly secret meeting where extraordinary measures will be deliberated and adopted Come my lad come on wild times are turning up but mind if you divulge a syllable. you die as sure as your alive By Heaven Man you die"

"And By G—d Denard if it is a stir I will not divulge so no more about it forward for I am so agitated that I dont know what I do—I say man dont think that I am mean spirited. because I abominate pride"

"No I guess if you [are] like many a man else do what you hate—But on man time is precious"

Then the two entered their carriage and drove headlong to the Hotel.

They were shown into a large Drawing Room the interior of which produced an awful effect being hung and festooned with blood red velvet Brass rods confined the hangings and a long green table ran down the centre of the floor. there were gathered round seated on sophas 30 or 40 Gentlemen with thoughtful faces and in earnest coversation But a little after Wentworth took his place fo[u]r or five whom he supposed the Belials and Molochs[33] of the company entered from some inner consultation with Satan himself at their head. Wentworth was the first who rose at this Advent for As he beheld the high solemn form in deep black with the Diamond broach and palid serious face. he recognised the vision of his youth Lord Elrington—Lord Northangerland. —this Man was liker than the person he saw yesterday though still they were the same.

Percy advanced to the head of the table and stood for a moment with his hands upon it searching into the faces of every body present. Wentworth felt the colour come into his cheeks when he fancied a sneer as he looked at him then Northangerland folded his Arms and began

"These are wild times Gentlemen! and wild measures m[u]st be had recourse to in order to meet them—[34] Kingdom is ranged against kingdom and nation against Nation—let men be ranged against both—Yes oer a sufficient time has Might ruled over right but now the time is past by. The lion and the Bear are fighting for the fawn let the fox come in between and deprive both of their prey.

Country men I think you know what we have resolved to do. with two thirds of the population of this city organised and arranged upon our Side and under our banner. it is fixed that we Erect upon some stated and favourable Day the blood red Banner of Revolution! But in hope of aid from others suppressing for a moment the watch word of a Republic! though shouting in defiance of Earth and heaven for LIBERTY! LIBERTY! Aye This is our intention and must be our labour But when is the Dawning of that great and important Day? —Keep it in your hearts but bar it from your tongues. Monday the 26 of June—Now shrink not from the near approach of so mighty a contest but listen to my reasons for bringing it near

The Hideous Mass of corruption which though dead yet speaketh and though abhorred by all yet rules over all. the Reform Ministry Has called Parliament together on that Day in order to avert the threatnings of Wellington and the Tyrant of the North. Now likewise on that day the poor fool Fidena will be near the City with 30000 men. Then mark me. —

There is a glorious but Mistaken Man now struggling with a hundred Adversitys one hundred miles distant in the East There he possesses yet an Army of 50000 well trained soldiers and his Enimies are now striving to get round upon his flank and rear so that his van toward Verdopolis is comparitively open. I will Now send a person to him with this Letter.

Arthur.

We are mutual enimies perhaps but united Against one power that power will be desperatly attacked upon Monday the 26th of June. At all

---

33 Probably a reference to Milton's *Paradise Lost*, Books I and II.

34 The following section consists of a two-page manuscript fragment in the Brotherton Collection, erroneously catalogued as "Northangerland's Address to the Angrians before the Revolution."

risks be you there to Destroy it Then if you and I should contend over the prey D—l take the Hindmost.

Yours offended and offending

Northangerland.

That Man has a most quick and fiery Mind he will grasp at the matter and improve on it. Aye he will take his seat with his Peers and Commons upon that Glorious Day!

Let us hear no more but Arrange our forces Let every one set his shoulder to the wheel and the carriage of state shall topple into the Mud And[sic] end now is approaching to all old Institutions and authoritys and opinions. They who were founded by the sword shall have a Milatary[sic] funeral. with Banners of Red and Scarlet and garments rolled in gore. —But for you my enslaved countrymen and fellow workers in the work of salvation though a night must close upon Despotism and Idolatry A morning shall arise upon you. Liberty LIBERTY like the Sun of Righteousness shall rise with healing under its wings!"[35]

What past besides at this meeting of the heads of the revolution I cannot tell. But. as I must now conclude this volumn let me remark that. (should Zamorna turn round upon the City to take his seat there will be all the great parties again drawn to feirce contest within our Metropolis and nothing but a dreadful commotion rises in the clouded and stormy future. Heaven preserve Africa from Revolutionary Tyrranny[sic] But our prospects are terrible indeed and now in the words of Lord Byron

> Hark through the silence of the cold dull night
> The hum of Armies gathering rank on rank
> Lo! Dusky masses steal in dubious sight
> Along the leaguered wall and bristling bank
> Of the Armed River while with straggling light
> The stars peep through the vapours dim and dank
> Which curl. in changing wreaths—How soon the smoke
> Of Hell shall pall them in a deeper cloak

> Here pause we for the present as even then
> That awful pause dividing life from death
> Struck for an instant on the hearts of men
> Thousands of whom were drawing their last breath
> A moment! and all will be life again
> The march the Charge the shouts of either faith

---

[35] Compare Malachi 4:2.

"Reform" or "Angria" and one moment more
The death cry drowning in the battles roar

Don Juan Canto VII[36]

P B Bronte—
June 22.
1836

---

[36] The last two stanzas of Canto VII, with "various" in l. 7 changed to "changing," and "Hurrah! and Allah!" changed to "Reform or Angria."

While Branwell composed the previous section of [**Angria and the Angrians**], he also composed the five following verse fragments, on three leaves, all of which have on the verso part of the draft of his letter to the Royal Academy enquiring about admission—see Barker Brontës, 226-27.

The Heart which cannot know another
Which owns no lover freind or brother
In whom those names without reply
Unechoed and unheeded die[1]

The heart which cannot know another
        Which will not learn to sympathise
In whom the voice of freind or brother
        Unheard unechoed sleeps or dies
Between whom and the world around
        Can stretch no life uniting ties[2]

A breeze embued with rich perfumes
Is waving younder sea of plumes[3]

---

[1]   The first of the five items by Branwell in a manuscript volume bound in green morocco, and attributed to Emily, in the BPM: Bon 147. These are trial lines for "The man who will not know another" in vol. III.

[2]   These lines appear on the third leaf, 9.9x6.6 cm, of Branwell's verse in Bon 147, and are also trial lines for "The man who will not know another," in vol. III.

[3]   These lines also appear on the third leaf of Branwell's verse in Bon 147.

May 17   The sunshine of a summer sun[1]
1836   Oer the proud domes of Elrington
Glows with a beam divinly bright
In one unquenched unvaried light
And high its arched windows rise
As if to invite the smiling skies
And proud its mighty columns shew
Between them ranked in haughty row
And sweet and soft the solemn shade
By the oerarching portals made
    The statly halls of Elrington
May fitly meet that glorious sun
For fetès and feasts are given to day
To Noble Lords and Ladies gay
And that vast City of the Sea
Which round us lies so endlessly
Has hither poured its proudest train
To worship mirth and fly from pain
    The sunshine of a summers sun
Glows oer the groves of Elrington
Where city girt spreads wide around
The flower and foliage laden ground
All round the Hot and glaring sky
Bespeaks a might city nigh
And through each opening in the shade
Palace and temple crown the glade
So here as an oasis stands
Mid the wide waste of Egypts sands
This glorious vision of a grove
With flowers beneath and fruits above
Lies in that Citys human sea
Whose streets stretch round so ceaslessly
    Oh who could pass unnoticed by
This scene of Natures royalty
Instead of Birds to warble there
Etherial music fills the air
Breathed from these Halls thrown open wide
To admit the ever changing tide
Of Earth and Africs hope and pride

---

[1]   This is the second item on the first page, 11.2x18.5 cm, of Branwell's verse in Bon 147.

There is something in this Glorious hour[1]
That fills the soul with heavenly power
And dims our eyes with sudden tears
That center all the joys of years
For we feel at once that there lingers still[2]
Like evening sushine oer a hill[3]
A Glory round lifes pinnacle
And we know though we be yet below
That we may not allways linger so
For still Ambition Beckons on[4]
To this a height that may be won
And Hope still whispers in our ear
Others have been—thou mayest be there

---

[1]   These lines appear on the second leaf, 11.2x11.5 cm, of Branwell's verse in
Bon 147, and are trial lines for ll. 58-70 of "How Eden like seem Palace Halls"
in vol. III. In the right-hand margin, Branwell has sketched an arm.
[2]   A canceled line follows:
"A Glory mid the scenes of life."
[3]   A canceled line follows:
"Oer the plains of dulness and valleys of strife."
[4]   The line originally read:
"Hope and Ambition pointing on."

[Angria and the Angrians]
III (a)[1]

P B Bronte
June 24
1836

To relate the awful scenes which I must here describe [a] preface is unnecessary
and therefore without delay I shall begin

On Thursday the 22. A rumour had reached every one in Verdopolis of
some dreadful confusion as certain to attend the Opening of Parliament. On
Friday the Mayor of the City General Grenville issued the order for the instant
calling out of the Metropolitan Volunteers. On Saturday Proclamations were
sent from the Treasury Office directing a General Arming of the Police and
commanding all Doors of every house to be closed at 8 in the Evening. On
Sunday 5000 cavalry under Sir John Fenton and 7 Regiments of foot in 3
Brigades Entered the West of Verdopolis from Edwardston and Zamorna while
100 Guns were drafted from the Island Fleet and ranged under guards at
Parliament Square. St Michaels Square and on the Citadel Hill. The Gates of
Twelves Bridge with every other in the City were closed and guarded while
regular patroles of Cavalry Sallied forth after Evening service and commenced at
Dusk to parade through all the Cheif streets of the city—And through all that
three days of portentous warning Verdopolis exhibited the aspect of Dull deep
threatning composure No Gathering in the streets for the police directly cleared
them no insults to the authoritys. But an anxious serious intensity of thinking
on what might come

On MONDAY—At Three o clock in the morning the Earl of
Northangerland entered his Breakfast room in D'Aubigne's Hotel and while
Shaver himself. was engaged in making ready the accustomed beverage of Hot
Green Tea dry toast and Brandy His Master walked about silent and thoughtfully.
stopping now and then at the large window to notice the still dull grey of the
city and the utter solitude of the streets below In heaven a few stars still twinkled
though the wind rising from a Bed of clouds to seaward was bringing a hazy grey
over the dawn As he stood gazing a sound of hoofs clattered onward and a troop
of Horse appeared passing down the square—the patrole making its rounds—a
sight which produced in his face a sort of sneering smile—They passed and
quietness returned till the approaching wheels of a carriage rattled on the ear and
one drawn by four horses drew up at the Door of the Hotel and from which after
the porter had appeared. a footman handed a Lady in a travelling dress

---

1   This section consists of a two-page fragment, 11.2x18.5 cm, in the
Brotherton Collection, catalogued as "Further Events Preceding the Angrian
Revolution."

Percy muttering something among which "She D—ls" was alone distinguishable and then remarked quietly as he sat down to Breakfast

"Its only 3 o clock James and I don't rise till 6."

The Earls Gentleman appeared to understand his master and departed from the room But in less than five minutes he returned

"My Lord the arrival is not what you expected. It his My Lady from Alnwick."

His master relinquished the bottle which he held with a frown saying "She might have known this no time—But don't keep My Mother waiting Sir!"

So James withdrew again after placing a Chair and ushering in Lady Helen who entered As her Noble Son arose respectfully to receive her

"Alexander" she said "What is this you are bent upon is it what I dread to name and must I again see my son the curse not only of himself but of his country? I cannot think that amid all the silence I for the last hour have driven through there exists a latent fire enjendred by you which may—but you know when and how it is to break forth. I saw you enter upon the preliminarys of 1829 and I saw you in consequence ruined and imprisoned I saw you carry through the insurrection of 1831 and you were forced to fly from society to regain power through robbery I saw you raise the rebellion of 1832 and then you narrowly escaped death by the confiscation of a noble fortune—will you tread the same ground over again Or Alexander is it untrue. this frightful—"

"True madam Every inch of it—every word and letter!"

"I cannot change you I see that is impossible but I must wait calmly as I have by this time learnt calmness from necessity—Alexander is it your intention to throw this City into horrible confusion and ruin the ancient order of things?"

"In SIX HOURS your Ladyship!"

"I have born long—long with you my son through forty years of unceasing vissicitudes I have seen you a Murderer an Outlaw a rebel and now I see you without one single freind. of the first half of your life but Myself. And I—I feel my affection for you as if a guilty one as if a crime to my country— You know Alexander that my character is one which clings most firmly to one I love through good report and evil report sacrificing every thing to the object of my affection—But there is a point beyond which I dare not go—I feel that I have been the cause of. dreadful evils to Africa and yet that I have never mourned over those evils because the hand which inflicted them was the hand of my Son but a gulph meets me now wider than any I have yet passed and at a time when the exertion of overcoming others leaves me less power to pass it. I dare not I must not acquiesce in your present designs—"

"Madam I seek for the acquiescence of None but those who have Hands and energies!"

This mean and wretched taunt Lady Helen firmly overlooked though her dark and reproachful eye shewed that she understood it

"Alexander I once hoped that I should not have to detest you as a monster. But I at last have in some moments doubted of my hope—for know that the cause of my Journey made to you was not to attempt to dissuade you from your aim for that I felt and feel to be impossible. not even so much to expostulate with you as—To show you a view perhaps not yet taken of those whom you were accustomed to Love—I have visited you because your Daughter is dying!"

The Earl who hitherto stood hastily resumed his seat seeming to wince under the gloomy sentence

"She saw that reconciliation between yourself and Her Husband was humanly impossible she feared or rather felt the final separation of herself. from Zamorna She beheld round her a present of Desertion and could see in the future only for Arthur Hate and strife and power overthrown and life hunted by those who thirst for his blood while you she knew though you might attain momentary greatness could not and would not feel its effects and might be certain of an utter overthrow It looked and still looks as if ten years hence all that she cares for must either be no more or more wretched than if they were buried in their graves Zamorna is too splendid in mind and person to be loved otherwise than with all the heart and she thinks he has cast her aside between carelessness we[a]riedness and revenge She cannot hate him for an instant and she cannot bow to fate—Her heart is far too warm her resolution too much lost in her feelings to admit for a day the comfort of resignation I know she is so much like you as to care for father and childern nothing when she thinks of him that she would lose all the world for him and yet she knows she is nothing to him—and then the vision crosses her mind of Zamorna ruined and persecuted and deserted. remembering her only as the troublsome cause of his downfall the agony is only exceded by that of Zamorna Victorious and Mighty. with herself forsaken and forgotten! Mary Percy was not formed to bear such evils coldly or resentfully from such a Being as Arthur. When she arrived first at Alnwick. she passed through the bright summer days a being most miserably different from what Mary Percy was before. Silently abstracted till thoughts and scenes and visions so overwhelmed her that she would burst into long and passionate fits of weeping she would lie for hours on a sopha at a great window that looks over the woods towards the east with her face leaned on her hand till as she caught the feeling of the noble prospect of sunshine and statly verdure. mingling with ideas of. that Magnificent Being now struggling with fortune beyond the eastern horizon. farther far farther from her than those bright clouds which rose and changed above the trees. with pictures of hours in his Halls and his arms which he had forbidden to recurr and which war and ruin might make impossible to return she would look hurriedly round while her breath faltered with the stifling depression of despair till those large eyes which used to look so cheerfully shone suddenly with the agony that burst in a flood of tears. But of late Alexander your Daughter sitting alone in the cold statly drawing rooms or wandering aimlessly through the park. alike looks wan and pale and wasting yet alike fevered with inward misery If you saw the wearied look of her eyes seeing no rest or comfort but so unnaturally dark and bright and unrecognising with neither a sign or a smile for anything or any one till Zamornas name is mentioned or his actions spoken of and then she breaks out into wild impatient questions and enquiries devouring with her soul the intelligence she hears about him forgetting herself in examination of its bearings and probability till the constant darkening of his face brings again miserable Ideas and one hour after she is more hopelessly melancholy than before

But—again mention his name and the clasped hands the upraised face the excited rapture of the glance shew that all her heart is with that ruined and mighty man—But now Alexander Mary is fast sinking and cannot possibly sustain her agony long though the Idea could she receive a letter from the Duke—one line one word will yet bring all the former brightness to her eye—If she could see him if she could hear him speak I believe she would rejoice to Die! YOUR name she hardly mentions for she must know that her ruin is owing to you But she loves you far too strongly to dare to murmur at you

According to his 1837 volume of poems (see vol. III), Branwell composed the first draft of **Lines**—"Now heavily in clouds comes the day"—in June of 1836. Since the last four lines of the poem begin section (b) below, which begins at the top of the manuscript page, the rest of the poem was part of the missing section between (a) and (b).

[Angria and the Angrians]
III (b)[1]

Thy flower deprived of warmth. will withering die
Thy Store is squandered and thy well run dry
While **HE** whose glory chased the clouds of woe
Thy dearest freind is now thy deadliest foe!"
All very fine! But—when will it strike 10! there is a finer climax than freinship turned to enmity—Oh that I could forsee myself at 10 this night! —Daughter Mother Wife Monarch good day to ye all. and now for buisness! —"

He rung for Shaver who appeared and marshalled his master toward his dressing room

But while he was absent. in a seemingly unnaccountable manner every door of the house began to pour in twos threes of Gentlemen who filled a suite of rooms laid out for Breakfasts with great rapidity and while they gathered in knots together their threatning looks betrayed some storm gathering somewhere Some dropped out as quickly as they dropped in others. moved inward to a. vacant and library like apartment These were such as Bernadotte Naughton Wharton Denard Lord Clairmont and the like

Here in half an hour they were joined by the Great Master Spirit of conspiracy. Attired in Black. the Black of Elrington with the broad red ribbon and "Brood of chickens" alias half a dozen pocket pistols. his advent was like the signal for exhibiting a simalar[sic] decoration on the breasts of each of his associates He came toward them bowing to the number collectivly and with intirely his usual countenance he said

"Now Gentlemen our buisness to day is to throw this Metropolis into the utmost confusion to attack and slaughter every soldier or sailor we can— meet to storm the Government Offices and Houses of parliament to plunder the Ministerial Mansions and to over turn the—present constitution with that last word comes victory and then a Provisional Government with a General Republic

---

1   This section consists of four manuscript pages, 11.2x18.5 cm, at two libraries. The first portion consists of pp. 17-18 of the manuscript at the HRC noted on p. 278, n. 1.

so as the time approaches to your Tents O Israel.[2] —News Gentlemen reached me last night of the Approach of Zamorna upon Edwardston. ere now he must have taken his position—perhaps his conflict is begun. let yours then commence for it is time Come go away! and rejoin me at the Parliament Square but dare not to appear without each of you brings 10000 men! there are 20000 Arabians Africans and French in this city these are not to be beaten by words there are 1200 cannon in the Rover these will beat with more than words there is a man in office now who is using more than words—Listen there are some of his deeds!"

As he spoke a troop of cavalry were filing past under the windows. french and in number 15 or 16 hundred. feild peices followed. and a gloomy mob brought up the rear. as all were looking on Northangerland remarked those fellows want work. they have no object but let them wait one hour. —Gentlemen only one hour. So Now then OFF to your stations.!"

Before the Earl had concluded fresh arrivals of Gentlemen began to fill the rooms with a stern. muttering Multitude and Sdeath silently entered the Library rigged out in those Ancient Garments whose rusty black has survived the storms of a century his knife was sticking from his waistcoat and a hundred demons glittering in his eyes

"Naa" said he "Naa fort my lads Naa fort!"

P B B
June 30th
1836

On this this Mighty and Eventful Morning a Cabinet Council was gathered in the Treasury Offices Great St Georges Street. the Marquis of Ardrah himself being present. in the Chair. where he sat his elbow resting on a quire of paper. one hand holding a pen and the other convulsivly grasping his own bony and whiskered cheeks covering his face as he <leant> till only his cold keen searching eyes wandered free under the light neglected hair just now and then such a frown would pass across his brows as [he] cast his eyes into one deep and threatning shadow opposite to him at the bottom. of the table sat his Foreign Secretary with Herculean Chest expanded and Brawny arms laid over it while his eyes twinkled in his massive countenance with a glee that was at such a time far from intelligible but if Ardrah turned from him the look was changed it became that of a vulture watching his yet living prey The Noble Chancellor of the Exchequer with Lord Strafford Mr Goat and Colonel Luckyman stood all apart drawn together and except the first clouded with bitter rage but Macara's palid visage knew no change save to increased paleness and his distorted squinting eyes seemed as likely to threaten every body as any Body Next the Marquis of

---

2   Compare I Kings 12:16.

Wellsely reclined on a setee Mr Tree at hand to flatter him and Harlaw Elphinstone Douglas Musselburgh and Haines on the side of the premier closing their lips in imperimable[sic] hatred—Save too in this case the first who rolling his eyes round at the ornaments of the ceiling or looking at the winds of heaven occupied his hands in stuffing his maw with quids and his cheeks in rolling them to purpose But in spitting forth the longest something came along with it for he broke forth poising on his centre

"Its a comical plan this—it is. And Aw nevver knew such jars to answer except in a decent Buttery Hatch. Ha Ha—Well 'Aw knaw a tale that would fit us to a hair—!"

"Aye Ha. Man" roared Montmorency "One with forked sting at the end of it—"

"My Lord Marquis's tales" —said Macara "are seldom furnished with a sting—save one which hurts the brandisher."

"Naw it isnt fair to be badgered this way. and for the life of me Aw dawnt knaw what ye're driving at."

"Then if you dont." broke in the Premier "you have no right to speak and how dare you Sir how dare you to interpose your buffoonery among the deliberations of an hour like this"

"Aw'll be hanged if it is Buffoonery but yew see theres an Old Fellow. a rum old blade I'll be <buid> such an one as the Duke of Wellington and he has a score or so of. Sons creditable sticks just as. the marrow to myself And aw— and you see he being on his last anchor and leaking. 9 feet water in the Hold—"

"Dropsey Heh Harlaw?"

"9 feet. Be quiet aw say noan of your jaw.! Where was I—Oh—"

"None of yours sir" cried the Premier rapping the table with his knuckles None of yours Sir" and then he was swirling the pen and quire toward Montmorency—"you are blind in this matter blind or worse—I dare you to name such a compromise—I defy any one to name it. —the thing shall not be uttered and I assure ye that while I possess the power which I now hold sooner—"

"Stop My Lord Marquis" and Montmorency rose too "this is a little bit too fast our wits are none of the ripest and we are but childern when compared with an Admiral of the Fleet. But—still our nebs."

"—Sir I was speaking—"

"Well well and so was I. let us split the difference eh?"

"Split my timbers but thats a hit. and so the Old Fellow. —"

"Harlaw—! what was it I told you just now"

That was said in such a drawl as shewed the premiers desire to regain his usual coolness but it was impossible. as soon as Hector gave a grin the bitterness returned

"You shall not I say you shall not—Gentlemen you shall NOT—No compromise no concession no faltering is allowed here. —Sir if you concede you retire—Lord Macara I thought differently of you

"Oh My Lord I hope I have given your ideas no cause to alter. I really did merely mean in the plan I wished to be adopted—to retain the utmost quantity of power consistent with the welfare of the state and besides what I threw forth was simply a suggestion a a mere hint. really I would this moment withdraw such a trifle and as the questions seems[sic] fairly agitated I prefer to leave it open for discussion—"

"That was what you threw it out for Sir! I knew it. let no one attempt a falsehood.! —"

"Gad. if every one here were as sharp as you My Lord High. we should be a mere bag of nails a case of rasors. however Lofty shall be the Oil to smoothen. and sharpen them the more I defy any one to dissent from my propsals.

A Monarchy in future Elective

An Aristocracy made so instantly

Universal suffrage and

Down with the Establishment!

"Accursed Man—" cried the premeir again rising up "you cursed villain—Be silent. intrude not your anarchical pestilence here."
"Oh I will not be silent My Lord Marquis And its time to speak out. Northangerland is too strong his force too great the struggle is to near impending to admit of the rigid Naval stiff backedness you have hitherto adopted as your policy we must concede or we shall have nothing left to concede—This conscession will at once disarm him it will satisfy the people and it will carry out the grand principle of Reform. —who every[sic] knew a child born with a crown or a coronet on it[s] pate who thinks that a feild or a pigsty gives a man sense and discretion who will bear to be ridden by a pack of knaves who have regularly been found the most notorious wrangling greedy bloodthirsty villains that ever cursed the Globe—" I reckon nought on 'em" thats the voice of the people "Nor I nother" thats the voice of Montmorency. "You or they Go by G—d" thus speaks Northangerland— "Not we" say the Ministry. "well then they" roars his Lordship. "I'll die first." screams our premier. Northangerland clatters below with armed. men at his heels. Is that Jezebel[3] the Kirk to be Uphanded now. I—with her painted face and her tire on her head. Humph! —two or three Eunuchs look out—"fling her down" cries Jehu. and the Scarlet Lady plays plump on the grassplat like a frosty potato! thats my humor!"

"Hear Hear" cried Goat Strafford and Musselburgh in a breath while the Premier stood contorting his uncertain grey eyes with a countenance in which pride Rage and mortification contended for the mastery. He could [not][4] bear to behold his power and prospects dissolving in such confusion before him but ere he could give utterance to his harsh northern voice an Orderly man was brought into the room with despatches from Head quarters at Zamorna These Ardrah took opened and glanced over. his teeth fixed and he settled into his chair fastning

---

3   See I Kings, chapter 21.
4   The following section consists of two pages, 11.2x18.5 cm., in the Brotherton Collection, catalogued as "The Angrian Revolution."

grimly on the contents of the papers Montmorency still continued standing grinning at his superior and Macara silently watching both sides of the room at once. but likewise keeping an unapparant observation on the Foxy features of the premier. Strafford was beginning to give tongue but the High Admiral got up and rapped again on the table in his general Gunroom fashion

"Gentlemen I have received intelligence which out[sic] to bring a blush of Shame on your faces. wrangling among fires like these Hearken!

Zamorna June 27th
6 o clock a m.

My Lord Marquis

Arthur Wellesly with the van of his army of Rebels After suddenly breaking up from Angria have made their appearance on the Hills[sic] sides above Castle Feild and Church hill. near. 13000 strong Four Divisions follow comprehending all the insurgent Forces So I have arranged My own Men in such a manner as to prevent further progress toward their aim Verdopolis. A General Action is expected this Noon. Send me in as many Men as you can spare.

Yours faithfully
J J H De Bruce Maclarrin Macterrorglen

P S While I write the affair begins in a brisk fire beyond Girnington I'll take them and roast them and eat them before we've done with them—Be Gad! — "Yours J. M. Edwardston Hall is buttered to purpose! Battered I mean J M.

"Now then! —Dare you give in farther now?"

"Aye Aye Man Aye will we. what the D—l is not this a yet stronger argument in favour of concession—with an enemy without the gate who would think of fighting within we must close with the Earl and then have at. the Rebels!"

"Mr Montmorency I know you. your a traitor. you have always been a traitor You have betrayed Northangerland you have betrayed the Tyrant of Angria you would now betray me. but you shall not. you shall. not. Sir you are a traitorous Wretch I will keep terms with you no longer you are a desperate dissapointed man you would barter Your Sovereigns and your Government for a mess of pottage.⁵ Sir you are no longer among us. I will speak to the kings. —Harlaw silence—I will hurl you forth.! —"

"Heigho. where are we now I suppose I am to hear all this from a Great raw looking dishonest. Avaricious Scamp. a sort of Seal. on the Scurvy Service he proffesses. Aye a Lowlander⁶ indeed low as his father was before him. Ha you base bloody brutal—"

"My Dear Montmorency be in order. His Lordship certainly expressed himself with unbecoming severity but that is hardly a pretext for you to launch beyond the bounds of decency!"

---

5   Compare Genesis 25:29-34.
6   i.e., a lowland Scot.

"Baw! Nonsense. dye think I care for decency no no man never an inch more than you do but I care for my own life and it is handsomly jeopardised by the conduct of such a ragamuffin—itch be scratched Beggar as—"

Such language became unendurable to the Council bad as it was. Elphinstone and Douglas jumped over the table to seize upon the Speaker and his own side were none of them fighters but Mont had stood many a storm he still kept his Arms folded with Ardrah fronting him in a paroxism of silent hate. and Haines wiping the perspiration from his Forehead strove to calm the overwhelming confusion

"Cock a doodle do Haines hold your cant there and D—n our freind of the Helm here with all his Hypocritical crew Its much you care for the Nation when your slender wits cannot provide for yourselves—But Gad Hush! —" Montmorency held up his hand and Ardrah dashed his on the table

"Yon's 10 St Michaels is tolling. Oh the time is past the time is past!"

That was all that Ardrah said for each Man stretched for his hat and the chairs were overturned upon the Carpet Ten o clock was the hour appointed for opening parliament they were thus yet in Council and now while the Servants were opening the Doors. they heard the bells of the churches pealing up with a deafning clangor. All rushed forth to the open street where their Carriages were Drawn up and each hailed the breezy wind which met him as a soother of their fiery Agitation. A Regiment of cavalry was drawn up down the street to accompany them to the House and several Ministerial Peers Carriages Drew up to accompany them but the Premier ere he mounted his steps glanced round for Montmorency and Macara. neither was present both had staid behind. So had Strafford and Goat and Luckyman. Turning to His carriage he entered with features as white as a sheet. then called to Colonel Milner the commander of the Cavalry—

"Milner be ready for disturbance the bottom of the street looks doubtful."

"Yes My Lord" exclaimed the Soldier and the Marquis pulled his hat over his gloomy brows. giving the word "Forward" His Cavalcade Drove off and the Horsemen closed in around it

The Marquis is a Stern Iron man of inflexible courage but of an Ambition so intense and passions so deadlily[sic] excitable. the present situation of his Affairs was dreadfull beyond description and none need envy the feelings with which the Prime Minister of Africa rode down Georges Street to open the Houses of Parliament. He saw Fidena with a powerful Army nearing him on the one hand. Zamorna driven to desperation assaulting him on the other. He had just parted from a feirce personal quarrel and in a moment half his Ministry had deserted him. Then the design he was bent on was most uncertain in its results while All the City round him was known to be the Nursing plaace[sic] of some dreadful plot against the existence of his Government and with Northangerland for its Mover he knew not but it might be bursting forth that moment. Most certainly now that day was to meet a feirce political contest in the House unless he met before a dreadful warlike one out of it.

Ardrah only testified his feelings by repeated Commands to Drive faster and hasty glances cast on each side of him But as they were turning round St Peters Church where the pealing of its bells and the waving of flags and the Hurrahs of according Multitudes looked every way happy and prosperous. Som[e]thing like the sound of Trumpets came wafted from distant streets and presently long hoarse shouts rising like wind one after another taken up and prolonged into the remotest distance—Many of the Cavalry and most of the carriages stopped for an instant but those who saw. say that the Marquis jumped from his seat clenched his hand and shouted "Drive On you villians!" —So they pressed for ward with ears straining with affright—They passed the Rejiment and Guns on St Georges pavement. all there were still staid and ordinary they saw the Multitudes shoaling along in there[sic] wake all looked eager inquisitive and Noisy but. when they drew near Twelves Street. the music burst on them most audibly and every Beat of the Drums. made each heart knock against its owners Ribs

"Oh" said. Lord. Farnham "its the Military band in the Square" Ardrah replied "No" and as he spoke they turned round into Twelves Street itself. with the parliament Square in Advance nearly half a mile. Every thing halted for the Advance was. a Sea. an Ocean of human beings. Pikes Muskets Red Flags and Ribbons clustered till they nearly hid the long rows of Houses round. Drums thundered within the Masses and the blasts of Trumpet and bugle broke by gusts upon the Ear. —Here was no Mistake. The Noblemen in the Carriages sought for their fire arms and the Premier drew himself erect in his seat. Then the Cavalry pressed to the front. and Milner rode up for Ardrahs commands the Latter rising to overlook the crowd. said.

"Force a passage"
"Must we not rather send for fresh troops my Lord!"
"On your peril Sir"
Ardrah believed this to be a deceptive Mass of people and that they should soon get through them. the Capt[a]ins of the different companies forced upon their unwelcome buisness began to sign for the people to part which they began to do but in a while for hitherto the idea had not entered their minds many began to see this was the Premiers cavalcade. so A Hoarse howling roar rose from the formost in the tumult and as it spread down the street. the Soldiers pushed their Horses against the crowd. these cheifly unarmed people cast down and bewildered were rapidly giving way when something like a peal of THUNDER rolled Majestically upon the growing Confusion it seemed almost like the voice of an Earthquake and with a single break. broke forth more deep and thundering than before. Doubt fled before it and Ardrah with his own hand threw back the hood of his Barouche laid hold of his Surtout and put it on then. turning he called for a horse which a servant brought him. then he said. leaping from his carriage and mounting the steed

"Back My Lords—There is Treason here—Back! Soldiers give way"
The Earl of Carlington Lord. Cressingham. with Elphinstone and Douglas. All leaped from their Chariots and laid hold of Horses brought for

them. The Others turned their Horses heads and the Cavalry strove to keep the crowds from pressing onwards

Ardrah said with a loud calm voice. "Follow me to the Admiralty" So that way they turned at a measured pace hearing the deafning crash of Artillery bursting from Parliament Square

As they departed their place was occupied by thousands of people and then these swayed and ebbed till all the street took a determinate Motion downward. but this quarter and this scene was in a manner the covering of the real contest which developed gradually when the people filed off and ran before an unseen but terror scattering storm of Balls then. the long interminable lines of Grim

[Angria and the Angrians]
III(c)[1]

only from this time that every eyes[sic] was constantly to be fixed upon him. And next came the dreadful Insurrection in Sneachis Land which under him threatning again to plunge Africa into confusion was quelled by the united efforts of all the Governments till at Last was not the snake killed.—proscribed beggared and given over to outrageous drunkenness—No. Piracys again had recourse to brought in fresh additions of fortune He appeared among the cheif of Verdopolis. and sought and wooed and won. one of the Noblest and greatest Women of the Age He became LORD ELRINGTON. and amid henious drunkenness set to work increasing his power by the formation and vigorous prosecution of his Abominable ROBBERY ESTABLISHMENTS which after overrunning the whole Land in the space of a year were at length discovered and supressed their Leader escaping with a fine of 200 000 pounds. was He not now at least lost and degraded beyond remedy. No there was just one help for him of that most adroitly he caught hold. The Marquis of Douro was fast rising into a brilliant popularity. This rise would draw up what clung to him so Elrington straight became his Associate and. the War of Aggression followed. that ever memorable war! —Fidena was beaten Africa ruined Douro and Elrington saved it and and once more for a few days in the confusion Rougue saw himself on the summit of power but when matters righted themselves that power was to be given up with the Equivalent of an Earldom and a noble grant of money. all soon lost in the full Blaze of the premiership of the ANGRIAN KINGDOM. But again evil deeds and an evil mind soon hurled him from such an eminence. frowned on by his Insulted Sovereign we once more saw him powerless a self banished Exile in the Stumphses Isle. —In 2 short months again to return reaccept the seals. make a speech in the first Angrian Parliament which abused every earthly member of his Administration and then again threatened from above. fly to Verdopolis and Join himself with his monarchs foes Ardrah and the Reformers. His Monarchs vengeance followed in his terrible speech in the Verdopolitan Parliament Percy. straight declared himself a traitor to everyone. and fled into obscurity an insane public criminal. Now we thought He is cast off. his king His country his Old freinds his new freinds all have cast him off.! But Lo! Ardrah came into power Zamorna was determined to overthrow him he recalled Northangerland. who came and made the scarifying speech on the Southern Navy which with the bill founded on it caused a dissolution of Parliament where in the following election contest Northangerland triumphed beside his King appeared next Parliament sat silent while the contest for the

---

[1]   The following section consists of pages 19-20, 11.2x18.5 cm, in the manuscript at the HRC noted above. Pages 17 and 18 in the previous section and these two pages form a single sheet; therefore a half sheet to go with the two pages from the Brotherton in the last section is missing.

Liberty of Angria was fighting silently suffered imprisonment and liberation incurred the just suspicion of His King refused to aid his country and next escaping to France buried himself in a Idle dream of pleasure at St Cloud.[2] —The Thunder of Civil war awaked him and he found that His King his Countess his Daughter were all gone his party dissolving and his nearest associates stealing away? —Now he returned again attracted popular attention by ridiculous Theology organised a secret Association armed the populace and ON MONDAY the 26th of June 1836—the Day appointed for the opening of Parliamemt He AROSE with 50000 Armed men at his back. cocked His pistols and with one vast explosion blew Ministry and Constitution to the winds of HEAVEN

Let me describe the Evening of June 26 and shew the Hall of Conference between the two Houses of Legislature in parliament square. —where through the day had occurred the Hottest struggle between Tyrannous Despotism and ferocious Democracy

This Hall is a Spacious Domed building with vast folding Doors and staircases springing from a common flight opposite the great Enterance into two branches upward round the building to communicate with the Galleries of the Lords and commons

On the Common Landing place at the root of these two flights—Beside a Great Table stood several Gentlemen unbuckling swords and pistols which they placed upon that Table for a momentary respite, Wiping their foreheads and draining glasses of Brandy and water as if they had just escaped from a hot and ardous Labour Opposite to them flanking the Vast opened Doors A Strong Guard of Working Men and Mechanics Heavily armed kept the Enterance free from the crowds of people that thronged outside and beyond whom from the Elevation of the Landing place could be observed. many carts and waggons bearing off Loads of Dead or Wounded men and masses of Armed fellows stationary or moving among the Black Artillery of the battery erected by order of Government which had so materially contributed to create the scene of grim confusion around them Beyond this Square from within the Doors parts of Statly Houses might be noticed with windows battered and Doors smashed in peices and numbers of Blackened riotous looking men hurling from their upper stories a thousand costly articles among the mob beneath. Beyond these Scene[s] St Peters spire bore the Terrible RED FLAG OF LIBERTY(!) aloft into the sky and in completing of the picture that sky Hung Dull Heavy Electrical clouded with smoke and lowering with evening shadows

The Sounds distinguishable all were lost in a ho[a]rse discordant swell that changed or broke as shouts or shreiks or yells predominated till the long distant roll of musketry and the Deep dull Burst of Cannon from the Admirality Harmonised all with their awfully portentous bass

---

2   A town on the outskirts of Paris with beautiful gardens and a château that both Napoleon and Queen Victoria found very appealing.

I said that the Great Conference Hall itself was empty except of the Gentlemen round the table in the landing place But as the Square outside began to fill with people and a stream of flags and Ensigns to flow into it from Georges Street the Armed men in the portal parted and crowds flocked up the steps under the Archway. Presently while without the crowd of flags waved thicker and the hoarse sounds of Applauding increased. A vein as it were of Horsemen threaded the Horizontal strata of heads which gathering into a knot of cavalry beneath the pillared building Halted till All the Riders ranged in a guard round the formost and most Noted among them After this those up on the Landing place could see nothing but the flocking in of. Dusty Blackened Heavily armed Insurgents so that when thousands had just led into the mighty area tens of thousands blocked up the Square outside to arouse when Drums and Trumpets in concert with the Deafning peal of St Peters and St Georges Bells broke forth in Triumphant and exhilirating bursts of sound

A Lane was cleared up the flight of steps for a Man in Black who stopped in front of the Table and turned to address the people.

"IT IS FINISHED! That is a mighty sentence once used men say to announce the termination of a work of Redemption and regeneration of the world.[3] And now I say to you my fellow countrymen the second act. (perhaps the first.) of Redemption is FINISHED. though Mark me it is only begun! I say it is finished when I know that this day Tyranny and Ardrah are overthrown The Constitution and Superstition are annihilated all Old things are swept away. It is finished with the last blow and the last shout of the Victorious Verdopolitans for those Guns which you hear from the River are the insensate gaspings of a lifeless foe. But. It is only Begun when I look at the Rights to be granted the Laws to be formed and the New things to be brought in place of the old. This day we have only removed to morrow we must replace Tyranny is gone down to the Grave but Liberty is not yet set free from its prison we have undone everthing but Done nothing!

Africans this is the 27th of June 1836 at 10 o clock a m in the morning of which you arose in arms to the number of 60 000 men Attacked the Houses of Parliament the Ministry and the Government troops fought and defeated and captured them under the command of Alexander Rougue. your ancient Representative. for what did you do all this? What Have you required him to Do?

Why Listen!

All Africa is Declared one great REPUBLIC. The Republic of Africa!

All power and Government in this Republic is vested for the present in a PROVISIONAL GOVERNMENT till such time As a regular foundation of Laws and civil polity can be laid for the people to erect a Temple of VITALITY!

Look at the first foundation stone. the corner stone of the building.

All Titles of every rank and Degree save those military and belonging to Government Offices are to be Abolished

---

3   Compare John 19:30.

The Church shall be annihilated and her property confiscated to the State

The Parliament shall be formed into one Great NATIIONAL ASSEMBLY. every member of which shall be Elected by the people

And Every man in the Republic above the Age of 21 years shall Have a voice in the Election of his Representative

Whoever agrees not to these fundamental Rules must DIE and his property shall be devoted to the PROVISIONAL GOVERNMENT

Of this Government I for the present am constituted Head

And therefore I BID YOU TO ATTEND TO ME!

July
 1836   My Ancient ship upon my Ancient sea[1]
                    Begins another voyage—Nay thourt gone
                    But wither pending? who is gone with thee?
                    Since parted from thee I am left alone
                    Unknowing what My Rovers[2] fate may be
                    Into Its native world of tempests thrown
                    Lost like a speck from my diverted eye
                    Which wilder mightier visions must survey

                    Lost and unnoticed—far away the roar
                        Of Southern Waters breaking to the wind
                    With restless thunder rolling still before
                        As the wild gale sweeps wilder on behind[3]
                    And every vision of old Afric's shore
                    As much forgot and vanished out of mind
                    As the wild track though[sic] markedst so long ago
                    From those eternal waves which surge below

                    Gone—tis a word which through lifes troubled waste
                    Seems always coming and the only one
                    Which can be called the PRESENT. Hope is past
                    And Hate and strife and love and peace are gone
                    Before we think them for their rapid haste
                    Scarce gives us time for one short smile or groan
                    Ere that thought dies and new ones come between
                    It and our heart with some as fleeting scene

                    And yet there is or seems at least to be
                    A general hue of thought that colours all
                    So though each one be different all agree
                    In the same Melancholy shade like pall

---

1   The first of five items wrongly attributed to Emily in BPM: Bon 146,
bound in green morocco. On two pages, 11.2x18.5 cm. Branwell's initials above
the date have been erased. Although the speaker is Percy after his victory over
Zamorna at Edwardston, it is not clear whether the poem was actually intended to
be part of [**Angria and the Angrians**].

2   The name of his pirate ship—see **The Pirate A Tale** in vol. I.

3   A canceled line follows:
    "And <Genii> and Afric vanished out of mind."

Even as the shadows look the same to me
Though cast I know from many a varying wall
In this Vast city—Hut and Temple[4] sharing
In the same light and the same darkness wearing

Not that I deem All life a course of Shade
Nor all the world a maze of streets like these
From youth to age a mighty change is made
As from this City to the Southern Seas
For years through youthful hope our course is laid
For years in sloth a sea without a breeze
For years amid the stir of civil jar
For years within some silent. sleepless care

Changing and still the same yet swiftly passing
Tis here tis there tis nowhere oh my soul
Is there no rest from such a fruitless chasing
Of the wild dreams that ever round thee roll
Each as it comes the parting thought defacing
Yet—all still hurrying to the selfsame goal
Gone ere I catch them but their path alone
Stretching afar toward <u>one</u> for ever gone!

What have I written—nothing for tis over
And seems as nothing in the single cloud
That shadows it and long has seemed to Hover
Oer all the crossing thoughts that ever flowd
In this wrecked spirit Oh my ocean Rover
Well mayst thou plough the deep so free and proud
Thou bearst the uniting tie of ceasless dreams
The fount. the confluence of a thousand streams

  I do not see myself again
  A wanderer oer the Atlantic main
  I do not Backward turn my eye
  Toward sleepless sea and stormy sky
  Oh no these vanished visions rest
  In far woodlands of the west
  And there let Hesperus[5] arise
  To watch my treasure where it lies
    The present scenes the present clime

---

4   "Hut and temple" originally read "tower and cottage."
5   The evening star, Venus.

28   Forbid the Dreams of olden time
<u>28</u>   The present thoughts the present hour
56   Are rife with Deeds of sterner power
<u>14</u>   And who shall be my leading star
70   +Amid the howling storm of war.
<u>25</u>
95[6]   Hark Listen to the Distant Gun
    From the Battle feild of Edwardston
    It breaks upon the awful roar
        Which stuns my ears around
    And oh the shout of Victory
        Strikes with a Hollow sound[7]
    My struggles all are crowned with power
    And fortune gives a glorious hour
    Men who hate me kneel before me
    Men who kneel are forced to adore me
    My Name is on a million tongues
    <u>The Million</u> babbles of my wrongs
    And Twenty years of Tyrant pride
    Which strove this Modern God to hide
    At last have vanished in the rays
    Of his unquenched unclouded blaze
    Oh is not Jesus come again
    Over his thousand saints to reign
    While sin and Satan vainly spit
    Their venomed fury <from> the pit
    Where they may lie for<gotten>
    Till Heaven descends in <judgement down>
    Their reign is past their power <oerthrown>[8]
    For fallen is Mighty Babylon

---

6   The numbers and the "+" opposite l. 70 are Branwell's.
7   An unreadable canceled line follows.
8   Lines 91-94 are partially obliterated by an ink blot. The reference to "sin and Satan" echoes Branwell's reading of Milton's *Paradise Lost*.

Through the hoarse howling of the storm[1]
    I saw but did I truely see
One glimpse of that unearthly form
    Whose very name is VICTORY
Twas but a glance and all seems past
    For cares like clouds again return
And Ill forget him till the blast
    For ever from my soul has torn
That Vision of a mighty man
    Crushed into Dust! —

Forget him! —Lo the Cannon's smoke
    How dense it thickens till on high
By the wild storm blasts roughly broke
    It parts in volumns through the Sky
    That heavily are drifting by
Till the dread burst breaks forth once more
    With whitening clouds which seem to fly
Affrighted from that ceasless roar
And there it lightens! dashed with gore
The thick of battle rends in twain
    Whith[sic] their rough ranks of bristling steel
Flashing afar while Armed men
    In mighty masses bend and reel
Like the wild waters of the main
    Lashed into foam—Where there again
100*   Behold him!

---

[1]   The second item in Bon 146, (leaf 3, 11.2x18.5 cm.), these are trial lines for the poem beginning on p. 597 below. The "100" at the end is Branwell's. Presumably the "him" is Zamorna at the battle of Edwardston.

Yet oer his face a solemn light[1]
  Comes smiling from the sky
And shows to sight the lustre bright
  Of his uplifted eye
The aimless heedless carelessness
  Of happy Infancy
Yet such a solemn tearfulness
  Commingling with his glee
The parted lips the golden hair
  Cast backward from his brow
Without a single shade of care
All bathed amid that moonlight air
  Oh who so blest as thou!

---

[1] The third item in Bon 146, appearing on the same page as the previous item, these are trial lines for ll. 141-53 of the poem beginning on p. 588.

Memory how thy majic fingers[1]
    With a wild and passing thrill
Wakes the chord whose spirit lingers
    Sleeping silently and still
Fast asleep and allmost dying
    Through my days of changless pain
Till I deem those strings are lying
    Never to be waked again
Winds have blown but all unknown
Nothing could arouse a tone
In that Heart which like a stone
    Senselessly has lain
All seemed over Freind and Lover
    Strove to waken music there
Flow the strings their fingers over
    Still in silence slept the air

Memory Memory comes at last
Memory of feelings past
And with an Eolian blast
    Strikes the strings resistlessly

---

[1] The fourth item in Bon 146; it appears on the verso of the leaf containing the previous two items. For an earlier version, see the next page. Because the two previous items are trial lines for poems dated July 22 and August 8, these lines were likely composed in late July or early August.

Hours annd[sic] days my Heart has lain[1]
Through a scene of changless pain
As it neer would wake again
       Sad and Still and Silently

Time has flown but all unknown
Nothing could arouse atone
Not a single string would moan
       In replying sympathy

Memory memory comes at last
Memory of feelings past
And with an Eolian blast
       Strikes the strings resistlessly

---

[1]   These trial lines for the previous item appear on the recto (the verso is blank) of the first leaf, 10x10.5 cm, in a manuscript volume bound in green morocco, containing five items, four of which are misattributed to Emily, in the PML: MA 2696 R-V. Opposite the last stanza Branwell wrote: "I am more terrifically and infernally and Idiotically and Brutally STUPID—than ever I was in the whole course of my incarnate existence The above prescious lines are the fruits of one hours most agonising labour between 1/2 past 6 and 1/2 past 7 on the evening of Wednesday. July   1836." In the first line "Hours and days" originally read "Years and years."

Oh all our cares these Noontide airs[1]
 Might seem to drive away
So glad and bright each sight appears
 Each sound so soft and gay
And through the shade of yonder glade
 Where thick the leaves are dancing
Whith jewels rare and flowrets fair
 A hundred plumes are glancing
For there its palace portals rise
 Beyond the Myrtle grove
Catching the whitest brightest dies
 From the deep blue dome above
But here this little lonely spot
 Retires among its trees
By all unknown and noticed not
 Save sunshine and the breeze

---

[1] These lines appear on the recto of the second leaf, 7.9x11.2 cm, of the PML manuscript noted for the previous item. The similarities of paper, ink, and hand, and the dating of the previous item indicate that this fragment was composed at roughly the same time—late July/early August 1836.

PBB   Still and bright in twilight shining   Aug 8th 1836[1]
            Glitters forth the evening Star
            Closing Rosebuds round me twining
                Shed their fragrance through the air
            Slow the river pales its glancing
            Soft its waters cease their dancing
            Calm and cool the shades advancing
                Speak the hours of slumber near!
            Why this solemn silence given
                To the close of fading day
            Feels the earth the hush of heaven
                Can the expanse of nature pray
            And when daylights toil is done
            Gratful for summer sunshine gone
            Can it before the Almighties throne
                Its glad obeisance pay?

            Such a hush of sacred sadness
                Wide around the weary wild
            Oer the whirl of Human madness
                Spreads the slumbers of a child
            These surrounding sweeps of trees
            Swaying to the evening breeze
            With a voice like distant seas
                Making music mild
            Percy Hall above them lowering
                Darker than the darkning sky
            With its halls and turrets towering
                Wakes the wind in passing by
            Round that scene of wondrous story
            In their old ancestral glory
            All its Oak's so huge and hoary
                Wave their boughs on high.

            Among these Turrets there is one
            The soonest dark when day is done
            And when Autumns winds are strongest
            Moans the most and echoes longest
            So—On the steps that lie before

---

[1]   This poem originally covered pp. 18-24 of the manuscript notebook described on p. 444, n. 1 above, but is now split between two libraries. The first portion is at the PML: MA 2696 R-V, bound in brown calf with the poem beginning on p. 487. This poem was composed during the time Branwell was writing the section of [**Angria and the Angrians**] that follows—see p. 605.

A solitary arched door
In that lone Gable far away
    From sights and sounds of social joy
Fronting the expanse so dim and grey
    There sits a lonly boy
One hand is in his curling hair
    To part it from his brow
And that young face so soft and fair
    Is lifted heavenward now
On the cold stone he has laid him down
    To watch that silver line
Beneath the power of twilights frown
    In the wide west decline
For Heaven still guides his azure eyes
    Toward its expanse so wild
As veiled in darkness their[sic] he lies
    A little Angel Child!

Oh who has known or who can tell[2]
    The Fountain of those feelings high
Which while in this wild world we dwell
    At times will lift us up on high
    In a celestial sympathy
With yon blue vault yon starry dome
    As if the spirit deemed the sky
Was even on earth its only home
And while the eye is dim with tears
    The feelings wrapt in dreams sublime
How dead seem earthy hopes and fears
    How all forgot the course of time
And yet the soul can never say
    What _are_ the thoughts which make it glow
We feel they _are_ but _what_ are they?
    Tis this which we must never know
While lingering in this world of woe
Yet did Mans Soul descend from heaven
With feelings by its Maker given
All high all glorious all Divine
    And from his hand perfected gone
With such a bright reflected shine
    As the full moon bears from the sun

---

2   Compare this stanza with Wordsworth's *Ode on the Intimations of Immortality.*

But then—The Soul was clothed in clay
So straight its beauty passed away
And through a whirl of misery driven
Earths shadow came 'tween it and heaven
A darkned orb the moon became
Lost all its lustre quenched its flame!
Or entering on this mortal life
The clouds of woe the storms of strife
Continual passing veil it round
With gloomy wreaths of shade profound
So only shining fitfully
A single gleam of light we see
As part the clouds on either hand
To shew the clear calm heaven beyond
Yet as one moment soars our Soul
    Into these wayward dreams divine
Till back again the darkness roll
        And hide the uncertain shine

Yet shall a time come rapid on
When all these clouds that round us frown
From Heavens vast vault all past & gone
Leave the full moon in glory there
To shine for ever bright and fair
    When this dull clay is cast away
These THOUGHTS shall shine with cloudless ray
And we shall understand what now
But dimly is revealed below
In yon lone childs uplifted eyes
    Such dreams can scarc[e] be dim
So late upon those mortal skies
        The moon has risen to him
So late his soul has passed from Heaven
        That it can scarce forget
The visions bright whose haloed light
        Is round its musings yet
Silent he sits on the darkned stone
        With night around him falling
As if to him that hollows moan
        From the old tree tops were calling
He listens to the eerie wind
        Around his Fathers dwelling
Till faster following on his mind
        More glorious thoughts seem swelling
For both his little hands were stretched

In rapture to the sky
When wilder from the wilderness
Each blast came howling by
Toward clouds all southward resting wide
Above the Atlantic sea
While oer them far the darksome air
Is haloed lustrously
He gazes as some wondrous sight
To him were opening soon
Till, lo! —that sudden shining light
"The MOON the glorious MOON!"

Oh soft and sweet is the silver beam
That floods the turret high
While feilds & woodlands round it seem
All glinting gloriously
Each window glitters cold and clear
Upon the southern tower
And—though the shade is darker made
Around his lonly bower—
Yet oer his Face a solemn light[3]
Comes smiling from the sky
And shews to sight the lustre bright
Of his uplifted eye
The aimless heedless carelessness
Of happy Infancy
Yet such a solemn tearfulness
Commingling with his glee
The parted lips the shining hair
Cast backward from his brow
Without a single shade of care
But Bathed amid that moonlight air
Oh who so blest as thou!
The moon in glory oer the grove[4]
Majestic marches on
With all the vault of heaven above
To canopy her throne
And from her own celestial rest
Upon the dark woods waving crest
Serenly she looks down

---

[3] For earlier trial lines, see p. 584.
[4] The following portion is at the BPM: BS 118. For earlier trial lines, see p. 476.

Yet beaming still as if she smiled
Most brightly on that beauteous child
But what thought he as there he lay
       Beneath the arched door
Amid the ever trembling play
       Of moonshine through the bower
Gazing with blue eyes dimmed by tears
To that vast vault of shining spheres
       Till its mysterious power
Makes the bright drops unnoticed break
In dewy Lustre oer his cheek

    "Oh how I could wish to fly
Far away through yonder sky
Oer those trees upon the breeze
       To a paradise on high!
Why am I so bound below
That I must not cannot go
Lingering here for year on year
       So long before I die!
Now how glorious seems to be
Heavens huge concave stretched oer me
But—Every star is hung so far
       Away from where I lie!
I love to see that Moon arise
It suits so with the silent skies
I love it well but cannot tell
       Why it should make me cry!
Ist that it brings before me now
Those wondrous times gone long ago
When Angels used from Heaven to come
And make this earth theire[sic] happy home?
When Moses brought from Egypts strand
Gods favoured tribes through seas and sand
Victorious to the promised land!
When Salem rose her Judahs pride
Where David lived and Jesus died!
Ist that I know this very moon
Those vanished wonders gazed upon
When Shepherds watched their flocks by night[5]
       All seated on the ground
And Angels of the Lord came down
       And glory shone around?

---

5   Compare with the well known Christmas carol that begins with this line.

Ist that I think upon the sea
Just now tis beaming beauteously
Where I so oft have longed to be
   But never yet have been?
Ist that it shines so far away
On Lands beyond that Oceans spray
Mong Lonly Scotlands hills of grey
   And ENGLANDS groves of green!
Or ist that through yon Deep blue dome
It seems so solemnly to roam
As if upon some unknown Sea
   A vessels statly form
It oer the waves was wandering free
   Through calm and cloud and storm!
—I cannot tell but its in heaven
   And though I view it here
Till I am mouldring dust to dust
My parted spirit never must
   Behold its brightness near
I am crying to think that mighty throng
Of Glorious Stars to heaven belong
That they can never never see
A little earthly child like me
Still rolling on still beaming down
And I unnoticed and unknown
Though Jesus once in ages gone
   Called Childern to his knee
So where He reigns in glory bright
Above these starry skies of night
Amid his paradise of light
   Oh why might I not be!
Oft when awake on christmas morn
In sleepless twilight laid fo[r]lorn
Strange thoughts have oer my mind been born
   How he has died for me
And oft within my chamber lying
Have I awaked myself with crying
From dreams where I beheld him dying
   Upon the accursed tree
And often has my mother said
While on her lap I laid my head
She feared for time I was not made
   But for Eternity!

So I can read my title clear[6]
>To mansions in the skies
And let me bid farewell to fear
>And wipe my weeping eyes
Ill lay me down on this marble stone
>And set the world aside
To see upon its ebon throne
>Yon Moon in glory ride
Ill strive to peirce that midnight vault
>Beyond its farthest star
Nor let my spirits wanderings halt
>Neath Edens crys[t]al bar
For sure that wind is calling me
>To a land beyond the grave
And I must not shrink upon the brink
>Of Jordans heavenly wave
But Ill fall asleep in its waters deep
>And wake on that blest shore
Where I shall neither want or weep
>Or sigh or sorrow more
Oh Angels come! Oh Angels come!
And Guide me To my Heavenly Home!
Guide thee to Heaven!—Oh lonely Child[7]
Little knowest thou the Tempests wild
Now gathering for thy future years
There blighting floods of bitter tears
Little thou knowest how long and dread
Must be thy path ere thou art laid
Within thy dark and narrow bed
Or how thou then wilt shrink to be
Launched out upon Eternity
All these celestial visions flown
All Hope of Heaven for ever gone!
>This passionate desire for Heaven
Is but the beam of brightness given
Around thy spirit at its birth
And not yet quenched in clouds of earth
The inward yearnings of the soul
Toward its original and goal
Before that goal is hid from sight

---

6   These four lines are adapted from the first verse of Isaac Watts' hymn "When I can read my title clear."
7   The following portion is again at the PML.

Amid the gloom of mortal night
To thee just entering into Time
This world is like a stranger clime
Where—nothing kindred—nothing known—
Leaves thy young spirit all alone
To spend its hours in thinking on[8]
The Native home whence it has gone
          But—Oh at last a time will come
When Heaven is lost and earth is Home
Where pleasures glimmering in thy sight
As soon as seen shall sink in night
Whilst thou pursuest them through the gloom
Sinking like meteors to the tomb
This light shall change to lightning then
This love of Heaven to Hate of men
So if thou seekest a glorious name
Thy path shall pass through blood and flame
From crime to crime impetous hasting
Blasted thyself and others blasting
For that which from on high is thrown
Will always fall most rapid down
And sink the deepest. —So with thee
Thy quick and passionate heart shall be
But further plunged in misery
Then those around thee oft may find
Earth and its joys to suit thine mind
For dust to dust the sons of earth
Will love the land that gave them birth
Yet never thou or if thou dost
Too quickly thou shalt find it DUST!

He sleeps! —in slumber calm and deep
An Infants blest and balmy sleep
Dreaming of heaven those closed eyes
See glorious visions of the skies
And tremblingly their fringes lie
On the yong[sic] cheek of Infancy
The softened curls of golden hair
Just moving in the moonlight air
But his white brow so sweetly still
So free from every shade of ill!
Shall it be so for ever? —NO!
Who in this world would wish it so

---

8   For earlier trial lines, see p. 470.

Yon is the Image of a man
Destined to lead the formost van
Of coming time and in his land
The future chooses to command
Tis He whose never dying name
Shall set a future world on flame
PERCY! awake thee from thy sleep
Awake! to bid thy country weep[9]

P B Bronte
August 13 [th]
1836.

Begun and finished in
five days. [10]

---

[9] These last two lines originally read:
"PERCY! sleep on in happy <sleep>
Then awake! to bid thy country weep."
[10] Branwell first wrote "seven days," then changed to "five."

According to his 1837 volume of poems (see vol. III), Branwell composed the first draft of **The Battle Eve** on July 9, 1836. No manuscript has been found.

[Angria and the Angrians]
III(d)[1]

P B B
July 22
1836

Through the hoarse howlings of the storm[2]
I saw—but did I truely see
A Glimpse of that unearthly form
    Whose name has once been Victory
Twas but a glimpse and all seems past
    For cares like clouds again return
And I'll forget him till the blast
    For ever from my soul has torn
That vision of a Mighty Man
    Crushed into Dust! —

Forget him! —Lo the Cannon's smoke
    How dense it thickens till on high
By the wild Storm blasts roughly broke
    It parts in volumns through the sky
    With dying thunder drifting by
Till the dread burst breaks forth once more
And loud and louder peals the cry
Sent up with that tremendous roar
Where as it lightens broad before
    The thick of Battle rends in twain
With roughened ranks of bristling steel
    Flashing afar while armed men
In mighty masses bend and reel

---

[1] The following section consists of forty pages (2 blank), 11.2x18.5 cm., scattered over five libraries. The first portion consists of a manuscript of sixteen pages—4 sheets folded and laid inside each other but not stitched—in the Brotherton Collection, catalogued as "The Angrian Adventure."

[2] See the 1837 revised version, **Percy's Musing's upon the Battle of Edwardston**, in vol. III. See also the trial lines for the opening portion on p. 583.

Like the wild waters of the main
Lashed into foam! —where there again
Behold Him! as with sudden wheel
At bay against a thousand foes
He turns upon their serried rows
All heedless round him though they close
  With such a bloodhound glare
That eye with inward fires so bright
Peirces the tempest of the fight
And lightens with the joyless light
  Of Terrible Despair
He sees his soldiers round him falling
In vain to Heaven for vengeance calling
He sees those firmest freinds whom he
Had called from happy happy home
And for the prize of victory
  Over the eastern world to roam
He sees them lie with glaring eye
  Turned up toward him that wandering star
Who led them still from good to ill
  In hopes of power to meet with war
And fall from noontide dreams of glory
To this strange rest so grim and gory
When rolling on those freinds oerthrown
Wars wildest wrack breaks thundering down
Zamorna's pale and ghastly brow
Darkens with anguish—all in vain
To stem the tide of battle now
  For every rood of that wide plain
Is Heaped with thousands of his dead
Or shakes beneath the impetous tread
  Of foes who conquer oer the slain
  No! never must he hope again
Though still abroad that Banner streams
On whose proud folds the sun of glory gleams
  Though still unslaughtered round their Lord
His chosen cheifs may grasped[sic] the unvanquished sword
  Tis Hopeless! and He knows it so
Else would not anguish cloud his brow
Else would not such a withering smile
Break oer his hueless face the while
Some freind of years falls helplessly
  Yet still upon that eagle eye
Turning with dying ecstasy!
That Eagle eye the Beacon light

Through all the changes of the fight
Whose glorious glance spoke victory
And fired his men to do or die
On the red roar of Battle bent
As if its own wild element
And gazing oer each thundering gun
As he were wars unconquered son
That Eye! oh I have seen it shine
    Mid scenes that differed far from these
As Gambias woods and skies divine
      From GreenLands icy sea's
I have seen its lustre bent on me
    In old Adventure gone
With beam as bright and gaze as free
      As His own Young Angrian Sun!
When oer those mighty wastes of heath
      Around Elymbos' brow
As side by side we used to ride
    I smiled to mark its glow
I smiled to see him how he threw
    His feelings into mine
Till my cold spirit almost grew
    Like his a thing divine
I saw him in his Beautys pride
    With Manhood in his brow
The Falcon eyed with heart of pride
    And spirit stern as now
Almost as stern—For many a shade
    Had crossed his youthful way
And clouds of care began to mar
    The brightness of his day
I knew him and I marked him then
    For one apart as far
From the surrounding crowds of men
    As Heavens remotest star
I saw him in the Battles hour
    And conquered by his side
I was with him in his height of power
    And triumph of his pride
Tis past—But am I with him now
    Where he spurs feircly through the fight
His pride & power and crown laid low
    And all his future wrapt from sight
Mid clouds like those which frown on high
    Over the plains in purple gloom

With rain and thunder driving by
    To shroud a nations bloody tomb
And in the cannons ceasless boom
    The toll which wafts the parting soul
While heavens bright flashes serve to illume
    Like torches its funereal stole
Its Horrid funeral—Far and wide
    I see them falling in the storm
Mid clouds of Horse that wildly ride
    Above each gashed and trampled form
His Charger shot Zamorna down
Mong foes and freinds alike oer thrown!
Yet never may that desperate soul[3]
Betray the thoughts which oer it roll
Teeth clenched cheeks blenched and eyes that dart
A Boar like Feircness from his heart
As all the world was nought beside
The saving of his Iron pride
For every one on earth might die
And not a tear should stain that eye
Or force a single sob or sigh
    From him who cannot yeild
Yet stay one moment—tis but one
A single glance to Heaven is thrown
One frenzied burst of greif—Tis gone
    His Heart once more is steeled
That was a burst of Anguish—there
Blazed all the intensness of Despair
It said "Oh all is Lost for ever!"
All he loves to him is dead
All his hopes of glory fled
All the past is vanished
    Save what nought can sever
Ever living Memories
That shall haunt him till he dies
With things that he can realise
    Never Never Never

I said I saw his anguished glance
    Say he did think on me
Incendiary of Rebel France
    Parrot of Liberty

---

3   An unreadable canceled line follows.

> The wretched Traitor who let in
>   On Africs opened Land
> Deceit and craft and cant and sin
>   In one united band
>
> Who raised the Standard of Reform
>   And shouted "Earth be free"
> To whelm his country in the Storm
>   Of Rebel Tyranny
>
> Who called himself the good right hand
>   And Father of his king
> Only on his adopted Land
>   This awful curse to bring
>
> Aye it was I. and only I
>   Who hurled Zamorna down
> From Conquering glory placed on high
>   This day to be oerthrown
>
> I barbed the Arrow which has sped
>   To peirce my Sovereigns breast
> And Only on my guilty head
>   May All his sufferings rest!
>   174 lines.

Such were the feelings of the Lord President of the Provisional Government upon the subject which filled the minds of all men but in none so fully as his own!

But it befits us to take a short view of the present state of affairs in Verdopolis.

JUNE TWENTY SEVENTH. had altered the face of Africa. after the bloody and determined struggle of that Day. the Reform Ministry was no more but with it sunk. the Constitution the Church the Aristocracy and real Liberty. For all power was now Lodged in the Provisional Government under the controul of the Earl of Northangerland. Every one who Loved order and His Old and glorious Government. trembled for his Life since it was known that lists of proscriptions were preparing and several Noble families had already been placed under arrest while the propertys and Houses of all the Absent and refugee or Constitutional Noblemen with Wellington and Sneachi were Confiscated to the Revolutionary Government as well as that of. the Ministry. Likewise heavy contributions were levied on the City and great Licence permitted to the disorganised troops of the Insurgents Besides the constant preparations for levys of Men and the necessary preparations for a force of 100000 men which Northangerland declared his intention to raise. This mighty creator of the

Tempest Whenever He appeared in public was met by a roar of exulting Enthusiasm not a whisper dared be heard against him and not a power arose over him This was the shining surface. but within there abode rotteness. Half of his Government. Montmorency Macara. Strafford. and the like were his bitter and deadly foes Every respectable Individual in the city detested him at heart—Fidena with 50000 troops lay within 100 miles of the City Wellington was advancing with has[sic] many more over the western frontier. Ardrah with 20 vessels still hovered about the Niger Mouth and Macterrorglen Gloomy Neutral and Victorious with his 30000 lay close at hand in the East Massena expected exhorbitant remuneration if he should bring over his 30000—and Quashias 20000 and Medinas 10000 were a set of rampant and savage mercenaries. But within Himself it was that the blow fell most stunningly. A mighty press of Buisness overwhelmed him day and night so that his broken constitution utterly unable to bear it was beginning to fail with Sleepless Nights. hideous visions. feverish exhaustion utter loss of appetite and miserable melancholy He was become intolerably capricious so that no one could be with him half an hour without meeting with insult and parting in disgust He was ever tormented with the future. For Zenobia was still apart and irreconciliable. Mary was dying and his peace was broken by the intrigues of Lady Vernon. Lady Georgiana and. his own weak. balancing between them. Above all where was ZAMORNA the mighty the miserable King of Angria! First on the 27 of June this falling Monarch in a desperate attempt [to] meet his foes and dash toward Verdopolis had met a terrific defeat at Edwardston losing 18000 men and forced to fly chased by Macterrorglen. Jordan Massena and Quashia till all his splendid Army was dashed in peices his Generals dispersed and himself flying to Angria was taken alone and exhausted among the Warner Hills. then after detention and brutal insult from Simpson. Northangerland Bought him and had him conveyed to Verdopolis here lay imprisoned the most glorious Man of the Age under the Alternative of the surrender of all his supporters subjects and country or DEATH—But Northangerland was in torment he visited him and pressed him to assent to the Destruction of Angria and in freedom ascend to power with him! Zamorna sternly refused. and Percy his freind his father! had him that night placed in the ROVER under Sdeath who directly set sail to banish him 2000 miles off on the rocks of the Ascension Isle.

On the Evening after this Awful sentence had been put into Execution The Earl was to preside at a grand Entertainment in Elrington Hall. Most of the provisional Government with several Noble Adherents of his faction present Lady Louisa Vernon on the right hand of the Presidential Chair looking triumphantly Beautiful with her Raven curls waving and her wild black eyes flashing in the anticipated fullfilment of all her Hopes for she sat in the place of. the Countess of Northangerland—the Expected Punishment of Zamorna was the subject of conversation (For his actual sentence was yet unknown)

The Earl entered among servants for the Man assumes great state since his late exaltation. (it is in his nature). All eyes were fixed on him He Advanced slowly and rather bent with a face dismally pale and eyes sunk and glittering in their sockets while his rather gay dinner Attire contrasted disagreeably with his Sallow dejected countenance. but a grim cloud rested on his bald brow and he took his seat while the company all stood and the Orchestra struck up in moody silence Louisa spoke but he didnt answer She looked earnestly at him and beheld with suprise a tear quivering in his eye.

"How horridly low the louse looks" muttered Jordan at the bottom of the table to Strafford. who squeaked "He's going—I know—he's going!"

"Well" said Montmorency to Quashia who sat opposite stretching himself and exalting his deep voice that the Earl might hear him

"Well my lad—what was your scheme for the prisoner—Now lets have a good one—you guess mine's hanging by G—d I should like to see his long limbs grace a ropes-end, and then suffer dissection like this Gods head and shoulders—eh Man?"

Quashia was already half drunk. and his tones hardly needed exaltation

"Montmorency mind yourself. I'll not be mocked by you—Have him hung—! Hang yourself. Why Listen and Know what refined vengeance is you theif—I'd have him whole sound and hearty upright on his pins and standing at one end of a table. I'd have what I have had. Yes I'd have him only see what Me and Simpson has been doing Yesterday—no the day before yesterday. a darkish room but enough light to see ill with. a table I say and us beside. it the wind and rain blowing a racket without and not a soul around to care for him. Simpson holding HIM! Yes HIM I say (exalting his voice to a discordant Screech) "Earnest. aye his son his oldest. son. holding him in his arms just as if he were going to baptise him. the preist one Quamina I say. at hand and a bright red Iron in his paws. Whron.[sic] we stand. and here we go. have at it then in goes the Iron first into one eye and then into the other hissing and searing to the brain. off I whips the pitch cap. and we shakes him to the skies. —this is the way my Boys this is the torment!"

So the Demoniacal Black. seized a Handkercheif and wrung it about over his head shaking it with a feindish laugh but. the Earl had been a sullen looking hearkener with a brow clouded by passion. He rose and said.

"O Zamorna Zamorna might not this cup pass from you!"[4]

"From him by Dad Unch. bring him out to make sport for the philistines if we cannot. do the thing over again we'll act it for him and tell him IT IS DONE! Maew maeuw—"

So Quashia went on imitating the crys of a child. But Percy who had sat down again rose

"Gentlemen I see you are all earnest to know what is to be the punishment of Arthur Augustus Adrian Wellesly—He set sail for a voyage to the Ascension Isle at 1 o clock this Morning!"

---

4   Compare Luke 22: 42.

In the stern growl of dissaprobation which burst forth Louisa forgot herself. Springing up she Clasped the Earls hands and cried.

"Oh I'll never forgive you! You wretched Man!"

But his rage was terribly Sour. he threw one fearful squint at her muttering

"You stand on a pinnacle you think. Miss take care you dont fall.!"

And then was turning to Quashia with double threatning in his looks.

Vernons eyes looked too excited for caution in her anger She threw herself recklessly on the feelings of the Moment and was near crying with vexation

"Didnt you promise me his death? Didnt you swear it. I will put no faith in you your a treacherous vacillating man. gone to sea! Oh that I had known it sooner.!"

"Woman" said the Earl turning round "Dont trouble me" And Quashia cried

"At him ye D—l!" while Mont and Jordan with others joined at an insulting laugh over his weakness "Oh" said. Caversham "how the Scamp has diddled him. eh I would'nt be him for two pence"

"Percy" cried Vernon with a face like a pretty fury "you're a fool nor care I who hears it I'll leave you" "Not so said the Earl grasping her arm so that she gave a slight scream but he raised his awe inspiring voice

"Shall I be Baited thus. Madam you do not know yourself. By Heaven you shall pay dearly for this day and listen—Usher send for the Guard and a Carriage!"

"You ordered one and it is waiting my Lord!"

Vernon saw her fate had been predetermined. She was fallen at His Lordships feet in a swoon He raised Her and gave her into the hands of Her Ladies behind her chair while the Guard appeared in the Hall. Then he pointed to them and they escorted her born sensless while He turned from the sight with a convulsive movement of supressed Agony

"Death" he cried "Take Her to the TOWER!"

Now here be noticed an exact characteristic of his mind I am certain these Guards will die if they are not perished now!.

"Is ERNEST FITZARTHUR DEAD THEN?" was his last word for ere he had spoken it he was turned and. going from the room

Dinner seemed broken up. on his departure the Guests broke up into knots and Montmorency Quashia Strafford Carlington Denard and others spread the words "Fool" "half mad! D—n him" and the like in a way that Augured hatred ready any moment to break out in open revolt.

Never did Government stand on more slippery ground with their head nor the head with them!

But Oh tha[t] Fidena could free us from such Tyrant Dominion!

P B B ronte
July 23 1836

———

P B B
Aug 8th
1836

From the treachery and profligacy of the Revolutionary Government in Verdopolis let us turn our eyes for a while to the despairing struggles of Liberty among the Warner Hills

Angria might now be considered subdued under the power of its enimies who indeed showed it by an excerscise of that power in most wanton and cruel barbarity Every town in Zamorna Arundel and the inland parts of Angria was occupied with a French Ashantee Arabian or Northangerlandian Garrison in whose commanding Officers lay supreme powers of life and death to every inhabitant The Blacks ranged unmolested along the Etreia[sic] and Calabar save round the huge fortress of Gazemba where the Lion Enara lurked baffled but still unconquerable. Even upon the Gordon Mountains of Northangerland troops of "Sportsmen" as Simpson brutally termed them roved to shoot or capture the loyal peasantry of their trackless Heaths. Oppression raged most horribly through the Land for 100000 soldiers supported themselves upon the people wantonly wasting and spoiling as well as consuming while the Rapacious Massena exercised all his well known powers of grinding And Simpson And Jordan and Fenton each required and forced his tens of thousands from the life blood of this persecuted people. Vessels also detached from the fugitive Ex premiers Navy were regularly coasting along the shores landing at every favourable spot capturing goods and burning towns till the glittering Bayonets of Northangerland warned them back to the Ocean—While in this state of affairs the Great Dictator of Verdopolis turned his blue eyes toward his Vanquished Sovereigns land. Could not mercy be hoped from the companion of its King the father of its Queen its own former premier? —None! Not for an instant. He never thought of mercy and certainly there was no one to remind him of it But. He saw that it was a most excellent fund from whence to pay his hungry coadjutors and stop their mouths from grumbling and dissappointment So he Arranged for it a vice regal government

RICHARD NAUGHTY   Lord Lieutenant!!!!!!
Lord Macara Lofty   Cheif Secretary
Marshal Massena   Commander in cheif
M J Barrass   Treasurer of the Forces
Quashia Quamina Esqr   Governor of Zamorna
George Caversham Esqr   Governor of Arundel
Robert Patrick Sdeath Esqr   Governor of Angria
As a Grand Provisional Directory!

Than which for that country a more Horrible Government could not possibly be devised Every member of it was filled with a Demoniacal and vindictive Hatred of Angria they were all Brutal and bloody minded men needy too and grasping in disposition while their Head was a Man universally dreaded for his gloomy and revengful ferocity Ardrahs Court Martial was bad enough but this if possible was worse and its components[sic] parts seem selected too as persons who have personal hatred of the Fallen King Adrian which stamps the conduct. of Northangerland with a disgusting and hipocritical Malevolence for which his Mighty Exile can never forgive him

Well upon the First of August 1836 this New Government made a grand public Entry into Zamorna surrounded by an awful display of Military Force but proceeding through streets otherwise as desert[ed] as the grave—But let me transcribe Charles Wentworths Discription of that Entry—Since he accompanied them as Loftys Private Secretary

"After the Directory[5] had finished a long interview with the Lord President at the Palace in Elrington Square they formed in their carriages each one being drawn by Six white Horses with the Mocking Emblems of Peace and Liberty Sir Joseph Fenton with 2 French Regiments of Cavalry drawn up around them as a Guard of honour to the borders of the Kingdom We proceeded slowly through the city among immense crowds of Applauding spectators with the bells ringing troops presenting and cannon firing as in duty bound to the Redeemers of an oppressed nation But at last beyond Waterloo Palace where was stationed the last dense Multitude the City began to ebb away and the open country to appear (the First green feilds which I have beheld for a weary while) Ere I would have kept the carriage window open to look out. but His Lordship the secretary with whom I sat hastily ordered me to close it upon coming abreast of a large clump of trees beside the road and When We reached the frontier post of Angria He Muttered something about. "Extreme danger in these unsettled districts"— Squeezing himself into one corner of the Carriage and wrapping himself more closly in his cloak. I saw he was mortally afraid and Indeed the paleness of his face and his startled glance whenever he heard a distant gun go off. or any unusual sound from afar would not if he strove allow him to conceal it. —So I with his permission pretending faintness from close confinment Got out upon Horseback and gazed upon this Unhappy Land

It was a couple of miles in advance of Edwardston that I first beheld it and I may say that there my blood curdled with horror and indignation at the sight. We were driving at a rapid rate past. Edwardston Park. but the fences on the road side were gone soldiers in undress jackets cutting down the trees for sale and as a wide opening in the demolished woods gave an opportunity I beheld within the broad lawns torn up and covered with Cavalry Horses the stacks of. lopped trunks and branches piled over the paths and the huge unsightly Redoubt stretching its hideous mass. before the Great House statly and Aristocratic still though shattered by Balls and shadowed by the Red Flag of Liberty downward in the woods the smoke rose from the trees burning for charcoal and as it faded for a while hunderds of Barked and branchless poles whitned the groves of what should have been summer green Such a terrible system of ravenous devastation impressed me with the darkest gloom and depression of spirits but as yet I had beheld only the begginning of horrors—We hurried as fast as the cavalry could

---

follow Through Edwardston the young flourishing town of Edwardston Where had passed all the fury of the Battle of the 26 of June. Shattered to peices were half its houses showing the plastered or papered walls within Roof trees laths and lime mingled on the floors with streets encumbered by rubbish and torn up by cannon balls No Inhabitants were seen save a few wretches who had sworn fidelity to the new order of things and these were skulking about as if afraid of their own shadows. But the DEAD were to be seen! —Yes with horror I speak it When we had left the town All the March seemed strewed with dark. objects— the horribly putrefying carcasses of the Brave Angrians left by the commands of the Demon Simpson as he said to be an example—and now corrupting the whole air with their stench so that on this hot day the horses feeding on these Meadows half worried by the legions of flies that eat the Bodies were plunging and gallopping about over the horrid scene The river presented the same scene as underneath the Bridge we passed over a hideous mass lay. covering the water round with the many coloured oily matter of Decay! Such a relation I know is disgusting but I want to give an idea of the Horrors of Angria which we beheld more darkly developed the near[er] we approached the end of our journey— Nobody was to be seen but Soldiers. none haymaking in the feilds or marketing in the villages but at Ashfeild[6] a line of Twenty Gibbets supporting the rotten remains of martyred Patriots beyond we came past a troop of Africans conveying to Zamorna 50 prisoners from the south half clad. jaded and ready to drop with thirst these Gallant fellows were urged along by their brutal captors and Oh how I felt my cheek burn to see white men thus tormented by those half beastly Blacks but when I reflected that it was their fellow Whites who urged it on and approved of it that glow was changed into a blush for Human nature. I looked to see if my Superiors had any better feelings but in vain for they were jeering to each other on the fallen King and Kingdom As for the Prince Quashia I felt a sort of respect for him he at least had a right to laugh for with what contempt must he have thought upon his tools the Whites!

At Stavley[7] within a mile of Zamorna we came upon the commencement of a line of soldiers drawn forth to welcome our arrival in the city and which continued along the road in two ranks between which we passed to the very centre of the town. I computed there must have been 20000 men French Southerns and Ashantees. with their Bands all playing at Intervals and their Bayonets flashing in the air a Most warlike and noble spectacle considered in itself. But one which filled me with even contempt at the utter hop[e]lessness of the condition of Angria

The camp lay upon our left as we went along tremendously fortified with trenches Redoubts and masked or open Batteries showing a grinning front of Cannon both toward Zamorna the country and the Road. while on our right flanking the River we could perceive another long mound of works commanding

---

6   There are two Ashfields, one in Scotland and one in Suffolk.
7   Staveley is just north of Knaresborough in North Yorkshire.

the Olyimpian[sic] and the Meadows crowded with Cavalry and Baggage Horses of the Army this Warlike spectacle increased in grandeur as we filed up the Great Street of Zamorna but Alas for the Second City in this ruined Empire. How are the Mighty Fallen[8] Houses riddled with shot windows broken along twenty fronts at a time Interiors beheld naked of furniture and Owners. forsaken shops deserted streets these were the fillings up of the gloomy picture A crowd of Northangerlandians or Southerners being the only beings discoverable besides the Scarlet Soldiers We came upon the Central Market Square where all the Executions take place. and we beheld a hideous Shambles The Gallows. Macterrorglens favorite. rearing its dol[e]ful form above platforms and pens to keep the prisoners in there were indeed 10 Gallows and as usual a Human Corpse upon each And I caught in one place a crowd round a man whom the soldiers were lashing and in another four blacks bearing off a great crate with something bloody within while several soldiers were washing the pavement in the centre from clotted gore. Opposite two[sic] was the Sessions house where Simpson cries and sentences his victims and beyond that a great Hotel Girt by many hundred Cavalry and bearing the Yellow Banner of Reform above its Roof.

This was the Monsters den and here we were to alight. the Soldiers first forming a long row on each side and reining back their Horses in to a wide lane for our passage I stood on the Inn steps Beholding all round a Swelling sea of Plumes and Sabres and Bayonets with bloodred Flags waving to the Deafning Music of Kettle drums and Trumpets—No joyful populace no crowds of enthusiastic people all a warlike and Military show as if I had stood in an entrenched camp within an enemys country and not in the heart of flourishing young City Zamorna

I followed my superiors where they were led still among files of Red Coats into an Ante Room filled with Officers and from thence to the Audience Chamber of the General Himself.

So far Mr Wentworth but now to pass forward—This New Government Installed itself directly and a proclamation emanating no doubt from Elrington Hall. was issued the morning after their arrival Declaring the Intention and Determination of the Provisional Government of Verdopolis to Consider Angria as part and parcel of the new Grand Confederate Republican Union into whose ranks it invited every other Nation to come Telling the People of Angria that all they have to do is to come before the Military Authoritys of any town or station take the oath of Alleigance to the Provisional Government and enter themselves as A Citizen of Africa while all who neglected doing this All who appeared in arms against the Republic were sentenced to Instant death the moment they could be lighted on An immense List of proscriptions followed with rewards for capture alive or dead and a conclusion promising all the blessings of freedom and prosperity to the just enlightened world It was signed with the ominous name of RICHARD NA[U]GHTEN. Lord Lieutenant

---

8   See II Samuel 1:19 and 25.

Naughten is not a man of many words he is much fonder of acting than of speaking so he directly followed up this Manifesto with all possible promptitude Rest was denied to the Soldiers day or night they were up harrying capturing shooting and plundering through all the country every gallows was had in requisition every arcre[sic] of property was confiscated and every grain of corn or farthing of money was torn from the hand of a people already on the brink of Starvation till at length Slavery became to dreadful to be born and Insurrections and night attacks and revolts and suprises became more frequent than has been known Since the Storm of Adrianopolis

All this was vain a yet more terrible struggle was preparing for the unhappy land The Duke of Fidena was preparing at Freetown to throw 30000 troops upon the frontiers of Arundel. Warner among his native mountains was determined to cooperate with him So Northangerland Issued orders for the preparation of an overwelming Armament wherewith to crush at once Both these his deadly enimies

P B B
Sept 3
1836

I know not how it is but somehow during the whole course of my Former writing I have felt as if the Spirit and importance of my subject while it constantly increascd before me was as surely diminished on my pages till at last in the most momentous crisis it has withered intirly away I have mighty things now to tell but I am unable to speak.

But   Wide oer the warlike world hovers my mind

           To all its doings dead and cold and blind[9]

So that either I must fairly give up the pen or only while I am training for exertion employ it on a theme private confined and therefore light enough for my miserabley[sic] diminished strength So leaving the Awful excitement and mighty preparations of Verdopolis let us enter a little into the immediate ongoings in its Nucleus—Elrington Hall.

St Michaels Bell had just finished tolling twelve and though the principal Wing of the Palatial Building still blazed and sounded with the Whirl and brightness of Lordly dissipiation the Apartment now open to my minds eye was utterly silent and solitary Vast like all the gorgeous Rooms around it and lighted with one great Constellation of lights from the noble Lustre in its centre but the Aimless shining with no one to profit by it the luxuriant couches which spread themselves without an occupant the fires glowing for themselves and by themselves the far off din of Music and dancing that seemed to mock that Soundless Organ and unechoing ceiling produced so Solemn and melancholy a Solitude that not the then midnight Aisles of St Michaels could more have

---

9   These lines are likely Branwell's.

struck into the Mind This room was one of a Suite of Galleries And only seperated from the Grand Staircase by another so that the ceasless steps of Laqueys[sic] or Visitors ascending and descending there Sounded here with out intermission in a deep distant thunder reverberated from the enormous Central Dome Carriages arriving and drawing up without gave a similar sound and the Wind blending all together produced what I can only call a most wonderful and glorious tone

I call this great Room solitary though there came one person into it A Statly and beautiful Lady in full dress and retired as it seemed from the Dazzling confusion of the Grand Ball going on in the Eastern Wing. the folding Doors were closed Silent[l]y behind her and she looked as if expecting to meet with one who was not there. but this almost Sublime situation began to arrest her attention So she did not pass through to the other door but stopped under the Lustre with a smile at the contrast to the Gorgeous revelry she had left—There was something in this Ladys fair hair and luxuriant figure which told she was one more disposed for smiles than sighing but she could not help one heaving of the Bosom when turning toward the fire she looking up beheld on a sudden that Glorious Bust upon the Great Marble Mantel peice itself of White Marble and crowning the Classic pile of Sculpture far above her head but looking down on her with Sight[l]ess orbs that yet seemed to penetrate her very soul Who could see those Divine Features and the neck so regally set upon its snowy Shoulders and not feel within their souls it was the Eidolon[10] of The Mortal Phebus the Mighty Sun just set in such coming Clouds and Darkness. Lady Georgiana gazing up could not repress the involuntary aspiration "ZAMORNA" but started at the echoe of that. proscribed and forgotten name! —She looked at his Image till the Haughty inspired Brow seemed to contract in a melancholy frown and she felt as if she could look no more His Smile looked ominous first of the clouds ungathered when it was chiselled but at last she feared the lips would part in reproachful scorn at her So she turned round in undefined apprehension to mark the bright but lonly room it was open every where for her view save where the vast Mass of Curtains fell before the Cheif embayed Window so passing across the carpet she parted these in she knew not what sort of apprehension but then the view without arrested her a midnight Stretch of Verdopolis darkly visible in Starlight with the faint halos of a yet unrisen moon behind a Black Front of Building towering far off above the rest. —Wellesly House in Victoria Square! —No lights in those Windows now but gloomy as in Mourning for its Departed King! —Turning again with a mind yet fuller of him who is now as if he never had been (to the world at least for unnoticed there still survive hearts that mean to bleed for him) the exquisite taste of the Decorations and peices of art about her only suggested the idea were these things dictated by Zamorna? was all this the work of his varying genius which stooped or rose with unconcern because either in Ornamenting a House or a kingdom it was still doing the will of ADRIAN. And has he not been present here too has not his own Noble form stood face to

---

10 A phantom, apparition, or image.

face with that white Sculpture. the cold and lif[e]less shadow of the warm living and moving Divinity? —"Well!" she exclaimed "How Mad how frantically mad for the Man beneath whose roof I am to conspire against and join in overthrowing that glorious Being his King and freind and Son! —Would I have done this? could I have sent coldly and deliberatly sane into perpetual Exile a thousand miles over the Sea in anguish too and despair the only one and the one with whom to me to live and die would be a paradise beyond which I should ask for nothing—nothing more! —Now if I—but I must not say it the hope is Chimerical—though I wonder where Percy has gone—"

Georgiana turned as if to go but lingered still in the room sitting down again with her elbow leaned on a black Cabinet and with the white Fingers unconsciously moved in time to the Far Distant Ball room—Strains of Webers last Waltz[11] that rose and fell in measured cadence with an effect that doubly solemnized the melancholy sweetness. of this effusion of a Dying Swan—Music in so Vast a House sounds indefinate and Aerial for among a multitude of grand apartments its source can not be fixed on and accordingly it increased the present tone of this Lady's good natured and sensitive mind

"Well" she said again "if I could gain his recall I should bring a sun again in the world. but my Lord is so miserably impracticable I cannot tell what to do with him and that little witch Vernon with her ungovernable insolence will thwart me so—besides the Demons Montmorency Quashia Macara Jordan! Oh I shall never suceed—However I WILL try! So where is Percy!"

A Picture Gallery lead from this Room to the Lord Presidents Library and through it she hurried with a springing step and a bright cheerful look which one would have mistaken for Joy when it was only the general effect of her handsome dashing features and well developed form yet she was almost laughing at her own concern and earnestness when she opened the Library Doors—A Goodly Noble room and richly lighted but with some one at a Desk by the fire who had sunk forward from his chair till his face was buried on that Desk in his Folded Arms—and to him she ran.

Well! my Lord—fairly tired out! —but you are soon asleep though!"

A Slight yet convulsive shudder which seemed to pass through Northangerlands frame with the sigh that followed as if extorted by bodily pain told her that his Lordship was not slumbering though farther than this he neither moved or noticed her

"Now Percy dont give yourself up so too melancholy. raise your head and come now—be cheerful Ill give you a song and it shall be "drive Dull Care away!"[12] For in spite of all their intriguing and treachery. I'm sure you have a freind—at least one—left and she'll be sad my Lord when you're not merry! —let me see the light of your countenance—and hide not thy face from me O—but

---

[11] Likely a reference to Carl Maria von Weber's *Invitation to the Dance*, 1819.

[12] Probably a reference to the seventeenth-century air, "Begone dull care"; the final line of the second stanza reads "To drive dull care away."

this wont do its flat blasphemy to address in such terms a sensless statue for this can be no other—its as still as one—and as cold as one—and a good deal less pleasing than at least one that I have been looking at—Rouse thyself Man! ZAMORNA'S in Exile! —"

The last words only had effect in Georgianas musical awakening for Percy hastily rose from his reclining posture presenting a startling aspect of mental agony with tears on his hollow cheeks and more fast gathering in his eyes While his fine expansive forehead and trembling lips were both of the same deathly paleness—an Oath burst from his tongue with a hasty "Begone" But Georgiana was not so to be scared when she saw him in such despair She stood opposite almost frightened with parted lips and dovelike eyes fixed on the Earl and glistening at the appalling spectacle of Northangerland forced into real bitter tears

"What's the matter!" she exclaimed hysterically— "What—has anything happened? —Are you ill my Lord?"

"Ill! ha ha. —Georgiana. You've hit it. By Heaven I <u>am</u> Ill. DEATHS the matter—"

"What do yo[u] mean? —My Lord!"—

"Why look you there!"

He pointed to a letter and Lady Greville took it. reading till she cried. —"Is she dying then!"

"Aye as sure as you're living!"

"And to night you're called away!"

"And to morrow she is called away! —Oh this is horrible coming on me now! Myself just going to head Armies against My Kings existence. My Daughter going to die. for this and with a bitter horror of me. Arthur gone in to eternal exile The—My FRIENDS. —I <u>know</u> just plotting <u>My</u> Death. and so I must finish a cursed cursed life—! —What dye want with me Woman what am I that you should follow me here—Something so preminently Glorious and beatific that my face is life and paradise to your heart? —You'll do no good here!"

"Now dont speak so Percy! there's no body in this House cares a pin for you but me. and all the rest who care for you are gone—all gone. —Oh I'de give up my own prospects every one—to give you what you've lost. —My Lord. now do just hear me. Oh call back. Zamorna! She'd live then I'm sure she'd recover. and HE whould drive away your <u>Freinds</u>—he'd drive them into hell! —Yes! theres no one in this palace but ought to go there and will go there— they are a pack of heartless ferocious Demons already—Oh how I wish Zamorna were here! How his Noble Countenance would Shrivel there Frenchified hearts together and send with one glance of his eye the drunken beast Quashia and the Jaded Idler Jordan and the cowering Atheist Macara and the Wolfish hearted Montmorency down to the only place there fit for. and then Mary would revive to life and happiness directly. and you would be yourself again and I. why I suppose you would forget me because your Countess must come back—well she ought to—but its a bitter thought! —Percy do you hear? —"

"Georgiana I DO NOT! —No my Girl Wheres my Power and my Schemes and my Vengeance? —"

"They! They're nowhere. Your under the feet of your <u>Freinds</u>!"

"Aye—And I am far far above there heads. but stuff this is raving I am ready to shoot myself! —Georgiana Good night I must set off for Alnwick. —And then the—Funeral!"

The last sentence was hardly audible for with its horrid reminiscences. Percys very soul sickened and he became as white as ashes Georgiana running to him lest he should have fallen from the Sopha but he had not lost recollection so taking her hand with a wan smile he said

"You're a generous Girl Greville—you dont get your due from me—yet I cant forget you for these looks are not very common before me now adays—the feirce eyes and stamping of feet and fits of crying from one woman and whining and c[r]oaking and fawning from another and sickening coquettry from a third. and Squinting and staring and sneering and swearing from my Masculine supporters—Curse them! —Georgiana Good night!"

Clasping Lady Greville in his arms with a long parting Kiss he impressed this Farewell and She in tears with a beating Heart could hardly leave his embrace So as the momentary rapture left him and the Angrian of his heart returned on a sudden again he left her on the sofa and hurried abruptly from the room

P B B
Sept. 19
1836

At the same period in the night after that one last mentioned the Lord Presidents Carriage was driving swiftly over a smoothened road in the doubled darkness of a mighty grove. fourscore miles away from Verdopolis and still farther increasing his distance from a scene where his presence was the sole stay which held together his Schemes and his Power But though those to whom these were for a time Intrusted were just the men who most thouroughly[sic] hated him though the measures they would pursue were for the destruction of the only few who cared for him though Kingdoms were gathering in arms to overthrow him and enemies directed those who should support him Still the Earl of Northangerland seated alone in his chariot could forget all these forebodings of disaster for miseries which lay still nearer to his heart

The Night now far advanced was very dark and gusty so that the Huge trees over the road though nearly unseen groaned and swung without ceasing and an Autumn rain drifted past beating down the decaying leaves and shaking the Carriage Windows with a fitfull struggling till the Horses were Stopped near a lighted window and Percy called out impatiently

"Drive on ye D—ls!"

The coachman muttered to the porter for they were now at Alnwick Park gates

"God you neednt stare to see the nags smoke so for His Lordships has been cursing em all the road and I'm done if Ive eat or drunk to day—"

But the imperious voice again broke in with the command to hasten so the Servant flung open the gates and the Horses burst forwards but as the great Iron leaves flew back again to their places Percy heard their clash and started to think himself so near the House of Death though his pale lips compressed themselves directly and he folded his arms in stern resignation to await what in a few minutes occurred, The termination of his journey where he alighted in the dark night and beneath a gloomy front of [a] building among shining lamps and respectful crowds of Servants at hand but unnoticed for the tall statly figure enveloped in a black cloak with hat drawn sternly over his brow passed hastily through the lane preceded by Shaver and Steaton to the great interior staircase and hence into a Noble room where his Valet took the hat and cloak from his passive Master who then kept pacing the length and breadth of the apartment lost in thought and giving no directions to either of his Servants till at last he said abruptly—

"Is She alive?"

Shaver was too experien[c]ed in his Lords temper to dare to answer in words upon such a subject but bowed in silence Northangerland said again

"Who are here?"

Hesitation in the reply would at that moment have been a dissmisal so the Valet replied

"The Bishop of Hylle with Sir Ashton Cowper[13] and a consultation"

A withering and bitter "Faugh!" was the only acknowledgement of this intelligence in a while again he turned from them gloomily so they both directly left the room and he shortly went out by another Door through a lonly lighted gallery and to a solitary Marble Stair covered with thick matting unlighted and opening with a window upon the Midnight Skies which of all he had seen seemed alone to possess power over his attention for he stopped at the Balustrade resting his head on his hand in sight of the great tree tops now on a level with his eye and swaying darkly round the building as far as woods that mingled unseen with the rainy night which at last was abating into clouds flying across open spaces of starlight and toward the horizon over a Sky silvered by a Struggling Moon this lonly crescent driving through the Clouds at times showing her golden bow in a clear calm feild of air and then as soon obscured in the wild gusty shadows of the storm was quickly and dreamily associated in Percys singular mind with the end of his dying daughter he first watched the midnight rack into which it had dived and then saw it come quickly out till it stopped in that pure pearly grey there was nothing weak in this tendency of his mind it was just that he was struck with this swallowing in the clouds as a shadow of the burial in the grave and when the glorious orb came forth into the

---

13 Sir Astley Cooper was a noted surgeon, and the Duke of Wellington's neurobiologist. See Alexander EW, 46-47.

sky it looked to him like a Soul escaping from earth to heaven but as this idea belonged not to his creed it would not have lasted unless he had kept looking on what had caused it and it was so much too fair to perish that he still kept gazing through the Gothic Window at that bright bow as if the Soul of Mary and those clouds as the shadows of death in a while the Shadows accumulated faster the half hour of fair weather which had intermitted was over and the Moon was lost the darkness returned rain once more began to beat against the windows and Northangerland turned away as if a voice had said that as this storm had come so death should be with not an enterance into paradise but an ob[struc]tion of dark and eternal clouds—he turned and found all dark about him without a sound to break the Silence his own footsteps muffled by the Matting and his heart oppressed with the consciousness that this was the unnatural hush kept round a sick bed to lull and sooth the Dying The Duchess lay in this wing of the Building and Percy proceeding up the Stair came in a while to an Ante room where in silence as still as death several Ladies Her Attendants sat to be within call Here too was Lady Helen Percy who met her Son in silence for she knew so well what sorrow had been his lot that now to behold him raised up so many dreary recollections that she could not speak But he said

"You are aware I suppose that I cannot be now what I used to be—that I shall bear the approaching event without any very great display of sorrow it has not taken me unawares I could expect no other—Its all the same tale—all alike—all alike! —Your letter gives me to understand that—that—" he hesitated here and gave a restless gloomy glance at the attendants So Lady Helen knowing how little he liked any unconcerned persons to be a wittness[sic] to any expression of emotion on his part for indeed he is most singularly sensitive on this head signed for them to leave the room. when they were alone he continued

"You told me Mary could not live more than a day or two did you not—?"

"Now not more than an hour or two!"

Such a word was evidently a shock to the Earl he could not turn paler but he looked feircer as if to resent the stab But Lady Helen continued

"It is useless Alexander I know I speak severly but this Night must conclude the scene—you ought to know it and so I do not shrink from telling you of it"

"O mother" he said agonisedly "I have too too much to bear! —Despair without and within for do you know"—he went on with a harsher expression and bitterer tone— "I'm plotted against just now so that there can be no time for me to wittness the funeral of my child. I must back in a day. from Her deathbed to the feild of war—it is more than I can endure Can you tell me what to do? When I DO get back I shall see the City in a Hell and if I stay to the—funeral— Jeremiah Simpson must be my Judge on returning. I shall follow Mary soon enough—Has she spoken of me mother? would she recognise me?

"She has not Alexander!"

"And if her dying prayer be for—But I must be silent I can say Nothing on that head. She has spoken of <u>Him</u>?"

"Not one word for weeks!"
"Well Lead me in"

Percy <u>was</u> changed now from the man he had been once before As he neared the place where the flower of his hopes was dying no Stronger expression of agony no faltering step or altered voice betrayed an increase of mental despair But he stalked along tall thin sallow and gloomy with saturnine eyes and brow and hollow Whiskered cheeks in acid silence but with perfect self possession though as he muttered to himself when the Door was opening to admit him to the Chamber of Death. "It was like going into Hell!"

She who was Queen of Angria and Wife of Zamorna and Daughter of Northangerland. thus the owner of the three highest titles this World could bestow whose name had been Formost in the first rank of every thing bright and beautiful who two short years ago. appeared before our delighted eyes in such loveliness and splendour as if <u>She</u> were the real rising Sun or who though her glorious Husband rather claimed that distinction did to every one appear being His and Angria's Queen in that dayspring of hope and promise our one Bright MORNING STAR! —She was now—truely the same mortal being but except [for] personal identity—in What was she the same? —The Queen of Angria was exiled and throneless Her Kingdom the vast gory death bed of its people The Wife of Zamorna was divorced and discarded her Husband lying 2000 miles off a freindless and hopeless Exile the Daughter of Northangerland the young and lovely Mary Percy was laid in this Room wasted to a Shadow and just going to DIE! —When first I introduced to my Readers the name of Mary Henrietta Percy. it was to describe her. now three years ago as a beautiful Imaginative and cheerful hearted Girl walking with her Dog in a bright Autumn Evening among the glorious groves of Percy Hall far off in the West her own Dear Native Land![14] That was a Vision of brightness which crossed my own eyes but whose passing beauty I could not describe to another yet it was not long before my readers saw her too in a vast and dazzling ring of Splendour beneath the Mighty Dome of St Michaels before its High Altar and by the side of her countrys Glory KING ADRIAN'S chosen Bride! We all know the revolutions which have passed since then wherein one placed apparently so far above all the chances and changes of Fate has undergone more and more awful vicissitudes than ever fell to the lot of a Peasant Girl the Queen of Angria though risen in morning like the star I have compared her to was destined to dissapear before day Her Fathers cursed and infatuated conduct had alienated and enraged His King and He when opposed as he was in heart and feelings never hesitates on measures of retaliating vengeance if Percy strives farther Mary is to be forsaken—Percy heeded not the threat so when war came on Angria and while Zamorna was fighting for his life the Fiat of Vengeance passed and the Duchess was Queen and Wife no longer but banished to Alnwick She heard sucessivly of Adrians struggles and fall and capture and imprisonment and Exile through which not even the same wide land must hold

---

[14] See vol. I, pp. 336-38.

them any more that last act too was her fathers and such a blow from his hand she knew not how to bear. But indeed Mary never troubled herself with <u>Trying</u> to bear sorrow for she had neither Patience Nor resignation there never was a being more intirely of feeling and more utterly destitute of the sterner qualities of the mind. Her good and her bad qualities sprung from this single source—Through it she was warm hearted cheerful strong in affection and most earnest and ardent in Love by it nothing her father could do could shake her affection till he drew his sword against Zamorna who by it too was so much the one all sufficient Deity and Heaven of her heart that everything was nothing beside him and he was all in this world and the next to her.

This chamber of death was opened now in all its dreary Magnificence Lofty and Airy but hung and festooned with velvet so dark as to seem shadowy in despite of the softly shining silver Lamps that glistened from their white marble pedestals and centered their radiance on the Bed where lay the Shadow rather than the substance of the forsaken Wife and crownless Queen over her the Vast festoons of Drapery hung from the Coronetted Tester as if even they were mourning and on each side of her sat silently a fair young watcher in White whose dark western eyes and blooming figure contrasted strongly with that shrine of a departing spirit. upon a sopha retired into shadow the Venerable Prelate Dr Duncombe[15] and Sir Ashton sat as if their prescence and assistance was us[e]ful no longer and wanted no more but still lingering as unwilling to leave to the Destroyer a victim so young and fair But above these and right opposite Marys Eyes a wide and lofty Arch opened sublimly to the Sky its Curtains were drawn aside to display the full extent of [a] waste midnight Heaven and sad struggling Moon Trees waved too beneath this window which looked toward the South west where every thought every feeling of her Soul were hovering round the Ascension Isle What was she like for such things as I have hitherto mentioned were only auxiliarys in the picture Here was the principal figure Cold white and wasted supported by a pile of pillows with attenuated hands clasped and glassy eyes fixed in unutterable anguish All the once rich auburn curls were fallen back and parted in long locks from her brow which with her cheeks and lips was stricken with the glistening light of death—This was not like the death bed of her Mother there was no mingling of Heaven with earth nothing of that Angelic hope of glory that real triumph over death This was the end of a Child of earth all whose Soul and spirit were rooted in earth and perishing on being torn away from it Her thoughts were expressed plainly by her a day or two before this time

—It does not matter where I am going I know I <u>am</u> going and I know <u>from whom</u> I am going—

---

15 Branwell may have taken the name from Thomas Slingsby Duncome (1796-1861), aide-de-camp to General Ferguson, elected whig M.P. for Hertford in 1823, and as a radical for Finsbury in 1834.

Death in such a state is more terrible than any anticipations of the future can be

Into this Room then came Lord Northangerland preceeded by Lady Helen who walked and looked as if she was struck with awe for the unutterable miserys of her Son the Hand of providence itself seemed laying such burdens upon him and she stood aside as if from something consecrated to sorrows when he walked past stern and grimly with clenched teeth suppressing every visible sign of the Anguish tha[t] worked within yet it was only on a sudden and visibly by an effort that he could force himself to look at Mary and certainly then the frightfulness of the change from the lovely and adored creature he had seen her last was such as to send in a moment the blood to his heart and the drops to his brow Still he said nothing except that as he stopped at the Bedside he muttered to Lady Helen "Mother send all out—" and when every one save her had left the room he seated himself on the vacant chair of a Watcher unable for a while to speak another word

Now Mary though dying was perfectly sensible and when after an ineffectual glance at those departing from the room whose stifled footsteps had roused her from abstraction she turned herself away to die amid her own miseries Her unsettled eyes caught the figure by the bed expressionless for an instant till Identity flashed on them and then her frame shuddered all over with an emotion which no words could describe thousands of things rushed to her heart on that look till she bowed her head to the pillow as if her feelings were too vivid to be born As for Percy when he looked at the wan cheek and white wasted Neck averted from him with the Arm cast back as if to motion him away when he dwelt on the sad faded figure of his dearest Child the iron entered his heart and a frown of trouble gathered more darkly over his brow. He strove to disipate it he tried to suppress it but the hot burning came on his eyes and he felt himself losing command of his features so he buried his face in his handkercheif while the disengaged hand took her Slender fingers tremblingly in his own But that grasp was electric that appeal was resistless turning at once with a single glance from the hand to the hidden Face a flood of tears sprung to her eyes and she stretched to clasp him crying "Father! Father!" Here the wild warm Spirit threw all its enthusiastic affectionate feelings into one word and action with a passion which hardly left strength for more but more did come for the spell was lo[o]sed and she burst forth with a plaintive wildness

"Oh you're come at last—when I thought all had left me I thought I should never see you again but I see you and feel you now!

Speak father for I am miserable and I cannot bear to Die! Oh If you knew what I have suffered If you could feel what I feel you would have come to me sooner you would not have left me so Let me see your face I must not see it long Let me hear you and that will bring back for a moment things and times that I never never shall know again.! —Oh father they have talked to me about Heaven they have been either trying to fit me for it or to pacify me with it But they know nothing or else they would think their. very souls well spent to buy back what I am going to lose for ever—and now you've come still in vain father!

its horrible to think your coming is all all in vain.! —Then must I relinquish must I at last give up the things—the—Oh I cannot I cannot let them go!

I do beleive in Heaven I know there is a God—But He has made me as I am and so I will not call it possible to part from where my heart is for the things I never knew though they be eternal and divine—I dont care how wicked how sinful be the thought I dont care what the world may call me but I dare not I cannot. I have not the power to die!

And this is what I feel though I know I am dying! —though there's no body and nothing to look to for an hour of hope though I shall never see that night change to morning or see sunshine in this room again!"

She could speak no more for a while but lay earnestly gazing at her fathers well known face then saying

"Oh I have looked up to that face with love ever since I could notice any thing but I did not know that he was to kill me who gave me life! I Never thought this blow should come from my Noble Father—but I cannot hate you father when I am gone. remember that I could never hate you!—"

From her fathers face her eyes wandered to the great window fixing a long dreamy gaze on the Glorious Gusty Skies! I call them glorious for that over cast and changing wrack of clouds with its drear melancholy winds spoke too thrillingly of times departed to be called any thing but almost insupportably divine! Not a blast that blew but called forth Angria! her country Angria the rain had the very beating sound. of that which when long since in her fathers Mighty palace she a bright and beautiful Girl heard. while thinking of the wars and tempests that then were raging round her Mighty Father and her future Lord. Often while Queen of Angria at the window of her Regal room she had sat looking out over the Calabar catching such gusts as these and thinking of the wondrous changes which made her her Noble Adrians Bride often she had been roused from such dreams by the embrace of him whom she adored and then with what a thrill she used to note the wild flash that brightened his eyes as he found what she was dreaming on and would for a moment himself lend to the dream— Now these long moaning Sighs came from a land of chains and graves from roofless halls and hous[e]less people now too. it swept over a desert of trackless Ocean from the rock bound coast that exiled Angrias King Only one of all she had held dear in life remained unwrecked and near her that one was the ruin of all and now bowed with anguish by her side—These were the things that filled her heart to bursting while she lay with unearthly eyes fronting that Stormy Sky—! As a yet drearyer Gust swept the midnight woods of Alnwick. she wildly cried

"O ADRIAN ADRIAN! Would to God you were here! Oh might I see you might I but see you before I die To hear that glorious voice to hear him speak One word to know that he did think of me that he did love me to know it from his darkned eyes and clasping hand—to know to feel that would be Heaven it would be paradise! —But to be parted. divorced. forgotten to be thousands of miles away to be severed—to be parted for EVER. is horrible and more than I know how to bear! —Father" she then said turning her face toward Percy—

"Father It was you who exiled him Remember theres none to aid him now[16] Remember he is aidless <and> hopeless So glorious a mind and so utterly so wholly given to despair! Oh can you Dare you WILL you destroy him in life [raise] up your hand for another stroke against him Will you henceforth as hitherto hunt his noble freinds from Hill to hill and wilderness to wilderness. thinned at each step and on every Altar leaving in sacrifice for their country some Patriot life—What are their wretched Destroyers to them What are they to you— your darkest deadliest Enimies are engaged in this work because while engaged they know they are exterminating the followers of your Great Your Only friend Oh My Father My Father. Ardrian[sic] Is your freind and you never had one but him! He is ruined now by you his people are ruined his Country is ruined I am ruined All All of his name and in his following are falling to ruin and Death finds all his employment in devouring them. For not I alone now die here for My Adrian but. hundreds nay thousands this night are dying for him in a far wilder scene and in more agonizing pain My Glorious Country can answer for this covered with blood the death bed and the grave of her sons—Father—what will yo[u] do with Angria?—"

"Mary—" he answered gloomily—" I may not long be able to do anything to Angria—"

"And oh will you still hunt the life of your King will you still seek to ruin Adrian—"

As she spoke she raised herself for a moment on one arm looking in the Earls face with an intense eagerness but not one ray of hope beamed from his stern troubled countenance and closing her dark eyes with faintness she sank back exhausted in silence As for him he could give no hope and therefore could say nothing to comfort so that this dead stillness became miserably painful A sign from Lady Helen seeming almost a releif to such blank despair the tick of the Timepeice began to intrude with unusual distinctness and this perhaps caught by Marys ear reminded her of the short short period now allotted to her in this world for looking to the face on which the hour hand stood between 12 and 1. she sobbed audibly with tears following from her eyes now turned again from the Earl to the Dark Autumn Sky

Now this utter silence on the Earls part is not [to] be wondered at for literaly he could say nothing He believed that his Daughter was passing from existence into Annihilation therefore he could not speak one word of hope for eternity and As his Schemes had put all aid of Zamorna utterly out of his power he could as little hold out a hope for time then he was sick at heart with despair himself so there was nothing wherwith[sic] to mitigate her awful despair and himself silent and her silent he sat in restless agony thinking each moment that ticked was bringing Death closer and yet nothing would rise that could give even a seeming of hope or relief there was a weight upon him as in a Nightmare and he felt as if he could never speak again The face upon which his eyes were fixed

---

16 The following section consists of the two pages, 11.2x18.5 cm., at the BPM: Bon 145.

was itself an index to the near approach of Death for a glistning <pale>ness had overcome the Ivory features and a Shadow as if it were that of the King of Terrors began to darken the eyes and brow those eyes wandered over the scene from the Opened Arch with a gloomy suffusion of Tears changing their expression alternatly and with wonderful vividness from ardent Enthusiastic Love to bitter trouble or biting blasting despair. What a heart must she have had to retain in this last moment of bodily pain or torpor such a warm extatic[sic] strain of mind and what passionate feelings were hers thus on the terrible brink of Eternity even when dashed and falling over never for an instant to turn her thoughts from the things and the beings she was parting with in Time it was no stupid insensibility no sordid meanness it was the thrilling intensity of Soul she inherited from the Mighty Man beside her which was the origin of all her defects and excellencys by which she both neglected so willfully and loved so well It was owing to this character that when before the Earl arrived she had taken farewell of her childern though she so wildly embraced and wept over them it was more by far through the ideas their dark eyes and curling locks brought of their Glorious father than from the warmth of a Mothers love to them this may sound unpleasant but its true the little wild dark bright complexioned beings were not so much present as the soul engrossing vision of him from whom they lived and for whom she died

So now it was the same vision which kept arresting into vacancy her glowing gaze and the far journeying hollow sounding winds to which she listened with so wrapt a soul seemed to her ear already able to hearken things unnoticed by the living ears of earth. as if speaking and bringing word of him

Who in that rocky Isle lay dark and lone

Amid the oceans everlasting lullaby[17]

Though now the Earl perceived with Anguish that the sight of his Daughter was growing dazed and uncertain unconscious of real objects and fixed on phantoms dilated also with an expression of delirium that communicated itself to her whole countenance till she broke that long and horrid stillness by a low unnatural laugh glaring round and saying hurriedly

"What a strange thing to spend the time I have done the hours and years of trouble to acquire a knowledge and an information so wretchedly soon to pass away—Ive been living and thinking and exerting myself—to shine was it? and to adorn and beautify the sphere I looked to move in—No to carry my Accomplishments and graces and taste and intellect inside the coffin into the grave for the converse and enlightning of the worms! Oh what vanity is there in Life with all this laboured training to die to become extinct. at Twenty-one! Music studied so enthusiastically Languages spoken so admirably. —for I may praise myself now father—person so much decorated—and—look at the end!- then why did I form such affections—why did I cling to my glorious West why so fondly love you Why so much mourn for Angria when for so short a time only these things were to be mine—Wouldnt it have been wiser to pass through

---

[17] These lines are likley Branwell's.

Life as one little stage of the journey only making passing acquaintances and slipping them all off when parting with a single shake of the hand—Can I do this now—? Can I shut my eyes on that dear native far off land My Home my child hoods home Can I forget my delightful walks there with a heaven of feelings round me and in the pages I read all the Mighty Spirits of this world present in a communion of kindred thoughts—I cannot I cannot do this So Oh Can I forget for one instant. the Realization of all these Dreams the Incarnation of all I had ever delighted in dreamed of or hoped for nay whose existence I did not hope. for surely never in this world had their lived so perfect an embodyment of the visions and feelings and yearnings that will fill a mind like mine I saw him and I could not but love him—! Love him father!" And here she clasped her hands together with thrilling voice and a spirit that soared quenchless above her weakness— "Love I Adored I do adore him and Because he has left me Because he has forgotten me Because we are parted and I must never see him again I will die—I will give up this wretched life with a scorn of that from which all life has evaporated I will care not wither I go to but I'll stop no longer here!

WE HAVE PARTED so Father God bless you! My Noble Father of whom a world like this is not indeed worthy God bless you But its bitter to part from you No whatever you have done or May do I cannot cease to think of you—And fare you well Lady Percy his mother and in what you have done and suffered and watched for me well may I call you mine for my Childern I leave them to him who if he cares for me will protect them and if he does not I hope they may DIE! My Country is in the hands of Demons but there are Hearts within it which while they beat will never without an effort know it wronged So God bless Angria and Warner its Noblest Son—But theres one beyond you all ADRIAN May God look on thee! —Oh for a look for a word of you a single look over that dark far off sea! —"

The dying Eyes again were wildly bent on the Night and the hands momently raised to heaven The grand Idea of her soul had rushed upon her and in it she was to be born away with a mingled ecstasy of Despair and Love the lovely orbs swam and beauteous lips quivered but losing their hue and meaning both at once closing with a struggling whisper that seemed like Zamornas name then Her Hands dropt beside her and with a miserable groan Percy threw himself on the Body of his Departed Child[18]

Thus then has departed from among us a being In whom surpassing loveliness of person was united to a corresponding beauty and brilliance of mind all In such mingling as to render her worthy of being what she was the Daughter and Wife of the Two greatest men in this world. —She is gone now and though

---

[18]   This section consists of pages 3-4 (1-2 are blank) of a five-page manuscript fragment, 11.2x18.5 cm., in the private collection of Roger W. Barrett in Chicago. The two blank pages suggest that Branwell may have planned to describe the funeral, but did not get around to doing so. For Charlotte's reaction to the death of her heroine, see Alexander EW, 153-56.

and Wife of the Two greatest men in this world. —She is gone now and though I have hinted at her character in the pages before yet it would not be amiss to take a farwell over her grave with a single glance at her character and one word upon her destiny

Mary Percy was the only daughter (as far as his feelings were concerned) of One whose intensely warm passions concentered in affection upon her as the memorial of his adored departed wife She was born with most warm and active feelings herself and these were fostered by unlimited indulgence in to a most headstrong uncontrollable spirit which refused the slightest governance except from its own natural dictates she was therefore wilful capricious and sometimes unreasonable in all her thoughts and actions living and hating laughing and crying without rule or reason regardless of consquences in whatever she said or did yet utterly unable to endure the slightest reverse or pain But over all this character her sweet soft and elegant mind threw a charm which removed far away rudeness boisterousness or masculine impetuosity far was it from her to ride a hunting drive tandem or henpeck a husband. intuitive elegance forbade the wish to do this and the helplessness of indulgence was unable to practice it Indeed for good and bad she was nearly what the character of Woman would be in a bright estate with a soul and Imagination given from one to whom these gifts by their very intensity proved a curse and a generosity and warmheartedness that if it was not natural assuredly came down from heaven

Such was the being of faults and beauty that Lord Elrington three years since brought with him from the West to Verdopolis and such an one so acomplished and lovely as she was could not long escape the Falcon eyes of the youthful Hope of Africa—Douro saw her and marked her for his own She saw him and who could not anticpate the result.? Heart mind soul feelings Ideas every thing were were filled directly with that Form Divine that realization of all her unbounded hopes could dream of nor long did she wait for their fulfillment for returning from a sucessful war the Companion of her Mighty Father this Imperious God dashed down all opposition to his will and made her his WIFE and presented to her the crown of Angria There happy was her lot for a while as anything in this world could be surrounded by a glowing glittering court amid a noble rising Empire its bright centre of attraction and in the arms of Adrian her King But Adrians Premier her father was a Mortal Lucifer cursed in heart and blighted by sorrows he <insanely> enraged his Sovereign by a course of duplicity and treachery which changed a freind as devoted as could be to a stern relentless foe no warning would suffice no threats and Zamorna was not a man to threat[en] in vain so when upon the grand attack made on Angria Northangerland hung back and deserted. Zamorna issued his command and Mary was discrowned and discarded to bear this was with her impossible Anguish brought on Consumption and this was fast bringing on Death But the ruin of Angria the destruction of Zamornas power his own captivity and exile from her fathers <fiat> brought on Despair and these three together tormented out of existence one who had no defence

She is gone then now. and after a life like a short splendid vision is herself become a vanished dream.! —The feelings which this certainty bring on my mind accustomed as I have been to the splendour of her court and to the charms of her prescence are distressing and overwhelming nor can I without difficulty persaude myself that such a terrible change has taken place. But it is so. and she has died amid sights and sounds of Ruin She has died in a land torn by intestine war with a hundred convulsions passed or passing and countless storms of trouble just beginning to arise—the fair Ladies with whom she shone and smiled are fled into the protection of Strangers from their burning Halls. the Noble Gentlemen who rallied round to defend and adore her—All either lie with bloody breasts buried in feilds of defeat or lurk outlawed among wintery mountains to watch for the return of a freedom which has set as if it would never rise Her father though nominaly high in power is betrayed and plotted against by his freinds and surrounded by a thickening cloud of Enimies Her Husband. Her All. is an EXILE crownless companionless and Hopeless. She herself is Dead and amid such a gathering storm of trouble has the earth been heaped over the corpse of the fair young Queen of ANGRIA

Reader I cannot do otherwise than drop a tear to her memory for recollect that I it was whose pen first brought her to your notice who from her rising to her setting have so long recorded the different phases of her glory. I wrote on the Brilliant Morning of Angria I described its coronations and its meetings and its short champaign of Victory I told of the troubles as they came till fallen Angria is now lost in falling Africa—So come then this mournful ending is only suited to so Darkened a time and knowing that if I looked around the prospect would only still be graves I am losing no time and forgoing no pleasure in dropping a farwell tear over this early Grave that our parting may be in tune with our company let it be in the words of the Noble Poet of strong and troubled feeling

> Thus lived thus died she never more on her
>> Shall sorrow light or shame she was not made
> Through years on years the inner weight to bear
>> Which colder hearts endure till they are laid
> By age in earth her days and pleasures were
>> Breif but delightful such as she had not staid
> Long with her destiny But she sleeps well
> In that wide land wherein she loved to dwell[19]

                        P B Bronte
                        Nov 11 1836
                        Haworth

---

[19] Compare Byron, *Don Juan*, Canto IV, stanza LXXI.

P B B[20]
Nov 19th
1836

I Have detained both myself and my Readers too long from watching the progress of that torrent which is sweeping so wildly over our distracted country But the scenes upon which I have detained are not only in themselves momentously mournful but form as it were a branch of the main Tide as deep and as impetous as it in their flow I have been certainly lingering round the Grave of one among Millions But that Grave is the Grave of Old and Dear Associations to two of the Mightiest Rulers of the Storm in it buried and the last ties which bound them together and from it will spring thorns that may tear the hearts of either with a useless but bitter war Perhaps those two Mighty Hearts formed so for each other now that She who joined them is gone may only throb in mutual strife till one yeilds its last blood to the other or till both yeild to the frost of Death

Now at last Mary is buried and so let us turn our faces to the Approaching Awful Strife of War and to this we may turn without difficulty since as quickly even He her Miserable father was for[c]ed without heart or spirit for it to turn likewise though from the very brink of the Vault which held his buried Child and toward confusions and plots and treacheries which required for their disentanglement the clearest and most disengaged and unoppressed brain. While above the gathered group of Mourners In Alnwick Minster the Requiem was still sounding and the gilded Coffin still open to the Eye a Packet was thrust into the Earls hand that when upon his return to the castle he opened it disclosed such a scene of treacherous confusion in Verdopolis and Gathering Dangers without as compelled even his half dead and desolate spirit to rouse though with the feeling which actuates the start of the reeling horse when it feels the spur dashed to the head into its panting and reeking side without a word to anyone living the Earl flung himself into the readiest Carriage and hurried from his wood girt Mansion with the headlong speed of desperation

It was very late at night when Northangerlands Carriage halted in Elrington Square Verdopolis But though a sort of rest seemed at last to have fallen over the Giant City round it—No rest no slumber existed here And when His Lordship alighted a bitter thrill shot through his heart to think how he must directly enter upon an endurance of the harry and turmoil of that Great Blazing Pandemonium before him.[21] To see its vast front of sparkling light and the Chaos of its Carriage Crowded Square to know that all this Blaze of frantic Extravagance was kept up from his resources for the Appetite of a hundred insatiable Vultures who under the mask of freindship were gnawing the heart out

---

20   This portion consists of two pages at the BPM: Bon 143.
21   Again Branwell seems to be echoing his reading of *Paradise Lost*.

of his bosom that there he must meet and hear and speak to through night and day was a prospect so horrible as to whiten yet more his ghastly wearied face He stood a minute wrapped in his Mourning cloak like a statly wreck the Midnight rain beating on that grand but careworn form Silent and neglected Servants round who never stopped before him for it was not he who was their Master not a freind coming out to welcome him—he stood one moment thinking he was—A Desolate Man But the Awful Shadow of Percy could still somewhat awe the Harpies of Democratic Tyranny the Great Doors were opened and a crowd of servants in a while lounged forth to admit the Ruler of Verdopolis into a Palace hardly his own

Shaver marshalled his Master toward his Library through galleries that echoed the far off sounds of Revellry and when it was reached Percy careless of anything about him threw himself upon a sopha beside the cold sparkless fireplace refusing to allow the Valet to uncloak him and covering his face he gave himself up to all the bitterness of unavailing sorrow He was not think[ing] of the Insolence of his Adherents or the Discomfort and wearieness of his frame the Cold he felt was nothing to the Icy coldness of his Soul and the single Taper on the Table was at least lighter than the[sic] Its rayless gloom. Even Shaver because he knew well the plots laid against his power the wishes pointing at his life the foes that were gathering and the dissapearance of freinds even he could not on gazing at his Mighty Master refrain from a passing shade of emotion which he expressed by adjusting the cushions on the Sopha lighting the lustre and and muttering an Oath on those who had neglected the room and fires. However the Earl murmured a wish that he should leave him and the Valet tripped off with all his stock of flippant carelessness again about him though he did think. "Curse him he'll need the Countess enow!"

Five minutes then passed away fifteen half. an hour. a whole one yet nothing more approached to distrub the solitude of that Lofty Library its owner was still laid on the Cushions with his eyes closed and his hand over them suffering a thousand passing torments of mind and in a state of great bodily pain for the excitment and restlessness of the last four days had brought on his usual complaint Angina Pectoris so that every now and then the splendid statuesque features else so utterly still were crossed with the troubled convulsion of acute anguish his lips being closer compressed and his breath drawn in gasps till the fit passed off and the pale forehead cleared into calm despair for of late years continual trouble and the incessant torments of an utterly broken constitution have so inured him to pain that he can bear without speaking without changing in features what makes the drops start to his forehead and the iron enter into his soul

As St Michaels great Bell tolled ONE the Earl opening his eyes looked round but there was nothing to comfort him for the Curtains being undrawn each window showed an utter blackness of midnight and every taper shook with its lengthened neglected flame uncertain Shadows flickered in the far off extremities of the Apartment a motion without sound and creating phantasms in his disordered eyes but from afar through the Grand Saloons of this Enormous Palace a confused sound of Music and Revelry was born with the roar of wheels in the Square and a hollow toned wind from the Sea directly he caught quick and light footsteps approaching from the Ante room then the Door was flung open and in came the warm living luxuriant Georgiana Greville Her ladyship was shawled and Bonneted looking as cheerful and cheering as Youth beauty and blooming cheeks and fair clustering curls could make her yet there was a visible concern in her large sympathising eyes and that deepened into indignation when she beheld the cold discomfort of the room she had entered

"My Lord" she cried "Hows this! What have they done or why dont I see you in a different situation. Why what are the Insolent Rascals about do they mean publicly to proclaim their rotten Ingratitude Oh Ill make them feel it"— ringing the bell with violence— "Come now My Lord you do wrong to give yourself up so to misery. had I been in you should have had better welcome But I've only just returned from Charing Square and now the wretch Vernon is just behind me—youll be plagued to death to make amends for this wanton neglect —"

A servant here made his Appearance in answer to her call

"Why you pitiful wretch doesnt this room fall to your care and is this the manner in which you fullfil your trust?

"Really dont know mi Lady—"

"Whats that—What do I hear—To your work slave! right the Library this moment if it take thee all night to do it Come my Lord rise and leave this room—Come! How cold you are!"

As she took his hand to entice him from his lonely dejection another person came running in A dark haired little Lady in a ball room dress and with eyes flashing from the excitment of flatteries and distinctions she had been playing Lady <Protectoress> in the Saloons and hearing that Lady Greville was gone to See the Earl just arrived she had hurried breathless to be in at the <death> before her So hasting to him with an aspect in which pride and passion and Jealousy and Triumph had almost quenched the very appearance of tenderness and Sympathy she motioned Lady Greville impetously aside and burst forth without mercy[22]

"I never expected to see you again and I could not but be astonished my Lord when you left us without even speaking to me or your child—but you are come back at last so I will forgive you and now dont be cast down so but leave off greiving for what cannot be avoided and though I do greive with you in the melancholy loss you have suffered but its unavailing and there are brighter prospects opening—come will you not see your Caroline—"

"You pitiful creature" cried Georgiana impatiently and red with contemptous Indignation

---

[22] The following portion consists of leaf 3 of the manuscript in the Berg Collection, catalogued as "Elegant Extracts"; the title actually applies only to leaf 1.

"you pitful wretch bringing forward your dirty little slut of a daughter to occupy and fill up the place of Zamorna's Wife—Ha you know that Now a mighty property lies vacant and ready for the first snatcher you think that now at last my Caroline will be heiress so I must take care and remind him of her existence which otherwise he would most likely have forgot—"

It was only the excess of rage which prevented Louisa Vernon from breaking in sooner upon this lovely exposition of her intentions her light frenchified figure quivered with an agony of wrath and her slender fingers clutched as they would tear out the heart of her handsome Rival

"Worthless Upstart" she said stamping with her fairy foot "Do you dare to insult me any more—I thought I had warned you of that—What are you here for and what I ask. What portion have you in my Husband—

"Ha Ha Ha—laughed Lady Greville with joyous scorn Brightning at the unguarded slip and exposing the hasty anticipation

"What you've made so sure of him have you that you have already settled the marriage portion and passed through the ceremony—that My Lord that is the Idea which has been running through this Opera Dancers head—"

The passive victim for which this struggle was contesting hardly answered to the appeal by a dreary smile but Vernon gave no time for furthur word for she boldly dashed in to correct her error

"You think vile woman that you have hurt me by that pitiful sneer but if I rip up all your secrets and reveal all your Anticipations your head wouldnt be on your shoulders another day—do you think that you hang so fast on Percys heart you mushroom creation of a day do you think that he feels for you—it [is] only his wretched apathy that makes him endure you for a moment—"

"for shame Louisa Vernon for shame to pester with your prescence and unruly temper the only hour of rest which has passed over Percy during the many days that you've been assisting the plots against him—My Lord She vexes you with her insolence leave her Im sure this room has no comfort for you come my Lord—"

"Touch him if you dare woman!"

"And what then pray?"

"Ill kill you! stupid sorceress!" and thereupon poor Louisa burst out into crying mingling her passionate sobs with feirce lookes from her tamless eyes and an impetous shake of her raven curls but her Rival stood by Percys Sopha in triumphant consciousness of superior strength of Arm   [23] if a conflict were begun and fired with a really generous impulse to think how this disgracful scene was harrassing the misery of the wearied Northangerland till only her regard for his peace prevented her from taking her fiery litte Antagonist by the waist and carrying her from the room

"If you stop here" she said "It shall be to answer for your conduct—who was it that hired Ruffians to set upon my carriage the other night—who was it

---

[23] Branwell canceled two words here, but provided no replacements.

that burst out a laughing when th news came that the Queen of Angria was dead—"

"You Liar"

"Who was it that when I told her that Percy had spoken to me last before he set out for Alnwick ran to Montmorency's and threw herself head over ears into the plot against him who was it

"Vile wretch. —she lies percy—I did not they had planned it before—I only wanted them to lead off the Army for a little while—

"Lead off the Army Madam—" said Percy breaking sternly in and rousing on a sudden as if at the sound of a trumpet He rose and faced the trembling Vernon and the astonished Greville—

"What is that she says Greville?"

"My Lord I had intended to tell you when I came in but she interrupted me—My Lord you are beset with treachery They have been tampering with the Army

"Who?"

"The Provisional Government. —Madame Tallien[24] bribed Steaton to put into her possession all your ready money and Montmorency wiled it out of her and then He and the rest distributed it among the new <levies>

"Where is Montmorency—"

"With the Army—"

The Earl started as if an adder had bit him

"And Jordan and the Prince and Macara and Naughten

"All with the Army

"Now on my Soul" muttered Rougue between his teeth "this is terrible—"

"She Lies she lies" cried Louisa—she is the plotter she imitated you at the great fete last night and ridiculed you she's been conferring with Warner—"

Georgiana not being the most patient Woman on earth snatched up her antagonist and ran with her throwing her on to an ottoman in the next room but the the Vixen rushed back with an aim at her face which Percy stopped by raising each by an Arm and holding them off from him Conflicting thoughts at the same time stabbing into his soul

"Oh" he said "Women women you have ruined me and in my worst distress you rise to worry me—part—part directly each to your rooms—"

Then he himself departed to his own or at least another room but forgetting to shut the door stood with it in his hand in a moments dismay. The Army which ever since his rise to power he had been collecting on the frontiers of Angria and exerting his utmost energies to bring to perfection was composed of all his best most tried and most thourough bred Democrats men who adored his Name and arrayed and disciplined in such numbers that with them and with

---

[24] One of the "Merveilleuses," the ironical name given to the leaders of female fashion in Paris during the Thermidorian and Directory periods, she was the most notorious leader in the later 1790's, and mistress of Barras.

them only he had hoped to withstand and crush both Warner and Fidena and Ardrah and his own Co rulers were these vast forces corrupted would they be of no avail now when the great stuggle was just coming on Fidena in full march from Freetown Warner in full Gathering at Seaton—yet it was so The very Demons of the pit were among them. He was here alone worried with the vindictive quarrels of two impetous and imperious women—But such accumulations of evil had at last roused the true Rougueite Tyger That name I have not had occasion to use of late but it was up. for Rougues very voice called from that door in tones which would be obeyed and when Shaver hastily appeared his Master ordered him to be ready in a moment have out the Carriage again put on fresh horses and tell him so soon as it was done. till that time he continued pacing the room with a Brow of bitter gloom and on the reapearance of his valet with his hat and gloves he hurried forth threw himself into the Just vacated Coach and sickened and wearied as he was with the days journey—directed the. Coachman to drive with all haste for Northangerland Hall. the Head quarters of the Provisional Army

P B B[25]
Nov 29
1836

By the end of the first week in November there were gathered in a line from Zamorna to Cornshaw moor extending along twenty miles of the frontier of Angria and dipping from the Verdopolitan Valley N. W. to the Olympian S. E. nearly 150.000. Soldiers arrayed under the blood red banner of Percy and Revolution This huge force had in part been collected by the late Premier Ardrah but revolting to the conquerer now gave him all the aid he could derive from wild and wanton Cruelty treachery and disorganisation for the rest the ever stirring sea of Verdopolis had thrown up froth and foam sufficient of late to furnish 80000 Recruits from among those whose hearts had leaped to the voice of Rougue and Naughten

This great force the Lord President had taken care to dispose as follows 26000 men under Gen Sir H Macterrorglen alias Jer Simpson at the South end of the line round Zamorna and in a situation where even their defection could not materially injure him because these were very many of the Scotch and Southern Reformers at heart hating him and lead by one who had from his youth upwards been Percys Evil Genius—after all indeed this force had never even recognised Percys authority!— The second or. middle division and the leading one in the Army was composed of 40.000 French stationed in and round Edwardston protected by the Morena River fortified with an immense array of entrenchments bristling with cannon and lead on by that bold Determined tyrant General Massena As this was the strongest post and which if carried would ruin the

---

25 The following section consists of one leaf at the BPM: Bon 145(2).

whole army and throw Verdopolis open Percy had placed in advance of it a curtain to break the force of blows 14000 Africans Ashantees and Negroes under the Prince Quashia Quamina planted about Stuartville and Girnington an advanced guard for the whole Army and its grand provision foragers—Then farthest N. W. and the left wing about Northangerland and Cornshaw moor lay 42000 real Blood red Destructives from the populace of the Metropolis commanded by the only man who could command them Richard Naughten the Earls strong right hand—Besides—flung forward over all the Olympian Hills ranged 8000 wild Arabs of the Desart a flying Cavalry headed by the Sheik Medina alias the Earl of Jordan who burnt destroyed and slew both foes and freinds the froth the top the beauteous exhalation from this huge mass of ferocity and turbulence—

Here then was the grand Army of Angria composed of Six Nations and 130000 men. with a rese[r]ve of 20000 under M Bernadotte in the Eastern lines of Verdopolis. It was at present lying in active but destined for the utter destruction of the Insurgent Patriots and their Allies the Sneachians and Wellingtonians under John Duke of Fidena it was the great stay of the Lord President and it was commanded by HIMSELF.

But surrounded by the intrigues and dissipation of Verdopolis and hurried from thence to a scene of Death and despair Percy had never as yet visited or assumed the direction of this Mighty thunder bolt. Naughten was his Lieut[en]ant his Co rulers were the Generals and plunder and barbarity seemed the sole object of their Assembling so that when Montmorency Macara and Strafford formed their plan for deposing their mighty head they beheld in this Army an admirable means of attaining this object

I resume my Story of Civil Warfare then at a period. early in November when corruption had crept into the ranks of this grand stay of Northangerlands power. under the mask of his nearest companions and Co rulers. when Warner was just decending[sic] to revenge his Sovereign from the brows of his native mountains. when Fidena though without his request was advancing too with a noble force from Freetown the rendezvous of Conservative alliance. and when as for Angria itself. it was lying beneath its conquerors trodden in to a mire of blood ground down devastated depopulated and left without the barest form of a civilised and inhabited land

Daylight was just dawning over the grand Battle feild of Africa with a sky heavy comfortless and covered with clouds an horizon whose long grey mists portended coming rains and a sullen sound of brooks and waters that spoke loudly of those which were gone. Round the villiage of Northangerland in Turton Vale[26] leafless Woods stretched dull with mist and shaking their bare branches to the morning winds which swept raw and coldly from the Gorges of the Olympian Hills and on those surrounding summits the smoke of watch fires yet mingled with the vapours and sent down from the bosom of their wreaths

---

[26] Turton Bottoms is today part of Greater Manchester.

now and then the chance report of a musket and constantly the far of calls of Sentinels in the last watch of morning

There is a public house which stands outside the villiage of Northangerland on the road leading down toward Edwardston and here it was evident this morning that some persons of importance were assembled for early as it was not only an armed sentry was posted on each side of the Door but three or four grooms were walking as many chargers on the front and two handsome Barouches waited before the steaming stables. likewise and this formed the strongest feature in the scene at a stones cast from the house before a decaying fire half a score of wild brown men clothed in eastern Garb with bare sinewy limbs and raven beards all armed with slim curving scymitars rested on their firelocks beside their ready steeds A group of Real Arabs of the Desart—true Sons of the Sahara as rude and remorseless as its unpitying sands they had come in from plunder and they were prepared at any moment to start off again on such an errand for when a Horseman followed by two attendants dashed past them toward the Inn. as he reined up and shouted something to them in their own tongue they all sprung to horse and brandishing their peices over head with a wild cry scoured away on the scent which he had informed them of.

This Horseman was a tall wiry man in a top coat terribly swarthy and as he sprung from his smoking steed his two satellites took it under hand. a couple of lusty blacks with swart faces shining and yellow eyes rolling under the influence of Jamaica Rum. their master turning from them with a word of instruction strode sharply toward the door swaggering out a round oath in return to the obedient salutation of the sentrys and greeting the servant who hurried to receive him from within. with another commination

"D'rat it" he cried in a rough sharp voice "help me off with my disguise fellow! but egad if you did it properly you'd do it with a stomach pump Odd rabbit it it isnt the coat which disguises me its something better and hang me if a single drop doesnt operate in such a raw morning like a thumping bottle on [a] warm summer night curse me man put the thing on a pin where I can find it when I go out and this whip on the top of it—premising by Dad that I first lay it on the top of you! —"

As he spoke the Gentleman made it whack over the flunkies shoulders till the man turned in evident disrelish of such a salute but it was only to behold another preparing so he een took to his heels for it and the rampant stranger after him till he dashed against a door check fell full against the portal and burst it open breaking his own nose in the fall. at such a headlong enterance those within were heard to start up and a a great strong looking personage came laughing into the passage calling out

"Hey my Cock of the midden is it you. and a very suitable enterance you've made—could have sworn it was no other but come my heart cease your piping!"

In fact the speaker had reason to say so for the fallen was now up on his legs again a wild dark brown figure in black. (the top coat being deposed) bleeding from his mahogany Nose and swearing till the whole House rung again—The PRINCE was in every tone of that voice and now two or three more heads were thrust from the door to welcome the advent of his Highness who pushed into the room lighted up—for as yet within the house it was darkish. —and smelling nobly of Gin twist and Tobbaco smoke—it will not be inferred[27] that in this apartment were gathered the elite of Angrias Tyrants but it was the sanctum of the head quarters of the Army of the north. King Richard. himself pressed with his Elephantine bulk the great easy chair Lord Jordan had been stretching his luxurious limbs on the chintz covered settle Lord Lofty was shrunk like a rotten filbert into the Arm chair opposite Naughtens Marshal Massena's seat was at the thick of the spirit bottles and next him by the table the child like innocent—Montmorency had been occupying a three legged stool propped up in lack of a fourth limb by a kitchen poker. the multitude of Jugs tumblers and squeezed Lemons on the table with the well moistened spittons beneath shewed that they all had either been making a night or a morning of it probably for economys sake both in one but now that the jovial glee was broken into by the stir kicked up by the Truculent prince of the blacks all were forced to get onto their legs to assist in pacifying the innocent Ivory though Macara alone kept his place desirous of avoiding such another thwack as he had heard resound from the back of the waiter and muttering meanwhile

"This will never do—a pretty state to enter into such deliberations as ours!"

"Just the right state!" returned Montmorency behind his back and enjoying the spectacle "Just the right state my Boy—and we shall never see daylight into the buisness till we are all in a like pickle Gad he'll beat us all yet penetration and discrimination are just at their height Reason and judgement at high water mark—Hah my lad a stiff glass of toddy melts the difficultys and dangers into thin thin air!" then he turned to the Prince clapping him on the shoulder "Steady now my sweetie—take and sup. theres plenty of sugar in thats[sic] a dear sit thee down now and tell us thy story!"

"Stories!" cried the Prince wiping his bloody nose "I'll tell no stories it shall be truth. plain fact and so hand me over that Usquebaugh.[28] Now Gemmen listen to a plain tale! —He's coming thats fact and another with him But as I was saying to my tale Blast me if I know what I'm to tell!"

"Nay if thats the humor on't—"
"Now do be quiet its your own fault. What did you send me out for as far as Zamorna. at dead of night fleeing over bogs and among Boggards[29] to tell him to come here as if I was a common courier. I'll have no more on't"

"Nay But" interposed Massena "consider the importance of the thing we could not disclose—"

---

27   This section consists of leaves 8, 9, 15, 14 in Ashley 187 at the BL.
28   "Water of life"—whiskey.
29   A spectre, goblin or bogy, a local goblin or sprite supposed to haunt a particular gloomy spot, or scene of violence.

"Let him alone" said Mont handing out a soothing tumbler to the Prince "let the lad tell it his own way go on dear"

"I have gone on and I'll go no more to send me out on such a night and then just because I've got a drop or so of liquors into me to keep me alive. abusing me and knocking me down in the passage—and—and—Drat it!—"

"Now" said Naughten rising with a thundrous tone and menacing aspect "Now are our lives to be jeopardi[s]ed and our designs made nought of by such a drunken Rascal as that Hold thy clatter there man and If you cant tell us your news at least let us talk about our own goings on—Mont youre a fool to be heartning him on that gate youre always for making your cursed nonsense when youve gotten a matter of a gill of brandy into you! leave of I say!"

Mont winked with his eye at the Giant but said nothing though he would have been answered ere half his speech was over if the Prince had not been otherwise engaged leaning over a chair brewing a stiff tumbler of Grog with the assistance of Hector Matthias who added sugar and whiskey till a spoon might almost have stood up in the middle of it "there's thy porridge my boy" he said "sup it off" and as soon as the Moorish Infant had obeyed he burst out again

"What you old skinflint Because I'm at your charges you wont let me drink of a glass of liquor But I dont value you the crack of a louse I'm my own master and I can draw off my men or draw them onto the enterprise like an old black stocking" yes he repeated "I have ye there A good 20000 as regular born feinds as ever shook at doing your nasty work—ye beggarly ungratful Dogs—Ill levant If I am a man and Ill levant this minute blast you am I to be insulted i this gate—Says Jerry "Quashia youre drunk. when were you sober last?"—was that a Question to ask a Gentleman Says he—How am I to trust you for carrying word from me to your gang up there in this state—Jerry says I heres sommat to sup your liquor with so I walked over [to] his table with cold pork and hot steaks and rotten cheese and rum toddy—take your breakfast out of that says I So says he getting his tobbacco pipe and sitting amid the greasy stuff as if nought was the matter—your warm Quash this morning but its natural for the Blacks to hiss when they are thrown into cold water—If I am alive Ill draw my men off this blessed day HE never used to insult me this a way I'll see your hide flead for you ye dead alive in the corner there Dod I'de do it myself this minute for a sixpence—"

"Now my Lad" said Montmorency pulling him down onto a seat "I want to have a bit of talk with thee—"

"Mont" interrupted Naughten "curse you let the black beggar alone—sin I first knew him he has not been worth a flea's hide and he never will be—whats the use of heartning him on that gate!"

"Oh" cried Jordan who had upon his settle been choking with silent laughter "Quacco be mad for Massa him get a tree whip and a four whip all of his Bum but him more prouder the more him get from Massa—Oh Quacco banga de Congo?"

Jordan probably intended to have gone on but a great brown fist dashed into his face effectually stopped him and before he could gather up his lazy limbs for the combat the insulted Prince with a loud howl had rushed from the room almost overturning his wet Nurse Hector and kicking open the out door with his foot he absconded before another word could be spoken

"Well Gentlemen" said Macara breathing more freely in the abscence of the drunken Moor "I think we are well rid of him. hand across the Gin Massena and now were it not more prudent to proceed to buisness you know what we have on the anvil and though I will allow that Nature never intended me to be candid—I am sorry for the jades negligence yet I think I can in this prescence afford to say plainly that as we are met to rid Africa of a Monster the sooner we set about it the better—"

"Now Mac—returned Mont leaning with both arms on the table and looking round with the cheerfulness of a tipsy feind "Ive a thought—is it true that you and Louisa Dance are more nearly related than you would have us think. eh!"

"Why what makes you think so my dear Sir—"
"Ive been a poring over that lovely face of thine my Duck and you bring me to mind that when I used to look at Madam.—I always thought that as you say Mother Nature had someway forgot to insert the slightest trace of good in her very snivelling and uncandid physiognomy—heres her health—and so now I'll be dished if theres a ray of christian decency in thine my freind—your's too—and you've both that nice easy way of talking of your own defects and amusing people with a show of plainness and so forth which covers—Lord love us we'll say no more about it! —"

"Yes but Hector if that similarity in abscence of all good in our faces leads you to suppose a relationship between me and the Marchioness theres a something in your face which tells me you are her father at the very least—

"Now cried Naughten impetously "Did ever any one hear such fudge Jabbering about each others drunken faces when we are no such buisness as this no wonder that Rougue has kept the head of the table so long leave off or I'll go"

"Macara answered "Naughten's quite right but I thought that as the morning had begun in such folly as it did it might as well carry through with a shew of consistency—"

"Fudge again Im tired of your sinvelling[sic] nonsense that a plain downright man to understand it would have to learn a new A B C over again and forget his old one—consistency bonny consistency when we are met only to eat up our words and draw back our comradship and—

"Gad" said Massena "this is a game why were like so many scorpions this morning stinging each other to death I bear nothing but fair hits that character and conduct—"
"as if" interrupted Mont "we had either of those valuable qualities to aim at—"
"What strike again Mon?"
"Now said Macara "this is too bad had we not better my freinds far better direct our blows at the common enemy—But stay that[s] Simpson coming
As the worthy young Noble was sliding out his words a noise of Horses feet and much loud talking became audible without which increased as the Inn door was

opened and was followed by footsteps in the passage stamping of feet shaking of great coats and many elegant and well twanged oaths. the carpet in the parlour being meanwhile raised up and shook by the blast which driving in from the opened door and howling through the house shewed how intemperate the weather had become outside The party. within were all recharging their glasses for a freindly incountre when the door flew open and Sir Henry Macterrorglen alias Jerry Simpson entered his vast Grim ungainly stature aided behind by a battered tattered and most decrepid figure whose unlooked for advent made the heart leap to the throats of every one present as they one and all cried out

"Sdeath! what! Old Robert come alive again!" to which freindly greeting the resuscitated Ancient speedily answered dashing his Ghost of a hat sideways with the briskness of a 5 year old

"I be dad! and aw em alive agean and providence be thanked that as uphodden me old body through as mony skillets and scrimmages as would as wad a taen the best on ye to win ower wi ought like auther mense or dacency!—" It was plain that the veteran had lost in his voyages not an ounce of either ease or assurance but for his reappearance all eyes demanded an account from his apparent patron

"Naw" said Jeremiah pushing to the fire and rubbing his huge hands over the revivified embers now I never was so plagued in my born days as I have been on this ride with that old battered scare crow he'd be dear of a tenpenny rope if it were not a blessed riddance of him—Silence ye hanged rascal and let me hear myself. Hes been cast up I fancy somewhere off the french coast. neither Rover nor ought else visible as far as I know I supposed the sea would not entertain such a land wreck but however the Paris Government handed him over to me and I wanted to heave him across to his old master to curry favour but the Old dog's too cunning for me he knows when a ship leaks as well as another and said he was dashed before he'd come near that fooil of all foils as long as he had hand or finger to work for his jocks with—I soon found that yon Driveller had no charms remaining for his humble servant so I brought him along—Hold your tongue ye scamp—I brought him along with me to try if you could pump ought out of him about his elegant charge that was—I cant—"

"And yaw cannot cannot yaw and yaw donnat knaw yere mother English do yaw and yaw're aboon spaking to an owd body are yaw but aw'll tent ye and thaw's see wether this frail carcase downt bide as mich sense as your chimbley sweep Namscull—me ats defied wind and weather for five score years an's been perilled on th raging ocean wi the company of sich fearsome boggards as awve seen noon sa long sin swallowed in the Bawels of the deep—its fair scandalous that a frail worn aat delicate crature like mysel sud be sent o' sich errands as is fitter be far for the like o ye swearing tearing nonsenses. Rumble i yar Bellies owd fooils rumble i yor bellies and bite yer toe nails to think o' yor shameless impidence. for all yar minded Aw mud nother a supped not bitten this morning and now when aw come o' yowr errends yaw willn't as mich as club for an odd glass for an owd crature ats been shipwrecked wi Boggards in yawr sarvice—"

"Lord" cried one of the company "if thats what the old fellow is driving at let him have one or we we shall be deafened by his clamour!"

"No" returned Simpson "let every body here pay for his share I'll spend none of my brass on such an accursed brute—and now I'll go and see wether or not I cannot get hold of something to grub at my Belly feels cursed queer this wild morning Gad he'll be dinner and supper to ye while I'm off an you let him go on"

As the Grim ex Lord Lieutenant moved off upturning toward the kitchen Air his smoky feature. the old tatterdermalian[30] he spoke of. fronted him with a look of terrible gravity and ere he had done speaking turned short about on him spat quick and short into the fire and dashed his quid to the floor with such an air of magnificent and unendurable scorn as forced a peal of laughter from his stricken auditors So with his amiable temper no way sweetened by such peculiar applause he cocked his crownless hat yet more over his grizzled eyebrows plunged both fists into his depending coat pockets and recommenced with a flood of eloquence that meant to drown whatever opposed itself to it

"Dash me carcase! I reckon nought on't. I'll be stivered as small as taty pillings afore I'll be longer wi' sich catsmuck. —Aw hev a character to lose if you hev'nt and aw'll noan submit to take at chucky stones wi't i this a way. Shame upon ye Shame upon ye! —But ye'd rattle i your jackets if ye'd seen what aw've seen. the end of all sich scandals to a Christian country Aw've seen the like's o' ye yes just like the likes o' yaw owd Johnny Jordan! —wallowing i' the water a thaasand fit atween hivan and t' tother spot striking as yaw mud a heard em ower both wind and waves and picking up as mich salt water Owd Hector as ivver yaw picked up rum or brandy—there was me hodding fast on by the gunrails and aw calls aat to him ats goan "Yi how" says I wer sins are uncommon hard but Loard forgie us and them thats past repentance curse me if they sall'nt goo owerboard. —Yes Be Gow in the varry hurly o'th storm and tempist when nother the hivens nor the yearth wor presint but nobbut a mash of yeasty froth brasting the ship sides and lopping off the masts like cornstocks Aw take the liquor i' tone hind and drives tother toward him. standing fornent him thus And Be Gow I does rake him ower a screed of doctrine "Blast thee" I holloas "Blast thee! but where are thy misdoings now then scorner! Wheres her as yaw turned ower to dee like as one mud say at the back o'the dyke where is shoo now thaw mud as wealst a kept on another twalmonth shoo waddnt a troubled thee longer and to see what thaws getten by the Exchange! Loard deliver me Aw roared. fro the spoiler and fro the bloodthirsty mon—Yah How ma Lad whats thee looking tat gate for eh?—See'st thaa tother. Thinkst ta of her. cursed be the betrayer and the Desolator and Loard! what thinkst thaa is to do wi her? Tha's taen a third awm hoping for thy seconds noan long for tis part—Yeh be how! Aw says steady me Lad yee bean she't goan—Hollow ony commands for t'far spot Tho's goan dee'd at one this morn calling o'yaw and blaspheming her blessed Maker. Hilloo my Lad where's thy colour goan. after her—eh drat. whats

---

30   A person in tattered clothing; a ragged or beggarly fellow.

to do wi her father—gad we's Nick. him we's Nick him Theys me on the rest's going to do him naa nead he's mazed wi this latter knock me daan! Yes <u>thaw</u> may perish i the tempest but AW am resarved to be a curse and a plague upon his sons. —Hilloo'a Earnist thy fathers a coming Ha ha

"Capital" cried Mont. "but by G—d thou shalt have thy skinful old Boy. Drink it up and here's another to wash it down with. Blast me if I ever heard a sermon like yon Jordan my glass man and thine Maccy. nay not thine neither it'll be rank poison but thine Massena its sure to be good stuff and thine old clubb man. now there my Old Cock. Sup em all off. and thou's have some more! By G—d I say Gents what are we to believe of this!"

"Believe Nothing at all" said Naughten "but that He'll be on you before youre aware on it—I'll be hanged if I think. he's either dead or dying—and Mont if you go on brewing your glasses that gate you'll be as drunk as a puncheon afore we can get to buisness"

"Buisness" returned the Demagogue "D—n buisness!" and as he spoke he leaned back with a glorious shimmer in his eyes superbly warmed as he said into his very soul and extending his Herculean Arms he drew Sdeath toward him with a most loving embrace. The spectacle was so inimitable as to throw them all into a burst of laughter roused again and again as the two one reclined the other standing with hands clasped and glasses to their mouths eyed one another with a look in which it was hard indeed to tell wether Drunken glee or cunning malignancy most predominated. Monts figure alone was worth a hundred. that strong broad Herculean chested rascal leaned gloriously back. with his massy features haloed by their orange whiskers and shining with his repeated potations till the Diamond cut grey eyes glinted underneath their dark penthouse with a laugh that needed no assistance from the stern muscles of the face Sdeaths physi[o]gnomy was almost as much worth a perusal. only Jeremiah was now come back from Breakfast wiping his mouth with his handkercheif and strong as a Giant refreshed with swipes[31]

Clapping his hands on his paunch and shrugging up his mountain shoulders he said chuckling to himself.

"Now be gad there Ive been thrang taking a snack while youve been jabbering to that old corkscrew. and now Ive had the best picking both of the cold ham and round of Beef. Drat who d'ye thinks in the kitchen. why Quashy what the D—l have ye done to him he swears he wont come near ye—what now Mont where going—and is as drunk—nay stay lad—"

"Dad and leave a brother to roast in misery that way. never" So saying Mont swerved past out of the room to comfort a brother in Affliction not forgetting as he got up to grasp a bottle and two glasses for mutual solace and improvement.

"Well" went on Simpson settling himself onto an armchair. and drawing the sugar and spirits within his reach for an active champaign though

---

31 Poor weak beer; beer in general.

Massena grumbled out as he drew them over the table "What all my pretty chickens"

"Well" he chuckled out "Ive hit on a good un no need of our plots and schemings—all edge tools—we must work with softer materials on such an elegant peice of goods as his Lordship—I was thrang looking over what there was for Breakfast when—Bye the bye. why had not we servants of our own with us. —only cot-tamn. we must be secret. well in comes as sweet a wench as. but I dare say Jordan there as seen her afore now—A'nt she Johnny. she's the Daughter of mine Host. Gad I do think he's an Angrian I've half a mind to strap him up! Well. you know. I know a thing or two about our old freind at Verdopolis. and thats the reason he's so mad at me. I just thought as she stood at hand. —Why thats the very snare to take him with. a few sovereigns in hand and sommut better in expectation and she's ours. now those. Vernons and Grevilles and such trash. Dad I'll have none of them they are as obstinate [in] their own way as so many swine and I cannot get round em to floor him completly for the fools are always thinking of half measures. getting him into our power but saving him for themselves No no thats not my way. By the Bye. Dance might adone it but. he would none of her. no no I know him it must be a different cut creature. something of a form and shape—G—d D—n now if Augusta had been alive—stop a thought hits me—"

He got up and went to the door and Hallooed—

"Mont. and Quashy you take care of that lass. She's for none of you. Come your ways here!"

"Now—" returning to [the] fire and rubbing his vast hands over it— "Now a real form something slightly. like the old Daubers.[32] hits were or just such as. that cursed Countess old Hecate as I call her. there was a cut for ye if she'd only been Honest Lord he's clean dazzled by such an one and this shes a strapper. five foot nine at least. Such a shape. your Daubers talk. of your swelling outline and curve of beauty Gad. she's the thing itself. and with such a bold killing look—now that lassy wouldnt mind chopping of her old Dad or Mam's head to get at their savings. She's ambition is that one. She was in her silks and curls thus early because she thinks she can catch some on you—O' Drat. we must make her pro temp Lady Northangerland. I wish he would come this very minute By G—d I do If I dont may I—but However if he did come I'll be cursed if she wouldnt think herself fit for him what an Arm she has its Just like one of those knick knacks I got at the spoil of the Sultans Seraglio at Adrianopolis there theres a figure would just tally with this—such a step too—I call Greville a good figure of a woman but this beats her to nothing—and what I look most at is—she'd kill—aye she['d] do anything she['d] poison him when alls done! She'd betray him to our measures and neer fash her thumb[33] about it

---

[32] i.e., old painters.

[33] To give oneself trouble or not take the slightest trouble—Scots and northern dialect.

Why she throws her head back already like a Queen—Mont—I say come back and the Prince with ye!"

"Coming" cried the Demagogue from without and then entered with one arm round the neck of the truculent African now rather far gone and perfectly persuaded by the liquid eloquence of the Western Orator Mont as he came past flourished his now emptied bottle over his head. saying

"None of ye could have appeased wrath this way But I—Lord love us whats the use of talking on't I could do anything—except marry—What was't you were shouting at us Old Jerry Quash. thought it was for us to keep of the brandy flask. and he pulls me by the sleeve and says says he "Dont hearken him Mont dont hearken him" A Lass quotha. I'm not bound to thy bidding about Lasses my mon. now sit thee down Quash. sit down we cant do with any more stirs Sit thee down and hearken my boys. —he—he—hem I'm in no voice but howsever I'll begin

Sing Hey for Cock Robin in regular verse
How he harnessed Old Dobbin one day to the hearse
For a marvel had happened that could not be holpen
His wifes mouth was shut! and the graves mouth was open

To the Grave they went gravely with groaning and sighs
And Bob headed them bravely with tears in his eyes
The Mourners in black and the Parson in white
Were he couldnt help thinking a mighty fine sight

A Lady was there and her face looked so fair
That each look he cast on her dried up a tear
Lord he said if its greivous a[n] old wife to bury
Why sure the best cure is a new one to marry

If I lost my Old Horse say shouldnt I try
A new one of course directly to buy
And isnt a woman as good as old Dobbin?
Sing Ho and Hiero for my Jolly Cock Robin!

Cock Robin is kneeling devout at the Altar
To furnish his thrapple again with a Halter
'For richer for poorer for better for worse'
Odd he thinks is it this way Ide buy me a Horse?

Then he says to the Preist If a man take a wife
Is he bound with that one to remain all his life?
'Yes certainly Brother" —And if he dont marry
He's not bound at all— "No" —Then by the Lord Harry!

Since I see when a mans wed he's wedded to one

And that he may wed twenty if he will wed none
Ill bid for the twenty the folly's too great
When the world has such plenty to stick too one mate
And wed without trying and rue it too late!

I tried all his paces ere I bought Old Dobbin
Sing Ho and Hiero for my Jolly Cock Robin![34]
Now if that be'nt a good one—Well we'll say no more about it Here goes"—
standing up with a thud on the table—

"Gentlemen we are met here this morning for a purpose which
among the many freaks and amusments of innocent and childlike minds has as
yet been neglected and apparently forgotten. We are all men—and some of us a
little bit besides. We cannot bear slavery—except we are the slave Drivers—
we—we own no master—Except Old Harry. and this I am sure of—we hate
Tyranny just as much as we hate Sin! —Now my lord Lazy mind from the Land
of Sin in silver slippers And My Lord false of heart and eye from the City of
Malice by the river of Cold Blood. you Good General Bloody Hand Leader of the
Legions of Darkness. worthy Mr Envy Brother of Goliath. even he of Gath.
worship[f]ul young Master H—l fire from the Pit of Tophet. and you too
Venerable Mr Satans cast off clothes ferry man over the River of Death. I
beseech your attention for some breif space of time while I lay before you the
reasons and causes of our present downsitting—first youll allow me however to
brew a little of our congenial beverage which the Angels term Liquid fire and
distilled D—tion—"

So while the worthy statesman was concocting a stiff tumbler of
whisky toddy He really and seriously plunged into the Buisness they were met
about. The scene which I have given above was not the opening of this Secret
conclave they had met over night and by appointment in this out of the way
Change House where their plans and proposals had been mentioned and met till
Montmorency proposed refreshment and after it was brought in that is from 2 to
7 oclock in the morning little had been done except drinking swearing and
edifying conversation But light as might seem their conduct their intentions were
of the deepest import and both in mental powers and personal influence these
evil men were competent to the deeds they aimed at the Overthrow of Lord
Northangerland and the establishment of a grand Septumvirate. Jeremiah
Simpson detested Percy because He was aware in what light Percy regarded him
and as while in his power His head was not safe a day he brought to the
enterprise his own shrewd. and cruel heart backed by 30000 renegade Reformers
The Sheik Medina alias Lord Jordan was wide awake to the fact that his master
would rather see his severed head anyday than 10000 sovereigns and being
naturally more than sufficiently malevolent he lent his luxurious selfishness

---

[34] Despite the reference throughout to a well-known folk figure, the text would
seem to be Branwell's.

with 8000 Africans Richard Naughten had times without number born the sneers and superciliousness of the President. till his Rude gloomy dissapointed heart which only beat to cherish its remembrance of wrongs had accumulated such a store of Insult as moved his Giant bulk and giant influence with the lower orders into the thick of this Conspiracy General Massena thought Percy had been playing the fool of late and deeming his the weaker side wisely stepped over to the aid of his congenial accquaintances with 30000 veteran Frenchmen Hector Montmorency having suffered wrong from Percy in early life and having betrayed him in latter times being moreover generally very uncomfortable in his freinds prescence and desirous as he this morning observed of washing his toe tops in his blood being likewise hard up for want of cash and grasping at any means to come by it seemed the most zealous of all the conspirators Lord M Lofty's aid I can in no wise account for save from that natural spirit of his which would always lead him from the duty of defence of another to the pleasure of tearing another to peices he was a downright Atheistical Republican and as the world was not with him he espoused any change which might bring it nearer his sentiments The Prince Quashia Quamina was with them but for this I can give no reason except. drunkeness and faithlessness with a dim notion that his New freinds hated Zamorna more than his old one. besides the whole set of them hungered for power and thirsted for wealth this was a labour of love and they set to work on it with demoniacal delight. for Percys fall was not to be their ultimate object The demolition of Orders rank and property the murder of their private enemies the annihilation of Angria a land they agreed to hate and finally each in his own private mind held such a concealed hope of ultimate dominion for him self. that backed by Ability of mind and means such as few could attain to the conspiracy was one most formidable in character and terrible in its prospects

There were they sitting round the table in a lighted smoky Inn Parlour Seven heads such as once seen would be remembered above a thousand Montmorency leaning forward over the table with both arms upon it and twirling a crusher between his fingers with massy expressive features changing to every expression of scorn or hatred or reckless hilarity and the high stern forhead streaked with thin brown hair shining in the light of seven tumblers of most comfortable toddy He was talking in a deep rapid voice to Jeremiah Simpson who had leant back on his seat with hands plunged into his breeches pockets his satyr lips disposed to a brutal sneer and his Iron grey countenance mingling as it were with his touzled steely hair. Lord Lofty was listning for the moment resting his head on his elbows and glancing his distorted optics first to one speaker. and then to another though it always happened that he seemed eyeing the silent man instead of the speaking one As for Naughten that vast mass of feature that mountain brow of Eld. all lowered upon them in one gloom of bitter brooding thought speaking little but evidently ready for terrible action And Mr Sdeath—HE—carved in the thud end. with tumbler and bottle on the hob looked upon all in the room with an eye of utter contempt and only intimated his knowledge of what the[y] said with after each speaker had finished a grunt of unutterable scorn he had a companion in the armchair opposite—the Prince. very badly drunk. and enveloped in a cloud of tobbacco smoke but every now and then from his perfumed canopy flourishing a clenched fist and bursting out with something not at all to the purpose that Mont generally hushed by getting up patting his wild black locks and looking tenderly to the state of his hard used tumbler Massena sat cheek by jowl with Simpson and Medina lay in the window seat picking his teeth and sometimes clapping three yards of clay into his mouth with a reek which Sdeath by no means could by no means put up with but ever and anon he expressed his disrelish of the outlandish instrument by as he gazed acerbly on the disguised Italian. venting between a grunt and a mutter "Humph fooil of all fooils"— "Tom Nod" — "A bonny seight tha art.!" and "I reckon nought ont!" the last uttered with an impatient aversion of his bodily man from the noxious spectacle.

And though this group were so dissimilar in look and action yet in one thing they all chimed together when any Body Mont or Jerry especially put any low joke or pointed a sneering allusion to Northangerland all the party joined together in one well pleased laugh As the Democrat and the Banker from knowing their victim master so long were nobly furnished with stories and falshoods to exercise their wits upon it never lay idle for five minutes and in the Irishmans hands was always going in some ridiculous turn or other—But the deeper subject matter of the discussion was now Shall the Leaders of the Army obey Northangerland in an engagement with Warner before they shewed openly their intentions toward him There were two sides to the question first Angria was so thouroughly the object of their Hatred that it would be a pity indeed to spare a blow levelled at it. and if they did under Percy suceed in quashing it still the benifit in its ruin would remain with them after Percy himself was ruined But Secondly on the other hand a victory over Warner gained under Percy would in the worlds estimation be gained by Percy—so would it be advisable thus to strengthen his power by letting him shine forth so brightly the moment before they meant to quench him for ever? —Mont was agitating the question but as he spoke the wind and rain had increased to such a degree without that Jordan drew back the curtain to look forth upon the storm but he had no sooner taken a glance than he laid down his pipe gathered up his limbs and tramped with great speed out of the room

"Where are ye going?" shouted Mont and Quash after the fashion of one in his liquors made a flourishing attempt to get up and after him without knowing the why and wherefore but old Sdeath cried scornfully

"Nivver heed him—theres more tint at Flodden!"[35]
And so Hector himself rose went to the window and looked out to see what was the matter after which turning suddenly round and slapping his arm he cried

"Its like to be horrid stormy today Gents!" and then looked sternly at the door. Those who went to the window saw a carriage standing in the rain and

---

[35] The site at which in 1513 James IV of Scotland was defeated by the English.

directly from the opened door a mournful and boisterous howl of wind that blew the smoke out of the chimney into the middle of the room but while those nearest the fire were hastily rising to get out of the reek and before Montmorency had time to finish one warning sentence

"Stand to your tackle men! —"

A gentlemanly looking person opened the door and stood sideway for a superior to pass in—A man in a black surtout of stature so lofty that he had to bow slightly in entering under the door way and whose bald beautifully arched forehead and wan careworn physiognomy upon removing his hat apprised even the ecstatic Quashia of his awful Identity But utterly fearless of the appalling apparition Montmorency and Simpson had advanced their huge bulks to an instantaneous rencontre and were just breaking forth with brazen tongues when the wonderfully kindled eyes and brightened brow of their great Antagonist spoke to theire[sic] senses even before his voice though as he rested a wan hand on Sdeaths chair back he said sternly and at once—

"Have done! Let me hear nothing—My Lord Macara Mr Montmorency Betake yourselves to the carriage without there and drive off instantly to Verdopolis—Richard—"

Montmorency with a face dark red with rebellion interrupted him

"I'm sorry my Lord that your loss has unsettled your ideas but you seem to forget that our motions are as free as—"

"Then go while they are free Sir!"

"And" burst in Simpson blackening like a thunder cloud "you ought to be aware that in this state you are unfit as I have known before for—

And Montmorency again resumed

"That we are as free as yourself my lord free as Kings and for Souls good Lord! why we have a little sense. maudlin sentimentality has not done us clean into holyhood!"

"Blast him" cried Jeremiah "is he drunk. Confound your impudence Sir!"

"Mr Montmorency" cried Macara very white and squinting greatly "This will do no good let us go my Lord your suspicions are unjust Hector give me your arm—"

Indeed his Lordship was very glad of such assistance in passing by the silent Earl But Mont seemed inclined to bluster for as he stood near the door—he had edged so far out—he fronted Percy with

"I demand by what right is this done I demand—"

Percy was in no mood for trifling he suddenly grasped at Hectors collar and thrust him out of the door with a grim "G—d D—n you begone! —" and Mathias muttering "Confound it!" sourly obeyed[36] for as he stumbled into the passage his eye caught a glimpse of some soldiers standing by the out door corner He shouted after them with a sneer as he was getting into the coach

"Capitulate its no use just now! Obey!"

---

36 This section consists of page 2, then page 1 of Bon 145(3) at the BPM.

"Aye. aye" roared Jeremiah back again "Give him rope and.! What's your pleasure Alexander—?"

Without answering him Northangerland said

"I move upon the insurgents to morrow evening You are off your posts Generals and now resume them. Richard commence immediatly an advance upon Cornshaw moor to receive Fidena. Medina scour the Hills before us with your cavalry to intercept or Harass the Angrian outposts Massena down now to Edwardston and concentrate your Frenchmen upon the Morena Quashia—But go thou and vomit thy Liquors drunken brute. Wharton" —turning to the Gentleman at the door "collect my staff directly—Gentlemen you know your orders."

"Hilloo" said Jeremiah through his nose "your memorys impaired by your distresses sir You've forgot me What must I do recollect I had an odd 30000 at your service—?"

"Go you to H—l!" was the savage reply whereat the great brute shrugged his huge shoulder bones and sticking his tongue in his cheek stood with his coat tails under his arm and his back to the fire watching with a demon sneer his companions troop off to their destinations Naughten in a deep gloom. Jordon pulling a scornful face as he went out Massena stopping to drain off a half full tumbler of half and half. Quashia rising up and directly sitting down again with his eyes rolling and one fist struck on his knee as if something prodigious were forthcoming Northangerland stood quite still and Sdeath sat utterly unmoved by all the suprises and discord. his face turned to the fire in noble content a pipe in his cheek. and at the conclusion of what each person had to say emitting a loud expectoration with an expressive grunt of scorn

"Well now" cried the Prince again rising "I'll be dished! To think now! Lord! what a move—I say you there—you Sir and you. I say. Rat me I say its Its very stormy and moreover. Be gad—I'm no where steady—D—nation!"

With this beautifully lucid oration he concluded a first parallel or zigzag between the fire and the door then upon his second angle he cried

"You two—you two there—you and you—you'd better clear up them cursed alegar[37] faces rive my nightcap! what a couple. G—d d—n!"

That last emphatic expression concluded the second move which carried the Prince with a reel into the passage where he was first to thud against the wall in an attempt at his Great Coat and next blasting out of doors at his servants because he could not get feasably settled on to his Nag—Simpson went to the window where he laughed to see the area filled with carriages Mont and Macara driving townward Naughten Massena and Jordon each on a different direction but not without exchanging preliminary nods at each other. Wharton breaking furiously from among them on Horseback to collect the Lord President's Staff. Quashia reelling on his wild charger as if in a gale at sea and A terrible storm of wind and rain covering all with shining wet and harmonizing the threatning sudden departures

---

[37]   Sour ale.

"Gow!" said Jeremiah "I'm off too—hows your Daughter?" Then with a loud laugh he left the room and as he went Sdeath too reared his majestic bulk. knocking the last ashes from his pipe and draining the last drop of his toddy

"I've getten a character! And th' raams noan so wholsome! There is as isnt varry respectable company!" Then when he had acheived the out passage he exclaimed

"Him 'at's behind 'll pay th'shot!" and made a speed retrograde toward his venerable Nag

Percy was alone again with a terrific coming conflict to think off and remember that he had never rested since he had stood by his Daughters Grave

In the course of half an hour Military Gentlemen on horseback began to gallop up and ere long these with their servants crowded all the Inn Sir John Denard being among them who signifyed to the Earl that his Staff were round him to accompany his ride to the central Division and Percy answering with an inclination of the head re[e]ntered his carriage which surrounded by its Warlike attendance whirled off through the pelting November storm

P B B
Decr 16th
1836

From the interview between Greville and Percy in Elrington Hall my Narrative has gradually been enlarging its scope till last chapter wherein I presentd to view the Leader of a mighty army And now I must give a sight of an Army itself. —

The ARMY OF VENGEANCE the last sole defence of trodden and trampled Angria the revenge of her murdered childern and her exiled King

My Readers then must imagine a wide elevated tract of Upland covered with bent grass. the summit of the Olympian Hills and beneath the unpitying skies of November its whole face covered with a gathered host of stern warworn but well Armed men all their out posts flanked with cannon and pickets planted far around down the gorges of the valleys but this main mass gathered in attentive silence here thousands together leaning on their blackened Muskets with eyes whose desperate fire had fixed for the time in deep stirless attention for the Gusty winds through that wild day had raged themselves at last into an Evening calm and now a clear grey sky arched far above them down to the pale watery orange of the west and away to the one lone star that quivered in that silent dome

Not a drum nor a voice could be heard but the countless figures toward the outskirts ranged themselves black and sharp edged against the skies each bayonet point or feather distinguishable against the lucid grey while a great stone amid them was mounted by a single Gentleman and surrounded by a host of military men of distinction—That Gentleman was a slight and slender figure dressed in the deepest mourning who stood up took off his hat holding it before his face for an instant as if in prayer and then giving it to one beneath he turned to the multitude wiping the thin light hair from his brow What a sublime ascendancy has mind over body and how wholly at times can some souls shake of the defects and feebleness of their mortal coil.![38] That pale slender little man though he stood coughing for a minute before he could speak and held one hand pressed against his side stooping as from pain so soon as he had overcome the fit looked round with a calm enthusiasm that wrapt his features out of the expression of this weary world the light restless eye kindled as it glanced over the martial scene and the firm serious lips as he looked to the sky softened into one strange seraph smile just such a look would have had the face of a dying Martyr when as he felt the steel in his heart he turned to that heaven wither he was starting to fly just so that little wan figure in the cold moveless air gathered an unearthly dignity when it fronted the gaze of his own adoring thousands

"My fellow countrymen!" he said "My freinds the hour that calls us together is so solemn that you must forgive me one moments pause A look into that Heaven reminds me too well who are there!—"

He could hardly proceed for the high sweet earnest voice was choked with an irresistible and thrilling emotion no pause in the most sacred music could be so impressive as that one after the clear emphatic tones which all heard amid the complete stillness of the scene But it was plain the Spirit that spoke was too strong for its febble frame hardly less troubled than his short silence was his earnest face when he looked from above again to address his soldiers

"But!" —I cannot give the thrilling *soul* of his expression— "But—IF we fight for those who are above all earthly aid though we cannot defend them longer our duty is to Revenge! And though God has taken to himself what he gave us he has yet left a shadow of their presence in our memory of those who are gone! And when Revenge is only a just Retribution when it but gives to the Destroyers the doom of those they destroyed—you will attend although beneath the almost unobstructed prescence of God I call you to shed the blood of those whose farther punishment must remain with him—On the threshold of Battle and addressing you perhaps for the last time ere I or thousands of yourselves may leave this world for ever permit me to gaze a little after my departed freinds. when they are in the very place whither you and I may go! —When those we love die in the natural course of events on the bed of disease or sickness we feel however we may sorrow that they are only arrived at their journeys end But when they die amid their own blood or of greif for private ruin and a dying country then we sorrow as one without hope for they seem taken from us before their time—And surely before her time has died Our Queen—our Pride! —"—The voice stopped again in its own earnestness—

"When first I saw her I thought she was destined "Long to reign over us" and my mind conjured up around her the vision of many happy years But I thought too that my country was destined to a different fate and—mark the weakness of human foresight—Death was even then by her side and ruin was close upon us!

---

38 Compare Shakespeare's *Hamlet*, III, i, 66-67.

yet it is difficult recollecting what she was for me. to imagine that one world holds us both no longer and that I who amid all my struggles for my King and Country looked with Joy to the Idea that her heart would rejoice in all my sucesses and approve of every blow I gave—that I who looked for those smiles and that approval must look for them no more. —That should to morrow give us a victory however great and glorious her ears are closed to the intelligence and her heart is dead to any reply! —[39] And surely too died before his time that child of Hope and promise! —The Noble Boy! —My heart stops my voice when I remember his end—passing from this world in torment—mangled and bloody from the grasp of Men worse than Demons His death shreik wrung from agonies which no one has ever born and lived and—even while with little hands clasped he looked wildly to those feirce faces for mercy—the Burning Iron was thrust into his dying eyes! —But—My countrymen—God who has given him rest shall give him vengeance. And there is one waiting on that day to receive him and with whom he now is who saw in Ernests death his own! The last groan echoed by scornful laughter the last look. wandering on faces raging with Hatred—and like himself he knows that Child was a stainless spotless Lamb! —He called upon his father when he died. I have knowledge too that he called upon me—His Noble Father was far away But dayly and hourly do I sorrow that I did not answer to his call—Oh had I—had I but been present then this week body should have fallen peirced with a thousand wounds or his little heart should have throbbed in safty pressed to mine—But this is useless talk. all is over and this misery more is added to the countless troubles of your Exiled King I who ought to have clasped him safe from harm have only held in my hands dabbled with his hearts blood his cold corrupting Clay! Not for worlds would I live over again the Hour when I hung over the white silent face and the gory Eyes turned sightlessly to mine—For what Angrians was that murderous dead perpetrated. why did these men thus hasten their own headlong speed toward hell? —It was that they might stab your monarchs heart through that of his Darling child They knew that unlike them he had a heart and soul and feelings they wanted to harrow those to madness and those who laughed at the dying struggle of Ernest now for the same reason rejoice over the untimly end of Mary one end is answered by all each deed gives Zamorna another pang—Alone Aidless Exiled. on the rocky shores of the Ascension Isle Every wind wafts toward that Noble spirit the death toll of a departed freind He always looked to his own heart and hand for deliverance but they are chained and prisoned now. to whom can he look then to whom ought he to look.? —Angrians! he looks to YOU! —To morrow with these ten thousand Arms for a few hours seconded by courageous hearts and He has deleverance he regains his kingdom your Destroyers themselves destroyed and your Debt of Vengeance paid!—What is the price you must pay for such a glorious day—3 or 5000 lives of men—But should these men struggle for another when on the issue of that struggle they must know nothing and when

---

[39] This portion consists of two pages in the Brotherton Collection, catalogued as "Events succeeding the Angrian Revolution."

they shall never look upon the faces of those they have saved more than on those of those they avenge? —And shall they not And must they not.? —is Death a sleep is heaven a dream is the Eternal world a grave is Immortality decay? — Angrians over me this hour there stretches one great grey sky the stars shall be its distance posts and along that path they number millions of million[s] miles Can heaven be beyond them if beyond them be only stars? Heaven my countrymen is neither there nor here but it is with US The moment we leave our clay—What is that Heaven what is that other world? —Oh Angrians Advance boldly to the thick of the coming Battle oppose your breast[s] to the cannon and Bayonet sustain one short pang and—you shall Behold the Eternal world!— When I think upon this—when I know that there is but one step between me and such a knowledge—such an existence I wish I long to DIE! —Long long before my time those have died to this world who have been the glory and worship of my thoughts—But they live They shine in glory—I shall one day be with them and—My work finished my country saved my King restored. and I care not How soon I go!—"

The little wan looking man had now completely lapsed into soul that only in its brightest lights glanced from his extatic eyes he looked again upward and beaming with lofty joy like a prophet beholding visions of regenerate happiness turned round to his Hearers

> "Why should we mourn departed freinds
> Or shake at Death's alarms?
> Tis but the voice that Jesus sends
> To call them to his Arms![40]

Why did the tears come into my eyes when I looked upward with. with thoughts that gone for ever from me were the Beings I had honoured and loved so well. And—" Apparently now forgetting his Audience for both his thin hands were folded and tears running down his shining cheeks— "Could I weep for thy death my Noble Boy Could I greive to see thee removed from a world of sorrow whose ceasless and wearing troubles were indeed unfit for a soul so high as Thine! — Often I loved to watch that spirit unfolding its infant buds of thought and feeling whose wondrous beauty bore full promise of flowers too glorious for this barren world I thought if this tree shall possess hardihood as beauty it shall overshadow my country with a greater than its fathers shade but I knew it was unfit for earth and do I mourn that God hath transplanted it to Paradise? —

No the fevered struggle of thy dark departure is not forgot in the Great Redeemers Arms A crown of glory is thine who felt the worthlessness of an Earthly crown Creation itself lies open to the ardent gaze that sought from me in earth knowledge often more than I could give and thy warm feelings and affections shall meet with just return where every Angel round thee is so like to Thee! —has a heart like thine! —There she who sleeps in this world in her now covered grave. Has waked to companionship with her blessed mother and with

---

[40] The first stanza of Hymn 3 in Book II of Isaac Watts' *Hymns and Spiritual Songs*. Watts has "departing" rather than "departed."

his whose heart was her Heaven below She yet shall look on my endeavours if this life blood flows for Adrian and Angria The drops by her own eyes numbered may be registered on the Almighty's page! —And though these feet through this winter have on every path trodden over the dying and the dead. each heart around this wide land that has bled for its country shall not wholly die but shall beat again where God shall wipe the tears from our eyes—Have not I wept for freinds departed and is not my Mother dead whose spirit indeed was worthy of companionship with her sons departed Queen! —My heart brings back a childhood past with her away My eyes have dimmed over the decaying letters of her stone my memory only enshrines the shadows of her form—But though my body with hers shall one day moulder in the dust my soul shall yet again stand face to face with her own!— This night as well as fifty years hence I may walk with those over whose paths Archangels wander with whom worlds systems are halting places—Creation their study. Christ their companion and Heaven their HOME!"

Warner turned and stretched his arm to his people crying

"Where is the dastard now that cares for death? The coward breath[e]s not round me who can now shrink back from fight—You all know the Alternatives the salvation of your King and country or the wings and the world of Angels—in one word—Life or immortality Earth or Heaven! —

Angrians your Destroyers with all their leaders scorpion like divided and raging within themselves spread down beyond the Hollows of these very Hills they detach half their force to intercept Fidena while the other Half may devour us. —I shall strike in between the two the Duke will as his couriers have given us knowledge to day fall upon one division with twice the force they anticipate I and you now attack the southern wing and God to his own will give in time the Victory Now my country men if ever arouse yourselves. now look at this land of graves now think upon your exiled Monarch now rally under the flag of Vengeance Now at last and resistlessly ANGRIA ARISE!"

These last words were spoken with the force of a clarion And ere they had died off. 10 thousand voices shouted back the echo in one thundering ARISE That shout roared round the moor and rattled against the surrounding summits till the Dark. dying twilight absorbed its last echo into silence then just as Warner again prepared to speak from afar off a single deep roll broke upon the solemn pause those nearest him say his feathers quivered and that one word of heroic delight burst from his lips unconsciously—But with a clear high voice unbroken by exhaustion he called

"Let us now my freinds praise God for the mercies he has conferred and together intreat for the mercies to come

As the one hundredth Psalm
Shine on us God of Angria shine
Oh round us pour thy light divine
For sailing oer a stormy sea

> Through life to death we trust in thee![41]

As he gave out these noble words a burst of music rose thrilling from the Regimental Bands with long protracted swell of trombone and trumpet till from the symphony an ocean of manly voices took up the religious strain and that Sacred Psalm rose up in thundering chorus to the again lowering twilight skies as each stanza sunk its awful sound the single silver voice struck the ear with wonderful contrast So earnestly and enthusiastically giving them the words that again rose up in a solemn storm of sound

P B Bronte
Decr 17th
1836

---

[41] Compare with the lines on p. 206.

[Angria and the Angrians]
III (e)

All[1] of course the sole other Governors for his Monarchy was by no means Despotic and all united in the idea of carrying forward their Arms and victorys.

Quamina on his part boiled with Indignation to behold the encroachments and increase of the few poor scoundrels who had besought his fathers protection not 5 years before Assembling his Cheifs together He deliberated upon instant war—a war of extermination and gathering forces to the amount of 20 or 30000 men he commenced it by hostilitys along the western banks of the Niger But I have already spoken of the Abilities of young King Arthur and now they were exerted to their utmost He pushed several different companies of men under his 12 hardy and desperate. confederates into the very vitals of his enimies country stormed and burnt Acrofcroomb and Lancomfoodia Advanced upon the Cirhala and at last concentered his troops within sight of Coomassie. which great and Ancient city was doomed to the same fate as all savage tribes have suffered when they let in the stern European like a snake upon their heaven[2] The watchword of the 12 was Revenge for Fredric! —and their endeavour was to storm and destroy the Capital. On the Night of August 19 1786 it fell after a desperate conflict carried on beneath its walls and through its streets While Quamina was stabbed in his palace by conspirators who wished to ensure their own safety by the betrayal of their country. but the Rough Grim Twelve were not so to be humbugged They hung these followers along with the Loyal Nobles. set fire to the city and massacred every soul with in it out of a stern but cruel policy.

So fell under Arthur W—the Empire of Ashantee. for after this time though the Blacks still kept up a predatory warfare among their farthest frontiers nothing material remained to stop the conquerors from penetrating from the Senegal to the Etrei[3] And speedily they began the buisness founding towns in

---

[1] This portion of text consists of leaves 10, 12, 16-19, (11 pages), 11.2x18.5 cm., in Ashley 187 at the BL. Although Wise included these leaves with the Angrian material in his Ashley volume, the material is not directly part of the saga. Branwell seems to have set out to review the history of the Confederacy and of Angria at the same time that he composed III (d); the dates overlap completely.

[2] Presumably a comparison with the entry of the serpent into Eden.

[3] Again Branwell's geography is somewhat fanciful. The Senegal and Gambia Rivers are well north of traditional Ashanti territory, while the Rio Elrei lies well to the south of it. In short Branwell claims a huge section of West Africa for the Glass Town Confederacy, an area that roughly corresponds with the 1826

various eligable[sic] situations exploring lands and shooting the Negroes. While still increasing ship loads of Emigrants filled the harbour of VERDOPOLIS with the seeds of. something mighty to come

The rising nation was becoming to large for one man to govern at least so thought the leaders of the Band they concerted among themselves for some time at last coming to the determination that the land should be divided into 5 parts and one being held in reserve each of the other four should be given to him most qualified to keep it. Who was he? here was a question such as has seldom been decided without blood and that desicion was looked for here but the people to whom was left the determination thought the merits of. W—. Sneachie. Parry & Ross. so preeminent that they almost unanimously concurred in assigning to each of them that quarter he was most fitted to rule.

But the Land its divisions and constitution we must describe in our third chapter as follows

CHAPTER III^d

I said in the commencement of my last division that the most firtile[sic] portion of Africa was comprehended between the Gambia and the Calabar. and so it was but listen to the detail and forget the falsitys received in the world about it[4]

This portion of Africa then is in its general features very like England. placed under the sky of Italy. at least the flowers the woods the animals are European through their luxuriance agrees rather with their Equatorial Situation than the stern and rigid North. This Land. Beginning westward from the mouth of the Gambia to Cape Palmas and from the Senegal to the Sea[5] is a grand expanse of. Woodland and cultivable champaign well watered diversified with hills and laid out in a noble park like scenery probably not a palm or Exotic about it but. clothed with the Elms the Oak. and the Ashes of England with the Myrtles the Cypress and here and there the Olive of Italy. Always canopied by the divine Southern Sky and now spotted with the Halls of Old England. from Palmas to Cape St Pauls and up northward to the Cong Mountains it is yet more open flat and hotter. but now covered with corn or majestic pasture ground From St Pauls along the mouths of the Niger and hence to the Calabar it is still like England Deified but the Verdopolitan valley elevates the country into a table

---

map in *Blackwood's*—see p. 305, n. 19—and with Branwell's map in **The History Of The Young Men**—see vol. I, p. 137 and Alexander EW, 33.

[4] The 1826 *Blackwood's* article notes that "The discovery of a water communication between the Gulf of Guinea and the most populous, fertile, and civilized (if we may use the term) portions of Central Africa, is of great importance to the world, and more especially to Africa itself"(707).

[5] Branwell's geography is rather confused; the Senegal lies north of the Gambia, Cape Palmas south of the Gambia.

land and beyond is the region which used to be called Soudan.[6] Heath towers over Heath hills beyond Hills ending at length in the huge snow clad summits of the Branii Hills the Robbers Peaks and Sovereign Grey Garach. far beyond him all again is Africa the hills sink into plains and the streams are lost in the burning deserts so round Eastward to the Calabar and the Etrei which flows among tropical palms and African sands and hither it was in 1790 where the Defeated Africans fled among their neighbour tribes of Negroes to come forth again only after long lapse of years

In such a land. at the cheif Mouth of the Niger and 50 miles from the open Atlantic Verdopolis was built the capital of the rising Nation but. we must now tell the divisions and the Constitution which were conferred on that Neucleaus[sic] of a World

Firstly the country was divided into four kingdoms of which the westernmost. was the kingdom of.

I[st] Senegambia
Arthur W———— King
was declared to extend from the mouth of that river to the banks of the upper Niger. 400 miles in length and hither flocked the Irish as their monarch was a Native of the Emerald Isle

II[d.] Parrisland
Edward Parry King
reaching from thence to the Cape St Pauls and stretching its habitable part. along the sea coast with excellent Harbours whence and as the Sovereign was a sailor and an Edinburgh man the Scotch and the Maritime emigrants settled

III[d] Rossland
John Ross King
lying in the same direction Eastward under the Elbow of the last. and as the Monarch was of the same occupation and country so its settlers were all Scotch and Merchants

IIIIth Sneachies land Alexander Sneachi King
whose southern border lay parallel but 200 miles from the sea for twice that distance E and W elevated mountainous and covered cheifly with heath and snow which pointed it out as the fit kingdom for the Perthshire man Sneachi and accordingly all its settler[s]. were Highlanders or men of the Isles

---

6   Again some of Branwell's geography is fanciful, but the sub Saharan area north of the Niger River and its tributaries was known in the early nineteenth century as Soudan or Nigritia.

Vth Nigritia[7]

Stretching along the sea from Rossesland to the Calabar and bordered northward by Sneachisland. This is No Kingdom but it contains the great capital Verdopolis and its bearing on the others I must here proceed to explain

The Constitution

The first four of the Divisions above enumerated were Kingdoms Hereditary and limited for though there could be no power exercised within them but from the King and though his Authority in every case was the last appeal within the realm which without further provision would give a despotism and completly dissever each division from the other. these evils were all avoided by a Fifth Division that of Nigritia common to the rest under control of none but governed by a Union of all for the Sovereigns of this Division were the MINISTRY Appointed by a majority of the Kings officiating as the Government of all the Union and exercising that authority in Verdopolis where they reigned the Kings of a PARLIAMENT divided as in England into two Assemblies the Lords and Commons likewise common to all the Kingdoms and possessing jurisdiction over all The Navy and the Army were Each. under control of the Kings who elected their Heads by a majority But the parliament had their purse in hand and the Ministry their conduct The church (which was that Established in England) was under the control of the Kings too and its property lay in grants from the Legislature. The whole affair was a wheel where Each great power was satisfied by possessing the name of King and the form of a kingdom While all being so united by a common rule and a single head gave a Union and Solidity to the severred Nation and from every power in the Monarchy though it were composed of several men still going by a majority of those it gave them as much consistency as in One King the Judgement extracted from different conflicted ideas could do Then Tyranny and Despotism were prevented by a Parliament Chosen from All countrys by all the people that yet could not swerve into anarchy from being governed by a Ministry chosen by the Kings. So the chain wound round the Confederacy binding all together in the common name of
THE VERDOPOLITAN UNION.
Verdopolis its capital Nigritia its Nucleus its kingdoms four but its nations one

CHAPTER IVth P B B—te
                                                        Aug 20th
                                                        1836

So soon as the land assumed a settled and regular form of Government its prosperity began to encrease with amazing rapidity All men extolled the newborn

---

7   This name is a new addition to Branwell's geography. For the source of the name, see the previous note.

Constitution and Old decayed sinking Europe looked toward the south as if all the world was to be revivified in Africa

Europe was certainly falling rapidly in to decay. The boldest noblest and most daring of her sons were embarking for Verdopolis Spain & Italy furnished thousands But England and Ireland and Scotland almost millions For Noble families and men of the greatest wealth and consequence were every day shipped of to Africa the Irish generally settling in Senegambia the Scotch in the other three Kingdoms and the English in the Independancy of Nigritia Spain and Italy sent their quota to the Gambia. But France Determined upon a settlement of its own

2 Islands of great <size> had been discovered lying opposite the coasts of Guinea the western most 300 miles and in itself 200 long the Easternmost 500 and 300 long these Islands were Tropical in character and began to be settled by Englishmen from the East and West Indies So the Verdopolitan Union took possession of them by [the] name of Fredericia and Menzies Isle giving the first to Frederic Hume the last to James M Hume. each being crowned King and taken in as component parts of the Union upon exactly the footing of the former Monarchies

But the French seized upon a Third Island lying South of Nigritia and in its northernmost coast touching upon the East Arm of the Niger[8] large in size European and cultivable They began to colonize it and name[d] it FRANCE building upon a New SEINE their dear loved PARIS wither all true Parisians flocked with eager wing But the Verdopolitan Government disputed their possession of the soil and War directly arose which was carried on for several years in a feirce heat neither party losing or gaining a deal—till On the termination of that Mighty Conflict which for 18 years had been desolating Europe its Actors released from war and beholding the wretched wreck of Ancient Thrones flocked in double numbers to the new found Canaan then The French Emper[or] being exiled to Helena fled to the nearest coast of the new FRANCE whereon his devout soldiers commanders and people crowded after him till France was literally drained into this Island and here transplanted it has since grown unshaken

So now I must strike into a new path for one comes upon the stage of whom I know not wether this world be worthy

In 1791 about 9 years after the foundation of the Verdopolitan Union Mr Edward Percy of Raistrick Hall Northumberland the Gentleman of whom we spoke in our first page after keeping his eyes long upon the Gambia determined to leave his country and settle upon its promise giving shore

---

8   Branwell is once more revising his history of the African settlement; these were formerly Stumps and Man and Wamons Islands. The islands presumably correspond to what were in fact Fernando Po, Sao Tome and Principe.

After the departure of Mr King in 1782. he had run into so headlong a course of dissipation as shockingly to impair both his health and his fortune So when Old King returned upon his second visit with the 4 Yorkshire people in search of recruits for his adopted country he had determined to return with him when that wretch fell into the hands of the Laws upon His way to Raistrick. such an event changed Percys mind and he ran on a while longer till King got his liberty from jail. upon which Master and Man both levanted to Ireland for the purpose of pouncing upon a victim to supply them with means for the wished for voyage in a long course of profligacy and Gambling they ran down the Earl of M——.[9] King Arthur of Senegambias father But M—— found out their duplicity and treachery so he took measures for the recovery of some thousands that Percy had won from his victim but a dark mystery ensued. M—— was found dead near his horse one morning between Dublin and Wicklow Sdeath had passed on the road during the night and Percy was discovered to have left his House for the port of Cork. in the South of Ireland In fact he and his servant had plotted M——s death and now with nearly 100 000 of plunder and his young wife Lady Helen—of the Beresford family—Mr Percy embarked for the dominions of the son of him whom he had destroyed

He landed in 1792 at Arthurston the Capital of Senegambia and bought a Noble Estate about 20 miles from the metropolis which he called The Woodlands while the Hall which adorned its park he christened Percy Hall and then settling there with his Lady and Establishment he beheld his property incre[a]se in value as emigration increased till his heart contracted and darkened into avaricious cruelty. But Old King stood at this time in a different situation from the one he held 10 years before he was no longer the cheif and leader of the expedition but as unknown and unregarded as a Yorkshire Drover well might be Their *Majestys* Arthur. or John or Edward or Alexander held no communion with the low bred drunken scoundrel Sdeath so Sdeath revenged himself in his own mysterious soul by consorting with a set of Demonaical Blackguards of the West in hopes to poison them to the degree of exciting trouble in the land

This however is anticipation. Mr Percy had in December 1792 a son born to him whom he named.

ALEXANDER PERCY!

And then let the child grow on and play on unknowing of the Man he should hereafter be. This child in the first years of his life was a beautiful angelic looking being with golden hair and blue eyes and musical voice and of a soul capricious passionate indulged and bent with amazing devotion toward the science of Music for which he discovered a passion in his earliest infancy that only strengthened as he grew into a soul wrapping sort of Idolatry—He lived on music and Dreaming for when disengaged from his grand pursuit he wandered about or laid himself down for hours on hours in the statly park or girdling woods beneath the glorious skies of an African summer Afternoon. The rich luxuriance of Nature the Deep blue of Heaven the gold and brightness of its

---

9   Mornington. See the **Life of Alexander Percy**, p. 95, n. 10 above.

clouds the dazzling effulgence of its Sun filled his unreasoning but sensitive spirit with a delight which he could not express or attempt to name It was the same when he accompanied his Mother to her cottage on the shores of the Atlantic where seated on her lap he would gaze for hours at the wide <welking> waving sea. The same at night when he stole out of the crowded and dazzling rooms of his fathers Hall to look at the Moon or Stars in the Midnight Sky it was that feeling too which led him to be for ever talking about religion the Bible and Heaven or whishing that to go there he might die but with opening youth came other feelings too a most ungovernable spirit wilful passionate and resentful embroiling him constantly with his hard heartless and bilious looking father but throwing him straightforward into the acquaintanceship and paths of the Drunken Demon old Robert Sdeath whose hardened soul being fired on him would not leave him but drew him on from one thing to another till even his Noble but Indulgent mother could not shut her eyes to the excesses of Her darling son

As young Alexanders time was passed among the very highest circles of Society in what was then the Loftiest and the most Dissolute city in the Union he eternally got himself entangled in the worship of some fair Divinity or other Having allways sense enough to keep out of the Fudge of Platonism[10] He in nine cases out of ten brought himself into serious predicaments with his idolatries But never surely did any one less care for peculiar situations than the wild thoughtless and enthusiastic young African who was himself considered a God in the temples where he worshipped paying very little attention to advice or consequences he dashed fairly into a course which as his father swore would D—n him before he was 5 years older

Among the many noble and beautiful stars in the Court of King Arthur there was one who shone preeminent. a sort of Lucifer a bright but fallen star. This was Lady Augusta Romana Di Segovia an Italian of the highest birth and most easy morality who as her parents were both dead held in guardianship the immense property of her young Brother the Earl of Jordan Her Establishments and dissipations being upon the most princly style of expenditure were with unscrupulous freedom defrayed from the coffers of her relative Creditors did the rest and farther she neither knew nor troubled herself about Being Eminently Beautiful and inspired by a most warm passionate and excitable soul she very soon arrested the gaze of the equally southern Alexander and knowing that so yo[u]ng magnificent looking and imaginative [a] lover was a prize not easily to be slighted she could not hinder herself from repaying him with real and ardent love. She was older than him this only gave her the more dominion and though he was wide awake to her profligacy and impetouosity[sic] he regarded her with feelings too warm to unhesitating to spend a thought about such trifles in other words he was only 18 years old a handsome indulged Boy with a spirit as reckless as corrupted and as unprincipled as the oldest scoundrel in Arthurstown and far far higher and impassioned than any there or elsewhere old or young—

---

[10] i e., the doctrine or practice of Platonic love.

However the result was his marriage with Lady Segovia at her Palace in the metropolis whereupon his father burst into a paroxysm of rage laid hold of him by force and conveyed him away into the University of the Philosophers Isle where he was forced to enter upon his studies with the other Academicians

Swearing Revenge and distracted with dissapointments Percy gathered a knot of dissipated young Westerns formed a s[e]cret society of Atheistic Republicans began to laugh at religion and rebel against the heads of college stud[y]ing only in secret and idling all day. But the Authoritys were not to be bearded the[y] investigated his affairs discovered his infamous Association brought him and his followers to trial and fined him in 100000£ or banishment for ever to the Ascension Isle. Now not a stiver of this enormous sum would Mr Percy senior disburse nor could his son by any possibility of himself discharge it so he applied to his freinds at Arthurston Lord Caversham a villainous Old Nobleman and Jeremiah Simpson a Demonaical Banker to whom he owed enormous sums already which in case of his banishment they never could receive these two were Augustas freinds and she used all the power she had to prevail upon them but a far more powerful argument was their own intrest So they drew up a stipulation by which upon their paying off his prodigious fine they should be able the moment he entered into his fathers estates to come upon them for an equivalent with single and compound interest of 10 per cent a claim which would sink the property almost to the shades but young Percy stuck at nothing he signed the agreement paid his money passed his examination the first man of his year and with spirits broken and principles departed flew back to his Goddess Augusta

On the day of his arrival His father being out hunting received a fall from his Horse which caused him to be conveyed home sensless. Caversham Simpson Montmorency and Vernon upon receipt of the intelligence hasted to the Segovia Palace where Lady Augusta fairly met them by a proposal for the murder of Mr Percy—she wanted to revenge herself and enter upon his property they wanted their share of the money which would accrue on the event Old R P Sdeath Mr P—s servant heartened them on with a word in season and the result was that he should do it in his own way on the following morning Young Percy coming in during their discussion assented to the deed and early next morning as agreed on while Caversham Vernon and Montmorency were calling to know how Mr Percy Did Sdeath being alone with his Master throttled him and cried out saying (a likely thing in reality) that while in a violent fit of passion Mr Percy had received a stroke of apoplexy. Whatever Lady Helen thought on the subject she was much too devotedly attached to her son to dare to implicate him openly She bore the awful event in silence and Mr Percy was carried to the grave with pomp and procession but no eye wept for him—who never wept for another

Alexander now entered into possession of his fathers Estates but his right was hardly more than nominal more than half of them was due His Creditors. though indeed Augusta intreated him to refuse payment of his vast Debts to Caversham and Simpson because she knew they dared not come upon him in a court of Law that would rip up things rather unpleasant to a Peer of the

Realm and a wealthy Banker However Augusta was too open and daring in her suggestions they came to the ears of the Demonaical creditors and henceforward Her doom was sealed. Sdeath was hired to put her out of the way and he did it by poison. So Percy almost distracted by the event and broken by the payment of huge Debts upon Gambling transactions found no rescource but to bow to his creditors and think afterwards of revenge He paid away 150000£ in all and then threw himself outwardly into fresh dissipation and inwardly into awful musing and bitter melancholy.

But he was more captivating and interesting than ever in his person so He kept all his station in the world of fashion and there in Arthurston at the court of his Majesty meeting with Mary Henrietta Wharton Daughter of Lord George Wharton of Alnwick in Nigritia A light seemed anew to break upon his soul She was a young and lovely creature with generous heart and quick warm feelings with an imagination that spoke in the lustre of her eyes and a heart that could hardly beat without freinds and freindship round it. She saw this statly melancholy and suspicious Gentleman. so her susceptibility or sentimentalism was touched. She found his vastness and ardour of soul so could not help loving [so] grand a man. he found all he hoped in her and gave her his hand in 1814. After which they both lived in a sort of paradise together among their statly groves of Percy Hall or in the grandest circles of African Nobility at the Paris of the West. She presented her Lord with 2 sons but his capricious temper hated the idea of looking on men as his children so he comissioned the hoary Bloodhound Sdeath to destroy them. but the villain only secreted them and Mary though filled with anguish could not speak against her God on earth She bore the sorrow in secret till she gave birth to a daughter and this he received as the image of its mother and his hope in years to come. But Mary fell into a consumption and wasted away through summer while Horrible Anguish fell upon her Husband till she died in his Arms and then he mourned as if without hope [H]is warm feelings were so torn by the blow as never to recover He in a manner flew from the scenes of past enjoyment. came to Verdopolis and commenced there a run of hollow heartless dissipation. Entered the Army and followed His King in a campaign against the Blacks where he planned in conjunction with Sdeath a gross conspiracy against his superior officer Earl St Clair in order to remove him from competition for the hand of a Beautiful Heiress in the North[11] Happy was it for that lady that this treachery exploded for wedded to so heart broken a profligate only misery through life could be hers he was tried condemned and confined for 6 months in the tower but on his release he Eloped with the Lady of H Montmorency Esqr a wealthy young Barrister and one of his darkest Associates The Injured Husband commenced proceedings against him the lady forsaken in a while fell into a fever and died.[12] Percy could not tell where to turn for to add to his troubles debts were again accumulating and the two Usurers

---

11 Lady Emily Charlesworth—see p. 189, n. 3.
12 Harriet O Connor.

Caversham and Simpson pressed hard for another 100000£. Percy turned on them fought a Duel with the old Earl whom he slew and now at last utterly surrounded by difficulties he gathered together a knot of young broken and dissipated profligates of fashion hard up like himself. procured a fleet vessel and with Sdeath his servant set sail from Africa with the resolution of never returning again—

But once out on the open sea his active unprincipled mind began to speculate upon some method of retreiving his broken fortunes Piracy with his men and means seemed the likliest way so crossing the Atlantic Northward to the seas of Europe he entered on the lawless and bloody trade taking and cruelly destroying many vessels till his Name the "ROVER" became a terror of the sea Coasting along America and thence to the West Indies he tracked again toward Norway through the British seas. in the Mediterranean and finally almost exhausted with melancholy and restless as Cain[13] he ordered his vessel home under Sdeath and landed alone on the coast of Sidon. How he wandered through Palestine or how he returned toward Africa is not known for he will never tell it but in 1824 He appeared on a sudden at Percy Hall before his mother and his child after an abscence of 6 dark and bloody years

CHAPTER VI[th][14]   P B B
                                                    Aug 24
                                                     1836

During these years which we have passed in detailing the scenes of Percys eventful life the African Union was rising with immense rapidity to population weal[t]h and glory Citys towns villages were rising and settling Nobilitys honours and offices creating the 12 enjoyed almost despotic sway and the people opened up their striking Character of Reckless warmth and intrepid daring No intestine tumu[l]ts occurred to disturb the Government but war with the Blacks or the French served to establish their southern fire into a mettled warlike Disposition—So it had been but a change was coming over the spirit of this dream

Percy in his loneliness had not let time fly away without thinking he had returned to Africa determined to make Ambition do the work of Passion since Passion seemed to have raved itself to an eternal sleep He was become through a thinking which found no end to difficulties a hopeless Atheist and of course an Anarchical Republican he Hated those above him because the Authorities had so often controled his lawlessness he calculated upon making the 12 feel his mighty[sic] and he set about commencing a grand idea which was matured in his mind—First Percy knew that He was such an one as if seen could

---

[13] See Genesis 4:12-14, and also Montgomery's *The World Before The Flood*, Canto I, ll. 9-10.
[14] Branwell seems confused about his chapter numbers.

not be unnoticed so he determined upon being seen.but by whom The Aristocracy could not be moved they had no complaint—the Democracy could for they were bold and reckless so He laid out thousands of his Gory gains in enormous stocks and set up an immense concern in Horses and Horned cattle. Travelling through the Different kingdoms of the Union attending all the Great Fairs and carrying along with him his Lieutenant Old Sdeath and a desperate dissolute company of partners. the dregs of the Western Aristocracy. his companions of the Rover and men lost to kindred country and religion in riotous debauchery with such a set and with such a SOUL Percy of course became King and Emperor among all the Drovers Cow jobbers Cattle dealers pasturers and farmers of Africa they could not tell what to make of him but they worshipped him and wondered at him Among the Thousands who attended the great fairs at Fidena Denard and Selsden in Sneachisland or Pequena Rossendale Freetown and other such marts in the East and South He was monarch in the market place and Hotel made speeches instilled corrupt and Revolutionary Ideas increased and confirmed adherents and in fo[u]r years time became an object of alarm and suspicion to the scarcly awakened Government. they hit on bad means for suppressing him resolving on private ruin which they might have known would only make one like him more desperately dangerous They incited His creditors to fall upon him for Percy had been attending far more to the spread of his power and opinions than to the amassing [of] a fortune in his journeys his rooted profligacy which then was incorrigible had likewise involved him in serious scrapes so he lay open to attacks of the bloodsuckers who fastened on him and led on by his foe Simpson and the injured and malevolent Montmorency threw him into jail. and sold of his Estates and property. Percy Hall went to the Hammer but Lady Helen bought it in. Percy almost died with misery but his Associates having no one else to depend on so exerted themselves that th[ey] freed him from prison and the star of the west came forth a broken Bankrupt. bitter in heart and cursing God and man He flew to Gambling and swindling cheated great sums and recommenced his career as Apostle of Anarchy arousing the people with the idea of his being a persecuted saint and Martyr of freedom sounding the watchword of Liberty and gathering his meetings of thousands howling for Reform. The 12 and Government quite unused to such a spirit again committed an error They determined to quash the spreading evil by instant force it was used too prematurly and indiscriminatingly only giving Percy a fresh handle which he grasped and thereby roused the populace of Verdopolis to a furious Insurrection in the Spring of 1830 wherein the Kings and Ministry in the first burst were forced to fly from the Capital and Alexander was made President of the Provisional Government But the Constitution and Monarchy was yet to this New Power as a[n] Elephant to a flea They recoiled upon the Revolutionists and instantly retook the City and its power. Percy fled to France in company with his cheif Adherents. He knew the storm just past was not more than a premature prelude of the storms to come so he was not a whit daunted but with many disaffected Atheists in that Island commenced a coresponding mission of Liberty in Paris and thence levanted to Sneachies land which in consequence of its enormous moors and pasturage had always been the cheif scene of his cattle dealing journeys. at Fidena which was the seat of the greatest fairs in Africa and the depot for all the stocks of the Highland he formed his Headquarters leaving his leading supporters to agitate there while [he] avoided [the] pursuit of Government among the wild and inaccessible peaks of the Robbers Hills but when the plot thickened and his supporters increased he showed himself rallyed his comrades of the Rover armed the people and erected the Standard of Revolution through all the moorlands of the North. Sneachies Government despatched large forces under the young Prince John Marquis Fidena and King Arthur furnished his quota of Allies from the Banks of the Senegal while the General Government in Verdopolis exerted all its energies in amassing still further means for crushing the revivified outbreak [of] Anarchy Yet so great was Percys influence in the North that for some time he triumphed in his capital of Fidena but at length cooped up by his Enemies and weakened by division in his own camp he hazarded a general Engagement upon the Banks of the Red River where he was routed with the loss of several thousand men after which event Fidena surrendered the Highlands subsided and people thought no more would be heard of the Rebellion in Africa

It was a foolish thought to harbour at the Begginning of the Rebellion but time was soon to teach us better—Percy—knowing that to re erect his power money and money only would avail him set about endeavouring to procure it he gathered his dissolute and daring companions joining with them a great Ally Richard Naughten a Gigantic and Aged soldier whose vast strength of body and relentless inflexibility of mind had given almost sovereign power over the lower orders in Africa. He instituted a grand organization of Apparently trading firms but really the covers for a scheme of universal Robbery. dividing his followers into different bands with centres of communication one in each of the kingdoms but only openly as Mercantile Houses in Parrystown. Menziestown and Humestown which different companies were known as the firm of Rougue (his new name) Sdeath and Co—Employing vessels and dealing in. their stolen goods the scheme was such as could only have answered in our wild half natural Union but here it was well and deeply laid plundering on sea and land with eminent sucess. the leader residing cheifly at Verdopolis where he dashed into dissipation with unabated desperation often practising the vice of intoxication and exhibiting now in his once iron constitution the marks of rapid and premature decay But still Lucifer was bright though fallen he still shone as a man not blended with the common herd and as such attracted the attention of one whose mind and feelings were as high and as distinguished as his own I mean—

Lady Zenobia Elrington only Daughter and supposed Heiress of the emmensly[sic] wealthy old Western Peer the Earl of Elrington a statly and magnificent Lady distinguished in the first rank of fashion as the most reckless learned and haughty woman in the Union possessed of a grand Roman person and dark Italian Beauty imbued with very Atheistic principles and then chafed and rendered doubly reckless by the ruinous failure of a long ardent and devoted attachment. mention of which brings us forward to a name the second trumpet note of warning for a change in the world! a Man whose deeds were to produce works in Africa which could only be emulated by him whose course I am in the midst of describing. A man in short the brightest perhaps the most transitory meteor that has ever flashed across the Earth—

Arthur Adrian Augustus W———y

The Eldest Son of His Majesty Arthur of Senegambia and heir to the throne of that kingdom was born A D 1813 at his fathers seat in the West. And before he was three years old became the hope and glory of his future people He was a wonderfully beautiful child with Large eyes and dark brown hair warmly affectionate to those who loved him but increasing daily in wilfulness and headstrong passions more especially as there was then at Court the Grandson of Quamina a young Moor. Quashia by name whom His Majesty retained about him as if he were another son but the young prince Arthur (or as his title went the Marquis of D—)[15] looked with most jealous eyes upon the indulgence of this prince of the blacks they hated one another till at last when D— was but 16 years old after a desperate affair in which they had nearly slain one another the King was compelled to send Quashia from Court. but before that time D— had grown up into youth a being hardly looking of this earth so Nobly almost Divinely beautiful was his face and form Impetous passion could not shine brighter than from his lustrous eyes nor could anything seem so winning as his smile if it were not for this warm heartedness the Court would have thought him intolerably vain but such generous and unshaken affections as his wiped away the coxcombry of Spanish dress and lace collars The young Marquis was of course indulged beyond endurance and as I believe he did not possess the firmness to avoid hurt from it indeed he had no firmness but what proceeded from a soul and a constitution produced under an Equatorial Sun Tropical and luxuriant in all manner of feelings and Affections throwing all his being into the feeling of the moment hate or love amusement or study by turns engaged his whole existence and so in each he attain[ed] surpassing excellence. Quashia Prince Arthur of Parrisland the young Marquis of Harlaw. each knew how he could hate his astonished Tutors knew the extent of his learning his fathers foresters his Grooms. and two or three Horsedealers and fancymen found employment enough in administering to his amusements. and as too his Love there were who knew about that and some to their dying day! So Glorious a Creature could not live up to 17 or 18 in the bosom of the proudest the most reckless Court in Africa without creating an Idolatry whose object was himself and whose votaries were the very flowers of the land. votaries and victims as well for this Divinity delighted in human sacrifices requiring from his worshippers their heart and soul—

Ere the young Marquis had attained his 17th year among the many rumours current of him one was that he was involved over head in an "affair of the heart" with the Daughter of one of his fathers Retainers Edward Laury and

---

15 Douro.

upon its coming to the ears of the Duke himself as he knew his Sons headstrong temperament how in the matter of the moment every thing else was lost sight of and how he might any day do something which could never be undone he caused strict search to be made after this matter whereupon the young prince was found to have left the metropolis for a wild woodland solitude where upon the northern Gambia dwelt his Beautiful young Mina Laury. His Dearest and Devoted freind John the Prince of the North and Marquis of Fidena was despatched to save him from some rash step of youthful folly but neither he or the Duke himself could tame their fugitive who upon being startled thus fled and threw himself wildly into the arms of. —no other than the Western Drover! —he wanted to fly the country as a comrade of this Traitor but Percy valued his life too much to countenance such a step and D— was compelled under pain of dishineriting to return to his fathers palace. However nothing in the warm wild west could cure his impetuosity so he was ordered for correction to the stern Presbyterian Court of the North where it was intended to negotiate a marriage with the Princess Lady Maria Sneachi But Arthur was not [to] be controlled he existed very well for a while because Prince John his companion was the freind of his very heart but in a little while he was off no one knew whither among the no[r]thern Highlands shooting with Percy on the moors. then actually entering as a Minister into a secluded parish where he stayed till the Synod ejected him for sundry scrapes or the like with (as it is said) his fair parishioners and then determined not to return to the west he enlisted as a private in the 11th Regiment of Highlanders in which he was captured by Percy at Fidena upon the close of that insurrection he made his escape and now ensued an affair which changed in a degree this warm impassioned headstrong soul. out of a desperate freak he put him self off for an expected suitor to the hand of a Beautiful young Heiress in the North Lady   .[16] but upon seeing her was so struck with her loveliness that he disclosed to her his real name and as a matter of course bore her off from lovers relatives or freinds They were married and there just opened an hour of glorious enraptured bliss when alone together the[y] lived yo[u]ng beautiful impassioned as if nothing but such hours were to come But Arthur forgot his stern father who when he heard this given instance ordered his son instantly to the Philosophers Isle and ere he were well returned Lady   on whom all his Godlike soul had hung was dead.! leaving an infant. Ernest Fitzarthur that beautiful but ill fated child! Young D—s agony for a while almost overcame his reason but that singular characteristic then first appeared which has since so strongly marked him whereby Nothing which can happen however he may feel it will crush him so long as he retains <u>himself</u>. SELF is with him all in all so now he apparantly reentered into all the gaitys of life and ere long was known as the Lover of Marian Daughter of a stern old Twelve his Grace the Duke

---

[16] The blank here and below is Branwell's. The lady in question is Helen Victorine Gordon.

Alexander Hume of   [17]. Marian Hume was a young lovely devoted being all whose thoughts were his but her mild guileless heart was as different from Prince Arthurs as the evening star from the Noonday sun. yet he loved her most fervently and she adored him as an Incarnate Divinity His mother and the Duke both in time countenanced their marriage and Marian received his hand as Marchioness of D— this event brings me round upon my subject

    Lady Zenobia Elrington from Arthurs earliest years had been his constant companion and devoted freind as he grew up into youth his wild heart fixed upon many attachments yet retained strong freindship for her. She with a heart almost as warm as his being innocent of Platonism—[18] could not carry on such a feeling to the magnificent young Prince of Senegambia her childish freindship was changed insensibly and involuntarily to a deep rooted love upon which she hung nourishing hopes and feelings which when upon Arthurs first marriage were blasted at once nearly threw her into the grave But so high and Roman a woman recovered [from] the shock and these treacherous temptations again engirdled her Arthur was again married and Zenobia hasted half wild from Verdopolis over the whole extent of Africa to meet him walking in happiness with his Bride the shock was too much for her insanity followed from which she recovered into haughty recklessness. and now in Verdopolis seeing the former Drover Demagogue Pirate and Robber the subject and Author of such wonderous change his mighty fortunes and grand Aristocratically handsome form so suited to her own chafed but Noble spirit that she felt toward him as he did toward her Admiration that kindled into Love

    Mr Percy was then in Verdopolis living openly and without fear upon his nefarious gains in a style of splendid magnificence He cared about nothing apparently and was known to be involved in the most desperate profligacy but he knew his power that it was not dead and upon this occasion took care to exert it. He married Lady Zenobia and she procured him the title of LORD ELRINGTON a Nominal dignity of Nobility but which did not affect his seat in the House of Commons where he continued laying the foundations of a party and policy. Lady Zenobia had unbounded control over her aged fathers property She gave her Ambitious Husband Her Noble mansion in Elrington Square and he immediatly enlarged it into the most splendid Palace (Royalty excepted) in all Verdopolis the most splendid and most celebrated for here the two kindred spirits one in Pride and Ambition kept up a scale of magnificence unparrall[el]ed in the land.

    But this Union laid the foundation of another more portentous far. Lady Elrington still continued the firm devoted freind of the Marquis of D— they were often together and hence arose an intercourse between Arthur and Lord Elrington no wise amicable truely but more so than ever they were aware off.

    Verdopolis was at this time in a state in which it has never been since. The Marquis of D— had become the Leader of the fashion on one hand and Lord

---

[17] Again the blank is Branwell's. Hume was the Duke of Bady or Badey.

[18] See note 10 above.

Elrington its leader on the other So stimulated by the rivalry of these two spirits Luxury Magnificence and dissipation attained a height the like of which had never been known before D— Villa was the focus of all the young dashing and reckless Nobility of Africa all looking up to a Leader as youthful as reckless as any of themselves Elrington Hall was the headquarters of the Older and more cunning roués. those whose increasing years could not tame their wildness but could direct it to an aim with Douro followed young Castlereagh young Lofty young Molineux Abercorn Roslin with Elrington Gordon Montmorency FitzArthur O Connor Quashia The first were the hope of Africa the last its fear but both lead it and in a dance of dissipation such as it has had no time for since.

Now Douro though he was the Prince of so brilliant a reign In himself seemed or assumed the character of a singularly Gentlemanly and courteous young Nobleman very little addicted to buisness though one of the Ministry but a most devoted admirer and a most munificent patron of the Arts and Sciences Poets Painters Sculptors Architects all followed flattered and in truth almost worshipped him as he really felt at home with them for never was there a man created with a finer sense of the sublime and beautiful than him. But Elrington held these things at arms length sneering at them with morose disdain HE. was all hauteur insult and scoffing depravity his Imagination was satiated now and his youthful heart was gone But shocking Intoxication horrible swearing and [a] sort of partial insanity marked his whole conduct and demeanour. I cannot tell what to attribute it [to] but insanity when he took upon himself to act the Methodist Preacher prayed ranted and held forth to immense congregations which he really did D— chiming in with affected gravity—But what most singularly marked the plans of these two singular beings was the ELYSIUM. a secret Association of both parties meeting in a suite of magnificent Apartments at regular intervals but always in the dead of night to transact scenes of the wildest debauchery and lose and win thousands on thousands at every species of Gambling Elrington was President Douro Vice Lofty treasurer Montmorency secretary Sdeath Door keeper. the very elitè of the youth fashion and nobility of the land members all unknown to and without reach of the laws or constitution only guided by Demons (for at times even D— was a Demon) and evidently pursuing the shortest route to Hell At such times though feeling to each other as John and Simon did in Jerusalem[19] the two Rulers of the Institution felt drawn by the attraction of their mighty minds into closer and closer communion each found in the other the only heart which could feel with him or appreciate his vast ideas and highly wrought feelings they would swear at each other and fight. in drawn battles to stimulate their followers and D— would exultingly laugh to behold his Antagonist reel past him in the street at midnight before his Tail (as Rougues gang were called) horribly Drunk and falling with his huge length into the very kennel and Percy would sneer at D— as a young coxcomb and abuse him for a witless and helpless child of nobility but after all many and mary a time did each take his Horse. on a wild windy night. escape from the city and be

---

19   See the Acts of the Apostles, chapters 3 and 4.

found side by side on the Banks of the broad Guadina in Communions which were the Germs of prodigious things to come!

At this time Percys grand stay for support in the station he held was his nefarious and widly ramified Robbery scheme but upon one occasion 5 or 6 of his Instruments were taken in the act upon a moor in Sneachies land. brought to Verdopolis and confined for trial but only on suspicion of their being mere private Robbers however they threatened to Percy that if they were not lib[e]rated they would impeach him so he was forced to hazard in prevention of this dreadful event. an attack by night upon the principal jail in the City which though sucessful for the moment was supressed by D— at the head of a Rejiment of cavalry and now Government enquiring into the case discovered a part of this vast and iniquitous scheme Percy ran the greatest danger for a while but ultimatly escaped with a fine of 200000£ but even this huge sum could not now injure him so vast had proved his gains from his "firms" and indeed he had some time before bought back all his fathers and his own former property so now he only entered the more feircly onto the attack against his as he termed them tyrannical persecutors. he spoke vehemently in parliament and employed all his tail in seconding his cry for Liberty. so upon the Election in the Autumn of 1833 nearly every man in the Tail was returned as a Member for some town or county under their leaders influence He associated a Jacobin Club at Paris formed of his Adorers and creatures. then planned a great effort for Revolution[20] which the Jacobin Club was to begin they rose but. the Emperor suceeded in quelling them and Percy lost a main limb of his enterprise so he grew reckless <broke> his plot and measures and turned about for something new to rise and overcome by—this was presented to him in the stern scenes that must now be detailed.

P B B
Aug 31
1836[21]

---

20 Nine lines of canceled text follow here.

21 The initials and date signal the beginning of a new section that was not carried further.

Forgotten one! I know not when nor how
    Thou diedst—for even thy very tomb is dead
The stone that covered thee so long ago
    Itself by weeds and grass is overspread

Forgotten one I know not now
When thou diedst or where or how[22]

---

[22] The verso of leaf 19 in Ashley 187—see note 1 above—contains these lines, accompanied by four pen and ink portraits, at least one of which is a self portrait, l. 34 of Book I of *The Illiad,* and the words "Thalassa, Thalassa" in Greek. In l. 4, "overspread" is written after "covered"; neither is canceled.

Oct 4 1836[1]

P B B

Behold the waste of waving sea
    In stormy shadow lying
As vast and shoreless stretched away
    As the clouds above it flying
As rough and restless and as free
    As the wild winds oer it sighing
There mingled with the ocean gale
    I hear the sea birds crying
As through the unmeasured Heaven they sail
    Some far off rest descrying
And oft their white wings glittering forth
Till lost amid the stormy North
And still from out the Atlantic surge
    The heavey vapours rise
Whence darkly gathering they diverge
    Around the dusty skies
And ist the Heaven to Ocean speaks
    Or Ocean back replies
That such a mournful music breaks
    And swells and falls and dies
For as the wild winds wilder sound
More hoarse the surges murmur round
Till they are rolling oer the deep
    With such a thundering roar
As might arouse from fastest sleep
    The Dwellers on the shore
And waken many in anxious start
    For those who never more
To some yet warm and yearning heart
    Such tempests shall restore
Each Gust still calling it to mourn
For one who never can return
Look How the tumbling ridges swell
    And roll in restless agony
The very burning lake of Hell
    Could scarce more rough and raging be!
Black billows ever rising round
And hurried on toward oceans bound
Till if a blast more strongly sweeps

---

[1]This poem covers pp. 25-28 of the manuscript notebook described on p. 444, n. 1, at the BPM: BS 119.

It tears the waters from the deeps
Whose boiling crests of tortured spray
Are torn and shivered oer the sea
While that white foam eternally
    Brewed in the tempests feircest wrath
    As on the bit steeds champ their froth
Mounts on the broken blast and scatters to the sky
    Yet—What is that—which mid the spray
    Scuds like a mist wreath oer the sea
    Now bending downward through the surge
    Then as its dripping sides emerge
Cast back upon the waves or forward born away

    A Ship! A Ship! She bends her side
        Rejoicing to the seas
    Beneath a cloud of canvass wide
        That stretches in the breeze

    The bristled poles which rise above
        Are glancing through the rain
    And bow beneath the tempests breath
        With many a sudden strain

    So wild the blast so dense the press
        Of canvass oer her prow
    That on her decks the tempest breaks
        Like flying clouds of snow

    And yet—as if her desperate crew
        Had maddened in the gale—
    Though driving past as whirlwinds fast
        Swells forth another sail!

    And yet another!—Till she bends
        The boiling deeps below
    Where every dash the water sends
        In flashes from her bow

    One moment stopping on her course
        As doubtful what to obey
    & Then with unresisted force
        Born forward oer the sea

    Her crew with dark locks oer their brows
        Amid the tempest streaming

To each wild eye a spirit rouse
    That fires its fitful gleaming

And breif words mixed with breifer smiles
    Are passed from man to man
As for a moment from their toils
    The[y] pause their cheif[2] to scan

He stands upon the rocking prow
To see the surges boil below
And mark his vessel plough her path
Through Heavens and Oceans feircest wrath
And then he lifts his wild blue eye
To note the changes of the sky
Then through the storm a glance he flings
As if to search for unseen things
Since—failing even that eagle gaze
To peirce the ever varying maze—
His seamen start to hear him hail
"All Hands aloft and crowd all sail"
    Tis grand to view his Noble brow
Confront the breezes while they blow
Aside his curls of Auburn Hair
That forehead leaving free and fair
To change with the resistless light
    Which flashes from his Azure eye
Now softened like the calm moonlight
    Now troubled as that stormy sky
    Now feircly daring to defy
The deepest gulph those waves could form
The loudest piping of that storm
And loud that storm does pipe and vast
The foam white waves are roaring past
And stands he on his streaming deck
    As chiding even the flying gale
Till Lo! the restless vapours break
    A wild wide waste of waves to unveil
    There forward fleets a distant sail
Tossed in distress—And eagerly
That storm tost ship these sailors eye
With such a shout as through the sky
    Oer powers the tempests wail
"Hurrah she heaves in sight again!

2   Alexander Rougue/Percy.

Now merrily haste we oer the main
    Though from us she flew
    Like the fleet sea mew
As like lightning we follow her speed were in vain!"
"Heave Ho—my Hearts" the Boatswain cries
"Now draw your lots and chuse your prize!"
And back an Ancient Mariner
His Answer shouts with ruthless sneer
    "Lets leave 'em their sails their shroud to be
Their ship their coffin their grave the sea"

That Sailor was a hoary man[3]
Tottering on lifes remotest span
But still his step was on the seas
And still his grey locks faced the breeze
Not one of all that desperate crew
With eye more quick or hand more true
Not one with oaths more terrible
Could speak the mother tongue of Hell
His ragged garments scarce might warm
His blighted carcase in the storm
Yet those mean limbs had forced a way
Where thousands trembling stood at bay
And though so rough his cursing tongue
His oaths had mid a palace rung
Tutor and Oracle in crime
To Serf or Lord who wished to climb
    And blithly now his Wolfish eyes
Sparkle to behold the promised prize
While cool between his toothless jaws
A Glittering knife he grimly draws
Feels its keen edge and laughs to mind
The deeds it did in times behind
And to his comrade watching nigh
Slowly he turns his tyger eye
    That comrade was of statlier form
As yet scarce battered by the storm
Youth still oer him her beams had flung
If not in sins in seasons young
Wild rose the locks above his brow
And brown his cheek's unfading glow
His eye rolled ever feirce and free
As fits a spoiler of the sea

---

3   Sdeath.

His pirate vest was dashed aside
For that wild breast would scorn to hide
The beating of its lawless pride
And loud and carelessly he sung
As reckless in the shrouds he hung
Riot in peace and spoil in war
Were all O Connors hope or care
    But standing by a silent gun
Behold another darker one
A man of crime whose eyes had neer
Been clouded with a single tear
Hard were those eyes and black the brow
That shadowed oer their tiger glow
Though scathed by storms an Age might pass
With all its winters oer his face
Yet never clear away the frown
Which called revenge in bloodshed down
Nor might His Cheiftan brook that scowl
Save that he trusted Gordons soul
However black the path he trod
Would never bid him leave the road
              [Unfinished][4]

He[5] sits at the end of the first bench in front His dress is the simplest consisting of a blue frock coat and plain white trousers His attitude is singular With his arms folded <his> head sunk on his breast his hat slouched over his eyes and his legs stretched out to their full length on the floor he would appear to be asleep to all that is going on but if you watch his mouth you will perceive he is engaged in deep thought and he frequently rises and proves he has been So by delivering a plain energetic and vigourous John Bull speech redolent of short arguments and unanswerable facts

---

4   Branwell's comment.
5   These lines appear after the end of the poem.

PBB
Decr 10th
1836

QUEEN MARY'S Grave[1]

I stand beside Queen Mary's grave neath Alnwicks holy Dome
With sacred silence resting on the marble of her Tomb
The Organs thunders hushed to sleep the mourners passed away
All left to her the sepulchre the coffin and the clay
The Vault is closed the stone is placed the inscription only tells
Within that dark and narrow house whose corpse corrupting dwells
And one with those who passed from Earth forgotten years ago
From theirs around by sight or sound that tombstone none might
    know
So I may stand to think a while oer things for ever gone
And drop one tear to memory dear above this funeral stone
    What seek my eyes they rest not on the columns arching oer me
Nor the storied windows shimmering round nor the sculpture piled
before me
They are watching through its prisoning tomb the cold corrupting
    clay
They are wandering oer the eternal gloom of deaths unfathomed sea
Not the wintery winds which moan without in such a mourning tone
Have so wild a path or so far a flight as the[y] gaze on a spirit gone
    How strange seems now that vanished Past reflected to my eye
That pride of rank that pomp of power that blaze of Royalty
Collecting all their brightest beams around a single brow
Yet paling all their borrowed light Neath Beautys native glow
    How strange to know that She to whom I bent my willing knee
Among a thousand round her throne who joyed to kneel with me
Is now so near me—All alone! with arms clasped oer her breast
Lying clothed with white in an endless Night of everlasting rest
Her lovely limbs stretched stiff and still her ey[e]lids closed for ever
And her white lips in silence pressed no more on earth to sever
And her pale brow surrounded now with wild flowers withering
Like her to a long long winter snatched from a short and sudden
    spring
My mind retraces back the path of this quenched and fallen Star
To that bright morn when first its light shone oer the Calabar
Companion of our Country's Sun in his refulgent rise
The chosen and the only one beside him in the skies
And farther back upon her track to the hour remembered well
When Loves first word upon her heart like whispered Thunder fell

---

[1]   This poem follows immediately after the date at the bottom of p. 624, covering the latter part of p. 4 and p. 5 of the manuscript.

Her fathers Palace roof above its glorious Halls around
When her cheek first flushed and her bosom beat to hear that awful
  sound
War settled to triumphant peace and DOURO home returned
Crowned with the crest of victory that oer its hero burned
But brighter in unborrowed beams that form magnificent
Above the chosen of his pride its kingly stature bent
What darkning curls oer hung the brow whose smoothness seemed to
  be
Like the oerpowering stillness of a deep but treacherous sea
The imperious eyes half closed to hide the lurking feind within
The proud lips curled in a witching smile of decked and gilded sin
For not in garb more Angel like to Eve appeared the Devil
Nor the winged Dragons gilded Mail hid thoughts of deadlier evil
Nor the words that changed our Earth to Hell like sweeter thunder
Than that deep voice whose Organ tones his love in music told
Oh shook not younder[sic] gorgeous Hall when words so eloquent
Delivered oer one beauteous Bride to lonely Banishment
And gave another one short flash of loves celestial light
To end in such a frightful change of deaths eternal night

   He says he has grasped her fathers hand their freindship sworn to
     share
And that each summoned by his band of conquerors fresh from war
With all the youth of Afric round could dare a thousand dangers
Their hands creators of their power their arms their own avengers
He opens up a dazzling dream where parting clouds of glory
Disclose a land of paradise unknown to former story
His own white finger points the place of realms that are to rise
And his own deep voice prophetic speaks of coming victories
Till she surveys that glorious brow whose crown has just been won
And knows in its refulgent glow Creations rising Sun
Her heart is in her eyes and they with burning tears run over
For who unmoved could hear the voice of such a glorious Lover
Not that bright form of beauteous youth whose thoughts unutterable
Thrill wild through veins of Percyian blood with feeling none can tell
Oh none but one who had been like her a child of Poetry
If round him youths romantic dreams arose—reality!
And he had heart and soul to thrill with joys so wonderous wild
Oh none but such could know the thoughts of Percys lovely child
And when he speaks again and says of all the world that she
Alone is meet Zamorna's bride and Angrias Queen to be
Even if his looks of light at once had changed to Satans frown
The eloquence of her mute reply must seal her for his own
The Auburn curls from her kindled brow in inspiration flung
The whole heart and spirit in that vow which trembles on her tongue

But straight his own curls bent oer hers are mingling with their
    tresses
And his royal lip with a burning Kiss the cheek of beauty presses
And his Statly limbs on the cushions thrown are straight her own
    beside
That to her ear more sweetly false his poisoned words may glide

Glossary of Glass Town/Angria Persons and Place-names

Abercorn, James, Marquis of: A member of the Council of Elysium, Rougue's secret society. He sees military action during the War of Encroachment under command of Elrington and Douro, being recognized, along with Molineaux, as a "reckless, iron hearted wild bloodied young office[r]," and at the battle of Loango.

Acrofcroomb: A city and province of Ashantee, home to a tribe of cannibals ruled by ten brothers. After its inhabitants attack Glass Town, the city is razed by the Twelves in an act of revenge.

Adrianopolis: Capital city of the new kingdom of Angria, on the banks of the Calabar, 150 miles from Verdopolis, "a city destined to rule the world."

Alanna, King: King of the Inward tribes and an ally of Quashia during the invasion of Angria.

Alnwick: A large town about fifty miles west of Verdopolis which becomes the temporarary seat of Government after Verdopolis is evacuated during the final stages of the War of Encroachment.

Alnwick Hall: The "Noble second country residence" of Rougue Elrington in Sneachiesland, this "huge Hall" becomes home to the Council of Six during their evacuation from Verdopolis in the War of Encroachment. It is the ancestral home of the Percy family and the Earl of Northangerland, where Zamorna sends, his wife Mary when Northangerland, he father, begins the Revolution. Branwell has her die there, but Charlotte rebels against her death; she has Mary wasting away, but transformed at the last moment by a letter from Zamorna assuring her he is alive.

Ancient Britons: According to tradition, "some thousands of years" before the Twelves arrived in Ashantee (West Africa), twelve men of gigantic size from Britain, and twelve from Gaul came to the area, but after years of continual war, they returned to their respective countries.

Angria: The kingdom created for Zamorna in 1834 after his heroic defense of the Verdopolitan Union against the French and Ashantees: it has seven provinces: Zamorna, Angria, Douro, Calabar, Northangerland, Arundel, Etrei. He appoints his Father-in-law, Northangerland, Prime Minister, but the latter leads a rebellion against his son-in-law; in the ensuing war Angria is ravaged, Zamorna driven into exile, only to return triumphantly and put an end to Percy's political ambitions.

Aornos: A tall mountain near Glass Town, reputedly home to the Genii and therefore regarded as the "Olympus" of the Glass Town Confederacy.

Ardrah, Marquis of (Arthur Parry): Prince of Parrisland and leader of the Reformers in Verdopolis, Commander of the Verdopolitan Navy. Opposed to the creation of Angria as an independent state and enemy of Zamorna, his forces invade Angria and defeat Zamorna's, but is then overthrown by Northangerland.

Arundel, Earl of: See Lofty, Viscount Frederic.

Arundel, Edith, Countess of: The oldest daughter of the King of Sneachiesland.

Ashantee: Located on the African Gold Coast, identified with Guinea; Ashantee consists of a series of countries extending 1700 miles from east to west, and 500 miles from north to south. To the east of Ashantee lies the desert; to the west the Atlantic; to the south the Gulf of Guinea; and to the north the Gibbel Kumri Mountains (the Mountains of the Moon). It has been chosen by the Chief Genii to be "the seat of all Grandeur Fame and Glory."

Ashworth, Brother: An alias Northangerland assumes when preaching at the Wesleyan Chapel.

Badey (Bady) Dr. Alexander Hume: One of the Twelves. A large "exceedingly ugly" man who dissects corpses stolen by his accomplices, but an excellent surgeon and physician to the Duke of Wellington; father of Marian, Douro's second wife.

Barras: A leading member of the "Faction du Manege" who works to bring about the downfall of the Emperor Napoleon. He is later imprisoned in the French State Prison by Napoleon for his part in the attempted coup d'état, but reappears as an envoy to Verdopolis and friend of Northangerland. During the occupation of Angria he is appointed Treasurer of the Forces.

Bellingham, James: A "rich English banker" who travels through the Glass Town territories with the Marquis of Douro, Charles Wellesly, and Young Soult, and whose escapades during Glass Town's revolutionary times are narrated in **Letters From An Englishman**. As a result of approving a £13 million loan to the Glass Town government, intended to finance its counter-revolutionary effort, he is imprisoned and threatened with death by the leader of the insurrectionary forces, Rougue. He later plays an important role in Zamorna's Angrian Wars, supporting him in the way that the Rothchilds supported Wellington's Peninsular Wars. See Alexander CB, I, Part I, 213.

Bernadotte: Insurrectionist against the Emperor Napoleon, and one of the leading members of the "Faction du Manege." After successfully (but only temporarily) ousting Napoleon from office, he is elected Chief Consul of France, and assumes the title of His Highness of the New Republic of Frenchyland. Upon Napoleon's successful counterattack, he is imprisoned in the State Prison. Later he becomes an ally of Ardrah and Northangerland in the campaign against Angria.

Bobbadil, Thomas Beresford: As Major General of the Army of Wellingtonsland, he maintains order at the Hustings during the heated Glass Town elections. During the War of Encroachment he serves as Brigadier General, placed in charge of 8,000 men.

Branii Hills: A vast mountain range to the north of Sneaky's Land, "savage and barren"; home to the Highlanders.

Bravey's Inn (later Hotel): named after William Bravey, its corpulent landlord and one of the original Twelves, it is an important meeting place for the Young Men and for Glass Town politicians and literati.

Bud, Captain John: An eminent Glass Town political writer and historian, author of **The History of the Young Men, The Life of Alexander Percy,** and other works, the greatest prose writer of early Glass Town; a pseudonym of Branwell, and a friend of Lord Charles Wellesley. See Alexander CB, I, 126-27.

Bud, Sergeant: Son of Captain Bud, "a sharp thin Lawyer like looking young man," publisher and bookseller, who executes a writ on behalf of the Duke of Wellington requesting the presence of Alexander Rougue before the court of Admiralty to answer charges of piracy. He also acts as Government prosecutor in the Glass Town trial of five men convicted of robbing a Government courier of certain Government Dispatches. See Alexander CB, I, 128.

Calabar: The river on which Adrianopolis is situated.

Carey: A member of the Council of Elysium, Rougue's secret society. He is entrusted by Rougue with minor charges, participates in the fleecing of Castlereagh, and brawls with O Connor.

Cashna Quamina: The king of the Ashantees at the time of the Twelves' arrival. A "mild old king" who trades and communicates "amicably" with the new Glass Town settlers until his death, he is succeeded by his son, Sai Tootoo Quamina.

Castlereagh, Frederic Stuart (Viscount Castlereagh and Earl of Stuartville): A young and wealthy visitor to Verdopolis from Ireland, he is initiated into the secret society, Elysium. Although he believes himself the political protégé of Rougue and Montmorency, their real intention is "to fleece him of all his property then cast him off." Castlereagh loses his estate in gambling debts, but when he subsequently rescues Lady Julia Montmorenci from an unwelcome marriage to Lord Thornton Wilkin Sneaky, he is granted the post of Secretary of the Foreign Office (worth £50,000) by the Marquis of Douro, and subsequently marries Lady Julia. He later takes an active part in the War of Encroachment, distinguishes himself in battle, becomes a member of the Council of Six and subsequently an Angrian minister and close friend of Zamorna.

Caversham, Fitzgerald, Earl of: An associate of Edward Percy (senior) and father of Frederic; he lends money to Alexander Percy, and connives with Augusta Percy in the death of Alexander's father.

Caversham, Viscount (later Baron) Frederic: A Colonel in the Dragoons during the War of Encroachment, and an associate of Alexander Percy, who murdered Caversham's father in a duel at Percy Hall.

Charlesworth, Lady Emily: Bravey's niece; abducted by Percy on the eve of her marriage to St Clair, but eventually married to him.

Coomassie: The Ashantee capital, located by "a deep and rapid river" near Rossendale Hill. The city of 500,000 inhabitants is destroyed in an attack by the Twelves. Later visited by the author of **Letters from an Englishman**, it is described as a majestic ruin, "desolate and inhabited by tigers and owls."

De Lisle, Sir Edward: An eminent Glass Town portrait painter patronized by both Earl St Clair and the Marquis of Douro, and later by Edward Percy.

De Segovia, Augusta: Alexander Percy's first wife, who plots to kill Percy's father, but is then herself poisoned by her accomplices for counselling Percy not to pay his debts.

Denard, Sir John: A friend of Wentworth and close associate of Alexander Percy.

Di Enara, Henri Fernando: Commander-in-Chief of the Angrian forces, known as "The Tiger."

Douro, Marquis of: See Wellesly, Arthur

Dundee, George (later Sir John Martin Dundee): A popular artist of "the sublime," associated with the nineteenth-century painter, John Martin.

Edwardston: The chief manufacturing town in Angria, where Zamorna is defeated by the Reformist forces.

Edwardston Hall: Country estate of Edward Percy in the Verdopolis valley.

Elrington, Dowager Countess: The mother of Rougue. A "stately Old Lady" with a "Most majestic and almost regal deportment." She is one of the few persons to command "the least glimmer of respect and attention" from Rougue.

Elrington Hall: The Percy family residence in Verdopolis.

Elrington, Lady Zenobia: The proud, haughty daughter of the old Earl of Elrington, she is first attracted to the Marquis of Douro; their relationship is a complex one: they admire each other's mental and physical abilities, but when she tries to become a rival for Marian Hume, their relationship cools. But this "Majestic Lady with fine Italian features" is also admired by Rougue/Percy who, after capturing her on his pirate ship, marries her. Although largely excluded from her husband's illicit activities, she maintains a prestigious Salon, and devotes much of her time to reading classical authors "in the original," engaging in literary discussions, and writing letters. She is also known for her pride and choler, and her dress indicative of a decadent background—see Alexander CB, I, 286, n. 2.

Elrington, Viscount: See Percy, Alexander.

Elysium or "Paradise of Souls": A Secret Society in Verdopolis (also known as "Pandemonium"). Members must be worth over £5000 a year, be over the age of fifteen, and must have slain a man. Rougue serves as its President, and the Marquis of Douro as its vice-president; its champions include Pigtail; and its members include Montmorency, John Flower, Castlereagh, and others. The club's main activities appear to consist of drinking, gambling, and brawling.

Evesham: A city on the Cirhala which is fortified by Northangerland's Revolutionary forces, then taken by General Thornton in the last major battle in Zamorna's return to power.

Faction du Manege: A secret society in France dedicated to the overthrow of the Emperor Napoleon. The Society is given financial support by an unamed faction in Glass Town, presumably Rougue's.

Fidena: A "noble city" of "tall monuments and shining domes" and capital of Sneachiesland, which Rougue targets as a strategic key to victory in the Revolutionary War: "Gain Fidena and you will gain Africa."

Fidena, Marquis of: See Sneaky, John Augustus.

Flower, Captain John (later Viscount Richton and Baron Flower, Verdopolitan Ambassador to Angria): An eminent scholar in Verdopolis, author of **The Politics of Verdopolis, Real Life in Verdopolis, The Wool is Rising** and other works. Loyal to the Twelves, he stands as a Constitutional candidate, is later appointed Secretary of the War Office, and subsequently plays an active role in the War of Encroachment when he is promoted to the rank of Colonel of Foot Soldiers, and principal Staff Officer to General the Marquis of Fidena. One of Branwell's pseudonyms.

Freetown: A large town of strategic importance during the War of Encroachment: "Gain Freetown," states Sir John Flower, and "the road to Verdopolis is easy."

Gambia: River on which Glass Town (Verdopolis) is situated.

Gazemba: A town and plain on the banks of the Calabar where Zamorna reviews his troops before the battle of Evesham.

Genii: The presiding spirits of Ashantee, who assume various guises, and exhibit supernatural powers. The Chief Genii are Talli (Charlotte), Branni (Branwell), Emmi (Emily), and Anni (Anne). Guardians and protectors of the Twelves, they use powers of shape-shifting and transformation to aid the Twelves in times of crisis.

Gifford, John (Professor, R.A.S.): Lawyer and antiquarian, and later Chief Judge of Glass Town; a learned historian whose research aids Captain Bud in writing **The History of the Young Men.**

Girnington Hall: The rambling gothic country house of General Thornton in the valley of Verdopolis.

Glass Town: A confederacy of four kingdoms—Wellingtonsland, Sneachiesland, Parrysland, Rossesland—formed by the Young Men in Ashantee. Its capital is the Great Glass Town, later Verdopolis.

Glasstown (Verdopolis) Valley: Traversed by the River Niger, the valley consists of "mighty and Fertile" plains which house vast cornfields and "a hundred stately parks and a thousand stately Mansions."

Goat, John James, Esq.: The Under Home Secretary in St Clair's cabinet during the War of Encroachment, and Speaker of the House of Commons during Ardrah's premiership.

Gordon, Captain Julian: One of the "dark-malignant scowling Gordons"; a confederate of Percy.

Gordon Mountains: Located one hundred miles from Verdopolis, these mountains are home to "fourscore thousand Africans" who threaten to join forces with the Emperor of France against the Confederacy.

Gravi, W: Arch Primate of Verdopolis.

Greenwood, Mr.: The organist at St Michaels in Verdopolis, who seeks a new post in Angria.

Grenville, Thomas: Speaker in the House of Commons, member of St Clair's Cabinet, and a Major General in the War of Encroachment, taking command of 38,000 men to serve as a force against Marmont's French division. Also an eminent mill-owner in Angria and father of Ellen Grenville who marries Warner Howard Warner.

Guadima: River which flows over the plains of Dahomey and on which Verdopolis is built, site of a great loss of life during the War of Encroachment. Probably based on the River Guadiana in Spain, scene of much action during the Peninsular War.

Guelph, Frederick (King Frederick I): One of the Twelves, he is also the second son of George III of England, the Duke of York. He is later elected first king of Glass Town.

Harlaw, Marquis of: Son of the King of Rossesland, and Home Secretary in Ardrah's Government. .

Hartford, Colonel (later General): An Angrian nobleman and military leader, friend of Sir John Flower, Lord Richton.

Hastings, Captain Henry: A popular Angrian soldier and author who later degenerates into a drunken murderer; cashiered for shooting his superior officer, he joins the Revolutionary forces, and eventually becomes involved.in a plot to kill Zamorna. A pseudonym of Branwell's before his desertion of Zamorna.

Hume, Marian: Daughter of Alexander Hume Bady, second wife of the Marquis of Douro, always presented as "an angel" and an ideal heroine.

Jack, King: Alias Quacco Camingo, one of the black commanders in Quashia's army.

Jordan, Earl of: Profligate brother of Augusta di Segovia. Later as Sheik Medina, he and his troops participate in the occupation of Angria.

King, R P: See Sdeath.

Kumriis: Gibbel Kumri or Mountains of the Moon; see Ashantees.

Laury, Mina: The daughter of Ned Laury and Faithful mistress of Zamorna, who lives at the Cross of Rivaulx, the lodge of Hawescliffe Estate.

Laury, Ned: Glass Town villain, poacher, and body-snatcher; rival of Young Man Naughty; "noted servant of the Marquis of Douro."

Leaf, John: The Glass Town Thucydides, originally sent from England by Pitt's ministry in 1782 to sue for assistance from the Twelves in the war against Napoleon. He subsequently becomes one of the first historians of Glass Town, keeping records, transcribing speeches, and writing "The Acts of the Twelves." Unfortunately, his history is "much mutilated."

Leyden: Scene of Zamorna's most famous victory over Northangerland's forces after his return from exile.

Lofty, Edith: See Arundel, Countess of.

Lofty, Lord Macara; The scoundrelly younger brother of the Earl of Arundel and Ardrah's Chancellor of the Exchequer. Later, he is Cheif Secretary of the Government Percy installs in Angria, but eventually turns against both Ardrah and Percy.

Lofty, Viscount Frederic, Earl of Arundel: a close friend of the Marquis of Douro, an accomplished horseman, and a highly popular General. Presumably slain at the Battle of Velino, he is "resurrected" by Sdeath—see Alexander CB, II, part ii, 78-79.

Macterrorglen, Sir Jehormam Henry: See Jeremiah Simpson.

Manfred: The head of the University on the Philosopher's Island.

Manns and Wamons Isles: A pair of islands "just off the coast of Frenchyland" which belong to the Glass Town Governments. Possession of these islands is demanded by the newly-armed Emperor of France, and the War of Encroachment ensues.

Marmont: The French Commander of 30,000 troops which are to move "100 miles south of Verdopolis" in order to keep a footing on the coast, and eventually join forces with the French commander, Massena, in a final push toward Verdopolis.

Massena: Commander of a large French force of 40,000 men which, according to the French plan of action, is to move "nearly 200 miles north of Verdopolis," and from thence attack southward, eventually joining forces with Marmont in a final push against Verdopolis. Later, he joins forces with Ardah and Percy against Zamorna, and becomes Percy's Commander-in-Cheif in Angria.

Medina, Sheik Abdallah: See the Earl of Jordon.

Molineaux: A member of the Council of Elysium, Rougue's secret society, and a patron of the boxing ring, who is described as "wild dissipated." Under the command of Elrington and Douro during the War of Encroachment, he is recognized, along with Abercorn, as a "reckless, iron hearted and wild blooded young office[r]."

Montmorency, Hector Matthias Mirabeau: A Verdopolitan nobleman, banker, and "familiar" of Alexander Rougue, but for a time bears a deep hatred for Percy for absconding with his wife, Harriet. He has two daughters, Julia and Harriet. He wishes to arrange a politically advantageous match between Julia and Lord Thornton Wilkin Sneaky, but his daughter eventually marries Castlereagh. He later takes an active role in ousting the ruling Aristocrats during the War of Encroachment, and becomes one of the Council of Six replacing the ousted Ministry. He is Foreign Secretary for Angria, then in Ardrah's Reform government, but turns against both. Similarly he initially supports Northangerland in the campaign against Angria, but then turns against him.

Montmorency, Lady Julia: A young lady "of 17 or 18" of lively disposition, she is, with her sister, Harriet, a new arrival to Verdopolis. Her father wishes to arrange her marriage with Lord Thornton Wilkin Sneaky, but she is rescued from this fate by Castlereagh who fights a duel on her behalf. She subsequently marries Castlereagh.

Morely, Thomas Babbicome: Returned as a Constitutional Candidate for Glass Town; he is later made Colonial Secretary; is loyal to the Twelves. Later, he is Colonial Secretary for Angria.

Murat: During the War of Encroachment, Murat leads a regiment of French horsemen at the Battle of Little Warner against Douro's troops, but despite engaging in courageous personal combat with Thornton, he and his regiment are repulsed. He is killed by a stray rock thrown during the turmoil of battle.

Musselburgh, Lord Viscount: Politically affiliated with the Vacillators, he is also Chancellor of the Exchequer in St Clair's government during the War of Encroachment, and therefore indirectly responsible for the government's withholding of funds from the military during this crisis. Later he becomes Paymaster of the Forces in Ardrah's Reform government.

Naughty, "Young Man": Glass Town villain and body snatcher, as well as "champion of the poachers." Of gigantic stature, cruel and ruthless disposition, he is a follower of Rougue Elrington, and supports him during the Great Rebellion of 1831, and again during Percy's campaign against Zamorna, as leader of the People's (Destructives) Party. He is appointed Lord Lieutenant of Angria and Commander of Northangerland's forces.

Niger: The river that forms the boundary between Angria and the Verdopolitan Union.

Northangerland, Earl of: See Percy, Alexander.

Northangerland, Zenobia, Countess of: See Zenobia Elrington.

O Connor, Arthur: A member of the Council of Elysium, Rougue's secret society, he is also one of Rougue's Colonels. Described as "a mind and person originally of the highest order," he has, however, been "degraded by the use of everything mean and low." His fate is sealed when, in command of Rougue's rebel army, and contrary to Rougue's instructions, he orders a retreat while in a drunken rage, thereby causing the deaths of 30,000 men. Although he attempts to take his own life rather than face a dishonourable execution, he is strung up on the gallows by Rougue's order, but then mysteriously reappears.

O'Connor, Harriet: Sister of Arthur O'Connor, seduced by Percy, later unhappily married to Montmorency, elopes with Percy who deserts her, and she dies a sad, lonely death.

Parry, William Edward: One of the Twelves, King of Parrysland and father of the Marquis of Ardrah. .

Pelham, Sir Robert Weever: Coming to Verdopolis from Lancashire, England, after having inherited "vast wealth," he contributes £50,000 to Rougue's political activities, and is returned as a member of Rougue's Democrats party. Engaged to Mary Percy, but rejected by her in favor of Zamorna.

Pequena: A strategic location for the defence of Glass Town during the War of Encroachment. It becomes the focus of attack by Napoleon's force of 90,000, and is the site of action between Fergusson and Massena.

Percy (also Rougue), Alexander Augustus: First wife, Maria di Segovia—son William Etty. In 1814 he married Lady Henrietta Wharton: three sons—Henry, Edward, William—whom he orders Sdeath to dispose of, but Sdeath saves Edward and William, and one daughter, Mary Henrietta::; wife dies of consumption; heartbroken, he leads a dissipated life; involved in the 1831 and 1832 rebellions, he is captured and executed, but brought back to life again in 1833; returns as Colonel Alexander Augustus Percy, abducts Lady Emily Charlesworth, trying, unsuccessfully, to get rid of he fiance, Lord St Clair; elopes with Harriet (O Connor) Montmorency; forsaking her, he spends sixteen years on "The Rover" as a bandit and pirate; seizes Lady Zenobia Elrington and her father on their ship, woos and marries her and returns to Verdopolis as Lord Elrington; assists the Marquis of Douro in the War of Encroachment against the French and Ashantees; helps Douro (now the Duke of Zamorna—Percy is now Earl of Northangerland) become King of Angria; becomes his father-in-law and Prime Minister; helps Ardrah defeat Zamorna and occupy Angria, then turns on Ardrah to try to establish a republican government in Verdopolis, with himself as Lord President of the Provisional Government. He sends Zamorna into exile on Ascension Island, thereby bringing about the death of his daughter, Zamorna's wife. On Zamorna's successful attempt to regain his country, Percy is allowed to live, provided he lives quietly as a private individual. His mistresses include Harriet O Connor, Lady Georgina Greville, Lady St James, Lousia Dance (Vernon), Miss Pelfe, Madame Lalande.

Percy, Edward: Unpleasant eldest son of Northangerland, given at birth to S'Death to be destroyed but saved by him; saves the Marquis of Fidena's life; becomes a leading industrialist in Angria, MP, Lord Viscount Percy and rises to the post of Secretary of Trade in Angria; fights a duel with the Marquis of Ardrah, and marries Maria Sneachie, whose family had arranged for her to marry Ardrah.

Percy Hall: The Percy family residence in Wellington's Glass Town, located in a pastoral region twenty miles east of the city.

Percy, The Honourable Miss Mary Henrietta: The daughter of Rougue Elrington and Lady Mary Henrietta Percy, she has inherited her mother's gentle manners, and is much beloved by her father, Rougue, as well as by the tenantry and local peasants. In addition, she is courted by Glass Town's high society owing to her father's "wealth power and vast consequence," but does not relish this kind of attention, preferring, instead, to discourse with thoughtful souls on literary and philosophical matters. She is initially egaged to be married to Sir Robert Pelham, but marries Zamorna and becomes Queen of Angria.

Percy, Lady Mary (Maria): The soft spirit who charmed Percy/Rougue away from his evil genius; after her death from consumption Percy becomes a desolate man, his "life and motives utterly perverted."

Percy, William: Northangerland's second son, also given to S'Death to be destroyed and saved by him. He rises to the rank of Lieutenant General in the Angrian army and becomes Sir William.

Philosophers Isle: Where the young nobility of Glass Town receive their early schooling and training. Manfred is President of the University on the island.

Quashia Quamina: Son of the Ashantee King, Sai Tootoo; adopted by Wellington after Sai Tootoo's death at the Battle of Coomassie and brought up with his children; becomes leader of the Ashantees and incites them to rebellion against the Verdopolitan Union; allied with Northangerland and Zamorna's sworn enemy, he murders Zamorna's son Ernest and sacks Adrianopolis.

Ross, Captain John: King of Rossesland and father of Edward Tut Ross, the Marquis of Harlaw, and supporter of Ardrah.

Rougue, Alexander (Viscount Elrington): See Percy, Alexander.

Ross, John: One of the Twelves; "frank open, honest" and brave; he is killed on Ascension Island, but later magically restored. He is one of the founders of Glass Town and King of Rossesland and friend of the Marquis of Ardrah.

Rossendale Hill: "[A]bout the size of Pendle hill in England," and located on the outskirts of Coomassie, it is the site of the Battle of Rossendale which Captain Bud calls the Twelves' "battle of Marathon." Here King Frederick I meets his death at the hands of Quashia Quamina. Subsequently, a small temple, which eventually becomes a pilgrimage site, is erected to commemorate these events.

Scroven, Tom: One of the "Rare Apes,"a poacher of intimidating mien: "8 feet high, bony, haggard and lean," with a "sinister, malignant expression," companion of Ned Laury and Young Man Naughty.

Sdeath, Robert Patrick (also King): A pirate and murderer—according to Captain Flower, a "little hideous bloody old man"—his name is derived from the oath "God's death." He is the "usher" of Elysium, and acts as partner and servant of Rougue/Percy. He possesses supernatural powers, for although capable of being wounded, he cannot be killed.

Simpson, Jeremiah: A banker and associate of Montmorency. As "Macterrorglen" he joins Medina and Quashia in support of Northangerland in the occupation of Angria, but later turns against him.

Sneaky (Sneachie), Alexander: King of Sneachiesland.

Sneaky (Sneachie), Prince John Augustus: Duke of Fidena, eldest son of Alexander Sneachie, King of Sneachiesland; one of Zamorna's most respected and trusted friends. Foreign Secretary and later Major General and Commander-in-Chief during the War of Encroachment.

Sneaky (Sneachie), Maria: Daughter of the King of Sneachiesland; her family arranges her marriage to the Marquis of Ardrah, but she rebels and marries Edward Pery.

Sneaky (Sneachie), Lord Thornton Wilkin (later General Thornton): Son of the King of Sneachiesland. Although he is unsuccessful in his bid to marry Lady Julia Montmorency, and humiliated when he is wounded in a duel with his rival, Castlereagh, and although his Parliamentary career is jeopardized when he is named as one of Rougue's criminal conspiritors, and he is disowned by his family, he later exonerates himself during the War of Encroachment by distinguished action on the battlefield, and becomes a member of the Council of Six, and a distinguished military leader in the campaign against the Ashantees. Later, Commander-in-Cheif of Angria's army.

St Clair, Earl: Prime Minister and Leader in the House of Lords during the War of Encroachment. He is executed by Rougue after he and his party, the Arisocrats, withhold financial support from the army, but is revived later and marries Lady Emily Charlesworth.

St Michaels Cathedral: Like the Tower of All Nations, a landmark of Glass Town, visible from afar. Its great dome gives a view of the entire spread of the city.

Stanhope, Charles: Primate of Angria.

Stumps Island: An island off the coast of Africa to which Northangerland retires after Zamorna dismisses him as Premier of Angria.

Sydney, Lady Julia: Niece of the Duke of Zamorna and wife of Edward Sydney, Lady Julia belongs to a circle of ladies "of high rank, beauty and fashion" who regularly attend society events in Glass Town.

Sydney, Edward, Geoffrey Stanley (Lord Strafford):   Initially a Member for the populous borough of Freetown, his successful political bid earns him the hatred of Rougue. Although he enters Parliament "unknown young [and] little tried," he makes a spirited speech opposing Rougue's attempt to bring division and discord into parliamentary proceedings. He marries Lady Julia, the niece of the Duke of Wellington, and by the time of the War of Encroachment, fills the office of Home Secretary and Leader in the Commons. He supports Ardrah and Northangerland.

Tower of All Nations: Landmark in Glass Town, modeled on the Tower of Babel or Babylon, it rises 6,000 feet and is the home of Crashey, the great patriarch.

Tree, Captain: Famous Glass Town prose writer and pseudonym of Charlotte.

Tree, Sergeant: Glass Town's chief publisher, printer, bookseller, a "clever lawyer and a great liar."

Twelves, The: Originally Branwell's toy soldiers; they become the discoverers, explorers, and settlers of Ashantee, forming the Glass Town Confederacy. The original Twelves who board the "Invincible" for Ashantee in 1770 consist of: Butter Crashey, the Captain, aged 140 years; Alexander Cheeky, the surgeon, aged 20 years; Arthur Wellesly, a trumpeter, aged 12 years; William Edward Parry, a trumpeter, aged 15 years; Alexander Sneaky, a sailor aged 17 years; John Ross, the Lieutenant; William Bravey, a Sailor, aged 27 years; Edward Gravey, a sailor, aged 17 years; Frederick Guelph (the Duke of York), a sailor, aged 27 years; Stumps, a midshipman; Monkey, a midshipman, aged 11; Trackey, a midshipman, aged 10 years; and Crackey, a midshipman, aged 5 years. The first Twelves later form the House of Lords of Glass Town; the second Twelves form the House of Commons; four of them—Arthur Wellesly, Sneaky, Parry and Ross became kings of their respective countries: Wellingtonsland, Sneachiesland, Parrysland and Rossesland.

Velino: A range of hills outside of Vedopolis, and close to Freetown, housing a small village of the same name. This "wild Little" village affords a retreat to Fidena's army and becomes the general's new headquaters during the War of Encroachment.

Verdopolis: Capital of the Glass Town Confederacy—first called Glass Town, then Verreopolis, then Verdopolis; on the river Guadima; center for government, "high life," and commerce; "a splendid city rising with such graceful haughtiness from the green realm of Neptune," with walls, battlements, a cathedral, the domed Bravey's hotel, the Great Tower, and many fine streets with fine shops. It is later sacked by the French army during the War of Encroachment. See also Glass Town.

Vernon, Caroline: Daughter of Northangerland and his mistress, Louisa Vernon.

Vernon, Louisa, Marchioness of Wellesly: Married first to Lord Dance (or Vernon), then to the Marquis of Wellesly, the brother of the Duke of Wellington. Later she is the mistress of Northangerland and Lord Macara Lofty.

Warner Hall: Residence of the millionaire, Warner Howard Warner Esq.

Warner Hills: A long ridge of isolated mountains north of Verdopolis; site of the first military engagement in the War of Encroachment, and of a subsequent mutiny in the Glass Town army by its "three best" regiments, which is henceforth known as "the Mutiny at Little Warner."

Warner, Mr. Warner Howard: A reclusive millionaire "from an ancient and distinguished family" whose property includes a significant "part of Angria." He commands "4000 armed devoted tenantry," and an additional body of 8,000 men. On condition of full repayment, he offers the Glass Town Government troops and financing during the War of Encroachment, as well as full hospitalities to the 5,000 casualties of the Battle of Little Warner. He also makes a decisive speech in Parliament castigating the ruling Aristocrats for their "hideous blindness" and "willfull insanity" in refusing to support the army, and calling upon members to "hurl from office the whole present Ministry." He subsequently becomes a member of the Council of Six. He becomes Zamorna's Chancellor of the Exchequer and Home Secretary, and succeeds Northangerland as Prime Minister. Credited with the gift of second sight.

Wellesly, Arthur: One of the Twelves (originally a trumpeter aboard the "Invincible"), and a co-founder of Glass Town. "Ardent for all military glory and fame," he is chosen by the Genii to return to England to help in the war against Napoleon. He becomes the "champion of Europe," and is awarded "the title of DUKE OF WELLINGTON." Upon returning with 3,000 of his "brave soldiers" to Glass Town, Frederic II relinquishes his crown in favour of Wellesly who is "formally installed 'King and ruler of the 12s town and of all its inhabitants.'" Later, however, with the refusal of the ruling Ministry to support the army during the War of Encroachment, he secedes his kingdom, Wellingtonsland, from the Confederation of the Twelves, thus "dissolving that Mighty Body". Upon the forcible removal of the Ministry, he, "form[s] a 7th. councillor" to the Grand Council of Six. He is the father of the Marquis of Douro and Lord Charles Wellesly.

Wellesly, Arthur Augustus Adrian: Wellinton's eldest son, Marquis of Douro, later Duke of Zamorna and King og Angria. He marries Lady Helen Victorine Gordon—one son, Ernest Fitzarthur; Marian Hume—one son, Arthur Julius, Marquis of Almeida; Mary Henrietta Percy—six sons and a daughter. His mistresses include Rosamund Wellesly, Mina Laury, Caroline Vernon. After the War of Encroachment he is awarded his own kingdom of Angria, there builds his capital, Adrianopolis, and makes Percy his Prime Minister. He is opposed by Ardrah and his Reformist army from Verdopolis. Percy turns against him, defeats him and sends him into exile, then turns on Ardrah's forces. In the meantime, Zamorna's wife, Mary dies at Alnwick. Helped by Warner Howard Warner, Zamorna returns from exile and retakes his kingdom, demoting Noethangerland to the status of private individual.

Wellesly, Ernest Edward Fitzarthur: Son of Lady Helen Victorine, he is murdered by Quashia during the invasion of Angria.

Wellesly, Lady Julia: Cousin of the Marquis of Douro, who marries first Edward Sydney, then General Thornton.

Wellesly, Lord Charles Albert Florian: Precocious son of Arthur Wellesly, Duke of Wellington, and brother to the Marquis of Douro (whom he despises as a "sour puritanical milk sop"). As the young author of various literary libels and tracts, including "Something about Arthur," he is the subject of Captain Bud's **The Liar Detected** in which he is "unmasked" as "a Boy uterly destitute of all common understanding Foolish and Inconsiderate in the extreme But with a few small marks of some sort of a genius." While travelling with his brother, Young Soult and James Bellingham, he is captured by Rougue during the revolutionary insurrections, and wounded although not fatally. As Charles Townshend, he is the author of a number of works by Charlotte, including **The Green Dwarf, Corner Dishes, The Spell, My Angria and the Angrians.**

Wellesly House: Residence of the Marquis of Douro.

Wentworth, Charles: Another of Branwell's pseudonyms, he becomes private secretary to Lord Macara Lofty.

Zamorna, Duke of: See Wellesly, Arthur.

INDEX OF FIRST LINES AND TITLES

As some titles have been derived from the first line, neither titles nor first lines have been inverted, so definite and indefinite articles have been treated as keywords in alphabetization and occur at the beginnings of lines.

Titles of manuscript volumes and of stories and poems have been printed in italics. First lines of stories and poems, including poems that occur within stories, are printed in roman type in quotation marks. Titles in italics and quotation marks indicate story titles derived from the first line of text.

When there are several installments of one story, these have been placed in chronological order. Dates heve been included in square brackets where necessary to distinguish two or more items with the same titles.